THE PAPERS OF
General Nathanael Greene

*Nathanael Greene, 1742–1786; oil painting by Charles Willson Peale,
from which most later likenesses were copied or derived
(Independence National Historical Park Collection)*

THE PAPERS OF
General Nathanael Greene

VOLUME VIII
30 March–10 July 1781

Dennis M. Conrad
EDITOR

Roger N. Parks
SENIOR ASSOCIATE EDITOR

Martha J. King
ASSISTANT EDITOR

Richard K. Showman
EDITOR EMERITUS

Assisted by Elizabeth C. Stevens and Nathaniel N. Shipton

THE UNIVERSITY OF NORTH CAROLINA PRESS
Chapel Hill and London

Published for the
RHODE ISLAND HISTORICAL SOCIETY

To the memory of Richard K. Showman, 1913–1995

© 1995 The University of North Carolina Press
All rights reserved
Manufactured in the United States of America

The paper in this book meets the guidelines for permanence
and durability of the Committee on Production Guidelines for
Book Longevity of the Council on Library Resources.

99 98 97 96 95   5 4 3 2 1

Library of Congress Cataloging-in-Publication Data
(Revised for vol. 8)

Greene, Nathanael, 1742–1786.
   The papers of General Nathanael Greene.
   Secondary editors vary.
   Vol. 6– includes maps.
   Includes bibliographical references and indexes.
   Contents: v. 1. December 1766–December 1776—
[etc.]—v. 7. 26 December 1780–29 March 1781—
v. 8. 30 March–10 July 1781.
   1. Greene, Nathanael, 1742–1786—Manuscripts.
2. United States—History—Revolution, 1775–1783—
Sources. 3. Manuscripts, American. I. Showman,
Richard K. II. Rhode Island Historical Society.
III. Title.
E207.G9A3 1976   973.3'3'0924   76-20441
ISBN 0-8078-1285-4 (v. 1)
ISBN 0-8078-1384-2 (v. 2)
ISBN 0-8078-1557-8 (v. 3)
ISBN 0-8078-1668-X (v. 4)
ISBN 0-8078-1817-8 (v. 5)
ISBN 0-8078-1993-X (v. 6)
ISBN 0-8078-2094-6 (v. 7)
ISBN 0-8078-2212-4 (v. 8)

TABLE OF CONTENTS

ILLUSTRATIONS

MAPS

For locating a place-name on a given map, see listing in the index.

INTRODUCTION

Volume VIII of the *Papers of General Nathanael Greene* traces events in the Southern Department from 30 March through 10 July 1781, a crucial time in the Revolutionary War in the South, as Greene brought his army back to South Carolina to challenge the British for control of that state and Georgia. Included in the volume are 843 letters and orders, of which 652, or 77 percent, have been abstracted, or calendared. The abstracted letters and orders are those that the editors have judged to be of less significance or that repeat information found in other documents; letters written by Greene are also more likely to be printed in full than are letters to him. The abstracts or calendars of the letters are complete, omitting nothing of substance. The same is true of Greene's orders, though the parole, sign, countersign, and names of the officers of the day have always been omitted. If a portion of a calendared letter is judged to be highly significant or somehow unique, that portion is quoted verbatim. A microfilm or electronic edition of the full transcripts of all documents in this volume is planned.

The volume opens with Greene preparing to execute his plan to break off pursuit of Lord Charles Cornwallis's army and to abandon North Carolina by moving the Southern Army into South Carolina. This was a brilliant strategic decision, but a risky one, for Greene was violating established military principles by leaving an enemy army virtually unchallenged in his rear. Greene realized both the risk and the unorthodoxy of the maneuver, writing to James Emmet, a North Carolina officer, on 3 April: "Dont be surprisd if my movements dont correspond with your Ideas of military propriety. War is an intricate business, and people are often savd by ways and means they least look for or expect." Greene's decision appeared even riskier when Cornwallis, contrary to Greene's expectations, did not follow the American army into South Carolina but soon afterward marched toward Virginia instead. (The situation in that state, which was also part of Greene's command, is discussed below.)

Greene's plans for a South Carolina campaign were further unsettled when, upon his arrival at Camden on 19 April, he discovered that a quick capture of that post was impossible. The fortifications were even stronger and the garrison larger and better supplied than he had been led to believe. With his army too weak to take Camden by storm, Greene took a position nearby and tried to cut the flow of supplies into the post, hoping eventually to starve the garrison into submission. He was only partly successful, for his army was too small to surround Camden completely, and men and supplies continued to slip into the enemy's post.

Greene had known before he left North Carolina that he would have trouble taking Camden, and he had asked Thomas Sumter, the commander of the South Carolina militia, to join him with a sizable force of militiamen to assist in the operation. Upon his arrival at Camden, Greene modified these orders, asking Sumter to take a position to cut off supplies coming to the post from the west and southwest. Sumter never complied with the orders, citing difficulties in gathering his force. This episode was the first in what became a troubling pattern: Greene would request support or assistance from Sumter, only to have the South Carolinian ignore his orders or offer excuses as to why compliance was impossible. Sometimes Sumter was truly unable to do as Greene requested; it appears, however, that just as often he refused to follow orders because he had decided that his forces could be better employed elsewhere or because he was loath to limit his independence by serving with the Southern Army. The correspondence between Greene and Sumter in this volume reflects their increasingly strained relationship.

Although Greene was not completely successful in his attempt to cut off supplies, Lord Rawdon, the British commander at Camden, soon became concerned that his command would be isolated and forced into a disadvantageous tactical situation. The threat to Rawdon's position was a result of a campaign that Greene had initiated before he left North Carolina when he ordered Henry Lee to precede the army and join forces with the South Carolina partisan leader Francis Marion in attacking the British support posts along the Santee River. These small forts protected supply lines between Charleston, the center of British power in the lower South, and Camden, the northernmost post in the British defensive perimeter. Lee and Marion began a siege of Ft. Watson, the largest of the posts, on 15 April and captured it eight days later, thanks in part to their use of an ingenious siege machine, the Maham tower. Even before Rawdon learned of the fall of Ft. Watson, he had decided that he must either destroy Greene's army or face eventual defeat. On 25 April, he led his garrison out of Camden to challenge Greene's army. At Hobkirk's Hill, Rawdon defeated the Southern Army in a battle that was marked by bad luck for the Americans and bad decisions by Greene and some of his subordinate officers. The outcome of the battle did not, however, change the strategic situation. Rawdon had not dispersed Greene's army and thus continued to face the prospect of eventual isolation and defeat. Although a reinforced Rawdon tried one more time to engage Greene's troops, he had decided before the engagement to evacuate Camden and did so on 10 May.

With Rawdon in retreat and anxious to protect Charleston against a possible attack by Greene's army, Marion, Sumter, and Lee were able to move against the remaining British support posts. Quick sieges or negotiated surrenders led to the capture of posts at Orangeburg, McCord's Ferry (Ft. Motte), and Friday's Ferry (Ft. Granby). Two other posts, Georgetown and Nelson's Ferry, were evacuated, so that by early June the Americans had reclaimed the northern and central parts of South Carolina for American arms. Greene now moved his army against the fort at Ninety Six, which had been the western anchor of the British defensive perimeter. Rawdon and Nisbet Balfour, the British commander at Charleston, had already decided to draw their perimeter closer to Charleston. They had ordered John Harris Cruger, the Loyalist commander at Ninety Six, to evacuate the post, but all of their messages to Cruger were intercepted. Aware of the orders to evacuate the post, Greene confidently marched his army to Ninety Six and initiated a siege on 22 May.

Meanwhile, sieges were also in progress against three British forts in and near Augusta, Georgia: Ft. Dreadnought, Ft. Grierson, and Ft. Cornwallis. These operations, which were directly linked to Greene's, were conducted by Andrew Pickens, the South Carolina militia leader, and Henry Lee, whom Greene had sent to Augusta with a detachment from his army. The Americans captured Ft. Dreadnought on 21 May and Ft. Grierson the following day. The surrender of Ft. Cornwallis on 5 June broke the British hold on the interior of Georgia.

A few days after the fall of Ft. Cornwallis, Greene sent Joseph Clay, a Georgian and the Southern Army's paymaster, to reestablish state government in Georgia. Greene's decision to become actively involved in resurrecting state government there sprang from two motives. The first was to end the chaos that had given rise to a particularly brutal civil war in the state and led to the murder of the British commander of Ft. Grierson while he was a prisoner in American hands. Greene believed only a duly established government could impose order. The second motive, which was tied to the first, was to honor a request by certain Georgia officials that Greene intervene in the state. A short time later, an even more compelling reason to reestablish state government in both Georgia and South Carolina arose. Greene learned that mediation to end the war had been proposed and that preceding the negotiations there would likely be a truce based on *uti possidetis*—the principle of combatants retaining the territory they held at the cessation of hostilities. It became imperative, therefore, for both Georgia and South Carolina to have governments in place before any negotiations commenced. (This proposal of mediation would also greatly affect Greene in his conduct of operations in the South during the later summer and fall of 1781.)

Ironically, while Greene was working to end the lawlessness and chaos in one way, he contributed to civil unrest in another. Shortly after the capture of Ft. Granby, he had approved implementation of Sumter's plan to confiscate slaves from Loyalists and offer them as a bounty to new enlistees in the South Carolina state troops. Although Greene ordered that the confiscations be carried out according to established legal procedures, in the end the practice resulted in looting, murder, and Loyalist retaliation.

This instance involving "Sumter's law" was an exception to Greene's conduct of the war, however. The bloody and internecine nature of the conflict in the South appalled even as hardened a soldier as Greene, who wrote his wife: "My dear you can have no Idea of the horrors of the Southern war. Murders are as frequent here as petty disputes are to the Northward." Greene tried, with limited success, to lessen the brutality that characterized the southern war. He was generous in paroling prisoners of war, worked to arrange a cartel to ameliorate the situation of prisoners on both sides, and passed up opportunities to retaliate against British violations of the rules of war. He also advocated lenient treatment for Loyalists who wished to return to American jurisdiction.

Even as Augusta fell, the siege of Ninety Six proceeded more slowly than Greene had expected. Once again, he found a fort to be stronger and better defended than he had anticipated. His small army was severely taxed by having first to dig siege lines and then defend them against frequent sallies by the fort's defenders. To hasten the post's surrender, the besiegers tried various tactics that had proved successful in earlier sieges. They attempted to ignite the roofs of the buildings in the fort, for example, and also constructed a Maham tower on which cannon were mounted and sharpshooters posted. Each time, the post's commander was able to check the temporary advantage gained by the besiegers. Despite the spirited defense of Ninety Six, though, Greene's men moved closer and closer to the walls of the fort and would certainly have captured it had not a British relief force arrived from Charleston.

Rawdon found himself able to mount this expedition when reinforcements intended for Cornwallis's army arrived in Charleston from Cork, Ireland, on 3 June. Four days later, Rawdon marched with some 2,000 men to relieve Ninety Six. Greene had left orders for Sumter and Marion to combine and slow any British force that moved toward Ninety Six, but both partisan leaders let other concerns slow their response to Rawdon's movements. As a result, the British column successfully avoided the partisans and brushed aside the few American units that did gain its front. On 21 June, two days after Greene had launched a desperate and unsuccessful attack on the fort, Rawdon relieved the beseiged post.

In explaining to Congress his inability to capture Ninety Six, Greene blamed the state government of Virginia. He contended that by countermanding his order to send 2,000 Virginia militiamen as reinforcements, Virginia had denied him the troops he needed to complete the siege. A disgusted Greene then raised the question of whether state officials under the Articles of Confederation had the right to ignore or countermand the orders of a Continental department commander. What might have been a precedent-setting debate on national versus states' rights was avoided when Congress chose not to address Greene's concern.

Greene did not press the matter because his campaign and his reputation were vindicated when the British decided to implement their original plan and abandon Ninety Six. Again, it was a case of Greene's superior strategy overcoming a tactical defeat. As at Camden, Rawdon realized that as long as Greene's army remained intact, Ninety Six was vulnerable to a renewed siege. He decided, therefore, to abandon the post and evacuate the Loyalists from the area.

To accomplish the evacuation, Rawdon divided his army. Greene, seeing an opportunity to defeat the British piecemeal, spent the final days covered by this volume in attempting to draw his forces together and engage Rawdon before the British commander could reach safety. An American force did succeed in destroying Rawdon's cavalry, but Rawdon reached Orangeburg and was reinforced there before Greene could assemble his forces for an attack. By July 1781, Greene had decided not to assault Rawdon's position and had chosen instead to withdraw his army into a camp of repose in the High Hills of the Santee.

While these events took place in South Carolina and Georgia, the situation in Virginia—which was part of Greene's Southern Department command and had been the mainstay in supplying men and supplies to Greene's army in the opening days of his command in the South—went from devastating in the spring to somewhat more hopeful by July. This volume opens with the denouement of an unsuccessful Franco-American attempt to capture a British force operating in Virginia under the command of the American traitor Benedict Arnold. The Franco-American expedition against Arnold had been thwarted when a British fleet turned back its French counterpart at the mouth of Chesapeake Bay in an indecisive battle on 16 March. Accompanying the British fleet was a detachment of 2,000 reinforcements from New York commanded by Gen. William Phillips. These troops united with

Arnold's raiders on 26 March, more than doubling the size of the British force in Virginia. To oppose them, Baron Steuben, Greene's increasingly unpopular commander in the state, had only an army composed of some 1,300 unreliable militiamen and a handful of equally unreliable regulars. Steuben's ragtag force was all that prevented the British from cutting the supply lines providing Greene's army with a small but necessary flow of stores from Philadelphia and the upper South.

Not surprisingly, Greene wrote to both Washington and the Marquis de Lafayette to ask that the detachment that Lafayette had brought as far as Maryland in anticipation of the expedition against Arnold be allowed to continue southward. In April, Lafayette received permission to join Greene. But by then Phillips had begun an invasion of the Virginia interior and Cornwallis had begun to march his army toward a union with Phillips at Petersburg, Virginia, so Lafayette remained in Virginia to oppose them.

The union of the two British armies at Petersburg on 20 May was particularly devastating, for Lafayette by then was powerless to do more than try to limit the scope of British raids while avoiding a general engagement. With Greene's encouragement, he made it his first priority to keep his army intact. Even after he was reinforced by Gen. Anthony Wayne's Pennsylvania Continental troops on 10 June, Lafayette wisely remained on the defensive.

In late June, Cornwallis recalled his raiders and moved toward the coast in anticipation of sending part of his army to reinforce the British garrison at New York City. A puzzled, though happy, Lafayette followed what he grandly and inaccurately termed Cornwallis's "retreat" and looked for opportunities to strike at the British as they moved. This new aggressiveness led to Wayne's falling into a cleverly laid British trap at the battle of Green Spring Farm on 6 July. Only a heroic effort by the troops of Lafayette's army prevented a crushing defeat. At the close of the period covered in this volume, a more cautious Lafayette continued to trail Cornwallis as the British commander marched toward the coast.

Throughout this period, Greene received reports from his commanders in Virginia but was so far removed from that theater of war that he felt inadequate to offer more than the most general advice. As the situation in Virginia deteriorated, he considered going there himself, but his failure to capture Ninety Six and, later, word that Washington was planning to move with his army into Virginia led him to remain in South Carolina.

By July, Greene and the Southern Army, with the help of the partisans, had wrested control of most of the South Carolina and Georgia hinterland from the British. While those areas were still vulnerable to

British incursions and Loyalist raids, they would never again be subject to British control. Greene was now faced with the task of driving the British back into Charleston. In doing so, as will be seen in Volume IX, he would employ basically the same tactics that he had used in freeing the backcountry. During the remainder of the summer, he and his army would also play an important ancillary role in the siege of Cornwallis's army at Yorktown, Virginia, undertaken by the combined armies of Washington and the Comte de Rochambeau. Though Greene was not yet aware of it, by July the tide of war in the South had turned, and his small, ragged, underequipped Southern Army had been the driving force behind the Americans' changing fortunes.

Providence, R.I.   DENNIS M. CONRAD, *Editor*
October 18, 1994

ACKNOWLEDGMENTS

In each volume of the *Papers of General Nathanael Greene* we have acknowledged the institutions, foundations, and many individuals who have helped to sustain the project over the years. We take the opportunity again to thank those who have assisted the project in various ways. This volume marks the first in which the name of Richard K. Showman, our editor emeritus, does not appear at the top of the title page. We would be remiss if we failed to acknowledge the great debt that we owe to Dick, not only for reading through the manuscript pages for this volume but also for being an on-call editorial and administrative resource in his retirement. More importantly, Dick has set a high editorial and scholarly standard for us to follow. We are likewise grateful for the assistance of Mary MacKechnie Showman, whose contributions to this volume and throughout this documentary edition are too numerous to list.

The National Historical Publications and Records Commission has continued to support the project with indispensable funding. We greatly appreciate the time and consideration given to us by commission members, who generously serve without compensation. The staff of the NHPRC has been unfailing in its help and support, and we owe much to Executive Director Gerald George, Nancy Sahli, Roger A. Bruns, Richard N. Sheldon, Don Singer, Timothy Connelly, and others who have helped from behind the scenes.

The preparation of this volume and preceding ones was made possible in part by a grant from the Program for Editions of the National Endowment for the Humanities, an independent federal agency. We thank Sheldon Hackney, who chaired the Endowment during the preparation of this volume, and we gratefully acknowledge the contributions and help provided by Douglas M. Arnold, our program officer at the NEH.

The project would also like to thank the state of Rhode Island for its long and continuing financial support. In particular, the secretaries of state have been great and valued friends. Institutional sponsors that have provided matching funds for the NHPRC and NEH grants are listed on the opening page. Their officers and staffs are among the unsung heroes of the Greene Papers project. Among those who should be mentioned by name are members of the Society of the Cincinnati, including past president general Frank Mauran of Providence, Rhode Island, who has been a supporter of the project since its inception. Individuals who have been instrumental in the continued support of the sponsoring groups to which they belong are Frank S. Hale II and Ray H. Durfee of the Sons of the Revolution and Robert A. Greene and Col. Anthony Walker of the Sons of the American Revolution.

Listed also on the page of institutional sponsors are the officers of our own Rhode Island Historical Society and members of its publications committee. We remain obligated to the society's staff, only a few of whom can be mentioned by name. Director Albert T. Klyberg initiated the project and has helped to guide it ever since. The administration of various grants and financial recordkeeping have been the responsibility of Associate Director James K. Mahoney and Business Manager Patricia Mende. Librarian Madeleine Telfeyan and her professional staff have always been ready to make the resources of the Historical Society's library available.

We extend thanks to the staffs of the Brown University Libraries, especially to Peter Harrington of the John Hay Library. We are indebted to the Computing Center of Brown University for the use of their optical scanner and to Geoffrey Bilder, who oversaw the scanning of documents for this and later volumes.

For help with the maps in this volume several people should be noted. Charles T. Cullen, president and librarian of the Newberry Library in Chicago, provided and permitted us to use the base maps for Lester Cappon's *Atlas of Early American History* (Princeton University Press, 1976). Lawrence E. Babits of East Carolina University kindly assisted us in locating obscure places. The finished maps were prepared by Lyn Malone of Barrington, Rhode Island.

We also wish to thank several private collectors who have furnished copies of letters for this volume: Peter Agnew, David Coblenz, Louis R. Lau, and Horace J. Stepp.

Finally, there are many other persons who support the Nathanael Greene Papers in various ways. We are indebted to James C. Kochan, Donald Londahl-Smidt, Elizabeth Nuxholl, and Todd W. Braisted for their help in locating sources and answering our research questions. We also acknowledge the help of Eric Deudon, who provided us with a translation of a letter written in French. Finally, we are indebted to John C. Dann, Mrs. Thomas Casey Greene, Thomas Casey Greene, Jr., Thomas Enoch Greene, and Robert Allen Greene for their continued assistance.

EDITORIAL METHOD

Arrangement of Materials

Letters and documents are arranged chronologically. Letters written over a span of several days have been placed at the last date indicated by the writer. If two or more related items are dated the same day, they are arranged in sequence; if unrelated to each other, they are arranged as follows:

1. Military orders and documents (as opposed to letters)
2. Letters from NG, alphabetically by recipient
3. Letters to NG, alphabetically by sender

Undated Items

If a date omitted by the author can be determined, it is printed in brackets, and the item takes its place chronologically. A doubtful conjecture is followed by a question mark.

If a precise day cannot be established, the shortest conjecturable time span is placed in brackets and the item arranged as follows:

Conjectured Time Span	Chronological Arrangement
[10–18 December 1779]	Placed at 18 December 1779
[April] 1780	Placed at end of April 1780
[November 1779–February 1780]	Placed at end of February 1780
[1780]	Placed at end of 1780
[1779–81]	Placed at end of 1781
[before 12 June 1781]	Placed at end of 11 June documents
[after 20 July 1780]	Placed at end of 20 July documents

All such conjectures are explained in footnotes. If no time period can be conjectured, the item will be placed at the end of the last volume of the series.

Misdated Items

If a correct date can be determined for a misdated item, it follows the incorrect date in brackets; if a date is suspected of being incorrect, a question mark in brackets follows.

Form of a Letter

The form of a letter is rendered as follows, regardless of the original:
1. Place and date are at top right.
2. Complimentary close is set continuously with the body.
3. Paragraphs are indented.
4. Author's interlineations or brief additions in the margin are incorporated into the text silently unless of unusual significance, when they are explained in a footnote.
5. Scored-out or erased passages are not included unless mentioned in a footnote.
6. Address sheet and docketing are normally omitted.

Calendared Items

Many less important items are calendared, with an abstract of the contents set within brackets. The item is arranged according to date. We often quote from a document, either to retain the flavor and characterize the author or because the quotation is more accurate than any paraphrase could be. The writer's original wording is set off by quotation marks, or if in a lengthy passage, by indentation.

MANUSCRIPT TEXTUAL POLICY

In earlier volumes, following the practice established by Julian Boyd, Leonard Labaree, and others, manuscripts were rendered in such a way as to be intelligible to the present-day reader while retaining the essential form and spirit of the writer. In Volume VII, the Greene Papers have moved closer to a literal rendering of the manuscripts, with the editors using brackets to indicate changes made to clarify the text. In a very few cases, spelled out below, the editors alter the text silently.

Spelling

Spelling is retained as written. If a misspelled word or name is not readily recognizable, the correct spelling follows in brackets. Names are correctly spelled in notes and index.

Inadvertent repetitions of words are corrected silently.

Capitalization

The author's capitalization is followed, including the eighteenth-century practice of capitalizing words within sentences, except where necessary to conform to the following rules:

1. All sentences begin with initial capitals.

2. Personal names and titles used with them, honorifics (such as "His Excellency"), geographical names, and days of the week and months are capitalized.

Abbreviations and Contractions

1. Shortened word forms still in use or those that can easily be understood (as "t'was" or "twixt") are rendered as written.

2. Those no longer readily understood are treated thus: "cmsy [commissary]" or "warr[an]t."

3. Abbreviations of names or places—forms known only to the correspondents or their contemporaries—are also expanded in brackets, as in S[amuel] A[dams] or Chsn [Charleston].

Symbols Representing Letters and Words

When any of the following symbols are expanded they are done so silently:

1. The thorn, which by 1750 had been debased to "y" as in "ye," is expanded to "th." Such abbreviations as "ye," "y^t," or "y^m" are rendered as "the," "that," or "them."

2. The macron is replaced by the letter(s) it represents—as in comͬission, which becomes commission, or hap̄en, which becomes happen.

3. The 𝇐 sign is expanded to the appropriate letters it represents (e.g., per, pre, or pro).

Punctuation

Where necessary, punctuation is changed to conform to the following rules:

1. A period or question mark is placed at the end of every sentence.

2. Dashes used in place of commas, semicolons, periods, or question marks are replaced with appropriate punctuation; dashes are retained when used to mark a suspension of the sense or to set off a change of thought.

3. No punctuation is used after a salutation.

Missing or Indecipherable Passages

If such passages cannot be conjectured, they are indicated by italicized editorial comments in brackets, such as [*mutilated*], [*indecipherable*], [*several words missing*], [*remainder of letter missing*].

If missing or indecipherable portions can be conjectured, they are treated in one of the following ways:

1. Any missing letters that are conjectured are inserted in brackets. If there is some doubt about the conjecture, it is followed by a question mark: Ch[arleston?].

2. If such portions can be supplied from a variant version of the manuscript, they are set in angle brackets: ⟨Washington⟩.

3. A blank left by the author is so depicted.

PRINTED MATERIAL

In reprinting documents from printed sources, the capitalization, spelling, punctuation, and paragraphing have been faithfully followed.

SOURCE NOTE

An unnumbered source note directly follows each document. For manuscript material it consists of a symbol describing the type of manuscript, followed by the symbol or name of the repository that owns the document, or the name of an individual owner. Pertinent facts or conjectures concerning the manuscript are added when required. A list of manuscript symbols and a list of the Library of Congress repository symbols follows the section on annotation below.

ANNOTATION

The editors have set several goals for themselves in annotating the documents. The most important is to explain a document sufficiently to make it intelligible to the modern reader who may be unfamiliar with the subject. In a sense, the editor puts the reader in the place of the eighteenth-century recipient of a document by alluding to facts that were unknown or unknowable to them. Another goal is the correction of errors in a document, since many a myth has found its source in "documentary evidence" that was false or inaccurate. Then, too, for the reader's convenience, the editor should relate the document at hand to other documents or notes in the series by the use of cross-references. And there is a final goal: to provide continuity and understanding to the reader by filling significant gaps in the documents.

A few procedural points need emphasis:

1. Identification of persons is usually made at the first appearance of their names and is not repeated. References to these biographical notes are found in the index. Identifications are omitted for such

leading figures as Washington or Franklin, as well as for obscure persons who played an insignificant role in NG's career.

2. Cross-references to an earlier volume are designated by volume and page number, as in "See above, vol. 6: 418." Otherwise, cross-references to documents in the current volume are by date, as in "See above, NG to Washington, 11 January." If the document is from a different year, the year is also given, as in "See below, NG to Sumter, 9 February 1782."

3. When a page number does not appear in a citation, the reader can assume the work is in dictionary form.

DESCRIPTIVE SYMBOLS FOR MANUSCRIPTS

Following are the symbols employed in source notes to describe the kinds of manuscripts used in the texts.

AD Autograph document
ADS Autograph document signed
ADf Autograph draft
ADfS Autograph draft signed
AL Autograph letter
ALS Autograph letter signed
D Document
DDf Document draft
DS Document signed
Df Draft
DfS Draft signed
L Letter
LS Letter signed
LB Letter book copy
FC File copy
Cy Copy (made contemporaneously with original)
ACy Autograph copy
ACyS Autograph copy signed
Tr Transcript (later copy made for historical record)
[A] Indicates some uncertainty about the autograph
[S] Indicates signature has been cropped or obliterated
(No symbol is given to printed letters or documents.)

LIBRARY OF CONGRESS SYMBOLS OF REPOSITORIES

The following institutions have provided copies of manuscripts that are printed, calendared, or cited in Volume VIII:

CLjC Copley Library, La Jolla, Calif.

CSmH	Henry E. Huntington Library, San Marino, Calif.
DLC	U.S. Library of Congress, Washington, D.C.
DNA	U.S. National Archives and Records Service, National Archives Library, Washington, D.C.
DSoC	Society of the Cincinnati, Washington, D.C.
GU	University of Georgia, Athens, Ga.
ICU	University of Chicago, Chicago, Ill.
IHi	Illinois State Historical Library, Springfield, Ill.
InU-Li	Indiana University, Lilly Library, Bloomington, Ind.
MB	Boston Public Library, Boston, Mass.
MH	Harvard University, Cambridge, Mass.
MdHi	Maryland Historical Society, Baltimore, Md.
MiDbEI	Edison Institute, Henry Ford Museum, and Greenfield Village Library, Dearborn, Mich.
MiU-C	University of Michigan, William L. Clements Library, Ann Arbor, Mich.
N	New York State Library, Albany, N.Y.
NHi	New-York Historical Society, New York, N.Y.
NN	New York Public Library, New York, N.Y.
NNC	Columbia University, New York, N.Y.
NNPM	Pierpont Morgan Library, New York, N.Y.
Nc-Ar	North Carolina State Department of Archives and History, Raleigh, N.C.
NcD	Duke University, Durham, N.C.
NcU	University of North Carolina, Chapel Hill, N.C.
NjGbS	Glassboro State College, Glassboro, N.J.
NjMoHP	Morristown National Historical Park, Morristown, N.J.
NjP	Princeton University, Princeton, N.J.
O	Ohio State Library, Columbus, Ohio
OClWHi	Western Reserve Historical Society, Cleveland, Ohio
OMC	Marietta College, Marietta, Ohio
PEL	Lafayette College, Easton, Pa.
PHC	Haverford College, Haverford, Pa.
PHi	Historical Society of Pennsylvania, Philadelphia, Pa.
PPRF	Rosenbach Foundation, Philadelphia, Pa.
PWacD	David Library of the American Revolution, Washington Crossing, Pa.
RHi	Rhode Island Historical Society, Providence, R.I.
RNHi	Newport Historical Society, Newport, R.I.
RPAB	Brown University, Annmary Brown Library, Providence, R.I.
ScC	Charleston Library Society, Charleston, S.C.
ScU	University of South Carolina, Columbia, S.C.
Vi	Virginia State Library, Richmond, Va.

ViHi   Virginia Historical Society, Richmond, Va.
ViU   University of Virginia, Charlottesville, Va.
WHi   State Historical Society of Wisconsin, Madison, Wis.

SHORT TITLES FOR WORKS FREQUENTLY CITED

"Annual Register—1781"
    "Annual Register—1781." In *Rebellion in America: A Contemporary British Viewpoint, 1765–1783*. Edited by David H. Murdoch. Santa Barbara, Calif.: Clio Books, 1979.
Archives of Md.
    Archives of Maryland. Edited by William H. Browne et al. Baltimore: Maryland Historical Society, 1883–.
Bartholomees, "Fight or Flee"
    Bartholomees, James B., Jr. "Fight or Flee: The Combat Performance of the North Carolina Militia in the Cowpens-Guilford Courthouse Campaign, January to March 1781." Ph.D. diss., Duke University, 1977.
Bass, *Marion*
    Bass, Robert D. *Swamp Fox: The Life and Campaigns of General Francis Marion*. New York: Henry Holt and Co., 1959.
Bemis, *Hussey-Cumberland Mission*
    Bemis, Samuel F. *The Hussey-Cumberland Mission and American Independence*. Princeton: Princeton University Press, 1931.
Biog. Directory of S.C. Senate
    Biographical Directory of the South Carolina Senate, 1776–1985. Edited by N. Louise Bailey et al. 3 vols. Columbia: University of South Carolina Press, 1986.
Boatner, *Encyc.*
    Boatner, Mark Mayo, III. *Encyclopedia of the American Revolution*. New York: David McKay Co., 1974.
Boyd, *Jefferson Papers*
    Jefferson, Thomas. *The Papers of Thomas Jefferson*. Edited by Julian P. Boyd et al. Princeton: Princeton University Press, 1950–.
Brown, "Memoirs"
    Brown, Tarlton. "Memoirs of Tarlton Brown." Edited by Charles Bushnell. *The Magazine of History with Notes and Queries*, extra no., 101 (1924), 11–43.
Brunhouse, *Pennsylvania*
    Brunhouse, Robert Levere. *The Counter-revolution in Pennsylvania, 1776–1790*. Philadelphia: University of Pennsylvania Press, 1942.
Burke Microfilm
    Burke, Thomas. *The Thomas Burke Papers in the Southern Historical Collection of the University of North Carolina Library*. Edited by

Clyde Edward Pitts. 5 reels. Chapel Hill: University of North Carolina Library Photographic Service, 1967.

Burnett, *Congress*
Burnett, Edmund Cody. *The Continental Congress.* New York: The Macmillan Co., 1941.

Calendar of Va. State Papers
Calendar of Virginia State Papers and Other Manuscripts, 1652–1781, Preserved in the Capitol at Richmond. Edited by William P. Palmer et al. 11 vols. Richmond, 1875–93.

Cann, "Siege of Ninety Six"
Cann, Marvin L. "War in the Backcountry: the Siege of Ninety Six, May 22–June 19, 1781." *South Carolina Historical Magazine* 72 (1971): 1–14.

Caruthers, *Revolutionary Incidents*
Caruthers, E. W. *Interesting Revolutionary Incidents: And Sketches of Character, Chiefly in the "Old North State."* Philadelphia, 1856.

Cashin, *King's Ranger*
Cashin, Edward J., Jr. *The King's Ranger: Thomas Brown and the American Revolution on the Southern Frontier.* Athens: University of Georgia Press, 1989.

Cashin and Robertson, *Augusta*
Cashin, Edward J., Jr., and Heard Robertson. *Augusta and the American Revolution: Events in the Georgia Back Country, 1773–1783.* Augusta: Richmond County Historical Society, 1975.

Chase, "Steuben"
Chase, Philander D. "Baron von Steuben in the War of Independence." Ph.D. diss., Duke University, 1973.

Chesney, "Journal"
"The Journal of Alexander Chesney, a South Carolina Loyalist in the Revolution and After." Edited by E. Alfred Jones. *The Ohio State University Bulletin* 26 (October 1921).

Clinton, *American Rebellion*
Clinton, Henry. *The American Rebellion: Sir Henry Clinton's Narrative of His Campaigns, 1775–82.* Edited by William B. Willcox with an appendix of original documents. New Haven: Yale University Press, 1954.

Coleman, *Revolution in Georgia*
Coleman, Kenneth. *The American Revolution in Georgia, 1763–1789.* Athens: University of Georgia Press, 1958.

Conrad, "Southern Campaign"
Conrad, Dennis M. "Nathanael Greene and the Southern Campaigns." Ph.D. diss., Duke University, 1979.

DAB
Dictionary of American Biography. Edited by Allen Johnson and

Dumas Malone. 21 vols. New York: Charles Scribner's Sons, 1928–36. 5 supplements: 1944, 1958, 1973, 1974, and 1977.

Dann, *Revolution Remembered*
The Revolution Remembered: Eyewitness Accounts of the War for Independence. Edited by John C. Dann. Chicago: University of Chicago Press, 1980.

Davies, *Documents*
Documents of the American Revolution, 1779–1780 (Colonial Office Series). Edited by K. G. Davies. Dublin: Irish University Press, 1972–.

DeMond, *N.C. Loyalists*
DeMond, Robert O. *The Loyalists of North Carolina during the Revolution.* Durham, N.C.: Duke University Press, 1940.

Dictionary of N.C. Biography
Dictionary of North Carolina Biography. Edited by William S. Powell. Chapel Hill: University of North Carolina Press, 1979–.

Draper Microfilm
Draper Manuscript Collection. 123 reels. Teaneck, N.J.: Chadwyck-Healey, 1980.

Dull, *French Navy*
Dull, Jonathan R. *The French Navy and American Independence: A Study of Arms and Diplomacy, 1774–1787.* Princeton: Princeton University Press, 1975.

Duncan, *Medical Men*
Duncan, Louis C. *Medical Men in the American Revolution, 1775–1783.* Carlisle Barracks, Pa.: Medical Field Service School, 1931.

Eckenrode, *Revolution in Virginia*
Eckenrode, H. J. *The Revolution in Virginia.* Boston: Houghton Mifflin Co., 1916.

Ewald, *Journal*
Ewald, Johann. *Diary of the American War: A Hessian Journal.* Translated and edited by Joseph P. Tustin. New Haven: Yale University Press, 1979.

Ferguson, "Pickens"
Ferguson, Clyde R. "General Andrew Pickens." Ph.D. diss., Duke University, 1960.

Fitzpatrick, *GW*
Washington, George. *The Writings of George Washington, from the Original Manuscript Sources, 1745–1799.* Edited by John C. Fitzpatrick. 39 vols. Washington: U.S. Government Printing Office, 1931–44.

Freeman, *GW*
Freeman, Douglas Southall. *George Washington.* 7 vols. The last volume by John C. Alexander and Mary W. Ashworth. New York: Charles Scribner's Sons, 1948–57.

Gibbes, *Documentary History*
> Gibbes, R. W. *Documentary History of the American Revolution: Chiefly in South Carolina, 1764–1782.* 3 vols. 1853–57. Reprint. Spartanburg, S.C.: The Reprint Co., 1972.

Gillett, *Medical Department*
> Gillett, Mary C. *The Army Medical Department, 1775–1818.* Washington: Center of Military History, U.S. Army, 1981.

Gordon, *History*
> Gordon, William. *The History of the Rise, Progress, and Establishment, of the Independence of the United States of America.* 4 vols. 1788. Reprint. Freeport, N.Y.: Books for Libraries Press, 1969.

Gottschalk, *Lafayette*
> Gottschalk, Louis R. *Lafayette and the Close of the American Revolution.* Chicago: University of Chicago Press, 1942.

Graham, *Morgan*
> Graham, James. *The Life of General Daniel Morgan.* New York, 1856.

Greene, *Greene*
> Greene, George Washington. *The Life of Nathanael Greene, Major-General in the Army of the Revolution.* 3 vols. 1871. Reprint. Boston and New York: Houghton, Mifflin and Co., 1897–1900.

Gregorie, *Sumter*
> Gregorie, Anne King. *Thomas Sumter.* Columbia, S.C.: R. L. Bryan Co., 1931.

GWG Transcript
> George Washington Greene Transcript.

Haiman, *Kosciuszko*
> Haiman, Miecislaus. *Kosciuszko in the American Revolution.* New York: Polish Institute of Arts and Sciences in America, 1943.

Heitman, *Register*
> Heitman, Francis B., comp. *Historical Register of Officers of the Continental Army during the War of the Revolution.* 1914. Reprint. With addenda by Robert H. Kelby. Baltimore: Genealogical Publishing Co., 1967.

Higginbotham, *Morgan*
> Higginbotham, Don. *Daniel Morgan, Revolutionary Rifleman.* Chapel Hill: University of North Carolina Press, 1961.

Idzerda, *Lafayette Papers*
> Lafayette, Marquis de. *Lafayette in the Age of the American Revolution: Selected Letters and Papers, 1776–90.* Edited by Stanley J. Idzerda et al. Ithaca: Cornell University Press, 1977–.

James, *Marion*
> James, William D. *A Sketch of the Life of Brig. Gen. Francis Marion and a History of His Brigade.* 1821. Reprint. Marietta, Ga.: Continental Book Co., 1948.

JCC
Journals of the Continental Congress, 1774–1789. Edited by Worthington C. Ford et al. 34 vols. Washington: U.S. Government Printing Office, 1904–37.

Johnson, Dictionary
Johnson, Samuel. A Dictionary of the English Language. 2 vols. 1755. Reprint. New York: AMS Press, 1967.

Johnson, Greene
Johnson, William. Life and Correspondence of Nathanael Greene, Major General of the Armies of the United States. 2 vols. Charleston, S.C., 1822.

Johnson, Traditions and Reminiscences
Johnson, Joseph. Traditions and Reminiscences Chiefly of the American Revolution in the South. Charleston, S.C.: Walker & James, 1851.

Kennett, French Forces
Kennett, Lee. The French Forces in America, 1780–1783. Westport, Conn.: Greenwood Press, 1977.

Kirkland and Kennedy, Camden
Kirkland, Thomas J., and Robert M. Kennedy. Historic Camden. Part One: Colonial and Revolutionary. Columbia, S.C.: The State Co., 1905.

Klein, Unification of a Slave State
Klein, Rachel N. Unification of a Slave State: The Rise of the Planter Class in the South Carolina Backcountry, 1760–1808. Chapel Hill: University of North Carolina Press, 1990.

Lambert, South Carolina Loyalists
Lambert, Robert Stansbury. South Carolina Loyalists in the American Revolution. Columbia: University of South Carolina Press, 1987.

Lee, Campaign of 1781
Lee, Henry (1787–1837). The Campaign of 1781 in the Carolinas; with Remarks Historical and Critical on Johnson's Life of Greene. 1824. Reprint. Spartanburg, S.C.: The Reprint Co., 1975.

Lee, Memoirs
Lee, Henry (1756–1818). Memoirs of the War in the Southern Department of the United States. 2 vols. Philadelphia, 1812.

Lipscomb, "S.C. Battles"
Lipscomb, Terry W. "South Carolina Revolutionary Battles." In Place Names in South Carolina 23–38 (1976–81).

Lossing, Field Book
Lossing, Benson J. The Pictorial Field-Book of the Revolution. 2 vols. New York, 1860.

McCall, History of Georgia
McCall, Hugh. The History of Georgia: Containing Brief Sketches of the Most Remarkable Events up to the Present Day (1784). 1811–16;

1909. Reprint of 1909 ed. Atlanta: Cherokee Publishing Co., 1969.

McCrady, *S.C. in the Revolution*
McCrady, Edward. *The History of South Carolina in the Revolution, 1780–1783*. New York: The Macmillan Co., 1902.

McHenry Letters
A Sidelight on History: Being the Letters of James McHenry, Aide-de-camp of the Marquis de Lafayette, to Thomas Sim Lee, Governor of Maryland, Written during the Yorktown Campaign, 1781. 1931. Reprint. New York: The New York Times and Arno Press, 1971.

Mackenzie, *Diary*
Mackenzie, Frederick. *The Diary of Frederick Mackenzie*. 2 vols. Cambridge: Harvard University Press, 1930.

Mackenzie, *Strictures*
Mackenzie, Roderick. *Strictures on Lt.-Colonel Tarleton's History of the Campaigns of 1780 and 1781, in the Southern Provinces of North America*. London, 1789.

Mackesy, *War for America*
Mackesy, Piers. *The War for America, 1775–1783*. Cambridge: Harvard University Press, 1964.

Madison, *Papers*
Madison, James. *The Papers of James Madison*. Edited by William T. Hutchinson et al. Chicago: University of Chicago Press; Charlottesville: University Press of Virginia, 1962–. Publication by the University Press of Virginia began with vol. 11.

Mitchell, *Hamilton*
Mitchell. Broadus. *Alexander Hamilton: Youth to Maturity, 1775–1788*. New York: The Macmillan Co., 1957.

Morris, *Papers*
Morris, Robert. *The Papers of Robert Morris, 1781–1784*. Edited by E. James Ferguson et al. Pittsburgh: University of Pittsburgh Press, 1973–.

Moultrie, *Memoirs*
Moultrie, William. *Memoirs of the American Revolution, So Far as It Related to the States of North and South Carolina and Georgia*. 1802. Reprint. 2 vols. in 1. New York: New York Times and Arno Press, 1968.

NCSR
The State Records of North Carolina. Edited by Walter Clark. 26 vols. Raleigh, 1886–1907.

Nelson, *Gates*
Nelson, Paul David. *General Horatio Gates: A Biography*. Baton Rouge: Louisiana State University Press, 1966.

Nelson, *Wayne*
Nelson, Paul David. *Anthony Wayne: Soldier of the Early Republic.* Bloomington: Indiana University Press, 1985.
O'Donnell, *Southern Indians*
O'Donnell, James H., III. *Southern Indians in the American Revolution.* Knoxville: University of Tennessee Press, 1973.
OED
Oxford English Dictionary
Palmer, *Steuben*
Palmer, John McAuley. *General von Steuben.* 1937. Reprint. Port Washington, N.Y.: Kennikat Press, 1966.
PCC
Papers of the Continental Congress. Unless otherwise noted, all citations are from Records Group 360, M247, National Archives and Records Administration, Washington.
PRO
Cornwallis Papers, Public Record Office, London.
Rankin, *N.C. Continentals*
Rankin, Hugh F. *The North Carolina Continentals.* Chapel Hill: University of North Carolina Press, 1971.
Rankin, *Swamp Fox*
Rankin, Hugh F. *Francis Marion: The Swamp Fox.* New York: Thomas Y. Crowell Co., 1973.
Records of Georgia
The Revolutionary Records of the State of Georgia. Compiled by Allen D. Chandler. 3 vols. Atlanta: Franklin-Turner Co., 1908.
Records of the Moravians
Records of the Moravians in North Carolina. Edited by Adelaide L. Fries. 5 vols. Raleigh: North Carolina Historical Commission and North Carolina Department of Archives, 1922–41.
Risch, *Supplying*
Risch, Erna. *Supplying Washington's Army.* Washington: U.S. Government Printing Office, 1981.
Robinson, *Davie*
Robinson, Blackwell P. *William R. Davie.* Chapel Hill: University of North Carolina Press, 1957.
Schenck, *N.C., 1780–81*
Schenck, David. *North Carolina, 1780-'81. Being a History of the Invasion of the Carolinas by the British Army under Lord Cornwallis in 1780-'81.* Raleigh, 1889.
SCHGM
South Carolina Historical and Genealogical Magazine/South Carolina Historical Magazine

Selby, *Revolution in Virginia*
  Selby, John E. *The Revolution in Virginia, 1775–1783.*
  Williamsburg: Colonial Williamsburg Foundation, 1989.
Seymour, "Journal"
  Seymour, William. "A Journal of the Southern Expedition, 1780–
  1783." *Pennsylvania Magazine of History and Biography* 7 (1883):
  286–98, 377–94.
Simcoe, *Military Journal*
  Simcoe, John Graves. *Simcoe's Military Journal.* 1784. Reprint.
  Toronto: Baxter Publishing Co., 1962.
Smith, *Letters*
  Letters of Delegates to Congress, 1774–1789. Edited by Paul H.
  Smith et al. Washington: Library of Congress, 1976–.
Stedman, *History of the American War*
  Stedman, Charles. *The History of the Origin, Progress and Termina-
  tion of the American War.* 2 vols. London, 1794.
Steuart, *Maryland Line*
  Steuart, Reiman. *A History of the Maryland Line in the Revolutionary
  War, 1775–1783.* N.p.: Society of the Cincinnati of Maryland, 1969.
Steuben Microfilm
  The Papers of General Friedrich Wilhelm von Steuben. Edited by
  Edith von Zemensky. 7 reels. Millwood, N.Y.: Kraus Interna-
  tional Publications, 1982.
Stevens, *Clinton-Cornwallis Controversy*
  *The Campaign in Virginia, 1781. An Exact Reprint of Six Rare Pam-
  phlets on the Clinton-Cornwallis Controversy with Very Numerous Im-
  portant Unpublished Manuscript Notes.* Edited by Benjamin
  Franklin Stevens. 2 vols. London, 1888.
Tarleton, *Campaigns*
  Tarleton, [Banastre]. *A History of the Campaigns of 1780 and 1781,
  in the Southern Provinces of North America.* 1787. Reprint. [New
  York]: Arno Press, 1968.
Virginia, Council of State, *Journals*
  Journals of the Council of the State of Virginia [1776–88]. Edited by
  H. R. McIlwaine et al. 4 vols. Richmond: Division of Purchase
  and Print, 1931–67.
"Von Bose Journal"
  "Journal of the Honourable Hessian Infantry Regiment Von
  Bose." Typescript and translation of the original by John Muller,
  courtesy of Guilford Courthouse National Military Park.
Waddell, *New Hanover County*
  Waddell, Alfred Moore. *A History of New Hanover County and the
  Lower Cape Fear Region, 1723–1800.* 1901. Reprint. Bowie, Md.:
  Heritage Books, 1989.

Ward, *Delaware*
   Ward, Christopher L. *The Delaware Continentals, 1776–1783.*
   Wilmington: Historical Society of Delaware, 1941.
Ward, *War*
   Ward, Christopher. *The War of the Revolution.* Edited by John
   Richard Alden. 2 vols. New York: The Macmillan Co., 1952.
Ward, *Weedon*
   Ward, Harry M. *Duty, Honor, or Country: General George Weedon
   and the American Revolution.* Philadelphia: American Philosophi-
   cal Society, 1979.
Ward and Greer, *Richmond*
   Ward, Harry M., and Harold E. Greer, Jr. *Richmond during the
   Revolution, 1775–83.* Charlottesville: University Press of Virginia,
   1977.
Waring, *Fighting Elder*
   Waring, Alice N. *The Fighting Elder: Andrew Pickens, 1739–1817.*
   Columbia: University of South Carolina Press, 1962.
Wharton, *Revolutionary Diplomatic Correspondence*
   U.S. Department of State. *The Revolutionary Diplomatic Correspon-
   dence of the United States.* Edited by Francis Wharton. 6 vols.
   Washington, 1889.
Wickwire, *Cornwallis*
   Wickwire, Franklin, and Mary Wickwire. *Cornwallis: The Ameri-
   can Adventure.* Boston: Houghton Mifflin Co., 1970.
Willcox, *Clinton*
   Willcox, William B. *Portrait of a General: Sir Henry Clinton in the
   War of Independence.* New York: Alfred A. Knopf, 1964.
Wright, *Continental Army*
   Wright, Robert K., Jr. *The Continental Army.* Washington: Center
   of Military History, U.S. Army, 1983.
WRMS
   War Department Collection of Revolutionary War Records, Rec-
   ord Group 93, National Archives and Records Administration,
   Washington.

A GLOSSARY OF MILITARY TERMS

ABATIS	A barrier of felled trees, with limbs pointing toward the enemy, usually temporary.
ACCOUNT	A financial record.
ACCOUTREMENTS	Soldiers' outfits, usually not including clothing or weapons.
ARTILLERY PARK	An encampment for artillery.
ARTILLERY TRAIN	An army's collection of cannon and material for firing them.
BARBETTE	A platform or mound of earth for artillery, usually separated from a main fortification.
BASTION	An outward projection of a fort enabling gunners to fire along the wall of a fort at an enemy.
BATEAU	A light, flat-bottomed river craft with raked bow and stern.
BATTALION	See Regiment.
BOMB, BOOMBE	A powder-filled iron sphere that is fired from a mortar and fused to explode after falling.
BREASTWORK	An improvised fortification, usually consisting of a trench and earthen barrier.
BRIGADE	A formation of two or more regiments.
BROADSIDE	The firing of all artillery on one side of a warship.
CANISTER	A tin cylinder containing metal balls that scatter when fired from a cannon.
CARCASS	An incendiary device fired from a cannon at wooden structures or ships.
CARTOUCHE	Cartridge made of a paper cylinder, containing powder and lead ball.
CHANDELIER	Wooden frame filled with fascines, for protection where earth could not be dug.
CHEVAL-DE-FRISE	Used usually in the plural; a portable defense barrier bristling with long, iron-tipped wooden spikes. An underwater version consisted of a rock-filled wooden frame, on which sharpened timbers were set at an angle to rip the hull of a vessel.
CIRCUMVALLATION	Works made by besiegers around a besieged place facing outward, to protect their camp from enterprises of the enemy.

COLOURMAN	Traditionally, a soldier who assisted in preparing a new camp site; also often used for one who was responsible for disagreeable cleaning and sanitation tasks.
DIVISION	A unit of two or more brigades.
DRAGOON	Once a mounted infantryman, by 1775 the term was used interchangeably with cavalryman.
DURHAM BOAT	A shallow-draft boat developed to transport iron ore. Varying in length from forty to sixty feet and about eight feet in width, it could carry a company of troops and was usually poled.
EMBRASURE	An opening through which cannon were fired.
ENFILADE	To sweep with gunfire along a line of works or troops from end to end.
EQUIPAGE	Camp equipage is equipment that is needed for an encampment. Field equipage is equipment needed to facilitate the movement of an army.
FASCINE	A firmly tied bundle of wooden sticks or small limbs.
FATIGUE	Manual and menial duty performed by troops.
FIREBOAT	A vessel filled with combustibles for burning enemy vessels.
FLECHE	An outwork of a fort, shaped like an arrow, the point toward the enemy.
FOSSE	A ditch or dike surrounding a fortified place.
FRIGATE	A two-decked warship built for swift sailing, mounting twenty to thirty-eight guns on the upper deck.
GABION	A cylindrical wicker basket to be filled with earth for use in fortifications.
GLACIS	A bank sloping away from a fortification.
GRAPE-SHOT	Iron balls, held together in a rack or bag, that scatter when discharged from a cannon.
GRASSHOPPER	A field carriage for a three-pounder. It had no wheels, but was transported on the backs of horses or in a wagon. Two long tail pieces, placed at an angle from each other, served to absorb recoil and probably gave the carriage its name.
GRENADE	A hand-thrown metal device that exploded when the lighted fuse reached the powder inside.
GRENADIERS	Once hurlers of grenades, by 1775 an elite corps.

GUN	Although technically used to describe a cannon, the term was also regularly used in America for a musket or rifle.
INVALIDS	Disabled soldiers who were assigned to limited duties.
JÄGER	German light infantry chosen for their marksmanship with the German rifle (not the German-American long-barreled rifle).
LABORATORY	A place for the manufacture of arms and ammunition; an arsenal.
LIGHT INFANTRY	Lightly equipped, highly mobile troops.
MARÉCHAUSSÉE	Mounted provosts, responsible for policing a camp.
MARQUEE	A canvas tent designed especially for officers; also, a cover for another tent.
MATROSS	Assistant to an artillery gunner.
MORTAR	A short-barreled cannon used for lobbing shells, bombs, etc., over an obstacle.
MUSQUETEER	Soldier armed with a musket.
ORDNANCE	Military equipment and supplies.
OUTWORK	A defensive work outside a fort.
PALISADE	Timbers set in the ground, close together and sharpened at the top.
PAROLE	A prisoner's oath on being freed that he will not bear arms until exchanged.
PETTY AUGER	An open, flat-bottomed boat, generally two-masted, carrying some thirty tons.
PICKET, PICQUET	An outguard to warn of an enemy's approach.
PIKE	Wooden spear of varying length, with a steel point.
PIONEERS	Men responsible for digging trenches, repairing roads, preparing fortifications, etc.
PLATFORM	A wooden bed upon which a cannon was placed.
PRIVATEER	A privately owned armed vessel commissioned to capture enemy merchantmen as prizes.
RECRUIT	A newly enlisted or drafted member of the army; to rehabilitate, particularly horses.
REGIMENT	During this period, regiment and battalion were used interchangeably. Usually composed of eight companies and at full strength numbering from 520 to 780 men.
RETURN	A listing of men or materials.
REVETMENT	A wall to sustain an earthen rampart or the side of a ditch.

ROW GALLEY
: A low, flat vessel with one deck, varying in length up to 130 feet, manned by oarsmen and carrying several small cannon.

SCHOONER
: A small fore-and-aft rigged vessel with two masts.

SCOW
: A flat-bottomed boat with square ends.

SHIP
: A large sailing vessel with three masts.

SIX-POUNDER
: Artillery piece so designated because it could fire an iron ball weighing six pounds; these guns were low angle, relatively high velocity, were about 509 pounds in weight, and had a bore of 3.66 inches.

SLOOP
: Small, one-masted vessel.

SNOW
: Generally a two-masted vessel with a small mast behind the main mast.

SPONTOON
: A spear used as a weapon and as a badge of rank.

SUBALTERN
: Commissioned officer below the rank of lieutenant.

SUTLER
: A provisioner for an army camp who operates for profit.

THREE-POUNDER
: Artillery piece so designated because it could fire an iron ball weighing three pounds; these guns were low angle, relatively high velocity, were about 286 pounds in weight, and had a bore of 2.91 inches.

TRANSPORT
: A vessel for carrying troops.

VEDETTE
: A mounted sentinel stationed in advance of the pickets.

NATHANAEL GREENE CHRONOLOGY

1781	29 March	NG ends his pursuit of Lord Cornwallis's army in North Carolina and prepares to lead his army into South Carolina.
	29 March	The Virginia Executive Council votes to send a militia reinforcement to NG but later rescinds its order after a British army commanded by Gen. William Phillips invades the interior of Virginia.
	6 April	Washington orders the Marquis de Lafayette to join NG. Lafayette will proceed only as far as Virginia, where he will take command of the American forces opposing the British invasion.
	6–19 April	NG's army marches from Deep River, N.C., to Camden, S.C., but finds the post at Camden too strong to storm.
	7 April	Cornwallis's army, in retreat since the battle of Guilford Court House on 15 March, reaches Wilmington, N.C.
	18–30 April	Phillips, who brought 2,000 troops to Virginia on 26 March, moves up the James River, conducting raids and advancing to the vicinity of Richmond. Finding Richmond defended by Lafayette, he sails back down the river.
	23 April	Gen. Francis Marion and Col. Henry Lee capture Ft. Watson, S.C., the first British fort taken in the "War of the Posts."
	24–25 April	Cornwallis's army leaves Wilmington, marching north toward a junction with Phillips.
	25 April	Lord Rawdon defeats NG in the battle of Hobkirk's Hill but suffers heavy casualties and soon decides to abandon Camden.
	8 May	Agreement is reached on a general exchange of prisoners in the Southern Department.

10 May	Rawdon evacuates Camden, retreating toward Charleston.
11 May	Gen. Thomas Sumter captures the British post at Orangeburg, S.C.
12 May	Ft. Motte, S.C., falls to Marion and Lee.
13 May	Phillips dies of typhoid fever; Gen. Benedict Arnold succeeds him.
15 May	Lee negotiates the surrender of Ft. Granby, S.C., angering Sumter, who had begun the siege of the post.
17 May	NG approves Sumter's plan to use confiscated slaves as a bonus for enlisting in Sumter's South Carolina state troops.
20 May	Cornwallis's army joins Arnold's in Petersburg, Va.
22 May	NG begins the siege of Ninety Six, S.C.
26 May	Pennsylvania Continental troops commanded by Gen. Anthony Wayne march south from York, Pa., with orders to join NG.
28 May	The British garrison evacuates Georgetown, S.C., after Marion arrives to begin a siege.
3 June	Col. John Harris Cruger rejects NG's demand to surrender Ninety Six. A British fleet brings reinforcements to Charleston the same day.
5 June	Gen. Andrew Pickens and Lee capture the last of three British forts in and near Augusta, Ga. The Loyalist commander of one of the forts is murdered soon afterward while a prisoner.
5 June	At Point of Fork, Va., Baron Steuben abandons quantities of stores to British raiders.
7 June	Rawdon, now reinforced, marches from Charleston to lift the siege of Ninety Six.
9 June	NG sends Joseph Clay to Augusta to reestablish civil government in Georgia.
10 June	Wayne's Pennsylvania troops join Lafayette; they will remain in Virginia.
16–20 June	After destroying supplies and other property in and around Richmond, Cornwallis's army retreats toward the coast of Virginia.

19 June	NG makes an unsuccessful attempt to storm Ninety Six, after efforts to delay Rawdon or assemble a force to oppose him had failed. The siege is ended.
21–27 June	Rawdon reaches Ninety Six. He briefly pursues NG but then returns to implement his plan of evacuating the post.
29 June	Rawdon marches toward the Congarees, leaving part of his force at Ninety Six. NG issues orders to intercept Col. Alexander Stewart, who is bringing reinforcements to Rawdon.
1 July	NG decides to pursue Rawdon, who reaches Ft. Granby on this date.
4 July	Unable to rendezvous with Stewart at Ft. Granby, Rawdon moves toward Orangeburg.
6 July	In Virginia, Wayne narrowly avoids a trap set by Cornwallis in the battle of Green Spring Farm.
7 July	Stewart eludes Marion and joins Rawdon at Orangeburg. Finding that the combined British force is too strong to attack, NG soon decides to suspend his campaign and move his army into a camp of repose in the High Hills of the Santee.
10 July	Cruger evacuates Ninety Six, taking both the garrison and the Loyalist families from the area with him.

THE PAPERS OF
General Nathanael Greene

To the Board of War

Camp on Deep River

Gentlemen   Col Ramseys [N.C.] March 30th 1781[1]

It gives me pain that things are in such a disagreeable train in this
quarter that I cannot furnish the Board with regular returns. But my
situation has been such, and the confusion which has prevail'd has
been so great that it has been utterly out of my power. I shall take every
measure in my power to keep the Board regularly informed of the state
of things in this quarter; but the department is so extensive and the
operations so various in the different States & so distinct one from
another as well as the force employed so fluctuating and uncertain &
the demand for Stores so extensive from the nature of the service & the
Militia orderd into field from such different Authority and supplied
through such different channels, that it is utterly impossible to tell
what force there is[,] how employed or how supplied either with
provisions or Stores, nor can I tell what we have on hand. I have taken
every possible step to prevent the issues of Stores coming for the use of
the Southern Army from being issued at the different posts on the
route but I have not been able to effect it.[2] The demands have been so
pressing and the difficulties attending the service so great that no
general arrangment could be made but that at times has been subject
to partial inroads; and I fear will be the case until a more permanent
and respectable Army can be formed for the protection of the Southern
States. The Service here is infinitely more severe than to the northward and the consumption of stores unavoidably much greater &
besides which they are subject to much greater embezzlements. I find
it has been the custom heretofore in the Southern States to employ
generally for equiping the Militia both Continental and State Stores
indiscriminately and the waste which has arose from this mode as well
as from the difficulty of recovering the Stores delivered into the hands
of the Militia have renderd the consumption and waste almost incredible. This I have indeavord to check as much as possible; and shall
continue so to do. But while the force employed in the field is orderd
out from such different Authorities great irregularities must and will
prevail.

The moment I took command in the Southern department nay
before I arrivd at Head Quarters I gave written instructions to General
Gist for Maryland and Delaware[,] Baron Stuben for Virginia[,] General Sumner for North Carolinia to call the officers together belonging
to each of those States and for them when convened to determin who
were to continue in service and who to retire as supernumerary and
that business should be conducted agreeable to the resolution of Congress and that reports should be made to the Board of War and to me.[3]

[3]

But neither has yet reported.[4] After I got to Camp I wrote in to Charlestown to General Moultrie to collect the same account of the officers belonging to South Carolinia and Georgia officers to which I have recievd no answer.[5] The moment I get the reports they shall be forwarded to the Board.

The circumstances of the Southern States with respect to men are so widely different from those of the Northern States that it is utterly impossible to get men by the same scale of pay as they can be had to the Northward and all the Staff business in the Q M Generals department as well as the Commisaries will be at a stand unless the heads of those departments have a latitude of discretion subject to the controul of the commanding officer.[6] We are now distressed exceedingly on this very subject. If the operations here continue as active as they have been the Soldiers will require a double quantity of Shoes and indeed almost every other article of cloathing. Our poor fellows are now naked and destitute of almost every thing necessary to render them comfortable. I hope the Board will forward us all the Cloathing that can possibly be spard from the Northern Army. Stores of every kind is wanting and particularly Military Stores. Col Harrison has had instructions to make a return of the Military Stores in this department to the Board as well of the articles on hand as those wanted; which I hope will be forwarded accordingly.[7] Inclosed are the returns of the Army.[8] The Military operations in this quarter I must beg leave to refer the Board to my letters to Congress. I have the honor to be with great respect your most obed   N GREENE

N B Hallifax in North Carolinia is appointed for the place of rendezvous for the Invalids in the Southern Department which I hope will meet the Boards approbation.[9]

ADfS (MiU-C).

1. NG's army was camped at the mill of Col. Ambrose Ramsey on Deep River, near the mouth of Rocky River; it would remain there until 6 April.

2. See, for example, NG to Gen. Jethro Sumner, 19 January, and Capt. William Pierce to Maj. John Mazaret, 13 March, both above (vol. 7: 148, 429). NG discussed the problem further in a letter to the board dated 2 May, below.

3. See NG's letters to Gen. Mordecai Gist, 10 November 1780; to Baron Steuben, 20 November; and to Sumner, 15 December, all above (vol. 6: 472, 496–97, 580).

4. Gen. William Smallwood discussed the lack of an arrangement of Maryland officers in his letter of 4 May, below. Delaware did nothing about reorganizing its line until summer. (Wright, *Continental Army*, p. 273) Steuben did not complete an arrangement of the Virginia line until 21 April. (Steuben's General Orders, 21 April, Steuben Microfilm) Sumner had sent NG an arrangement on 27 January and was bemused when NG found it inadequate. (See NG to Sumner, 18 February, above [vol. 7: 312].)

5. NG's request to Gen. William Moultrie has not been found.

6. The board replied to NG's request on 11 May, below.

7. Neither NG's instructions to Col. Charles Harrison nor the return of military stores he was to prepare has been found. In one of his first letters to NG, Capt. John Pryor, who

had been appointed commissary of military stores by Steuben, wrote that he would try to collect returns of military stores in Virginia. (See Pryor to NG, 11 May, below.) This suggests that Harrison had not completed a return.

8. The return has not been found.

9. The board's instructions regarding the corps of invalids is in its letter to NG of 2 January, above (vol. 7: 41).

*   *   *

¶ [TO COLONEL WILLIAM DAVIES. From "Col Ramseys Deep River," N.C., 30 March 1781. NG has received Davies's letter "of the 20th," which accompanied the "warm[,] friendly and respectful" address of the Virginia Continental Officers.[1] He disagrees with the officers' view of Gen. [George] Weedon, whose situation they "altogether misunderstood." General officers belong "to the Continental line at large," so Virginia has no more claim to Weedon than any other state.[2] Moreover, as NG remembers it, the decision of the board of general officers [in 1778] "was not to the prejudice" of Weedon but was simply that Congress "could not delegate powers to change the standing of officers of the same grade." NG believes that Congress has never had this power, nor has any "potentate in Europe ever exercisd" it.[3] His sentiments, however, will have "no influence on the matter," as he will be governed by the decisions of Congress and Washington, to whom the address was sent.[4] ADfS (MiU-C) 2 pp.]

1. Davies's letter of 20 February is above (vol. 7: 322). The address, in which the officers sought to have Weedon removed from the Continental service, is discussed there.

2. Davies replied on 18 April, below.

3. The general officers' report at the time Weedon left the service in 1778 did not explicitly deal with the question of Congress altering the seniority of officers. From a letter that he wrote Weedon at the time, though, it is clear that NG saw congressional interference as the crux of the issue. (See above, General Officers to Washington, 4 March 1778, and NG to Weedon, 27 April 1778 [vol. 2: 297, 362–64].)

4. The Virginia officers sent a copy of their address to Washington, who refused to give an opinion, replying that it was "a matter intirely dependant upon the pleasure of Congress." (Washington to Steuben, 1 May, Fitzpatrick, *GW*, 22: 19) Davies also sent a copy to Congress, which took no action. (PCC, item 78, vol. 7: 367, DNA; Ward, *Weedon*, p. 174)

*   *   *

To General Mordecai Gist[1]

D[r] Sir   Head Quarters Deep River [N.C.] March 30th 1781

I had the pleasure to receive your letter of the 14th ultimo, and from the measures which the Assembly of Maryland had taken, to raise their quota of regular Troops, expected that before this time a sufficient number would have been collected and equiped to form a respectable detachment for the southern Army, but from a late account which has been communicated to me, I learn that as late as the 13th inst no progress was made in that very necessary business.[2] The state of the

Treasury may be calculated to answer the exigences of War, if the powers of Government are exerted with proper energy; & however unwilling the Legislature may be to press the importance of this Truth upon the inhabitants it is neither impossible nor improbable that a visit from the enemy may bring conviction to the door of your Capitol, & expose the State to ten times the expence that would have secured her Tranquility by keeping the War at a distance. Means are not wanting, & measures must of necessity be taken to prosecute the War vigorously. Your activity affords me a hope that nothing will be deficient on the part of the Military. Let your detachment be well equiped, armed & officered before they leave the State, otherwise they will be incumbrances to the Army.

The want of officers in the Maryland Line, has been of very material prejudice to the service this campaign. If the arrangement is not settled, you will please to order five or six Captains and twice that number of subalterns, to come to Camp with the next Detachment, which I hope will not be long coming; indeed it would not be improper for a much greater number of Officers of every Rank, to join the Southern department of the Army, as those who have served the preceeding Campaign & the present, are almost destitute of every article of cloathing & convenience, and by their patient perseverance deserve to be indulged if the service would possibly permit. Your presence here will be necessary as soon as you have put our military matters in a proper channel in the State, and I hope you will not suffer yourself to be delayed by any impediments, that the recruiting business may meet with.[3]

Your conduct respecting the Artillery Company under Captain Brown has my entire approbation, I hope the General Assembly are convinced of the impropriety of interfering their civil authority with military operations.[4]

We rejoyce that the confederation is completed & confirmed by the compliance of the State of Maryland.[5] It deprives the enemy of one vain hope & will undoubtedly strengthen our credit with our friends.

I thank you for your good wishes and accept them as a tribute of your Esteem. Want of time obliges me to refer you to the accounts published by Order of Congress for information respecting our southern operations. I am with sentiments of the highest respect & esteem my Dear Sir Your most Obedient & most Humble Servant

NATH GREENE

LS (MdHi).

1. Gist was in charge of recruiting men and forwarding supplies from Maryland and Delaware. (See NG to Gist, 10 November 1780, above [vol. 6: 472].)

2. The source of the "late account" is not known.

3. Gist replied on 28 May, below, that he would march the Maryland recruits to NG's

army in "a few weeks." These troops did not leave the state until late August, when they were sent to join Washington's army in the siege of Yorktown, Va. (Fitzpatrick, *GW*, 23: 109, 134)

4. For more on Capt. William Brown's decision to delay his artillery company at the request of Maryland officials, see Gist to NG, 14 February, above (vol. 7: 287–88).

5. On Maryland's ratification of the Articles of Confederation, see William Sharpe to NG, 30 January, above (vol. 7: 223, 224n).

To Catharine Greene

Col Ramseys Deep River North Carolinia
My dear   March 30th 1781
The time approaches which you have fixed for setting out for the Southern World. Beleive me my dear this is a land of trouble and your humanity cannot bear the shocking scenes to which you will be exposd nor is your constitution and delicasy fitted to the rude manners and hard fare which you will meet with on this side Virginia. Nothing would give me greater pleasure than the happiness of seeing [you] could I be indulgd without exposing you to every thing that is shocking to humanity. I tremble when I reflect on your determination; and was you fully acquainted with the real situation of things in this Quarter I am confident you would never think of exposing your self to such rude attacks as you will frequently meet with on your jou[r]ney. In Virginia you will be receivd with politeness; but if you attempt to come farther you will have great reason to repent it. Could you be content at home, I am perswaded you would be much better of[f] than you will be to the Southard. But as I promised to leave you at liberty, I shall say nothing farther on the subject.

Should you come on let me know it by every opportunity, and how far you propose to come.[1] Yours aff

AL (MiU-C).
1. Catharine Greene did not set off from Rhode Island to join NG until December 1781.

To Samuel Huntington, President of the Continental Congress

Head Quarters Col° Ramsays
Sir   Deep River [N.C.], March 30th, 1781
I wrote your Excellency on the 23ᵈ from Buffaloe Creek.[1] Since which we have been in pursuit of the Enemy, and tho' without Cannon I was determined to bring them to Action again.[2] As most of the Inhabitants between Pedee and Haw River are disaffected we found the greatest difficulty in procuring supplies and obtaining intelligence. Our reconnoitering Parties were frequently shot down by the Tories, while they

furnished the Enemy with a plenty of every thing, and doubtless gave them good intelligence.

On the 27th we arrived at Rigdens Ford twelve Miles above this, expecting the Enemy would have crossed the Day before and that we should have found the River fordable, and that we could have fallen in with the Enemy at the junction of the Roads 12 miles beyond the ford. But on my arrival there I found the Enemy had not crossed, but still lay at Ramsays Mill, from which I expected they meant to wait an attack. I left our Baggage on the ground and put the Army in motion without loss of time. But we found the Enemy had crossed some Hours before our arrival, and with such precipitation that they left their dead unburied on the ground.[3] The want of provision and the greater part of the Virginia Militia's time of service being out prevented our further pursuit. Our Men had suffered so much for the want of provisions that many of them fainted on the march. The Enemy are on their route to Cross Creek, and Wilmington.[4]

I have it from good authority that the Enemy suffered in the Battle of Guilford 633 exclusive of Officers, and most of their principal Officers were killed and wounded.[5] They have met with a defeat in a victory.[6]

On Monday all the Virginia Militia return home, and once more I shall be left with a handfull of Men exposed to a superior force, and be obliged to seek security in a flight.[7] These are some of the disagreable effects of a temporary Army. The greatest advantages are often lost by the Troops disbanding at the most critical moment. Never was an Army in greater distress than the British, they were loaded with their wounded, and must have fallen a sacrifice had not the Tories given them support. Many have joined the Enemy, and many have fallen off.[8] Nothing but blood and slaughter have prevailed among the Whigs and Tories, and their inveteracy against each other, must if it continues depopulate this Country. We have been exposed to incredible difficulties in subsisting the Army, and the manner of doing it has been distressing to many of the Inhabitants.[9]

I hope when the difficulties are taken into consideration which I have had to encounter it will appear I have done every thing which could be expected from a Person in my situation.

It will be impossible to support the southern War with Militia, the obstruction to business and the waste attending the service will soon put it out of the power of the States to make farther exertions. Virginia has made great exertions upon the present occasion, and the spirit of the Inhabitants does them the greatest credit.

It gives me great pleasure to hear the confederation is compleated and have published it in general orders agreable to the order of Congress.[10]

I do myself the honor to transmit to Congress a copy of a Letter which I received from General Lillington, containing an account of an Action which happened at the Great Bridge on the 9th between a detachment of the Enemy from Wilmington, and the Troops under his command.[11]

Inclosed is also a copy of a Proclamation issued by Lord Cornwallis after the Battle of Guilford. His sudden retreat must render the proclamation rediculous.[12]

Since we have recrossed the Dan River we have taken at different times upwards of a hundred and twenty Prisoners and several Officers.

By late accounts from Charles Town I learn the Enemy have droped their scheme of raising two Negroes Regiments, and are turning their whole attention towards the Militia, who they are endeavoring to engage by every means in their power.[13]

From the support which Congress promise me I flatter myself I shall be able to baffle all the Enemies attempts for the subjugation of these States if the States themselves will but heartily second the measures of Congress. Most of our Men are naked for want of Overalls. Indeed they are destitute of all kind of Cloathing and the operations here are so exceedingly severe that the Men wear out more than double the usual quantity of Cloathing. I have the honor to be with the greatest respect Your Excellencys most obedient & most humble servant

NATH GREENE

P.S. We found 70 of our Wounded in the hands of the Enemy. Except these they have taken but few Prisoners, not so many as we took of theirs notwithstanding they kept the ground.

LS (PCC, item 155, vol. 2: 17, DNA).

1. NG's letter of 23 March is above (vol. 7: 464–65).

2. NG's artillery, consisting of four six-pounders, had been captured at the battle of Guilford Court House. (See NG to Huntington, 16 March, above [vol. 7: 435].)

3. Banastre Tarleton later wrote that Lord Cornwallis halted his army at Ramsey's "for the benefit of the wounded, and to complete a bridge over Deep river." (Tarleton, *Campaigns,* p. 279) A rudimentary bridge, constructed during the two days that the British remained at Ramsey's, allowed Cornwallis to cross the rain-swollen river as NG's army drew near. The bridge was then partially destroyed to delay pursuit. (Caruthers, *Revolutionary Incidents,* pp. 182–84; "Von Bose Journal," p. 53)

4. Cornwallis had not intended to march to Wilmington but discovered upon reaching Cross Creek on 30 March that Maj. James Craig had been unable to open a supply line up the Cape Fear River or to send the supplies that Cornwallis's army needed. Cornwallis then decided to march to Wilmington, some ninety miles southeast of Cross Creek. He arrived on 7 April. ("Von Bose Journal," p. 54; Cornwallis to Lord George Germain, 18 April, PRO 30/11/5)

5. Cornwallis reported his casualties as 532 killed, wounded, and missing. (PRO 30/11/103) His army suffered heavy losses among its officers, officially listing five killed and twenty-four wounded, some mortally. (Ibid.)

6. NG's opinion that Cornwallis had suffered a "defeat in a victory" was shared by contemporary British observers. Charles Stedman, Cornwallis's quartermaster, later

described Guilford Court House as a victory of "the most honorable kind," but wrote that "the expense at which it was obtained rendered it of no utility." (Stedman, *History of the American War*, p. 344) Charles Fox reportedly said in Parliament that "another such victory would destroy the British army." (Quoted in Henry S. Commager and Richard B. Morris, eds., *The Spirit of 'Seventy-six: the Story of the American Revolution as Told by Participants*, 2 vols. [Indianapolis: Bobbs-Merrill, 1958], 2: 1160)

7. NG was not "obliged to seek security in a flight." As seen in his letter to Washington of 29 March, above, he was planning to "carry the War immediately into South Carolina." (Vol. 7: 481)

8. Cornwallis wrote Sir Henry Clinton on 10 April that during his retreat from Guilford to Cross Creek, "Many of the inhabitants rode into camp, shook me by the hand, said they were glad to see us and hear that we had beat Greene, and then rode home again, for I could not get one hundred men in all the Regulators' country to stay with us even as militia." (Davies, *Documents*, 20: 107)

9. Henry Lee would later recall that the army was "without money to purchase" supplies and thus "depended upon compulsory collection from the country through which" it marched. (Lee, *Memoirs*, 1: 362)

10. On the adoption of the Articles of Confederation, see William Sharpe to NG, 30 January, above (vol. 7: 223, 224 and n). Huntington had directed NG to announce the adoption in general orders. (See Huntington to NG, 6 March, above [vol. 7: 404].)

11. NG enclosed an extract of Gen. Alexander Lillington's letter of 21 March and Lillington's account of the battle of Heron's Bridge. (See above, vol. 7: 457.)

12. In his proclamation of 18 March, Cornwallis announced that his army had achieved a "compleat victory" over the "rebel forces." He called on all "loyal subjects to stand forth, & take an active part in restoring good order & Government," promising pardons and protection to all rebels—murderers excepted—who surrendered and turned in their arms and ammunition by 20 April. (PCC, item 155, vol. 2: 25, DNA) This proclamation has been called "the last serious British effort to rally the American Loyalists." (Paul H. Smith, *Loyalists and Redcoats: A Study in British Revolutionary Policy* [New York: W. W. Norton Company, 1972], p. 153)

13. In a letter to Washington of 28 February, above, NG had reported that the British were preparing to raise two regiments of slaves. (Vol. 7: 370) As noted there, the information was false. Nothing is known about the reported attempt to recruit men into the Loyalist militia, but according to one historian, that force was never revitalized. (Lambert, *South Carolina Loyalists*, p. 176)

*   *   *

¶ [TO COLONEL NICHOLAS LONG.[1] From "Camp on Deep River," N.C., 30 March 1781. NG wants Long to send immediately a ton of powder, two tons of lead, and as many flints as possible to Hillsborough. If necessary, he should impress teams. Long is to "use all possible industry in repairing the Arms" in his possession, as the "service creates perpetual demands." Shoes are also greatly needed, and NG asks Long to enlarge his "manufactories if possible." The army must make "long and hasty marches" and needs a double supply. Col. [Edward] Carrington will send a list of quartermaster stores that are required, and Long should "forward if possible" the rum that the governor promised to provide.[2] If Long needs money, Mr. [Joseph] Clay can supply him with $100,000, but this fund was sent "for the relief of the Army," and he should draw on it only for "the most pressing necessity." In order to see "how our affairs stand in the Southern department," NG wants a return of the stores in Long's hands. He also wants the manufacture of cartouche boxes to continue, but "upon the new plan," for which Long should get a pattern.[3] NG adds: "You may think I require a great deal of you. It is true I do. Our situation demands it, and the circumstances of your State require it. Without support your State is inevitably lost; with it I am in hopes the enemy will gain no great advantage." The British were defeated at Guilford Court House, even "tho they kept the ground." NG's army was preparing to attack them again when they "suddenly retird" on 18 March, leaving seventy of their wounded. NG pursued them to this place, which they abandoned hastily, leaving their dead unburied; he must give up "further pursuit for the present," however. Long's "virtue and exertions" will be needed to keep North Carolina from falling to the enemy, who "will persevere."[4] ADfS (MiU-C) 4 pp.]

1. Long was deputy quartermaster general for North Carolina.

2. In a letter of 29 March, above (vol. 7: 480), NG had asked Gov. Abner Nash to provide twenty hogsheads of rum for the army. (See also, Nash to NG, 3 April, below.)

3. Cartouche boxes were improved during the "early 1780's" by "the inclusion of a tinned iron tray for gun flints which lay under the wooden cartridge block." (Harold L. Peterson, *The Book of the Continental Soldier* [Harrisburg, Pa.: The Stackpole Company, 1968], p. 68) This may have been the "new plan" to which NG referred.

4. Long replied on 18 April, below.

¶ [**TO THE MARQUIS DE MALMEDY**. From Camp on Deep River, N.C., 30 March 1781. Malmedy's regiment of "Light horse and mounted Infantry" is to join Gen. [Alexander] Lillington immediately.[1] NG outlines a route of march, but Malmedy should change it if his troops are in danger of "a surprize." He should order Capt. [Pleasant] Henderson to join him after Henderson has finished "at Cross Creek and upon Cape Fear."[2] Malmedy should inform NG by express of anything important that he learns on the march. ADfS (MiU-C) 2 pp.]

1. Lillington commanded a militia force near British-occupied Wilmington. NG expected Lord Cornwallis to march his army there. (See NG to Huntington, this date, above.)

2. On Henderson's mission, see NG to Henderson, 26 March, above (vol. 7: 468–69).

*   *   *

To Joseph Reed, President of the Pennsylvania Council

Head Quarters Col Ramseys Deep
Dear Sir   River [N.C.] March 30th 1781

I am happy to find by a resolution of Congress that the Pennsylvania line is annexed to the Southern department.[1] No army ever wanted reinforcements more than ours, nor was there a Country ever in a more critical situation than these Southern States. I flatter myself with speedy and effectual support from Pennsylvania both of Men and supplies: its resources being very extensive and easily commanded.

I shall not undertake to enumerate our wants, I have only to observe that we are in want of everything. But there is a greater and more pressing demand for Shoes than any other article. We are obligd to perform such long and rapid marches that there is a great call for shoes, nor are they to be had in sufficient numbers in this quarter.

Indeed the confusion which prevails in North Carolinia puts almost a total stop to all business. The Inhabitants are in the greatest distress and their calamities call aloud for protection.

I must beg leave to refer you to my letters to Congress respecting the operations of the two Armies in this department. I am with Sentiments of the most perfect esteem Your Excellencys most Obed᛭ humble Ser

NATH GREENE

ADfS (MiU-C).

1. Congress had notified NG of the addition of the Pennsylvania Continental line to the Southern Department. (See Samuel Huntington to NG, 20 February, above [vol. 7: 323 and n].)

To General Thomas Sumter

Head Quarters at Col° Ramsays
Dear Sir   Deep River [N.C.], March 30th 1781.

I wrote you from the Iron Works near Guilford, of the Battle which happened on the 15th at that place.[1] We lay within ten miles of the Enemy three Days after the Action preparing ourselves to make another attack. On the 18th they retired to the New Gardens, and from thence to Bells Mills leaving upwards of 70 of their Wounded at our mercy. We have been in pursuit of them ever since, and they left this ground with such precipitation as to leave their dead unburied. They are on the rout to Cross Creek, and probably will fall down the Country as low as Wilmington, but this is not certain. The greater part of our Militia's term of service being out will prevent our farther pursuit; especially as the difficulty is very great in procuring provisions. Indeed it would be impossible to subsist the Army in the Pine Barrens; and as we are obliged to halt a Day or two to collect provisions at this place, it will give the Enemy such a start of us as leave no hopes of overtaking them if they choose to continue their flight, nor can we fight them upon equal terms after our Militia leave us. All these considerations have determined me to change my route, and push directly into South Carolina. This will oblige the Enemy to give up their prospects in this State, or their posts in South Carolina; and if our Army can be subsisted there we can fight them upon as good terms with your aid as we can here. I beg you will therefore give orders to Genls [Andrew] Pickens and Merion [Francis Marion] to collect all the Militia they can to co-operate with us. But the object must be a secret to all except the Generals; otherwise the Enemy will take measures to counteract us. I am [in] hopes by sending forward our Horse and some small detachments of light Infantry to join your Militia, you will be able to possess yourself of all their little out posts before the Army arrives.[2] Take measures to collect all the provisions you can: for on this our whole operations will depend. I expect to be ready to march in about five Days; and perhaps we may be in the neighbourhood of Camden by the 20th of next Month, or earlier.[3] You will please to inform me of your prospects, and the probable force I may expect to co-operate with us.[4] I am with the greatest respect Your most ob[t] humble serv

NATH GREENE

LS (Sumter Papers: DLC).
    1. NG's letter, dated 16 March, is above (vol. 7: 442–43).
    2. On 12 April, below, NG ordered Henry Lee to join and cooperate with Sumter.
    3. NG's army left Ramsey's Mill on 6 April and was near Camden, S.C., by the 19th. (See NG's Orders of 5 and 19 April, both below.)
    4. Sumter replied on 7 April, below.

*   *   *

¶ [CAPTAIN NATHANIEL PENDLETON TO COLONEL ANTHONY W. WHITE. From Deep River, N.C., 30 March 1781. As a superior cavalry provides "an essential advantage" in "this Country," NG wants White to equip and send "fit" men and horses to Col. [William] Washington and the Southern Army.[1] ACyS (MiU-C) 1 p.]
    1. White's dragoons were in Virginia for refitting. They remained there when the Marquis de Lafayette decided to detain them for service with his force. (See Lafayette to NG, 18 May, below.)

¶ [FROM GOVERNOR THOMAS JEFFERSON OF VIRGINIA, "In Council" [Richmond, Va.], 30 March 1781. Has NG's letters of 16 and 23 March. Congratulates him on "the Effects" of the battle of Guilford Court House. NG may have left the field, but the enemy's retreat "best shows which party was worsted." The council has ordered out militia from eleven counties to replace those now serving with NG. There are "always considerable Deficiencies," so it has called for "about half as many more" as the 1,500 men NG requested.[1] Most of the counties north of the James River have not had to provide militia, so Jefferson assumes they have finished raising their "New Levies."[2] When the militiamen serving with NG return, the "residuary Counties"—excluding the eleven now sending militia—will also be ordered to provide recruits. The eleven "must be spared" because the law for raising levies "cannot be executed in any County in the Absence of any considerable proportion of its Militia." The state's commissary fears he will fall short of expectations in "bringing in stall fed Beeves." He is feeding 2,000 and has a number of individuals working to prepare them to send to NG.[3] Jefferson will "give constant Attention" to the matter. Everything that can be spared will be sent to NG, but quantities will have to be "abridged" as additional Virginia troops are called out to counter the enemy "Reinforcement" at Portsmouth.[4] LB (Vi) 1 p.]
    1. NG's request is in his letter of 23 March, above (vol. 7: 466). As seen at Steuben to NG, this date, below, the Virginia Executive Council had decided to order out a new force of militia after rejecting a proposal from Steuben to send 2,000 militiamen who were already in the field to North Carolina. Steuben disgustedly predicted that it would be at least two months before the new troops reached NG. (Steuben to the Marquis de Lafayette, 29 March, Idzerda, *Lafayette Papers*, 3: 424) As it turned out, most of them never left

Virginia. Seven of the eleven counties that had been ordered to furnish men applied for exemptions, and the militiamen who did turn out reported slowly and in far fewer than the expected numbers. (Jefferson to Arthur Penn, 4 May; Robert Lawson to Jefferson, 1 May, Boyd, *Jefferson Papers*, 5: 598–99, 583–84) By early May, as Lord Cornwallis's army marched to Virginia from Wilmington, N.C., most of the then-collecting troops were ordered to remain in the state. (Jefferson to Lawson, 8 May, ibid., pp. 613–14)

2. In his letter to Lafayette of 29 March, Steuben reported that only seventy of the 500 expected recruits were at the rendezvous site. (Idzerda, *Lafayette Papers*, 3: 424) As a result of Cornwallis's invasion, none was sent to NG.

3. Jefferson also sent a copy of the report from John Browne, the Virginia commissary of purchases, to Col. William R. Davie. (Jefferson to Davie, 30 March, Boyd, *Jefferson Papers*, 5: 290) Jefferson issued an order for "seizing live Cattle," but the animals that were obtained either fell into the hands of the British or were used to feed American forces in Virginia. (George Mason to Jefferson, 14 May, and Jefferson to Speaker of House of Delegates, 10 May, ibid., pp. 647, 627)

4. The arrival of British reinforcements under Gen. William Phillips is discussed at Washington to NG, 21 March, above (vol. 7: 459n).

¶ [FROM COLONEL STEPHEN MOORE, Charleston, S.C., 30 March 1781. Moore remains a prisoner, and the exchange of militia has been "retarded."[1] NG's "genteel treatment" of Moore's property on the Hudson River leads him "to expect notice as a public sufferer."[2] Names six militia officers who have been paroled. Excerpt from Stan. V. Henkels, *Catalog #1074, Supplement* (1912)]

1. Moore had written NG on 5 December 1780, above, to seek the exchange of militia prisoners at Charleston. (Vol. 6: 528–29). Such an exchange was part of the cartel agreed to in May. (See note at NG to Huntington, 10 May, below.)

2. Property belonging to Moore had been taken to build the fortress at West Point, and NG had helped him to obtain reimbursement from Congress. (See above, vol. 5: 208 and n.) On Moore's situation as a prisoner, see also Edmund M. Hyrne to NG, 1 August, below.

¶ [FROM THE MEMBERS OF THE NEW GARDEN MONTHLY MEETING NEAR GUILFORD COURT HOUSE, Guilford Court House, N.C., 30 March 1781. They have received NG's letter of 26 March and will do what they can to assist.[1] They cannot help as much as they would like, for the "Americans have lain much upon" them and the British have recently plundered them. Nearly 100 people are now living at their meeting house, with no means of support. They will nevertheless share as long as they "have anything," for their duty as "true Christians" is to help those in distress, regardless of "party" or "cause." Reprinted from *The American Friend* 2 (Third Month 28, 1895): 307]

1. NG had asked the members to provide "for the relief of the suffering wounded at Guilford Court House." (See above, vol. 7: 469.)

¶ [FROM BARON STEUBEN, Chesterfield Court House, Va., 30 March 1781. Colonel Morris has informed him of NG's "wishes and intentions," which are in keeping with a plan that Steuben revised after writing NG on 27 March, to bring 2,000 men into North Carolina via Halifax, N.C.[1] Believing that the French had landed at Cape Fear, N.C., he tried to persuade Virginia officials that Lord Cornwallis's army could be pressed "from three different points" and forced to "retire towards" Camden, S.C., if his proposal were implemented.[2] He presented letters of endorsement for the plan from the Marquis de Lafayette, General Weedon, and Colonel Gouvion; Morris also tried to help win its approval. "After a debate," the officials "came to the Resolution," a copy of which Steuben encloses. He has "not a word more to say."[3] He has now come "here to fulfill the first objects" for which he "was left in this State." Complains that wherever he turns he finds "difficulties & disappointm^ts." There are only seventy recruits at Chesterfield Court House. He has sent an express to the rendezvous sites to find out why so few men have been sent but fears that it is because of the "number of Militia orderd out."[4] "Col° Davis [William Davies]" has been appointed Virginia's Commissioner of War. Davies is the "properest person" for the post and will "render much Service." Steuben is disappointed that Davies is already serving in his new post but has persuaded him to assist in "the business on hand" until a successor is named.[5] Steuben will remain in Virginia until matters are in a "proper train to fit out the recruits." He will then march with the first detachment to join NG, "for you may be assured I am not less tired of this State than I believe they are of me."[6] He will detain Morris one day longer to "inform him more fully of what may be expected" from Virginia. Col. [Anthony W.] White has just arrived. Steuben is afraid that the cavalry will give "much trouble"; indeed, he is "at a loss" to know "how they are to be remounted."[7] Cy (NHi) 4 pp.]

1. NG had sent Col. Lewis Morris, Jr., his aide, from camp on 22 March to consult with the Marquis de Lafayette. (See NG to Lafayette, 22 March, above [vol. 7: 460].) After learning that Lafayette had returned to Annapolis, Md., Morris gave up on trying to meet with him. (Morris to Lafayette, 29 March, Idzerda, *Lafayette Papers*, 3: 423) Steuben's letter of 27 March is above (vol. 7: 473–74).

2. The French expeditionary force had returned to Rhode Island after being turned back at the entrance to Chesapeake Bay. (See above, vol. 7: 468n.)

3. Steuben had convened a council of war and solicited the written opinions of the three officers. (His proposal, dated 27 March, and the supporting opinions of Lafayette and Col. Jean-Baptiste Gouvion of the engineers are printed in Idzerda, *Lafayette Papers*, 3: 419–21. Gen. George Weedon's letter to Thomas Jefferson of 27 March, supporting Steuben's plan, is in Boyd, *Jefferson Papers*, 5: 267.) The Virginia Executive Council, which considered Steuben's proposal on 29 March, concluded that "the number of arms such Detachment would necessarily carry with them bearing a very great proportion to what will afterwards remain in the State, it will be a measure unjustifiable in the present circumstances of Affairs[,] the enemy having lately received a great reinforcement." (Steuben Microfilm) The council resolved instead to send militia reinforcements to NG from eleven Virginia counties. (See Jefferson to NG, this date, above.)

4. Steuben wrote Lafayette on 29 March that he had expected to find 500 recruits at Chesterfield Court House. (Idzerda, *Lafayette Papers*, 3: 424)

5. Upon the removal of the ineffectual George Muter as Commissioner of War on 22 March, the council immediately offered the post to William Davies, the commander of the Continental post at Chesterfield Court House. (See *Calendar of Va. State Papers*, 1: 587; Jefferson to Davies, 22 March, Boyd, *Jefferson Papers*, 5: 204–5; Davies to NG, 2 April, below.) After consulting with Steuben, Davies accepted the offer and was named to succeed Muter on 27 March. NG enthusiastically supported the appointment. (NG to Davies, 11 April, below) In a letter of 30 March to Jefferson, Davies discussed his agreement with Steuben concerning the "business on hand." Steuben, he wrote, "expressed to me yesterday in such strong terms the great importance of the post at Chesterfield, and urged so strenuously his idea of the necessity of my continuing my superintendance at that place till the march of the new raised troops shall be over, that it was in vain I represented my opinion of the impracticability of discharging my duty towards it, or the fatigue and trouble to which I should subject myself. I was therefore

obliged to consent, and purpose whenever my business will permit here [i.e., at the Virginia War Office], to attend at that place on Saturdays after noon and Sundays." (Boyd, *Jefferson Papers*, 5: 290)

6. Steuben, who never joined NG, had indeed alienated many members of the Virginia government and Continental line. (Selby, *Revolution in Virginia*, pp. 266–67; see also Lafayette to NG, 4 April, and Davies to NG, 17 June, both below.)

7. As seen at Pendleton to White, this date, above, White's regiment had been sent to Virginia to be re-equipped and remounted. As Steuben expected, this created problems. The Virginia legislature had passed a law requiring state purchasers to pay no more than £5,000 each for cavalry horses. (For more on the law, see Jefferson to NG, 24 March, above [vol. 7: 467 and n].) Steuben wrote Washington on 15 April that such a sum was "inadequate to the purchase of the meanest wagon Horses." (Washington Papers, DLC) White had to resort to impressment. (See Jefferson to Lafayette, 29 May, Idzerda, *Lafayette Papers*, 4: 145, 146n.)

¶ [TO MAJOR ROBERT FORSYTH. From "Head Quarters[,] confluence of Deep and Haw River," N.C., 31 March 1781. Has his letter of 25 January.[1] Forsyth's prediction of "scanty supplies" has been confirmed to a degree that can "scaresely be conceived." NG understands that "necessary supports" cannot be obtained unless the states comply fully with the "requisitions of Congress." The "deranged State" of Forsyth's department requires his "immediate" presence with the army.[2] In a postscript, refers him to the "public accounts" for details of the army's operations. Df (MiU-C) 2 pp.]

1. The letter from Forsyth, the Southern Army's deputy commissary for purchases, is above (vol. 7: 196).

2. Forsyth replied on 20 April, below.

¶ [TO JAMES HUNTER. From [Deep River, N.C.], 31 March 1781. Hunter deserves "every thing of his Country," and NG's only excuse for failing to answer his letter "before this" is "the innumerable difficulties and perplexities that have for some time surrounded" him.[1] Hopes this reply "will prove seasonable and advantageous." Is "under great obligations" to Hunter for offering to furnish "such Articles as the Quarter Master may think necessary."[2] Encloses an order on Maryland for $200,000, as Hunter requested.[3] Refers him to the newspapers for "all the circumstances of our movements & operations"; adds that "the Enemy have fled precipitately before us, & are now on their way to Cross Creek and Wilmington." Df (MiU-C) 2 pp.]

1. Hunter, who operated an ironworks in Fredericksburg, Va., had written NG on 24 December 1780, above (vol. 6: 608).

2. On Hunter's dealings with Col. Edward Carrington, the deputy quartermaster for the Southern Army, see Carrington to NG, 29 December 1780, above (vol. 7: 24).

3. In his letter of 24 December, Hunter had also asked NG to draw funds for him on the state of Virginia. Carrington had applied for the money in NG's name, but the state was slow to provide it. (See Carrington's letter of 29 December.)

¶ [TO SAMUEL HUNTINGTON, PRESIDENT OF THE CONTINENTAL CONGRESS. From Headquarters, Deep River, N.C., 31 March 1781. Urges Congress to take "immediate notice" of the "irregular and deranged situation of the Hospital department in the Southern States." Hopes it will make a "permanent and regular establishment" and that it will return Doctor Fayssoux, who "waits upon" it, to the army "as soon as possible."[1] Recommends

Dr. "Robert Johnson" as "a very deserving Officer" who was "left out of the northern arrangement"; Congress should decide whether to include him in this one.[2] LS (PCC, item 175, vol. 2: 35, DNA) 1 p.]

1. In response to an earlier request of NG's, Congress on 22 March had approved a number of "additional Regulations" for the hospital department in the South. (Huntington to NG, 15 April, below; JCC, 19: 292–94; see also NG to Huntington, 14 January, above [vol. 7: 119–20].) On 15 May, after receiving this letter, Congress appointed "officers in the hospital department for the southern army," including Dr. Peter Fayssoux as chief physician of the hospital; eight days later, it voted Fayssoux partial "arrearages of pay" so that he could "repair to the southern army." (JCC, 20: 506, 529; for more on Fayssoux and his mission to Congress, see Pendleton to Browne, 1 April, below.)

2. In its resolution of 15 May, Congress appointed Dr. Robert Johnston a hospital physician in the Southern Department. (JCC, 20: 506)

* * *

To Governor Thomas Jefferson of Virginia

Sir   H^d Q^{rs} Deep River [N.C.] March 31st 1781.

The time of service of the Militia under General Lawson and General Stevens is expired, and they are discharged having honorably performed their duty agreable to contract.[1] It was unfortunate that their term of service expired at the time it did; but we could ask no more of the Men than they were bound to perform, nor would it answer any purpose as they cannot be prevailed on to continue in a disagreable service longer than they are bound by agreement.

General Lawson will do himself the honor to present your Excellency this Letter; and to him I beg leave to refer you for the state of all matters in this quarter.

If more Militia are ordered out which will be indispensably necessary if the regular forces are not ready to take the field, there is no Man has a better claim to the command than General Lawson or Stevens. They are both valuable Officers.[2]

I beg your Excellency to pay the greatest attention to the manufacturing of Shoes. More depends upon this than you can readily immagine. I am much afraid our supply will be very unequal to our demands.[3] My greatest dependance is on Virginia for support, and without her exertions I cannot keep the field. The business of transportation is an important object, and on which the whole operations depend. Unless your State accomodate their Laws to the demands of the service, the Army must inevitably fall a sacrifice, as this State is too much exhausted to give any considerable aid to the Army upon the most pressing emergency.

I have long endeavored to impress upon the different Legislatures, the impossibility of accommodating the operations of the Army to civil convenience; and the more serious they grow the less practicable the measure. Indeed civil polity must accommodate itself to the emer-gencys of War, or the People submit to the power of the Enemy. There is no other alternative.[4]

We have had a great struggle and our prospects are mended if seasonably supported; without which we shall soon have the same path to tread over again; and I cannot flatter myself with an equal degree of success; nor will the temper of the Army under its present difficulties enable me to make equal exertions. Send us Men, and support the different branches of the Staff, and I am not without hopes of keeping the War at a distance from you in this quarter: At least my endeavors shall not be wanting.[5] I have the honor to be with the greatest respect, Your Excellencys most ob^t humble serv^t

NATH GREENE

LS (Vi).

1. Generals Robert Lawson and Edward Stevens had commanded the Virginia militia forces that joined NG's army shortly before the battle of Guilford Court House. Their troops fought well there. (See NG to Huntington, 16 March, above [vol. 7: 434–35].) For more on the return of the militia and the two generals to Virginia, see NG to Jefferson, 27 March, above (ibid., p. 471).

2. Neither Lawson nor Stevens returned to the Southern Army. (See above [vol. 7: 472n].)

3. On the army's need for shoes, see also NG to Board of War and NG to Long, both 30 March, above.

4. According to Julian Boyd, this letter "epitomizes the differences" between NG and Jefferson. NG "believed the entire civil polity should subordinate and adjust itself to the needs of the military," Boyd has written, while Jefferson "insisted upon the right of the civil power to decide how far its republican principles should be compromised in order to meet military demands." (Boyd, *Jefferson Papers*, 5: 302n) Boyd, however, went too far in his contention that NG would sacrifice government to the needs of the military. Time and again, NG willingly subordinated the army to civilian direction and control and scrupulously adhered to the instructions of those in civil power despite disagreeing with those policies and instructions and with the view of governmental responsibility for the army that underpinned them. (See, for example, the note at NG to Jefferson, 28 February, above [vol. 7: 367–68n].)

5. Jefferson's reply has not been found.

*   *   *

¶ [TO GENERAL WILLIAM SMALLWOOD. From [Deep River, N.C., 31 March 1781][1] Knowing that Smallwood was "fully" aware of the Southern Army's "distressing and critical situation," NG had expected his "extensive influence" in Maryland to result in "a considerable reinforcement" for the army. NG was therefore "astonished to hear" recently that "not even an arrangment of the Officers had taken place, nor a single soldier raised."[2] He is "at a loss to account for this very extraordinary delay" and entreats Smallwood "to forward the recruiting service all in your power." No country was ever "in a more dangerous or critical situation"; if "disagreeable consequences" result, "those States will be answerable who have neglected to give seasonable sup-port." Only "good fortune" has kept the army "from ruin" thus far. NG hopes his "friends will not desert" him or leave him "to fall a sacrifice in an unequal conflict."[3] ADfS (MiU-C) 2 pp.]

1. The date was taken from the docketing, the place from other letters of this date.

2. Smallwood had left the Southern Army in December 1780 in a dispute over rank and had returned home to Maryland, where he was expected to "hasten" troops and supplies to NG. (NG to Samuel Huntington, 28 December, above [vol. 7: 9]) As noted at NG to Gist, 30 March, above, the source of NG's information about the situation in Maryland is not known.

3. In his letter to Gist of the previous day, NG had been less severe in his remarks about the lack of reinforcements than he was here. (See ibid.) Smallwood reported on his activities in a letter to NG of 12 April and replied to this letter on 4 May, both below.

¶ [GENERAL GREENE'S ORDERS, Headquarters, "Ramsey's Mill on Deep River," N.C., 1 April 1781. Announces the results of a court-martial held on 31 March. Capt. William Lytle, accused of disobeying orders, was acquitted. Three enlisted men charged with desertion or with deserting and joining the enemy were found guilty and sentenced to receive 100 lashes each; two were also sentenced to "make good the time" they were absent. Greene Orderly Book (CSmH) 4 pp.[1]]

1. The designation of this orderly book at CSmH is the "Greene Orderly Book." Neither the name of the officer who kept it nor the unit to which he belonged is known.

¶ [CAPTAIN NATHANIEL PENDLETON TO DOCTOR JAMES BROWNE.[1] From Headquarters, Deep River, N.C., 1 April 1781. Reports that Dr. [Peter] Fayssoux and "several other" surgeons who were exchanged have arrived from Charleston, S.C. Considering the "extent of the southern Department" and the number of physicians employed, NG thinks an "immediate arrangement" of the hospital department is "indespensibly necessary." Browne is to furnish Fayssoux with a list of surgeons serving with the Southern Army, giving their ranks and any "temporary appointments" they have received. Fayssoux is going to Philadelphia to acquaint Congress "with all the claims" so that a "permanent, & productive arrangement" can be made that will prevent future complaints or "Contests."[2] Capt. [William] Pierce acknowledges Browne's letter of 28 March and will answer "very shortly."[3] ADfS (MiU-C) 2 pp.]

1. Browne was chief physician and surgeon of the Southern Department. (Duncan, *Medical Men*, p. 321)

2. For more on Fayssoux's mission to Congress and the arrangement of the hospital department in the South, see NG to Huntington, 31 March, above.

3. Neither letter has been found.

¶ [COLONEL OTHO H. WILLIAMS TO GENERAL ROBERT LAWSON.[1] From "Camp at Ramseys Mill," N.C., 1 April 1781. The Virginia militia commanded by Lawson have served six weeks "according to their engagements." They are discharged by NG's order and with NG's thanks for their "faithful services and patient perseverance in times uncommonly difficult."[2] ALS (NcD) 1 p.]

1. Next to his signature, Williams added "D[eputy] A[djutant]. Gen'."

2. For more on the discharge of the militia, see NG to Jefferson, 31 March, above.

¶ [TO JAMES MADISON. From Headquarters, "Confluence of Deep & Haw Rivers," N.C., 1 April 1781. Thanks him for his letter of 13 January.[1] NG may have already replied but fears that Madison's letter "was put up without being answered" during the "hurry" of the campaign. NG's "situation must plead" his apology for any neglect. Df (MiU-C) 1 p.]

1. Madison was a member of the congressional committee appointed to correspond with the commander of the Southern Army. His letter, reporting the mutiny in the Pennsylvania Continental line, is above (vol. 7: 116–17).

¶ [TO MAJOR ARNOLDUS VANDERHORST. From "Col Ramseys on Deep River," N.C., 1 April 1781. This is the first opportunity NG has had to reply to Vanderhorst's letter of 20 February, which he received "some days since."[1] If NG's appointment pleases his friends "in this quarter," he hopes his conduct will also warrant their approval. He will do all he can "to relieve this distressed land, but the means are very unequal to the end," and the prospects are "gloo[m]y." NG is "accustomed to encounter difficulties," however, and is "not without hopes of surmounting them." The army has had a "hard struggle," including "one general action," in which "We were not as successful as we ought to have been." The enemy nevertheless "sufferd so greatly" that they have been "unwilling to fight us again"; NG's army has "pursued them upwards of seventy Miles."[2] Vanderhorst can get "further particulars" from "Col Wyly Jones," who has been with the army.[3] Regrets Vanderhorst's losses, "but if we can preserve our liberties, and breath[e] once more in a free air, with the blessings of peace, these little losses will be forgotten." ALS (PHi) 3 pp.]

1. The letter is above (vol. 7: 326).
2. On the battle of Guilford Court House, see NG to Huntington, 16 March, above (vol. 7: 433–36).
3. "Col Wyly Jones" was Willie Jones, of Halifax, N.C., a delegate to Congress. (See NG to Henry Lee, 5 March, above [vol. 7: 395].)

¶ [CAPTAIN NATHANIEL PENDLETON TO DOCTOR ROBERT WILSON.[1] From Headquarters, Deep River, N.C., 1 April 1781. At NG's direction, he acknowledges Wilson's letter of 15 March [not found]. NG is "sensible" of the difficulties Wilson encountered "in the removal & attendance of the sick." NG is satisfied that Wilson spent the money frugally and is "happy" that Wilson could obtain it. ADfS (MiU-C) 1 p.]

1. The recipient's name was taken from the docketing. As noted above (vol. 6: 541n), Wilson was a purveyor for the hospitals in the Southern Department.

*   *   *

From Governor Thomas Jefferson of Virginia

Dear Sir   Richmond [Va.] Apr. 1 1781.

Obliged in my public character to be the pipe of communication to the sentiments of others, I must beg leave once to address you as a private man on a subject which has given me uneasi⟨ness. My⟩ letter by Colo [Lewis] Morris inclosed some resolutions of assembly requiring that all horses impressed & valued to more than £5000 should be returned to their owners.[1] This was in fact requiring them all to be returned. Should this be complied with fully, I apprehend that it must have the most fatal effe⟨ct⟩ on your operations which depend so much on your superiority in cavalry. I dare say you will think (if it be true that some of our most valuable studd horses were impressed & estimated, as has been said, to what they were worth as co⟨ver⟩ing horses) that reasonable oeconomy requires that ⟨they⟩ should be restored, and that the taking them was ripping up the hen which laid the golden eggs. But as to the great groupe of those impressed, notwithstanding they may have been valued high, yet they will be cheaply bought if they enable you to strike your enemy & prevent being stricken by him. To return them, have them revalued as the resolutions propose, ⟨&⟩ pay the damages to the owners would subject th⟨e pub⟩lic to a great & certain burthen for nothing. Reports which ⟨were⟩ circulated that those employed in impressing had ⟨been⟩ so indiscreet as to seize ⟨the⟩ fine covering horses & ⟨c⟩astrate some of them (which rend⟨ered it⟩ impossible to use them for the sudden emergence [i.e., emergency?] which alone justifies impresses) were probably what in some measure induced the assembly to take up the business. But to this I believe an error was added. They entertained an idea that the furnishing horses to our two regiments of cavalry was the separate expence of the State, a very strange error, which ⟨I should not⟩ have credited had not the Speaker [Richard Henry] Lee assured ⟨me of⟩ the fact. The assembly was then up, so that it was too late for me to set them right when I received that information.[2] My purpose in writing thus confidentially is to suggest to you the expediency of your rectify⟨ing⟩ any abuses which you may find to have been committ⟨ed⟩ by unreasonable & imprudent impresses, and as to the rest, if you think it inconsistent with the public good, as I expect it is, to comply with the resolution, that you should take the trouble of remonstrating on the subject, which will give me an ⟨opp⟩ortunity of laying the matter again before the assembly who are to meet the first of the next month, and who I cannot but believe will be glad to have an opportunity of correcting what they did when the error they were under shall be made known to them.[3] I throw myself on your discretion & shew my confidence in it, when I th⟨us v⟩enture to write in a private character, what seems to co⟨ntradic⟩t my public duty. I wished you to be made acquainted with facts, which cannot be always & fully collected from public ⟨votes alone⟩. I am with very real estee⟨m & respect Sir Your most obed^t humble serv^t ⟨TH: JEFFERSON⟩

L[S] (DLC). The LS is damaged; the words in angle brackets, including the signature, were taken from a GWG Transcript (CSmH).

1. Jefferson's letter to NG of 24 March is above (vol. 7: 467). The controversy over impressment of horses in Virginia and the measures taken by the legislature in response are discussed there.

2. The "strange error" was the legislators' assumption that horses furnished to the

Southern Army would not be counted against their yearly quota of funds for the national government.

3. NG replied to Jefferson's letter of 24 March on 6 April and to the present letter on 11 April, both below.

*   *   *

¶ [FROM GOVERNOR THOMAS JEFFERSON OF VIRGINIA, Richmond, Va., 1 April 1781. Has NG's letter of 27 March.[1] Jefferson informed NG "by Colo Morris" that militia reinforcements have been called out to join the Southern Army but will not arrive in time to replace the militiamen now with NG "if they leave you so early."[2] Hopes "the knowlege that a releif is coming" will keep those troops from leaving NG "in a state which may soon give us all to do over again." Those militiamen who are "under the regular orders of government" will be treated as deserters "if they withdraw without orders." All of the militia, moreover, are under the orders of county lieutenants, "which are as obligatory as those of the Executive."[3] Jefferson will send the new draftees as soon as possible, knowing it is "more practicable to carry on a war with militia within our own Country than out of it."[4] Morris will have informed NG about Virginia's "preparations against [Benedict] Arnold." Adds: "An enemy 3000 strong, not a regular within our state, nor arms to put into the hands of the militia, are circumstances which seem to promise difficulties." Jefferson, however, realizes it is "essential" to do everything possible to "prevent the return of Cornwallis's army." LS (Greene Papers: DLC) 1 p.]

1. See above (vol. 7: 471–72).

2. Col. Lewis Morris carried Jefferson's letter of 30 March, above, to NG. As noted there, most of the militia reinforcements remained in Virginia.

3. On the militiamen's return to Virginia, see also NG to Jefferson, 31 March, above. It appears that few, if any, of the returning troops were punished as deserters. (One county lieutenant's reasons for not taking action are given in George Skillern to Jefferson, 14 April, Boyd, *Jefferson Papers*, 5: 450.)

4. As noted at Jefferson to NG, 30 March, above, the "new levies" were not sent.

¶ [FROM THE MARQUIS DE MALMEDY, "Sprowels Ferie [Spruill's Ferry]," N.C., 1 April 1781. Sends a "man of a suspicious conduct" to headquarters, who was caught "trying to swim the river down this ferie." The man, who threw his papers away before Malmedy "met with him," first claimed that NG had sent him to Hillsborough for provisions the "day before yesterday." Malmedy gives reasons for considering that explanation implausible. The man has since claimed "he belongs to Colonel [Anthony W.] White." ALS (MiU-C) 1 p.]

¶ [GENERAL GREENE'S ORDERS, Ramsey's Mill, N.C., 2 April 1781. Gives an extract from the minutes of Congress, taken from the *Pennsylvania Packet* of 13 March, paying tribute to Gen. [Daniel] Morgan and the officers and men of his command for their victory at Cowpens over a "select and well appointed Detachment" of British troops. The delegates have resolved to present a gold medal to Morgan, silver medals to Colonels [William] Washington and [John E.] Howard, a sword to [Gen. Andrew] Pickens, and brevet commissions to Maj. Edward Giles and Baron de Glaubeck. The commander of the Southern Department is to publish these resolutions in general orders. NG has not "receiv'd the above order Officially, But does not doubt of its authenticity; therefore, with pleasure, communicates the Resolves."[1] Greene Orderly Book (CSmH) 5 pp.]

1. Congress had passed the resolutions on 9 March. NG had apparently not yet received Samuel Huntington's letter of 10 March, above [vol. 7: 432], communicating the resolutions and directing him to publish them in general orders.

¶ [TO THE BOARD OF WAR. From Headquarters [Deep River, N.C.], 2 April 1781. Asks the board to "confirm or disapprove" an enclosed request from the captive officers of North and South Carolina to alter their uniforms.[1] Df (MiU-C) 1 p.]

1. The enclosure, which has not been found, had been sent with Gen. William Moultrie's letter to NG of 2 February, above (vol. 7: 239).

*   *   *

To Baron Steuben

Dear Baron   Deep River Col° Ramsays [N.C.] April 2ᵈ 1781.
    This moment your Letters of the 25th and 27th have come to hand.[1]

I am exceedingly mortified at your disappointment.[2] To do justice to the British their exertions do them honor. They are now victorious upon the Sea and greatly superior by Land. In this situation of things considering the critical state of affairs to the Southward I cannot see the propriety of the Marquis's drawing off his force to the Northward especially as the Enemy are reinforced here; and their force lessened to the Northward. I have written to him on the subject and advised him to march immediately for Richmond, by the way of Alexandria and Fredricksburg. At Richmond he will be at a point either to operate in the lower Country or to operate farther southward as occasion may require. I have not given him a possitive order, but the manner in which I have recommended this measure amounts to an order; and I will take upon me the blame, if Genˡ Washington should disapprove thereof.[3]

I am not of opinion that the French fleet will attempt any thing to the southward. On the contrary I am led to beleive they are gone to New Port.[4]

I see and feel for your disagreable situation, and any thing that is in my power to grant you, you may command. But if you leave Virginia all things will run into confusion; but I am so far from thinking that you are disgraced by your command in Virginia that every body allows you to have acquired great credit. And tho' it is not of the splendid kind, it is nevertheless very honorable, and is founded upon the same line of conduct from which General Washington has justly acquired so much honor: I mean that of guarding against misfortune.[5]

My greatest expectations of support are from Virginia, drawn forth under your regulations and arrangements. If you leave them State policy and partial views will counteract all the support we may expect from that quarter, and we shall all fall together to the Southward. Nothing in my power shall be wanting to do justice to your reputation, and I feel my obligations to you for your exertions.

Should you continue to wish to join this Army you shall most readily have my consent, for I am greatly in want of your Aid here as well as there, but it is my opinion that you can be more extensively useful there than here.

I wrote you by Col⁰ Morris and referred you to him for the military operations in this quarter since the Battle of Guilford.[6] We pursued the Enemy to this place which they left with such precipitation on our approach as to leave their dead unburied. The Virginia Militia claiming their discharge obliged us to discontinue the pursuit. The last account I had from the Enemy they were at Cross Creek, and I think it is possible they may fall down to Wilmington: but this is not probable; or at least not certain.[7]

From a persuasion that the Enemy wish to get full possession of this State, and are making every effort to effect it; and as their advance northward secures their possessions Southward I think it will be our true plan of policy to move into South Carolina, notwithstanding the risque and difficulty attending the manoeuvre. This will oblige the Enemy to follow us or give up their posts there. If they follow us, it will releive us in this state. That whether they go or stay an advantage must result from the measure. Besides this advantage, it will keep the Enemys force divided and enable us to employ a greater body of Militia against them, and also to fight them to more advantage, as the force of the Militia don't encrease with the regular troops in the same proportion as their numbers encrease; on the contrary the militia constantly losses their compaᶦᵗive force as their numbers are augmented.

From these considerations I am determined to march immediately into South Carolina, being persuaded that if I continue in this State the Enemy will hold their ground in the southern States; and this also. Another advantage may result from it, which is we shall live upon the resources which the Enemy have at command; and the boldness of the manoeuvre will make them think I have secret reasons which they cannot comprehend. If I can get supplies and secure a retreat I fear no bad consequences.

Captain [Anthony] Singleton has just returned from Prince Edward [Va.], who I sent after more Cannon, and reports that we are in the most disagreable situation respecting Lead. I beg my dear Baron that you will take every measure to get a supply in your power. Write to the Board of War and Congress, and purchase or impress all you can. Also urge the Governor of Virginia to employ as many People as he can to get a supply from the lead Mines; if the vein is not run out. To be out of ammunition will be ruinous, especially as there will be a great demand for it in all probability.[8]

If the Pennsylvania Line comes on let them take the upper route by the Saura Towns, Shallow Ford, and Charlotte; unless the Enemy should go down to Wilmington; in that case they may take their route by Hillsborough, Bells Mill, Colston, and Camden, taking care to send forward and advice me of their approach and also guarding against any sudden movements of the Enemy into the upper Country.[9] The Cloathing I advised you to send to Hillsborough; let it go by the upper route to Oliphants Mill on the Catawba.[10] Indeed all the Stores coming to the southern Army should go by that route.

I am persuaded the Enemy will make great exertions to subjugate the southern States and we must exert ourselves accordingly. The many disadvantages we labor under give us bad prospects for obtaining glory, but the more difficulties we surmount the greater the glory in the end. The Enemy got the ground the other Day, but we the victory. They had the splendor, we the advantage, and tho' it is not glorious for me it is beneficial to the community. With real esteem I am dear Baron Your mo: ob[t] humble serv[t]   NATH GREENE

LS (NHi).

1. The two letters are above (vol. 7: 467–68, 473–74).

2. Steuben's "disappointment" was the failure of the Franco-American expedition against Benedict Arnold. (See note at NG to Lafayette, 29 March, above [vol. 7: 429n].)

3. NG's letter to Lafayette, dated 3 April, is below; before it arrived, Lafayette had received orders from Washington to remain in the Southern Department. (See Lafayette to NG, 17 April, below.)

4. The French expeditionary force had indeed returned to Rhode Island after it was turned back by a British fleet at the entrance to Chesapeake Bay. (See Washington to Rochambeau, 31 March, Fitzpatrick, GW, 21: 397.)

5. In his letter of 27 March, above, Steuben had asked to leave his post in Virginia and join NG. (vol. 7: 473–74) He remained in Virginia, but Lafayette's presence there and the dislike that many public officials and citizens felt toward Steuben left him isolated and nearly forgotten. (See Davies to NG, 17 June, below.)

6. See NG to Steuben, 22 March, above (vol. 7: 463–64).

7. Finding that he could not obtain the necessary supplies there to refit his army, Lord Cornwallis left Cross Creek on 1 April and marched toward Wilmington. (Cornwallis to Clinton, 10 April, Stevens, Clinton-Cornwallis Controversy, 1: 397; "Von Bose Journal," p. 54)

8. Steuben gave Gov. Thomas Jefferson a copy of this part of the letter. (See Jefferson to the Virginia Delegates in Congress, 15 April, Boyd, Jefferson Papers, 5: 440.) Even before he received the extract, Jefferson, who was well aware of the shortage of lead, had taken steps to obtain a supply. On 27 March, he wrote Col. Charles Lynch, the manager of the lead mines, urging him to "employ a much larger number of hands," as the mines needed to be "worked to the greatest extent." (Ibid., p. 263) On 6 April, Jefferson wrote the Virginia delegates to ask that lead be sent from the North; Steuben sent a similar plea to Washington. (See ibid., p. 367; Steuben to Washington, 14 April, NHi.) A short time

later, the vein of lead was rediscovered in the Virginia mines, ending the crisis and bringing the "prospect of a very abundant Supply of Lead." (David Ross to Jefferson, 4 May, Boyd, *Jefferson Papers*, 5: 600)

9. NG assumed that the Pennsylvania line was already on its way to the Southern Department. As noted at Washington to NG, 1 June, below, those troops did not leave York, Pa., until 26 May. In the meantime, NG had decided to keep them in Virginia. (See ibid. and NG's letters to Lafayette of 1 and 14 May, both below.)

10. See NG to Steuben, 22 March, above (vol. 7: 463). Map 1 includes places listed in this paragraph.

*   *   *

¶ [DOCTOR JAMES BROWNE TO CAPTAIN WILLIAM PIERCE, JR., Guilford, N.C., 2 April 1781. Has had "the Misfortune of loosing your Capt[n] Fautleroy. Barret is in a fair Way to recover."[1] General Stevens left for home yesterday; Browne could not persuade him to stay any longer.[2] As directed, Browne is sending [Dr. Charles] Warfield and [Dr. Reuben] Gilder to camp. "The wounded at [Col. Peter] Perkins's [in Pittsylvania County, Va.] are all in a fair Way of Recovering. The wounded at this Place will not recover so fast from the Badness of their Wounds." Dr. Wallace has left nothing undone "for their Relief."[3] Browne hopes his own decision to remain with the hospital and with Barret will meet with NG's approval. Asks for a ream of paper, which both hospitals lack. Capt. [John] Davidson's health requires him to "visit the warm Springs"; he then wants to go to Maryland until he learns "what Regiment he will be arranged in."[4] Asks what to do with "those Soldiers who have been receipted for, and are recovered of their Wounds"; there will soon be many of that sort.[5] The hospital at Perkins's is well-supplied with provisions; the one at Guilford, he fears, will suffer from "the Ignorance, and Inaction" of Mr. [James?] Hunter, whom Col. [William R.] Davie appointed to supply them. Browne hopes to be in camp in a "Fortnight." ALS (Greene Papers: DLC) 2 pp.]

1. Griffin Faunt le Roy and William Barret had been wounded at Guilford Court House. (See Nathaniel Pendleton to Washington, 17 March, above [vol. 7: 445 and n].)

2. Edward Stevens had suffered a leg wound in the battle. He was leading troops in Virginia by early June. (Lafayette to La Luzerne, 16 June, Idzerda, *Lafayette Papers*, 4: 188)

3. NG had sent Dr. James Wallace to care for wounded American prisoners immediately after the battle of Guilford Court House. (See NG to Cornwallis, 16 March, above [vol. 7: 433].)

4. NG's reply has not been found, but Davidson was in Maryland in early June. (*Archives of Md.*, 45: 464)

5. The wounded who were "receipted for" were probably British soldiers whom Cornwallis had left behind when he began his retreat to Cross Creek. Pierce's reply has not been found.

¶ [FROM COLONEL WILLIAM DAVIES, Chesterfield, Va., 2 April 1781. Col. [Lewis] Morris will inform NG of the "footing" upon which Davies has agreed to head the Virginia war department.[1] NG is aware of the importance of the post and that it has previously been conducted on a "principle" that "will forever prove ruinous." The Assembly, after "displacing" the former head, directed that a plan for running the department be submitted at its next session. The governor, "who will resign as soon as they meet," has referred the matter to Davies, who believes the department "stands upon a very insufficient footing."[2] The state's quartermaster department, which is vital to the Continental quartermaster department and to the Southern Army, is also in a "deplorable and indeed ridiculous situation." At Davies's recommendation, Capt. [Henry] Young has been appointed to head it. Davies is sure that the advantages of having Continental officers at the head of state departments "will soon be evident."[3] He has received permission from "the Executive" to forward money to pay the Virginia line and has fourteen wagonloads of hospital stores and rum ready to send to NG's army. His "principal attention," though, is directed to the "removal of a numerous artillery and a large quantity of military stores" belonging to Virginia, "which are scattered every where along the water, as if intended for the enemy. The Government are almost entirely ignorant of the state of their stores, and cannot give me any tolerable account of them." Davies gives the whereabouts of more than fifty cannon but says removing them will be difficult.[4] The state has only thirteen wagons in its service, and they have been "foolishly dispersed upon the most trifling purposes."

Directs NG's attention to "the article of lead." The miners have "lost the vein," and none is to be had. Yesterday, Davies received a "demand" for lead for [George Rogers] Clark's western army that exceeds the amount the state possesses. Davies has delayed releasing lead to Clark until he learns about NG's situation; he will make sure that NG is "first supplied." Suggests that NG make an "official application for a large quantity . . . at once, otherwise the back woods will get it all, for my silly countrymen are exhausting the whole resources of this state in their ridiculous thirst for, I can hardly tell what, in the back country."[5] He asks for orders from NG if he can be of service and says "there is no person more devoted" than he is to NG's "interests." ALS (Greene Papers: DLC) 3 pp.]

1. For more about the "footing" on which Davies agreed to head the state's war department, see Steuben's letters to NG of 30 March, above, and this date, below.

2. The Virginia legislature, in separate resolutions of 20 March, called for the removal of George Muter as head of the war office and ordered the governor to submit a "State thereof before the next Session." ("Journal of House of Delegates, March 1781 Session," *Bulletin of the Virginia State Library* 17 [January 1928]: 41, 43) By the time the legislature reconvened on 10 May, the invasion by a British force under Gen. William Phillips had made it "impracticable" for Davies to submit his reorganization plan. (Jefferson to Speaker of House of Delegates, 10 May, Boyd, *Jefferson Papers*, 5: 626–27) The British advance also caused a delay in Thomas Jefferson's departure from office and in the naming of a successor. (See note at NG to Jefferson, 27 June, below.)

3. Capt. Henry Young, a Virginia officer who continued to hold his Continental commission, arrived at Richmond on 31 March to begin serving as state quartermaster. Within a week, he was so "disheartened at the distracted situation of affairs in his department" that he decided to decline the appointment. (Davies to Steuben, 4 April, Steuben Microfilm) Davies then turned to Baron Steuben, who wrote Young a gracious letter that persuaded him to serve. (Steuben to Young, 4 April, ibid.; Boyd, *Jefferson Papers*, 5: 389n)

4. In his reply of 11 April, below, NG advised Davies not to send money to pay the Virginia line. Some of the cannon that Davies had discovered belonged to North Carolina. In a letter to Richard Caswell of 11 April, below, NG ordered them moved to safety.

5. As seen in his letter to Steuben of this date, above, NG had made an "official

application" for a large supply of lead; in a reply to Davies of 11 April, below, he asked that 20,000 pounds be reserved for the Southern Army.

¶ [FROM COLONEL JAMES EMMET, "Camp at Stewerts Creek near Avery's," N.C., 2 April 1781.[1] Has reliable information that the British left Cross Creek "yesterday" on the road to "Rockfish."[2] Emmet, who has asked Colonel Malmedy to leave Capt. [Pleasant] Henderson's detachment with him, is marching to Cross Creek and will be "happy to receive" NG's orders.[3] ALS (MiU-C) 1 p.]

1. Emmet added after his signature that he was "Col° of the [Cumberland] County."
2. Rockfish Creek flowed into the Cape Fear River from the west, a few miles below Cross Creek.
3. As seen in his letter to NG of this date, below, the Marquis de Malmedy complied with Emmet's request.

¶ [FROM GENERAL ROBERT LAWSON, Hillsborough, N.C., 2 April 1781. The wife of a British surgeon, who was left behind in Hillsborough because of illness, seeks permission to rejoin her husband. Lawson has referred her to NG and is sure he will grant her request if possible. ALS (MiU-C) 1 p.]

*   *   *

From Colonel Henry Lee, Jr.

My dear Gen[l]   April 2[d] &c [1781][1]

As you have been pleased to honor me with your confidence, I take the liberty to communicate to you my Sentiments respecting your plan of operations.

I am decidedly of opinion with you that nothing is left for you, but to imitate the example of Scipio Africanus.[2]

This conduct may eventually undo the Successes gained by the enemy the last campaign, & must probably render abortive every effort of his Lordship [Cornwallis] to establish himself in this state [i.e., North Carolina].

Thousands of difficultys oppose your success, & yet as I said before, no other System can promise you naught, but loss to the United States, & disgrace to your arms. I am conscious that no General in any period undertook an enterprize more glorious. I am also conscious that no General ever commanded troops worse appointed or worse supplyed, than those which form your present army.

These numerous & material difficultys will require the utmost wisdom & decision to be counteracted.

I think the following matters claim your immediate attention.

The passage of the Pedee, Supply of ammunition transported in such a manner, that it cannot be damaged, an extra pair of shoes per man, the 1st rgt of cavalry to be collected & to join the troops left in this State, the most cautious instructions to the com[manding] officer of the Pen: division, least his ignorance of the mode of warfare in this country may expose his troops to ruin: a proclamation pardoning deserters, pointing out the delusion of the Tory[s], breaking up paroles given to inhabitants taken from their houses by the enemy & recommending union & zeal to all orders of the people.

I am certain that good consequences must result from a proclamation at this period: perhaps it may be proper for government to do something of the same sort.

I think it would be politic in government to attend to measures for the forming a public press as the proper communicatur of events would tend very much to stir up the patriotism of the people. It would also be politic to apply to their religious feelings & the influence of preachers.[3] By steps of this sort the govern[ment] might probably put the State in a posture of defence, during the absence of your army.

I shall be happy to hear what news you may have by the last dispatch & am most aff[y] Your obdt   HENRY LEE JUN[R]

Tr (GWG Transcript: CSmH)

1. No place was given.

2. During the Punic Wars, Scipio Africanus abandoned the Italian peninsula to Hannibal, the Carthaginian general who had defeated several Roman armies and was marching unchallenged through Roman territory. Scipio moved instead to attack Hannibal's home base at Carthage, on the North African coast. His audacity was rewarded when Hannibal was forced to leave Italy and return to defend his homeland. Scipio defeated him in battle there. (*Columbia Encyclopedia*, 3d ed. [New York: Columbia University Press, 1963])

3. NG had already taken steps to address some of the matters Lee mentioned. These included securing boats to cross the Pee Dee River, extra shoes for the troops, a supply of ammunition, and assembling the First Continental Regiment of Dragoons. (See Wade to NG, this date, below; and NG to Singleton, 27 March [vol. 7: 472–73]; NG to Board of War, 30 March; and Steuben to NG, 2 April, all above.) NG worked later on such other matters as attempting to set up a "public press." (See NG to Walters, 10 July, below.) It does not appear that NG ever sent the "cautious instructions" to the commander of the Pennsylvania troops or issued the proclamation that Lee recommended, although he did press the North Carolina government for a policy of leniency toward the state's Loyalists. (See NG to Alexander Martin, 9 October, below.)

*   *   *

¶ [**FROM COLONEL CHARLES LYNCH,**[1] "Camp W[m] Daniels," N.C., 2 April 1781. Hearing that they were to march to headquarters, 100 of Lynch's men left for home without his knowledge and without officers. They left "Publick" muskets, which Lynch sends to NG, and some cartridge boxes. The only excuse Lynch can offer for the men is that they are "Poor," anxious to get home, and "Comeing by Hed Q[rts] woud Keep them two Days Longer." He has sent someone to "try to Collect" and march them "in good Order Least they Shou'd Do somthing Wrong on their Way." For this reason, he will be unable to "Wait on" NG. ALS (MiU-C) 1 p.]

1. Lynch commanded a detachment of militia from Bedford County, Va.

¶ [**FROM THE MARQUIS DE MALMEDY**, Cape Fear [River], N.C., 2 April 1781.[1] Believing he "could not decline" Col. [James] Emmet's request, Malmedy has left Capt. [Pleasant] Henderson's company with Emmet, who has received word that the British evacuated Cross Creek.[2] Malmedy will move as quickly as possible to join Gen. [Alexander] Lillington. ALS (NNPM) 1 p.]

1. Malmedy was with Emmet, whose letter to NG of this date, above, placed him at Stewart's Creek. The creek runs into Rockfish Creek, a tributary of the Cape Fear River.

2. See Emmet to NG, this date, above.

¶ [FROM GENERAL WILLIAM MOULTRIE, [Charleston, S.C.], 2 April 1781. He has sent Congress copies of his correspondence with Col. [Nisbet] Balfour about the sending of prisoners of war to the West Indies.[1] Tr (GWG Transcript: CSmH) 1 p.]

1. See Moultrie to NG, 3 April, below.

¶ [FROM COLONEL ROBERT MUNFORD, "Richland," Va., 2 April 1781.[1] Is "much obliged" to NG for the "permit to return Home." He has recovered enough from his "Indisposition" to be able to carry out NG's orders again.[2] ALS (MiU-C) 1 p.]

1. Munford, a Virginia Continental officer, had commanded a detachment of militia that joined NG before the battle of Guilford Court House. "Richland" was the name of Munford's plantation in Mecklenburg County, Virginia.

2. As seen in his letter of 4 March, above (vol. 7: 390), Munford had suffered an attack of gout.

¶ [FROM BARON STEUBEN, Chesterfield Court House, Va., 2 April 1781. Col. [Lewis] Morris will deliver this letter and inform NG of the situation in Virginia; Steuben regrets that the report will not be more "satisfactory."[1] If Steuben could follow his own inclinations, he would immediately set out to join NG—such is his desire to serve with NG and his disgust with his situation in Virginia. It is his duty, however, to remain in Virginia until he can bring on the "first Detachment," which he is doing his "utmost" to assemble. Hopes it will number 500 infantry and sixty to eighty cavalry.[2] Capt. [Nathaniel] Irish's artificers have marched to Prince Edward Court House. Steuben has asked [Richard] Claiborne to find "proper" working space for them and has requested that "Government" send them 12,000 pounds of powder, 6,500 pounds of lead, and sixty reams of paper. Irish can make 300,000 musket cartridges with those supplies. That is all the ammunition that Steuben can send NG, as he does not have enough cartridges for the militia now "under Arms."[3] Morris also brings Col. [William] Davies's plan for operating the Virginia War Office. Steuben believes "much good" will come from Davies's heading a department that "has hithe[r]to been absolutely neglected."[4] It is up to NG, who must exercise his "power for the good of the Service," to reconcile Davies's appointment with the "System laid down by congress."[5] Steuben wants to appoint "Capt. Prior" as commissary of military stores. The office has previously been held by the senior artillery officer in the department and has passed "from one hand to another, as these officers may be absent or present." Assures NG that Pryor is "active, and intelligent." While serving under a "temporary appointment of this nature" from Steuben, Pryor has provided "the resources" that Steuben has received from the state.[6] Steuben proposes that supplies coming from the North be sent to Pryor. They can then either be used to outfit the troops marching to NG or, if needed by NG, can be shipped directly to the Southern Army, where a deputy commissary can distribute them in accordance with instructions from Col. [Otho] Williams, the assistant inspector.[7] Steuben has ordered the cavalry to rendezvous at Petersburg. He has sent staff officers there to outfit the cavalry; they are not to issue anything, however, without instructions from Davies.[8] Only in this way can Steuben prevent "the partial and improper distributions which have hitherto taken place." NG should make this arrangement known to the army and prohibit corps commanders from sending officers to receive "particular Articles for their Corps." As nothing will be delivered to the officers, it can now "only serve as a pretext for absenting themselves from the Army and neglecting their Duty."[9] LS (MiU-C) 4 pp.]

1. On Morris's mission in Virginia, see note at Steuben to NG, 30 March, above. Morris brought this letter with him when he returned to the army. (See NG to Steuben, 15 April, below.)

2. Neither Steuben nor the detachment joined NG.

3. Gov. Thomas Jefferson reported to the Marquis de Lafayette on 24 March that 10,900 pounds of powder and 6,000 pounds of lead had been sent to Irish, who had 18,000 cartridges on hand and was making 3,000 per day. Jefferson said he was sorry to inform Lafayette that the state's "Stock of Lead will not employ him [i.e., Irish] much longer even at this slow rate." (Boyd, *Jefferson Papers*, 5: 232)

4. On the appointment of Col. William Davies to head the Virginia War Office, see note at Steuben to NG, 30 March, above.

5. Steuben alluded to Davies's desire to serve as head of the state's war office without resigning his commission in the Continental army. (Davies to Steuben, 23 March, Steuben Microfilm) NG replied on 15 April, below, that the rules of Congress only prohibited the holding of more than one Continental office at the same time.

6. NG agreed to John Pryor's appointment. (Ibid.) As seen in Pryor's letter to NG of 25 July, below, however, the Board of War had already named another man to fill the post.

7. NG approved Steuben's proposal in his reply of 15 April, adding that Capt. Anthony Singleton had been serving as a deputy commissary of military stores with NG's army and that all issues had been made under the supervision of Otho Williams.

8. Steuben's decision came as a result of NG's prodding. He wrote Gen. Peter Muhlenberg on 1 April that NG "presses me to compleat the Cavalry but how I am to procure either Men Horses or Equipment I know not." (Steuben Microfilm) On the same day, Steuben ordered Richard Claiborne, the Continental quartermaster in Virginia, to "lay in" accoutrements and supplies for "300 horses" and a "large Magazine of Forage." (Claiborne to Jefferson, 2 April, Boyd, *Jefferson Papers*, 5: 319) A few days later, Steuben recalled Armand's Legion from the lines at Portsmouth and instructed officers of the First and Third Continental Dragoons to take some of the new recruits to fill their units. (Steuben to Muhlenberg, 5 April, and White to Steuben, 5 April, Steuben Microfilm) Steuben's efforts were not successful, however. Only a small number of recruits arrived from the rendezvous points, and Claiborne found it impossible to obtain the needed supplies. (Claiborne to Steuben, 4 April, ibid.) Finally, the renewal of offensive operations by the British in Virginia and their great superiority in mounted troops caused Lafayette to cancel plans to send the dragoons to NG. (See Lafayette to NG, 18 May, below.)

9. NG approved Steuben's plan in his reply of 15 April.

¶ [FROM COLONEL THOMAS WADE, Haley's Ferry, N.C., 2 April 1781. The order to "Brigadier Gen[l] Caswell" was not complied with until 18 March, nor were any horsemen provided.[1] To remove the stores, Wade marched directly toward "this Place" with four wagons, but upon reaching the Cape Fear River he heard "Canonadeing" and discovered that the enemy were at Ramsey's Mill. He crossed the river thirty miles below the British and pushed for Haley's Ferry by forced marches but was attacked near Cole's Bridge by 300 Loyalists and 100 British soldiers. Only twenty of Wade's men "Stood to Fight"; if the other seventy-five had not run away, he thinks he could have "Repulsed" the attackers. Some of his men, who were captured and paroled, report that Wade's casualties were three killed, two wounded, and seven taken prisoner. The enemy, who suffered four killed in the attack, captured the wagons, some carts, a wagonload of Col. [Abel] Kolb's household goods, and some of Kolb's slaves, who were accompanying it. They likewise captured all of the horses. The slaves, household goods, and horses were "Made Plunder of"; the wagons were "Burnt Instantly." Some British and Loyalist troops are said to be marching toward Haley's Ferry from Snow Island, S.C., where they freed some prioners. Kolb's men have "Chearfully" gone to join Gen. Marion in an attack on these troops, who now are reportedly heading toward Camden.[2] As wagons are scarce "here," Wade has asked "Gen[l] Polk" for some to move the supplies.[3] He has only twenty men with him; "the Rest Run home." In a postscript, he reports that boats have arrived at Haley's Ferry from "Spinkses," guarded by people of "this County."[4] ALS (MiU-C) 2 pp.]

1. Ichabod Burnet, one of NG's aides, had sent the orders to Gen. William Caswell on 9 March, above (vol. 7: 414). Burnet asked Caswell to provide fifty infantrymen and twenty-five cavalrymen for Wade.

2. An enemy force under Col. Welbore Ellis Doyle had captured and destroyed Gen. Francis Marion's base at Snow Island in late March, while Marion was occupied elsewhere. (For background on the raid, see note at Wade to NG, 19 April, below.) Doyle also freed twenty-six British prisoners who had been confined at Snow Island. (*Royal Gazette* [Charleston, S.C.], 31 March–4 April) After destroying Marion's base, Doyle's men began foraging the plantations in the area. They advanced up the Pee Dee River in the direction of Haley's Ferry but were soon recalled to Camden by that post's commander, Lord Rawdon, who had learned that NG was marching to Camden. (Bass, *Marion*, pp. 157–62; Rankin, *Swamp Fox*, p. 177; Rawdon to Balfour, 12 April, PRO 30/11/5)

3. Thomas Polk, who would remain a colonel, apparently did not send the wagons. As seen in Wade's letter of 10 April, below, most of the meal stored at Haley's Ferry was damaged; the rest was sent in wagons, which NG provided, to feed the Southern Army on its march to Camden.

4. The boats were probably ones that Col. Thaddeus Kosciuszko had had built while NG's army was camped near the Pee Dee in January. (See NG to Kosciuszko, 1 January, and Lewis Morris to Kosciuszko, 1 February, both above [vol. 7: 35, 232].) NG sent instructions to Wade on 8 April, below.

¶ [**GENERAL GREENE'S ORDERS**, Headquarters, Ramsey's Mill, N.C., 3 April 1781. The wagonmaster general and his deputies may enlist anyone from the army who is not "engaged for more than three months." Troops are to "Wash and clean themselves to Day, to get their arms in good order and be prepared to march at a short warning." Greene Orderly Book (CSmH) 1 p.]

¶ [**TO JOSEPH CLAY**.[1] From Camp, Ramsey's Mill, N.C., 3 April 1781. Has his letter of 20 March [not found]. Clay is to have all the osnaburg cloth "on hand made into Overalls" for the troops and is to purchase as many shoes as he can. He should avoid "No care or expence," as those articles are "indispensibly necessary to the operations of the army as well as to the comfort of the Troops." He is to secure the public stores in his possession by "removing them into the upper Country"; Hillsborough would be a "good post for the present." Clay should then make his report and await further orders.² Cy (MiU-C) 1 p.]

1. Clay was paymaster and a purchasing agent for the Southern Army.
2. Clay replied on 11 May, below.

¶ [TO COLONEL JAMES EMMET. From Camp, Deep River, N.C., 3 April 1781. Has his letter of 31 March [not found]. Emmet should move to a place where he can gather intelligence "conveniently and with the least risque" and send it to NG and Gen. [Alexander] Lillington. Adds: "Dont be surprisd if my movements dont correspond with your Ideas of military propriety. War is an intricate business, and people are often savd by ways and means they least look for or expect." NG will do all he can to protect "this Country" but must keep the "manner" to himself. Emmet should place as many spies as possible "in & about the enemies Camp"; they are his "most effectual security." To avoid being surprised, he should "never stay more than one day" in any place "within twenty or thirty miles" of the British. He should also post along the major roads "trusty fellows," who know the country, "have no Arms," and can reach him quickly if the "enemy pass." Expects the British to try to "surprise the Militia" if they remain "many days" at Cross Creek and are able to cross the [Cape Fear] river. Emmet should take precautions. "Dont suppose your selves more secure by days than by nights." He is to remove "from the neighbourhood of the River" any horses fit for cavalry service and is to notify NG "immediately" if the British "move farther down the River or towards the Pedee."¹ ADfS (MiU-C) 3 pp.]

1. Emmet sent reports on 2 April, above, and 4 April, below, that the British were moving "down the River" towards Wilmington.

*   *   *

To the Marquis de Lafayette

Head Quarters Col Ramseys
Dear Sir   Deep River [N.C.] April 3ᵈ 1781
    This day your letter of the 25th of March was deliverd me; and two of the 25ᵗʰ & 27th of from Baron Stuben, by the last of which I find the British fleet continue masters of the Sea.¹ The Baron thinks the French fleet have come to Cape Fear, this I can hardly suppose.² He also adds that you had set out for Anapolis with an intention to return to the Northward.³ I cannot think this will be advisable for you to return, as the enemy are greatly reinforced in Virginia, and superior by far to the southward.⁴ The Northern Army must be secured by the detachments which is made from New York to the Southward; and the Northern States will certainly have reinforced Genⁱ Washington before this; therefore I cannot apprehend any thing for the safety of the Northern

Army; and to this may be added the plan of the Ministry is to push the war to the Southard and not to the Northward.[5] These reasons and the very critical situation of the Southern States and the fatal consequences that must attend your drawing off your force if the enemy push their operations as they most undoubtedly will induces me to wish you to March your force Southward by Alexandria & Fredricksburg to Richmond which will be a point from which you can cooperate either with me or the Militia in the lower Country [of Virginia], as the movements of the Enemy may render necessary. As we cannot effect any thing splendid it is necessary to guard against a misfortune. I am confident General Washington will approve of the measure and from this perswasion venture to give you this advice until His Excellencys pleasure can be farther known.[6] It is impossible for the Southern States with all the exertions they can make under the many disadvantages they labour to save themselves. Subsistence is very difficult to be got and therefore it is necessary that the best of troops should be employed that a less number may answer. Every exertion should be made for the salvation of the Southern States for on them depend the liberty of the Northern.

It will be our interest to keep the enemy as much divided as possible for many reasons: As our force is composed principally of Militia we can avail our selves of a much greater number when they are divided than when they act collectively. We can also fight them to much more advantage divided than collected as the force of the Militia dont increase from the increase of numbers in the same proportion as the force of regulars does.

For these reasons I have determined to carry the war into South Carolinia to prevent Lord Cornwallis from forming a junction with [Benedict] Arnold, and expect by that movement to draw him immediately out of the State,[7] and if you follow on to support me it is not impossible but we may give him a drubbing, especially if General Wayne comes up with the Pensylvanians.[8] But if you go immediately to the northward Virginia will not be able to send us another man; and the dangerous and critical situation they will be left in, will prevent them from making the necessary exertions raising the Continental troops.

The last accounts I had from the Enemy they were at Cross Creek, and probably they mean to take post there, but I am rather inclind to think they will fall down to Wilmington; however this is quite uncertain.[9]

It would afford me great pleasure to have you with the Southern Army and here is a sufficient field to exercise your genius and gratify your ambition. I kindly thank you for your affectionate and friendly address upon our misfortunes at Guilford. I did all I could to obtain victory and with the pride of a republican feel a conscious superiority to that black torrent of censure that ever follows (for a time) the unfortunate.[10] With esteem and affection I am my dear Marquis Your most obed humble S[r]   N GREENE

ADfS (NNPM).

1. Steuben's two letters are above (vol. 7: 467–68, 473–74); Lafayette's has not been found. Steuben, in his letter of 27 March, had reported the return of the British fleet to the Chesapeake, along with ships bringing enemy reinforcements from New York.

2. Lafayette informed NG in a letter of 4 April, below, that the French fleet, which the British had turned back near the entrance to Chesapeake Bay, had returned to Rhode Island.

3. Lafayette, intending to return to the Northern Army after plans to attack Gen. Benedict Arnold's force were abandoned, had gone to Annapolis, Md., where he had earlier left his troops to wait for transportation to Virginia. (See ibid.)

4. The British reinforcement in Virginia consisted of troops who had recently arrived from New York under the command of Gen. William Phillips. (See note at Washington to NG, 21 March, above [vol. 7: 459n].)

5. NG meant that the British transfer of troops to the South had made the Northern Army's situation more secure. As noted at Washington to NG, 27 February, above (vol. 7: 365n), hopes for a significant addition to the Northern Army through enlistment were not realized. In November 1780, a delegate in Congress had sent NG intelligence obtained by John Adams in Paris that the British ministry was planning a vigorous prosecution of the war in the South. (See John Mathews to NG, 27 November 1780 [vol. 6: 508].)

6. Washington wrote Lafayette on 6 April, rescinding his orders to return to the North and instructing Lafayette to march his detachment "as speedily as possible" to reinforce NG's army. Washington believed the augmented British force in Virginia was likely to "cooperate with Lord Cornwallis" and thereby place NG in a precarious situation. (Fitzpatrick, GW, 21: 421) Lafayette, in a reply to NG from Baltimore on 17 April, below, described the difficulties he had encountered in trying to equip and prepare his detachment for its altered mission and outlined his plans to march southward.

7. On the decision to "carry the war into South Carolina," see NG to Washington, 29 March, above (vol. 7: 481–82). Instead of following NG into South Carolina, Cornwallis took his army to Virginia.

8. Because of the growing threat from the British in Virginia, Lafayette did not join the Southern Army. NG sent him orders on 1 May, below, to take command of military operations in that state. Gen. Anthony Wayne was to bring a division of the Pennsylvania Continental line to the South. As noted at Washington to NG, 1 June, below, they did not march until 26 May—and then only as far as Virginia.

9. As NG surmised, Cornwallis did move his troops from Cross Creek to Wilmington, N.C.

10. Lafayette's "address" must have been in his letter of 25 March. For more on the battle of Guilford Court House, see NG to Huntington, 16 March, above (vol. 7: 433–36). It is not known what "censure" NG had in mind. Public reaction to news of the battle and NG's conduct was generally favorable. (See, for example, La Luzerne to NG, this date, below.)

*   *   *

¶ [CAPTAIN NATHANIEL PENDLETON TO COLONEL NICHOLAS LONG. From Headquarters, Deep River, N.C., 3 April 1781. Long's letters of 12 and 22 March have arrived, along with the "Stores enumerated, except two halters & a pack saddle or two."[1] NG thanks him for sending the stores and asks him to continue his exertions. NG especially wants an account of "all the powder & lead" in North Carolina that Long "can possibly Command." Pendleton fears the army will "feel the want of" this "article of the last importance"; asks Long to do all he can to increase the supply.[2] ADfS (MiU-C) 1 p.]

1. Long's letter of 12 March has not been found. In that of 21 March, above (vol. 7: 457–58), Long had enclosed an invoice for three wagonloads of stores that he was sending to the army.

2. See also NG to Long, 30 March, above. Long's reply to Pendleton's letter has not been found.

*   *   *

To Governor Abner Nash of North Carolina

Head Quarters Col Ramseys
Deep River [N.C.] April 3^d 1781

Sir

By letters just receivd from the Marquis de la Fyette and Baron Stuben I find that Admiral Arburthnot with 6 Ships of the line and a considerable reinforcment of land forces had arrivd in Chessapeak Bay; and had beat off the french fleet coming into the Bay after two pretty smart actions.[1] The Marquis is also on his March to join the Northern Army.[2]

The enemy are surrounding you on all sides and reinforcing in every quarter. In this your very critical situation you have nothing left but to exert your selves equal to the occasion. From the oppressions of the enemy and the cruelties of the tories you see what you have to hope without it.

There are four things necessary which claim the attention of the Legislature on their first meeting. First Make a law which will draw out your regular troops, and whether drafted or enlisted, there should be a great penalty against any person who harbours or conceals a deserter.[3] Secondly put your Militia upon a better establishment and subject them to the same dicipline while in service as the Continental troops. Without dicipline they will ever disgrace themselves and the state to which they belong.[4] I am not acquainted with the mode in which your Militia are officerd but the officers should be appointed either by the Governor or the commanding Officers of the different Districts. The Militia should all be obligd to find themselves with a Cartouch box; for want of which there is more than treble waste of Ammunition necessary for the service. If you dont raise your regular troops and put your Militia upon a better footing your state cannot be defended. It is not numbers that is wanting it is dicipline, and good government.[5]

The third thing which claims the attention of the Assembly is the Comissarys department. I recommended Col Davie for a superintendant to be invested with certain powers for appointing Commisis-saries and providing provisions. He has been acting under an appointment from the Governor; but wishes his appointment to be confirmed by a law and as the task is arduous there should be a hansome consideration annexed to it.[6]

The fourth thing is the transportation business. I can add nothing new upon this subject, having given my sentiments fully on this matter in a letter written at Pedee last winter.[7]

In one of my letters written last winter I requested to be vested with powers to call out such Militia to reinforce the Continental Army as the service might require. I have frequently seen the necessity for these powers nor can I take proper measures for your security without them.[8] It is in vain to expect protection from the Army unless you give effectual support. I flatter myself I have given you sufficient proof of my zeal to serve you, tho I have not been as fortunate as I could wish nor shall any thing on my part be wanting to promote the welfare of the state and secure it against the inroads of the enemy. But you must support me or I can do nothing. I have innumerable difficulties to contend with; and I hope the Legislature will be disposd to lend me all the assistance in their power.[9] I have the honor to be with great respect your Excellencys Most Obed^t humble Sr NATH GREENE

Since my last I have receivd a letter from Col Polk who refuses to act under the Commision you were pleasd to send him. Nothing short of a Brigadiers commision will be accepted. Your Excellency will take such measures in the matter as you may think the public good may require.[10]

Col Jones has servd with the army for some time past, and from his observation can give your Excellency many intimations respecting reformations wanting in the Militia establishment; which will be worthy the attention of the legislature. I cannot help recommending Col Jones as a person worthy of high command in the Militia service and I am perswaded the honor and interest of the State would be greatly promoted by it.[11] I have the honor to be with great respect Your Excellencys Most Obedt humble Sr N GREENE

ADfS (MiU-C).

1. On the letters from Lafayette and Steuben, see NG to Lafayette, this date, above. The turning back of the French by a British fleet commanded by Adm. Marriot Arbuthnot near the entrance to Chesapeake Bay is discussed at Steuben to NG, first letter of 4 March, above (vol. 7: 386–87n). One of the "pretty smart actions" that Steuben reported turned out to be thunder. (See Steuben to NG, 25 March, above [ibid., p. 468 and n]; Lafayette to NG, 4 April, below.) The reinforcement consisted of a detachment of 2,000 troops from New York commanded by Gen. William Phillips.

2. Lafayette was preparing to return to the Northern Army when Washington ordered him to join NG. (See note at NG to Lafayette, this date, above.)

3. As seen at Malmedy to NG, 10 February, above [vol. 7: 275n], the North Carolina

legislature had recently enacted a law for filling the state's Continental battalions; as noted at NG's letter to the legislature of 17 February, above, little came of the effort. (Ibid., p. 304n) Nash wrote NG on this date, below, that drafts for the Continental service were "going forward" and the "Law is being patiently submitted to." On the state's efforts to prevent the harboring of deserters, see note at NG to Caswell, 11 April, below.

4. NG and other Continental officers had been disturbed by the prevalence of desertion among North Carolina militiamen—officers included—from the Southern Army. (See, for example, Andrew Pickens to NG, 20 February and 5 March, and NG to Nash, 6 March, all above [vol. 7: 325, 399, 402].) Most of the state's militia force at the battle of Guilford Court House had deserted. (NG to Huntington, 16 March, above [ibid., pp. 437–39n]) In his letter of this date, below, Nash said the state was moving to "Subject the Militia Men who shamefully deserted their colours" at Guilford Court House to service as Continental soldiers "during the war." NG, replying to Nash on 13 April, below, called the "penal laws" Nash enclosed the "first of the kind" he had ever seen and "best calculated to render the Militia useful."

5. The North Carolina legislature appointed generals and field-grade officers. (NCSR, 10: 1008) Under the recent law establishing the Council Extraordinary, the governor, acting "with the advice of" the council, was also empowered "occasionally" to appoint or suspend "all militia officers." (Ibid., 24: 378) Company-grade officers were usually elected by the members of their units and were typically drawn from a community's upper classes. (Bartholomees, "Fight or Flee," pp. 74–75) The "disgrace" of the North Carolina militia had occurred at the battle of Guilford Court House; NG blamed his army's defeat there on the militia's performance. (See NG to Nash and NG to Washington, both 18 March, above [vol. 7: 448, 451].)

6. As noted at Alexander Martin to NG, 5 January, above (ibid., p. 54n), North Carolina governors "continued" Col. William R. Davie's appointment as superintendent commissary general during the next two years.

7. NG's request was in his second letter to Nash of 17 January, above (vol. 7: 137–38). As noted there, the legislature had taken no action in January on NG's specific proposals relating to transportation, nor did the lawmakers deal with this issue when they met again, in June and July. (The laws passed during that session are in NCSR, 24: 384–412.)

8. In his letter to Nash of 7 January, above, NG had suggested that someone who was with the army be empowered to call out militia reinforcements as needed. (Vol. 7: 63)

9. Nash's reply has not been found. NG enclosed a copy of this letter with the one he wrote to Nash on 21 May, below, saying he feared the original "may have miscarried."

10. For more on NG's unsuccessful efforts to obtain the command of the Salisbury militia district and a brigadier general's commission for Col. Thomas Polk, see Polk to NG, 8 March, above (vol. 7: 413 and n). In a letter to Polk of 7 April, below, NG said he had informed Nash that Polk would not serve without the commission. As seen in NG to Nash, 9 June, below, the militia appointment went to Col. Francis Lock.

11. On Willie Jones, see note at NG to Vanderhorst, 1 April, above.

*   *   *

¶ [TO COLONEL THOMAS POLK.[1] From Headquarters, "Deep River at Col Ramseys," N.C., 3 April 1781. Has his letter of 30 March [not found]; is "sorry the Militia are so hard to get into the field and still more so" that Polk's "appointment is not confirmed."[2] Col. [William R.] Davie, who will deliver this letter, will inform Polk of NG's "intentions." NG has "calculated largely" on the Salisbury militia and cannot effect his plans without them. Hopes "every exertion will be made" to call them out and wants Polk to command them, even though his appointment has not been confirmed. NG expects to march "by to morrow or next day" and will move rapidly. Polk can join the army on the west side of the Pee Dee River, "some where near Colstons or Masks Ferry."[3] He should form a "Magazine" of provisions near Charlotte and another at Oliphant's Mill; the militia should also bring a ten days' supply with them, as nothing is available in the country through which they will march and the army cannot supply them. Asks Polk to let him "know how matters stand and your final determination" by express.[4] ADfS (NcU) 2 pp.]

1. NG addressed Polk here and in many subsequent letters as "General." On the unsuccessful attempt to obtain a brigadier general's commission for Polk from North Carolina officials, see Polk to NG, 8 March, above (vol. 7: 413), and NG to Nash, this date, immediately above.

2. As noted at his letter to NG of 8 March, Polk was never appointed to command the Salisbury district militia.

3. On the date of the Southern Army's march, see NG's Orders of 5 April, below. NG hoped to bring the Salisbury militia force to South Carolina and put it under the command of Gen. Thomas Sumter. (NG to Sumter, 7 April, below)

4. Polk's reply has not been found. In a letter of 7 April, below, NG again inquired about the force he wanted Polk to collect. As seen by NG to Polk, 14 April, below, Polk did not bring the reinforcements.

¶ [CAPTAIN NATHANIEL PENDLETON TO DOCTOR JAMES WALLACE.[1] From Headquarters, Deep River, N.C., 3 April 1781. Has his letter of 27 March [not found]. NG has referred Wallace's request for supplies, "accomodation," and help with "the sick & wounded" to another physician, who will make the necessary arrangements. Those militiamen who are able to go home may do so, but the Continentals are not to leave, "except those who may probably be unfit for farther service." ADfS (MiU-C) 2 pp.]

1. Wallace, a surgeon, was tending the wounded from the battle of Guilford Court House. (See Browne to Pierce, 2 April, above.)

¶ [FROM LORD CORNWALLIS, Headquarters [near Elizabethtown, N.C.], 3 April 1781.[1] "Captain Brodrick [Henry Broderick]" has informed Cornwallis about the negotiations for a prisoner exchange. Cornwallis's "feelings for the Captives" make him anxious to conclude an agreement, but he considers some of NG's demands to be "manifestly unreasonable" and would think himself "criminal in agreeing to them." He must conclude that NG does not seriously want an exchange if he continues "to insist on them."[2] The first objectionable demand is NG's call for " 'mutual Choice of the Subjects of Exchange.' " That is "unprecedented" and would be "unequal to" the British, who hold more officers than the Americans; it would enable the Americans to choose those officers "most usefull" to them. The exchange must be by "dates of Captivity." A second demand of NG's, that officers " 'who cannot be exchanged' " be granted immediate paroles, "has not been the practice" and would favor the Americans, but Cornwallis will agree to it "in this district during our respective Commands, after an Exchange has taken place." Thirdly, NG has stipulated that prisoners " 'not be sent from the Continent.' " The "Feeding & guarding" of prisoners is not a "great expence or trouble" for the Americans, but is for the British. It has never been Cornwallis's intention, however, to send prisoners away while there is hope for an exchange, and he will agree to keep "the balance of" the American prisoners in Charleston, S.C., as long as a cartel is observed.[3] Finally, NG's proposal that officers be permitted to remain with captive prisoners at the request of " 'the party to whom they belong' " is unprecedented and would cause "inconvenience" and "disputes." Cornwallis cannot agree to it. Cornwallis has "acted openly & very far from any design of gaining an advantage" in "this transaction"; he hopes it is apparent to prisoners on both sides that he "does not wish to prolong the Distresses of the unfortunate." If NG is "inclined to close the Negociation by removing" these obstacles, Cornwallis proposes that the commissioners meet on 16 April at Cross Creek or any place along the Cape Fear River that is "more convenient" for NG.[4] Cy (PRO 30/11/91) 3 pp.]

1. The place was taken from another letter written by Cornwallis on this date. (PRO 30/11/85)

2. The conditions to which Cornwallis objected are in NG's instructions of 11 March, above, to Col. Edward Carrington (vol. 7: 425).

3. Cornwallis had threatened to send American prisoners from Charleston to the West Indies unless a general exchange were negotiated. (Cornwallis to NG, 4 February, above [ibid., pp. 250–51])

4. NG replied on 9 April, below.

¶ [FROM THE CHEVALIER DE LA LUZERNE, Philadelphia, 3 April 1781. Has learned that a "second squadron" will be sent to the United States. Does not know exactly when it will arrive, but the date should "not be very far distant."[1] This news is "in confidence"; NG can bolster "the courage of our fellow citizens" by assuring them of French assistance "without explaining the nature of the succours." The king "is determined to make the greatest efforts" to support the "cause of independance," but the states must also prepare themselves "to make vigorous efforts." Gov. [Abner] Nash should put North Carolina "in condition to co-operate in every thing we shall be in a situation to undertake."[2] If all is ready when the French forces arrive, the next campaign "cannot fail of being decisive." Sacrifices made now will save citizens from "losses which a prolongation of War cannot fail to bring." La Luzerne is not sure what the effect of England's declaration of war on Holland will be, but the British must not be given time to "form alliances" that could alter the state of affairs.[3] The situation is now "advantageous" for the allies, who must all "redouble" their efforts to "profit of it." He has received news of the battle of Guilford Court House and tells NG: "You have the modesty to call it a defeat, but it appears to me that the general Opinion is, you displayed on that occasion, those military Tallents, which have determined the Republic to confide to you, the command of its forces to the South."[4] Cy (MiU-C) 3 pp. The LS, which is in French, is also at MiU-C. The copy, in English, is in the hand of Nathanael Pendleton, NG's aide, who undoubtedly did the translation. As NG did not read French, he would have consulted Pendleton's copy.]

1. Writing on 4 April, below, the Marquis de Lafayette informed NG that he had received letters from the Comte de Vergennes and the Marquis de Castries, the French foreign and naval ministers, giving "Every Reason to Hope that Vigorous Measures will Be Adopted for our Relief in the Course of this Campaign." James McHenry, Lafayette's aide, elaborated on that statement in a letter to NG of 9 April, below, saying that the French force was expected in late April or "sometime" in May. "The land force will be

considerable, and the marine will ensure a complete superiority." La Luzerne had most likely received his information from the same "cabinet" sources as Lafayette. News arrived in May, however, that because of unsettled conditions in Europe, plans to send the second division of the French expeditionary force to America had been canceled. (Kennett, *French Forces*, p. 104)

2. See NG to Nash, 23 June, below.

3. On Great Britain's declaration of war against the Dutch, see Washington to NG, 21 March, above (vol. 7: 459). The British gained no allies.

4. The battle of Guilford Court House is discussed at NG to Huntington, 16 March, above (vol. 7: 436–41n).

¶ [FROM MAJOR JOHN MAZARET,[1] Prince Edward Court House, Va., 3 April 1781. Apologizes for "troubling" NG, but has become "a supernumary" officer after five years "in the Continental & State service." As "an Old Soldier, and having the satisfaction of seeing the Laurels in full bloom, success at the door," he longs for "an equal proportion of them as a true American."[2] He was told some time ago that NG intended to give him an appointment, but has heard no more about it. As NG ordered, Mazaret has established a "Larborato[ry]" at this Post." He will willingly "act in any capacity," but would give anything to serve with NG. He will send between 15,000 and 16,000 cartridges on 25 April and more every week thereafter while "materials last." Asks where "to get a fresh supply" of the needed items "before wanting." He will be unable to send the cartridges "agreable to orders" if all the covered wagons are detained at headquarters. Asks for directions.[3] With NG's approval, he can furnish shirts and overalls to "50 Soldiers here" who are "Starck-na[ked]" but otherwise fit for duty. LS (MiU-C) 2 pp.]

1. Mazaret commanded the post at Prince Edward Court House.

2. The recent arrangement of the Virginia officers, under which Mazaret had been declared a supernumerary, is discussed at NG to Davie, this date, below.

3. No reply has been found, but Mazaret, "several captains," and "a guard of about twenty" were reported to have passed through Salem on 30 April, taking ten "baggage and ammunition" wagons to the army. (*Records of the Moravians*, 4: 1692) As seen in Nathaniel Pendleton to Mazaret, 26 July, below, Mazaret returned to Virginia to oversee the production of ammunition for the army. On 24 August, below, NG informed him that his appointment in the ordnance department had not been confirmed and gave him permission to return home immediately.

¶ [FROM GENERAL WILLIAM MOULTRIE, Christ Church Parish, S.C., 3 April 1781. Sends copies of two letters from Col. [Nisbet] Balfour, the commandant at Charleston, and Moultrie's replies concerning the sending of American prisoners of war to the West Indies.[1] Also encloses a copy of the proceedings of a British court of inquiry involving two American officers charged with "a breach of Parole" and the complaints of two American captains against the British assistant commissary of prisoners. If NG finds the papers "right," Moultrie asks him to "Signify" by the bearer.[2] LS (Greene Papers: DLC) 1 p.]

1. On the threat to send American prisoners to the West Indies, see Cornwallis to NG, this date, above.

2. The enclosed documents, numbered one through ten, are with Moultrie's letter in the Greene Papers, DLC. On the charges against one of the American officers, Col. John F. Grimké, see NG's Orders of 29 June, below.

¶ [**FROM COLONEL ROBERT MUNFORD**, Richland, Va., 3 April 1781. Asks NG to obtain the exchange of a prisoner, the bearer's son, who formerly served in Munford's regiment. ALS (MiU-C) 1 p.]

¶ [**FROM GOVERNOR ABNER NASH OF NORTH CAROLINA**, New Bern, N.C., 3 April 1781. Has received NG's letter reporting Lord Cornwallis's "precipitate retreat over Deep River"; the "event does the highest honour" to NG's "little army."[1] North Carolina must still look to NG "for safety & protection"; NG "may depend on" the state making "every exertion" to "support" him. The draft is "going forward," and Nash believes the "Law is patiently submitted to."[2] With the "advice & aid" of the Council Extraordinary, the state is also "endeavouring to Subject the Militia Men who shamefully deserted their colours in the action of Guildford Court House, to the Condition of Continental Soldiers during the war. The Law warrants this measure & their crimes deserve it." Hopes to get "at least one Batalion in this way."[3] Nash will send the rum NG requested "as soon as possible." Asks for wagons to transport it but will forward the rum by any "possible means of conveyance." Nash thinks NG did not request enough rum and therefore plans "to procure a much larger quantity."[4] Has also "demanded a contribution of one fifth part of all the Bacon & other salted meat in the state" for NG's army and is "taking measures" to collect cattle.[5] On his way home from NG's headquarters, Nash ordered the quartermaster at Harrisburg to send NG a wagonload of turkeys, chickens, fresh butter, turnips, etc., which NG should have received by now.[6] Nash can find no "English cheese" but promises to send NG the "first that comes in here." Adds: "I beg you at all times to let me know what will be agreeable to you in Camp as I shall take a perticular pleasure in procuring any thing for you in my power." Doubts reports that [Gen. Benedict] Arnold has been reinforced. A British naval force did arrive in Virginia, but Nash does not think it brought troops. Nothing has been heard about them, and they would have certainly landed before the British fleet sailed to attack the French, which it did with considerable loss.[7] Encloses, as a matter of "great curiosity," letters that passed "some time ago" between Maj. [James] Craig and Gen. [Alexander] Lillington. Wonders if "such bare faced Lying" as Craig's is "deemed a fare & Honourable stratagem in war."[8] Adds in a postscript that he is sending the proceedings of the Council Extraordinary "respecting the Deserters & defaulters."[9] ALS (NHi) 2 pp.]

1. See NG's letter to Nash of 29 March, above (vol. 7: 480).

2. On the state's efforts to fill its Continental battalions, see note at NG to Nash, this date, above.

3. William Hooper wrote James Iredell on 29 March that under an order of the Council Extraordinary, "*every man who abandoned his post in the last action should be enrolled in the Continental Army for twelve months.*" (Griffith J. McRee, *Life and Correspondence of James Iredell*, 2 vols. [New York, 1857–58], 1: 497; on this subject, see also Eaton to NG, 4 April, below.)

4. NG wrote Nash on 13 April, below, that he could not send wagons and said that the quantity of rum he had asked for was "less than we want."

5. According to the biographer of William R. Davie, NG's commissary and commissary of purchases for North Carolina, supplies began to arrive at collection points from all parts of the state by May. (Robinson, *Davie*, p. 110)

6. Nash had presumably been at NG's headquarters shortly after the battle of Guilford Court House. (See NG to Nash, 18 March, above [vol. 7: 448].) In his reply of 13 April, below, NG thanked Nash for his "good intentions" but said he had not received the provisions.

7. On the British fleet in the Chesapeake, see note at Lafayette to NG, 4 April, below. In his letter to Nash of 29 March, NG had warned that the reinforcement of the British army in Virginia would "change all our prospects in that State" and make the Southern Army even more dependent on North Carolina for support. He wrote Nash on 13 April, below, that the report of the reinforcement was true.

8. The enclosures were no doubt copies of the same correspondence that Gen. Alexander Lillington had sent with his letter to NG of 21 March, above (vol. 7: 457). On 9 March, Maj. James Craig, the British commander at Wilmington, had sent Lillington an ultimatum to surrender his force at Heron's Bridge, claiming that the Americans were completely cut off from escape and that Col. Banastre Tarleton's troops would be "upon" them "in a few hours." Craig's assertion was undoubtedly the "bare faced Lying" to which Nash referred. (Copies of the letters, which NG had sent to Congress when he wrote Samuel Huntington on 30 March, above, are in PCC, item 172, vol. 1: 113, DNA; on the action at Heron's Bridge, see Lillington to NG, 21 March.)

9. Nash referred to the effort, which he had outlined earlier in this letter, to draft militia deserters from the battle of Guilford Court House into the Continental line.

¶ [FROM VIRGINIA OFFICERS SERVING WITH THE SOUTHERN ARMY,[1] Camp [Ramsey's Mills, N.C.], 3 April 1781. They "observe the disadvantages" of their current situation—"in detachments & not Regimented." These include "inattention" of the officers to the soldiers, a "desire to Retire from Camp," and a decline in "discipline and subordination." Detached commands "are temporary & uncertain, & the duty of the officers unequal and unjust"; when regiments are formed, the "absent officers" will be more accountable to their commanders. In the arrangement that has taken place at Chesterfield Court House, Va., the regiments "have enjoyed equal Privileges, & as their is a proportion of the officers of every Regiment now in the field, we think it just and right that the first Regiment should be immediately Compleated, by ordering out all the officers belonging to it, to receive the soldiers now in Camp." The other regiments should be completed "in Rotation, as soon as the men are raised." Under the arrangement, there are to be proportionately more officers in the regiments than is now the case in detachments.[2] Cy (PHi) 3 pp.]

1. The letter was signed by thirty officers of the Virginia line.

2. In response to this letter, NG asked Col. William Davies to complete the first two Virginia regiments. (See immediately below.)

* * *

To Colonel William Davies

Dear Sir   Deep River [N.C.] April 3ᵈ 1781

The disagreeable situation of the detachments serving with this army from the State of Virginia, and the complaints of all ranks of officers from their not being Regimented induces me to wish that the first and second Regiment should be immediately formed, and the

Officers sent forward without loss of time. While the troops act by detachment and the officers uncertain whether they will comand the same men, they will not pay that attention to the dicipline of the troops which the good of the service requires.[1] Major Hill & Major Ridley consider themselves as supernumery officers and are impatient to get home; and if they are really so, it is but a piece of justice that they should be immediately relieved.[2]

I should be glad to be favord with a copy of the arrangment as soon as possible with every other information concerning the Recruits now drafting.[3]

The critical situation of the Southern States renders it absolutely necessary that reinforcements should be forwarded to this Army as soon as possible. I must entreat you to use all imaginable diligence in collecting and forwarding the recruits.[4]

There was three officers which left us at Pedee upon very unjustifieable principles and such as must be looked upon as little less than disgraceful. I have not had time to represent their conduct to the Governor. I am told they were not content with depriving us of their services at the most critical moment; but have been endeavoring to instill into the Minds of the Virginia line in order to justify their return home that there was great prejudices against them at Head Quarters. The insinuation was as illiberal as it was unjust. I defy the most malevolent to produce an instance of an unequal conduct to any part of the Army; and nothing but arrogance and ignorance could have given birth to such a sentiment. I encourage and reward merit where ever I find it, and censure sloth and negligence. If those Gentlemen comes under the latter description they may think they have reason to charge me with partiallity. However as I have little or no acquaintance with the Young Gentlemen and as the report respecting their insinuation may be groundless, I shall take no further notice of the matter than to assure you that what ever they may have said upon the matter it is altogether without foundation.[5]

Nothing would give me greater pleasure than to have you with the Army, being confident your example would have a happy influence.[6] Great application and industry is necessary to dicipline troops in such an active service. I am with Sentiments of the most perfect esteem & regard Your Most Obed[t] humble Ser   NATH GREENE

ADfS (MiU-C).

1. NG was reacting to the petition of Virginia officers serving with the Southern Army, immediately above. Davies replied on 16 April, below.

2. Thomas Hill and Thomas Ridley were supernumerary officers who had won NG's thanks by serving with the army after they could have gone home. (See NG to Hill, 20 June, and NG's Orders of 28 May, both below.)

3. The Virginia officers who petitioned NG on this date apparently had either seen a

draft of the arrangement of the Virginia Continental line or had received much earlier reports about the completed document than NG did. As seen at Davies to NG, 20 February, above (vol. 7: 322n), a board of officers had begun the task of arrangement on 10 February. Davies wrote Baron Steuben on 10 March that the "long and complicated" document was not yet "fairly copied." Most of the work was apparently completed by 21 March, when Davies sent an extract to Steuben, with the suggestion that it be published. (Steuben Microfilm; the extract was most likely a list of assignments of officers then with the Southern Army and at Chesterfield Court House, Va.; Steuben published it in general orders of 21 March. [Ibid.]) Replying to NG on 16 April, below, Davies said that Col. Lewis Morris had brought NG a copy of the arrangement. As seen in Steuben to NG, 2 April, above, Morris had not yet returned to camp from Virginia. NG acknowledged receipt of the arrangement in a letter to Steuben of 1 May, below.

4. Davies wrote NG on 18 April, below, that he continued to give "as much attention to the new levies" as his "other duties will permit."

5. Three Virginia officers are known to have submitted resignations to NG in January 1781, during the Southern Army's encampment near the Pee Dee River in South Carolina: Capt. William Eppes and Lieutenants Samuel Jones and Tarpley White. (See above, vol. 7: 164, 194.) In his letter of 16 April, below, Davies told NG that every officer who had recently returned to Virginia had expressed "the fullest confidence" in and "the warmest attachment" to NG.

6. Davies, who had recently been named to head the Virginia War Office, remained in Virginia. (See Davies to NG, 2 April, above.)

* * *

¶ [**GENERAL GREENE'S ORDERS**, Ramsey's Mill, N.C., 4 April 1781. "The most active Men & the best Arms & Accoutrements" in the North Carolina militia brigade are to be formed into four companies numbering 200 rank and file under the command of Col. [James] Read. The Virginia troops are to be divided with "great equality" into two regiments. The North Carolina detachment and the Virginia regiments are to "parade" at 4 P.M. All troops are to receive two days' provisions, which they should cook. The army should be prepared to march "Tomorrow Morning." The quartermaster and commissaries are to take with them "as great a stock of Provision and Forage as can be Transported." In after orders, the march is postponed "till further orders."[1] Greene Orderly Book (CSmH) 3 pp.]

1. See NG's Orders of 5 April, below.

¶ [**TO THE BOARD OF WAR**. From Colonel Ramsey's on Deep River, N.C., 4 April 1781. "The importance of the Cavalry in the Southern Department and the constant demand for their services" make it "absolutely necessary" that they receive new clothes before their old ones "decay." Col. [William] Washington's regiment has had its present clothing for almost nine months; "in this severe service," it will not last more than twelve. Lt. [Ambrose] Gordon, the bearer of this letter, carries a return of Washington's regiment and a list of "articles wanted." Gordon will take charge of the clothing when it is provided. NG hopes that the critical situation of the southern states and the need for a "well appointed Cavalry" will excuse his "solicitude."[1] ADfS (MiU-C) 2 pp.]

1. Gordon did not return to the army until after 31 August, when he was reported to have reached Charlotte with eight wagonloads of clothing for Washington's regiment. (See Hamilton to NG, 31 August, below.)

¶ [**CAPTAIN WILLIAM PIERCE, JR., TO JOSEPH CLAY**. From [Camp, Deep River, N.C.], 4 April 1781. NG orders Clay to provide Lt. [Ambrose] Gordon with $60,000.[1] ADS (MiU-C) 1 p.]
1. On Gordon's mission, see NG to Board of War, immediately above.

¶ [**TO GOVERNOR THOMAS JEFFERSON OF VIRGINIA**. From [Camp, Deep River, N.C.], 4 April 1781. Requests payment to Capt. Patrick Fitzpatrick of $14,500 for 110 gallons of whiskey, which Fitzpatrick furnished to the army. Cy (MiU-C) 1 p.]

*   *   *

To Colonel Henry Lee, Jr.

Dear Sir   Camp [Deep River, N.C.] April 4th 1781
   We march tomorrow morning at 7 oClock.[1] You will take your route towards Cross Creek and pass the Pedee at Haleys Ferry or higher or lower as you may think necessary either for your own security or to effect a surprise upon the enemies posts on the Santee. The post garrisoned by Watsons Corp, is the only one which I think you will have a chance to strike at.[2] I have detached Capt Oldhams company to join your Legion, which I hope will enable you to accomplish the business.[3] But you must govern yourself by the intelligence you may get. You have only to remember that our force is small, and that we cannot afford to waste men without a valuable object in contemplation.
   I dont mean that you should march far towards Cross Creek; but only such a distance as you may think necessary to mask our real designs.
   It will be of importance if it can be easily accomplished to have all the Boats and Craft securd upon the Pedee from the great bluff upwards.[4] This may delay the enemy should they attempt to follow you or us; and will give time to effect our designs.
   You must also govern your self by circumstances in crossing the Santee. Should the Enemy pursue us pretty close out of this State, it will not be advisable for you to be seperated from us. Give me constant information of your Movements, and of the intelligence you may get. I will transmit you a copy of figures to write to me by, and shall write to you by the same table.[5] All good horses fit either for the Waggon or Dragoon service, which falls in your way, and which may fall into the hands of the enemy, you will take on with you, giving the owners proper recepts therefor.
   Remember that you command Men, and that their powers may not keep pace with your ambition. I have entire confidence in your prudence, and flatter myself that nothing will be left unattempted which may promote the honor or interest of the American Arms. I am dear Sir Your Most Obedient humble Ser   NATH GREENE

ALS (IHi).

1. NG's army left its camp at Ramsey's Mill on 6 April. (See NG's Orders of 5 and 6 April, both below.)

2. Lee's Legion and Gen. Francis Marion's partisans laid siege to Ft. Watson on 15 April. (See Marion to NG, first letter of 23 April, below.)

3. Capt. Edward Oldham was a Maryland Continental officer. (Steuart, *Maryland Line*, p. 117)

4. The "great bluff" was undoubtedly Mars Bluff, S.C., on the Pee Dee River, some sixty miles south of Haley's Ferry, N.C.

5. Lee asked for a copy of the code in his first letter to NG of 5 April, below.

*　　*　　*

¶ [FROM COLONEL HENRY LEE, JR., [Near Deep River, N.C., 4 April 1781].[1] Lee's troops were ready to move when he received NG's letter [not found] announcing that the army would not march for another day. Lee's infantry will proceed eight miles toward Cross Creek tomorrow; his cavalry will follow the next day. Suggests that Capt. [Edward] Oldham's company take the "direct road" from Ramsey's Mill to Cross Creek and meet Lee's infantry at McIntosh's.[2] Extract (Greene, *Greene*, 3: 234)]

1. No place or date was given, but the contents establish the date and indicate that Lee was still near the army's camp at Deep River.

2. As seen in the letter immediately above, NG had assigned Oldham's company of Maryland Continentals to serve with Lee.

¶ [TO COLONEL HENRY LEE, JR. From [Camp, Deep River, N.C.], "Wednesday Evening 10 oClock PM [4 April 1781].[1] Capt. [Edward] Oldham will "march in the morning" to the place Lee mentioned.[2] The militia light horse have gone with "Capt Conners [James Conyers]" to collect cattle for the army.[3] NG regrets Lee's "bargain" with the riflemen; their tour of duty is for three months, although they pretend it is only six weeks.[4] Encloses "the best route to surprize Watsons Corps." It was suggested by Conyers, who will send a guide to meet Lee at the Pee Dee River.[5] ALS (IHi) 1 p.]

1. Neither the date nor the place was given. The letter was docketed 6 April, but Wednesday was the 4th, and that date is consistent with the contents. The place was taken from NG's other correspondence of 4 April.

2. See Lee to NG, immediately above.

3. See NG to South Carolina Militia Officers, this date, below.

4. Lee discussed his "bargain" in a letter to NG of 5 April, below.

5. The enclosure has not been found. As seen in Lee to NG, 10 April, below, Conyers himself met Lee's detachment.

¶ [TO GENERAL FRANCIS MARION. From Camp on Deep River, N.C., 4 April 1781. The bearer, "Capt Conniers [James Conyers]," will inform Marion of NG's plans and give him a "full history" of the army's operations, including the battle of Guilford Court House. Following the battle, Lord Cornwallis was obliged "to run lustily." NG hopes Marion will assist Conyers in collecting provisions for the army.[1] NG's troops will march "to morrow."[2] NG hopes Marion and General Sumter, to whom NG has also written, will be prepared to support the army "with a considerable force."[3] ADfS (MiU-C) 1 p.]

1. Conyers wrote NG on 14 April, below, that he was setting out to find Marion the next day. That same day, Marion joined forces with Col. Henry Lee, who undoubtedly

informed him of NG's plans and operations. (Marion to NG, first letter of 23 April, below) Conyers did join Marion, who assisted him in collecting provisions. (Marion to NG, 21 April, below)

2. As noted above (NG to Lee, first letter of this date), the army did not march until 6 April.

3. NG's letter to Thomas Sumter, dated 30 March, is above.

*   *   *

To Colonel Timothy Pickering

Head Quarters Col Ramsay's Deep River [N.C.]

Dear Sir   April 4th 1781

Your Letter of Feby 4th was duly received.[1]

I am sorry for the embarasment which took place from the appointment of Major Claibourne. I have a high esteem for both him & Majr Forsyth. I did not think of recommending the former, because he was but little known in Virginia, and I considered that as essential in the discharge of the duties of his appointment: however, I believe no difference has taken place respecting Forsyth's appointment; and Majr Claibourne succeeds in business as well as can be expected, when he is so much dependant on the legislature, who it is difficult to impress with the importance of giving aid timely, as well as effectually.[2]

Lieut Colonel Carrington's appointment is only a field Deputy, but I can assure you it is absolutely nec[e]ssary, both for the honor and interest of the Quart. Mast. Generals Department, as well as for the Army and public in general, that his Commission should extend to all the southern Department. There is such a necessary connection in the business, not only in providing Supplies, but in establishing Posts, and marking out Routes, & many other things; that it is absolutely requisite, that the deputies belonging to the States should be subject to his Orders and controul: & without it the Army cannot be supported. It is also necessary to check abuses and to facilitate the operations of the Army, that he should have those Powers, nor will he serve in the department without them. Were you here, you could both see the propriety & necessity that it should be so. He is an Officer of extensive abilities and great resource, and no man has the honor of the Department or the good of his Country more at heart. He thinks the deputies should be subject to him, and he and the Deputies subject to you. I think him an honor to your department, and cannot tell who you can get to fill his place, if he should leave the business.

The War here is upon a very different Scale to what it is to the Northward. A man of great resource is essential to the operations; and without one your office will fall into disrepute, and the Army be brought into the greatest distress, if not total ruin.

I beg leave therefore to recommend giving the Colonel an appointment for the Southern Department. It will by no means diminish your authority, nor give any check to your particular Orders.[3] On the other hand it will afford a double check upon the deputies and greatly facilitate all the business of the southern Department. If you expect the same scale of doing business here will answer that will to the northward, I assure you, that you are greatly mistaken; business must be accomodated to the circumstances of the Country, and its resources, or the operations here stand still; and after all much will depend upon force: nor can the Army be supplied without. Money has but little influence, and agents are difficult to be got. This department will be unavoidably expensive, from the extent of the operations, nor will it be in the power of Government to Contract them, without giving up the southern States. I shall do every thing in my power to curtail expence, & have chose rather to let the inhabitants suffer, than swell the public expenditure, in compensating them for damages. The powers of Government are feeble in North Carolina, and their Property is held by the most precarious tenure.

I have recommended such matters both to this State and Virginia as I think concern your department, as well in matters of oeconemy, as in the business of aid and support.[4]

As Lieu^t Col^o Carrington writes you from time to time respecting the State of the department, it is unnecessary for me to be more particular.[5] I thank you for your good wishes and readiness to give me all the aid in your power. And am with respect and esteem Your most Obedient Humble Servant   NATH GREENE

LS (RG 93, WRMS, Misc. Mss. #23075: DNA).

1. The letter from Pickering, the quartermaster general, is above, dated 3 February. (Vol. 7: 248–49)

2. On the appointment of Richard Claiborne as deputy quartermaster for Virginia, see note at Pickering to NG, 5 November 1780, above (vol. 6: 467–68n). In his letter of 3 February, Pickering had protested Edward Carrington's role in the appointment and pointedly observed that Carrington, as deputy quartermaster for the Southern Army, had no official "connection" with the state deputies. Carrington wrote a spirited defense of his involvement in the appointment of Claiborne in a letter to Pickering of 30 April. (Boyd, *Jefferson Papers*, 5: 574–77) Robert Forsyth, who NG had recommended for the post of deputy quartermaster, was serving as deputy commissary of purchases for Virginia. In his letter of 3 February, Pickering implied that Forsyth had wanted the quartermaster appointment and was disappointed in not receiving it.

3. On 21 October, below, NG wrote Pickering that he had informed him "some time last summer" of "the light in which Col Carrington viewed his appointment; and that he could not be prevailed on to serve unless he was vested with those powers and right of jurisdiction which appeared to him necessary to discharge the duties of his office. To this letter I have never receivd any answer, nor was it very necessary as it was only a matter of information the better to enable you to govern your own conduct." (NG's "summer" letter has not been found; his comments in that of 21 October contrast sharply with his statement here.) Carrington also asked Pickering on 30 April for "an early answer." (Boyd, *Jefferson Papers*, 5: 577)

4. As seen in NG to Carrington, 4 December 1780, above (vol. 6: 516), NG had ordered a complete overhaul of the quartermaster department in Virginia. He also took an active role in North Carolina, explaining the state deputy's duties to him and recommending wholesale changes in the organization and powers of the department. (See NG to Nicholas Long, 18 January, and NG to Abner Nash, 17 January, both above [vol. 7: 140–41, 137–39].)

5. It appears from what NG wrote Pickering on 21 October, below, and from Pickering's register of letters that Carrington did not correspond regularly with Pickering. (RG 93, WRMS, vol. 89: 44, DNA)

*   *   *

¶ **[TO THE SOUTH CAROLINA MILITIA**. From Camp on Deep River, N.C., 4 April 1781. Orders "Officers or privates" of the militia to assist "Capt Conniers [James Conyers]" in collecting and driving "stock." Anyone who refuses will be "tryed for disobedience of orders and punnished accordingly."[1] ALS (MH) 1 p.]

1. Conyers was collecting cattle and horses for NG's army. (See NG to Lee, first letter of this date, above; Conyers to NG, 14 April, below.)

¶ **[TO BARON STEUBEN**. From Colonel Ramsey's, Deep River, N.C., 4 April 1781. Encloses an "address" of the Virginia officers.[1] Their "observations are so well founded, and the necessity is so great for accomplishing what they propose" that Col. [John] Green has agreed to go to Richmond, Va., "to have it effected as soon as possible." After tending to this business and "matters respecting cloathing," Green has NG's permission "to retire to the Springs," as he is "grievously affected with the Rheumatism."[2] NG has written "Colº Davis" about the need to form the two regiments and send their officers to camp as soon as possible.[3] Wants Steuben to "give an order on this matter" as soon as Green arrives, as the Virginia detachments will be "in a bad way untill they are formed into Regiments."[4] LS (NHi) 2 pp.]

1. See the letter from Virginia Officers Serving with the Southern Army, 3 April, above.

2. On the "matters respecting cloathing," see Green to NG, 11 April, below.

3. See NG to William Davies, 3 April, above.

4. On Steuben's response, see Green to NG, 11 April, below.

¶ **[FROM GENERAL THOMAS EATON**, "Halifax Town," N.C., 4 April 1781. After he returned from [Speedwell's] Iron Works, Eaton met with the members of the North Carolina Council Extraordinary, who "directed" him "to wait there determination" instead of proceeding as NG ordered. Eaton embodied the militia as soon as the council reached a decision and has sent 138 men under Col. [William] Linton "to serve twelve months as Continental Soldiers."[1] Eaton will "spare no pains" to collect the militia deserters who remain "in the several Countys" and will send them to NG with "dispatch."[2] ALS (MiU-C) 1 p.]

1. After the battle of Guilford Court House, NG had sent Eaton to collect the North Carolina militiamen who had deserted during the battle and those men who were to serve the next tour of duty. (See NG to Eaton, 17 March, above [vol. 7: 444].) As seen in Nash to NG, 3 April, above, the council decided to punish the deserters by drafting them into the Continental service. Those in Linton's detachment were the first to be

collected. Linton marched them to Chatham Court House and turned them over to the Continental officer in charge there. (Eaton to Jethro Sumner, 13 April, *NCSR*, 15: 438)

2. As seen in Gen. Jethro Sumner's letters to NG of late April and May, below, the few deserters who were drafted into the Continental service were collected slowly. Eaton does not seem to have played a role in the process.

¶ [**FROM COLONEL JAMES EMMET**, "Campbleton," N.C., 4 April 1781. The bearer will acquaint NG with everything he may wish to "be inform'd of." Emmet received NG's letter of 3 April and will do his best to follow NG's "prudent instructions." The enemy are moving by "rappid marches, seemly toward Wilmington." They reportedly reached Elizabethtown at noon yesterday and halted "to settle the Business" of NG's flag of truce and bury Col. [James] Webster, who died during the march.[1] Emmet fears they will overtake Gen. [Alexander] Lillington, who reportedly crossed the river on 2 April. He has written Lillington once and would have done so again, "but knew not where."[2] Capt. [George] Fletcher, the commissary, reports that he and the county commissioner have NG's orders to collect provisions and forage. They are "to demand assistance" from Emmet, who has assigned Capt. [Pleasant] Henderson and the "County light Horse" to that duty.[3] Emmet has been able to collect only a few "Foot militia," who are now at Avery's Ford. "The English[,] according to custom, have left the small Pox behind them," and Emmet therefore cannot bring his men into town. Asks NG for a flag of truce so that he can go to recover "some Negroes that several here, with myself, have lost" and can carry "some hard money" to a friend, who is a prisoner with the enemy.[4] ALS (MiU-C) 2 pp.]

1. On NG's flag of truce, see Cornwallis to NG, 3 April, above. Webster, who had been wounded at Guilford Court House, died a few miles outside of Elizabethtown on the evening of 3 April. He was buried on a plantation near town on 4 April. ("Von Bose Journal," p. 53; Schenck, *N.C., 1780–81*, pp. 370–71 and n.)

2. As seen in Lillington's letter of 9 April, below, the enemy did not overtake his troops.

3. NG's instructions to Fletcher have not been found.

4. NG's reply has not been found; his response of 14 May to a similar request from Fletcher is below.

¶ [**FROM THE MARQUIS DE LAFAYETTE**, Annapolis, Md., 4 April 1781. NG will have heard about the engagement between the fleets before this letter arrives.[1] The enemy were superior in "force and numbers." The French fought "very well" but have returned to Rhode Island, while "Arbuthnot Has Retired to the Point which we intended to Attack." Lafayette thus has "Nothing to do But to Return to the Grand Army."[2] His "Bad luck" included not seeing Col. [Lewis] Morris, who arrived near Williamsburg, Va., just after he left. Lafayette would have liked to have news from NG even though he is unable to "Help you, (as my instructions are *As soon as the Enterprise Has either Succeeded or miscarried to Return immediately to the Grand Army* and the latitude afterwards Added to them Was in the supposition of a *Naval Superiority and Cooperation with the french*)."[3] There was only one engagement between the fleets, thunder having "been mistaken for a [second] Cannonade." The report that the French anchored off Cape Fear, N.C., is likewise false.[4] One French ship is "much damaged" but will soon be repaired. "By every Account Even from Portsmouth the Enemy Have not gained the Honor of the day." Hopes the French fleet will soon be reinforced.

Although Lafayette would have liked to bring his "Excellent detachment" to NG, he has now given all the help that he could. In the expectation that NG needs ammunition, he is sending four six-pound field pieces, with 1,200 rounds of ammunition and nearly 100,000 musket cartridges. Maryland will provide horses for the field pieces and will send NG a detachment of troops. Lafayette will ask Gov. [Thomas] Jefferson and Baron Steuben to make sure that the cannon are safely transported through Virginia. On his return to Pennsylvania, he will try to hasten the march of the Pennsylvania Continentals, who, he fears, will be "on the Rout at a time when they May be wanted in Both Armies."[5] Letters from the Comte de Vergennes and the Marquis de Castries give "Every Reason to Hope that Vigorous Measures will Be adopted for our Relief in the Course of this Campaign." Wants NG's opinion and "Accurate Accounts" of NG's situation, so that he may know "what Measures" could "Best" be taken.[6] Lafayette hopes that plans can be "Built upon the Expectation of a Naval Superiority." He is glad to hear that Lord Cornwallis is "Retreating." By abandoning his wounded, Cornwallis "Acknowledges Himself to Have Been Severely Handled." From intelligence that Lafayette has obtained, however, it would have been better if the enemy had retreated towards Camden, S.C. "Duty to the Public, and Affection" for NG lead him to say that "the Executive of the State of Virginia Appear to Be disatisfied with Baron de Stubens." That may "throw New Embankments" in NG's way. Sends his compliments to NG's aides and various officers in the Southern Army. Tr (GWG Transcript: CSmH) 2 pp.]

1. For more on the battle between British and French fleets near the entrance to Chesapeake Bay, see note at Steuben to NG, first letter of 4 March, above (vol. 7: 390).

2. The ships that had arrived at Portsmouth, Va., were not part of Adm. Marriot Arbuthnot's fleet. They were the flotilla that had brought Gen. William Phillips's detachment from New York to reinforce Benedict Arnold. (See note at NG to Lafayette, 29 March, above [vol. 7: 479n].) The defeat of the French naval force ended plans for a Franco-American expedition against Arnold. Washington's "Grand Army" would remain in winter quarters in the Hudson Highlands of New York until 1 June. (See Fitzpatrick, GW, 22: 151.)

3. Lafayette no doubt realized that Morris had been sent to persuade him to remain in the South and join NG in case Washington's orders permitted him to do so. (See NG to Lafayette, 29 March, above [vol. 7: 478].)

4. NG had received both erroneous reports. (See Steuben to NG, 25 March [vol. 7: 468] and 30 March, both above.)

5. Lafayette did not return to Pennsylvania. As noted at NG to Lafayette, 3 April, above, Washington sent Lafayette orders while he was still in Maryland to join forces with NG. In saying that the Pennsylvania Continentals would be "wanted in both Armies," Lafayette was anticipating a plan by Washington for an attack on New York City. (Lafayette to Washington, 8 April, Idzerda, Lafayette Papers, 4: 14)

6. On the "Vigorous Measures," see La Luzerne to NG, 3 April, above. NG apparently did not send the information.

¶ [FROM LIEUTENANT WILLIAM PENDERGAST, Prince Edward Court House, Va., 4 April 1781. He has not let NG know where he "retired to" until now because of the "movements of the Army" and his belief that NG is involved with "business of greater importance."[1] He would have returned to camp "some time since" but has been "detained" by Maj. [John] Mazaret, who says he is not to leave "till further orders." Pendergast has asked Col. [Otho] Williams for orders and whether he should bring his accounts if he returns to camp.[2] ALS (MiU-C) 1 p.]

1. Pendergast, who had been serving as a contractor for the army, had presumably "retired" because of illness. (*NCSR*, 14: 641)

2. Mazaret commanded the post at Prince Edward Court House. Neither Pendergast's letter to Williams nor Williams's reply has been found.

¶ [FROM CAPTAIN MATTHEW RAMSEY,[1] Chatham, N.C., 4 April 1781. Forwards dispatches to NG from Generals [Jethro] Sumner and [John] Butler; hopes they arrive safely.[2] Supposes that Butler will inform NG of the enemy's movements. Reports that Lord Cornwallis "Four Days ago" was at a plantation on the Neuse River and has divided his army: "one Division is gone to take the Stores at Kingston, & another to Cross Creek."[3] Ramsey will send "News better authentikated" when his express returns from Halifax. He has collected "a Large Quantity of hides" that the army left behind. ALS (MiU-C) 1 p.]

1. Ramsey was a quartermaster who had been in charge of the post at Cross Creek.

2. The letters have not been found.

3. Cornwallis's army had already left Cross Creek; in a letter of 3 May, John Johnston reported to James Iredell that an enemy "party of Infantry and horse" had marched to Kingston "in order to take the Magazine there, which being removed, they returned." (*The Papers of James Iredell*, ed. Don Higginbotham, 2 vols. [Raleigh: North Carolina Department of Archives and History, 1976], 2: 234)

¶ [FROM COLONEL THOMAS WADE, Haley's Ferry, N.C., 4 April 1781. He arrived at "this Place" on 30 March and found the provisions safe. Repeats the account given in his letter of 2 April, above, of his detachment being ambushed. He has asked [Thomas] Polk to replace the wagons that were lost and will use them to send provisions to NG if a "Passiage Could be Open between this" and NG's army. Adds: "for God Sake lets have no more Low Land Militia Guards to guard Public Property." Asks for news from Virginia and Wilmington, N.C., saying that "it would be Very agreeable to the Good men hear to Know how things that Way are Likely to go" and what route Lord Cornwallis will take if he is not "totally Routed."[1] Between the militiamen Wade has called out and those he expects from Colonel Kolb's regiment, he hopes to have 300 to 400 horsemen "to Reduce those Torys to Order between Drowning Creek & Cape Fear, when we Perhaps shall pay you a Visit."[2] ALS (MiU-C) 2 pp.]

1. NG sent news of enemy movements in a letter to Wade of 8 April, below.

2. As seen in his letter of 10 April, below, Wade's men did move against the Loyalists, although he was stricken with rheumatism and was unable to go. The militiamen, led by Col. Abel Kolb, twice dispersed parties of Loyalists who had assembled in the Drowning Creek area. Kolb was mistaken, however, in thinking that he had intimidated the Loyalists. On 28 April, a party of about fifty Tories surrounded his house. After a fierce fight, Kolb, who had had a reputation for cruelty in dealing with the Loyalists, reportedly accepted an offer to surrender but was shot and killed when he emerged from his house. (Rankin, *Swamp Fox*, pp. 197–98) Kolb's death seems to have further emboldened the Loyalists in the area. A North Carolina militia colonel who marched from NG's army after the battle of Hobkirk's Hill recalled that when he tried to pass through the area he found it "in a state of insurrection and parties of armed Tories spreading themselves in

every direction." (Guilford Dudley's narrative, in Dann, *Revolution Remembered*, p. 225) In June, Gen. Francis Marion, attempting to restore peace to the region, negotiated a treaty with the leader of the Loyalist militia in the Drowning Creek area. (Moultrie, *Memoirs*, 2: 419–21)

¶ [**GENERAL GREENE'S ORDERS**, Ramsey's Mill, N.C., 5 April 1781. The troops are to be furnished with provisions and will march "tomorrow" at 7 A.M. Certain officers are assigned to "do duty" in Col. [Richard] Campbell's regiment.[1] A return of overalls "wanting" in each corps is needed immediately. Lamar Orderly Book (OClWHi) 1 p.[2]]

1. On the reorganization of the Virginia troops serving with NG, see NG's Orders of 4 April, above.

2. This orderly book was kept by William Lamar, a lieutenant in the First Maryland Regiment.

¶ [**TO THE BOARD OF WAR**. From Deep River, N.C., 5 April 1781. Lee's Legion needs 200 cloaks, 20 pairs of boots, 200 pairs of shoes, and 200 pairs of "drill Breeches." NG asks the board to forward these items as soon as they are obtained.[1] Df (MiU-C) 1 p.]

1. Another draft of this letter contains the following sentence: "I send a Sergeant on to receive them, if the Board of War may think necessary to furnish him with them." (MiU-C) William Grayson replied for the board on 11 May, below.

*   *   *

To Major Ichabod Burnet

Dear Sir   Head Quarters Deep River [N.C.] April 5th 1781

In my last I gave you a hint that I was going to take a bold and I believe an unexpected measure.[1] We march tomorrow directly for South Carolinia. This will oblige the Enemy either to follow us or give up their posts there. If the former takes place it will draw the war out of this State, if the latter we shall gain more than we can lose. Should [we continue?] in this State and follow the enemy down towards Wilmington, they will hold their ground in both States; for strange as it may appear the Enemy by moving northward secure their conquests southward. If we can oblige the enemy to retire into South Carolinia we shall just undo all that they have been doing all winter, at such an expence of blood and treasure. Another reason for my moving into South Carolinia is the enemy have now almost the entire command of the supplies of that State, and by going there we shall be able to share it with them at least.

Our golden prospects are at an end in Virginia; and if we continue in this State, Lord Cornwallis will form a junction with [Gen. Benedict] Arnold upon the Roanoke if he pleases.

The last account I had from the Enemy, they were about thirty Miles below Cross Creek on the march towards Wilmington, to which place it is not improbable they will go.[2]

Col Morris has not yet returnd nor have I heard from him since the

25th.[3] It is said the Pennsylvania line under General Wayne, are on the march, and far on their way to the Southward. It is certain they have had orders to march, but where they are I know not.[4]

To be prepared for any thing that may happen, I am ordering a Magazine to be formed at or near Olliphants Mill on the Catabaw, and all our heavy baggage & Stores are directed to that place.

The Continental troops and 400 North Carolinia Militia will march with me. Col Greene is gone to Virginia, and the three detachments are formed into two Regiments. Lt Col [Samuel] Hawes commands one, and Lt Col Cambell [Richard Campbell] the other.[5]

The family are pretty well. Major Hyrne has joined the Army, but has not been able to get a proper state of the prisoners. He carried safe to Winchester upwar[ds] of 400 men.[6] All that deserted or made their escape, had done it, before that he joined them. Philips that commanded the Guard, deserves hanging or something worse.[7]

God bless you with better health, and restore you speedily to the Arms of the family, where you are much wanted, and where you will be most cordially received.[8]

My best respects to D[r] Browne.[9] Yours most Aff   N GREENE

ALS (NjMoHP).
1. NG's earlier letter to Burnet has not been found.
2. As seen at NG to Huntington, 30 March, above, Lord Cornwallis's army reached the outskirts of Wilmington on 7 April.
3. Lewis Morris, one of NG's aides, had gone to Virginia to meet with the Marquis de Lafayette. For more on his whereabouts, see Steuben to NG, 30 March and 2 April, both above.
4. As noted at Washington to NG, 1 June, below, the Pennsylvania Continentals did not march until late May.
5. NG discussed Col. John Green's return to Virginia in his letter to Baron Steuben of 4 April, above.
6. Maj. Edmund Hyrne was the Southern Army's commissary of prisoners. For more on the prisoners he "carried safe" to Virginia, see NG to Hyrne, 25 January, above (vol. 7: 194).
7. Col. James Phillips, a militia officer from Surry County, N.C., had commanded the troops guarding the prisoners at Salisbury. (See NG to Phillips, 7 January, above [vol. 7: 67].)
8. In a letter of 3 April from "Col. Perkins's" hospital in Pittsylvania County, Va., Burnet informed another of NG's aides that he expected the "obstinate and disagreeable" stomach ailment from which he was suffering to keep him confined for ten more days. (Burnet to Nathaniel Pendleton, 3 April, MiU-C)
9. As seen in Browne to Pierce, 2 April, above, Dr. James Browne was in charge of the hospitals that had been set up to care for the wounded after the battle of Guilford Court House; Burnet was staying in one of them.

*   *   *

¶ [TO GENERAL JOHN BUTLER.[1] From Camp, Deep River, N.C., 5 April 1781.[2] Using the militia that NG leaves "behind," he is to take a position "in this Neighbourhood" and is to collect and organize the militiamen who have been called into service. Those who ran away from Guilford Court House are to be "tryed" and formed into companies "agreeable to the Continental establishment" and under the command of Continental officers. They are to be sent to NG with arms and ammunition.[3] If more officers are needed to train and form these troops, Butler should obtain them from Gen. [Jethro] Sumner. He is to collect "a good quantity of provision at or near this place" and send it to NG's army with guards and escorts by routes that NG will direct. He is to keep spies and patrols near the enemy and send the "earliest information" of any movement toward NG. He should be careful to "guard against a surprise." ADfS (MiU-C) 2 pp.]

1. Butler, who commanded the Hillsborough militia district, was an experienced military officer, having led troops in several major engagements, including the battle of Guilford Court House. (See NG to Samuel Huntington, 17 March, above [vol. 7: 434].) He had settled on the Haw River in North Carolina before May 1763, and by 1768 was sheriff of Orange County. During the Revolution, he was a political as well as military leader, serving several terms in both the provincial congress and the North Carolina legislature. Butler remained in North Carolina after NG moved his army into South Carolina. Later in 1781, during the Loyalist uprising in which Gov. Thomas Burke was captured, he led outnumbered militiamen against David Fanning's force in the battle of Lindley's Mill. He died in 1786. (*Dictionary of N.C. Biography*, 1: 290–91)

2. According to a note at the bottom of the letter, these orders were "Given at Camp"—i.e., after a meeting between NG and Butler.

3. The "Continental establishment" was the Congressional plan, implemented 1 January 1781, which called for five sergeants, four corporals, and sixty-four privates in each company. (Wright, *Continental Army*, pp. 157–58)

¶ [TO GENERAL ALEXANDER LILLINGTON. From Deep River, N.C., 5 April 1781. NG wrote earlier that he had sent "Col Malmody [the Marquis de Malmedy]" to join Lillington.[1] He has learned since then that the enemy are marching toward Wilmington from Cross Creek, and he was informed "Yesterday" that Lillington planned to cross the Northwest Cape Fear [i.e., Cape Fear] River. Such a move would leave Lillington "exposd." NG hopes he has not crossed the river and recommends that he keep "out of the way of the Enemy and avoid if possible a surprise."[2] Will write again "in a short time." ADfS (MiU-C) 1 p.]

1. See NG to Lillington, 29 March, above (vol. 7: 479).

2. After receiving NG's letter, Lillington, who was still on the east side of the Northwest Cape Fear, moved away from the river and successfully avoided contact with Lord Cornwallis's army. (See Lillington to NG, 9 April, below.)

¶ [FROM GOVERNOR THOMAS JEFFERSON OF VIRGINIA, "In Council" [Richmond, Va.], 5 April 1781. Virginia formerly required warrants from Congress for funds advanced to Continental officers in the state. Since the war has been "transferred to the Southward," the calls for money have become "so apparently indispensible" that the state has not waited for warrants; however, it must still get NG's "Sanction for the Monies after paiment of them." Sends Major Claiborne's receipt for money he received from the state without "previous Authority."[1] Adds that Virginia cannot provide NG with £5,000 "hard Money" but has given Claiborne a warrant for £500,000 "current Money," subject to NG's order alone.[2] Suggests that NG have "hard Money" purchased in Philadelphia, "to be paid here."

To give NG an idea of the "Indiscretions" that have "occasioned a dissatisfaction in the Impresses of Horses," Jefferson sends affidavits concerning the activities of "a Mr Rudder employed in that business."[3] Instead of "soothing the Minds of the People, and softening the harsh Act," impressments were frequently accompanied "by defiance of the civil Power, and Circumstances of personal Irritation." It may be "tedious" to explain to every person the need for exercising such "disagreable Powers," but "free People think they have a right to an Explanation of the Circumstances which give rise to the Necessity under which they suffer." The impressments caused such a "General Irritation" that the council has "been obliged to authorise the County Lieutenants to restrain them under the Directions of the resolutions of Assembly." LB (Vi) 1 p.]

1. The receipt has not been found, but in a letter to Jefferson of 6 April, Claiborne acknowledged that he had received a warrant for two million pounds. (Boyd, *Jefferson Papers*, 5: 358)

2. NG had requested the £5,000 in November 1780. (See above, vol. 6: 494n.) A collapse in the value of the Virginia currency in early May would have made it impossible to purchase specie with such a warrant. (See Madison, *Papers*, 3: 109n.)

3. The "papers," which have not been found, undoubtedly included a letter to Jefferson from Col. Abraham Buford, dated 20 March, concerning the activities of Lt. Epaphroditus Rudder, an officer in the 3rd Continental Light Dragoons. (Boyd, *Jefferson Papers*, 5: 187) For more on the controversy and the legislature's action, see Jefferson to NG, 24 March, above (vol. 7: 467).

¶ [**FROM COLONEL HENRY LEE, JR.**, 5 April 1781.[1] Asks for the "table of cyphers" and wants to be informed of NG's "different stages" so that Lee "may know where to communicate precisely" with him.[2] Expects to cross the Santee River about the same time that NG crosses the Pee Dee; thinks this will be "proper."[3] NG has Lee's "best prayers." ALS (MiU-C) 1 p.]

1. Lee did not give his location. As seen in his letter of 4 April, above, he was on the march from Ramsey's Mill, N.C., toward Cross Creek.

2. On the "cyphers," see NG to Lee, first letter of 4 April, above. NG's "different stages" were the places he planned to stop during his march to Camden, S.C.

3. For more on Lee's mission, see ibid.

¶ [**FROM COLONEL HENRY LEE, JR.**, 5 April 1781. The troops that NG "attached" to Lee's command insist their tour of duty is for ten weeks, four of which have "elapsed." Lee thinks the twelve men who have agreed to serve with him "will render more service than the whole company."[1] ALS (NNPM) 1 p.]

1. In his first letter to Lee of 4 April, above, NG had complained about Lee's agreement with the men.

¶ [**FROM COLONEL GEORGE WALTON**,[1] Philadelphia, 5 April 1781. Clothing for the Georgia militia is being sent in a "brigade of Continental waggons" that is en route to NG's headquarters. NG is asked to insure that it is delivered to the "eldest Colonel" in the Georgia militia.[2] "*We need not suggest, how necessary it is, that these articles scanty as they are, should be delivered for their intended uses.*" Excerpt (A. S. W. Rosenbach, *The History of America in Documents*, 3 vols. [Philadelphia: The Rosenbach Co., 1949], 2: 84)]

1. Walton, a delegate to Congress from Georgia, was writing on behalf of the state's delegation. (Smith, *Letters*, 17: 187n)

2. NG wrote the Georgia delegates on 22 June, below, that the clothing had been turned over to Elijah Clarke, "the eldest Colonel then in the State."

¶ [GENERAL GREENE'S ORDERS, "Head Quarters Evans Mill," N.C., 6 April 1781. The army will encamp "here" tonight and march "by the Right tomorrow at Noon."[1] Lamar Orderly Book (OCIWHi) 1 p.]

1. In his regulations for the army, Baron Steuben mandated that the infantry "on all occasions encamp by battalions, as they are formed in order of battle," with an open space in front for the troops to form. (Joseph R. Riling, *Baron Von Steuben and His Regulations* [Philadelphia: Ray Riling Arms Books Co., 1966], p. 77) When the troops assembled, they were to form "on their respective parades"—i.e., the open areas in front of their encampments. When the signal to march was given, they were to "wheel by platoons or sections, as shall be ordered, and begin the march." (Ibid., pp. 68–69) "By the Right" meant that they would wheel to the right of the direction in which they had been facing. If they had been encamped facing east, for example, their movement would be toward the south.

*   *   *

To Governor Thomas Jefferson of Virginia

Sir   Head Quarters on Deep River [N.C.] April 6th 1781

I receivd last Evening your Excellencys two letters of the 24th and 30th of March. The first upon the subject of the Cavalry and the last upon the Militia orderd into service.

I am sorry if any of the Officers sent out with the impress warrants have misbehavd. In some instances I beleive they have, but in most I perswade myself they have not. Those horses of very high value as covering horses or breding Mares, I had given orders should be returned before the recept of your letter; and at the time of the officers going out upon the business of impressing I gave written instructions not to impress such, as well to avoid expence, as to prevent the complaints of the Inhabitants.[1] There are only two or three that have been brought to Camp which comes under this description. Such I have given particular directions about. Most of the horses that have been impressed are rather inferior than superior in their quallity requisite for the service. Superior Cavalry is of the greatest importance to the salvation of this Country and without them you would soon hear of detachments being cut to p[i]eces in every quarter. It is not only necessary that we should be superior in number but in the quallity of the horses. This will prevent the enemy from attempting surprises at a distance from which so many disagreeable consequences happened last Campaign. The Militia can only be useful with a superior Cavalry and hundreds and hundreds of them would have fallen a sacrafice in the late operations had it not been for the goodness of our Cavalry and the great activity of the Officers commanding those Corps. Without a fleet Cavalry we can never reconnoiter the enemy[,] attempt a surprise, or indeed keep our selves from being surprisd. The use and value of them has been but little attended to in the Southern Department. I observe the price fixed for the purchase of the horses is very low. At the rate that they are now selling in Virginia it would not purchase by voluntary sale a horse that I would trust a dragoon upon; and it would little be less then [deserting?] the Men and supplying the enemy with implements to mount them on such Cattle.[2] The difference between good[,] midling and bad horses can only be known to those who have a particular knowledge of the service. No man wishes to promote oeconemy more than I do, or sees a greater necessity. But furnishing bad horses for the Cavalry is neither consistent with good policy or the principles of true oeconemy.

I am on the march for South Carolinia, and I hope Virginia will not lessen her exertions from my being more remote from her borders. Should this be the case you will soon bring the war to your doors again; I am in hopes to keep it at a distance if you support me in this quarter.

The Enemy are at or near Wilmington and I expect will follow us as soon as they discover our intentions. One of two things must happen[.] They must either give up their posts in South Carolinia, or return and support them; in either case our purpose will be answerd, as it will be undoing all they have done the whole campaign. I had the present plan in contemplation at the time I wrote for the uper Country Militia. Your Excellency does not mention where they are to rendezvous. Charlotte in North Carolinia would be a proper place; and they should bring out as much provision as possible without which we shall starve all together.[3]

I have written to the Marquis de la Fyette and desird him not to think of leaving Virginia in her present distresses but to march his Infantry by Alexandria[,] Fredricksburg to Richmond.[4] By taking this interior route he will be better able to direct his motions to any point where the enemy may attempt to operate, than if he took a route lower down, and will be less liable to misfortune. I perswade my self as the enemy are detaching from New York, his Excellency General Washington, would agree to the measure; and upon that presumption have venturd to assure the Marquis that I will take all the blame upon my self.[5] The Enemy are making great exertions for the subjugation of the Southern States, and ours must be proportionable or they must fall. The Inhabitants must be taught to bear the burthen with patience. One great misfortune is the Southern world dont appear to be well acquainted with their own strength. Their pride induces them to wish to be thought powerful but not being so, from the Nature and circumstances of the Country, they deceive themselves and others. I have the honor to be your Ex^s   N GREE[NE]

ADfS (MiU-C).

1. See NG's letters of 17 February to Henry Lee and William Washington, both above (vol. 7: 301–2, 305).

2. The legislature had mandated a maximum valuation of £5,000 in Virginia currency— about £37 in specie—for an impressed horse. (Jefferson to NG, 1 April, above; as seen there, Jefferson recognized that this low valuation was a problem that needed to be rectified.)

3. As noted at Jefferson to NG, 30 March, above, most of the militia who were ordered out never joined NG.

4. See NG to Lafayette, 3 April, above.

5. As noted at ibid., Washington ordered Lafayette and his detachment to remain in the South.

To Baron Steuben

Dear Sir   Head Quarters Deep River [N.C.] April 6th 1781

Yours of the 30th of March came to hand last evening. I am exceeding sorry that the marquis is going to retire to the North. I have written him that it is against my opinion he should; and as I wrote you before, advised him to march for Richmond.[1] I observe your project has failed. Present evils will always govern measures which are only calculated to guard against those, which are more remote; notwithstanding they may be much more extensive. From this general principal I foresaw you would fail.[2] One point is absolutely necessary to be settled by Congress, which is, whether the militia or State Troops shall be under the Orders of the continental officers or not. If the views of a State are opposed to the general plan of operations, and the force in the field can only be employed at such points as they shall think proper, no Officer can be safe in his measures; nor can the War be prosecuted upon a general Scale, where partial views have an undue influence.[3] However, my Dr sir, when you consider this critical and disagreeable situation I am in, the little prospect I have of acquiring glory, and the almost certain disgrace that has and will accompany my manoeuvres, from the nature and constitution of our Army, and from the many difficulties I have to Combat and compare your situation with mine, you may think yourself happy, that you are not in as perplexing a State as I am. I wish both our prospects were better, but mine of all mens is the most disagreeable. Let us labour & faint not. Happily we may get through the thorny path in due time, and by ways & means, not very clear to either at present.

Lord Cornwallis has retired towards Wilmington, and from the last accounts I had from them, they were upwards of forty Miles below Cross Creek.[4] We march this morning for South Carolina. I am Dear Baron Your most Obedient Humble Servant   NATH GREENE

LS (NHi).

1. See NG to the Marquis de Lafayette, 3 April, above. As noted there, Lafayette remained in the South.

2. For Steuben's plan to bring a force of militia into North Carolina to assist NG, see his letter of 30 March, above. As seen there, the Virginia Executive Council did not allow him to march the militia out of the state.

3. NG put the issue of control over the militia before Congress in his first letter to Samuel Huntington of 9 June, below. As noted there, Congress considered the question but did not adopt any regulation or make any recommendation to the states.

4. NG's intelligence was two days old; by 6 April, Lord Cornwallis's army was seventy-five miles below Cross Creek and within fifteen miles of Wilmington. ("Von Bose Journal," p. 54)

*   *   *

¶ [FROM GENERAL RICHARD CASWELL, Kingston, N.C., 6 April 1781. Caswell left New Bern "yesterday." Both houses of the legislature lacked a quorum, but he expects them to meet by the end of "next week."[1] NG's "Account" of 29 March is the most recent that the governor has received.[2] To "keep up a more regular Correspondence" with NG while the legislature is in session, Caswell has been asked to assign four horsemen to ride between New Bern and the army; one of them should reach NG's camp every second day.[3] Accounts from Virginia are "vague," but he has a reliable report that the French fleet has engaged and defeated a British fleet and is now "at or within the Capes." The Marquis de Lafayette is reportedly in [Gen. Benedict] Arnold's "neighbour Hood," but it is "uncertain" whether Lafayette's troops have "got down."[4] Says "Most of our people" are busy "geting out Men to Compleat our Continental Battalions." Lists the sites at which the six militia districts are to hold their musters and "receive the Men on the 20th Instant"; asks NG to send an officer to each.[5] ALS (Greene Papers: DLC) 3 pp.]

1. The Assembly did not convene until 23 June, at Wake Court House. (*NCSR*, 17: 877)

2. NG's letter to Gov. Abner Nash is above (vol. 7: 480).

3. The chain of riders does not seem to have functioned long. On 15 April, Caswell reported to Nash that the second rider had returned with a letter from Gen. John Butler after learning that NG's army had marched. Caswell wondered to Nash about the "propriety of Continuing" the riders. (*NCSR*, 15: 439)

4. As seen by Lafayette to NG, 4 April, above, this information was false.

5. In a letter of 11 April, below, NG instructed Gen. Jethro Sumner, the Continental commander in North Carolina, to send officers to each of the musters.

¶ [GENERAL GREENE'S ORDERS, Evans's Mill, N.C., 7 April 1781. The troops will be issued one day's provisions, which they should cook "immediately." Lamar Orderly Book (OClWHi) 1 p.]

¶ [TO GENERAL ROBERT LAWSON. From Evans's Mill, N.C., 7 April 1781. Finding it "impossible to injure" the enemy, who have "fallen down towards Wilmington," NG has decided to march immediately to South Carolina. "As I had had this in contemplation, in expectation that the Enemy would retire into the lower Country I called for the Militia of the upper Counties in Virginia some time since to second our operations."[1] NG wants Lawson to take command of the 2,200 militiamen who have been ordered out and to hasten their march. Asks him to write the governor for permission to "arrange" the men, who should rendezvous at Salisbury, N.C.[2] Laswon should send as many provisions there as possible.[3] NG's situation requires Lawson's "utmost exertions." Wants to know as soon as possible when the militia will take the field and when they will join the Southern Army.[4] Hopes "the same Gentlemen may come out with" Lawson as before. Thinks "we shall vex Lord Cornwallis if not beat him." Adds that Generals [Thomas] Sumter, [Andrew] Pickens, and [Francis] Marion are collecting their forces to cooperate with NG. Sends his compliments to Lawson's "Lady, and the happy circle." L (NcD) 2 pp. Although unsigned, this version of the letter appears to be the one that was sent to Lawson.]

1. See NG to Jefferson, 23 March, above (vol. 7: 466).

2. Lawson decided to see Jefferson about the equipping and arranging of the militia force. (See Lawson to NG, 20 April, below.)

3. In a draft of this letter at MiU-C, the rendezvous point was given as Charlotte. In the copy sent to Lawson, Charlotte was erased and Salisbury written in its place. In his letter to William R. Davie of 14 April, below, NG explained why he changed the rendezvous point.

4. Lawson wrote NG on 20 April. In the end, he remained in Virginia, as did most of the militiamen. (See note at Jefferson to NG, 30 March, above.)

¶ [TO GOVERNOR THOMAS SIM LEE OF MARYLAND. From "Head Quarters," Evans's Mill, N.C., 7 April 1781. NG received Lee's letter of 19 March the "day before yesterday."[1] He had learned about the order "some time since" and had incorporated the new regiment into the Continental line and sent its officers home.[2] When NG met with the Maryland legislators, he was assured that his army would be reinforced as soon as possible and that he "might rely upon all the support they could give."[3] He is "not a little disappointed that succour is so long acoming" and has had the "mortification" to learn that as of 13 March "not a man was raised." The army's distresses are even greater than NG has represented them to be. "Had it not been for the very great exertions of Virginia, the Southern States must have fallen." Virginia, however, cannot continue to "give effectual aid" while "a large body of the enimy" is in its "bowels." Reminds Lee that Maryland has not complied with any part of NG's requisition.[4] The army is in desperate need of the wagons, cavalry horses, and especially the money, of which NG has not received "a shilling." Adds: "In this situation you may readily conceive my difficulties." Maryland has the ability to "relieve" NG. He asked very little of the state, but it has given nothing. Hopes it does not wait too long to act. If the enemy succeed in "reducing" North Carolina, Lee "may depend upon Virginia and Marylands falling next." The enemy will shift large numbers of troops "from this quarter if they establish their Government." NG is on his march to South Carolina but cannot hold his ground unless he is immediately reinforced. He is told that the "old German Regiment" has been halted in Maryland to guard prisoners of war.[5] "This I am surprised at, while we are so weak here, and Militia would answer that service there." Refers Lee to the "publications of Congress for a state of the southern operations."[6] ADfS (MiU-C) 3 pp.]

1. See State Council of Maryland to NG, 19 March, above (vol. 7: 455).

2. See Mordecai Gist to NG, 14 February, and NG to Commissioned Officers of the Maryland State Regiment, 10 March, both above (vol. 7: 287– 88, 422).

3. NG's meeting with the legislators had taken place on 10 November 1780. (See NG to Lee, that date, above [vol. 6: 473].)

4. For NG's requisition, dated 10 November 1780, see ibid., p. 474.

5. The German Regiment had been raised by direction of Congress in Maryland and

Pennsylvania in 1776. It was disbanded as part of the reorganization of the Continental Army on 1 January 1781. (See above, vol. 7: 288n.) On 20 February, the Executive Council of Maryland ordered that Marylanders still in the regiment be sent to Frederick, Md., to guard the enemy prisoners captured at Saratoga in 1777. (Maryland Council to Phillip Thomas, 20 February, *Archives of Md.*, 45: 320) Sometime between then and 10 April, when the prisoners were ordered to be moved, these troops were reassigned, probably to join the Marquis de Lafayette's detachment. (See Maryland Council to Moses Rawlings, 10 April, ibid., p. 388.)

6. By "publications of Congress," NG meant letters of his to Congress that had been printed in the newspapers. As seen in NG to Lee, 11 April, below, this letter was intercepted by Loyalists, and NG had to send another copy.

¶ [TO COLONEL THOMAS POLK. From "Head Quarters Evans Mill on Rocky River," N.C., 7 March [i.e., April] 1781. The bearer, who is on his way to see Gen. [Thomas] Sumter, will visit Polk to learn the size of the militia force that will be sent from the Salisbury district to "operate" with NG's army.[1] NG also wants to know the "time[,] place" and how these troops are to be supplied with provisions and ammunition. Asks Polk to get them "in the field" soon.[2] NG has informed Governor Nash that Polk will not serve unless he receives a brigadier general's commission.[3] Tells Polk that provisions "will be wanted" for the 2,000 militia from Virginia who are to assemble at Charlotte, N.C.[4] ADfS (MiU-C) 2 pp.]

1. As seen in NG to Sumter, this date, below, the bearer was Maj. Edmund Hyrne, who was acting as an aide to NG.

2. Polk's reply of 11 April has not been found, but NG's letter to him of 14 April, below, gives a sense of its contents.

3. See NG to Abner Nash, 3 April, above.

4. As seen at NG to Lawson, this date, above, NG changed the rendezvous point to Salisbury, but only a few of the militiamen ever left Virginia.

¶ [TO GENERAL EDWARD STEVENS. From Evans's Mill on Rocky River, N.C., 7 April 1781. Was "very happy" to learn "yesterday" that Stevens has recovered enough to ride and that his wound was not a "greater misfortune."[1] NG would be "exceeding happy" if Stevens could "take a command" with the Virginia militia forces that have been ordered out. Knows, however, that he is not well enough to do so. Cannot expect as much from the militia without him. NG has asked Gen. [Robert] Lawson to join him and will be "in the greatest distress" if Lawson does not.[2] The battle of Guilford Court House "has given us a great advantage over the enemy," who have been forced to retreat with "evident marks of disgrace." The Southern Army's "present advantageous situation" is in "great measure owing" to the actions of Stevens and Lawson, and NG is "under the highest obligations" to them. Stevens has NG's "cordial thanks" and his wish for a "speedy recovery." ADfS (MiU-C) 2 pp.]

1. Dr. James Browne reported in a letter to William Pierce of 2 April, above, that Stevens had left the hospital at Guilford to ride home to Virginia.

2. See NG to Lawson, this date, above.

¶ [TO GENERAL THOMAS SUMTER. From Evans's Mill, Rocky River, N.C., 7 April 1781. The bearer, Maj. [Edmund] Hyrne, has been sent to learn what force Sumter can collect to assist NG's operations. "General Polk" is trying to collect militia in the Salisbury district.[1] NG plans to put these men under

Sumter's command, along with the 400 to 500 well-armed North Carolina militia who are already with the army. The enemy were within thirty or forty miles of Wilmington by last report.[2] "If we can get provisions, and you can raise a considerable force to co-operate with us, I think we shall perplex the enemy not a little, and perhaps do them an irreperable injury." They must either give up their posts in South Carolina or abandon North Carolina, and the American cause will benefit either way. This plan is the only one that promises any advantages. NG informed him earlier of his intentions; hopes that Sumter, who is to give Hyrne a candid estimate of his prospects, is prepared.[3] If "no misfortune attends us on the March," NG hopes to reach Camden, S.C., by 20 April.[4] Reports that 2,000 Virginia militia will be in the field in "a few days." They are to collect at Charlotte, N.C.[5] LS (Sumter Papers: DLC) 2 pp.]

1. See NG to Col. Thomas Polk, this date, above.

2. NG's reports were two days old. By 7 April, Cornwallis's army had reached the outskirts of Wilmington. ("Von Bose Journal," p. 54)

3. See NG to Sumter, 30 March, above.

4. The Southern Army was within a few miles of Camden on 19 April. (See NG's Orders, 19 April, below.)

5. For more on the expected reinforcement by the Virginia militia, see NG to Lawson, this date, above.

¶ [FROM GOVERNOR ABNER NASH OF NORTH CAROLINA, New Bern, N.C., 7 April 1781. Sends the bearer to "have an opportunity of hearing from" NG and to inform him that Nash has sent a "Cart" with "Loaf Sugar[,] Coffee[,] Spirits, Cheese &c" for NG and his aides.[1] Regrets that "the poverty of the place affords nothing better at this time." Was unable to get "good Tea"; hopes Col. [Nicholas] Long has sent NG a "few pounds." Also sends a "packett of York Gazetts," which a recently captured "Schooner from York" was carrying.[2] Nash has learned that the British in Virginia have been reinforced by 1,200 to 1,500 men.[3] Hopes the American force can "take care of the Enemy in that State." Nash has "no fears for this [state] as long as you stay with us and possess the peculiar Art of making your Enemies run away from their Victories leaving you master of their Wounded and of all the fertile part of the Country." Not enough legislators have arrived to "make an Assembly," and Nash begins to fear a quorum will not be achieved. That would be a "great misfortune, as "further provision" should be made for NG's support. The safety of the state "depends entirely" upon it.[4] Nash plans to visit NG's camp within a few weeks.[5] Sends his compliments to NG's aides. In a postscript, adds that he just received NG's letter of 6 March.[6] ALS (NNPM) 2 pp.]

1. On the riders who were supposed to facilitate communication between New Bern and NG's camp, see Caswell to NG, 6 April, above.

2. The "York Gazetts" were copies of James Rivington's *Royal Gazette*, published in New York City.

3. For more on the reinforcement, which numbered 2,000 men, see note at Washington to NG, 21 March, above (vol. 7: 459n).

4. As noted at Caswell to NG, 6 April, above, the legislature did not meet until 23 June.

5. Nash apparently did not visit NG.

6. NG's letter is above (vol. 7: 401–2).

¶ [**FROM WILLIAM SHARPE**, Philadelphia, 7 April 1781. Is "the more thankful" for NG's letter of 18 March because he knows NG has "little time to correspond with individuals."[1] Is pained by the army's "sufferings, distresses and losses." Assures NG that Congress has done everything in its power to provide relief, "altho our embarrassments are infinite." Adds that the conduct of NG and his army is "not only universally approved" but "even admired." Sends intelligence, which he "can scarcely believe," that Sir Henry Clinton plans to "come into the Delaware." If Clinton does so, it may be to divert the Pennsylvania line, which is ready to march to the South after being paid "37,000 dollars new emissions."[2] NG will have heard of the operations of the French and British fleets. "The former, altho disapointed, deserve great praise."[3] Congress has heard nothing about the second French division or the clothing and stores for the army. Encloses an uncertified, but "true," copy of an inquiry of the Board of Admiralty, showing that neither Congress nor Dr. [Benjamin] Franklin is to blame for the delay in sending supplies.[4] "Of this the Army and the Legislature ought to be acquainted." Congress has heard nothing about the effects in Europe of England's declaration of war on the Dutch. Sharpe thinks the Dutch navy "must be greatly weakened" by the capture of "so many seamen as England must take" before the Dutch "can look about them."[5] The express is waiting; sends his compliments to NG's officers. ALS (MiU-C) 2 pp.]

1. The letter to Sharpe has not been found.

2. The enclosures, which have not been found, were undoubtedly copies of letters to Samuel Huntington from Gen. David Forman and Gov. William Livingston, dated 2 and 5 April respectively, reporting that an embarkation from New York for New Castle, Del., was imminent. (See copies in Washington Papers, DLC.) Clinton had considered sending a force to the Delaware River to disrupt American supply lines and rally the large number of Loyalists reported to be in the area. He decided against such a move after learning that Lord Cornwallis was moving into Virginia. (Opinions of General Sir Henry Clinton on Operations in Chesapeake [26 April], and Clinton to Lord George Germain, 9–12 June, Davies, *Documents*, 20: 120–22, 154–55; see also St. Clair to NG, 6 May, below.) The diversion of the Pennsylvania line was not a consideration. As Sharpe indicated, the Pennsylvanians would not march until they were paid. The state issued interest-bearing certificates to its troops in mid-April, but they marched only as far as York, Pa., where they remained until 25 May. (Nelson, *Wayne*, pp. 127–30; on their eventual march to the South, see note at Washington to NG, 1 June, below.)

3. For more on the battle between British and French fleets near the entrance to Chesapeake Bay, see note at Steuben to NG, first letter of 4 March, above (vol. 7: 390n).

4. The Board of Admiralty's findings, dated 28 March, are in *JCC*, 19: 316–20. On the question of Franklin's role, see note at Ralph Izard to NG, 19 January, above (vol. 7: 152n).

5. The Dutch were able to put their fleet to sea sooner than expected. To counter that force, the British had to divert vessels from other stations. (See Mackesy, *War for America*, pp. 392–96.)

* * *

From General Thomas Sumter

D^r S^r   Catawba River [S.C.] 7th Ap^l 1781

I Received by Capt Miles [Jonathan Mills] Your letter of the 30th Ulti^{mo} And am extreemly Glad to find that our Insulting Enemy are obliged once more, to Seek Secourity by flight, and although the Route they have taken May Secoure them from your farther Persuit yet, Should they March through So an inhospitable a Country Round by the Way of Wilmingtown it will almost Amount to a Defeat.[1]

But I am apprehensive they Mean to turn in to So. Carolina by the way of the Cheraws if Not Prevented. Circumstanced as you are I am of oppinion that Your Plan of opperation to the South Will Disconsert and Injure the Enemy More than any other You Coud have thought of.

And you may Rely upon my unremitted endeavours to Promote & facillitate Your Designs.

This I may be the better enabled to Do by having falen upon a Plan of Raising Some Cores [i.e., Corps] of horse to Serve under Continental Articles for Ten Months.[2] This I was obliged to Do, at any Rate, or at once abandon the State. I am happy to be informd by Cap[t] [John] Hampton that You approve of the Measure, the Disoluteness of the People has of late Given the Enemy Great advantages over us, and thereby Distroying the happy effects that Might have Resulted from your Successfull oppossission.[3] Three Regim[ts] in my Brigad is left without a field off[r], a Number of other off[rs] & Men Kild[,] taken & Paroled, by their Imprudently Going upon private & Disgracefull business.

Nevertheless I expect to have Six or Seven hundred Men belonging to My Brigade in the field before the 20th Ins[t], But it at present appears that I Shall be obliged to Move to the Westward for a few days.

The Enemy has by Detachments from Camden[,] Congerees[,] 96 & Tories Collected a body of about Eight hundred men Near the Fish Dam Foard. Some late Movements indicates their having a Design to Cross to this Side.[4]

By Some unexpected opposission from Certain off[rs] in North Carolina I Shall, or is lightly [i.e., likely] to Loose a Number of men that is ingaged in the ten Months Service[.] The Reasons they asign for their Conduct are in My oppinion Very Trivel & Exceedingly impolitick, & altogether Contrary to the intent & meaning of the laws by which they pretend to act. The true Cause of the objection is, those Who May Want a Substitute Will have to give More to procoure them. A Number of the people Ingaged with Me before I Knowd any thing of the Continental Draft taking place. However this Matter I Submit to your Determination.[5]

I Shall make No use of those enlisted or Suffer any more to be ingaged untill I Know your pleasure. By Thursday Next I Shoud have had five hundred ten months men in the field. Cheifly So well Mounted as to perform tollerable Service, and from the activity of the enemy & indiscression of our Militia, I think all the Men that Can by any Justifiable Method be Procoured, will Not be two many.

Gen[l] Pickens Men are Much Scattered. He will have but few Out that is in any Short Time.

I expect fore or five hundred will be Ready to Join you out of Gen[l] Marians Brigade. I have Requested him to take a position high up Black River if it Can be Done with Safety to prevent the enemy from foraging that way & to have as Much provision as possible Provided.[6] I have Wrote Co[l] Marshell to the Same effect.[7]

I will do every thing in my power in that way, but all the Corn the Country afoards Lies between the Enemies posts. The Post at Co[l] Thompsons is Broke up & the Troops Removed to the Congress, Where there is five Two pound peices of artillery, & one Wal peice.[8] The Enemy are useing every Possible Means to Raise a Number of horse. Many of our Country men Downward Gives them Great assistance both by furnishing with Good horses & by Subscriptions.[9]

Nothing in the Summit of my Power Shall be Neglected that may in the least tend to further your opperations against the Enemy. I have the Hon[r] to be D[r] Sir Your Most obedt Hble Servt   TIIO[s] SUMTER
NB Please to excuse inaccurcies. I am obliged to Write in Great haste as by holding the pen long Renders my hand useless.[10]

ALS (MiU-C).

1. As seen in the next sentence, Sumter assumed that Lord Cornwallis would return to South Carolina from Wilmington, N.C.

2. Some historians have concluded that Sumter, in his plan for raising ten-month men, was making the best use possible of a situation— plundering—that was already beyond control. (See, for example, Gregorie, *Sumter*, pp. 146–48.) Others, such as Rachel N. Klein, have argued that Sumter's use of "slave bounty payments . . . made robbery from loyalists official policy and tempted numerous militiamen to rob from whigs as well." (Klein, *Unification of a Slave State*, p. 103) Under Sumter's plan, those who enlisted were to receive a certain number of slaves taken from Loyalists. Payment was to vary by rank, from "one grown negro" for a private to "three grown negroes and one small negro" for a regimental commander. In addition, each company was to receive "two-thirds of all articles captured from the enemy except negroes and military stores; and salvage allowed them for all the articles belonging to our friends which we may capture from the enemy." (Richard Hampton to John Hampton, 2 April, Gibbes, *Documentary History*, 3: 48) Sumter seems to have initiated "Sumter's Law," as it came to be known, reluctantly. In a letter to Francis Marion, who refused to have anything to do with his plan, Sumter wrote:

> The dissoluteness of our pretended friends, and the ravages committed by them, are as alarming and distressing, as that of having the enemy among us. It is therefore necessary immediately to discriminate who are enemies, and who are real friends; the former treated as their baseness and perfidy authorize, the latter to be known only by their conduct, that is, by bearing arms and doing duty when thereunto required by proper authority, and in case of refusal or neglect, both person and property to be treated and dealt with accordingly. Nothing can be more unwise or impolitic than to suffer all the wealth of our country to be so basely and unfairly appropriated, for the sole purpose of accumulating our mis-

fortunes, and finally completing our ruin, when it is in our power at once to check, if not totally prevent the evils and disadvantages resulting therefrom, to which end I propose raising several Regiments of Light Dragoons. . . . (Gibbes, *Documentary History*, 3: 45)

Sumter was unable to enlist as many men under this plan as he anticipated. Instead of five regiments, he ended up with only three, which were undersized. After the war, the South Carolina legislature passed an act relieving Sumter and Andrew Pickens of any liability for actions taken under the plan. Nevertheless, a series of lawsuits continued until 1792. (McCrady, *S.C. in the Revolution*, pp. 144–48, 145–47n)

3. Although NG no doubt approved of Sumter's efforts to recruit, he tried to make sure that the process did not degenerate into outright plundering. (See his letter to Sumter of 15 April, below.)

4. As seen in his letter of 13 April, below, Sumter ordered Pickens to take a position near Fishdam Ford and sent him four regiments from Sumter's brigade.

5. NG did not answer Sumter's query directly, but in a letter of 10 April, below, he told Col. Wade Hampton, one of Sumter's subordinates, that he did not want the plan to "interfere" with the raising of Continentals in North Carolina and could not "authorize" any activity that was contrary to that state's laws.

6. In his letter to Marion of 28 March, Sumter had ordered Marion to take a position "higher upon Black River, which is very necessary to not only prevent the stock from being drove to Camden, but also to facilitate my plans and designs on the west side of the Wateree. The more speedy your movements are, the better they will answer." (Gibbes, *Documentary History*, 3: 46) According to his biographer, Marion "resented" these "arbitrary orders" and sank into a dark mood, in which he considered abandoning the low country of South Carolina and giving up his militia command. (Rankin, *Swamp Fox*, pp. 181–82)

7. Sumter's orders to Col. John Marshel have not been found, but NG said nothing about the latter joining him when he wrote Marshel on 15 April, below.

8. When the British abandoned their post at Belleville, Col. William Thompson's plantation, they moved to the plantation of Mrs. Rebecca Motte, about a mile away. Motte's estate was strategically located, near the confluence of the Congaree and the Wateree, and stood on more defensible terrain than Thompson's. According to Henry Lee, however, the installation lacked artillery. (Lee, *Memoirs*, 2: 74; for more on Ft. Motte, see Lipscomb, "S.C. Battles," *Place Names in South Carolina* 35 [Winter 1978]: 28–29.) A wall-piece was "an enlarged firelock or firearm mounted on a swivel, and placed in the walls of a fort or other fortified place." (*OED*)

9. In early June, Lord Rawdon reported to Cornwallis that the inhabitants of Charleston had "made a subscription amounting to near three thousand guineas" for "equipping a corps of dragoons." (Gibbes, *Documentary History*, 3: 90)

10. Sumter was still suffering from the wound he had received the previous November. (See above, vol. 6: 581n.)

*   *   *

¶ **[FROM COLONEL HENRY LEE, JR.** [After 7 April 1781][1] Offers an "anecdote," which throws "light on the British plan of operations for the present campaign." After news of the battle of Guilford Court House reached Charleston, S.C., Gen. [Charles] Scott was given permission to return home on parole, subject to approval by Lord Cornwallis. He was accompanied by Maj. [George] Benson, a British officer.[2] After crossing the Black River, Benson inquired about "the nearest route to Petersburg," Va., but was told "he might meet with Lord Cornwallis much nearer." He thereupon "betrayed in his passion his disappointment, & treated the commandant with contumely."[3] ALS (MiU-C) 1 p. At least one page is missing.]

1. The place and date are missing; an approximate date was determined from the information discussed in note 3, below.

2. Scott, a general in the Virginia Continental line, had been captured at Charleston in May 1780. He received permission to leave for home "around the end of March." (Harry M. Ward, *Charles Scott and the "Spirit of '76"* [Charlottesville: University Press of Virginia, 1988], p. 81) Scott wrote NG from Haley's Ferry, N.C., on 13 April, below, reporting that he was on his way to see Cornwallis and requesting a "passport" for Benson's "return."

3. Lee presumably concluded that Cornwallis had been planning all along to proceed to Virginia after the battle of Guilford Court House. The reasons for Benson's alleged "disappointment" are not known but almost certainly had nothing to do with British plans to invade Virginia. By at least 24 March, Col. Nisbet Balfour, the British commandant at Charleston, was aware that Cornwallis was en route to Cross Creek, N.C., to try to resupply his army. (Balfour to Lord George Germain, 24 March, Davies, *Documents*, 20: 96) According to Sir Henry Clinton, Balfour detached Benson, his military secretary, on 7 April to inform Cornwallis "of the distressed state" of affairs in South Carolina as a result of NG's invasion and to ask Cornwallis to return there. (Chesney, "Journal," p. 10n; Clinton, *American Rebellion*, pp. 284–85n) Cornwallis's army reached the outskirts of Wilmington on the 7th. (See note at Emmet to NG, 9 April, below.)

¶ [**TO COLONEL JAMES EMMET**. From Camp [Wilcox Iron Works, N.C.], 8 April 1781.[1] NG is "on the march for South Carolinia" and wants to know the "enemies movements in consequence thereof." He begs Emmet to keep spies near the British and send word as to "which way they move." He details his army's route of march, cautioning Emmet not to give even his "most particular friends" a hint of NG's "route and intentions." ADfS (MiU-C) 2 pp.]

1. The place was taken from NG's other letters of this date.

¶ [**TO GENERAL JETHRO SUMNER**. From Camp, Wilcox Iron Works, N.C., 8 April 1781. NG has learned that several North Carolina counties are drafting "regular troops agreeable to the late Law."[1] Sumner is to collect the draftees "immediately," organize them, and send them to NG's army. They should be equipped and well-armed, as the army has no muskets to spare. Sumner is "well acquainted" with the situation in the Southern Department and should need no persuasion to "exert" himself.[2] The army is marching to South Carolina but cannot "support" itself there without reinforcements. The draftees should be sent via Charlotte, where they will receive further orders. As the route to Charlotte could become unsafe, he should keep himself informed of "the enemy's motions." Adds that the officer bringing this letter wants to join the army "with the first company." Says in a postscript that "the route, & situation of the Army" are "a profound secret," which is not to be shared with anyone. LS (NcSoC) 2 pp.]

1. On North Carolina's efforts to fill its Continental battalions, see Nash to NG, 3 April, and Caswell to NG, 6 April, both above.

2. In a letter to NG of this date, below, Sumner discussed his plans to send the recruits to the army.

¶ [**TO COLONEL THOMAS WADE**. From Wilcox Iron Works, N.C., 8 April 1781. NG, who had heard nothing from Wade since learning of his defeat, is glad to find by his letter of 4 April that Wade is safe.[1] The enemy have been retreating ever since the battle of Guilford Court House. They were heading toward Wilmington and are probably there by now.[2] NG is marching to Camden, S.C., by way of Colston's, N.C. His army is "greatly distressed for want of provisions." Asks Wade "to forward to the mouth of Rocky River" meal and all the livestock he has collected.[3] NG will send ten or twelve wagons to the Cheraws for meal; wants Wade to prepare a quantity, so there will be no delay. Thinks it "highly probable" that Lord Cornwallis will follow the Southern Army when he learns what NG's route and intentions are.[4] "All the provision in and about the Cheraws" should therefore be sent to the army to keep them out of the enemy's hands. "Capt Conners" was sent to collect cattle west of the Pee Dee River.[5] NG would have informed Wade of this earlier but "could hear nothing" of him. If there is any bacon at Colston's, the army will take it, so Wade need not concern himself further about it. Asks him to secure all the boats between the "great bluff" and Mask's Ferry to prevent the enemy from crossing the river if they go that way.[6] NG has ordered "General Marian" to join the Southern Army when it crosses the Pee Dee; hopes he will bring "a considerable force."[7] In a postscript, tells Wade to "Keep a good heart and fear not." ADfS (MiU-C) 3 pp.]

1. On the defeat that Wade had suffered, see his letter to NG of 2 April, above.

2. As noted at NG to Sumter, 7 April, above, Cornwallis's army had reached the outskirts of Wilmington on that date.

3. Colston's, where NG had established a magazine of provisions, was at the mouth of the Rocky River. (See note at NG to George Fletcher, 8 January, above [vol. 7: 72n].)

4. Cornwallis did not follow NG's army into South Carolina.

5. For more on Capt. James Conyers's mission, see NG to Marion, 4 April, above.

6. On the location of the "great bluff," see note at NG to Lee, first letter of 4 April, above.

7. NG's letter to Gen. Francis Marion, dated 4 April, is above.

¶ [FROM GENERAL THOMAS PERSON,[1] Goshen, N.C., 8 April 1781. Asks NG to suggest "the most Elligable plan for the Accommodation & Support of the Army." That will be the "Great Object" of the legislature's "present meeting." Person is sure that NG's recommendations will be "well receivd," as the legislators have a "high Sence" of his "Military Skill & abillities."[2] Congratulates NG on the news, "whether True or otherwise," that a French fleet is at the mouth of the Cape Fear River.[3] Person will not "be wanting" in his efforts to support the army. ALS (MiU-C) 2 pp.]

1. Person was a North Carolina militia officer and a member of the legislature. As seen above (vol. 6: 504n), NG had stayed at his home while en route to join the Southern Army.

2. As noted at Caswell to NG, 6 April, above, the legislature did not meet until 23 June. NG's reply has not been found, but in a letter to Gov. Abner Nash of 3 April, above, he had outlined the actions he thought North Carolina should take in the army's behalf.

3. The report was false. (See Lafayette to NG, 4 April, above.)

¶ [FROM GENERAL ANDREW PICKENS, Camp, Enoree River, S.C., 8 April 1781. Pickens marched south immediately after he wrote NG "from the Catawba."[1] He met "Colonel Clark [Elijah Clarke]" of Georgia at the Broad River. Clarke was then retreating from the Long Canes, where on 23 March he had fought a "smart action" with an enemy party of about ninety men commanded by Maj. [James] Dunlap. Clarke's force was twice that size, but a number of his men were unarmed. He attacked "with vigour and resolution" in two divisions, and his "Militia Horse" quickly put a larger number of the enemy's regular cavalry to flight. The enemy infantry "retreated to some Houses" but soon surrendered.[2] "The Enemy loss was great for the Amount of Men; their Horse being chiefly killed in the flight and great part of the Infantry before they surrendered."[3] The prisoners are being sent to Virginia "by way of the Mountains."

Pickens is "exceeding sorry" to report an "inhuman action" that followed Clarke's victory. Dunlap, while a prisoner, was killed at Gilbert Town, N.C., by "a set of Men chiefly unknown," who "forced the Guard and shot him."[4] Pickens has offered a reward of $10,000 for the apprehension of the one known perpetrator.[5] He has also sent a "Flag" to Col. [John Harris] Cruger, informing him "with what horror and detestation American Officers looked on the act." At the same time, Pickens pointed out to Cruger that "barbarous massacres" of captured Americans—especially the "murder" of an officer while he was under the "sanction of" a flag of truce—had "actuated those persons to that mode of redress." Pickens has misplaced his letter to Cruger but encloses a copy of the latter's reply, which reveals Cruger's "sentiments."[6]

Reports that the "Country here" is greatly distressed by the enemy and is "broken up" by "marauding and plundering parties." Thinks the entire area "would have been evacuated by our Friends" if it had taken him any longer to reach the Tyger River. On 31 March, Cruger, reinforced by Innis's corps, marched some 300 regulars and 200 Loyalists to "Harrisons Store on Fair Forest" Creek to establish a garrison.[7] Pickens gathered some South Carolinians and took the Georgians with him "to risque an Action." He was informed, though, that Cruger had retreated to Ft. Williams, "fifteen Miles this side Ninety Six."[8] Pickens will do all he can to "prevent their return," but it will be difficult to maintain even a small party for lack of provisions. He has already written Gen. [Thomas] Sumter for help and will do so again; does not know "the probability of success."[9] Asks NG to send intelligence, "as there is no certainty to be learnt here of any Event."[10] Repeats in a postscript that unless he is "speedily assisted," he cannot "make a stand this side" of Ninety Six. Has sent NG "three receipts" for "officers Servants" who were captured at Cowpens.[11] LS (NcD) 4 pp.]

1. The letter to which Pickens referred has not been found. In orders that Pickens remembered as being "only general," NG had detached him from the army and sent him with a militia force to his home district near Ninety Six. (NG to Pickens, 8 March, above [vol. 7: 410]; Pickens to Henry Lee, 25 November 1811, Draper Microfilm) Pickens reached the Catawba River by 20 March. (Ferguson, "Pickens," p. 195) He recalled in 1811 that a short time later he received orders from NG to "harass the foraging parties at Ninety Six and Augusta [Ga.] and as much as possible encourage the desponding inhabitants." (Pickens to Lee, 25 November 1811, Draper Microfilm)

2. Dunlap, who commanded the cavalry at Ninety Six, was on a foraging expedition with a party of Loyalists and British dragoons. (Cornwallis to Balfour, 16 November 1780, PRO 30/11/82; Ferguson, "Pickens," p. 196) In the engagement, which took place at Beattie's Mill on the Little River, Capt. James McCall of Clarke's militia captured a bridge to prevent a retreat. Clarke, meanwhile, attacked the mill and outbuildings, in which Dunlap and many of his troops had taken refuge. (Waring, *Fighting Elder*, p. 68)

3. A note at the top of the letter gives enemy casualties as thirty-four killed and forty-two captured.

4. It has been speculated that Dunlap was killed either by his guards "or by some one with their connivance." (McCrady, *S.C. in the Revolution*, p. 128) A Loyalist officer from the North, he had become "infamous" for "his barbarity" even before going to the South. He had served with Maj. Patrick Ferguson prior to the battle of Kings Mountain, and his "severities" had "incensed the people against him." (Ibid., p. 19) Historians have suggested that fear of revenge had kept him from surrendering until many of his men were either dead or wounded. (Ibid., p. 127; Waring, *Fighting Elder*, p. 68)

5. The perpetrator was apparently never caught. Historian Edward McCrady has written that Pickens's response to the killing of Dunlap reflects a "high sense of honor [that] revolted against such turpitude." (McCrady, *S.C. in the Revolution*, p. 128) Certainly, in taking the steps that he did, Pickens must have acted in spite of strong personal feelings toward Dunlap. The latter had raided Pickens's own plantation in late 1780, "burning and destroying his buildings and crops" and insulting his family. (Waring, *Fighting Elder*, pp. 41–42) That act of Dunlap's led Pickens, then a prisoner on parole, to declare the terms of his parole broken and return to the field. In doing so, he became subject to execution if he were recaptured. (Ibid., p. 42; on Pickens's renunciation of his parole, see also vol. 6: 558n and vol. 7: 33n, both above.)

6. Cruger was the British commander at Ninety Six. A copy of what is undoubtedly his reply to Pickens, dated 3 April, is in the Greene Papers, DLC, where it is identified as a letter from Cruger to NG. In that letter, Cruger told Pickens that his "abhorrence & detestation of the horrid ⟨act of⟩ murdering" Dunlap did honor to his "feelings as ⟨a⟩ Man & a Soldier." (The words in angle brackets were taken from a GWG Transcript, CSmH.)

7. "Innis" was Col. Alexander Innes, a South Carolina Loyalist. (Chesney, "Journal," p. 83).

8. Ft. Williams served the British as an advance post for Ninety Six. (Lipscomb, "S.C. Battles," *Place Names in South Carolina* 34 [Winter 1977]: 13)

9. Sumter wrote NG on 13 April, below, that he had sent four regiments to Pickens and had asked Pickens to take a position near the Fish Dam Ford.

10. NG replied on 15 April, below.

11. The receipts are not with the letter, but ScU has copies of five receipts, dated 24 January and addressed to Pickens as "agent for the american Troops," concerning eight "negroes" taken at "Tarltons Defeat." The individuals giving the receipts were to hold the "negroes" until "Called on for them" and were to be held accountable for them unless they should die, run away, or "by some unavoidable accident Should fall into the hands of the Enemy."

¶ **[FROM GENERAL JETHRO SUMNER**, [N.C.], 8 April 1781.[1] He has arranged to have Continental officers "receive the drafts of the several districts" in North Carolina and march them to a general rendezvous at Hillsborough. "The distress'd condition of that neighbourhood, the probable Rout[e] of the enemy, and the supply of Armes, would make" a general rendezvous farther "to the eastward more convenient for provisions, more in the way of the Enemy, and in all probability get sooner supply'd with arms &c."[2] But Sumner's recommendation is based on a supposition that the arms will be borrowed from Virginia, as Col. [Alexander] Martin of the Council Extraordinary gave him to understand.[3] Nothing will deter Sumner "one hour" from equipping the draftees for the field.[4] He has "not realy, twenty dollars" at his command and asks for an order on the Southern Department's deputy paymaster for "the Arrearage due" him and other officers.[5] ALS (NNPM) 2 pp.]

1. Sumner did not give his location.

2. NG replied on 19 April, below, giving Sumner latitude in determining the rendezvous site.

3. The Council Extraordinary had sent Allen Jones to borrow arms from the state of Virginia, but he was informed that Virginia had already sent all its surplus arms to NG's army. (Rankin, *N.C. Continentals*, p. 342) Sumner then turned to the Continental officers in Virginia and requested the arms from Baron Steuben and the Marquis de Lafayette, who were able to send him a supply in July. (Sumner to Steuben, 29 June, Steuben Microfilm; Lafayette to NG, 4 and 5 July, below)

4. Despite Sumner's pledge, the North Carolina draftees did not join NG until early August. (Rankin, *N.C. Continentals*, p. 346)

5. NG advised Sumner to try to obtain the pay from the state, "as the military chest is very low." (See NG to Sumner, 19 April, below.)

¶ [GENERAL GREENE'S ORDERS, "[Widow] Cottons," N.C., 9 April 1781. Wants a count of the number of portmanteaus needed to furnish each officer with one. In After Orders, the army is to camp "here" and march at sunrise. Lamar Orderly Book (OClWHi) 1 p.]

¶ [TO LORD CORNWALLIS. From Headquarters [Widow Cotton's, N.C.], 9 April 1781. He received Cornwallis's letter of 3 April on the evening of the 6th. NG is not "justly chargeable with either proposing or insisting upon any unreasonable terms." His "object" was to bring "the most speedy and effectual relief to the unfortunate captives in the hands of both Parties." All of his conditions are "mutual," and "accidental circumstances" should not influence the settlement of a cartel. The Americans now have more officers in captivity than the British, but that may not always be the case; with "Privates," the advantage is "evidently" on the side of the British. However, to show that he is "desireous of effecting an exchange," even in the face of "political inconvenience," NG agrees that officers will be exchanged "according to the dates of their captivity"; those who remain prisoners will be paroled and not recalled unless they violate their paroles or one of the parties breaks the terms of the cartel. NG cannot understand why allowing officers to reside with rank and file prisoners is objectionable. He finds "want of a precedent" an insufficient objection; hopes Cornwallis will agree to this "measure" but will "not insist upon it."[1] If Cornwallis finds these conditions acceptable, "in addition to those already agreed to," NG proposes that the commissioners meet at "Mr Pegees on the Pedee" on 24 April to complete the negotiations.[2] ALS (PRO 30/11/91) 2 pp.]

1. For the terms of the cartel, see note at NG to Huntington, 10 May, below.

2. As seen in Carrington to NG, 8 May, below, "Mr Pegees" was Claudius Pegues, whose residence was near Cheraw, S.C. Cornwallis replied on 15 April, below.

¶ [FROM COLONEL WILLIAM R. DAVIE, Salisbury, N.C., 9 April 1781. Is pleased to report that the "Continental quotas" for "this District" are "completing very rapidly." Expects most of the new troops to "take the field" by 24 April.[1] The officers have been "so ingaged in this business that they have forgotten the Delinquents from the last three months Service."[2] Col. [Francis] Lock and several other aspirants seem "wounded by the Appointment of General Polk."[3] Davie finds "this country almost entirely exhausted"—not by the "two grand armies," but from "frequent Bodies of Militia," which have been "supported with so little oeconomy." Transportation is the "principal

Difficulty here" and "in every other place"; the lack of a quartermaster "embarrasses" Davie "exceedingly."[4] On "Friday last [6 April]" he sent an express to Col. [Thomas] Wade, whom he learned was at home.[5] Has received reports that "Lord Rawdon is moving with a small Body" towards the Pee Dee River; asks "if this will effect my Operations."[6] Despite the difficulties, he hopes to send 1,400 bushels of meal and all the livestock that can be collected to the Pee Dee by 16 April.[7] Twenty-four British prisoners have been brought to Salisbury; Lock wants to know where to send them.[8] ALS (NcU) 4 pp.]

1. The "quotas" were draftees for the state's Continental line. According to an undated letter from Gen. Jethro Sumner to an unnamed correspondent, the Continental officers in the Salisbury district received 180 draftees. (NCSR, 19: 910) NG sent orders about the conscripts in his letter to Sumner of 11 April, below.

2. The "delinquents" were militiamen who had failed to turn out when summoned in early March. (See Polk to NG, 13 March, above [vol. 7: 430].)

3. As noted at NG to Nash, 3 April, above, Thomas Polk, who had demanded a brigadier general's commission as a pre-condition for taking the post, never received the appointment as commander of the Salisbury militia district; Lock was named to the command instead.

4. Transportation was one of the responsibilities of a quartermaster.

5. Wade received Davie's letter on the 8th and discussed it in his to NG of 10 April, below.

6. Rawdon was still in Camden, S.C. On the detachment that had been moving up the Pee Dee, see note at Wade to NG, 2 April, above.

7. On the forwarding of the provisions, see Davie to NG, 23 April, below.

8. If NG sent instructions regarding the prisoners, they have not been found.

¶ [FROM COLONEL JAMES EMMET, Campbelltown, N.C., 9 April 1781. Has NG's letter of 8 April and will "observe" its contents. Emmet's letter to NG of 4 April may not have been delivered. Emmet knows the express and thinks error, not "deceit," was involved.[1] Reports that the British reached Wilmington on "Friday last."[2] Lord Cornwallis was "much displeas'd to find the Mills here dismantled, and several of his Gentlemen were so nettled, that they could not help shewing it to the Ladies, who were left in town[.] They said, they repaird Bridges & Mills too for Mr Green, & wondered he should do things in so small a way." Emmet has received a report from the Pee Dee, which, if true, shows "exceeding" cruelty. A Colonel "Culp, thro' a Zeal, more like a madman, than an Officer, & Gentleman, is burning & distroying every kind of Property, perticularly Provision of all kinds, nor does his cruilty stop at that, for every one he sees, and has the least conjecture of there being unfriendly to their cause, he immediately tortures with the most cruel death." Emmet believes it is possible to be "a true friend to his Country, without shewing so much violence, & persicution." He does not know the colonel and makes "this complaint" only out of "feelings of humanity." If the reports are true, he hopes that NG can "put a stop to it."[3] Emmet has delayed the express, whose horse was "much tired," in the hope of receiving more timely information "before Evening." Encloses a letter from an officer who has offered to gather intelligence for NG and who, Emmet believes, will "hazard much." ALS (MiU-C) 2 pp.]

1. Emmet's letter is above. As it is among NG's papers, NG probably received it.

2. "Friday last" was 6 April. According to the journal of the Von Bose Regiment, Lord

Cornwallis's army arrived on the outskirts of Wilmington on 7 April. ("Von Bose Journal," p. 54)

3. Colonel "Culp" was no doubt Col. Abel Kolb, whose forays against Loyalists in the area of Drowning Creek—also known as the Little Pee Dee River—are discussed at Wade to NG, 4 April, above. As seen there, Loyalists attacked Kolb's house on 28 April and killed him, reportedly after he surrendered.

¶ [FROM GENERAL ALEXANDER LILLINGTON, "Camp at R[utherford's]: Mills," N.C., 9 April 1781. "Agreeable to" NG's last letter, Lillington left "the Bridge" and retreated sixteen miles to "Rutherfurs Mill."[1] Has heard that Lord Cornwallis himself is in Wilmington, but does not know if Cornwallis's army has yet reached town.[2] When it does, Lillington will "Push for Kingston," as it will be unsafe to remain where he is. As NG ordered, Lillington sent "light horse" to drive off cattle near Wilmington. A party of those troops, who "would not Obay their Officers," was surprised by the enemy; eight were bayonetted to death, and two others were wounded.[3] Lillington's men have "brought off" 150 cattle, and Colonel Malmedy, who reached camp "Last Evening," will be sent to collect more.[4] Lillington has 500 militiamen but cannot keep them for long, as provisions and especially grain are scarce. Wishes to hear from NG.[5] ALS (MiU-C) 1 p.]

1. See NG to Lillington, 5 April, above. Lillington had been camped at Heron's Bridge, on the North East Cape Fear River.

2. Cornwallis's army was encamped some three miles outside Wilmington, on a bluff overlooking the North East Cape Fear River. ("Von Bose Journal," p. 54)

3. For another perspective on this episode, see Rowan to NG, 18 April, below.

4. NG had sent the Marquis de Malmedy to join Lillington. (See NG to Malmedy, 30 March, above.)

5. As seen by his reply of 21 April, below, NG did not receive this letter until the 20th.

* * *

From Doctor James McHenry

Baltimore [Md.] 9th April 1781.

When I left Annapolis, my dear General[,] the Marquiss was writing you a melancholly tale of his misventures.[1] I was then too much indisposed to add a line of thanks for your letter of the 22d of March.[2] The detachment went from Annapolis by water to the Head of Elk, where it now is on its return to New Windsor.[3] On bursting of the bubble the mortification I felt on your account was beyond that on my own, although I had flattered myself with the pleasure of encreasing the number of your family.[4] This is now at an end.

I long to hear from you and Cornwallis.[5] The people here begin to find out who it is they should praise; but then as is almost always the case with the herd of mankind, they expect more than what is proper. I endeavour to reduce their ideas on this head to what is reasonable, and to shew them that both the country and the militia, you have for your support and manouvres, are essentially different from those which assisted in the reduction of Burgoyne.[6] Let me add—your public letters have a great deal of merit and do not want for admirers. They will continue to please while you put into them nothing but good sense and judicious observation, and do not embrace much ornament. The latter dress was never designed for official dispatches, written under your circumstances, and I see that you have wisely reserved the glase of it for other occasions.

Perhaps the Marquiss has told you all he knows respecting our expectations of a French armament. If he has not you shall know all that I do. There are letters from the cabinet which leave us to look for them the latter end of this month or sometime in the next. The land force will be considerable, and the marine will ensure a complete superiority.[7] The old object of attack should these get here without diminution or accident will be the hobby horse for another campaign.[8] So you see upon what you have to depend. We must be disappointed in the Strength of the succour, successful or defeated before any part of it be turned your way.

As I do not move from this place till the campaign to the Northward begins to shew itself, I shall enquire at every express which comes through here from your quarter for something for me.[9]

I embrace you my dear General. Be only as successful as I wish you to be, and then you will be as great as you deserve. But be this as it will you will always deserve to be great. In the utmost and truest friendship adieu   JAMES M^CHENRY
Phillips I suppose with his detachment (said to be at Hampton Road) either came as a counterbalance to that under the Marquiss, or to support Cornwallis.[10] If the former he will return to New York. Perhaps he is to take the command to the Southward—and Cornwallis is to repair to New York as Commander in chief—Clinton retiring. Conjecture.[11]

ALS (McHenry Papers: DLC). The addressee was not given, but the contents clearly establish that NG was the recipient.

1. See Lafayette to NG, 4 April, above.

2. NG's letter is above (vol. 7: 462). The nature of McHenry's illness is not known.

3. As seen in notes at NG to Lafayette, 3 April, above, the detachment did not return to New Windsor, N.Y.

4. McHenry had hoped to serve as an aide in NG's military "family."

5. He meant that he wanted to hear more about NG and Lord Cornwallis.

6. British Gen. John Burgoyne's army had been captured at Saratoga, N.Y., by a force of militia and Continentals in 1777.

7. On the hoped-for reinforcement from France, see notes at La Luzerne to NG, 3 April, above. Lafayette had discussed the expected assistance in his letter to NG of 4 April.

8. The "old object of attack" was New York City, the capture of which Washington continued to believe was the key to winning the war. (Freeman, GW, 5: 288)

9. Soon after his arrival in Baltimore, McHenry had been named president of the Baltimore Board of War. He served in that post until he left to join Lafayette's army in

Virginia on 9 June. (See Lafayette to NG, 17 April, below; McHenry to Thomas Sim Lee, 9 June, *McHenry Letters*, pp. 16–17.)

10. As noted at Washington to NG, 21 March, above (vol. 7: 459n), William Phillips's detachment, which was then at Portsmouth, Va., had been sent to support Cornwallis's and Gen. Benedict Arnold's operations.

11. McHenry's *"Conjecture"* was wrong. Clinton continued in the post of commander-in-chief, while Cornwallis remained in the South. Phillips served in Virginia until his death from a fever in May.

*　　*　　*

¶ [GENERAL GREENE'S ORDERS, "Camp at Kimboroughs on Little River," N.C., 10 April 1781. The troops are to receive one day's provisions and a "jill" of rum per man; they are to be ready to march at 9 A.M. "tomorrow." A "General Court Martial" is to sit "tomorrow." Lamar Orderly Book (OClWHi) 1 p.]

1. A "jill," or gill, was one-fourth of a pint. (*OED*)

¶ [TO COLONEL WADE HAMPTON. From "Head Quarters at Cottons," N.C., 10 April 1781. Has just seen Hampton's letter of 7 April to Gen. [Isaac] Huger and is pleased that General Sumter's plan to raise "Militia for a term of 10 Months" is "so successful."[1] It is NG's wish that recruiting under Sumter's plan "not interfere" with the raising of regular troops in North Carolina; any interference may have "bad consequences" and delay a procedure that the state has "with difficulty come into." Thinks "the most active young Men" may yet enlist in Sumter's regiments after the regular troops have been raised. NG wishes that North Carolina had exempted from the draft those who had enlisted with Hampton. As the recruiting of ten-month militia interferes with the raising of regular troops in North Carolina, however, he is not "at liberty to authorise" Hampton's recruitment, "nor indeed to give any order in the matter."[2] ADfS (MiU-C) 2 pp.]

1. Hampton's letter has not been found. For more on Gen. Thomas Sumter's plan for raising ten-month men, see Sumter to NG, 7 April, above.

2. Sumter, too, had complained about North Carolina taking the recruits and had asked NG to intervene. (See his letter to NG of 7 April.)

¶ [FROM LIEUTENANT NATHANIEL LAWRENCE, New Windsor, N.Y., 10 April 1781. Has just been released from "a very long and disagreable captivity." Wants to know if he has been included in the "late arrangement" of the North Carolina Continental line. He is a "native" of New York, and a journey to North Carolina would be an "unnecessary expence" if he has been "left out of the army."[1] ALS (MiU-C) 1 p. The letter is torn, and several words are missing.]

1. William Pierce, NG's aide, replied on 18 August, below, that Lawrence's status was unclear because the arrangement of the line had not been completed. In that letter, NG gave Lawrence permission to remain in the North until the line was arranged. Lawrence next served as an aide to Gen. Robert Howe. (Hugh Williamson to Alexander Martin, 17 September 1783, Smith, *Letters*, 20: 686) His status was still in question as late as September 1783. (Ibid.)

¶ [FROM COLONEL HENRY LEE, JR., [On Pee Dee River, S.C., 10 April 1781].[1] He reached "this place" before noon. Plans to cross "in the morning" and move on to the Santee River. Col. [John] Watson is said to be "near Brittons Ferry" with 500 men and two artillery pieces. Marion is reportedly "close" to Watson, but the intelligence that has been received is "not the most accurate."[2] There are only fifty enemy troops in Georgetown; the regiment formerly posted there was sent to Camden.[3] Lord Rawdon has 400 men.[4] Lee believes "the posture of affairs is favourable." It is thought by some that Watson is on his way to join Lord Cornwallis, and Lee has just received a report that Watson crossed the Pee Dee on 7 April.[5] Will send additional intelligence when he is better informed. Captain "Connuer [James Conyers] got here yesterday."[6] Either Conyers or his men "published" Lee's coming; nothing is being said about NG's army. Following his signature, Lee adds that his opinion of cavalry being stationed with the North Carolina militia is "more & more pres't."[7] Cy (MiU-C) 1 p. Several words were rendered in a number code, with the translation given above.]

1. The place was derived from the contents, the date from Lee's statement that he would cross the river the next day. Lord Rawdon reported on 13 April that Lee had crossed the Pee Dee "two days ago." (Rawdon to Nisbet Balfour, 13 April, PRO 30/11/5)

2. Watson, in pursuit of Gen. Francis Marion, crossed the Pee Dee at Britton's Ferry on 7 April but broke off and returned to Georgetown upon learning of NG's march into South Carolina. (Rankin, *Swamp Fox*, pp. 181, 185)

3. Balfour reported to Lord Cornwallis on 20 April that the garrison at Georgetown was "86 Inf^y with twenty mounted." (PRO 30/11/5) That was before Watson's arrival.

4. The garrison at Camden numbered about 500 men. (Johnson, *Greene*, 2: 68–9)

5. As seen in note 2, above, Watson was not on his way to join Cornwallis. The enemy force that had crossed the Pee Dee was that of Col. Welbore Ellis Doyle, whose movements are noted at Wade to NG, 2 April, above.

6. For more on Conyers's mission, see NG to Marion, 4 April, above.

7. By "pres't," Lee may have meant prescient. His opinion about stationing cavalry with the militia is not known.

¶ [FROM MAURICE SPILLARD, "Mr Dixon's near Dan River," N.C., 10 April 1781. Hopes his last letter answered any questions about his "coming round with the Army"; assures NG that "this Country has nothing to apprehend" from his activities.[1] Because he lacks a change of clothing and is in great "distress," he asks permission to go to Camden, S.C., to get his baggage, which was never forwarded by Gen. [Thomas] Sumter. Spillard's health is "much impar'd" from an "unhealthy situation" and "Anxiety of mind." If NG will not allow him to go by land to Boston, he asks permission to go to Charleston.[2] ALS (MiU-C) 1 p.]

1. Spillard's earlier letter has not been found. Ichabod Burnet, NG's aide, had written Andrew Pickens on 5 March, above, that Spillard, who had come out with the "British army," was "certainly a bad character." (Vol. 7: 395)

2. William Pierce replied for NG on 18 April, below.

¶ [FROM COLONEL THOMAS WADE, "Haley's Ferry," N.C., 10 April 1781. Has received NG's letter of 8 April; will carry out the instructions as quickly as possible, although he has been "bed Riden this ten Days with the Rumeties." He also received an order from "Col° David" on 8 April to provide 40,000 "Rashers."[1] Wade's "people" are out pursuing Loyalists, so it will be difficult "to get things Ready" by 14 April.[2] "Meal and Cattle" are now "on the way up," and Wade has also "Ordered up Corn"; the mills are grinding. Wagons and teams are scarce, and it will be "very Sutable" for NG to send some. Most of the barrelled meal at "this place" is damaged. Expecting that NG would march to South Carolina, Wade had previously sent drovers to collect cattle and take them wherever NG might direct. He will visit NG as soon as he can ride. ALS (NcU) 1 p.]

1. Col. William R. Davie sent the order to Wade. (See Davie to NG, 9 April, above.) Rashers were thin slices of bacon. (Johnson, *Dictionary*)

2. On the expedition against the Loyalists, see Wade to NG, 4 April, above.

*   *   *

To General Richard Caswell

Sir   H^d Quarters Little River [N.C.] April 11th 1781

Your Letter of the 6th I had the honor to receive last Evening.

Before this you will have been informed of the disappointment that has taken place in Virginia. The Enemy are Masters of Chessapeak Bay and General Philip[s] has arrived there with a very considerable reinforcement of land forces. Col° Morris one of my Aids returned last Evening from Virginia, where I sent him to consult with the Marquis [de Lafayette] upon a plan of operations. He informs me that by private intelligence obtained the Enemy are preparing to form a junction with Lord Cornwallis by the way of Albemarle Sound.[1] All public stores upon the sea coast should be moved into the interior Country. At Edenton I am told there are a large number of fine heavy Cannon. Those should be sent as high up the Roanoak as they can be transported by Water. By leaving the Towns naked of public property we render them a less object for the E⟨nemy⟩. But whatever is done in the business ⟨must be done⟩ immediately.

I am ⟨not with⟩out hopes that our movements will disconce⟨rt the⟩ Enemys plan; but if it should not it would have ⟨been ut⟩terly impossible to prevent the Enemys forming in the way they propose.[2]

If the Marquis de la Fayette marches to the Southward as I have desired him, and the Pennsylvanians and Marylanders get up in time, and Virginia and your State furnish any considerable proportion of their regular Troops, the Enemy will get little by their junction.[3]

Should the Enemy push their operations seriously to the Northward and this Army cannot be actively employed to the Southward, I shall leave it and join the Northern Army now forming in Virginia.

I have given directions to General Sumner to collect all the Continental Officers, and to send some to each place you recommend to receive the recruits.[4] Arms, Cartouch Boxes, and all other matters will be wanting to equip your Men. Every exertion should be made to provide for the Troops, that they may be able to take the field on the shortest notice.

I am very glad you h⟨ave esta⟩blished a plan for communicating intelligence. ⟨It is very n⟩ecessary, & I presume will be very useful, ⟨and you⟩ shall hear from me by every opportunity.[5]

I beg leave to refer you to Mr Wyley Jones for further information respecting my plan and reasons for the present movements. Letters being frequently intercepted prevents my being more particular.[6]

I had all my riding Horses stole a Night or two past. If the state could furnish me with a couple they would oblige me greatly; and for which I will be accountable.

At the first opening of the Assembly there should be a severe Law made against harbouring Deserters; without which I fear the Army will be little benefited by the drafts.[7] I have the honor to be with great respect Your most obedient humble serv^t   NATH GREENE

LS (NcU). The letter is damaged; portions in angle brackets were taken from a GWG Transcript (CSmH). Caswell apparently sent this letter to Gen. Jethro Sumner, whose papers it is with, for Caswell added a note just below the place/date line in his own hand that "the express says Kimboro's 10 Miles from Masks Ferry on Peedee—RC." NG's orders of 10 April, above, gave Kimborough's as the army's location.

1. Col. Lewis Morris's "private intelligence" was incorrect. Lord Cornwallis was making plans to join Gen. William Phillips in Virginia. (See Wickwire, *Cornwallis*, pp. 319–21.)

2. NG hoped his move into South Carolina would force Cornwallis to follow him.

3. In a letter of 3 April, above, NG had "desired" Lafayette to remain in the Southern Department.

4. NG's letter to Sumner of 8 April is above. See also NG to Sumner, this date, below.

5. Caswell discussed his "plan" in his letter to NG of 6 April, above. As seen in the notes there, the operation did not last long.

6. On Willie Jones, see NG to Nash, 3 April, above.

7. In its January session, the North Carolina legislature had added a section on the harboring of deserters to its act for raising the state's quota of Continental troops. The section stipulated that anyone knowingly harboring a deserter was to "be deemed a Continental Soldier" for the duration of the war and was either to serve himself or obtain and pay for a substitute during that term. If he refused to cooperate, the local militia commander was to obtain a substitute, who was to be paid with "the goods and chattels, lands and tenements, of the person so offending." (*NCSR*, 24: 370)

To Colonel William Davies

Dear Sir   Head Quarters Little River [N.C.] April 11th 1781

I had the pleasure to receive your letter of the 2^d of this instant.

Nothing would induce me to consent to your taking the direction of the war department; but a perswasion that you can render more important services to the public in general and not less to the army in particular by holding that office than without it.[1] However you must continue at times to assist all in your power to compleat the arrangment of the army. I believe no State abounding with such a plenty as

Virginia, ever experienced such a scarcity for want of order and a proper application of her supplies. From your abilities and application I am in hopes there will be a great reformation, but before you engage in this business give me leave to tell you it will be difficult under the best arrangment to keep pace with the demands of the service, and therefore dont get discouraged because you cannot at once effect what you wish and what is absolutely requisite.

History affords no instance of a nation, being so engagd in conquest abroad as Virginia is at a time when all her powers were necessary to secure herself from ruin at home. If they would seriously contemplate their situation, they must be convinced that by neglecting the Army here they hazard ruin and perhaps the State also.[2]

I agree with you that the appointment of Continental Officers into the State Departments will be attended with many advantages as they have one common interest with the Army and know its wants. On this consideration I approve of the appointment of Cap Young.[3] All that I would wish to recommend on this head is, that the business in all the appointments be so planed as not to interfere with the Continental establishment, but to give it all possible assistance.

Removing the heavy cannon you mention I think a very necessary measure. I have recommen[d]ed the Same to North Carolinia.[4]

Sending Money to the army to pay off the Virginia line I cannot think advisable. When the condition of an army is all upon one footing the soldiery will bear the hardships with a degree of patienc[e.] But when from a comparison one part finds the condition of others more eligible than their own, the same situation which would be tolerable when it was common would become insupportable when it operated unequally. For these reasons I think no payment should be made to the Troops of any State but through the paymaster general. Perhaps advances may be made to officers with propriety; but partial payments to the men I am confident would be productive of great confusion and discontent.

Upon the article of lead our situation is truly deplorable. With this Army we have not 20,000 spare Cartridges and very few in the Laboratory at Prince Edward; and no other dependance, nor is there lead enough at that place to make more than 60 or 70,000 if our returns are right; and I perswade myself they are. Some time past I wrote to Baron Stuben to secure all the lead he could and from the present appearances of an active campaign and the great waste of Stores by the Militia 20,000 weight is the least quantity which should be reservd for the use of this army and that army in the lower part of Virginia. Carolinia has got little or no ammu[ni]tion and both her Militia, and Continental troops if she raises any, must be supplied from the Magazine in Virginia. I think we shall have a bloody Campaign, and we ought to be prepard to meet our enemy upon the best footing we can; and after all we shall be under innumerable disadvantages.[5]

I thank you kindly for your profers of service and for your friendly attachment; and beg you to be perswaded that I feel no less esteem & regard for you than you for me.

ADf (MiU-C).

1. Davies had been named to head the Virginia War Department. (See Davies to NG, 2 April, above.)

2. NG referred to Virginia's activities in what later became the Northwest Territory.

3. In his letter to NG of 2 April, Davies had asked that Capt. Henry Young, a Continental officer, be permitted to become the state quartermaster.

4. See NG to Caswell, immediately above.

5. As noted at NG to Steuben, 2 April, above, the rediscovery of the vein of lead at Chiswell mines in early May ended the crisis and enabled Virginia to supply NG.

*   *   *

¶ [TO GOVERNOR THOMAS JEFFERSON OF VIRGINIA. From Headquarters, Little River, N.C., 11 April 1781. Has received Jefferson's letter of 1 April and is "obliged by the confidence" that Jefferson has shown on "the occasion"; assures him that "the hint shall only be improved."[1] Before he received the letter, NG had "written pretty fully on the subject" and "not widely different from the plan" that Jefferson proposed.[2] At the "first opportunity," he will write again "more fully on the matter, being more and more perswaded, that every measure which is taken to cramp the business of compleating the Cavalry has a direct tendency to sacrafice the Citizens."[3] ALS (MiU-C) 2 pp.]

1. The ALS gives the date of Jefferson's letter as "11 of this instant," but NG wrote "1st" in an ADfS (MiU-C). He was clearly responding here to Jefferson's first letter to him of 1 April, above.

2. NG had written about the plan in his letter to Jefferson of 6 April, above.

3. See NG to Jefferson, 28 April, below.

¶ [TO GOVERNOR THOMAS SIM LEE OF MARYLAND. From [Little River, N.C.], 11 April 1781.[1] Encloses a duplicate of his letter to Lee of 7 April; the original "unfortunately fell into the hands of the Tories." LS (MB) 1 p.]

1. The place was taken from other letters of this date.

¶ [TO CAPTAIN NATHANIEL PENDLETON. From Camp, Little River, N.C., 11 April 1781. Pendleton is to go to Virginia and give orders for the militia who have been called out to march immediately and rendezvous at Salisbury, N.C.[1] He is to send as many provisions as possible to Salisbury but is not "to interfere" with those "to be laid in at Olliphants Mill."[2] He is to give "farther directions in all matters" that concern "the service" and that further NG's "plan."[3] ADfS (MiU-C) 1 p.]

1. On the calling out of the Virginia militia, see Jefferson to NG, second letter of 1 April, above. As noted there, most of the militia never left Virginia.

2. As seen in his letter to Thomas Polk of 3 April, above, NG had ordered the establishment of a magazine of provisions at Oliphant's Mill, N.C.

3. The "plan" was NG's decision to march his army into South Carolina.

¶ [TO GENERAL JETHRO SUMNER. From "Camp Little River near the Pedee," N.C., 11 April 1781. Encloses an extract of a letter from Gen. [Richard]

Caswell, which NG received after writing to Sumner on the 8th. Caswell's letter indicates that the "drafts are raising fast in almost all the districts." Sumner is to send officers to take charge of the draftees, as Caswell requested.[1] He is also to fix a place to form the regiments and assign the Continental officers to their commands. He should "exert" himself "night and day" and inform NG of his progress. He is to "take measures" to procure arms and accoutrements, without which the draftees will be "of little use." The conscripts from Salisbury reportedly will be ready by 25 April, so "no time is to be lost in arranging the Officers."[2] LS (NcU) 2 pp.]

1. Below NG's signature, an aide copied the last part of Caswell's letter of 6 April, which is calendared above.

2. See Davie to NG, 9 April, above. Sumner replied on 23 April, below.

¶ [FROM GENERAL JOHN BUTLER, Camp, Ramsey's Mill, N.C., 11 April 1781. Maj. [Pinketham] Eaton will march "tomorrow" with 200 men who have been ordered to serve for a year because they fled during the battle of Guilford Court House.[1] They are not well-armed or well-equipped, but Butler is sending them on because they should be able to obtain what they need from Colonel Read's men, who will soon be discharged; there are no supplies available in Halifax.[2] Butler has asked Gen. [Jethro] Sumner to send officers to command these men.[3] The party that was sent to scout Lord Cornwallis's army has not returned, so there is no news of the enemy since they left Elizabeth Town.[4] The commissioner for Wake County has collected 15,000 to 20,000 pounds of bacon; Butler asks how much of it should be brought to Ramsey's Mill.[5] ALS (MiU-C) 1 p.]

1. For more on this detachment, see note at Eaton to NG, 4 April, above. Eaton wrote Sumner on 17 April that his troops "desert fast and complain heavily of the injustice done them, having never had a Tryall as they many of them declare." (NCSR, 15: 440–41) Eaton had only 140 men left in his detachment when he wrote NG on 17 April, below.

2. Col. James Read commanded a North Carolina militia force that had been serving with NG's army.

3. Butler wrote Sumner on this date that officers were needed for 240 deserters from the battle of Guilford Court House. (NcU)

4. Cornwallis's army had left Elizabeth Town on 5 April. ("Von Bose Journal," p. 54)

5. NG replied on 19 April, below.

¶ [FROM MAJOR GEORGE DAVIDSON, Rowan County, N.C., 11 April 1781. The enemy's invasion has "deranged" his department.[1] Some of the leather-producing "Yards" have been destroyed, and some of his shoemakers have left. Wants to use three or four "good Tradesmen" from the twelve-month draftees to make shoes. It is difficult to get artisans to work for the public, and the task "will not be done to so good purpose" without the conscripts. Davidson will forward the shoes that he has on hand. Asks NG to let him know about using the draftees and about any limits on the wages he can offer workmen.[2] ALS (MiU-C) 1 p.]

1. Davidson was commissary of hides in the Southern Department and superintendent of a shoe and boot factory at Salisbury.

2. NG's reply has not been found. Davidson's letter of 8 May, below, shows that he then had enough workmen.

¶ [FROM COLONEL WILLIAM R. DAVIE, Salisbury, N.C., 11 April 1781. There is a "tolerable" prospect of a "supply from this place"; hopes the shipment will reach NG's army by 17 April.[1] A woman who "lately" left Camden, S.C., reports that everyone is "starveing there; both the Families and Soldiers." Major Hyrne passed this place "yesterday."[2] No troops have been "collected here; but they seem serious in making up the Continental Quota." ALS (NcU) 1 p.]

1. Rains delayed the delivery of provisions from Salisbury. (Davie to NG, 21 April, below)

2. NG had sent Maj. Edmund Hyrne to consult with Gen. Thomas Sumter about NG's plans. (NG to Sumter, 7 April, above)

¶ [FROM COLONEL JOHN GREEN, Richmond, Va., 11 April 1781. He delivered NG's letter to Baron Steuben, who agrees on the need for "regime[nt]ing the troops" and has summoned the officers "for that purpose."[1] Green also saw the governor, who promised to supply the soldiers with clothing "if it costs all the money in the Treasury."[2] Col. [William] Davies, newly appointed to the Board of War, says he will do all he can to supply the troops. Davies gave him a list, which Green encloses, of clothing that was recently sent to the army.[3] Steuben, who is better informed than Green, can give NG the "news of this state." Wishes NG "Health & happiness & a Sucksesful Campaign."[4] ALS (MiU-C) 1 p.]

1. Green had carried NG's letter to Steuben of 4 April, above. For more on the issue of arranging the Virginia Continental line, see note at NG to Davies, 3 April, above.

2. NG had written Gov. Thomas Jefferson about the condition of the Virginia Continentals' clothing on 28 February, above (vol. 7: 367).

3. The list has not been found, but there is a return in the Steuben Papers, dated 26 March, of clothing sent to the Southern Army from Chesterfield Court House. The shipment included 235 coats, 226 overalls, 218 blankets, 675 shirts, 475 pairs of shoes, and 65 pairs of boots. (Steuben Microfilm)

4. As seen in NG to Steuben, 4 April, Green was not returning to the Southern Army.

¶ [FROM GENERAL DANIEL MORGAN, "Saratoga," Va., 11 April 1781.[1] NG's letter of "28th of March," which Morgan has received, gave him great satisfaction—both from its contents and the "mode of conveyance."[2] He has been "particularly happy" in his association with the Southern Army, and NG is "among the number" he esteems. NG's "good conduct" while Morgan served with him "created that esteem," and NG's "gallantry and good conduct" since then have "confirmed it." If NG gets his due, he will receive the country's thanks, for he has done "wonders, in repelling the enemy when the whole country stood trembling at their approach." Thinks NG's decision to give battle was "well-timed, and the disposition well concerted. Such conduct and bravery will seldom fail of success."[3] NG may consider this letter "flattering," but Morgan has always been pleased—and has always thought it right— "to give every one his due," for where else "is the grand stimulus that pushes men on to great actions?" He likewise gives "demerits" when warranted. He was not at home when NG's letter arrived, and the bearer did not await his return, but Morgan has sent the "standards on to Congress, and informed the President," as NG ordered.[4] He supposes that NG has overtaken Lord Cornwallis by now with a large enough army to "cope" with the enemy. He fears such an encounter, for he knows "what militia can do," but believes the British "must be dispirited" because of the way "they were handled in the last engagement." Hopes God gives NG "success." Morgan has been directed to send the Virginia Assembly's thanks to the men who fought with him at Cowpens. Asks NG to "put it out in orders."[5] Reports that the pain in his hip is gone but that he suffers the "same kind of pain" in his head, which leaves him "blind as a bat two or three times a day." A "cold bath seems to help," and he hopes to give NG some assistance "ere long."[6] Printed in Graham, *Morgan*, pp. 373–74.]

1. "Saratoga" was Morgan's new home near Winchester, Va. (Higginbotham, *Morgan*, pp. 172–73)

2. Morgan was referring to NG's letter of 20 March, above (vol. 7: 455–56). As seen there, a dragoon from Lee's Legion, who had been sent to take the battle flags captured at Cowpens to Congress, brought the letter to Morgan.

3. On the battle of Guilford Court House, in which NG used a battle formation similar to the one Morgan had employed at Cowpens, see NG to Samuel Huntington, 17 March, above (vol. 7: 433–36).

4. Morgan sent the battle standards to Congress on 28 March with a letter for Samuel Huntington, the president of Congress. (PCC, item 78, vol. 16: 159, DNA)

5. No such general order has been found.

6. In late May, Morgan was preparing to rejoin NG's army when he received a request from the Marquis de Lafayette to raise a detachment of riflemen for service in Virginia. He joined Lafayette on 7 July. (Higginbotham, *Morgan*, pp. 160–65)

¶ [**GENERAL GREENE'S ORDERS**, "Camp at Coleston's Ferry on Pee Dee," N.C., 12 April 1781. The troops are to wash their clothes and clean their arms "To-day." In a court-martial held on 11 April, Corporal Edward Decain of Lee's Legion was found innocent of illegally impressing a horse and "Plundering a Negro" from a North Carolina resident, but guilty of "receiving redemption Money for horses impressed for the Service, and for encouraging his Soldiers by his example in such practice." He was sentenced to 100 lashes and a reduction in rank, but the court recommended mercy. NG "is pleased to remit the Sentence." Lamar Orderly Book (OCIWHi) 2 pp.]

*   *   *

To Colonel Henry Lee, Jr.

Head quarters at the mouth of
Dear Sir   Rocky River [N.C.] April 1st [i.e.,12] 1781[1]
Your letter without date or place wrote at was handed me this

morning.[2] We got here Night before last and should have been 160 on

our 121 to day for 297 had we not been delayed for want of boats to cross the river.

Gen[l] Sumter   join us
311 will have 1000 Men to 94 63 by the 20th but he is going to take a
         Camden   Ninety Six
position between 297 & 298 about thirty miles from the former. If you

go over Santee   march   for Camden
68 170 299 you will fall in with him.³ We shall 121 directly 53 297 and
avail our selves of circumstances. If the detachment you mention low
             Peedee is   on   the   march for Wilmington   to   join Cornwallis
down 300 1 160 243 121 53   304   240 94 306, it is almost certain that
                                    scheme
he had no Idea of our 230.⁴ All things promise well as yet. Inform your
                                                                  Charlestown
self if possible whether any reinforcments have arrivd at 303. Col
Morris has arrivd from Virginia and says a report prevails there that
two Hessian regiments had arrivd from Europe. I dont believe it, but it
may be so.⁵

   Go on and prosper and let me hear from you as often as possible;
                  Lᵈ Cornwallis   on   the   march for Camden you   must join   the Army
and if you hear that 306 is 160 243 121 53 297 291 128 94 243 10
imly [i.e., immediately], that   we   may,   beat   us   junction with
   91   244 272 122 13 him before he gets 263 by a 96   287
other force joining
162 61 94ing him.
           Horse in   march for
   The light 77 85 Virginia shall have fresh orders to 125 53 North
Carolinia.⁶ Yours sinserely   310 [NATHANAEL GREENE]

ALS (IHi). The letter was written partly in cipher. In the manuscript, the
decoded words, which are in Lee's hand, appear above or below the corresponding code numbers. The only exception is the coded signature, for which
the editors have added "Nathanael Greene." The decoding as presented here
reproduces Lee's spelling. The editors have placed the decoded words above
their corresponding numbers.
   1. A draft of this letter at MiU-C carries the date "April 12th," which is consistent with
the contents.
   2. NG was replying to the letter from Lee that the editors have dated 10 April. (See
above.)
   3. See Gen. Thomas Sumter to NG, 7 April, above. Lee did not "fall in" with Sumter
but did join forces with Gen. Francis Marion to besiege and capture Ft. Watson, on the
Santee River. (See Marion to NG, first letter of 23 April, below.)
   4. As seen in notes at Lee to NG, 10 April, and Wade to NG, 2 April, both above, the
force probably belonged to Col. Welbore Ellis Doyle. It was not moving toward a
junction with Cornwallis. Doyle had already marched to Camden after being recalled by
Lord Rawdon, the commander there.
   5. NG was correct in assuming that no Hessian troops had arrived from Europe. A
Hessian regiment had been part of the force that accompanied Gen. William Phillips
from New York to Virginia. (Ewald, *Journal*, p. 294)
   6. The light horse was Col. Anthony W. White's corps of dragoons, which NG had
sent to Virginia to be refitted. (See NG to Jefferson, 26 January, above [vol. 7: 202].)
White's dragoons remained in Virginia.

                       *   *   *

¶ [FROM GENERAL WILLIAM SMALLWOOD**, Annapolis, Md., 12 April
1781. He has tried vigorously to get Maryland to raise its quota of men and

supplies.[1] After he arrived from the South, he addressed the General Assembly, but it adjourned soon afterwards "without effecting anything material." The governor and council are "perfectly disposed to aid the Service," but "their powers are incompetent." Smallwood has urged a reconvening of the Assembly, which the governor "inclines to do as soon as Circumstances" will admit.[2] Smallwood has also written "pressingly" to Gov. [Caesar] Rodney about Delaware's need to raise, equip, and forward its quota of Continentals, and has "prevailed on" Gen. [Mordecai] Gist to "wait on" Rodney and press "the expediency of the Measure."[3] Despite his efforts, Smallwood finds the "prospect of getting Men" to be "gloomy." Doubts that either state will come close to meeting its quota. No more than 300 men have been collected in the two states—and that includes deserters "who have been picked up." Smallwood wants to forward these men but thinks neither state has the resources to clothe and equip them. He has ordered Gist to seek assistance from the Board of War.[4]

Smallwood would have sent Gist to the Southern Army, "pursuant to" NG's orders, but Gist is "much indisposed."[5] Smallwood has ordered "some Officers" to go south and "fill the places of those killed and wounded in the late Action." When the detachment of recruits marches, he will send the remaining officers to relieve those "to the Southward who can be spared."[6] Has prepared two arrangements of the Maryland line: one is based on "Seniority and the other in that way which seems most agreeable to the Officers here." He will send both, so that the "sense of the Officers at large" can be obtained. Would have enclosed the arrangements but is waiting for the Board of War to send him a copy of the one for the Delaware line.[7]

The Marquis de Lafayette left Annapolis for Head of Elk "about seven days ago." Lafayette's "late Instructions" have given him "more latitude," so his troops can move "to this place" or to Alexandria, Va., or "the Southward as Circumstances may require."[8] A large enemy force, under the "immediate command of Sir Henry Clinton," is reportedly preparing to leave New York "for the Delaware." This intelligence is from "General Firman," whose sources are reportedly reliable.[9] The British seem to intend "vigorous and active Operations to the Southward." [Gen. William] Phillips's arrival with a force of "near three thousand as it is supposed will give them great Confidence and Superiority."[10]

"Refugee" Loyalists, under the "Patronage and Auspices" of [Gen. Benedict] Arnold, have "infested" Chesapeake Bay and Maryland's rivers, "plundering all before them[,] burning in some Instances the Houses and treating the Inhabitants with Savage and wantonly Cruelty. Contemptible as they are they pursue this impious practice with impunity from the Security derived from the command of the Waters." The raiders are now at Alexandria with a strong naval force and 300 men.[11] The LS (Greene Papers: DLC) is badly damaged, so the editors have used a GWG Transcript (CSmH) 4 pp. A few words were taken from the LS to fill gaps in the transcript.]

1. After receiving NG's letter of 31 March, above, Smallwood wrote again on 4 May, below, defending himself against NG's suggestion that he had not been active in the Southern Army's behalf.

2. The Maryland legislature had adjourned on 3 February. The governor set 10 May as

the date to reconvene, but the session did not begin until 28 May. (Maryland, General Assembly, House of Delegates, *Votes and Proceedings . . . October Session 1780* [Annapolis, 1781]; Maryland, General Assembly, Senate, *Votes and Proceedings . . . October Session, 1780 and June Session, 1781* [Annapolis, 1781])

3. See Gist to NG, 28 May, below.

4. On Gist's efforts to obtain help from the Board of War, see ibid.

5. Nothing is known about NG's orders concerning Gist.

6. As noted at NG to Gist, 30 March, above, no troops marched from Maryland until late August, when a force was sent to join Washington in Virginia.

7. In his letter to NG of 4 May, below, Smallwood said he had done nothing about arranging the Maryland line—first because of a conflict with Gist over seniority and then because it did not seem an "essential Object." He also asked NG for a copy of the arrangement of the Delaware line, as he had not received one from the Board of War.

8. On Lafayette's remaining in the South, see Lafayette to NG, 17 April, below.

9. "Firman" was David Forman, a New Jersey militia general. A copy of his letter of 2 April, communicating this intelligence to Samuel Huntington, the president of Congress, is in the Washington Papers, DLC. For more about the report that Clinton was bringing an army to the Delaware, see note at Sharpe to NG, 7 April, above.

10. As noted at Washington to NG, 21 March, above (vol. 7: 459n), the British reinforcement that Phillips had brought to Virginia numbered about 2,000 men.

11. For more on naval and privateering activities by the enemy in the upper part of Chesapeake Bay and the rivers flowing into it, see note at Gist to NG, 28 March, above (vol. 7: 477n).

¶ [**FROM COLONEL THOMAS WADE**, "Hayles Ferry," N.C., 12 April 1781. Wade is still feeling "very poorly" from rheumatism or gout and can barely move about his house. Discusses where and when the cornmeal, cattle, and hogs that are en route to the army will arrive. The boats carrying corn will not reach NG "in time," so Wade has halted them. He says forage is available on Rocky River, and NG's stay there will be short. The army's "beasts" have not yet recovered. Wade will hold them until the wagons return from the army and will then send them to NG at Camden by a much shorter route than that via Colston's. He can send "any other Article in the Middle Grounds" by the same route and can forward "a further Suply of Cattle." ALS (MiU-C) 2 pp.]

¶ [**GENERAL GREENE'S ORDERS**, "Camp at Colstons Ferry West Side of Pee Dee," N.C., 13 April 1781. The troops are to receive a two days' supply of provisions and be ready to march at 8 A.M. "tomorrow." Lamar Orderly Book (OClWHi) 1 p.]

*   *   *

To Governor Abner Nash of North Carolina

Head Quarters on the Pedee at the Mouth of
Dear Sir   Rocky River [N.C.] April 13th 1781

Your Excellencys letter of the 3d of April I had the honor to receive last evening. Before this you will have been informed of our march Southward. Letters being frequently intercepted prevents my being as particular as I could wish on this subject. Mr Wyly Jones can inform you of my principal object in this movement; and I hope it will answer my expectations, but if it should not I cannot help it, this measure appeard the most likely to afford relief to your State of any that I had it in my power to take.[1]

It affords me great pleasure to hear that your drafts for the Army are compleating. It will afford great relief to your Militia and give much greater security to the State.

I have only to lament that the business could not have been accomplished earlier as we are now in want of the force and it will be a month or two before the Men can be collected, formed, and equiped fit for service. I have written to General Sumner to collect the Continental Officers and use all possible industry in forming the recruits or drafts into Regiments.[2]

I am very glad the runaways at Guilford are to be made to serve in the Continental Regiments during the war. The penal laws you enclosed me were the first of the kind I ever saw; and in my opinion are the best calculated to render the Militia useful.[3]

The report of a reinforcement having arrivd in Virginia has been since confirmed and consists of about 1500 Men. It is also reported in Virginia that the enemy mean to form a junction with Lord Cornwallis by the way of Albamarle Sound and doubtless will effect it unless our movements should disconcert the plan, nor do I see how it could be prevented in the present situation of things.[4]

After the british fleet arrivd in Chessepeak, the Marquis de la Fyette began his march Northward, but I have written him on the subject, and desird him to march to Richmond.[5] If he complies with my wishes and the Pennsylvania line arrives and the Virginia drafts are speedily collected, I am in hopes there will be a sufficient force to counteract the enemy in that quarter; and to follow them into North Carolinia if they should move this way. It is said the enemy are constructing boats to move along the Sound.[6] All public Stores should be moved into the Country and the heavy Cannon of Edenton should be sent up the Roanoke as high as they can be transported by water. The Enemy can and will command the towns upon the seaside; and therefore as few temptations should be left in them as possible. When the seaports are without Stores they cease to be an object.

I thank your Excellency for the rum you promise us.[7] It is out of our power to send Waggons after it. If you cannot convey it to the Army we must do without it. It is true the quantity is much less than we want. The means of transportation is a distressing circumstance, and unless every aid is given, I fear it will soon be out of our power, either to move or subsist our army in fixed Camp. Draft horses are much wanted to supply the places of those that are dayly failing by hard service in collecting provisions. It would afford great relief to the Army if a couple of hundred could be sent us; and if the enemy should enter the State from the northward great care should be taken to move the horses out of their way.

We find it impossible to get a sufficient number of Dragoon horses from Virginia and Maryland; if you could furnish an hundred, it would enable us to keep the enemy from ravaging the Country much more effectually than we can without them. Our horses are dayly failing, and we shall soon be inferior to the enemy. We always have been in numbers, tho not in quallity.

On my March from the Haw to the Pedee I had the misfortune to lose all my riding horses; if you could furnish me with a couple that are strong and go easy they will be very acceptable; and for which I will be accountable.

I thank your Excellency for your good intentions respecting the Poultry from Harrisburg; but I had not the good fortune to receive any; and as you are obliging enough to offer to procure me any thing in your power, I will take the liberty to trouble you to procure for me a couple of quarter Casks of port or Claret wine.[8]

You shall hear further from me in a few days. I am with great respect Your Excellencys Most Obed[t] humble se[r]   NATH GREENE

DfS (MiU-C).
    1. On Willie Jones, see NG to Nash, 3 April, above.
    2. See NG to Sumner, 11 April, above.
    3. The "penal laws" are noted at Eaton to NG, 4 April, above. Nash had enclosed a copy in his letter of 3 April, above.
    4. The British reinforcement, which consisted of some 2,000 men under the command of Gen. William Phillips, is discussed at Washington to NG, 21 March, above (vol. 7: 459n). As seen there, Phillips was not planning to join Cornwallis by way of Albemarle Sound.
    5. NG's letter to Lafayette, dated 3 April, is above.
    6. The boats were being built in preparation for another British invasion up the James River. (Chase, "Steuben," pp. 216–17)
    7. On the rum, see Nash to NG, 3 April, above.
    8. Nash had written about the poultry in his letter of 3 April. His reply to this letter of NG's has not been found.

*   *   *

¶ [FROM GENERAL CHARLES SCOTT, Haley's Ferry, N.C., 13 April 1781. Encloses "Sundria" letters from Gen. [William] Moultrie.[1] Scott is on his way to see Lord Cornwallis and have his parole extended to Virginia. He is accompanied by Maj. [George] Benson, for whom he requests a "passport."[2] The long ride and Scott's "poor Cavilry" prevent him from visiting NG, but he has brought several messages and asks that NG send an aide "this Night" to receive them. Scott will remain in the area until NG replies.[3] ALS (OClWHi) 2 pp.]
    1. Scott presumably enclosed Moultrie's letters to NG of 2 and 3 April, both above; he also sent copies of two letters from Col. Nisbet Balfour to Lord Cornwallis. (NG to Scott, 14 April, below)

2. For more on Scott's journey and on Benson, see Lee to NG, after 7 April, above.
3. NG's reply, dated 14 April, is below.

*   *   *

From General Thomas Sumter

Dr Sir   Catawba [S.C.] 13th Ap^l 1781

On Tuesday night a party of horse & foot to the Number of a bout one hundred & fifty from Camden appeard in the Waxsaws, they Marched With Great precippitation as far as the Meeting house, Which they burnt together with Some other houses[,] Barns &C. They have Kild[,] Wound[ed] & Taken Several persons[,] Carried off all Kinds of horses, plundered the Settlement of as much as they Could Carry[.] As Soon as I Received Intelligence of Their approach, I Detached Col^{ls} Hampton & Taylor after them, but as they began to Retreat on Wedn[e]sday Night, Dont expect they will be overtaken.[1]

By accounts Just Received from Genl Pickens Who Wrote me about ten days ago that he had Collected a few Men of his Brigade and also a few Georgians, but was unable to attempt anything against the Enemy. I Give orders to the Co^{ls} Commanding four Regemts in My Brigade Wesward of Broad River to Join Genl Pickens, Which has been Done accordingly. I Requested Genl Pickens to Move Down & Take a position upon Tyger River Near the Fish Dam Foard to indeavour to Cover the Country & Collect Provision, & if hard presed by the enemy to pass Broad River to this Side, Rather than Retreat to wards the Mountains.

The enemy I find have Retreated to their forts at Williams & Ninty Six, Notwithstanding Genl Pickens is, as I am informd by the Barer Capt [Vardy] McBee, Moving upwards With the Men of these four Regem^{ts} already Mentioned, Which if With a Design to Take them on to Savanah River, will weaken Me Considerably. But as I Wrote Genl Pickens Very fully a few days ago, Wherin I Mentioned the Measures Necessary to be entered into in consequence of your Movements towards Camden. I am of oppinion that he Dont mean to go far, however.[2] I expect to have Near the Number in the field as Mentioned to Maj^r Herne, Shoud I Miss of these four Regem^{ts}. But as I intend to form a junction of all that are imbodyed on Tuesday Next Shall then be able to give you a More Satisfactory account. Which I Shall Do without loss of time.[3]

I apprehend that a Number of North Carolinans Might be Got out at this Time if the officers Were active. I am Dr Sir your most obedt Hble Servt   THO^s SUMTER

ALS (MiU-C).

1. "Tuesday" was 10 April; the "Meeting House" was presumably the Waxhaws Presbyterian Church, near present-day Lancaster, S.C. The enemy force was apparently

one commanded by Loyalist Maj. John Coffin. In a postscript to a letter of 15 April to Nisbet Balfour, Lord Rawdon wrote that Coffin had returned to Camden "the night before last. He killed fourteen of the Enemy, & took a few, without any loss." (PRO 30/11/5) Rawdon confirmed what Sumter had expected: that neither Col. John Taylor nor Colonel Hampton (three Hamptons were then serving as colonels in Sumter's brigade: Wade, Richard, and Henry) was able to overtake Coffin.

2. Andrew Pickens had discussed his movements in a letter to NG of 8 April, above. Sumter apparently did not know that NG had ordered Pickens to move toward Ninety Six and Augusta, Ga. (the latter of which was on the Savannah River) and lay siege to those posts. (See NG to Huntington, 14 May, below, and note at Pickens to NG, 8 April, above.)

3. As seen in his letter to Sumter of 7 April, above, NG had sent Maj. Edmund Hyrne to find out what force Sumter could provide for operations against Camden. Sumter next wrote NG on 25 April, below.

*   *   *

¶ [GENERAL GREENE'S ORDERS, "Camp at Colstons Ferry West-Side Pee-Dee," N.C., 14 April 1781. Wants a return of camp kettles "on hand, and wanting"; there should be one kettle for every twelve men and one for each officers' mess. Lamar Orderly Book (OClWHi) 1 p.]

*   *   *

To Colonel William R. Davie

Dear Sir   Head Quarters at Colstons [N.C.] April 14th 1781

I had the pleasure to receive your two letters of the 8th & 11th. In the last of which you inform me that your p[r]ospects are tolerable and that you will send on a supply of provision by the 17th.[1] At present our prospects are rather indifferent, not so much for want of provisions as the means of transportation.

We march to day for Mays Mill and from thence to Lynches Creek. You will direct your supplies on this route; and let them follow us as soon as possible.

We arrivd at the [Pee Dee] river on the evening of the 11th, and if a proper number of boats could have been had to cross the troops we should have been on our march the 13th.

The Virginia Militia coming to join this Army is ordered to collect at Salisbury. Some provision will be necessary to be made for their arrival. However they are directed to bring with them all the provisions they can. I first intended the place of rendezvous at Charlotte; but upon considering the matter more fully I thought provision could be got at Salisbury with more ease than at Charlotte whether collected from the Neighbourhood or brought from Virginia[.] This determined me to fix upon the former place. About 2000 Militia are orderd into service and will begin to come in, I expect in less than ten days.[2]

By intelligence I am perswaded our movements will be altogether

unexpected by Lord Cornwallis. I am with esteem dear Sir Your most Obed[t] humble Ser N GREENE
NB If you can procure us some fresh butter it will be very acceptable.

ADfS (NcU).
1. As seen at his letter to NG of 11 April, above, Davie was unable to forward the provisions by the 17th.
2. On the expected reinforcement, see Jefferson to NG, 30 March, above; as noted there, few of the militia ever left Virginia.

* * *

¶ [TO COLONEL THOMAS POLK. From Colston's, N.C., 14 April 1781. Has Polk's letters of 8 and 11 April [neither found]. Agrees that it is pointless to call out the rest of the three-month militia, especially as Gen. [Thomas] Sumter has enlisted "so many from Charlotte," and Continental troops are being raised there "with such facility."[1] NG does not know why the governor and council sent Polk a commission as colonel instead of general. "It is a pity that the public interest should be sacraficed to private resentment." NG recommended Polk for the militia command because he wanted a "good officer" who could help give "effectual protection" to the state and make the militia "as useful as possible. As to a popular Militia without dicipline I would not give a farthing for 20,000 of them. They are always coming and going and never in Camp when most wanted." NG has written the governor "fully" on the subject and has informed him once again that Polk will not "act without a brigader's commision." NG hopes the governor will give Polk the commission but "cannot help it" if he does not.[2] Meanwhile, if NG finds himself "hard pressed," he may give Polk "special orders" to call part of the militia into service. The army's means of transportation are "too small for the great distance we have to collect provisions & other Stores." Asks Polk to "engage twenty or thirty teams" to serve with the army for a month or six weeks. Those who enroll can "depend upon being dischargd" on time.[3] Warns that the army cannot "keep the field" unless the inhabitants give "all the assistance in their power." Is happy that Polk's son "has engagd with General Sumter" and only regrets "his not being in the Continental line."[4] ADfS (MiU-C) 3 pp.]
1. In a letter of 3 April, above, NG had asked Polk to call out the remainder of the three-month militia in the Salisbury district. As seen in Polk to NG, 8 March, above (vol. 7: 413), Polk had been helping Sumter raise a corps of ten-month men in the Charlotte area.
2. On the unsuccessful attempt to secure a brigadier general's commission for Polk, see note at Polk to NG, 8 March. NG's letter to Gov. Abner Nash, dated 3 April, is above.
3. Polk's reply has not been found, but he may have given it in person, for he apparently met with NG at camp a short time later. (See Polk to NG, 9 May, below.)
4. Polk's son, William, was to serve as a colonel in one of the ten-month regiments that Sumter was recruiting. (See Thomas Polk to NG, 8 March.)

¶ [TO GENERAL CHARLES SCOTT. From Headquarters [Colston's Ferry, N.C.], 14 April 1781. NG received Scott's letter of 13 April, with its enclosures, including the two letters from Col. [Nisbet] Balfour to Lord Cornwallis. Capt. [William] Pierce, the bearer, will decide if Scott should continue his journey to Cornwallis's army.[1] Df (MiU-C) 1 p.]

1. It appears from Scott's badly damaged letter to NG of 16 April and Pierce to Scott, 21 April, both below, that Pierce first decided to have Scott remain temporarily in the vicinity of Haley's Ferry, N.C. Then, in the second of those letters, Scott was permitted to proceed.

*   *   *

To General Thomas Sumter

Dear Sir   Colsons Ferry [N.C.] April 14th 1781
I receiv'd your letter dated the seventh instant, and am happy to understand that our plan of operations agrees with your sentiments.

You will collect your force with all possible speed, and endeavour to take a position, as mentiond by you to Major Hyrne, where you may be enabled to cut off, or interrupt the communication between Camden and the other posts of the Enemy, keeping it in your power to cooperate with, or *join* this Army, should the movements of Lord Cornwallis render such measures necessary.[1]

Our operations are very much retarded by a defficiency of teams. Could you procure about one hundred waggon horses to be sent to our assistance, it would greatly facilitate the movements of the army; but above all things endeavour to procure the best and earliest intelligence from Charles Town.[2] I am Dear Sir with great respect your most obedient humble servant   NATH GREENE

LS (Sumter Papers: DLC).
1. NG had sent Maj. Edmund Hyrne to consult with Sumter. (NG to Sumter, 7 April, above) As seen at NG to Lee, 29 April, below, Sumter did not comply with NG's orders. NG is said to have privately blamed his defeat at the battle of Hobkirk's Hill and his failure to capture Camden on Sumter's evasion of those orders. (See note at NG to Sumter, 30 April, below.)
2. Sumter was unable to send either the horses that NG requested or the intelligence from Charleston, S.C. (See Sumter to NG, 25 April, below.)

*   *   *

¶ [CIRCULAR LETTER FROM CAPTAIN NATHANIEL PENDLETON TO CERTAIN COUNTY LIEUTENANTS IN VIRGINIA, 14 through 19 April 1781.[1] NG has sent Pendleton to urge that the Virginia militia march immediately. Pendleton is sure the "importance of the object," the "probable consequences" of the enemy having "a superiority of force," and the "Zeal" of the lieutenants will "be sufficient motives" for them to act. The troops, "armed and accoutred," should carry enough provisions for a march to Salisbury, N.C. Gives the route to that place. Wagons should be used to carry baggage and provisions, but "Too many waggons encumber the March of the Troops." Owners can be assured that their wagons will be returned as soon as the men reach camp.[2] ADf (MiU-C) 3 pp.]
1. According to a table appended to the draft, copies of the circular were sent to eleven county lieutenants between 14 and 19 April. They were written from various locations,

which are listed in the table. According to an accompanying note, the lieutenant of Prince Edward County received his copy "in person" on 19 April.

2. As noted at Jefferson to NG, 30 March, above, most of the militiamen never left Virginia.

¶ [FROM CAPTAIN JAMES CONYERS, Col. [William] Thompson's, S.C., 14 April 1781.[1] Conyers visited Colonel Thompson, as NG ordered, but finds that militiamen have taken all of Thompson's horses. Conyers will seize the horses when he overtakes Gen. [Francis] Marion. He has asked Thompson to help obtain horses for the army and says "No man can or will be more Servicable." Thompson wants a "Special order" from NG to impress, care for, and send horses to the regiment "from time to time."[2] He is also willing to rehabilitate the army's unfit horses. His plantation, which is "as safe" as any, has "good Pasturage" and is in an area where forage is available. Thompson is sending two men to obtain horses and should soon have some for "our Dismounted Dragoons." One of these men "waits on" NG for instructions. Conyers suggests that two dragoons be sent to help feed the animals until they can be sent to the army. Has instructed Thompson not to deliver horses to anyone "except the 3rd Reg'" or by NG's "Special Order." Conyers is on his way to Marion, who "Marched Last Night"; will let no opportunity "Escape" him.[3] ALS (MiU-C) 2 pp.]

1. William Faden's map of South Carolina (1787) shows a Thompson's plantation on Thompson's Creek, a tributary of the Pee Dee River. Col. William Thompson was presumably living there at the time Conyers wrote, the British having turned his principal residence, at Belleville, into a fortified post. Thompson, who had been captured when Charleston fell in 1780, was on parole. A short time later, the British charged him with violating his parole and imprisoned him in Charleston. (*DAB*)

2. No "Special order" has been found.

3. On Conyers's purpose in visiting Marion, see NG to Marion, 4 April, above.

¶ [FROM THE MARQUIS DE MALMEDY, "Radefort[s] [Rutherford's?] Mill," N.C., 14 April 1781. He reached Gen. [Alexander] Lillington's detachment on 7 April and was immediately sent to scout "the Enemy[s] Lines at Wilmington." Reports that "british dragoons" arrived in Wilmington on 10 and 11 April and that Cornwallis's main force is said to be camped a short distance from town.[1] Malmedy had "but a trifling success on the Lines," as the enemy stayed "close in their works." Lillington therefore recalled him.

Malmedy's men will be discharged on 26 April. Although he may not have performed "Essential service" with them, he reminds NG of the "unfortunate circumstances & difficulties" he had to face. These included: the presence of the British in the district where he raised the corps; the "undiscipline & personal misconduct" of some of the officers and men, which "prevailed for a while"; and his being sent to suppress Loyalists, who "usually disperse at the sole sound of an American party."[2] He is unwilling to serve again with a two-month corps; wants a command of 200 mounted troops, raised "upon a regular Establishment" for nine months. NG proposed the establishment of such a corps to the last session of the North Carolina Assembly.[3] Malmedy does not dare ask him to repeat the request "this moment" but does await NG's orders.[4] Lillington has been absent from camp "for some days," leaving Malmedy in command. Malmedy is to fall back to "Limestone [Bridge] at the first movement of the british," who remained "still" as of "this morning." ALS (MiU-C) 3 pp.]

1. Lord Cornwallis's army remained in its camp there until 25 April. ("Von Bose Journal," pp. 55–56)

2. For more on Malmedy's corps and the problems and orders mentioned here, see Malmedy to NG, 10 February; Malmedy to Ichabod Burnet, 24 February; Malmedy to NG, 10 March; and NG to Malmedy, 18 March, all above (vol. 7: 274, 345, 424–25, 447–48).

3. On the proposal, which NG had made at Malmedy's request, see NG to Gov. Abner Nash, 13 January, above (vol. 7: 108). The Assembly's actions are noted there.

4. Malmedy again asked for orders in a letter of 11 May, below.

¶ [FROM GENERAL GEORGE WEEDON, Williamsburg, Va., 14 April 1781. Has NG's letter of 29 March [not found]. Congratulates him on "the noble Exertions made in the South" since NG took command. These do honor to NG's entire army. It is lamentable that NG's "defences and Supplies ware not adequate to the Activity and firmness" of his mind. The "events of war are uncertain and turns on so nice a point" that "changes of the most trifling nature" can disappoint "golden" hopes. "Had them Cursed NC Militia done their duty the head of the Serpent in the south would have been loped off. The tail might have quivered a while but our work both in that Quarter and this would afterward been easy."[1]

Weedon has "had many unhappy moments" on NG's account. He supported a plan, which was proposed after the "Expedition against Portsmouth failed," to take the "choicest part" of the Virginia militia "by forced & rapid marches" into NG's "Neighbourhood." Those troops would have given Lord Cornwallis "a Coup de grace" and then "returned immediately." Virginia would have been left "exposed but we could afterward have re established ourselves again with ease." The "Executive" of Virginia, however, was "too closly Attached to local Security" and balked.[2]

Weedon has been in Williamsburg since he last wrote NG and for a time was "in great expectations of Glory" in capturing Portsmouth. Adds: "You may judge how much we ware disappointed when on the Arrival of a Fleet in the Bay all our Aparatus for the work was set in motion, when behold instead of Mons[r] Le Touche, it turned out to be Arburthnot from Gardeners Bay! Thus all our golden hopes in this Quarter vanished and *Benedict* continues secure in his fastnings at Portsmouth."[3]

Encloses some letters concerning the Virginia field officers' address. That document astonished him "not a little," but Weedon knows his duty and the authority he has for "Carrying it into execution."[4] Assures NG of his support. He has urged the sending of assistance to NG to such a degree that some Virginians have called him "a madman for [having] Such Ideas at a time when the State was so powerfully Invaded." The new levies, who are coming in, will be forwarded "with all expedition."[5] Provisions are also going "forward." Baron Steuben "is very Active, and has been Exceedingly useful." Some "extravagant Accounts" of the size of NG's army have been received; Weedon never believed them, "tho' some came from those who might have been supposed good Authority." NG's "retreat, and Advance is equal in prudence and Gallantry to any on Military record and is highly approved by Congress, the commander in chief," and all of NG's friends.

After being left in command "in this Department," Weedon "opened a correspondence" with Gen. William Phillips about an exchange of prisoners. Sends letters from that correspondence.[6] Says the force that Phillips brought "is not very Considerable," numbering fewer than 2,500 men.[7] Weedon thinks they will "Attempt a junction with Cornwallis either by way of Cape Fear, or penetrating North Carolina."[8]

Weedon has invited Mrs. [Catharine] Greene to come as far south as Fredericksburg and wonders why NG is opposed to her doing so. Mrs. [Catharine Gordon] Weedon will be pleased to make her as happy as NG's "Absence" will allow, and Catharine can hear from NG more often at Fredericksburg than at home. Asks NG to reconsider.[9]

Has just received accounts of British ships being in the Potomac River. Weedon has orders to go and defend "that place" but not to take any troops "from hence." He will "set off tomorrow."[10] ALS (MiU-C) 4 pp.]

1. Weedon referred to the performance of the North Carolina militia at the battle of Guilford Court House, which is discussed at NG to Huntington, 16 March, above (vol. 7: 437–39n).

2. For more on the plan that Weedon described, see Steuben to NG, 30 March, above.

3. On the failure of the proposed Franco-American expedition against Benedict Arnold's force at Portsmouth, see Baron Steuben to NG, first letter of 4 March, above (vol. 7: 390). "Mons[r] Le Touch" was the Chevalier Destouches, the commander of the French naval force that was to have been a part of the expedition. Adm. Marriot Arbuthnot commanded a British fleet that was usually stationed at Gardiner's Bay, Long Island.

4. On the address of the Virginia Continental officers, protesting Weedon's readmission to the Virginia line, see Davies to NG, 20 February, above (vol. 7: 322).

5. The new levies never joined NG, who ordered them to remain in Virginia to assist the Marquis de Lafayette. (See NG to Lafayette, 14 May, below.)

6. Weedon was able to arrange the exchange of a few individuals but was thwarted in an effort to arrange a general exchange. (Ward, *Weedon*, p. 184)

7. As seen at Washington to NG, 21 March, above (vol. 7: 459n), Phillips's detachment numbered about 2,000 men.

8. The junction between Cornwallis's and Phillips's troops took place in Virginia.

9. As seen in his letter to Catharine Greene of 23 June, below, NG continued to oppose her traveling to the South.

10. On 10 April, Weedon received a report that Maj. George Tuberville had brought fifteen vessels into the Potomac. Weedon thereupon asked Steuben for permission to return to Fredericksburg to "remove his family" and defend Hunter's Iron Works and the arms factory there. (Weedon to Steuben, 10 April, Steuben Microfilm) Both Steuben and Gov. Thomas Jefferson rejected Weedon's request for troops. (Jefferson to Weedon, 17 April, Boyd, *Jefferson Papers*, 5: 483–84) By the time he arrived home on 21 April, the enemy had "all gone." (Weedon to Jefferson, 21 April, ibid., p. 529)

¶ [GENERAL GREENE'S AFTER ORDERS, May's Mill, N.C., 15 April 1781.[1] In after orders, tents are to be pitched and the troops furnished with three days' provisions and a jill of rum per man; the army will march "tomorrow" at sunrise. Lamar Orderly Book (OClWHi) 1 p.]

1. Only the army's location—"near Brown Creek"—was given in the general orders of this date.

¶ [TO COLONEL JOHN MARSHEL.[1] From Headquarters, May's Mill, N.C., 15 April 1781. NG asks him to provide intelligence about the British force at

Camden and about enemy movements in the Cheraws and in the area of Nelson's Ferry. Marshel is to get "the Mills to work agrinding Meal" for the army; if possible, he should also send NG "twenty or thirty good waggon horses." NG depends on Marshel's exertions and on his keeping "matters as secret as possible." ADfS (MiU-C) 2 pp.]

1. As noted above (vol. 6: 606n), Marshel was a militia officer in the Camden area.

¶ [TO GENERAL ANDREW PICKENS. From Headquarters, May's Mill, N.C., 15 April 1781. Has his letters of 23 March and 8 April, the latter of which arrived "this moment."[1] NG will report Colonel Clarke's victory to Congress; it "does him and his party the greatest honor."[2] Asks Pickens to convey NG's "thanks" to Clarke. Feels "sorrow" for the "inhuman attack upon Major Dunlop" following his capture. Is pleased that Pickens has taken "just and prudent measures to bring the criminals to justice."[3] It is "most fortunate" that Pickens "went into that quarter" when he did; his presence should "serve to spirit up the people."[4] Pickens has "been informed" of the battle of Guilford Court House. "The enemy got the ground, but their loss was so great" that they afterwards retreated "with precipitation." NG explains his decision to break off his pursuit of them and "march immediately for South Carolina."[5] He will be "in the Neighbourhood of Camden in four or five days."[6] NG has heard nothing of Cornwallis since beginning his march and is anxiously awaiting intelligence.[7] Gen. [Thomas] Sumter is collecting militia; NG hopes "in a few days to meet the enemy with a good face."[8] ADfS (MiU-C) 2 pp.]

1. Pickens's letter of 23 March has not been found.

2. Pickens had reported Col. Elijah Clarke's victory over an enemy party commanded by Maj. James Dunlap in his letter of 8 April, above. NG enclosed a copy of that report in his letter of 22 April, below, to Samuel Huntington, the president of Congress.

3. On the killing of Dunlap and the measures that Pickens had taken in response, see Pickens to NG, 8 April, above.

4. As noted at ibid., Pickens had been sent with a militia force to the Ninety Six district of South Carolina.

5. On the battle of Guilford Court House, see NG to Huntington, 16 March, above (vol. 7: 433–36). NG discussed his decision to abandon pursuit of Lord Cornwallis's army and return to South Carolina in his letter to Washington of 29 March, above. (Ibid., pp. 481–82)

6. The Southern Army was in the vicinity of Camden by 19 April. (See NG's Orders of that date, below.)

7. Cornwallis had retreated to Wilmington, N.C.

8. On Sumter's activities, see his letter to NG of 13 April, above.

¶ [TO BARON STEUBEN. From "May's Mill on the West side of the Pedee on Camden road," N.C., 15 April 1781. Col. [Lewis] Morris arrived with Steuben's letter of 2 April "a day or two" ago; NG is "anxious" for more current news from Virginia.[1] Is afraid the enemy will keep Steuben too busy "to think of joining this army," although his "presence would be exceeding agreeable." Hopes the "detachments of horse and foot" can be spared; NG's army greatly needs reinforcements.[2] Approves the appointment of Capt. [John] Pryor as commissary of military stores and of Pryor's handling the supplies sent from the North as well as those from Virginia. NG wrote the Board of War "a long time since upon the subject."[3] The army needs a field commissary, although

Capt. [Anthony] Singleton is performing the duty according to the "plan laid down by Congress"; all orders for arms and ammunition must be signed by Col. [Otho] Williams.[4] Is pleased that Col. [William] Davies is appointed "to the War office." The rules of Congress permit the holding of a state and a Continental office "at the same time" and only prohibit the simultaneous holding of "two offices under Congress."[5] NG has given Davies permission to accept the state appointment, subject to completing the arrangement of the Virginia line.[6] "His signing all orders for clothing will prevent much confusion."

It is "high time" for Capt. [Nathaniel] Irish's party to "get the laboratory in order."[7] Arms are "getting out of repair," and there are no armorers with the army. Even if there were, the troops move too rapidly "to repair the arms generally," but NG laments "the want of a few armourers for slight repairs." Thinks there will be an "insufficient" supply of ammunition unless "great attention is paid to this business." The army has "few cartridges," and NG fears there will not be enough lead; hopes Davies has "the power" to "reserve 20,000 weight at least," as NG requested.[8]

Encloses a return of Col. [William] Washington's cavalry. NG has asked Virginia for the supplies that were listed in the estimate Steuben sent with Morris.[9] "But the Southern service is so severe, and the difficulty of getting supplies so great, from the distance and length of time it takes, that I think there should be an additional number of every article, of at least one third the whole quantity; or else every accident will render a number of men useless." There should also be "a troop of spare horses constantly recruiting" to replace "those broken down in service." The two regiments of Continental dragoons have enlisted "upwards of 100 men for the War" from the "eighteen-months men" from Virginia. NG will write more fully about his "military operations" in a few days. As Petersburg, Va., is "so accessible to the enemy" he does not advise keeping "a great deposit of Stores" there unless they can easily be removed.[10] LS (NHi) 5 pp.]

1. Steuben sent another report on the military situation in Virginia on 25 April, below.

2. As noted at Steuben to NG, 2 April, above, neither Steuben nor the troops joined NG.

3. NG's letter on the subject has not been found.

4. Williams was the Southern Army's assistant inspector general. In his letter of 2 April, Steuben had suggested that supplies reaching the army from Virginia should be distributed by an assistant commissary of military stores in accordance with Williams's instructions.

5. In his letter of 2 April, above, Steuben had asked NG, as Southern Army commander, to decide if Davies could legally serve as both a Continental and a state officer.

6. See NG to Davies, 11 April, above.

7. Steuben reported in his letter of 2 April that Irish and his company of artificers had marched to Prince Edward Court House to establish the laboratory.

8. On the supplies of ammunition and lead, see Steuben to NG, 2 April, and NG to Davies, 11 April, both above.

9. A return of William Washington's regiment of dragoons is in the Steuben papers, dated 5 January 1781. (Steuben Microfilm) The estimate that Steuben sent NG has not been found.

10. As seen in Steuben to NG, 25 April, below, the British did move against American stores at Petersburg.

*　　　*　　　*

To General Thomas Sumter

Dear Sir   H Q^rs Mays Mill [N.C.] April 15th 1781

Your favor of the 13th was this moment handed me by Captain [Vardy] McBee. We are thus far on our way to Camden and expect to arrive there in four or five days. Lt Colonel [Henry] Lee is on his march from the Pedee to the Santee, and will cross that river some where near Nelson's Ferry and come up on the other side.[1] Perhaps you may make your movements co-operate with his and also those of Genl [Andrew] Pickens. You will keep in mind that our force when collected is very small; and therefore you should not lose sight of a junction should Lord Cornwallis move this way.[2] If he should not, and the Garrison at Camden is not well supplied with provision, it must fall in a few days. I have little hopes of the garrisons falling in any other way as we have no battering cannon, and too few troops to warrant a storm upon ⟨the post.⟩[3]

You will not fail to give me constant intelligence of your force and situation as matters may grow very critical by and by. If the Virginia militia come up I think we shall fight the Enemy to good advantage; but if not, we shall be weak.[4] It will be necessary therefore to have some measures taken to secure a retreat and a small quantity of provisions should be laid in on the Catawba up in the neighbourhood of the Waxaws. The Magazine need not contain provision for more than 3000 men for four days. Another collection should be made at Charlotte; however this I will attend to; and I have a magazine forming at Oliphants Mill at which place all our baggage and stores are collecting.

⟨Col Clarkes defeat of⟩ Dunlap will have a most happy effect; and if we are able to improve the blow, the Enemy will be in the greatest distress.[5]

The Pensylvania ⟨line⟩ and reinforcements ⟨from Maryland⟩ and Virginia are coming to join this army; but it will be some time before they can get up with us.[6] If we can hold our ground until their arrival, I make no doubt we shall have it in our power to drive the enemy out of the upper Country.

North Carolina is collecting its regular troops also, by drafts agreeable to the late law, and from present appearances promise a reinforcement of 1200 or 1500 men.[7] Encourage the people and let us do all we can, and if providence smiles upon our endeavours, happily we may have it in our power to give relief to this oppressed Country.

Much blood has been spilt, and more must be spilt, before this Country can regain its liberty. Have your Stores arrived from Virginia? You must be in great want of them.[8]

Altho' I am a great enemy to plundering, yet I think the horses belonging to the Inhabitants within the Enemy's lines should be taken from them; especially such as are either fit for the Waggon or Dragoon service. If we are superior in Cavalry, and can prevent the Enemy from equiping a number of teams it will be almost impossible for them to hold their posts, and utterly impossible to pursue us if we should find a retreat necessary. But indeed any horses, or any other kind of property whether taken from Whig or Tory, certificates ought to be given, that justice may be done to the inhabitants hereafter; and if any discrimination is necessary with the people, Government may make it when the certificates are presented for payment. I am dear Sir, your most obd[t] Serv[t]   NATH GREENE

LS (Sumter Papers: DLC). Words in angle brackets were taken from the ADfS (MiU-C).

1. When Lee reached the Santee, he joined Gen. Francis Marion in a siege of Ft. Watson, near Nelson's Ferry. (See Marion to NG, first letter of 23 April, below.)

2. Pickens joined Sumter briefly on 25 April. (Sumter to NG, 25 April, below) As seen in NG to Lee, 29 April, below, Sumter did not "co-operate" with the other American forces.

3. NG's attempt to capture Camden culminated in the battle of Hobkirk's Hill. (See NG to Huntington, 27 April, below.)

4. As noted at Jefferson to NG, 30 March, above, few Virginia militiamen came to NG's aid.

5. On Col. Elijah Clarke's victory over a force commanded by Maj. James Dunlap, see Pickens to NG, 8 April, above.

6. It would be many months before any of these reinforcements reached NG's army. (See notes at NG to Gist, 30 March; NG to Steuben, 2 April; and Steuben to NG, 2 April, all above.)

7. On North Carolina's efforts to fill its Continental battalions, see Nash to NG, 3 April, and Caswell to NG, 6 April, both above.

8. Gov. John Rutledge of South Carolina had promised to send some clothing and other items "stored up in Virginia" to Sumter and other militia commanders. Sumter wrote Gen. Francis Marion on 28 March that "what little there was, has been much pillaged." (Gibbes, *Documentary History*, 3: 46)

*   *   *

¶ [FROM DOCTOR JAMES BROWNE, General Hospital, Colonel Perkins's, Va., 15 April 1781. In response to an order of NG's [not found], he encloses a return of the hospitals under his direction. "The distant situations of the different" facilities made it "extremely difficult" to compile the return until all of the hospitals were brought "together at this place."[1] The "Derangements" in the Maryland and Virginia lines also made it impossible to give an accurate report of the companies and regiments to which the wounded soldiers belong. Wants to keep Mr. [William] McClure, who was ordered to join the army's "Flying Hospitals," to supply the facility that NG wants established at Charlotte, N.C.[2] Maj. [Ichabod] Burnet's "Complaints have proved tedious and troublesome to Himself[;] hope to restore him to you shortly, with the full Possession of his Health."[3] ALS (MiU-C) 2 pp.]

1. Browne enclosed two returns: for the hospital at Henry Court House "from March 1 to April 1," and for the one at Guilford, N.C., "from March 15th to April 2[d]." NG had

ordered Browne to combine the various hospitals in his department. (William Pierce to Browne, 22 March, above [vol. 7: 460])

2. NG's reply has not been found. For more on the hospital at Charlotte, see Browne to NG, 6 May, below.

3. On Burnet's illness, see NG to Burnet, 5 April, above.

¶ [FROM GENERAL JOHN BUTLER, Camp, Ramsey's Mill, N.C., 15 April 1781. Encloses two letters containing all the worthwhile intelligence he has received.[1] He sent men for further information after NG "left this place" and will advise NG of any intelligence they obtain.[2] ALS (MiU-C) 1 p.]

1. The letters, which gave information about British activity in the Wilmington area, were from John Whitaker and Thomas Owen and were dated 12 and 13 April respectively. (MiU-C) For more on this intelligence, see NG to Butler, 21 April, below.

2. NG had left Ramsey's Mill on 6 April.

¶ [FROM LORD CORNWALLIS, Headquarters [Wilmington, N.C.], 15 April 1781.[1] Has "just received" NG's letter of 9 April and "now" has the "greatest hopes" that a cartel can be agreed to on "fair & equal Terms." Will send a fully empowered commissioner to the place and on the date that NG proposed. Capt. [Frederick] Cornwallis will replace Capt. [Henry] Broderick, who cannot attend.[2] Cy (PRO 30/11/91) 1 p.]

1. As noted at NG to Sumter, 8 April, above, Cornwallis's army had reached the outskirts of Wilmington by 7 April.

2. Broderick had represented Cornwallis in the preliminary negotiations for a prisoner-exchange cartel. (See NG's instructions to Col. Edward Carrington, 11 March, above [vol. 7: 425].) On the outcome of the proceedings, see Carrington to NG, 8 May, below.

¶ [FROM SAMUEL HUNTINGTON, PRESIDENT OF THE CONTINENTAL CONGRESS, Philadelphia, 15 April 1781. Acknowledges NG's letters of 28 February and 10, 16, and 23 March; also one of 14 January, which Congress received on 22 March "by" Dr. [Nathan] Brownson.[1] Encloses an act of 22 March, giving regulations for the medical department and military hospitals.[2] Sends a copy of "Claypoole's Paper," containing intelligence about Great Britain's declaration of war against the Dutch. Huntington does not know if "what is mentioned relative to Portugal" can be depended upon; "what relates to the Empress of Russia" he presumes to be "Rivington-Like."[3] LS (PHC) 1 p.]

1. All four letters are above (vol. 7: 367, 433–36, 464–65, 119–20). In that of 14 January, NG had asked Congress to appoint Brownson purveyor for the hospital department in the South.

2. The act included an arrangement of hospital department officers in the South. (JCC, 19: 292–94)

3. Huntington enclosed the 14 April issue of David C. Claypoole's *Pennsylvania Packet*, containing reports on the British navy's attack on St. Eustatius, an outbreak of hostilities between Holland and Portugal, and diplomatic overtures toward Russia by the Dutch. (On the capture of Dutch-owned St. Eustatius by the British, see note at Joseph Clay to NG, 29 March, above [vol. 7: 483n]. The report of hostilities between the Dutch and Portuguese was incorrect; for more on relations between Holland and Russia, see Mathews to NG, 30 April, below.) James Rivington published the *Royal Gazette*, a Loyalist newspaper, in New York.

¶ [FROM DAVID WILSON, [Mecklenburg County, N.C.] 15 April 1781.[1] Is "Greatly Imbarshed in Managing the publick provisions" by Capt. [Joseph]

Marbury's seizure of two wagonloads of salt, which the [North Carolina] Board of War was sending to Wilson. Asks if Marbury was acting under NG's orders, as he claimed.[2] ALS (MiU-C) 1 p.]

1. Wilson was county commissioner for Mecklenburg County.

2. NG's reply has not been found.

¶ [GENERAL GREENE'S ORDERS, "Camp at Shoemakers, Deep Creek S. Carolina," 16 April 1781. Each man is to receive a jill of rum, each officer a quart. Arms and accoutrements are to be "well cleaned." The army will march at 7 A.M. on the "morrow." NG reports several recent victories, including that of Colonel [Elijah] Clarke over "a partizan Corps of horse and foot" and the defeat of a detachment from "Colonel [John] Watsons Reg[t]" by "Colonel Horrey."[1] Also reports that the rear of Lord Cornwallis's army "suffered considerably" from frequent attacks by the Bladen County, N.C., militia.[2] "These circumstances sufficiently evince the disposition of the Inhabitants of this Country, and may be considered as preludes to Victories, more decisive and more Glorious." Lamar Orderly Book (OClWHi) 2 pp.]

1. For more on Clarke's victory, see Pickens to NG, 8 April, above. Gen. Francis Marion sent an account of the engagement involving Col. Hugh Horry in his letter to NG of 21 April, below.

2. By contrast with what NG reported here, Banastre Tarleton wrote in his memoirs that the militia "did not appear in arms" when Cornwallis's army marched through Bladen County to Wilmington, although the militiamen did break down "some bridges over creeks, to retard the march of the royal army." (Tarleton, *Campaigns*, p. 281)

* * *

To Major Richard Claiborne

Dear Sir   Head Quarters Mays Mill [N.C.] April 16th 1781

I am sensible of the many embarassments you must meet with in the excutition [i.e., execution] of your duty as State Quarter Master. I was always of the opinion a system for the Q M Generals department was an idle thing. But as Congress were determined to have one, and would not leave a latitude to the Agents, I formed the best I could, but even this they mutilated in such a manner as embarasses the business by limiting its operation.[1] My advice to Col Pickering was to deviate from the plan where the public good requird it.[2] I give the same to you, and what ever principle the State adopts respecting Money I think will be a good rule of conduct for you; and must from the nature of it justify your conduct and pass your accounts.[3] Let me advise you not to get into any dispute with the commanding officer in Virginia. A little patience and a little attention will preserve proper harmony between you and him.[4]

I have lately written to Col Pickering, and informed him that it is impossible to get people to serve here, or do business upon the same scale that it is done to the Northward. You should write him on the subject.[5] Until you can hear from him, Lt Col Carrington will give you a power to act as circumstance may dictate to be necessary. With esteem & regard I am dear Sir Your Most Obed humble S^{er} N GREENE

ADfS (MiU-C).

1. On the quartermaster department "system," see headnote on NG's resignation (vol. 6: 150–55n).

2. NG most likely discussed this matter with Timothy Pickering in camp at Orangetown, N.Y., after the latter arrived in September 1780 to assume his duties as quartermaster general.

3. In a letter to Pickering of 3 April, Claiborne complained that although he was in possession of the plan for operating his department, it would be "chimerical" to imagine it could operate "without means." He said his department had numerous and expensive responsibilities, but no money, and that army officers and the public seemed to be ignorant of the rules Congress had established for issuing certificates for impressed items. (RG 93, WRMS, Misc. Mss. #25146: DNA) In counseling Claiborne to use the same rules for money as the state did, NG was presumably referring to the monetary value that Claiborne assigned to the certificates of impressment.

4. The "commanding officer in Virginia" was Baron Steuben. Claiborne discussed his relationship with him in a letter to NG of 2 May, below.

5. See NG to Pickering, 4 April, above.

* * *

¶ [TO COLONEL ANTHONY W. WHITE. From May's Mill, N.C., 16 April 1781. Two officers and some clothing are needed for fifty men who have been recruited for White's regiment from the Virginia line.[1] White should send them as soon as possible. Tr (GWG Transcript: CSmH) 1 p.]

1. In his letter to Baron Steuben of 15 April, above, NG reported that "upwards of 100 men" had been recruited from the "eighteen-month men" for the two regiments of Continental dragoons serving with NG's army. One of the regiments was White's First Continental Light Dragoons. White was in Virginia, recruiting for and refitting his unit. (See NG to White, 26 January, above [vol. 7: 204].)

¶ [FROM COLONEL WILLIAM DAVIES, Richmond, Va., 16 April 1781. The "jealousies" toward NG that "at first" disturbed officers in the Virginia line have been "totally removed." Officers who have recently returned from the army or have written to Davies "uniformly express the fullest confidence" in and "warmest attachment" to NG and say that suspicions "of slight and neglect" were mistaken.[1] Recruits have "come in," but not "expeditiously." Virginia's policy of short enlistments—a "system of absurdity"—has made "enlisting and deserting a kind of business." If the policy continues, so many will desert that it will be impossible to either raise men by draft or punish "delinquents."[2] Davies supposes that NG has received the proposed arrangement of the Virginia line from "Col^{o} [Lewis] Morris." This arrangement, adopted by the board of field officers, was the only "equitable" way to preserve the "officer's rights, particularly the subalterns." Suggests that NG send returns of "vacancies" in the line to the Virginia War Office; Davies will procure commissions for the replacements. Before he headed that office, officers would never communicate with state officials about matters relating to advancement. That was because of the executive's "ignorance" of "everything relative to rank" and a willingness on the part of government to do "injustice" to the Continental line. Davies is convinced that the officers hold "no jealousy" toward him and that they know his "attachment to their interests." They will readily see that what he is suggesting to NG is to "their own benefit" and that it will comply with the wishes of Congress.[3] ALS (MiU-C) 2 pp. The letter is torn, with large sections along the right margin of the first page and the left margin of the second page missing.]

    1. Davies was replying to NG's letter of 3 April, above.

    2. NG responded in his letter to Davies of 23 May, below.

    3. In his reply of 23 May, below, NG did not mention Davies's suggestion for filling vacancies among officers in the Virginia line.

¶ [FROM DOCTOR JAMES MCHENRY, Baltimore, Md., 16 April 1781. Now that NG has had the order reversed that called for the Marquis [de Lafayette's] detachment to return to the North, McHenry will "no longer wonder" how NG managed to baffle "poor [Lord] Cornwallis with a handful [of] men." NG has achieved the reversal despite a "strange spirit of [contraction?]" that seems to be affecting American "councils." McHenry marvels that NG "can work with such efficacy, [and pro?]duce such revolutions at the distance of [more than?] eight hundred miles."[1] Although he admires NG's "policies," he has "more than once ⟨pitied th⟩e Marquiss's situation." Lafayette's troops passed through Baltimore "yesterday[,] discontented almost to ⟨gener⟩al desertion—destitute of shirts and proper ⟨equipments,⟩ and in most respects unprovided for ⟨a⟩ march." Lafayette, however, has now managed to "reconcile" his men "to the service" by "binding himself to certain merchan⟨ts⟩" for "about two thousand" guineas to obtain shirts, overalls, and hats for the troops.[2] He has also tried "the power of novelty" by "giving to the march the air of a ⟨frolic.⟩" The troops will ride "in wagons and ⟨carts⟩"—at least as far as the Virginia border.[3]

    McHenry does not know what arrangement NG has made for Lafayette but supposes he will order the Marquis to place his force "before Portsmouth." In support of such a disposition, McHenry observes that "the Baron [Steuben]" and the state of Virginia "are not on good terms" and presumes that NG will "take the first occasion" to replace Steuben with an officer who "knows more of the manage[ment] of our public bodies than our Baron. [They?] must sometimes be cajoled into the [most benefi?]cial measures."[4] So that NG can carry out his campaign in South Carolina, the enemy troops at Portsmouth should be forced to remain there. That will require at least a large-enough force of regulars to be able to make "demonstrations of a land blockade." Confining the British there will give Virginia a better chance to provide its quota of men and supplies. If the enemy force at Portsmouth is sent to oppose NG, the Continentals can come to NG's support before "any danger can overtake" the Southern Army.[5] NG should write McHenry at Baltimore, where he will remain until he knows Lafayette's intention.[6] Wonders in a postscript: "Have we not been wrong in a certain affair since the beginning."[7] ALS (Greene Papers: DLC) 3 pp. The manuscript is torn along the margin, and portions are missing. Part of the letter was printed in *A Complete History of the Marquis de Lafayette* (Hartford, Conn., 1845), pp. 100–101; the words and letters in angle brackets were taken from that version.]

    1. On Washington's decision to keep Lafayette's detachment in the Southern Department, see note at NG to Lafayette, 3 April, above.

2. In a letter to NG of 17 April, below, Lafayette discussed the discontents among his troops and his use of his personal credit to supply them.

3. Lafayette wrote NG that he planned to advance to Fredericksburg, Va., by forced marches, impressing as many horses and wagons as he could. (Ibid.)

4. On Steuben's standing with Virginia officials, see Davies to NG, 17 June, below.

5. By the time Lafayette reached Virginia, the British had invaded the interior of Virginia. That placed him on the defensive, unable to consider placing his force "before Portsmouth." (See Lafayette to NG, 28 April, below.)

6. NG's reply has not been found.

7. The "certain affair" was NG's attempt—thus far unsuccessful—to secure a commission for McHenry. (See NG to Samuel Huntington, 30 October 1780, above [vol. 6: 445].) McHenry went on to discuss this matter, but key portions of the text are missing, and his meaning is unclear. McHenry wrote NG on 29 May, below, that Congress had voted him the commission.

¶ [FROM GENERAL CHARLES SCOTT, 16 April 1781. He has received NG's letter of 14 April. Is now twenty-five miles "below the place" at which Capt. [William] Pierce directed him to wait for further instructions; will comply with that order as soon as possible. Requests a small "Liberty," which would not compromise the Southern Army's operations.[1] ALS (MiU-C) 2 pp. The letter is torn, with large portions missing.]

1. For more on Scott's situation, see Scott to NG, 13 April, above.

¶ [FROM COLONEL THOMAS WADE, Haley's Ferry, N.C., 16 April 1781. Has learned that Lord Cornwallis was at Wilmington on 9 April. Also relays a report as to the whereabouts of "Merion [Gen. Francis Marion]." Excerpt from Anderson Galleries, *Catalogue #1213* (1916)]

¶ [GENERAL GREENE'S ORDERS, Camp at Lynch's Creek, S.C., 17 April 1781. Arms and accoutrements are to be inspected. Ammunition is to be issued to the troops, who are also to receive and cook a three-days' supply of provisions. The army marches "Tomorrow" at 8 A.M. Lamar Orderly Book (OClWHi) 1 p.]

¶ [TO GENERAL FRANCIS MARION. From "Head Quarters Widow Shoemaker," S.C., 17 April 1781. The army is marching to Camden and will arrive "next day after to morrow." NG is "in the dark" about "the enemies strength and situation in South Carolinia" and about Lord Cornwallis's "motions." Asks Marion to gather intelligence and send it to him and Col. [Henry] Lee, who is marching "towards the Santee."[1] Requests "a particular account" of Marion's force and an "official" report of Col. [Hugh] Horry's attack on a "party of Watsons detachment."[2] ALS (ScC) 1 p.]

1. Marion replied on 21 April, below.

2. As seen by his orders of 16 April, above, NG had received word of the engagement. Marion gave the report in his reply of 21 April.

¶ [FROM MAJOR PINKETHAM EATON, Little River, N.C., 17 April 1781. Is on his way to the army with 140 "Men from Halifax" who have been "turn[d] into" the Continental service for twelve months.[1] Asks about the route he should follow.[2] Will cross the Pee Dee River "tomorrow." ALS (MiU-C) 1 p.]

1. As noted at Eaton to NG, 4 April, above, these troops were former militiamen, whose punishment for desertion during the battle of Guilford Court House was to be drafted into the Continental service.

2. NG's reply has not been found.

¶ [FROM THE MARQUIS DE LAFAYETTE, Baltimore, Md., 17 April 1781. Gives a report of his "Movements," which he hopes will "Apologize" for his not having written sooner. He was preparing to march northward when he received Washington's order to "Return to Virginia." As Washington put it, the arrival of British Gen. [William] Phillips's force in Virginia necessitated "a Support of Continental troops," without which NG's situation could "Become Very Critical."[1] The day after Lafayette received these orders, NG's letter of 2 April arrived, spurring his "Exertions."[2] Congress and the Board of War, concerned about the "Peculiar Circumstances" of Lafayette's detachment [which he discusses later in this letter], advised him to delay his march until he heard further from Washington. Lafayette refused, saying that his orders "Could not Be Anhiliated by *Advices*" and that NG's situation obliged him "to Hasten."[3] After starting his march, he was "Overtaken" by a letter from Washington, confirming the previous orders and "Promising Every Relief" that Washington "Could Afford."[4] The Board of War, which Lafayette had asked to help supply his detachment, gives "A Very poor prospect." As a result, he has "di[s]charged" such "officers as Could not Conveniently[,] or to Speack with truth[,] Could not possibly Remain." Other officers will be sent to replace them. He has also sent one officer per battalion "to fetch Summer Cloathes" for their corps. Washington has recalled two of Lafayette's officers; another, who "Acted as Inspector is Dangerously ill," and his chief physician has had to return to Philadelphia. High winds during the crossing of the Susquehanna River and many other difficulties have slowed his troops' progress. They have just arrived "on the other Side of Elk Ridge Ferry" and will remain there one day "to Refresh and Clean" themselves.

Now, My dear General, I am Going to Give You An Account of Our Circumstances Which Are of An Uncommon Nature, and I defy they Can Be Exagerated.

When this Detachement Was ordered out Every Individual in it thought they were Going on a tour of duty of two or three days And Provided Accordingly. The Light Compagnies of Every Regiment (Newyork Excepted) which Consisted of 25 men were By Common Drafts from the Regiments Increased to 50 and to Complete the Number of 1200 (Which Was immense in Comparaison to our force then at West Point) the Jersay Line were Ordered to furnish a detachement. Thus Circumstanced our officers Had No Monney, No Baggage of Any Sort, No Summer Cloathes, and Hardly a Shirt to Shift. To these Common Miseries the Soldiers Added their Shocking Naked[ness and] a want of Shoes &c. &c. Having Been thus Conducted to Trenton, they were Hurried on Board of Vessels and Having Been Embarked at Elk they Arrived at Annapolis where the Hope of A Short Expedition Against Arnold Silenced Every Complaint and kept up their Spirits. They Had Hitherto Been in Houses or on Board of Vessels, So that it was Impossible they Would feel the Extreme Want of tents Which However Crouded with officers and Men Leave A Number of them to Sleep in Oppen Air. Camp kettles Could Be Borrowed in towns or from Vessels, and Blankets were Almost Unnecessary.

To this I May Add that Every farthing of Monney Has Been Spent, Every Shoe Worn out, and Many Hatts Lost in the Navigation, and that Want of Linnen Has given a dreadfull itch to a great part of our Men.

Every thing However Went on Very Well, and the troops Being Ready to March from Elk, Reconforted themselves with the pleasant prospect of Returning towards Home, Se[e]ing their Wives all of whom Had Remained, and Getting large Sums of Monney which You know the New England States Have Sent to their troops, When my Countermanding the Order was With An Amazing Sagacity Imagined to Relate to a Retrogade March to the Southward. The officers did not like it More than the Men, and the Men Whose discipline does not give them the Idea of Complaining Began to Desert in Great Numbers. This Disposition Was Increased By the part which Every Body took in their Misfortune and Desertion went to Such a pitch that out of the Rhodeisland Compagny which You know Very Well thirteen, I think, of the Best and Most trusty men Made their Escape. The New England troops Have taken An idea that Southern Climates Are Very Unwholesome and that of Carolina Mortal to them. Every officer Assured me that our detachement Would Soon Be Reduced to five or Six Hundred Men. Now, My dear General, that I Gave You an Account of our Situation, I Beg leave to Submit to You the Measures Which I thought proper to take.

Lafayette's first "object" was to get the troops across the Susquehanna River and to have deserters captured. He then addressed the troops. His address, "Enforced By the difficulty of Crossing" the river, ended desertion. "The Men Are Now on the other Side of Elk Ridge Ferry which is A New Barrier."[5] He will hang a recaptured deserter "to Morrow"; a second deserter and a soldier "who Behaved A miss[,] Will Be Disgraced So far as to Be Dismissed from this Corps." Because the "Brave and Excellent Men (for this Detachment is Extremely Good) are Shokingly Destitute of Linnen," Lafayette has borrowed on his own credit about £2,000 from the Baltimore merchants and will use it to obtain "a few Hatts, Some Shoes, Some Blanketts, and a pair of Linnen Over Alls and a Shirt to Each man." He also hopes "to Sett the Baltimore Ladies At work for the Shirts which will Be Sent after me, and the Over Alls will Be Made By our taylors." He hopes to have the loan added to the amount the French government will give the United States; if that attempt fails, he has agreed to repay the merchants personally, "With Interests in two years."[6] Adds that [James] McHenry, now the "President of the Baltimore Board of War," aided him greatly in "this Arrangement."[7] Thinks "these Precautions" will keep the detachment in "Good order." He will send NG an "Exact Return," but says he has "about thousand men Rank and file and a Compagny of Artillery."[8]

Baron Steuben has informed him that Phillips's detachment numbers 1,500 to 2,000 men; including Arnold's command, Phillips must now have a force of 2,500 to 3,000.[9] "Reducing it to 2000 men Philips Might operate With, it Becomes Essential that My detachement Should Advance as fast as possible."

For that reason, and because the "Common Way of Marching troops . . . Announces the Very day of our Arrival and Every one of our Stages to the Ennemy," he has decided to leave his tents, his sick, and his artillery under a small guard and to "make forced Marches" to Fredericksburg, Va., impressing "Every Waggon and Horse" he can find. Lafayette hopes to receive orders from NG at Fredericksburg, but if he does not, he will "March in the Same Way to Richmond" and act as he judges best until he receives NG's "positive orders."[10] Adds that his instructions from Washington "Are pointed towards Philips" and that NG's "plans" agree "with that Idea."[11] When he reaches Richmond, Lafayette will "prepare to Move Either Way Agreable to the dispositions you will make, and if General Philips appeared to Intend Such Motions as would Be of disservice to You I will Make it My Business to Be Ready to Check Him as far as it Can Be done with Such an inferiority of forces."

As "An affectionate friend," he finds NG's move into South Carolina highly pleasing and "A great piece of Generalship. Your Intention of Separating the Ennemy, and the Motives that Influence it perfectly Agree with My Own Opinion." Adds "an observation Upon the Detachement" that he commands:

On our Arrival at Richmond, Unless a Great Emergency Occurs, we must probably Wait for our Artillery, tents, &c Before we March to the Southward. General Waine Must Be Now on His Way to Your Army; I am not Certain He Has Marched, But Every Account Confirm it. I know He waited for Nothing But Monney which has Been Collected, So that He must By this time Have Marched or Be Ready to March from York Town—So that He will Be at Richmond a Very few days after us.

From what Has past Betwen the Jersay Soldiers we Have and those of New England, I foresee Great Inconveniences to join these to the Pennsylvanians. The More So as the last, *Because they Have Revolted* are well Clad, well paied. Their jonction with this detachement would Be attended with Disputes, and we are for the present Very well United.[12]

Our troops do not for the Present extend their Views farther than Virginia, and their Going farther Southward would Be attended with Real and Imaginary Inconveniences.

These Remarks, My dear General, Are far from throwing the Least objection to our Marching Southerly if a jonction of your forces Appears to you of Some Advantage. I Mean only to Say, that if You Are able to Effect Your purpose By dividing the Ennemy's forces, the New England troops would like Much Better to Remain in Virginia and would Easier get the proportion of Supplies from their States which the General Has promised to Send to them.

As to the love of Commands, paragraphs &c &c &c you Have So Little Ambition, My dear general, that you Could not [Conceive] my Wishes on those Accounts was it Not for the knowledge you Have Been able to Get from Our Intimacy. But these

Motives Are to Be out of the Question when public good is interested, and whenever it Can Be done With propriety, I know you
will Be glad to Gratify me. I will not only Mention that General
Philips's Battery at Minden Having killed my father, I would Have
No objection to Contract the Latitude of His plans.[13]

Asks if he should inform Congress, as well as NG, when "Something Worth
Mentionning" occurs.[14] Is "Happy" that he is to be under NG's command. In a
postscript, sends his compliments to NG's military family and to "other
friends." Adds: "Don't Believe that when I am alone my Schemes are So very
Bold as when I Submit them to the Examination of others."[15] Apologizes for the
"Lenght and Scribbling of this letter," but he will not take time to shorten and
re-copy it and will "Send it of[f] By the Chain day and night."[16] ALS (MiU-C)
8 pp.]

1. Washington's letter, dated 6 April, is printed in Idzerda, *Lafayette Papers*, 4: 8–9.

2. NG's letter, of 3 April, is above.

3. The correspondence between Congress, the Board of War, and Lafayette has not
been found, but Lafayette told Washington in a letter of 13 April: "Representations of
wants Have Been Made which they [the Board of War] Have Mistaken for objections
from me to our journey South ward." He added that his reply to the board might
"Appear Disrespectfull or Impolite—But Nothing Could stop Me in an Instance where it
Might Be suspected I objected to Your plans, or Even differed in Opinion." (Idzerda,
Lafayette Papers, 4: 29)

4. Washington's letter to Lafayette of 11 April is printed in ibid., pp. 24–25.

5. Elk Ridge Ferry was on the south side of the Patapsco River in Maryland.

6. In July, Lafayette signed a promissory note for £1,550 sterling, payable in two years
in bills of exchange on France. He offered his estate in France as collateral. Congress
resolved on 24 May to assume responsibility for the debt and on 23 November ordered
the financier, Robert Morris, to discharge it. According to the editors of the Lafayette
Papers, however, it was Lafayette who paid the note when it came due on 1 July 1781.
(Idzerda, *Lafayette Papers*, 4: 54n)

7. McHenry, who had served as Lafayette's aide, acted as a go-between with the
Baltimore merchants. (See extract of McHenry to Merchants of Baltimore, 6 March,
Archives of Md., 47: 116–17.)

8. The return has not been found.

9. Steuben's letter of 10 April is printed in Idzerda, *Lafayette Papers*, 4: 23–24. Sir Henry
Clinton wrote Lord Cornwallis on 30 April that Phillips's command numbered about
3,500 men. (Davies, *Documents*, 20: 129)

10. NG approved the plan in a letter to Lafayette of 1 May, below.

11. Washington told Lafayette in his letter of 11 April: "whether General Phillips
remains in Virginia or goes further southward he must be opposed by a force more
substantial than Militia alone." He directed Lafayette to write NG for instructions "as to
marching forward to join him, or remaining there to keep a watch upon the motions of
Phillips should he have formed a junction with Arnold at Portsmouth." Idzerda, *Lafayette Papers*, 4: 24–25.

12. On the revolt of the Pennsylvania line, see James Madison to NG, 13 January, above
(vol. 7: 116–18). In a letter of 4 May, Lafayette again wrote Washington that he did not
want the Pennsylvania Continentals in his detachment, as they would most likely "spoil
the Jersay Soldiers and fight first those or New England." (Idzerda, *Lafayette Papers*, 4: 83)
However, after Lafayette received NG's letter of 1 May, below, giving him permission to
retain the Pennsylvania troops—and upon learning that Cornwallis was marching

toward Virginia—he urgently requested Gen. Anthony Wayne to have the Pennsylvanians join him. (Lafayette to Wayne, 15 May, ibid., pp. 102–3) As noted at Washington to NG, 1 June, below, the Pennsylvania troops did not leave York, Pa., until 26 May.

13. Lafayette's father, a colonel in the French grenadiers, had been killed in the battle of Minden, in Germany, in 1759. (Idzerda, *Lafayette Papers*, 4: 41n)

14. NG replied on 1 May, below.

15. Despite this assurance from Lafayette, NG warned him in his reply not to let the "love of fame get the better of your prudence."

16. The "Chain" was a line of express riders between Baltimore and Richmond, Va. (See Lafayette to Jefferson, 17 April, Boyd, *Jefferson Papers*, 5: 477.)

¶ [FROM COLONEL THOMAS WADE, [Haley's Ferry, N.C.] 17 April 1781.[1] Forwards letters to NG. Has sent a man to the Cape Fear River and another down the Pee Dee to collect intelligence, which he will forward immediately. ALS (MiU-C) 1 p.]

1. Wade, who did not give his location, had written NG from Haley's Ferry on 16 April, above.

¶ [FROM COLONEL THOMAS WADE, [Haley's Ferry, N.C.], 17 April 1781.[1] Since writing to NG [immediately above], he has received intelligence that "Col° Watson" is encamped with 200 Loyalists on the east side of the Pee Dee River, about thirty miles below "Cheraw Hill." There are "no Troops in front of them," and the two largest companies in Colonel Kolb's regiment are with Gen. [Francis] Marion.[2] Col. [Henry] Lee and Marion have reportedly joined forces.[3] Wade has twelve wagonloads of meal "ready fresh ground and the mills going." ALS (MiU-C) 2 pp.]

1. On Wade's location, see note at the letter immediately above.

2. In regard to Col. John Watson's detachment and movements, see note at Wade to NG, 19 April, below. Col. Abel Kolb was the local militia commander.

3. Marion and Lee had begun a siege of Ft. Watson, the British post at Nelson's Ferry. (See Lee to NG, 18 April, below.)

¶ [GENERAL GREENE'S ORDERS, Headquarters, Lynch's Creek, S.C., 18 April 1781. The "Invalids, Spare Arms and heavy baggage" are to go to Salisbury, N.C., under guard. Women with children and "those unable to March on foot, must also be sent off; as none will be admitted to ride on Waggons or horses, on any pretence whatever." In after orders, given at Little Lynch's Creek, 5 P.M., the army is to camp "here" and march "at Sun-rise." Lamar Orderly Book (OClWHi) 1 p.]

¶ [CAPTAIN NATHANIEL PENDLETON TO JOHN BROWNE. From Prince Edward, Va., 18 April 1781. Pendleton is in Virginia at NG's order, for reasons that include forwarding provisions to the army.[1] Urges Browne to comply with resolutions adopted by the state's executive in January and February to execute the "Provision Law" and implement the plan of transportation.[2] According to those resolutions, each county is to deliver "a waggon and Team complete," together with provisions and forage, to designated Continental personnel. Pendleton also presses Browne to comply with the governor's "determinations" of 3 February to store a quantity of pork at the Roanoke River and to appoint county deputies "immediately."[3] The pork should be stored no lower than Dix's Ferry. Nothing having been done in the counties ordered to send militia to the Southern Army, Pendleton has had to resort to impressment. Urges Browne's "immediate attention" to the "procuring and delivering" of wagons to Continental quartermasters. The army is "absolutely dependant on Virginia for its supplies." The state abounds in provisions, has an "extensive Law" to collect them, and has appointed Browne to administer it. The army, therefore, should no longer be in want. If all orders from the Southern Army are to go through Browne, who lives far from many of his deputies, "it might be necessary to take some measures to obviate the difficulties."[4] ADfS (MiU-C) 4 pp.]

1. On Pendleton's mission to Virginia, see his circular letter to county lieutenants, 14 April, above.

2. Browne, the Virginia commissary general, had been directed in January to carry out the terms of the state's provisions act. (Boyd, *Jefferson Papers*, 4: 284n; for more on the act itself, see Carrington to NG, 29 December 1780, above [vol. 7: 23–24].)

3. Jefferson's letter to Browne is in Boyd, *Jefferson Papers*, 4: 508.

4. Pendleton wrote Browne again on 21 April, below, regarding transportation matters.

¶ [CAPTAIN WILLIAM PIERCE, JR., TO COLONEL WILLIAM FIELDS.[1] From Headquarters [Lynch's Creek, S.C.], 18 April 1781.[2] NG received Fields's letter and permits him to return to his family. Fields's "continuance" there will "depend entirely" on his "good behaviour." ADfS (MiU-C) 1 p.]

1. Fields was a "notorious" Loyalist from the Cross Creek area of North Carolina. (DeMond, *N.C. Loyalists*, pp. 48, 179)

2. The location of NG's headquarters was taken from his orders of this date, above.

¶ [CAPTAIN WILLIAM PIERCE, JR., TO MAURICE SPILLARD. From Headquarters [Lynch's Creek, S.C.], 18 April 1781.[1] Spillard's request to go to Camden or Charleston cannot be granted because it would "too materially interfere" with "military operations."[2] NG will forward a letter to Camden for him, however, and will forward any baggage of Spillard's that may be "sent out."[3] ADfS (MiU-C) 1 p.]

1. The location of NG's headquarters was taken from his general orders of this date, above.

2. See Spillard to NG, 10 April, above.

3. Spillard replied to Pierce on 27 April, below.

¶ [FROM COLONEL WILLIAM DAVIES, Richmond, Va., 18 April 1781. Davies is "obliged" by NG's attention to the objections raised against Gen. [George] Weedon's return to service but is sorry that NG does not agree with the "opposition."[1] Although Weedon's standing is "different" from that of officers of "inferior rank," the quota of troops to be furnished by a state "regulates the number" of the state's general officers. As the quota is now "diminished," the number of general officers should also be reduced. That is "immaterial," however, because "the long absence of any officer from service on account of private resentments or private business, ought to be a sufficient bar to his resumption of his former command."[2] Davies does not think NG would have granted this "indulgence" if Weedon had asked him for it. Washington has informed Davies that he does not know what transpired when Weedon left the service but was told " 'a special resolve of Congress' " was involved. Washington leaves it to Congress "to settle the dispute."[3]

The "great number of officers that are prisoners" makes it "almost impossible to form any thing like a compleat" regiment. Although "acting by detachment is very injurious," Davies proposes a solution that should "obviate the inconvenience": to divide every detachment into eight companies and assign one to each regiment in the Virginia line. Each company would be commanded by captains and subalterns of the regiment to which it is assigned. As soon as the companies arrive in camp, they would be combined with other companies in their regiments until "at length the regiments will be compleatly formed." Although the "field officers will not be at first annexed to the men" they are eventually to command, this situation will not last long or be "attended with any great inconvenience."[4] As Steuben requested, Davies is paying "as much attention to the new levies" as his "other duties will permit." He will "always be glad to render the public" any service he can and to "make the Interests of the Continent and State coalesce as much as possible."[5] ALS (MiU-C) 3 pp.]

1. See NG to Davies, 30 March, above.

2. Weedon had retired in a dispute over rank in August 1778. (See above, vol. 2: 305–6.) For more on the objections that Davies and other Virginia officers raised against his return, see Davies to NG, 20 February, above (vol. 7: 322).

3. See Washington to Davies, 24 March, Fitzpatrick, GW, 21: 367. By a resolution of Congress at the time of his retirement, Weedon had retained his rank and could be called back into service when the "difficulties" under which he "laboured" were removed. In June 1780, following the capture of much of the Virginia line at Charleston, Congress recalled both Weedon and another Virginian, Gen. Daniel Morgan, who had left the army in 1779 after being passed over for a command. (JCC, 17: 518) As noted at NG to Davies, 30 March, above, Congress took no action in the "dispute."

4. NG had written Davies about the problem of Virginia Continental troops "acting by detachment" and had asked for his plan of arranging the state's Continental officers. (See NG to Davies, 3 April, above.) Field officers were those who carried a rank of major, lieutenant colonel, or colonel. NG made no mention of the plan when he wrote Davies on 23 May, below, acknowledging receipt of Davies's letter.

5. On Davies's appointment as state commissioner of war and his continuing duties as a Continental officer, see note at Steuben to NG, 30 March, above.

¶ [FROM COLONEL HENRY LEE, JR., Scott's Lake, S.C., 18 April 1781. Lee took a position "before this place" upon his arrival at the Santee River.[1] He has "deprived" the post of water, which will force its surrender, "unless they can sink a well which is not very probable."[2] Believes there is a "great quantity of stores" in the post. Asks NG to send a cannon, which could reach Lee in a day and a half and would be in "no possible danger"; with it, Lee could "finish the business" in "five minutes."[3] Has intelligence that Lord Cornwallis "was at Wilmington [N.C.] & [Col. John] Watson had not recrossed the [Pee Dee] river on the 13th."[4] ALS (MiU-C) 2 pp.]

1. "This place" was Ft. Watson, which Gen. Francis Marion and Lee had placed under siege on 15 April. (See Marion to NG, first letter of 23 April, below.)

2. The British were able to sink a well. (Ibid.)

3. NG replied on 19 April, below.

4. As seen at Thomas Wade's second letter to NG of 17 April, above, Watson's detachment was on the east side of the Pee Dee.

¶ [FROM COLONEL NICHOLAS LONG, Halifax, N.C., 18 April 1781. Will pay "due regard" to NG's letter of 30 March, which just arrived. As NG ordered, Long sent stores for the army to Hillsborough and will continue to forward all that he obtains if he can get wagons. He has "classed the wagons in each County," and as soon as the governor and council meet "here," as he expects them to do any day, he will "indavor to get a resolve for that purpose."[1] Mr. [Joseph] Clay "readily supplide" Long with $100,000, as NG suggested. "The demands ware so great" that he has "only twenty-Eight dollar bills left." Is thankful for NG's "other order," as Long is "in great want at present."[2] LS (MiU-C) 1 p.]

1. As seen in Eaton to NG, 4 April, above, the North Carolina Council Extraordinary had met in Halifax in early April, but does not seem to have met there after Long wrote this letter. There is, moreover, no evidence that the council took any action concerning the registration of wagons.

2. Nothing is known about the "other order."

¶ [FROM COLONEL ROBERT ROWAN,[1] Campbelltown, N.C., 18 April 1781. Col. [Thomas] Wade has informed him that NG wants to know the movements of Lord Cornwallis's army. Sends intelligence, obtained by a man who tried to recover Rowan's "Negroes" in Wilmington, that the enemy began moving their camp across the river on "Wednsday evening last" and are now "on the heights back of the Town."[2] "The flux and other disorders rages amongst them, by which several die daily."[3] They are expected to make a "short" stay and "go off by water."[4] Enemy shipping in the harbor now "amounts only to twenty two."[5] Most "inhabitants" have gone into Cornwallis's camp and "acknowledged themselves british subjects."[6] Cornwallis sent an express to Camden, S.C., last Wednesday. Rowan reports an "inhuman piece of Barbarity," which an enemy party committed "the week before last, about nine miles from Wilmington." They surprised a party of ten "respectable people," who were "diverting themselves in a public house" at night, and put to death all but two, "notwithstanding they begged quarter, some of them on their knees."[7] Adds that General Lillington's force of 400 or 500 men, some 30 miles from Wilmington, is a "confused rabble."

Rowan hopes the shoes he sent to NG "arrived safe." Has more shoes ready, which he will send if he can get horses.[8] Cannot obtain more leather, as "the enemy destroy'd all that was here fit for working up, & the shoemakers went off with them."[9] Rowan, who was unable to move his family and belongings, "suffer'd very considerably by the enemy." He lost most of his property and had a child die of smallpox a few days ago; "two others [are] now dangerously ill." Would be glad to do business for NG "to the Northward, or elsewhere," as "little can be done here" and he needs "to get bread for a helpless family." Wishes NG "success" at Camden and says that "A few more such strokes" at the enemy as at Guilford Court House "will put a stop to their ravages." Supposes that NG has heard that the British were repulsed in an attack on French entrenchments "to the nor'ward."[10] ALS (MiU-C) 4 pp.]

1. Rowan was state clothier general for North Carolina. (See NG to Rowan, 26 December 1780, above [vol. 7: 4].)

2. "Wednsday evening last" was the night of 11 April. According to the journal of the Von Bose Regiment, "On the 11th, 12th and 13th April the Cape Fear River was twice crossed and we marched into camp a mile from Wilmington." ("Von Bose Journal," p. 55)

3. According to Cornwallis's biographers, 405 of his men were reported sick on 15 April. (Wickwire, *Cornwallis*, p. 455n)

4. Cornwallis's troops left Wilmington on 25 April, marching overland toward Virginia. ("Von Bose Journal," p. 56)

5. The ships were "row-galleys and provision ships." (Ibid., p. 55) As Cornwallis's army was not planning to move by water, the British flotilla that Rowan and others were looking for never arrived.

6. For more on Loyalist activity in the Wilmington area, see Rowan to NG, 5 May, below.

7. Gen. Alexander Lillington described the victims as American militiamen who had been sent to the Wilmington area to drive off cattle and were at the tavern contrary to orders. (Lillington to NG, 9 April, above) The incident came to be known locally as the "massacre of the eight-mile house." (Waddell, *New Hanover County*, p. 186)

8. Rowan discussed the shoes again in his letter of 5 May, below.

9. Campbelltown, from which Rowan wrote this letter, was near Cross Creek, where Cornwallis's army had stopped during its retreat to Wilmington.

10. The report was false.

*   *   *

From George Washington

My dear Sir   New Windsor [N.Y.] April 18th 1781

Your private letter of the 18th Ult° came safe to hand. Although the honors of the field did not fall to your lot, I am convinced you deserved them. The chances of War are various, and the best concerted measures, and the most flattering prospects may, & often do deceive us, especially while we are in the power of Militia. The motives which induced you to seek an Action with Lord Cornwallis are supportable upon the best military principles, and the consequences, if you can prevent the dissipation of your Troops, will, no doubt be fortunate.[1] Every support that is in my power to give you from this Army shall chearfully be afforded. But if I part with any more Troops I must accompany them, or have none to command, as there is not, at this moment, more than a Garrison for West Point. Nor can I tell when there will.

I am much pleased to find by your letter that the State of Virginia exerts itself to your satisfaction. My public & private letters strongly inculcate the necessity of this, and I have again urged Congress to use every possible means in their power to facilitate the march of the Pensylvania line, as also to recruit, equip and forward Moylans Dragoons to you with dispatch.[2]

I should be very sorry, on any occasion to hurt the feelings of the Baron de Steuben, whom I esteem as a very valuable Officer, but in the instance you have mentioned there is no cause for complaint; for if he will advert to his own letters to me he will find, that there was a great probability of his having marched with a detachment to reinforce you. Besides which, there was a necessity for sending a General Officer with the detachment from hence—and political considerations as it was to be a combined operation (depending upon critical circumstances) with a French land & Sea force, pointed to the Marquis. Add to this, I knew that the French Troops were to be commanded by an officer of Senior rank to either the Baron or Marquis. These are the facts, the knowledge of which must, I am perswaded, Satisfie the Baron.[3]

I am truly sensible of the merit & fortitude of the veteran Bands under your command, & wish the sentiments I entertain of their worth could be communicated with the warmth I feel them. It was my full intention to have requested you to thank Morgan and the gallant Troops under his command, for their brilliant victory; but the hurry with which my letters are often written, occasioned the omission at the time I acknowledged the official acc[t] of that action.[4] Your conjecture respecting the cause of the P—— M—— [i.e., Pennsylvania Mutiny] has more substantial ground for its support than the letter of the M—— C—— [i.e., Member of Congress], and I am mistaken if the licentious conduct of that line, was not more the effect of an over charge of Spirits on the first of January, than of premeditated design.[5]

I have the pleasure to tell you, that as far as I am acquainted with the opinion of Congress with respect to your conduct, it is much in your favor. That this is the [senti]ment of all the Southern Delegates I have great reason to believe, because I have it declared to me in explicit terms by some of them.* I hope the disorder of which you complained in your letter of the 18th was no more than the effect of over fatigue and that you are now perfectly recovered. That success equal to your merits & wishes may attend you, is the ardent desire of D[r] Sir, Y[r] affect[e] friend and obed[t] H[ble] Serv[t]   G[o]: WASHINGTON

PS. M[rs] [Martha] Washington & the rest of the family present their best wishes to you, and I have the pleasure to tell you that M[rs] [Catharine] Greene and your Children were well lately. Your letters to her, under cover to me, are regularly forwarded by the Post.

*Since writing the above I have received a letter from M[r] Custis dated the 29th Ult[o] in w[ch] are these words[:] "General Greene has by his conduct gained universal esteem, and possesses in the fullest degree the confidence of all ranks of People." He had then just returned from the Assembly at Richmond.[6]

ALS (PWacD).

1. NG had sent a report on the battle of Guilford Court House in his letter to Washington of 18 March, above (vol. 7: 451). For more on the battle, see NG to Samuel Huntington, 16 March, above. (Ibid., p. 433)

2. In a letter of 4 April, for example, Washington had urged Baron Steuben to turn his "attention again to the reinforcing Genl. Greene who will have occasion for every exertion that can possibly be made." (Fitzpatrick, GW, 21: 414) In a letter to the president

of Congress of 8 April, he had asked to have the Pennsylvania line's march to the South "facilitated" and Moylan's Dragoons "recruited, equipped and marched without delay." (Ibid., p. 431)

3. NG had warned in his letter to Washington of 18 March that Steuben might "think himself injurd" by the Marquis de Lafayette's superseding him in command. On Lafayette's original mission to Virginia and the failure of the plan to attack Gen. Benedict Arnold's army with a joint, Franco-American force, see Steuben to NG, first letter of 4 March, above (vol. 7: 390). Steuben had written NG on 22 February, above (ibid., p. 333), about his idea to join NG with a detachment of recruits from Virginia.

4. On Gen. Daniel Morgan's victory at Cowpens, see Morgan to NG, 19 January, above (vol 7: 152–55). Washington had acknowledged NG's report of the battle in a letter of 27 February, above (ibid., p. 363).

5. The mutiny of the Pennsylvania line is discussed at James Madison to NG, 13 January, above (vol. 7: 116). In his letter of 18 March, above, NG wrote Washington that although a member of Congress blamed the mutiny on the "cruelty of the officers," NG suspected it to be more a result of "indulgence" of the troops.

6. John Parke Custis was Washington's stepson. The letter has not been found.

* * *

¶ [GENERAL GREENE'S ORDERS, "Camp Sand Hills, four Miles from Camden," S.C., 19 April 1781. The troops are to receive provisions and rum. The army will march "Tomorrow" at 4 A.M. Maj. [Edmund M.] Hyrne is to be "respected and obeyed as a Volunteer Aid-de-camp." Lamar Orderly Book (OClWHi) 1 p.]

¶ [TO GENERAL JOHN BUTLER. From Headquarters [near Camden, S.C.], 19 April 1781. NG just received Butler's letter of 11 April. The army arrived within "three Miles" of Camden at 4 P.M. "this afternoon." NG has just heard from Maj. [Pinketham] Eaton, who is "on this side of Pedee," en route to the army.[1] NG is pleased that Eaton is coming forward, "notwithstanding the defect in his Arms," because [Col. James] Read's militia will soon be discharged. Advises Butler not to "form any large Magazine" in North Carolina, as "they become objects for the enemy." No more than a third of the bacon that is being collected in Wake County should be stored at Deep River; the rest should be sent to the army if Butler can get wagons.[2] ADfS (MiU-C) 1 p.]

1. Eaton's letter, dated 17 April, is above.
2. Butler replied on 26 April, below.

* * *

To Colonel Henry Lee, Jr.

Dear Sir   [near Camden, S.C.] 19th [April 1781]

We are here within two Miles of Camden and shall march to Log Town in the morning which is within half a mile of their advance works.

On our march I receivd your letter of yesterday, and Doctor [Matthew] Irvin is also arrivd. In your letter you request a field piece which the Doctor repeats. At present I am afraid the risque of sending it would be too great as we cannot afford a sufficient guard, the Garrison of Camden being much greater than I expected. If you could detach a guard for it, and no intelligence comes from Lord Cornwallis that forbids it, I will send a piece immediately; and it will be commanded by Capt [Samuel] Finley.

From Doctor Irvins account I think the field piece will not answer your expectations, and the only certain way of reducing the Garrison is to cut them off from Water.

Could you take the piece over the Santee with you should I send it, please to inform me?[1] I have heard nothing from General [Thomas] Sumter or Lord Cornwallis since the 9th. The latter was then at Wilmington [N.C.]. Col Watson was on the 16th moving up towards the Cheraws; and within thirty miles of it, but on the East side of the river.[2]

Doctor Irvin mentions a party on their march from Charles Town. Is there not a sufficient body of Militia on the West side of the Santee to prevent their approach.[3] Try to send intelligence to General Sumter on the West side of the Santee where he is [to] take a position upon the Congaree. Yours   310 [NATHANAEL GREENE]
We are short of Ammunition but will spare a little to General Marian if he cannot get a supply in any other way.

AL (IHi). NG used code for his signature.
    1. Lee's reply is in his second letter of 20 April, below. Lee and Gen. Francis Marion had captured Ft. Watson by the time NG decided he could safely send them a field piece.
    2. On Col. John Watson's detachment, see Wade to NG, 19 April, below.
    3. Col. Nisbet Balfour, the British commandant at Charleston, reported to Lord Cornwallis in a letter of 20 April that he had sent Maj. Archibald McArthur "with the Debris of the British to Pocotaligo, in order to cover that country." Balfour was now planning to have McArthur move to Dorchester, "where a post must be established to prevent the enemy coming to our gates." (PRO 30/11/5)

*   *   *

¶ [TO GENERAL JETHRO SUMNER. From "Camp 4 Miles from Camden," S.C., 19 April 1781. Has Sumner's letter of 8 April. Allows him to select a rendezvous site for the recruits. One that is "secure from the Enemy, and can best afford supplies" would be "the most proper and the most agreeable."[1] NG is confident that Sumner will "pay every attention" to collecting, organizing, and equipping the recruits as quickly as possible. "The present moment is big with importance to this Country, and while the tide of sentiment is in our favor, it should be industriously improved." If necessary, NG will advance two months' pay to those officers who are "arranged for immediate service." It would be better, though, if Sumner could obtain the money from the state, "as the military chest is very low."[2] LS (NcU) 2 pp.]
    1. An outbreak of smallpox complicated Sumner's efforts to fix a rendezvous site. (See his letter to NG of 1 May, below.)
    2. In his reply of 1 May, Sumner said nothing more about paying the North Carolina Continental officers.

*   *   *

To General Thomas Sumter

Sir   H^d Q^{rs} [near Camden, S.C.] April 19th 1781.

The Army has arrived and taken a position within three Miles of Camden. The Country is barren, and promises us no hope of support. My greatest dependence is on you for supplies of Corn and Meal. Both of these Articles are immediately wanted, and unless you can furnish me with them it will be impossible for me to keep my position.

I want to know very much your situation, and how you have disposed of yourself, so as to cooperate with our Army on any particular emergency.[1] I am sir with great esteem Your most hble serv^t

NATH GREENE

LS (Sumter Papers: DLC).
  1. To NG's consternation, Sumter did not reply until 25 April, below.

*   *   *

¶ [FROM GENERAL JOHN BUTLER, Camp at Ramsey's Mill, N.C., 19 April 1781. Has dependable intelligence that "the Enemy were Crossing Cape Fear [River] to Wilmington" about "5 or 6 days a go." Is not sure if this was the main body of Lord Cornwallis's army.[1] The commissioner of Cumberland County is "laying in corn" at local mills and expects to have 300 cattle collected soon. Butler has directed him to provide good grazing for the cattle until NG sends orders "for driving them."[2] Asks where to send five enemy prisoners captured by "Some of the good people of Bladen County as the Enemy marched Down."[3] ALS (MiU-C) 1 p.]
  1. As seen at Rowan to NG, 18 April, above, it was the main body of Cornwallis's army that had crossed.
  2. NG sent George Fletcher directions concerning the cattle on 14 May, below.
  3. NG's instructions concerning the prisoners have not been found.

¶ [FROM COLONEL ALEXANDER HAMILTON, Headquarters, New Windsor, N.Y., 19 April 1781. Has been "unpardonably delinquent" in failing to write before, but his "matrimonial occupations" have left him little "leisure or inclination for any other."[1] Does not know much about opinions "out of the army" but believes that NG's conduct is "universally approved" and his "reputation is progressive." How long this will last, "the wheel of fortune will have too much part in determining." Can say little of the army's prospects "here." Few recruits have arrived, so he fears the campaign in the North will "be a defensive one." [Robert Hanson] Harrison has left Washington's staff to become chief justice of Maryland.[2] Hamilton is about to leave, too. "This my Dear General is not an affair of calculation but of feeling." NG may "divine the rest" but should keep it to himself.[3] The enemy have become so proficient in intercepting the mails that Hamilton must be "cautious" for fear of seeing what he writes printed in "Rivingtons Gazette."[4] In a postscript, asks if there is anything worth his while in the Southern Army. "You know I shall have to be nominally a soldier."[5] ALS (Hamilton Papers: DLC) 2 pp.]
  1. As noted at NG to Hamilton, 10 January, above (vol. 7: 87), Hamilton had married Elizabeth Schuyler in December 1780.

2. Harrison had served as Washington's secretary since 1776.

3. Angered by a reprimand from Washington, Hamilton had resigned as his aide in February but was still performing some duties in Washington's military family. (Freeman, *GW*, 5: 259–60; Idzerda, *Lafayette Papers*, 4: 17n) A few days after writing this letter to NG, Hamilton left Washington's headquarters altogether. (Mitchell, *Hamilton*, pp. 241–42)

4. The captured letters of American leaders were often printed in James Rivington's *Royal Gazette*.

5. No reply from NG has been found. On 31 July, after threatening to resign his commission, Hamilton was given the command of a battalion of light infantry from the New York line. (Mitchell, *Hamilton*, pp. 244–46)

¶ [FROM ROBERT LANIER, Surry County, N.C., 19 April 1781. The "Commissioners appointed to Treat with the Cherokees and Chickasaws" have sent a message to the Cherokee chiefs, proposing a cessation of hostilities and a conference to arrange a prisoner exchange.[1] The Chickasaw will be invited to send an ambassador to the proposed conference. The commissioners believe "so great a business" requires "money in hand and Necessary Provisions and Stores." NG is asked to give the bearer instructions as to "where and to whom to apply" for the needed articles.[2] Denies a report that "the late rupture with the Cherokees was Occationed by the incroachments on their Lands." The Virginia government has documents that prove it was "a measur[e] of the British Generals."[3] Asks for "Intilijence" about the "progress" of American arms "towards Ninety Six [S.C.] & Georgia."[4] ALS (NcD) 2 pp.]

1. For more on the commissioners, see NG's letter of 26 February, above, appointing them. (Vol. 7: 351) As noted there, the conference took place in July. (See also note at Shelby to NG, 2 July, below.)

2. NG replied on 28 April, below.

3. The documents to which Lanier referred may have included a deposition from William Springstone, a Virginia trader, who asserted that a Cherokee chief named Raven had told him of receiving a "War Talk" from Thomas Brown, the British Indian commissioner. According to Springstone, Raven had agreed to "go to War immediately with the Inhabitants of Virginia and Carolina." (*Calendar of Va. State Papers*, 1: 446–47) Historians believe the attacks were incited by the British. (See, for example, O'Donnell, *Southern Indians*, p. 111.)

4. NG sent no intelligence in his reply.

*   *   *

From Colonel Henry Lee, Jr.

My dear Gen[l]   Scotts Lake [S.C.] 19th April [1781]

I wrote you yesterday, advising of my prospects here. A few hours after[,] I dispacthed Doctor Irvin to you, that no want of information might loose me the aid I asked.[1]

Three public reasons operate on my mind forcibly & makes me exceedingly anxious to reduce this post. 1st You entered this country to conquer. I wish not to contradict this intention in the least & shall be miserable if I am obliged to do it.

2d There are forty of the principal torys enclosed in the works. Their captivity would be attended with happy consequences to our distressed friends between the Santee & Pedee. 3 The sword^s pistols & other military stores which we must possess by conquest.[2] Lt Slator of Lord Rawdons Corps has the honor to bear this.[3] He will be exceedingly useful in his information. I have the honor to be most respectfully Your ob^t S^er HENRY LEE JUN

Col Watson on the 17th was marching up the Pedee & was at Hicory Grove.[4]

ALS (MiU-C).

1. As seen in NG to Lee, this date, above, Dr. Matthew Irvine had reached camp, as had Lee's letter.

2. As seen in Francis Marion to NG, first letter of 23 April, below, Marion and Lee did capture Ft. Watson.

3. A muster roll of Lord Rawdon's regiment, the Volunteers of Ireland, dated 24 February–24 April 1781 lists "James Slater" as quartermaster. (National Archives of Canada, RG 8, "C" Series, Vol. 1887) This officer's name was spelled various ways in muster rolls of the Volunteers of Ireland, but most commonly appeared as "Slater." (See ibid., vol. 1886, pp. 1, 3–4, 19, 30–31, 54–54A, 59; vol. 1887.) Marion also wrote NG concerning Slater—whom he called "Slater"—in his second letter of 23 April, below.

4. For a more detailed account of Col. John Watson's movements, see note at Wade to NG, immediately below.

* * *

¶ [FROM COLONEL THOMAS WADE, "Cherraws," S.C., 19 April 1781. Has NG's letter of 18 April. Reports that the party "under Watson," which had advanced to within thirty miles of Cheraws, has retreated, "Seemingly in Confusion," although "there wass no troops in front of them." They moved in such a hurry that they reportedly abandoned a wagon that had become stuck. Wade speculates that Watson retreated when he heard of NG's movements.[1] Reports that [Gen. Francis] Marion and Col. [Henry] Lee crossed Lynches Creek "last fryday"; their "Object is not Known."[2] Wade has discharged most of the militia from Anson and Richmond Counties, N.C., that he "ordered down" after hearing of Watson's advance. Has kept a few men to drive "Stock" to the army. He cannot get wagons to haul provisions to camp and is hard-pressed "to gitt them" for the mills. Promises not to detain any wagons that "comes for Supplys." Has sent his son, who is his assistant purchasing commissary, to aid NG. In a postscript, adds that the man he sent to obtain intelligence of Lord Cornwallis's movements has not yet returned. ALS (MiU-C) 3 pp.]

1. Col. John Watson's move up the Pee Dee had been the final, ragged conclusion to a badly coordinated attempt by the British to destroy Gen. Francis Marion's force. The plan involved a pincer movement in which Col. Welbore Ellis Doyle moved down the Santee River from Camden while Watson drove up the Santee, intending to trap Marion between them. The operation began in the first weeks of March and went awry almost from the beginning. Watson, moving toward Marion from Nelson's Ferry, endured almost constant sniping and several ambushes from Marion's partisans and decided to fall back to Georgetown and regroup. In the meantime, while Marion was occupied by Watson, Doyle successfully penetrated into Marion's "home" area and destroyed his

base at Snow Island. (For more on the raid, see note at Wade to NG, 2 April, above.) Before he could engage Marion himself or link up with Watson, Doyle was recalled to Camden by Lord Rawdon. As Marion belatedly redirected his troops toward Doyle, Watson's detachment, now reinforced, began a move up the Pee Dee River. Watson's advance coincided with a rising of the Loyalists in the area of the Little Pee Dee River, and Watson soon commanded a force estimated at 900 men. With nothing to impede him, he marched quickly up the Pee Dee, arriving at Catfish Creek on 9 April. There, however, he received intelligence that Henry Lee's detachment had arrived in the area, and he immediately began a hasty retreat. Watson, obviously frightened, abandoned his artillery, destroyed his heavy baggage, and fell back toward Georgetown by a round-about route, clearly demonstrating, according to one of Marion's biographers, how much he "dreaded" the partisan leader. (James, *Marion*, pp. 105–8; quote on p. 108) In his own account of the campaign, Watson said he had retreated quickly—covering fifty miles in one day—but contended that it was not fear for the safety of his detachment that led him to move to Georgetown. He claimed instead that he did it to help Rawdon, whom he believed to be in considerable danger, by trying to force NG to send troops in pursuit of Watson's detachment and thereby reduce NG's "collective force." (Watson to unnamed correspondent, no date, Clinton Papers, MiU-C) Watson received orders at Georgetown to join Rawdon in Camden and did so on 7 May. (For more on Watson's march to Camden, see Marion to NG, 6 May, below.)

2. "Last fryday" was 13 April; for more on the operations of Lee and Marion, see Marion's first letter to NG of 23 April, below.

¶ [**FROM ROBERT WALTON**, Prince Edward County, Va., 19 April [1781]. Returns NG's certificate and encloses a letter from the governor of Virginia explaining why the state has not paid the drafts that NG sent to Walton. Asks for drafts on Maryland and Pennsylvania instead. Walton is an agent for the Georgia delegates to Congress, who are required to return to their state by 1 May to stand for re-election and are "destitute of the Needfull to carry them" there.[1] If he has to wait for the Virginia Assembly to meet and "Squable a month or two before any thing is done," he may not get the money for six months, and that will not "answer the purpose." NG "will readyly see the Necessity" for granting Walton's request. The price of James River tobacco is 266 and 2/3 dollars per hogshead and much higher in the "Northen States"; the draft, if Walton can obtain it, will probably be paid in money rather than tobacco. Also requests a certificate and warrant "in the same way if Conveneant" for one of his neighbors.[2] ALS (MiU-C) 3 pp.]

1. In a letter of 1 April, Walton wrote Gov. Thomas Jefferson that he had sold horses to the army that had originally been purchased for the Georgia delegates; in payment, NG had given him a draft on Virginia for 126,000 weight of James River tobacco. (Boyd, *Jefferson Papers*, 5: 316–17) Jefferson replied the next day that he was not authorized to pay for horses until the Virginia Assembly reconvened. (Ibid., pp. 323–24)

2. NG replied on 30 April, below.

¶ [**FROM GEORGE WASHINGTON**, New Windsor, N.Y., 19 April 1781. Has NG's letter of 17 March, enclosing one to Congress of the 16th. "The motives which induced you to hazard a battle appear to me to have been substantial."[1] Is pleased to learn from NG's "subsequent letter to Congress, that the retreat of Cornwallis in circumstances of distress, corresponded with your expectations."[2] Washington still believes that NG's "affairs" are "critically situated." The enemy "are accumulating a large force in the Southern states," and there is news that "a further detachment is preparing at New York to be commanded by [Sir Henry] Clinton himself." This force is reportedly destined for Delaware Bay, but Washington thinks "it is much more probably for Chesapeak or Cape Fear."[3] The Marquis [de Lafayette] will have informed NG of his orders to march southward and act in "concert" with NG.[4] Gen. [Arthur] St. Clair says 900 Pennsylvania Continentals were to have marched from York, Pa., on 16 April.[5] "You may be assured that we give you all the support in our power. I wish our means were more adequate." Washington is waiting "impatiently" for "definitive advices from Europe." Has heard "nothing certain since the Dutch war."[6] The "precariousness of conveyances by the post would make it dangerous to enlarge confidentially."[7] LS (Hamilton Papers: DLC) 2 pp.]

1. NG's reports to Samuel Huntington and Washington on the battle of Guilford Court House are above (vol. 7: 443, 445).

2. Washington undoubtedly referred to NG's letter to Huntington of 23 March, above (vol. 7: 464).

3. For more on the report, see note at Sharpe to NG, 7 April, above.

4. See Lafayette to NG, 17 April, above.

5. As noted at Washington to NG, 1 June, below, the Pennsylvania troops did not march until 26 May.

6. As seen at Mathews to NG, 30 April, below, "definitive advices" arrived soon after Washington wrote this letter. On the declaration of war between England and Holland, see note at Washington to NG, 21 March, above (vol. 7: 459).

7. Loyalist bands were frequently capturing mail sent from Washington's camp. (See also, Hamilton to NG, this date, above.)

¶ [FROM GENERAL EZEKIEL CORNELL OF THE BOARD OF WAR, "War Office" [Philadelphia], 20 April 1781. The board has received NG's letter of 30 March. The members "feel" the army's distresses and will "chearfully lend every Assistance," but "present prospects are by no means flattering." They enclose returns of clothing and stores that have been sent "in good order" to NG's army.[1] The clothing is intended "Solely for the regular Troops," and they have "flattered" themselves that it will be adequate for the comfort of the men. They cannot clothe the militia and are "fully satisfied" with what NG has done "on this Subject." ALS (MiU-C) 2 pp.]

1. The return is not with the letter, but it may have been one prepared by Col. Christian Febiger, dated 21 March, of "stores sent to the Southern Army." There is a copy in PCC, item 39, vol. 3: 417, DNA.

¶ [FROM MAJOR ROBERT FORSYTH, Richmond, Va., 20 April 1781. He left Fredericksburg two days after receiving NG's letter of 31 March and is "thus far" on his way to the army. Has stopped only to purchase "a couple Pipes wine" for the army's use.[1] ALS (MiU-C) 1 p.]

1. A pipe was a cask equivalent to two hogsheads, or 126 gallons. (OED)

¶ [FROM COLONEL PETER HORRY, "Camp before Fort Watsone on Santee Lake," S.C., 20 April 1781. Gives "a Minute detail" of his "Conduct & Service" to prove that an injustice has been done and that he should be ranked senior to Col. [William] Henderson.[1] ALS (MiU-C) 5 pp.]

1. NG's reply has not been found.

¶ [FROM CAPTAIN NATHANIEL IRISH,[1] Prince Edward Court House, Va., 20 April 1781. Has moved the laboratory from Westham to Prince Edward Court House, as ordered; asks if he should establish it "on a permanent and extensive Plan" or if it is likely to be relocated again. He will do all he can to get ammunition and military stores "prepared," but NG will understand that after moving the laboratory "in so poor a Country," it will take "some time" to get "Business under way."[2] ALS (MiU-C) 1 p.]

1. Irish commanded the artificers at the laboratory. He also mistakenly thought that he held an appointment as commissary of military stores and added that title to his signature.

2. NG had been waiting impatiently for the relocation of the laboratory to Prince Edward Court House since sending orders on the subject to Col. Charles Harrison on 21 February, above. (Vol. 7: 327; see also NG to Steuben, 22 March, ibid., p. 463.) NG replied on 9 June, below.

¶ [FROM GENERAL ROBERT LAWSON, Prince Edward, Va., 20 April 1781. Captain Pendleton gave NG's letters of 7 and 11 April to Lawson on 18 April.[1] Lawson did not deliver NG's letter to the governor, as he promised he would, because the militia had already been ordered out by the time he reached home and he was "fatiegued & somewhat indispos'd."[2] Pendleton's arrival coincided with the "height of our Jubilee" and enabled Lawson to convince three of his field officers, who had decided they were "rather satiated with the repeat'd scenes of *Ease, & Tranquillity*" in Carolina, to agree to "farther Excursions." Pendleton will give NG the "minutia" of the affair. Lawson adds that he and his officers are "highly honor'd" by NG's "flattering approbation" of their conduct. Although service to their country induces them to "sacrifice (like others) domestick, & private views," their "greatest ambition" is to earn NG's "approbation." Lawson fears the militia will be slow to join NG because of "the very great difficulty" in getting wagons to transport provisions. He has "employ'd several persons" to obtain wagons and promises his "utmost exertions" to accomplish NG's wishes. He will see the governor about "equipment, & accomodation of the militia." Promises not to delay a moment "on this account" but wants to obtain the "accomodations" that the militia "have a right to claim, & such as the State can, or ought to supply." Promises to be at Salisbury, N.C., before the greater part of the militia arrive.[3] He will happily receive NG's orders. Hopes for the "completion" of NG's "grand object" and is honored to "participate." ALS (NjP) 4 pp.]

1. On the mission to Virginia of NG's aide, Nathaniel Pendleton, see NG to Pendleton, 11 April, above.

2. Lawson presumably was supposed to have delivered NG's letter to Gov. Thomas Jefferson of 27 March, above (vol. 7: 471). On the ordering out of the Virginia militia, see Jefferson to NG, 30 March, above.

3. As seen at ibid., few of the Virginia militia left the state. Lawson remained there to serve under the Marquis de Lafayette. (Lafayette to Lawson, 16 May, Idzerda, *Lafayette Papers*, 4: 493)

¶ [FROM COLONEL HENRY LEE, JR., "Scot[s] Lake," S.C., 20 April [1781]. Has written NG "thrice" from this place.[1] His goals in going there were to interrupt "communication" between the "lower posts" and Camden, to prevent "Col. W [John Watson]" from joining Lord Rawdon, and to "dispossess" the enemy.[2] Has already achieved the first two of those objects. Lee assumed that [Gen. Thomas] Sumter would be "adequate" in the Congaree area, as only "Col. [John] Small could be in his way."[3] Watson marched toward [Georgetown] on 17 April, but Lee thinks he may yet move toward "this place" or try to march up the west side of the Santee River.[4] Marion and Lee intend to follow Watson if he attempts either move. If Lord Cornwallis crosses the Pee Dee, Lee plans to join NG "in due season." Asks for 100 chosen riflemen and a company of regulars to assist in his plan.[5] ALS (MiU-C) 2 pp. Portions of the letter are in a number code. In most places, the translation is written over the corresponding number in the manuscript.]

1. Only two of Lee's previous letters from Scott's Lake have been found. They are above, dated 18 and 19 April.

2. It is not readily apparent from most of the letters Lee wrote NG from Scott's Lake that the siege of Ft. Watson was a joint operation, commanded by Gen. Francis Marion.

3. Col. John Small commanded a detachment stationed at Monck's Corner. It is not clear what Lee thought Sumter's force should have been able to accomplish. For more on the latter's activities, see Sumter to NG, 25 April, below.

4. Watson's destination was not decoded in this manuscript, but the letter immediately below indicates that it was Georgetown.

5. NG replied on 22 April, below.

¶ [FROM COLONEL HENRY LEE, JR., Scott's Lake, S.C., 20 April [1781], 10 P.M. Lee is "unhappy at the delay of the field pieces."[1] If he had them, "This post could be reduced in five moments" and all the other British installations "would share the same fate." He can cross the Santee with the cannon and promises to join NG "any where in season."[2] Col. [John] Watson, who is at Georgetown, "dare not move this side of the [Santee] river." Lee does not expect Watson to do anything until Col. [John] Small's detachment joins him.[3] Their combined force will number 600. If NG can send the requested reinforcements and some ammunition for [Gen. Francis] Marion's troops, who have fewer than two rounds per man, they will "beat Mʳ Watson and reduce Nelsons post where there is the greatest plenty of every article you want."[4] Thinks that "As to Lord Cornwallis, you will not hear of him in ten days time."[5] In a postscript, adds that no enemy reinforcements have arrived in Charleston and that Small has marched "this moment." Asks NG to write a "long letʳ" to Marion, who is feeling "[ne]glected."[6] Lee concludes: "Nothing can be done by me without the desired aid: much may be done with it." ALS (MiU-C) 3 pp. The letter is torn, and a portion of the postscript is missing.]

1. Lee's request for a field piece is in his letter of 18 April, above.

2. NG had asked if Lee's men could move the cannon across the Santee River. (See NG to Lee, 19 April, above.)

3. On Watson's movements, see note at Marion to NG, 6 May, below. Small, who commanded a force then at Monck's Corner, apparently did not join Watson.

4. As seen at ibid., Marion and Lee were unable to intercept Watson; nor did they capture the British post at Nelson's Ferry, some nine miles downstream from Ft. Watson. Before they could begin a siege, Rawdon marched to that post and evacuated and destroyed it. (See Marion to NG, 16 May, below.)

5. NG had agreed to send a field piece to Lee unless he received news that Lord Cornwallis was marching to South Carolina. (See NG to Lee, 19 April, above.) He wrote Lee on 22 April, below, that he was unable to send the artillery because of a sudden change of position that the army had had to make.

6. In a letter to Marion of 24 April, below, NG praised the South Carolinian's conduct.

¶ **[FROM COLONEL THOMAS WADE**, [Cheraws, S.C.], 20 April 1781.[1] Has sent 102 "fat," but "Small," hogs to NG at Camden. NG "mentiond" that he was sending Wade four wagons. Only three have arrived, and they have been "Dispatcht."[2] Wade could have used "Ten or a Dozen." Has no news. ALS (MiU-C) 1 p.]

1. No place was given, but Wade had written NG from Cheraws the day before.
2. NG's letter about the wagons has not been found.

¶ **[CAPTAIN NATHANIEL PENDLETON TO JOHN BROWNE.** From Prince Edward, Va., 21 April 1781. Needs forty wagons with drivers and teams to transport provisions to Salisbury, N.C., "agreeable to" NG's orders.[1] Pendleton believes it "proper" to call out wagons "agreeable to the plan of transportation adapted by Government" rather than impressing them.[2] Ten are needed immediately.[3] ADfS (MiU-C) 2 pp.]

1. As seen in Pendleton's Circular Letter of 14 April, above, the Virginia militia was to bring provisions when it marched to join NG's army. Only a small number of militiamen ever left Virginia.
2. On Virginia's plan of transportation, see Pendleton to Browne, 18 April, above.
3. By the date of this letter, British troops under Gen. William Phillips had begun an invasion of Virginia's interior, and state officials were hurrying to move public stores. The wagons that Pendleton requested were undoubtedly never sent.

¶ **[TO GENERAL JOHN BUTLER.** From "Camp before Camden," S.C., [21] April 1781.[1] Has Butler's letter of 15 April with its enclosures. Is sorry to hear the British have sent a detachment toward New Bern, N.C.[2] If they "push their operations that way," Butler should join forces with Gen. [Alexander] Lillington. NG has also asked Gen. [Jethro] Sumner to use Continental troops to protect "the Country."[3] If NG's "movements this way" do not "have the effect" that he "mentioned," he fears the British will "gain an advantage over us, as they are too strongly fortified at this place for us to storm it with the small force we have."[4] His "Maneuver," however, has "revived the sinking hopes of the people, and once more induced them to exert themselves for the recovery of their liberty." From Lillington's letter of 9 April, NG realizes that the army could not have been subsisted if it had tried to follow Lord Cornwallis to Wilmington; had it moved toward Halifax, moreover, "all the Southward would have given themselves up for lost." ADfS (NcU) 1 p.]

1. The date on the ADfS has been written over and appears to be the "28th." The editors have assigned 21 April as the date, based on the contents and a GWG Transcript. (CSmH)
2. One of the enclosed letters contained a false report that an enemy force from Wilmington had "salied on toward Newburn," with Lillington in pursuit. (Thomas Owen to Butler, 13 April, MiU-C)
3. NG's instructions to Lillington and Sumner are in letters of this date, both below.
4. On the "effects" that NG hoped his move into South Carolina would produce, see NG to Steuben, 2 April, above.

¶ **[TO GENERAL ALEXANDER LILLINGTON.** From "Camp before Camden," S.C., 21 April 1781. Is surprised that Lillington's letter of 9 April, which he received "last evening," was "so long on the way." Gen. [John] Butler reports that the British have sent troops "towards Newburn," N.C., so NG is ordering Butler "to move that way" and join Lillington.[1] He has also ordered Gen. [Jethro] Sumner to use the "Continental drafts" to aid Lillington.[2] NG finds by Lillington's letter—and was similarly advised earlier—"that an army could not be subsisted" near Wilmington. That would have kept him from "taking post" in the area. He moved "this way" because the people here "were so discouraged" and because he hoped to draw Lord Cornwallis after him. He also hoped to obtain better subsistence than was available in North Carolina, "unless we movd towards Halifax and that would have the appearance of giving up all the Southern world." NG does not have a large enough "force to storm this place" or "battering Cannon to beat down the works"; the "only way" to capture Camden "will be by starving them out which may be effected in time but it will be tedious."[3] ADfS (MiU-C) 1 p.]

1. See NG to Butler, this date, immediately above. As noted there, the report was false.

2. See NG to Sumner, this date, below.

3. In the letter immediately below, NG expressed doubt that he could starve out the garrison.

¶ [TO COLONEL THOMAS POLK. From "Camp before Camden," S.C., 21 April 1781. The garrison at Camden is "too large and the works" too strong to storm, nor can NG "starve" it out "without more men."[1] Asks Polk about prospects for a reinforcement from the Salisbury, N.C., district.[2] Wants a four-day supply of provisions laid in for 4,000 men at Charlotte. Is not sure if he gave Col. [William R.] Davie "instructions on this head"; if Davie has already given orders, Polk need not "trouble" himself further.[3] ADfS (MiU-C) 2 pp.]

1. On the strength of the garrison, see NG to Huntington, 22 April, below.

2. Polk's reply has not been found.

3. In a letter of 14 April, above, NG had ordered Davie to lay in provisions at Salisbury instead of Charlotte.

¶ [CAPTAIN WILLIAM PIERCE, JR., TO GENERAL CHARLES SCOTT. From Headquarters [before Camden, S.C.], 21 April 1781. NG has Scott's letter and permits him "to go on with Major [George] Benson to Lord Cornwallis."[1] NG wants to know the results of any negotiations between Scott and Cornwallis. ACyS (MiU-C) 1 p.]

1. Scott had written NG on 13 and 16 April, both above.

¶ [TO GENERAL JETHRO SUMNER. From "Camp before Camden," S.C., 21 April 1781. Since writing to Sumner "a day or two ago," NG has received word that an enemy detachment is moving toward New Bern, N.C.[1] If the report is true and these "operations" continue, Sumner is to collect all the Continental drafts from Hillsborough and the "lower district" for use "against the Enemy in that quarter." Urges him to "great activity and great industry." Sumner should inform Baron Steuben of his situation and apply to him for any equipment "that cannot be had" in North Carolina.[2] The garrison at Camden is "too large and the Works too strong" for NG's "little force" to storm, but the army's movements have "revived the hopes of the People." LS (NcU) 1 p.]

1. NG's letter to Sumner is above, dated 19 April. As noted at NG to Butler, this date, above, the information about the British movement was false.

2. Sumner replied on 1 May, below.

¶ [CAPTAIN NATHANIEL PENDLETON TO JOHN WATSON.[1] From Prince Edward, Va., 21 April 1781. Authorizes Watson, under NG's orders, to impress or obtain by other means 30,000 pounds of bacon, salted beef, or pork for the use of the Southern Army.[2] Watson should collect these provisions in counties as close to the Dan River as possible and have them delivered to Prince Edward in the wagons of "those who furnish" them. The wagon owners are to be told that they will be paid "ten Shillings specie, or the Value of the real depreciation p^r Day."[3] By the time these items are gathered, Watson is also to have 33,000 pounds of "good wheat flour, or Indian Meal" collected along the route between Prince Edward and Dix's Ferry, ordering the commissioners "under the specific tax Law" to provide them.[4] He should have wagons collected to "receive" these items, should load and take them "by the shortest road" to Salisbury, N.C., and should wait there for NG's orders.[5] Pendleton trusts in Watson's "Zeal" and hopes "the good People of Virginia, who have so freely spilt their Blood in the glorious Cause of America," will voluntarily "contribute every thing in their Power." If impressment is necessary, "as much gentleness and morderation as possible ought to be employed." ADfS (MiU-C) 3 pp. Subjoined to the letter is an order by Pendleton to the "County Lieutenants of the Counties near, as well as Prince Edward" to furnish Watson with "Necessary Guards."]

1. Watson was the deputy sheriff of Prince Edward County. (Herbert C. Bradshaw, *History of Prince Edward County, Virginia* [Richmond, Va.: The Dietz Press, 1955], p. 112)

2. On NG's orders, see NG to Pendleton, 11 April, above.

3. For more about the calling out of the wagons, see Pendleton to Browne, this date, above.

4. In regard to the commissioners, see Pendleton to Browne, 18 April, above.

5. As noted at Jefferson to NG, 30 March, above, most of the Virginia militia, for whom the provisions were intended, never left the state.

¶ [FROM COLONEL WILLIAM R. DAVIE, Charlotte, N.C., 21 April 1781. Fears "the rains have detained the supplies" from Salisbury.[1] Davie has just received NG's letter of 19 April [not found], informing him that the army is " 'Destitute of Provisions.' " Davie expected that there would be such a shortfall but "could not remedy" it; NG knows "how precarious and difficult a distant transportation by Wagons is." However, Davie will "put every thing in Motion" and join NG.[2] Asks that he be given the "earliest notice" if the army moves. Adds that "considerable collections might be made" along the Catawba River, in the vicinity of Rocky Mount "and between that and Camden," S.C. ALS (NNPM) 2 pp. Writing to NG on 26 April, below, Davie referred to "some dispatches from the Northward" that he had enclosed with this letter; they have not been found.]

1. On these supplies, see Davie to NG, 11 April, above.

2. Davie wrote NG on 23 and 26 April, both below, that provisions were on their way to the army. In the second of those letters, he again stated his intention to join NG.

¶ [FROM GENERAL FRANCIS MARION, "before Fort Watson Lake near Wright Bluff," S.C., 21 April 1781. Has just received NG's letter of the 17th. As soon as Capt. [James] Conyers arrived, Marion sent men to collect cattle for NG's army; Maj. [Alexander] Swinton has sent 100 head, and in three days NG should receive 100 more cattle and sixty hogs.[1] Hopes NG "will not want in future." Would have already told him of the enemy's strength "in this Country," but assumed that Col. [Henry] Lee, who joined Marion on 13 April, had informed NG of "every Surcomstance." Estimates the strength of various enemy detachments and garrisons, including Charleston, where he says there are fewer than 500 men. Encloses a letter from Col. [William] Harden, who has been "sent to the Southward with Seventy Choice men"; Harden's letter will "give the State in that part."[2] A "Small Detachment" that Marion sent to watch British "movements in Camden" has captured "a boat Loaded with Corn" and killed or taken the escort. The report that NG asked for is as follows: Marion sent Col. Hugh Horry across the Pee Dee with seventy men "to intercept" Loyalists attempting to join Watson. Horry's men "fell in with a party of thirty foragers & as many more to cover them." In a charge, they killed two and captured thirteen British, two Loyalists, and "two Negroes" without a loss. They had to retire "under a heavy fire" when enemy reinforcements arrived.[3] Swinton, who was left to watch Watson, reports that the latter is now marching toward Georgetown. Marion will send NG the earliest possible intelligence of British movements, "Perticularly from North Carolina." His own strength, including troops he has detached, is 300 men, but he expects reinforcements. He has been "in great want of Ammunition" for some time and would be "glad of a Supply." Wishes to cross the Santee River and "give the Inhabitants on that side" a chance to join him "if it woud not Interfer" with NG's plans.[4] LS (CSmH) 2 pp.]

1. On Conyers's mission, see NG to Marion, 4 April, above. On 21 April, Conyers wrote Capt. William Pierce that Swinton had sent fifty cattle and 100 hogs to Col. [Thomas] Wade. Conyers said he had given orders for the additional cattle and hogs collected by Marion's men to be sent "under a proper guard[;] those must be with you in three Days." (MiU-C)

2. As seen at Gen. Isaac Huger to Marion, 28 January, above (vol. 7: 208n), Harden was operating in the area south of Charleston. The enclosure was probably a letter that Harden had written Marion on 18 April, in which he reported several successful skirmishes with the enemy, culminating in the capture of Ft. Balfour. (The letter is printed in Gibbes, *Documentary History*, 3: 53–55.) Col. Nisbet Balfour wrote Lord Rawdon on 26 April that Harden "has over run all the Country to the Southward of Dorchester with a very few men." (PRO 30/11/6)

3. The enemy foragers belonged to Col. Welbore Ellis Doyle's detachment, which had recently raided Marion's base at Snow Island. (Rankin, *Swamp Fox*, pp. 176–77) NG had asked for information about the engagement in his letter to Marion of 17 April, above.

4. NG replied on 24 April, below.

¶ [GENERAL GREENE'S ORDERS, Camp before Camden, S.C., Sunday, 22 April 1781. "Plundering and Marauding are again positively prohibited." Only "properly authorised" personnel are to take horses or cattle from the inhabitants. Animals taken from the enemy or as strays are to be considered public property and turned over to the quartermaster. Individuals and units "exposed to any extraordinary risque or Danger in obtaining any article of Public Utility" will receive "competent recompense." Lamar Orderly Book (OClWHi) 1 p.]

* * *

To Samuel Huntington,
President of the Continental Congress

Sir   Camp before Camden [S.C.] April 22[d] 1781.

In my last I informed your Excellency of Lord Cornwallis's precipitate retreat from Deep River, of the situation of our Army for the want of Provisions, and of the Virginia Militia's time of service having expired, which reduced our numbers greatly inferior to the Enemys.[1] Finding that I had not a force to pursue them further, and that our Army could not be subsisted either on the route the Enemy had marched, or in the lower Country, I thought it most adviseable to push my operations into South Carolina to recover the expiring hopes of the People; to divide with the Enemy the supplies of the Country, of which they had the entire command, to break up their little posts of communication, and if possible oblige Lord Cornwallis to return to the State for their protection. This last was the great object of the movement, and had we a force to prosecute the plan, I persuade myself it would take effect, but for want of which the matter remains doubtful. Upwards of five Months have I been in this department with nothing but the shattered remain[s] of a routed Army, except the addition of Col° [Henry] Lee's Legion and a couple of small detachments from Virginia, amounting to little more than a Regiment, and those without discipline, or even Officers to command them. In this situation with a temporary aid of militia, we have been struggling with a very unequal force under every possible disadvantage, and surrounded with every kind of distress.

We have run every hazard and been exposed to every danger not only of being beaten, but of being totally ruined. I have been anxiously waiting for succour, but the prospect appears to me to be remote, except the temporary aid of Militia, which is too precarious and uncertain to commence any serious offensive operations upon.

The more I enquire into the natural strength of North and South Carolina, either to form, or support an Army, the more I am persuaded they have been greatly over rated. More of the Inhabitants appear in the Kings interest than in ours; and the Country is so extensive and thinly inhabited that it is not easy either to draw any considerable force together, or subsist them when collected. The Militia in our interest can do little more than keep Tories in subjection, and in many places not that. These States were in a better condition to make exertions last Campaign than this; the well effected last year spent their time and their substance in fruitless exertions, and finding themselves unequal to the conflict, and their family's being exposed, and in distress, hundreds and hundreds of the best Whigs have left the Country. Last year it was full of resources; this it is almost totally exhausted; and the little produce that remains lies so remote, and the means of transportation so difficult to command, that it is next to an impossibility to collect it.

The Enemy have got a firmer footing in the Southern States than is generally expected. Camden, Ninety Six, and Augusta cover all the fertile parts of South Carolina and Georgia, and they are laying waste the Country above them, which will effectually secure those posts, as no Army can be subsisted in the neighbourhood to operate against them. Below, they have a great many intermediate posts of communication, for the purpose of awing the Country and commanding its supplies. Nor can I see how we are to reduce those capital Posts but with a superior Army in the field. I wish Congress not to be deceived respecting the Situation of things in the Southern department, and therefore I hope they will excuse the freedom I take. If more effectual support cannot be given than has been, or as I can see any prospect of, I am very apprehensive that the Enemy will hold their ground, not only of the Sea Ports but the interior Country. The conflict may continue for some time longer, and Generals [Thomas] Sumter and Marian [Francis Marion] deserve great credit for their exertions and perseverance, but their endeavors rather serve to keep the contest alive than lay a foundation for the recovery of the States.

We began our march from Deep River on the 7th, and arrived in the neighbourhood of Camden on the 19th. All the Country through which we past is disaffected, and the same Guards and escorts were necessary to collect Provisions and forage, as if in an open and avowed Enemies Country.

On our arrival at Camden we took post at Log Town, about half a mile in front of their Works, which upon reconnoitering were found to be much stronger than had been represented, and the garrison much larger. The Town is upon a plane covered on two sides by the River Wateree and Pine Tree Creek, the other two sides by a chain of strong Redoubts all nearly of the same size, and independant of each other. Our force was too small either to invest the Town or storm the Works, which obliged us to take a position at a little distance from it.

Before we began our march from Deep River I detached Lieu^t Col^o Lee with his Legion, and part of the 2^d Maryland Regiment to join General Marian to invest the Enemys Posts of communication upon the Santee, and one of their Posts is now invested called Fort Watson, and must fall if not relieved by a detachment of Lord Cornwallis's Army.[2]

I have been greatly disappointed in the force I expected to operate with me. Fifteen hundred Virginia Militia were called for immediately after the Battle of Gilford, having this present movement in contemplation at the time, and the State gave an order for a greater number than was required, but the busy season of the Year, and the great distance they have to march, prevents their coming to our assistance in time, if not in force.[3] General Sumter also engaged to have 1000 Men in the field by the 18th to operate with us, but the difficulty of collecting the Militia from the disagreable situation of their Familes, has prevented their embodying yet in any considerable force. These disappointments lay us under many disadvantages to say nothing worse. The Country is extremely difficult to operate in, being much cut to pieces by Deep Creeks, and impassible Morasses; and many parts are covered with such heavy timber and thick under brush as exposes an Army, and particularly detachments to frequent surprises.

The service has been so severe that it will be absolutely necessary to give the Army some relaxation soon; and therefore I lament the Delay which is occasioned at this time for want of sufficient force to invest all the Enemys Posts of communication. Our numbers are so reduced by the different Actions and skirmishes which have happened, and by the fatigue and hardships of the service, that we have but the shadow of an Army remaining; and this we are obliged to divide, to push our operations to any effect, tho' it is attended with danger, and may prove our ruin.

I am extremely mortifyed at the disappointment, which happened in Virginia in the plan of co-operation against Portsmouth between our good Ally, and the Marquis de la Fayette.[4] Success there would have given us great releif here, and I am persuaded that nothing can recover this Country out of the hands of the Enemy, but a similar plan in the Southern States. At present the Enemy have as full possession of Georgia and almost the whole of South Carolina as they can wish. The last accounts I had from Lord Cornwallis he lay at Wilmington, and his Army it was said was getting very sickly.[5]

I do myself the honor to inclose Gen[l] Lillingtons report respecting the Bladen Militia, Gen[l] [Andrew] Pickens's report of Major Dunlaps defeat by Col[o] Clarke, and Gen[l] Marians report of a part of Col[o] Watsons detachment defeated by Col[o] Horee.[6] I have the honor to be with great respect Your Excellencys most obed[t] humble serv[t]

NATH GREENE

LS (PCC, item 155, vol. 2: 39, DNA).

1. See NG to Huntington, 30 March, above.

2. Marion and Lee captured Ft. Watson the day after NG wrote this letter. (See Marion to NG, first letter of 23 April, below.)

3. As noted at Jefferson to NG, 30 March, above, most of the Virginia militia never joined NG.

4. For more about the failure of the Franco-American expedition to capture Gen. Benedict Arnold's detachment at Portsmouth, Va., see note at Steuben to NG, first letter of 4 March, above (vol. 7: 390n).

5. Robert Rowan wrote NG about illness in Cornwallis's army on 18 April, above.

6. NG enclosed a summary from an undated letter of Gen. Alexander Lillington's; the letter itself has not been found. Lillington reported that the Bladen County, N.C., militia "fell with great Spirit on the rear of Lord Cornwallis's Army" as it was retreating to Wilmington, killing thirteen and taking between fifteen and twenty prisoners. (PCC, item 155, vol. 2: 165, DNA; on the performance of the Bladen County militia, see also NG's Orders of 16 April, above.) The enclosure also included summaries of Pickens to NG, 8 April, reporting Col. Elijah Clarke's victory over Maj. John Dunlap's detachment; and of Marion to NG, 21 April, with a report of Col. Hugh Horry's engagement with a party from Col. Welbore Ellis Doyle's detachment. (PCC, item 155, vol. 2: 165, DNA; both letters are also above.)

To Colonel Henry Lee, Jr.

Dear Sir   [Before Camden, S.C. 22nd April 1781][1]

Last night I was informed that Colonel Watson was on his march by unfrequented ways from the Pedee with a view of throwing himself and party into Camden. We made a sudden movement this morning from the uper to the lower side of Camden by a circuitous route with an intention to intercept the Colonel and his party and have sent out parties in all directions to see if we can learn any thing of them. We shall continue in this position until we get intelligence whether Col Watson is on his march for this place or not.[2]

Our march was so sudden this morning, that Capt Pearce [William Pierce] forgot to take the book of Cyphers with him which obliges me to write without them; and the baggage is orderd to Lynches Creek[,] too far to send for it[,] and our artillery is there also. They are both distant 20 Miles from us; and I have no way of either sending you a field piece, or ammunition.[3] I wish your operations was over below as an investiture cannot fully take place until your arrival, and storming must be the last resort. General Sumter I have not heard of but imagine he must be on the Congarees a little above you. I wish you could learn where he is and inform me.[4] I wrote you the evening we got in the neighbourhood of Camden that it would be impossible to send you either Artillery or ammunition; you dont mention the receipt of the letter from which I fear it has fallen into the hands of the enemy and what still renders it more unfortunate is it was not in cyphers.[5]

The Express that brought your letter says you are building a *mount* by which you expect to drive the enemy out of their post.[6] In my letter I desird to be informed whether you had any way of getting the field piece over the Santee if there should be a necessity for your crossing. I beg your answer to this point in particular.[7]

Lord Cornwallis was at Wilmington on the 13th. Whether he will move this way is quite uncertain. A detachment from Wilmington is gone towards Newburn and I am afraid will push on to that place. Reports say from Virginia that General Philips has left Virginia with 2000 troops and come farther south.[8] This will render it very necessary to get intelligence from Charlestown. I have no news from the North-ward; and am not a little impatient to hear from the Pennsylvania line which I expect must be on this side Virginia by this t[ime] and is commanded by General Wayne.[9]

Keep a good lookout for Lord Cornwallis and for Watson also for fear the latter should not be coming this way. Yours

I am this moment informed that Col Watson crossed Black River two days ago and is gone down towards Nelsons Ferry. The Express can give you further particulars.[10]

ADf (IHi).

1. The date, taken from the docketing, is confirmed by NG's letter to Lee of 24 April, below; the place was determined by the docketing and the contents.

2. As seen in Lee to NG, first letter of 23 April, below, Col. John Watson's detachment was at Georgetown, S.C. On 24 April, NG moved the army back to the "uper" side of Camden. (See NG's Orders of that date, below.)

3. NG soon changed his mind and decided to send a field piece to Lee and Francis Marion. (See NG to Lee, 24 April, below.)

4. Gen. Thomas Sumter sent NG an account of his movements and location in a letter of 25 April, below.

5. NG had discussed the field piece and ammunition in his letter to Lee of 19 April, above.

6. On the tower, designed by Col. Hezekiah Maham and used in the capture of Ft. Watson, see Marion to NG, first letter of 23 April, below.

7. In his second letter of 20 April, above, Lee had assured NG that he could cross the Santee River with the cannon and join him "any where" NG desired.

8. Reports about troops from Lord Cornwallis's army marching toward New Bern, N.C., and Gen. William Phillips moving his force out of Virginia were false.

9. The Pennsylvania Continental troops were still camped at York, Pa., and did not march until 26 May. (See note at Washington to NG, 1 June, below.)

10. As seen in Lee to NG, first letter of 23 April, below, the report was false.

*   *   *

¶ [TO GEORGE WASHINGTON. From Headquarters [before Camden, S.C.], 22 April 1781.[1] Encloses a copy of his letter to Congress, showing "the Miserable situation of our affairs."[2] LS (Washington Papers: DLC) 1 p.]

1. The place was taken from other letters of this date.

2. See NG to Huntington, this date, above.

¶ [FROM GEORGE WASHINGTON, New Windsor, N.Y., 22 April 1781. Has NG's letter of 29 March.[1] Remarks: "The sequel of Cornwallis's late movements do as much honor to you as discredit to him. He is so far baffled. 'Tis deplorable that the composition of your force did not enable you to make it more. The project you had adopted of endeavouring to transfer the War has many favorable sides. I am persuaded you have adopted it on sound principles."

Gen. [Arthur] St. Clair reports that "a disappointment in procuring Money" will delay the march of the Pennsylvania Continentals to join NG by at least "a fortnight from this time." The detachment will number nearly 1,000 men. St. Clair "does not give a flattering account of those that are to follow," as recruiting in Pennsylvania is "feeble and ineffectual."[2] Washington assumes that St. Clair keeps NG "punctually" advised "of his operations."[3] Hopes NG can find employment for "Major Mcpherson," who came south with the Marquis de Lafayette. NG knows McPherson's "merit," and the latter recently detected "a pretty extensive channel of supply to the enemy"—an "important" service, which he performed with "address and hazard."[4] LS (MiU-C) 2 pp.]

1. NG's letter is above (vol. 7: 481–82).

2. St. Clair reported that the detachment would number 960 rank and file. (St. Clair to Washington, 6 April, GW Papers, DLC) In the end, as noted at Washington to NG,

1 June, below, money problems and other difficulties delayed the march of the Pennsylvanians until 26 May.

3. As seen in NG to Lee, this date, above, NG had received no news of the Pennsylvania line. St. Clair wrote him on 6 May, below.

4. Maj. William MacPherson, a former officer in the British army, had used his knowledge of British personnel to persuade two Loyalists to reveal details of a supply network originating in the Maryland tidewater. (Lafayette to Washington, 8 April, Idzerda, *Lafayette Papers*, 4: 12) MacPherson remained with Lafayette, who hoped to get him the command of a corps of black troops that was being proposed to the Maryland legislature; when that idea was rejected, Lafayette placed him in charge of a small legionary corps. (Ibid., pp. 494, 499; Lafayette to NG, 27 June, below)

¶ [**GENERAL GREENE'S ORDERS**, "Camp before Camden near Kershaws Mill," S.C., Monday, 23 April 1781. The quartermaster is to "receive and brand all Public Horses" and distribute them, according to their "respective qualities," to the cavalry or wagon service. Premiums will be paid in "Spanish Milled Dollars" or their equivalent for horses that are taken from the enemy and assigned to the cavalry or wagon service. Horses taken from the "Inhabitants, or out of the Woods" are to be "delivered up"; persons caught "hereafter" with such horses "in their possession" will be "punished as Marauders." No "Negro is to be taken on any pretence unless he is armed or Serving with the Enemy, or as a Spy." All "Negro's so taken" are to be turned over to the provost guard and "disposed of as circumstances may require." Lamar Orderly Book (OClWHi) 2 pp.]

¶ [**CAPTAIN WILLIAM PENDLETON TO WILLIAM MCCRAW**.[1] From Peytonsburg, Va., 23 April 1781. Gives the route by which NG wants supplies sent to Salisbury, N.C., for the Southern Army. ADS (MiU C) 1 p.]

1. McCraw was an assistant deputy quartermaster, in charge of the "District of the Rivers, Dan & Stanton." His "principal post" was at Peytonsburg. (*Calendar of Va. State Papers*, 2: 159, 160) On the reverse side of this letter, Pendleton wrote: "Orders left at Peytonsburg."

* * *

To General Thomas Sumter

Dr Sir   Camp before Camden [S.C.], April 23^d 1781

I wrote you a day or two ago of our arrival in the neighbourhood of Camden, and desired to know your strength and situation, to which I have received no Answer, and am not a little afraid that it has fallen into the hands of the Tories.[1] Since I wrote you I have critically examined the fortifications of this place and find them much superior to what I expected. The Garrison from the best intelligence I can get is also much stronger than I expected; and I had the mortification to hear yesterday that the South Carolina royalists had the Day before thrown themselves into the place from Ninety Six.[2] Our numbers are not equal to a full investiture of the place without dividing our force too much to be secure from insult in any part. This will give the Enemy an opportunity to draw what reinforcements they please from other posts. I must depend entirely upon you to secure us on the quarter from Ninety Six & Charlestown on the West side of the Wateree, and General Marian [Francis Marion] on the East side from George Town and Charles Town.

General Marion and Col⁰ Lee are at Nelsons Ferry, they have closely invested the fort at that place upon the Lake, but for want of Cannon I am not a little afraid they will fail of success, as the Garrison appears to be well supplied with provision, and the situation don't admit of storming the Works.³

I long to hear from you that I may know how to take my measures respecting Provision and other matters.⁴ I beg you to keep two or three of your People constantly in Camp with us that I may have it in my power to forward you the earliest intelligence, and I beg you to get all the information you can from Charles Town as there are flying reports of General Philips having saild from Virginia to the Southward with 2000 Men. The arrival of this force, if it be true, is a matter highly interesting to the success and safety of our operations to be ascertained as soon as possible.⁵ With esteem & regard I am Dʳ sir Your most obᵗ servᵗ   NATH GREENE

NB. The reinforcement which came in yesterday was from the Congree's.⁶

LS (Sumter Papers: DLC).
1. Sumter did receive NG's letter of 19 April, above. (See Sumter to NG, 27 April, below.)
2. A detachment from the South Carolina Royalist Regiment had slipped into Camden from Ninety Six on 22 April. Lord Rawdon, the commander at Camden, wrote Lord Cornwallis on 26 April that he had been "obliged to abandon" the ferry across the Wateree River but had "fortunately secured the passage of that Corps into Camden." (PRO 30/11/6) The troops of this detachment served as Rawdon's reserve in the battle of Hobkirk's Hill on the 25th. (Ibid.) Sumter discussed his failure to intercept them in his reply of 27 April, below.
3. Ft. Watson, which Marion and Lee did capture, was at Scott's Lake, some nine miles up the Santee River from Nelson's Ferry, where the British had a small post. (On the capture of Ft. Watson, see Marion to NG, first letter of this date, below.)
4. Sumter wrote NG on 25 April, below.
5. The report that Gen. William Phillips's corps had left Virginia was false.
6. See note 2, above.

*   *   *

¶ [COLONEL ARTHUR CAMPBELL TO CAPTAIN NATHANIEL PENDLETON, Washington, Va., 23 April 1781. Has Pendleton's letter of 16 April.¹ It would give Campbell great "satisfaction to hear of the expulsion of the enemy from the Southern States," and he will do all he can to aid "our gallant Commander, whose late wise and patient conduct, must be the admiration of Ages." Campbell's county is in a "peculiar" situation, however. Two of its sides are "a frontier," and it is "Pressed hard by the Indians both from the

South and North." Counties that are more "secure" should provide their full quota of men. Gives a "hint" that Gen. [Daniel] Morgan "ought to be in the Army, to draw out, and give confidence to our Rifle men."[2] NG should know that the success of the negotiations with the Cherokee depends on cutting off their communications with the British agent at Augusta.[3] Several hundred of their women and children have moved into Georgia, where they are subsisted at British expense while the men steal large numbers of horses and murder "defenceless persons." The "savage war" now being fought did not originate with the frontiersmen, as Campbell understands "has been insinuated," but was "a scheme of the British General to mount his Cavalry &c and to employ some of our best Militia in opposing the Indians, in order to facilitate his operations in the low Country."[4] Notwithstanding their "disadvantages," the frontiersmen have sent a peace proposal to the "Chiefs" and employed an agent "to amuse and divide" the Cherokee nation. The outcome of those overtures will soon be known and will determine what kind of force Campbell can send to the army.[5] ALS (InU-Li) 3 pp.]

1. Campbell had received a copy of Pendleton's circular letter. (See Pendleton to Certain County Lieutenants in Virginia, 14 April, above.)

2. As seen in Morgan to NG, 11 April, above, Morgan was not yet well enough to return to the field.

3. A force of South Carolina and Georgia irregulars had already laid siege to the headquarters of Thomas Brown, the British agent at Augusta. (Cashin, *King's Ranger*, p. 130)

4. Robert Lanier wrote NG on 19 April, above, that the government of Virginia had documents to prove that the British were behind the renewal of hostilities with the Southern Indian tribes.

5. On the negotiations, see notes at Lanier to NG, 19 April, above, and at Shelby to NG, 2 July, below.

* * *

From Colonel William R. Davie

D[r] Gen[l]   Charlotte [N.C.] Ap. 23[d] [1781]

No person feels your situation more sensibly than I do, but I hope your distresses are in some measure relieved by the Arrivals from Salisbury and this place; as twenty eight waggons have moved off to the Army within these ten days past; taking the route by Lynches Creek no doubt has detained them.[1]

Twelve hundred bushels more will be put in motion from this place by Thursday next [i.e., 26 April], which has been borrowed with great difficulty, in small quantities thro the Country; when this is fairly under way, and a disposition made in the Back-country for a regular supply, I will join you immediately.[2]

This country is really exhausted[.] The distance to Wilks and Surry counties lying under the Mountains so great, and transportation so difficult, our supplies, while you are at that point will ever be precarious, being in a country that affords nothing itself.

Scarcity of Horses is always a natural consequence in every Country that has been the scene of war. This circumstance, with the busy season of the year, accounts for the difficulty of procuring transportation from these Counties: a good Quarter Master is much wanted at this Post.

The live-stock of this place are too poor for Service; I hope some may be procured in S° Carolina.

Much could be done—but *transportation*—no *transportation* is the grand difficulty. I am with sincere Esteem Dear Sir y^r hum^bl servn^t

WILLIAM R. DA[VIE]

ALS (NcU).

1. According to Henry Lee, "a comfortable supply of provisions" arrived at NG's camp on the morning of 25 April. (Lee, *Memoirs*, 2: 58)

2. In his letter of 26 April, below, Davie said he expected to be in camp on 29 or 30 April.

From Colonel Henry Lee, Jr.

[Scotts Lake, S.C.] 23^d April [1781][1]

Gen. Marion & myself agree in opinion that with a field piece, the addition of one hund^d chosen riflemen & fifty infantry we could in six days perform the most essential service.

I am miserable to find by your let^r of yesterday that no field piece is on the way. I am confident you are losing by its delay great & certain advantages. Watson is in Geo: Town & dare not venture toward^s Cambden.[2] When he joins Small he will have six hund^d men provided he evacuates G. Town[,] Nelsons & Biggin Church.[3] He will not do this & can have only 400 effectives. This force we can manage with the little assistance I request.

If you do not permit us to improve this opportunity you will get very little advantage by coming into this state, only the drawing Cornwallis after you.

Passive advantages will not arouse the people[.] I therefore wait your farther orders as I am unwilling to relinquish victory when so easily obtained,

As to the investiture of Cambden, my force can be of little service, & I do not believe they [the British] are destitute of provision.

Gen: Marion has four hund^d men here & has not four hund^d cartridges so I am destitute.[4]

No man ever was more deceived than you are concerning Watson. He did [not] even dare to cross Pedee but went forty miles out of his way across Wakemau & the bay.[5]

They are very desponding & viger on our part would accomplish great matters. Yours aff^y   HENRY LEE JUN

I got your let^r attended to. We can go any where with a six pounder.[6]

ALS (MiU-C).

1. As seen in Francis Marion's letters to NG of this date, below, Lee and Marion were at Ft. Watson, on Scott's Lake; the year was taken from the docketing and is confirmed by the contents.

2. Watson later marched 500 men into Camden to reinforce Lord Rawdon. (See NG to Sumter, second letter of 6 May, below.)

3. Col. John Small commanded a detachment, estimated to number 250 men, that was stationed at Monck's Corner. (Col. Nisbet Balfour to Lord Cornwallis, 20 April, PRO 30/11/5; Balfour to Maj. Archibald McArthur, 10 April, PRO 30/11/109) Small apparently remained at that post and did not unite with Watson.

4. Marion captured enough ammunition at Ft. Watson to resupply his men. (See Marion to NG, second letter of this date, below.)

5. NG told Lee in his letter of 22 April, above, that he had received information of Watson's detachment approaching Camden. According to Lee, Watson had marched to Georgetown in a northeasterly loop, across the Waccamaw River and down Winyah Bay.

6. In his letter of 22 April, NG asked Lee to scout for movements toward Camden by Watson and Lord Cornwallis and to obtain intelligence from Charleston. Lee had presumably "attended to" those requests.

* * *

¶ [FROM COLONEL HENRY LEE, JR., [Scott's Lake, S.C.], 23 April 1781. Gen. [Francis] Marion will report what has happened since Lee's other letter of "this day."[1] Lee apologizes "for the determination I took in consequence of the disappointment, which was neither more nor less than to sacrifice myself & my Infantry so as to gain a victory." While preparations were being made to storm [Ft. Watson], however, a "capitulation took place." He and Marion will march "tomorrow" for the High Hills of Santee. Prays for "the reinforcem[t] & Capt Finley."[2] Thinks Marion should move toward Georgetown to force the evacuation of that post, watch [Col. John] Watson, and "know" Lord Cornwallis's movements. Lee, at the same time, will operate on the west side of the Santee River with his "increased force & artillery" and will "communicate & act" with Marion. "Indeed," he would like to be formally under Marion's command "in some degree." That would "please" Marion, whom he admires. In a postscript, adds: "I press my opinion as to our employment. I recommend written instructions."[3] ALS (MiU-C) 3 pp.]

1. See Lee's letter, immediately above, and Marion's report of the surrender of Ft. Watson, immediately below.

2. Lee had requested a field piece and a reinforcement of regular infantry and militia riflemen in several letters. Capt. Ebenezer Finley was a Southern Army artillery officer.

3. NG replied on 28 April, below.

¶ [FROM GENERAL FRANCIS MARION, Fort Watson, S.C., 23 April 1781. After a "rapid," eight-day march from Ramsey's Mill, N.C., Col. [Henry] Lee joined Marion at the Santee River on 14 April. They marched to Ft. Watson the next day and "Invested it." The fort is on a "Small Hill forty feet high[,] Stockaded, with three rows of Abbatis around it, [and] no trees near enough to [provide] cover [for] our men." They had hoped to cut off the garrison's water supply but discovered on the third day that the enemy had successfully dug a "well near the Stockade which we could not prevent them from as we had no Intrenching tools to make our Approaches." They then decided to "raise a

Francis Marion, 1732–1795
(Reproduced from Benson J. Lossing, Pictorial Field-Book of the Revolution,
2 vols. [New York, 1860])

Work equal to the heighth of the Fort." After Maj. [Hezekiah] Maham completed that "Arduous" work "this Morning," they were able to make a "Lodgment" on the side of the mound near the stockade. An American party ascended the hill "with dificulty" and "pulled a way the abbattis[,] which induced the Commandant to Hoist a flag" of surrender.[1] Encloses the terms to which he and Lee agreed; hopes they meet with NG's approval.[2] American casualties were two militiamen killed and three Continentals wounded. Marion is particularly indebted to Lee for his "advice and indefatigable diligence" in this "tedious operation against as strong a Little post as could be made on the most advantageous spot that could be wished for." He also singles out Maham, whose tower was the principal reason for the post's surrender. Marion has had the "Greatest satisfaction from every one" in his command. Sends a list of prisoners and stores taken.[3] Will immediately demolish the fort and move on to the High Hills of the Santee to await NG's orders.[4] LS (MiU-C) 2 pp.]

1. In his memoirs, Lee was much more expansive than Marion was here on the subject of Maham's tower, which resembled a medieval siege engine, and on the capture of the fort. Maham, he wrote:

> proposed to cut down a number of suitable trees in the nearest wood, and with them to erect a large strong oblong pen, to be covered on the top with a floor of logs, and protected on the side opposite to the fort with a breastwork of light timber. To the adjacent farms dragoons were despatched for axes, the only necessary tool, of which a sufficient number being soon collected, relays of working parties were alloted for the labor; some to cut, some to convey, and some to erect. . . . Major Mayham undertook the execution of his plan, which was completely finished before the morning of the 23d, effective as to the object, and honorable to the genius of the inventor. The besieged was, like the besieger, unprovided with artillery, and could not interrupt the progress of a work, the completion of which must produce immediate submission.
>
> A party of riflemen, being ready, took post in the Mayham tower the moment it was completed; and a detachment of musketry, under cover of the riflemen, moved to make a lodgment in the enemy's ditch, supported by the legion infantry with fixed bayonets. Such was the effect of the fire from the riflemen, having thorough command of every part of the fort, from the relative supereminence of the tower, that every attempt to resist the lodgment was crushed. The commandant, finding every resource cut off, hung out the white flag. (Lee, *Memoirs*, 2: 51–52)

According to a journal that one of the post's British officers kept during the siege, it was "the Cowardly & Mutinous behaviour of A Majority of the Men [of the garrison,] having grounded their Arms & refused to defend the Post any longer," that forced the commander, Lt. James McKay, to capitulate. (British Headquarters Papers, DLC)

2. Under the terms of surrender, the captured officers were paroled and permitted to keep their sidearms and "private Baggage." The British prisoners were to march to Charleston and remain "out of service till exchanged"; captured "Irregulars" were to be treated as "prisoners of War." All stores were to be surrendered to the quartermaster of Lee's Legion. (MiU-C) NG "highly" approved the terms and sent a copy to Congress. (See NG to Marion, 26 April, and NG to Huntington, 27 April, both below.)

3. The list of prisoners has not been found, but a summary was appended to the copy of Marion's letter that NG sent to Congress. It included five officers and seventy-three British and thirty-six Loyalist rank and file. (PCC, item 155, vol. 2: 171, DNA). As seen in the letter immediately below, a large quantity of ammunition was also seized.

4. NG sent orders to Marion in a letter of 26 April, below.

¶ [FROM GENERAL FRANCIS MARION, Ft. Watson, S.C., 23 April 1781. He discussed the "Perticular force & Situation of the Enemy" in his last letter.[1] [Col. John] Watson cannot move toward NG; if Watson tries to come "this way," Marion's brigade, with Col. [Henry] Lee's detachment, "Can give a good Account of him." If NG sends them a field piece, they can "reduce the redoubt at Nelsons & Sᵗ Johns Church."[2] Marion has made arrangements that will enable him to "know" Lord Cornwallis's "first movements." He has a copy of the code, which he received from Lee, so NG can use it if he wishes to communicate anything "perticular." Recommends the bearer, "Mʳ Slater," a former British officer, who has "given Satisfaction" in his two months of service with Marion.[3] Says the ammunition captured at Ft. Watson "will be a

Sufficient Supply at present." Sends NG "a view of Fort Watson."[4] Facsimile (Robert F. Batchelder, *Catalog #71* [1989]) 1 p.]

1. See Marion to NG, 21 April, above.

2. Lee had also requested a field piece in various letters, including his first to NG of this date, above.

3. Lee had also recommended Slater when he wrote NG on 19 April, above.

4. The "view" has not been found.

¶ [FROM COLONEL JOHN MARSHEL, "Battiss Plantation," S.C., 23 April 1781. Gen. [Francis] Marion has ordered Marshel to send half of his regiment to Marion. "Last week," however, Marshel ordered all of his men to join NG. NG can send them to Marion if he "thinks proper." Col. [John] Watson has gone to Georgetown "as fast as he Can March." Marshel will stay where he is until he receives NG's orders.[1] ALS (MiU-C) 1 p.]

1. No reply has been found.

¶ [FROM GENERAL JETHRO SUMNER, [N.C.], 23 April 1781.[1] Sumner received NG's letter of 11 April on the 18th. He reports that some of the militia districts are "making their drafts" or are about to conduct them. Discusses the steps he has taken to collect the draftees, whom he will try to send to NG "without loss of time."[2] Is concerned about how to arm these men and has alerted the appropriate government officials to the need to act quickly. Does not know how to get arms to Salisbury conscripts but has decided to have the men wait there to receive them.[3] The arrangement of the officers will "be carefully done" at a general rendezvous, provided a return can be obtained of the "rank, and dates of the Officers Commissions in Captivity." Asks NG for such a return if he has one; fears that the one requested from Charleston, S.C., will be long delayed, as the flag vessel that is to take "Clothes &c" there has not sailed.[4] ALS (MiU-C) 3 pp.]

1. No place was given.

2. As seen in Eaton to NG, 17 April, above, and Carrington to NG, 24 April, below, the militia deserters who had been drafted into the North Carolina Continental line were about to join the Southern Army. Draftees from the Salisbury district were the next to arrive, about the end of June. (See NG to Armstrong, 21 June; NG to Pickens, 28 June, both below.) Sumner was still assembling other draftees when he wrote NG on 25 June, below. As noted there, he had marched them only as far as Salisbury by 14 July, and they did not reach the army until early August.

3. On the Salisbury draftees, see the preceding note.

4. NG's reply has not been found, but he was presumably unable to send the return. As noted at Lawrence to NG, 10 April, above, by late summer the arrangement had still not been completed.

¶ [GENERAL GREENE'S ORDERS, "Camp before Camden (North Side)," S.C., Tuesday, 24 April 1781. "General orders respecting passes are punctually to be observed"; corps commanders are the only officers who may grant them.[1] Roll is to be taken "at least three times" a day, "and absentees reported and punished." Officers are to "confine themselves" to their duties, "and every part of the army" must be ready "to stand to arms at a Moments warning." A general court martial will be held "Tomorrow Morning." Lamar Orderly Book (OClWHi) 1 p.]

*   *   *

To Colonel Henry Lee, Jr.

Dear Sir   Camp before Camden [S.C.] April 24th 1781

I wrote you by an Express night before last on the South side of Camden,[1] and soon after Doctor Irvin [Matthew Irvine] and Mr Winstead [William Winston?] set off to join you, and I desird Doctor Irvin to give you a particular account of things in this quarter, which I did not think proper to write. I informed you in my letter of the object of our movement, and of the situation of our baggage. Last night I got intelligence that Watson had gone to George Town,[2] the moment I receivd it, I sent an Express to Col Carrington who is with the baggage, to send you a field piece, and 100^{wt} powder & 400^{wt} of lead for the use [of] General Marians Corps, all which I hope will arrive safe; and I depend upon your taking such measures as will secure it in future.[3]

The post on the Congarees I have great reason to believe is evacuated as I am told the Garrison got into Camden the day after we got before the place by crossing the river in the rear of the town.[4] Camden a deserter says, is short of provision, and if we could invest it on all sides, it must fall in a few days perhaps a fortnight at most. But Lord Cornwallis has crossed the Cape Fear River, and is said to be on the move this way.[5] If this is true we shall not be able to accomplish all our purposes. General Sumter has not joined the operations as early by about a week as he promised, which lays me under many disadvantages.[6] Had he been down as early as was expected the Garrison of the Congarees could not have escaped. He is now collecting his Men, and will be down in a day or two.[7] I think the british have left their Stores on the Congaree. Will it not be well to send a party to see? Keep a good look out for Watson & [Col. John] Small, and also for Lord Cornwallis. If you fight the former, be sure to beat them if possible. Don't neglect to get all the good Dragoon horses you can meet with, and give Certificates for all both to Whig & tory, and let Government discriminate with regard to the discharging them hereafter.

I have orderd a Guard with the Field piece which is not equal to your demand, but its all I can spare at present; and I hope will answer your purpose. Compleat your business as soon as possible and keep me informed of all material intelligence.[8] Yours   N G

ALS (MiU-C).

1. See NG to Lee, 22 April, above.

2. Col. John Watson had indeed gone to Georgetown. NG received reports about this from several sources, including Lee, in his second letter of 20 April, above. As seen in NG's letter to Lee of the 22nd, NG had feared—correctly, as it later turned out—that Watson would move toward Camden.

3. Lee had first asked for the field piece in his letter of 18 April, above. NG had written him on the 22nd that he was unable to send it. From Carrington's letter to NG of this date, below, it appears that Carrington did not receive orders on the subject before at

least the 24th. Meanwhile, as Gen. Francis Marion reported in his first letter of 23 April, above, Ft. Watson had surrendered. Marion had requested ammunition in his letter of 21 April, above.

4. As noted at NG to Sumter, 23 April, above, the reinforcement was from Ninety Six, not Ft. Granby, "the post on the Congarees."

5. Cornwallis was not heading toward South Carolina.

6. NG had sent Maj. Edmund Hyrne to Sumter in early April to learn what support Sumter could give to the operation against Camden. (NG to Sumter, 7 April, above)

7. In a letter of 13 April, above, Sumter had detailed his efforts to bring a force together. As seen in Sumter to NG, 25 April, below, he would not join NG "in a day of two."

8. Lee had requested a reinforcement as well as the field piece. (See his first letter to NG of 23 April, above.) As mentioned in note 3, above, he had already completed his "business" in the capture of Ft. Watson.

To General Francis Marion

Dear Sir   Camp before Camden [S.C.] April 24th 1781
    Your favor of the 21st has just come to hand.

When I consider how much you have done and sufferd and under what disadvantages you have maintained your ground I am at a loss which to admire most your courage & fortitude or your address and management. Certain it is no man has a better claim to the public thanks or is more generally admird than you are. History affords no instance wherein an officer has kept possession of a Country under so many disadvantages as you have, surrounded on every side with a superior force, hunted from every quarter with veteran troops, you have found means to elude all their attempts, and to keep alive the expiring hopes of an oppressed militia, when all succour seemed to be cut off. To fight the enemy with a prospect of victory is nothing; but to fight with intrepidity under the constant impression of a defeat, and inspire irregular troops to do it is a talent peculiar to your self. Nothing will give me greater pleasure than to do justice to your merit, and I shall miss no opportunity of disclosing to Congress[,] the commander in Chief of the American Army and to the World in general the great sense I have of your merit & services.[1]

I thank you for the measures you have taken to furnish us with provisions and for the intelligence you communicate. A field piece is coming to your assis[tan]ce which I hope will enable you and Col Lee to get possession of the fort. With the Artillery you will receive 100wt of powder and 400wt of lead.[2] I wish my present stock would enable me to forward you a larger supply but it will not having sent you near half we have.

I have reason to believe the Enemy has evacuated their post upon the Congarees;[3] and if there is no object very important on the other side of the river it is my wish you should move up on this in order to enable us to invest Camden to more advantage[,] the Garrison of which I have good reason to believe is short of provisions.[4]

I have this moment got intelligence that Lord Cornwallis crossed the Cape Fear River last week in order to begin his march towards this State.[5] I beg you to take measures to discover his route and approach and have me constantly advisd of both.

Col Horees attack upon a party of Watsons detachment does him great honor.[6] With the highest respect & esteem I am dear Sir Your Most obed humble Ser   N GREENE

ADfS (MiU-C).

1. NG probably wrote this paragraph in response to Col. Henry Lee's suggestion that Marion's spirits needed bolstering. (See Lee to NG, second letter of 20 April, above.)

2. On the field piece and the ammunition, see NG to Lee, this date, immediately above.

3. As seen at ibid., the British had not evacuated their post at the Congarees.

4. After consulting with Capt. James Conyers, NG changed his orders as to where he wanted Marion to take post. (See NG to Marion, 27 April, below.)

5. The intelligence was false.

6. As noted at Marion to NG, 21 April, above, the British party that Col. Hugh Horry's men attacked was part of a detachment commanded by Col. Welbore Ellis Doyle.

*   *   *

¶ [FROM COLONEL EDWARD CARRINGTON, Upton's Mill, S.C., 24 April 1781, 9 A.M.[1] Has "just *now*" received NG's letter of the 23rd—the first news he has had from NG since they "parted"—along with the "instructions" mentioned therein.[2] Discusses the movements of his detachment and his efforts to ensure the safety of the army's baggage.[3] Major [Pinketham] Eaton's and Capt. [John?] Smith's detachments, totalling "about 220 men," have arrived and will march with the artillery.[4] Provision wagons will "move immediately" to NG, and Carrington will then "come on agreable to" NG's instructions. Reports that they are "well off for forage, & strong in Cattle." There is also a "tolerable supply of meal, & good prospects a head." Forwards several letters that he "intercepted" on their way to NG. He had not wanted to risk sending them on before receiving "some intelligence" from NG. He therefore broke the seals to see if they contained any important information that he could forward to NG "by message," as he did "yesterday" with "Rowans intelligence of Ld Cornwallis's situation."[5] ALS (MiU-C) 3 pp.]

1. According to a note by Carrington at the end of the letter, this location was "8 miles north of Little Lynches Creek Bridge."

2. The letter and the instructions have not been found. Nor is it clear from the contents of Carrington's letter whether the instructions were those NG had sent him to forward a cannon to Gen. Francis Marion and Col. Henry Lee. (See NG to Lee, this date, above.)

3. Carrington had the army's baggage and artillery with him. (Ibid.)

4. On Eaton's detachment, see note at Eaton to NG, 17 April, above. NG sent Eaton and his men to join Marion and Lee. (NG to Marion, 26 April, below) It is not known why Smith's party had been detached, but it may have been to escort the provision

wagons that Carrington mentioned later in this letter. Smith's company was with NG at the battle of Hobkirk's Hill on 25 April.

5. See Robert Rowan to NG, 18 April, above.

¶ [GENERAL GREENE'S ORDERS, [Camp before Camden, S.C.], 25 April 1781. The troops are to receive two days' provisions and a "gill of spirits" each "as soon as the spirits arrive." In after orders, given at "Camp before Camden (North Side)," the "Army having received a Slight repulse" is to camp "this Evening at the passes on Saunders and Suttons."[1] The orders were taken from Gordon, History, 4: 82; the after orders are in the Lamar Orderly Book (OClWHi). The latter are dated "24th April," but it is clear from the contents that they were given on the 25th.]

1. On the battle of Hobkirk's Hill, which was fought on the 25th, see NG to Huntington, 27 April, below. Saunder's and Sutton's were creeks just north of Camden.

*   *   *

Captain William Pierce, Jr., to Colonel Henry Lee, Jr.

Dear Sir   Camp before Camden [S.C.] April 25th 1781.

The Enemy advanced out of Camden this Morning and gave us Battle. They drove us from the field, but we sustained very little loss. It was in our power to have obtained a compleat victory, but many of our Troops behaved infamously; and prevented it. Col° [William] Washington made a timely charge and cut down a number of them besides taken about 40 Prisoners.[1]

We are now about 6 miles from Camden & may possibly have another touch with them in a Day or two. General Greene wishes you to be on your guard, as they may probably detach a party to releive the fort in consequence of their success.[2] I am sir Your very ob^t serv^t

W^M PIERCE J^R

ALS (CSmH).
1. On the battle of Hobkirk's Hill, see NG to Huntington, 27 April, below.
2. Lee and Gen. Francis Marion had already captured Ft. Watson. (See Marion to NG, first letter of 23 April, above.)

*   *   *

¶ [CAPTAIN WILLIAM PIERCE, JR., TO GENERAL THOMAS SUMTER. From Headquarters [before Camden, S.C.], 25 April 1781.[1] NG wants Sumter to collect his force and join NG's army "immediately." The Southern Army is "too small to maintain [its] ground before Camden," and it is therefore necessary to "form a junction."[2] The enemy "advanced out this Morning and gave us Battle. They drove us some little distance from the field, but we saved our stores, and took a number of Prisoners."[3] ALS (Sumter Papers: DLC) 1 p.]

1. The location was taken from the contents of this letter and from Pierce to Lee, immediately above.
2. As seen in his letter of this date, below, Sumter was not in a position to join NG.
3. On the battle of Hobkirk's Hill, see NG to Huntington, 27 April, below.

¶ [FROM GENERAL FRANCIS MARION, Capt. William Richardson's, High Hills, S.C., 25 April 1781.[1] An express reports that NG "moved entirely from Camden, where was not known. This is so misterious & Conjecturs various that we cannot tell what to conclude."[2] Wants NG to "clear up" the "Apprehension of Ill consequences." Marion has Col. [Henry] Lee's cavalry with him and expects Lee's infantry to join him "this morning." He will "make a Sudden movement" if he has not heard anything by "tomorrow Evening."[3] ALS (MiU-C) 1 p.]

1. As seen in his first letter of 23 April, above, Marion had decided to move his force into the High Hills of the Santee after he destroyed the works at Ft. Watson.

2. Contrary to the report, the Southern Army had not "moved entirely from Camden." On the army's movements in the days preceding this letter, see NG to Lee, 22 April, above.

3. NG replied on 26 April, below.

* * *

From Baron Steuben

On the Road from Petersburg to Chesterfield C° H°
Dear General   10 Miles from Petersburg [Va.] 25th April 1781

On the 24th I reconnoitred the Enemys Fleets then laying off Westover & consisting of Thirteen Top sail Vessells and twenty three flat bottom Boats full of Men. The whole number of Troops on board I judged to be about 2500—a Hessian Serjeant who deserted to us made them 3000. The same day the Fleet stood up the River. I therefore orderd General [Peter] Muhlenberg to move up as high as the Vicinity of Blandford and that Evening the Enemy landed their whole force at City Point which fully evinced that their first object was Petersburg. Being obliged to send large Detachments to the Neck of Land between James & Appomatox Rivers I had not more than One thousand Men left to oppose the Enemies advance. In this Critical situation there were many reasons against risking a Total Defeat. The Loss of Arms was a principal one, & on the other hand to retire without some shew of Resistance would have intimidated the Inhabitants and have encouraged the Enemy to further incursions. This last consideration determined me to defend the place as far as our inferiority of numbers would permit.

I made choice of Blanford for the place of Defence & the Bridge of Pocohuntas for our Retreat. The troops were disposed accordingly and passed the Night under Arms.

The Morning of the 25th I was informed that the Enemy were within three Miles of our advanced Posts and that Eleven flattom [flat-bottom] Boats were at the same time moving up Appomatox River. Towards Noon they came in Sight—formed & Displayed to their left but it was near three oClock before the firing commenced which continued from

Post to Post till past five, when the superior numbers of the Enemy & a want of Ammunition obliged me to order a Retreat & the Bridge to be taken up which was executed in the greatest Order notwithstanding the fire of the Enemy Cannon & Musketry. The troops with the same good order retreated to this place where they are just encamped.[1]

I am not yet able to Ascertain our loss but believe it not great. I do not think the Enemy took a Single prisoner. The Enemys loss I can form no judgement of.[2]

General Muhlinberg merits my particular acknowledgements for the good disposition he made & the great Gallantry with which he executed it. Indeed the gallant conduct of all the officers & the particular good behaviour of the Men must I am persuaded [have] attracted the admiration of the Enemy.[3]

I have the pleasure to say that our Troops disputed the ground with the Enemy Inch by Inch & executed their Manoeuvres with great exactness.

Gen[l] [George] Weedons Brigade is posted on both sides James River at Osborns.

With Gen[l] Muhlenbergs Brigade I shall march Six Miles above Chesterfield C[o] H[o] in which position I shall be able to cover Richmond to form a Junction with the Marquis [de Lafayette] or wi[th] Gen[l] Weedon according to Circumstanc[e].[4] With great esteem & respect I am D[r] General Your Very hum Serv[t]   STEUBEN

PS. So Soon as I get to my new position I shall detach 100 Horse & 200 Infantry on the other Side Appomatox to harrass the Enemy.

LS (MiU-C).

1. Gen. William Phillips, the new commander of British troops in Virginia, had taken time to strengthen the post at Portsmouth after bringing a reinforcement from New York in late March. (Ewald, *Journal*, p. 296; on the reinforcement, see note at Washington to NG, 21 March, above [vol. 7: 459n].) On 18 April, Phillips began to advance up the James River, carrying out instructions from Sir Henry Clinton to " 'move in force upon the enemy's communications between Virginia and North Carolina, at Petersburgh, in assistance to Lord Cornwallis.' " (Phillips to Clinton, 3 April, Stevens, *Clinton-Cornwallis Controversy*, 1: 377) The flotilla stopped at Burwell's Landing the next day. From there, troops fanned out to raid Yorktown, capture Williamsburg, and burn a shipyard on the Chickahominy River. Phillips then resumed his movement upriver, reaching Westover unopposed on the 24th. He then sent his main force up the Appomatox River toward Petersburg with orders to destroy the American stores there. (Simcoe, *Military Journal*, pp. 107–10; Selby, *Revolution in Virginia*, pp. 271–72) Steuben, who originally expected Phillips to join Lord Cornwallis in the Carolinas, had realized by 15 April that an invasion of the Virginia interior was imminent. (Steuben to Muhlenberg, 1 April, Steuben Microfilm; Steuben to Gov. Thomas Jefferson, 15 April, Boyd, *Jefferson Papers*, 5: 459) He ordered Muhlenberg and Gen. Thomas Nelson to follow the British up the river, gathering militia reinforcements along the way and harassing the enemy wherever possible. (Chase, "Steuben," p. 218) Not knowing whether the British would move against Richmond, as they had during Gen. Benedict Arnold's invasion in January, or against Petersburg, he directed Nelson to defend Richmond and Muhlenberg to halt near

Petersburg. He also ordered the public stores moved from both places and Chesterfield Court House. (Ibid.; Steuben to Richard Claiborne, 16 April, Steuben Microfilm) As seen by this letter to NG, Petersburg was the "first object" of the British; as can also be seen here, the American forces were not strong enough to do more than slow the enemy's advance. Following the engagement at Blandford, Phillips's troops continued to Petersburg, where they burned some 40,000 hogsheads of tobacco. (Chase, "Steuben," p. 222)

2. The Marquis de Lafayette informed NG that American losses were about twenty killed and wounded (Lafayette to NG, 28 April, below) According to Arnold, though, who was with the expedition, American casualties were thought to be "near 100 men killed and wounded," while the British lost "only one man killed and ten wounded." (Arnold to Clinton, 12 May, Davies, *Documents*, 20: 143)

3. Simcoe, who asserted that the Americans could have taken "many positions . . . to better effect," wrote in his memoirs: "The disposition of the enemy was not such as marked any ability in those who made it." (Simcoe, *Military Journal*, p. 113) Steuben's biographer contends that by making a stand at Blandford, he "managed to boost the morale" of Virginians. (Chase, "Steuben," p. 223)

4. As seen by Steuben's letter to NG of 5 May, below, Lafayette arrived in Richmond on 27 April.

From General Thomas Sumter

Camp at Davis', Broad River [S.C.],
Dr Sir   25th April, 1781.

My movements are very slow, which I fear will be attended with many disadvantages which would have been avoided if I had been down sooner.[1] The militia are coming in tolerably well now. I have also a number of waggons coming down & expect to be joined to-morrow by three more well-appointed troops from North Carolina.[2]

As I found some delay unavoidable, I marched into Mobley's, and Sandy River settlements, with a view to harrass the enemy, which has been effectually done, and will, I hope, in a great Measure relieve our friends in that part of the country from the unnatural cruelties that were daily exercised over them. Some small skirmishes have happened. I have lost no men. Several of the enemy have fallen; and many others taken prisoners. Upon the whole they have been pretty well scourged.

I shall send some large parties into the Dutch Fork to-morrow, to clear that place also, and call out the well-disposed inhabitants. I shall move on to-morrow, and the instant I am joined by these troops behind, march for the Congarees with all possible speed.[3]

I detached Col. [Henry] *Hampton* to the Wateree with a few waggons, which are to be loaded with provisions if to be got, and sent to you. He will also Keep back small parties of the enemy from going into, or coming out of, Camden, while there.[4]

Genl [Andrew] *Pickens* joined me to-day. He has none of his Brigade with him. Many men belonging to mine gone after Col. [James] McCall, who is in the neighborhood of Ninety Six with a considerable number of men with him. Genl *Pickens* will set off to-morrow with Col. *Hay's* regiment of my Brigade, to take command of the troops in that quarter.[5] The Georgians are gone into that State, and are joined, I am informed, by almost every man in the Upper Country.[6]

The enemy have burnt what works they had at Williams', and moving towards the Congarees.[7] Numbers of Tories hiding out until they Know what terms may be offered.

I find the country very bare of provision, and stripped of chief of the negroes and horses.

I mentioned by letter to Gen[l] [i.e., Col. Thomas] *Polk* and many others, the inhabitants of Mecklenburg, what straits you were in for provision; in consequence of which I am informed that twenty odd waggon loads were very soon collected, and to start yesterday.[8]

I hope by Saturday to Know how things are at the Congarees, and immediately after send you some meal and corn.[9]

The trouble and perplexity I have had to get the militia out inconceivable, but think them pretty well subdued.

I hope you have not suffered for supplies, and that your expectations and wishes may be fully and speedily answered. I am, D[r] Sir, Your most ob[dt] hb[le] serv[t]   THO[s] SUMTER

N.B. I have not as yet received any account from Charles Town. I should be very glad to Know where L[d] *Cornwallis* is.[10]

Tr (Draper Microfilm).

1. NG had asked Sumter to raise a force of militia and to assist the Southern Army in its attempt to capture Camden. (See NG to Sumter, 30 March and 7 April, and Sumter's letters to NG of 7 and 13 April, all above.)

2. In regard to the regiments of ten-month men that some of Sumter's officers had been recruiting in North Carolina, see Sumter to NG, 7 April, above. Thomas Polk reported to NG on 9 May, below, that there were 150 North Carolinians with Sumter.

3. Capt. William Pierce wrote Sumter on this date, above, that NG wanted him to join NG "immediately."

4. See Hampton to NG, 28 April, below.

5. Sumter wrote NG on 27 April, below, that Pickens had left for Ninety Six.

6. Georgia and South Carolina militiamen under Col. Samuel Hammond and Maj. James Jackson had placed Augusta under siege. (Cashin and Robertson, *Augusta*, p. 55; on the early stages of the siege, see also Pickens to NG, 3 May, below.)

7. Ft. Williams was an outpost of Ninety Six.

8. NG's commissary, William R. Davie, reported on 26 April, below, that twelve wagonloads were on their way to NG's army from Charlotte.

9. In a letter of 19 April, above, NG had asked Sumter to provide corn and meal for the army. Sumter wrote NG on 27 April, below, that he was having corn ground at the Congarees and would send some meal "in a few days."

10. As seen in his reply, NG sent Maj. Edmund Hyrne to brief Sumter. (Pierce to Sumter, 28 April, below)

*   *   *

¶ [**FROM LIEUTENANT JOHN TOWNES,**[1] Philadelphia, 25 April 1781. He has come from Charleston, S.C., to lay his "greviances" before Congress regarding a trial to which he was subjected as a prisoner.[2] Asks NG to forward the proceedings, which were sent to him, to the Board of War, which is "principally interested in the affair."[3] Hopes NG will do this "by the first dispatches," as Townes is "on great Expences."[4] ALS (MiU-C) 1 p.]

1. Townes, a Virginia officer taken prisoner at Charleston in May 1780, had been "lately released" from captivity. (Heitman, *Register*; Townes and Richard Worsham to Board of War, 22 May, PCC, item 148, vol. 1: 393, DNA)

2. The proceedings have not been found. In a letter of this date to Washington, Townes said that a panel of American officers, who were also prisoners, had sentenced him "to be cashiered"; Gen. William Moultrie, the ranking American officer at Charleston, had declined to approve the decision and had later given Townes permission to take his case to Congress. (Washington Papers, DLC).

3. NG enclosed the proceedings in a letter of 24 May, below, to the Board of War. The board's decision was presumably favorable to Townes, who stated in a letter to Congress of 13 August that the matter had been settled "ten or fifteen days ago" and that he was to return to the army. (PCC, item 78, vol. 22: 467, DNA)

4. In response to Townes's requests for expense money and back pay, Congress granted him $380 on 2 June and voted him and some other former prisoners six months' "nominal pay" on 13 August. (*JCC*, 20: 591; 21: 858)

¶ [GENERAL GREENE'S ORDERS, "Camp Sutton's Creek," S.C., 26 April 1781.[1] "The Action of yesterday," though unsuccessful, was not "decisive." The actions of Col. [William] Washington's cavalry, the light infantry commanded by Capt. [Robert] Kirkwood, the "Picquets," and the camp guards made the "advantage expensive to the En[emy]" and "merit the approbation" of NG and the "imitation of the rest of the Troops." NG also commends the conduct of the artillery officers. The army's loss is "so inconsiderable" that "it is only to be lamented that the Troops were not unanimous in a disposition to embrace so excellent an opportunity of obtaining a compleat Victory."[2] Orders a return of killed, wounded, and missing. Col. [John Eager] Howard is to replace the wounded Col. [Benjamin] Ford as commander of the Second Maryland Regiment.[3] Lamar Orderly Book (OClWHi) 3 pp. A list of men from the First Maryland Regiment who were wounded in the battle is appended to the orders.]

1. The entry is dated "25th Ap'" in the orderly book, but it is clear from the reference in the first sentence to the battle of Hobkirk's Hill having been fought "yesterday" that the orders were issued on the 26th.

2. For an account of the battle of Hobkirk's Hill, see NG to Huntington, 27 April, below.

3. The wound that Ford suffered during the battle later resulted in his arm being amputated. (Pindell to Williams, 26 May 1781, MHi)

*   *   *

To General Francis Marion

Dr Sir   Hd. Quar. before Camden [S.C.] April 26th 1781

I have to Acknowledge the receipt of your two Letters dated 23 & 25th Instant. I Congratulate you on your success against Fort Watson. The Articles of Capitulation I highly approve of, & feel myself particularly indebted to you, & all the officers & men under you, for their spirit, perseverance, & Good conduct upon the Occasion.[1] The Enemy Advanced upon us yesterday & Gave us battle. The conflict was Short & seemed once to promise us advantage, but we were Oblidged to retire & Give up the field tho' with no material Loss.[2] We are now within five Miles of Camden & shall Closely invest it in a day or two again. That we may be Enabled to operate with more Certainty against this post, I should be Glad you would move up Immediately to our Assistance, & take post on the North side of the Town.[3] I have detached a field Piece to your assistance, with an Escort of a few Continental Troops, under the Commd. of Major Eaton. I should be Glad you would send them a Guide, & Conduct them to your Army.[4] I am, Sir with Great Esteem & Respect, Your most obdt. hum Servt

NATH: GREENE

N.B. I should be Glad you would move up within 7 miles of Camden.

Tr (Force Transcripts: DLC).

1. Marion had sent NG a copy of the articles of capitulation with his first letter of 23 April, above, in which he reported the capture of Ft. Watson and asked NG if he approved the terms.

2. On the battle of Hobkirk's Hill, see NG to Huntington, 27 April, below.

3. NG revised these orders in a letter to Marion of 27 April, below.

4. Maj. Pinketham Eaton, hearing of the capture of Ft. Watson, halted and wrote NG for further instructions. NG first ordered him to rejoin the army but then sent him new instructions to join Marion. (See Eaton to NG, 27 April, and Pierce to Eaton, 28 April, both below.)

*   *   *

¶ [FROM LORD RAWDON,[1] Camden, S.C., 26 April 1781. During the "action yesterday," American dragoons "carried off" three British surgeons who were on the battlefield tending the wounded of both armies.[2] Rawdon has ordered that all captured American wounded be "received" into the British hospital. For this reason, he asks NG to release the surgeons. Believes their situation "should have exempted them from capture." If NG does not agree, Rawdon will request that "an equal number may be set at liberty from Haddral's Point."[3] ALS (NcU) 2 pp.]

1. Francis Rawdon-Hastings (1754–1826), known at this time as Lord Rawdon, was reputed to be " 'the ugliest man in England.' " He has also been described by the military historian Sir John W. Fortescue as the ablest British officer in America. A member of a noble Irish family, Rawdon had left Oxford for military service in 1774 and had been in America since before the battle of Bunker Hill. He was in the North until the spring of 1780, serving for a time as adjutant general of the British army; he also raised a Loyalist regiment, the Volunteers of Ireland. After he was transferred to the South, he took part in the capture of Charleston and fought at Camden. When Lord Cornwallis began his invasion of North Carolina in January 1781, he left Rawdon to command the post at Camden and maintain control of the South Carolina and Georgia frontier. At the time of his victory at Hobkirk's Hill, Rawdon was about twenty-seven years old. Most of his subsequent activities in South Carolina can be traced through this volume. Rawdon gave up his command for reasons of health in July 1781 but was captured by a French

Francis Rawdon-Hastings, Lord Rawdon, 1754–1826; engraving by I. Jones
after a painting by Sir Joshua Reynolds
(South Caroliniana Library, University of South Carolina)

privateer during his return voyage to England. In later life he commanded troops in the Napoleonic wars, served in Parliament, and was governor-general and commander-in-chief in India. At the time of his death, he held similar posts in Malta. (Boatner, *Encyc.*)

2. Col. William Washington's dragoons had captured a number of British support personnel during the battle of Hobkirk's Hill. (See NG to Huntington, 27 April, below.)

3. American prisoners of war were held at Haddrell's Point, near Charleston. NG's reply is immediately below.

¶ [TO LORD RAWDON, From "Head Quarters [before Camden, S.C.]," 26 April 1781. Rawdon's letter of "this Evening by a flag of Truce" has been received.[1] NG will permit the captured British surgeons to return to Camden in the morning, but they are not exempt from capture by "custom" or by "general principles of War"; he expects a like number of American surgeons to be released. Thanks Rawdon for taking American wounded into the British hospital and says he has extended "the same act of generosity and humanity" to the captured British wounded. Df (MiU-C) 1 p.]

1. Rawdon's letter is immediately above.

¶ [FROM GENERAL JOHN BUTLER, Ramsey's Mill, N.C., 26 April 1781. He received NG's letter of 19 April "yesterday." Hopes to hear soon of the surrender of Camden, S.C. Has a report that the enemy were in Wilmington "as late as the 21st" and that a number of vessels had come into the harbor there "under Ballast," supposedly to transport Lord Cornwallis's army.[1] Butler sent all the wagons he could to Wake County for "Barreled Pork & Bacon." Gen. [Jethro] Sumner reports that eight wagonloads of bacon have been sent to Ramsey's from Warren County. If the "teams are Sufficient," Butler will send them on to NG.[2] ALS (MiU-C) 1 p.]

1. The vessels at Wilmington were supply transports, bringing provisions, clothing, and military supplies to Cornwallis's army. ("Von Bose Journal," p. 55) "Severely wounded" troops were the only ones who left Wilmington by water. (Ibid., p. 54)

2. As seen in Potts to NG, 2 May, below, the bacon from Warren County was sent to Salisbury.

¶ [FROM COLONEL WILLIAM R. DAVIE, Charlotte, N.C., 26 April 1781. He wrote NG on 21 April, enclosing "some dispatches from the Northward." Twelve wagonloads of meal and flour were sent "this morning" and will reach NG's army on "sunday next" [29 April]. A commissary whom Davie sent to the Waxhaws "has made a tolerable collection; but wants waggons." Davie believes a considerable supply of provisions could be impressed in the Rocky Mount area. Public wagons and horses are scattered "thro this County," and several broken wagons "are lying in town"; concludes that "a Quarter Master is really much wanted" at Charlotte.[1] Has reports that NG "kill[ed] and captured a Detachment of t[he] British Army."[2] Expects to return to camp on Sunday or Monday "next" [29 or 30 April]. ALS (NcU) 2 pp.]

1. By the time NG wrote Gen. Robert Lawson on 10 May, below, there was an assistant deputy quartermaster at Charlotte.

2. Davie had probably received preliminary reports of the capture of Ft. Watson. (See Marion to NG, first letter of 23 April, above.)

¶ [FROM THE GEORGIA DELEGATES IN CONGRESS, Philadelphia, 26 April 1781.[1] "As the fate of Nations has sometimes depended, so that of States may now depend upon events appearing trifling." They have long been uneasy with the "irregular situation" of the citizens of Georgia. The "merit" of Georgians in opposing the enemy is "equal to any," and Georgians have "given tone to some of the most brilliant actions in that department upon the small scale"; but for want of "order and direction," the state loses the "credit of their exertions." To "remedy these evils, and to render their endeavors more useful," the delegates have "invested" Dr. [Nathan] Brownson with a

"Brigadier-General's commission, and given instructions for uniting our people under his command." They ask NG to "give the measure efficiency, by approving and protecting it."[2] LS (NcD) 1 p.]

1. The letter was signed by delegates George Walton, William Few, and Richard Howly.

2. Brownson, a former delegate himself, had gone to Philadelphia as purveyor for the hospital department in the South. In his reply of 18 July, below, NG expressed doubt that the "military characters" of Georgia would "readily" accept "the propriety of Doctor Brownsons appointment," but promised to write in support of Brownson. In the end, a compromise was worked out, by which Brownson was named governor and John Twiggs, a militia leader, became brigadier general. (Conrad, "Southern Campaign," p. 282)

¶ [GENERAL GREENE'S ORDERS, "Camp Saunders Creek [S.C.] Saturday 27th April 1781."[1] Announces the capture of Ft. Watson and its garrison.[2] "One or two Houses" have reportedly "been burnt by the Troops or Women of the American Army."[3] Threatens death to "Any Person hereafter detected in Such an Offence." The troops are to receive ammunition. Lamar Orderly Book (OClWHi) 1 p.]

1. The 27th was a Friday.
2. See Marion to NG, first letter of 23 April, above.
3. The reference was to women accompanying the army.

* . * *

To Samuel Huntington,
President of the Continental Congress

Sir   Camp Sanders's Creek [S.C.] April 27th 1781

I did myself the honor to address your Excellency on the 22d, and informed you that we lay before Camden, having found it impracticable to storm the Town with a prospect of success, and nothing left but to take a position to induce the Enemy to sally. We chose a Hill [i.e., Hobkirk's Hill] about one mile from the Town on the main road leading to the Waxhaws. It was covered with Timber and flanked on the left by an impassable Morass. The Country between that and the Town is covered by heavy Wood and under Brush. In this situation we lay constantly upon our Arms ready for Action at a moments warning.

About 11 oClock on the Morning of the 25th, our advanced Piquets were fired upon, who gave the Enemy a warm reception.[1]

The line was formed in an instant, General Hugers Brigade upon the right of the road, Colo Williams's Brigade of Marylanders on the left, and the Artillery in the centre. Colo [James] Read with a few Militia in the rear as a second Line. Captain Kirkwood and the light Infantry lay in our front, and as the Enemy advanced he was soon engaged with them, and both he and his Corps behaved with great galantry.[2]

The Piquets under the command of Captains [Simon] Morgan and [Perry] Benson, behaved with equal spirit and good conduct.

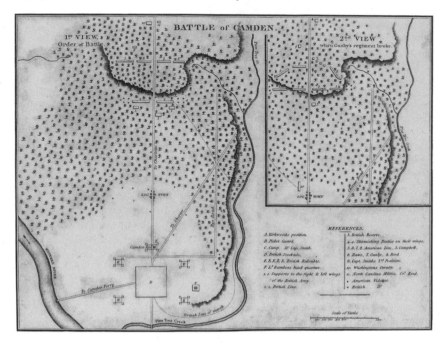

Battle of Hobkirk's Hill
(*Reproduced from William Johnson,* Life and Correspondence of
Nathanael Greene, *2 vols. [Charleston, S.C., 1822]*)

As the Enemy were found to be advancing only with a small front, Lieut[t] Col[o] Ford with the 2[d] Maryland Regiment had orders to advance and flank them upon the left, Lieut[t] Col[o] Campbell had orders to do the like upon the right. Col[o] Gunby with the first Maryland Regiment, and Lieut[t] Col[o] Haws with the second Virginia Regiment, had orders to advance down the Hill and charge them in front. Lieut[t] Col[o] Washington had orders to turn the Enemies right flank and charge them in the rear. The whole line was soon engaged in close firing, and the Artillery under Col[o] [Charles] Harrison playing on their front. The Enemy were staggered in all quarters, and upon the left were retiring while our Troops continued to advance, when unfortunately two Companies of the right of the first Maryland Regiment got a little disordered, and unhappily Col[o] Gunby gave an order for the rest of the Regiment then advancing to take a new position in the rear, where the two Companies were rallying. This impressed the whole Regiment with an Idea of a retreat, and communicated itself to the 2[d] Regiment which immediately followed the first on their retiring. Both were rallied but it was too late, the Enemy had gained the Hill and obliged the Artillery to retire. The second Virginia Regiment having advanced some distance down the Hill, and the Maryland line being gone the Enemy immediately turned their flank, while they were engaged in front. Lieut[t] Col[o] Campbells Regiment had got into some disorder and fallen back a little, this obliged me to order Lieut[t] Col[o] Haws to retire.[3] The Troops were frequently rallied, but had got into too much disorder to recover the fortune of the Day, which once promised us a compleat victory as Col[o] Washington found the Enemy both Horse and foot retiring with the utmost precipitation towards the Town, and took upwards of 200 Prisoners and ten or fifteen Officers, before he discovered our People had left the ground, more than fifty of which were brought off. The Colonels behaviour and that of his Regiment upon this occasion did them the highest honor.[4] We retired about two or three Miles without any loss of Artillery or Ammunition Waggons, the Baggage having been sent off at the begining of the Action.[5] The Enemy suffered very greatly.[6] Our force was not materially different; but had we succeeded from the disposition made, we must have had the whole Prisoners as well as full possession of Camden. Inclosed is the returned of the killed and Wounded.[7] Among the former is Captain Baty [William Beatty] of the Maryland Line, a most excellent Officer and an ornament to his profession.[8]

Our Army is in good spirits, and this little repulse will make no alteration in our general plan of operation. Inclosed I send your Excellency the conditions of the capitulation and surrender of Fort Watson, which I hope will be followed by others.[9]

I have been honored with your two letters of the 10th and 29th of March.[10] I have the honor to be with great respect Your Excellencys most obedient and most humble servant   NATH GREENE
P.S. The Horse and part of the Infantry at the close of the Evening charged upon the Enemy who retreated immediately into Town with precipitation.[11]

LS (PCC, item 155, vol. 2: 47, DNA).
1. In letters to Cornwallis of 25 and 26 April, Lord Rawdon explained his decision to attack NG's army. Believing that NG's troops greatly outnumbered his own, he said he decided to attack after hearing that Francis Marion, Thomas Sumter, and Henry Lee "were coming to Greene." Rawdon also had a report from an American deserter that NG lacked artillery at this time, having sent it "a day's March" to the rear, and that NG had recently "detached all" his militia to bring it back. Arming "our Musicians, our Drummers & in short everything that could carry a Firelock," Rawdon moved against the American army with "above Nine Hundred" men, including sixty dragoons. By keeping close to "the Swamp [Little Pine Tree Creek]," he was able to "get into the Wood unperceived; & by taking an extensive circuit," he managed to advance undetected until his forward unit "fell in with" the pickets of NG's army. (Rawdon to Cornwallis, 25 and 26 April, PRO 30/11/6) As Col. John Eager Howard remembered some years later, the latter troops were "not more than three hundred yards" in front of the army. ("Note by Col[o] Howard," n.d., MdHi) The effects of this surprise attack on NG's army and on the outcome of the battle have been much debated. According to Rawdon, the attack caused

"much confusion" among NG's men, but the Southern Army, "notwithstanding, formed; & received us bravely." At least one American officer, Col. John Gunby, whom NG held responsible for the defeat, argued that NG's troops never fully recovered from the surprise and attributed the loss of the battle to that fact. (Howard to unnamed correspondent, no date, MdHi) Howard recalled that because of the sudden attack, Gunby's First Maryland Regiment never "perfectly formed; our men were cooking & washing about the camp, and to the best of my recollection they had not all fallen in, but how many were absent I can not say though I think there were but a small proportion absent." (Ibid.) Other officers thought the surprise had little effect on the outcome, contending, as NG did in this letter, that the camp had been arranged in battle formation and that the troops were quickly formed, confident, and ready when the enemy advanced. (See, for example, William Davie's account in Johnson, *Greene*, 2: 95.) Even Howard, in a letter to Henry Lee in 1819, said the surprise "may not excuse the conduct of our men." (Howard to Henry Lee, 19 January 1819, quoted in Lee, *Campaign of 1781*, p. 262)

2. Gen. Isaac Huger's brigade consisted of the two Virginia regiments, commanded by Col. Richard Campbell and Col. Samuel Hawes. The two Maryland regiments, commanded by Col. John Gunby and Col. Benjamin Ford, were the components of Williams's brigade. Howard recalled that the right of Ford's regiment was "some distance, perhaps 150 yards, from the left of Gunby's," while "the left of Fords reg^t was a good deal advanced so as to form with the 1st reg^t [i.e., Gunby's regiment] almost a half moon. The ridge of high ground ran in that direction." (Howard to unnamed correspondent, no date, MdHi) Guilford Dudley remembered that the militia, which served as NG's reserve, had just returned to camp with the artillery and were ascending Hobkirk's Hill to take their "post in the line" when the American sentries opened fire. Otho Williams met them halfway up the hill and ordered them to " 'March to the right and support Colonel Campbell,' for there was not time to say more." The militia struggled up the sandy hill and were only "a third of the way" to their post when the Continentals opened fire. (Dann, *Revolution Remembered*, pp. 219–20) Capt. Robert Kirkwood's command supported the pickets and is credited with slowing the British advance enough to permit the American army to form. According to Rawdon, however, Kirkwood's force was easily brushed aside, and "the Piquets, tho' supported, were instantly driven in, & followed to their Camp." (Kirkland and Kennedy, *Camden*, pp. 231–32; Rawdon to Cornwallis, 26 April, PRO 30/11/6)

3. As seen here, NG decided to attack and planned a double envelopment of Rawdon's force. To prevent Rawdon's men from escaping, he ordered William Washington to attack the enemy's rear. Several writers have criticized NG for attacking Rawdon instead of maintaining a defensive position. (See, for example, Boatner, *Encyc.*, 506.) His decision to detach Washington has likewise been called both an example of the "deranging effects of unlimited confidence" and a "faulty tactical plan." (Lee, *Memoirs*, 2: 66; Boatner, *Encyc.*, p. 506) Quickly perceiving NG's intention, Rawdon extended his line, ordering regiments forward from his second line so that the first overlapped the American units facing it. (Rawdon to Cornwallis, 26 April, PRO 30/11/5; Boatner, *Encyc.*, p. 506) Despite Rawdon's adjustment, NG's plan seemed to be working when the American artillery, which Rawdon had not expected to face, opened up with grapeshot at short range and staggered the British advance. William Seymour, a sergeant serving with Kirkwood, observed in his journal that the cannonade "put the enemy in great confusion, having killed and dangerously wounded great numbers." (Seymour, "Journal," p. 381) Seymour credited Capt. Anthony Singleton for the fine performance of the artillery. He wrote that Singleton "signalized himself in levelling his pieces so well and playing with such impetuosity." (Ibid.)

The tide of battle quickly turned, however. NG had wanted his regiments to attack the

British line simultaneously with bayonets and without firing. As they began their advance, both Gunby's and Ford's regiments paused and fired a volley, although John Eager Howard would later remember that the enemy fire "was not severe." (Lee, *Memoirs*, 2: 61; Howard to unnamed correspondent, n.d., MdHi) Almost immediately, Capt. William Beatty, commanding a company on the right flank of Gunby's regiment, was killed, throwing that unit into disorder. Gunby then ordered the rest of his regiment to "rally by retiring to its right company." (Ibid.; quote taken from Lee.) Rawdon's troops, seeing confusion among the Americans, forged ahead. Their advance unsettled the First Maryland Regiment, which continued to retreat. At almost the same time, Col. Benjamin Ford, who was leading the Second Maryland Regiment, was wounded, and his regiment also broke. (Johnson, *Greene*, 2: 94) On the American right, Campbell's Virginians became unsettled and fled. Hawes's regiment was still advancing in good order, but the Marylanders' flight allowed the enemy to attack his flank. NG, who was with Hawes's regiment, was forced to order the Virginians to retire. (See NG to Lee, 28 April, below.) NG was so active and oblivious to danger in leading Hawes's troops during the battle that William Davie wrote of him: "General Greene exposed himself greatly in this action, expecially with Campbell's regiment; so much so, that one of the officers observed to me, that his conduct during the action resembled more that of a captain of grenadiers, than that of a major-general." (Johnson, *Greene*, 2: 95) Although Gunby's order began the chain of events, the confusion in Ford's and Campbell's regiments seems to have originated from other causes, and it seems unfair to place all the blame on Gunby. NG, however, as seen by his letter to Joseph Reed of 6 August, below, did hold Gunby responsible for the defeat. His opinion was supported by the findings of a court of inquiry convened at Gunby's request a few days after the battle. (For the convening and findings of the court, see NG's Orders of 28 April and 2 May, both below.)

4. Others have viewed Washington's conduct less favorably than NG did. (See, for example, Ward, *War*, 2: 806) After a long detour around dense underbrush that left him far behind the enemy's battle line, Washington encountered a number of British non-combatants, stragglers, and wounded. According to William R. Davie, NG's commissary, Washington's dragoons, instead of ignoring these "trumpery of an army," spent precious time "taking, securing, and parolling" them. Davie added that even British officers "acknowledged the unfortunate effect of the clemency of our cavalry, in waiting to capture and parol prisoners, when they should have cut them out of their way without stopping." Davie believed that Washington should have attacked Rawdon's second line "either before it moved up to extend the front, or while this manoeuvre was performing; and in either case, the charge would have been decisive." Instead, Washington's dragoons so encumbered themselves with prisoners that "they could do nothing." (Quoted in Johnson, *Greene*, 2: 83.) By the time the dragoons returned to the battle, the American army had broken, and Washington had to rid himself of his prisoners so that he could charge to protect the retreat. Rawdon acknowledged that Washington's presence prevented him from exploiting his victory. He explained to Lord Cornwallis in his letter of 26 April: "the Enemy's Cavalry greatly surpassing ours as to numbers, horses & appointments, our Dragoons could not risque much, nor could I suffer those Infantry to break their order in hopes of overtaking the fugitives" of NG's army. (PRO 30/11/5)

5. According to Guilford Dudley, it was only the American army's left wing that halted at Saunder's Creek, some two to three miles from the battlefield. The troops on the right wing, with which Dudley was serving, did not know what had become of the left wing or of NG, who "had greatly exposed himself during the conflict." The right wing retired "through the woods, over bog and morass, at a respecful distance from the [Camden-Charlotte] road," to a point beyond Sutton's Creek, some seven miles from Camden.

They then moved toward the road, where they "most fortunately met General Greene, who, as well as the left wing . . . were equally uncertain what had become of us." NG led the right wing to Saunder's Creek and reassembled his army there in the late afternoon. (Dann, *Revolution Remembered*, p. 220) Although NG did not mention it here, the American artillery was saved, as Rawdon put it, "by mere accident. It was run down a steep hill among some thick brush wood, where we passed without observing it, & it was carried off whilst we pursued the Infantry in a contrary direction." (Rawdon to Cornwallis, 26 April, PRO 30/11/5)

6. In a letter to Lord Cornwallis of 25 April, Rawdon gave his casualties as 220. (PRO 30/11/6) That total apparently did not include the missing. The official return gave total British casualties as 258—more than one-fourth of Rawdon's force. ("Annual Register— 1781," p. 857)

7. The return was prepared by NG's adjutant, Otho Williams, who reported 270 American casualties, nearly half of whom were listed as missing. Many of these, according to Williams, "had not understood the order to rally at Saunders Creek"; a third of the missing had since been "heard of" and would soon rejoin the army, he hoped. (PCC, item 155, vol. 2: 163, 167, 168, DNA; the quoted material is on p. 167.) It is not known how many returned, but Rawdon reported that a large number, whose retreat had been cut off, went into Camden and "claimed protection as Deserters." (PRO 30/11/6)

8. Williams commended Beatty in a letter to Beatty's sister, adding that NG had "mention'd him in very obliging Terms to Congress & Genl Washington. This is all the consolation his Friends can have. He died doing his Duty in a Gallant manner. Fame is the only Legacy a Deceasd Soldier leaves to his family." (Williams to Mrs. M. Stull, 4 May, MdHi)

9. On the capture of Ft. Watson, see Marion to NG, first letter of 23 April, above. The terms are noted there.

10. Huntington's letter of 10 March is above (vol. 7: 423). That of 29 March has not been found, but a note is attached to the letterbook copy of his letter to Dr. Nathan Brownson of the same date, stating that Huntington had written NG "A short letter" on the 29th to announce Brownson's appointment as deputy purveyor of hospitals for the Southern Army. (PCC, item 15, p. 254, DNA)

11. Rawdon withdrew to Camden shortly after the battle, taking most of his troops with him and leaving Maj. John Coffin to guard the battlefield with a force of dragoons and mounted infantry. William Washington, who was sent back to scout the area, lured Coffin into an ambush, in which the Loyalist cavalry commander lost twenty men and was forced to flee to Camden. (Johnson, *Greene*, 2: 34; Kirkland and Kennedy, *Camden*, p. 237)

To General Francis Marion

Dear Sir   Camp at Rughlys [S.C.] April 27th 1781[1]

Capt Conniers has just arrivd in Camp, and says that reports are below that we were routed and totally dispersed.[2] You will take measures to have the account contradicted and the public properly informed. By mistake we got a slight repulse. The injury is not great. The Enemy Sufferd much more than we did. What has happened will make no alteration in our plan of operations and therefore I wish you to pursue the same plan as you had in contemplation before.

In my last I desird you to move up within 7 miles of Camden, but Capt Conniers thinks that fifty Men below at the distance of fifteen or twenty Miles of it[,] all the supplies can be as effectually cut off as if you were at a less distance; and that if you cross the Santee you can take all the posts upon the Congaree and those posts that lies between Camden and that river.[3] I have therefore sent Cap[t] Conniers to conduct the Artillery to you which I was informed this morning by Express was on its return[,] Maj [Pinketham] Eaton having heard of the reduction of the fort.[4]

You will cross the river Santee or detach Lt Col [Henry] Lee and direct your force as information and circumstances may direct either towards George Town or elsewhere as shall appear to be necessary keeping me constantly advisd of your situation; and leaving a guard of about sixty Men at or about the High Hills of Santee to prevent supplies from going to Camden.[5]

Get all the good dragoon horses you can to mount our Cavalry[;] those for Col Washingtons Corps Capt Conners will take care of. This is a great object and I beg you pay particular attention to it.[6] I am dear Sir Your Most Obed[t] humble Ser   N GREENE

ADfS (Greene Papers: DLC).

1. NG was at the plantation of Col. Henry Rugeley, at Saunder's Creek, about four miles from Camden.

2. James Conyers, a South Carolina militia officer who had been serving in NG's army, had been sent to Marion at the time NG returned to South Carolina. (See NG to Marion, 4 April, above.) On the battle of Hobkirk's Hill, see NG to Huntington, this date, above.

3. The posts between Camden and the Congaree River were Ft. Motte, Belleville, and Ft. Granby. Marion was occupied for a time with concerns that Lord Cornwallis was returning to South Carolina and with an unsuccessful attempt to keep a British reinforcement from reaching Lord Rawdon at Camden. He and Lee began operations against Ft. Motte, the most important of the posts, on 6 May. (Rankin, *Swamp Fox*, pp. 197–201)

4. See Eaton to NG, this date, and William Pierce to Eaton, 28 April, both below.

5. See Marion's reply of 30 April, below.

6. NG's repeated requests for horses caused friction with Marion. (See NG to Marion, 4 May, and Marion to NG, 6 May, both below.)

*   *   *

¶ [TO BARON STEUBEN. From Camp before Camden, S.C., 27 April 1781. Gives a similar account of the battle of Hobkirk's Hill to that contained in his letter to Samuel Huntington of this date, above. Adds that he could not have stormed the fort at Camden, "as the Garrison was nearly as large as the whole of our force." The position he took outside Camden was "favorable either for defence or pursuing the Enemy should they sally." His troops, when forced to retreat from the battlefield, "retired skirmishing about 2 miles and a half." Col. [William] Washington's men were able to "get off only about fifty [prisoners], with six or eight Officers, and paroled five or six more." The Southern Army's casualties were "considerable tho' much less" than the enemy's. Adds that once his army had re-formed at Saunder's Creek, "the Horse and part of the Infantry [advanced] in the afternoon and drove the Enemy from the [Hobkirk's] Hill and obliged them to retreat into Town with precipitation." Concludes his account of the battle by saying: "Had it not been for the unfortunate orders of Col⁰ Gunby I am persuaded we should have been compleatly victorious, and in full possession of Camden, as it was impossible for the Enemy to have retreated into Town our Horse being in their rear. This repulse, if such it may be called, will make no alteration in our general plan of operations."[1] Reports the capture of "one of the Enemies posts upon the Santee" by Gen. [Francis] Marion and Col. [Henry] Lee.[2] LS (NHi) 3 pp.]

1. The battle and the role that Col. John Gunby played in it are discussed at NG to Huntington, this date, above.

2. On the capture of Ft. Watson, see Marion to NG, first letter of 23 April, above.

¶ [TO GEORGE WASHINGTON. From "Camp at Saunders's Creek," S.C., 27 April 1781. Encloses a copy of his letter to Congress; acknowledges one from Washington of "27th of March."[1] ALS (Washington Papers: DLC) 1 p.]

1. NG enclosed a copy of his letter to Samuel Huntington, this date, above. Washington's letter, dated 21 March, is above (vol. 7: 458).

¶ [FROM MAJOR PINKETHAM EATON, "Camp near Black River," S.C., 27 April 1781. He decided to stop and apprise NG of the situation after receiving accounts that Ft. Watson had surrendered and that Col. [Henry] Lee and Gen. [Francis] Marion had moved to the High Hills of the Santee.[1] Requests orders.[2] Gives the routes he can take to join Lee or to march to the army and tells where the express can find him. ALS (MiU-C) 2 pp.]

1. On the capture of Ft. Watson and Lee's and Marion's movements, see Marion to NG, first letter of 23 April, above.

2. As seen in Pierce to Eaton, 28 April, below, NG gave Eaton two sets of orders, the first of which has not been found.

¶ [FROM SHERIFF NATHANIEL HUNT, Halifax County, Va., 27 April 1781. As NG requested, he has received British prisoners "at Sundry Times" and sent them under guard to the place that NG directed. As there was no commissary or guard at that place, the local militia commander sent the prisoners on to Winchester.[1] Since then, the Halifax County militiamen who escorted the prisoners have been called out for three months' service with NG's army. They believe they have been wrongfully treated, their tour of duty as guards apparently counting for nothing. Hunt hopes NG will treat them as they "desarve from the above State of the matter."[2] ALS (MiU-C) 1 p.]

1. NG's orders to Hunt are above, dated 20 February (vol. 7: 321). As seen there, NG directed that the prisoners be marched to Charlottesville.

2. NG excused these militiamen from further service when they reached his camp in South Carolina. (See Wooding to NG, 10 August, below.)

¶ [FROM COLONEL HENRY LEE, JR., [High Hills of Santee, S.C.], 27 April [1781].[1] Sends an enclosure [not found], showing how often Lee has written NG and "how constantly" the expresses "have deceived" him. "There is a great opportunity for service on the other side [of] the Santee" if Lee can get a field piece and reinforcements.[2] He needs the former to "reduce" the enemy's posts and the latter "to fight the flying party⁵ and Watson[,] Small &c."[3] Thinks NG should "keep up appearances before Camden, never throw away men by storming, & act with vigor on the other side of the Santee." ALS (MiU-C) 2 pp.]

1. Lee was operating with Gen. Francis Marion, who wrote NG from the High Hills of the Santee on this date, immediately below.

2. The "other side [of] the Santee" was south and west of the river, where the British had several small posts.

3. "Flying party[s]" were presumably roving bands of Loyalist raiders. For more on the detachment commanded by Col. John Watson, see note at Marion to NG, 6 May, below. Col. John Small commanded the British post at Monck's Corner, and Lee incorrectly assumed that he would join Watson to relieve Camden. (See Lee to NG, first letter of 23 April, above.)

¶ [FROM GENERAL FRANCIS MARION, "W[m] Richardsons[,] High Hills [of] Santee," S.C., 27 April 1781. Has had no reply to three letters that he wrote to NG; fears NG has retreated.[1] If so, Marion and Lee are in a "Dangerous" situation, as Lord Rawdon is "superior to us." Sends intelligence that [Col. John] Watson crossed the Santee "Last Tuesday [24 April]" and marched for Monck's Corner, where Col. [Welbore Ellis] Doyle has 300 men.[2] Col. [Nisbet] Balfour "came out" of Charleston with 200 men. From the route that Balfour took, Marion thinks he is either going south—in pursuit of Col. [William] Harden—or is planning to "reinforce the Congarees or Camdan."[3] Marion awaits NG's orders with "great impatients." ALS (MiU-C) 1 p.]

1. NG wrote Marion on 26 and 27 April, both above. As seen in Marion to NG, 30 April, below, Marion received both letters.

2. On 26 April, Nisbet Balfour wrote Lord Cornwallis that Watson, who had been ordered to Camden from Georgetown, had crossed to the south side of the Santee "in order to proceed up towards McCords Ferry & there wait events as his crossing would be very dangerous untill we know more of Greene's Movements." (PRO 30/11/6)

3. Balfour reported to Cornwallis on 17 May that he had assembled in Charleston and had placed under the command of Maj. Archibald McArthur a force of 300 infantry and 100 cavalry, some of whom were "convalescents." Balfour sent these troops to "Eutaws" to "facilitate Lord Rawdons retreat, over the Santee." (PRO 30/11/6)

¶ [FROM MAURICE SPILLARD TO CAPTAIN WILLIAM PIERCE, JR., Caswell County, N.C., 27 April 1781. Has Pierce's letter of 18 April; encloses two letters, which NG has offered to forward for Spillard to Camden, S.C. Tells where to send his baggage if it "comes out." Spillard is obliged to NG for "his Generous endeavours" and awaits NG's permission to go "Northward."[1] ALS (MiU-C) 1 p.]

1. On 29 June, below, Spillard again wrote NG about his baggage and asked for permission to relocate.

* * *

From General Thomas Sumter

Broad River near Boyleys Ferry [S.C.][1]

D[r] Sir 27th Ap[l] 1781

I am Just favoured with Yours of the 23[d] Ins[t]. I Received Yours of the 19th and Wrote you immediately after Which I Sent to Col[l] Hampton then upon the Wateree to be forwarded to you.[2]

I Lament not having it in my power to prevent Maj[r] Fraziers [Thomas Fraser's] Detachment from Giting into Camden.[3] I have been under

Great perplexity. The Detachments from North Carolina & the uper Regim^ts in the South have Not Yet Joind me.[4] My force is daily increasing. I move Slow for that purpose. I have parties Dispersed through the Tory Settlements in Both forks to bring in the Militia, Collect Waggons & Horses & Disperce parties of Tories that are Lying out.[5] I Cant possibly assertain what forces I have[.] In a few days I May be able to do it more to your Satisfaction. But I am Convinced it will not be inconsiderable and have no doubt but I Can pervent your having any Interruptions from the South Side of the Wateree except a Very large force Shoud Come from Charles Town. I am Just inform'd that the Tories which have fled from above are embodying West of Saluda River. I have prepaird a proper party to Send after them, Which if Dispersed will leave all the Back Country open and Secoure, quite to 96.[6] So that the Inhabitants Can have No Good excuse for Not Turning out. Genl Pickens Set out yesterday for 96 Where there is a Number of men emboyed [i.e., embodied] under Co^l [James] McCall. He will Cut of[f] all Supplies from the Garrison as Soon as he arives.[7]

I have Nothing Certain from Charles Town yet. A Report prevails there that Genl Phillips is Coming to Virginia With three thousand men.[8] I have Corn Grinding at the Congrees and Shall be able to Send a Quantity of Meal to you in a few days. I am D^r S^r your most obed^t Hble Servt   THO^S SUMTER

NB. I have nether paper[,] wax or Wafers[.] If you have any to Spare Shoud be Much ob[l]iged to you for Some by any oppertunity. I Will have proper person engaged for Carrying intelligence.   T S

ALS (MiU-C).

1. Sumter was apparently at Brierly's Ferry.

2. See Henry Hampton to NG, 28 April, below.

3. In his letter of 23 April, NG had expressed "mortification" that a party from Ninety Six had slipped into Camden. He had wanted Sumter to cut off all supplies and reinforcements coming to the garrison at Camden from the west and south.

4. The "Detachments from North Carolina" were ten-month men who had been recruited around Charlotte. (See Sumter to NG, 7 April, above.)

5. By "Both forks," Sumter presumably meant the Dutch Forks area, where the Saluda River flowed into the Broad, and the area known as the Congarees, where the Congaree and Wateree rivers combined to form the Santee.

6. As seen in Andrew Pickens to NG, 3 May, below, the Loyalists who had collected in the Saluda area retired into the British post at Ninety Six before Pickens could overtake them.

7. In ibid., Pickens discussed his activities after leaving Sumter.

8. In his letter to Sumter of 23 April, above, NG had reported the rumor that Gen. William Phillips was bringing 2,000 men to South Carolina from Virginia. As noted there, the report was false.

*   *   *

¶ [GENERAL GREENE'S ORDERS, "Camp at Rugeley's," S.C., 28 April 1781. Appoints Gen. [Isaac] Huger, Col. [Charles] Harrison, and Col. [William] Washington to a court to "enquire into the Conduct of Colonel [John] Gunby" at the battle of Hobkirk's Hill.[1] Wants a return of camp kettles and knapsacks "on hand and wanting."[2] Lamar Orderly Book (OClWHi) 2 pp.]

1. For background on the court of inquiry, see notes at NG to Huntington, 27 April, above. The court's decision is given in NG's Orders of 2 May, below.

2. NG wrote Henry Lee on this date, below, that the only stores his army had lost at Hobkirk's Hill were "a few of the Soldiers Knapsacks and blankets."

¶ [CAPTAIN WILLIAM PIERCE, JR., TO MAJOR PINKETHAM EATON. From Rugeley's, S.C., [28 April 1781].[1] Eaton is to disregard NG's earlier letter of this date [not found] and go instead with Capt. James Conyers to join Gen. [Francis] Marion.[2] Df (MiU-C) 1 p.]

1. The date was taken from the docketing.

2. For background on this order, see Eaton to NG, 27 April, above.

* * *

To Governor Thomas Jefferson of Virginia

Sir [Camp near Camden, S.C. 28 April 1781][1]

Since I wrote your Excellency in answer to the resolutions of your Assembly relative to the conduct of the Cavalry Officers, and the measures pointed out to supply this Army in future with Horses, I have been considering more fully the tendency and consequences that would attend it.[2]

It is to be lamented that Officers will not exercise more discretion and prudence when entrusted with the execution of an order which seems to invade the rights of a Citizen not perfectly conformable to the Laws and constitution of the Land. And it is equally to be lamented that a Legislature should from a resentment for the misconduct of a few individuals, bring upon an Army employed in their service inevitable ruin, and upon the community disgrace and distress.

I was very particular in giving my orders to guard against the evils complained of, a copy of which is inclosed; and I have no wish to screen a single Officer who has wantonly invaded the property of the People, or offered any insult to the Inhabitants; but I wish the improper conduct of a few Officers may not be made to operate as a punishment upon the whole Army.[3] Particular situations and particular circumstances often make measures necessary that have the specious shew of oppression, because they carry with them consequences pointed and distressing to individuals. It is to be lamented that this is the case, but pressing emergencies make it political and sometimes unavoidable.

When we retired over the Dan our force was too small to stop the progress of the Enemy, or mark the limits of their approach. We appealed to the only means left us to save your Country, and prevent the destruction of a virtuous little Army. Men were called for, they turned out with a spirit that did honor to themselves and their Country; Horses were wanted to mount our Dragoons, they could not be procured but by virtue of impress Warrants. You was convinced of this fact and therefore furnished me with the Warrants for the purpose.[4] I took the most adviseable, and as I thought the most effectual means to have the business conducted with propriety; and I cannot but think the Gentlemen generally who were entrusted with the execution of my orders, were governed entirely by a principle of public good. Some mistakes and several abuses appear to have happened in impressing Studd Horses instead of geldings, but those mistakes arose from the necessity of mounting our Dragoo[ns] in such a manner as to give us an immediate superiority over the Enemy, as well in the quality of the Horses as their number. The People complained, I was willing to redress their grievances; some of the most valuable covering Horses were returned, and I shall direct some others to be restored notwithstanding the great inconvenience which must inevitably attend this Army by it.[5]

The Assembly of your State appear to have taken up the matter from a principle tho' acknowledged to be virtuous, yet from its tendency, must be allowed to be impolitic. The rights of Individuals are as dear to me as to any Man, but the safety of a community I have ever considered as an object more valuable. In politics as well as every think [i.e., thing] else a received and established axiom is, that greater evils should in every instance give way to lesser misfortunes. In War it is often impossible to conform to all the ceremonies of Law and equal justice; and to attempt it would be productive of greater misfortunes to the public from the delay than all the inconveniencies which individuals may suffer.

Your Excellency must be sensible of the innumerable inconveniencies I had to labor under at the time, and the variety of difficulties that still surround us. Nothing but light Horse can enable us, with the little Army we have, to appear in the field; and nothing but a superiority in Cavalry can prevent the Enemy from cutting to pieces every detachment coming to join the Army or employed in collecting supplies. From the open State of this Country their services are particularly necessary, and unless we can keep up the Corps of Cavalry and constantly support a superiority it will be out of our power to act or to prevent the Enemy from overruning the Country, and commanding all its resources.

The Assembly I fear by their resolves have destroyed my hopes and expectations on this head. Under the Law as it at present stands it is certain nothing can be done.[6] By limiting Dragoon Horses to the narrow price of five thousand Pounds it amounts only to a prohibition, and cuts off the prospect of any future supplies. At this moment the

Enemy are greatly superior to us, and unless Virginia will spring immediately to the most generous exertions they will indubitably continue so. It is in vain to expect protection from an Army which is not supported, or make feeble efforts upon narrow principles of prudence or economy; they only serve to procrastinate the War, and tire out the patience of the People. Already have we experienced in many instances, the ill consequences of neglecting the Army when surrounde[d] with difficulties and threatened with ruin. Great expence of blood and treasure have attended this policy and to redress the grievances of a few Individuals when it will entail calamity upon the Community, will be neither political or just.

If Horses are dearer to the Inhabitants than the lives of Subjects or the liberties of the People there will be no doubt of the Assembly persevering in their late resolution, otherwise I hope they will reconsider the matter and not oblige me to take a measure which cannot fail to bring ruin upon the Army, and fresh misfortunes upon the Country.

Df (MiU-C).
1. The date was taken from the docketing, the place from another of NG's letters of this date.
2. NG's letter, dated 6 April, is above. Jefferson, writing to NG on 1 April, above, had advised him to send a letter "remonstrating on the subject" and providing Jefferson with "an opportunity of laying the matter again before the assembly."
3. See NG to Henry Lee and NG to William Washington, both dated 17 February, above (vol. 7: 301, 305).
4. For more on the impressment warrant, see NG to Jefferson, 15 February, and Jefferson to NG, 19 February, both above (vol. 7: 289, 317).
5. See NG's letters to Lee and Washington, cited in note 3, above.
6. The Assembly's resolutions are discussed at Jefferson to NG, 24 March, above (vol. 7: 467).

To the Chevalier de La Luzerne

Sir   Camp near Camden [S.C.] April 28th 1781

I had the honor to recieve your Excellencys letter of the 21st of January some little time since.[1] It was a long time on the way as it frequently happens with despaches coming from the Northward.

I am greatly mortified at the disappointment of the intended plan of operations against Portsmouth.[2] I have not seen the particulars of the Sea engagement; but the Enemy in Charlestown give the highest honor to the conduct of the french fleet upon the occasion.[3] God grant the second division may soon arrive and relieve this distressed Country which I am sure cannot struggle much longer without more effectual support; and I am perswaded will never be effectually relieved but by a Naval operation in their favor.[4] They may struggle a little while longer but they must fail and I fear their fall will lay a train to sap the Independance of the rest of America.

I have agreeably to your Excellencys advice impressed the States all in my power with a sense of their danger but they have not the means to make the necessary exertions.

I must beg leave to refer your Excellency to my public despaches to Congress for the situation of things in this quarter.

We fight get beat rise and fight again. The whole Country is one continued scene of blood and slaughter. I have the honor to be with great respect Your Excellencys Most Obed[t] hum Serv   N GREENE

ADfS (MiU-C).

1. La Luzerne's letter is above (vol. 7: 167).

2. On the failure of the planned Franco-American operation against the British force at Portsmouth, Va., see Lafayette to NG, 4 April, above.

3. For more on the battle between British and French fleets near the entrance to Chesapeake Bay, see note at Steuben to NG, first letter of 4 March, above (vol. 7: 390n).

4. As noted at La Luzerne to NG, 3 April, above, the long-awaited second division of the French expeditionary force never was sent to America. The presence of a French naval force from the West Indies, however, later made possible the capture of Lord Cornwallis's army at Yorktown, Va., and helped to free the upper South from the threat of British domination.

*   *   *

¶ [TO ROBERT LANIER, [Camp near Camden, S.C., 28] April 1781.[1] Has received Lanier's letter of 19 April. Cannot empower him to draw "any considerable Sum of Money without the consent" of Congress. Lanier may "draw on" Virginia for £150 in NG's name, and NG will also write Congress "for liberty to extend the draught." NG is happy to do what he can "to promote and facilitate a peace" and to bring about an exchange of prisoners with the Chickasaw and Cherokee.[2] Df (MiU-C) 1 p.]

1. The place was taken from another of NG's letters of this date; the draft is dated "Ap[i] 10th," but the docketing and a GWG Transcript (CSmH) both date the letter the 28th, which is consistent with the contents.

2. One historian has termed NG's offer "laughable," pointing out that in the opinion of another peace commissioner, William Christian, £200,000 was needed for supplies and gifts for the proposed peace conference. (O'Donnell, Southern Indians, p. 118; Christian to Jefferson, 5 July, Calendar of Va. State Papers, 2: 199–201) No evidence has been found that NG wrote Congress to ask for additional money for the commissioners. They successfully petitioned the state of Virginia for the £200,000, however. (Virginia, Council of State, Journals, 2: 357)

¶ [TO COLONEL HENRY LEE, JR. From [Camp near Camden, S.C., 28 April 1781]. Has Lee's letter of 19 April, two more of 23 April, and two of the 27th. "You know best your own situation and your own wishes, but you are not well informed of mine. I have run every hazard to promote your plan of operations, as well to oblige you, as from a perswasion the public service would be benefited by it." Gives a detailed account of the battle of Hobkirk's Hill, which is similar to the report in NG to Huntington, 27 April, above, with such additions as follow. The American artillery, from "the advantage of position was doing great execution." Col. [Samuel] Hawes's regiment was advancing "in tolerable order, within forty yards of the Enimy, and they in confusion in front, but from the enimies having gained their flank . . . I was obliged to order them to retire also, to save them from being cut to pieces. I was with this Regiment my self, and they sufferd more than all the rest." Col. [Richard] Campbell's regiment became "disorderd" at the same time as the Marylanders but was rallied through the exertions of Campbell and NG's aide, Capt. William Pierce. All the regiments rallied at "different times, but not in such order or with such spirit as to recover the misfortunes of the day." Only "a few of the Soldiers Knapsacks and blankets" were lost in the retreat. Col. [William] Washington "never shone upon any occasion more than this." He took 200 prisoners and "in the course of the day made several charges, and cut to pieces their dragoons."[1] American casualties were 150 killed and wounded, including Col. [Benjamin] Ford, who was wounded in the arm. "A considerable number of straglers have not yet come in, but we have heard of them."

Lee should "undeceive the people" about the "consequences" of the battle. NG has ordered that a field piece be sent to Lee—if Lee and Gen. [Francis] Marion "think it will be useful."[2] They should cross the Santee River "together or act separate, as occasion and intelligence may dictate, but dont run great risques." Congratulates Lee on his "success."[3] Adds that Col. [Otho] Williams was "very active and greatly exposed" in the battle. ADf (IHi) 4 pp.]

1. As noted at NG to Huntington, 27 April, above, Washington's victory over enemy dragoons occurred after the battle of Hobkirk's Hill.

2. NG's orders are in Pierce to Eaton, this date, above. As seen in Lee's letter of this date, below, the field piece did figure in his plans. (Virginia, Council of State, *Journals*, 2: 357)

3. The "success" was the capture of Ft. Watson by Marion and Lee. (See Marion to NG, first letter of 23 April, above.)

¶ [TO COLONEL THOMAS POLK. From Camp at Rugeley's Mill, S.C., 28 April 1781. Orders "General" Polk to proceed to Salisbury and collect the "Continental Troops drafted from the Militia."[1] Polk is also to call on the other counties in the Salisbury district for their quotas of men and request that each county arm and equip its levies.[2] He is to provide fifty wagons and teams for the army by a "demand on each County [in the district] according to its ability."[3] Df (MiU-C) 1 p.]

1. Polk never received the promotion to general that NG anticipated here. (See Polk to NG, 15 May, below.)

2. See also NG to Read, 29 April, below.

3. Polk reported on his progress in a letter to NG of 9 May, below.

¶ [TO LORD RAWDON. From "Head Quarters" [Rugeley's Mill, S.C.], 28 April 1781. British treatment of Capt. [John] Smith of the Maryland line, who has been "closely confined," differs so markedly from American treatment of British officers captured in the same battle that NG requests an explanation.[1] Df (MiU-C) 1 p.]

1. Rawdon's response is in Doyle to NG, 29 April, below.

¶ [CAPTAIN WILLIAM PIERCE, JR., TO GENERAL THOMAS SUMTER. From Rugeley's, S.C., 28 April 1781. NG has received Sumter's letter of 25 April and thanks him for his "exertions." As Maj. [Edmund] Hyrne has been sent to brief Sumter, NG "declines" saying anything about the army's situation, which, except for the move "up to this place," is unchanged since Hyrne left camp.[1] In a postscript, reports the capture of Ft. Watson, with "6 Officers & 109 Privates."[2] ALS (Sumter Papers: DLC) 1 p.]

1. For more on Hyrne's discussions with Sumter, see NG to Sumter, 30 April, below.
2. On the capture of Ft. Watson, see Marion to NG, first letter of 23 April, above.

¶ [FROM GENERAL JOHN BUTLER, Ramsey's Mill, N.C., 28 April 1781. Sends intelligence, thought to be reliable, that Lord Cornwallis has crossed the North East Cape Fear River and plans to march through Duplin County and recross the river near Campbelltown.[1] Butler is trying to obtain "more Certain information" of the enemy's movements. In a postscript, acknowledges receipt of NG's letter of 21 April. ALS (MiU-C) 1 p.]

1. On the movements of Cornwallis's army, see note at Emmet to NG, this date, below.

¶ [FROM JOHN COMPTY, Carter's Ferry, Va., 28 April 1781. Has ten wagon-loads of ammunition and fourteen more of clothing for NG's army.[1] Has lacked guards for the wagons since "Frederic town."[2] Will move on to Hillsborough, N.C., where he hopes to receive instructions from NG; asks specifically if he should proceed past Hillsborough without guards. ALS (MiU-C) 1 p.]

1. According to a return, Compty had left Philadelphia on 30 March with 8,449 dozen musket cartridges and "fixed ammunition" for the artillery. (PCC, item 39, vol. 3: 417, DNA; see also Compty's invoice, dated 29 March, MiU-C.) The clothing included 1,775 coats, 1,272 shirts, 374 pairs of shoes, 234 linen overalls, and 10 pairs of dragoon boots. (Invoice, dated 23 March, MiU-C)
2. Compty's wagons could have gone by way of Frederick Town, Md., but it is more likely that he meant Fredericksburg, Va., which was on the direct route from Philadelphia.

¶ [FROM COLONEL JAMES EMMET, Campbelltown, N.C., 28 April 1781. He received reliable intelligence "last night" that part of Lord Cornwallis's army moved on "Tuesday last" to a point "about ten miles from Wilmington on the E. side of the N E. River." They are to be joined there by the rest of the army, except one corps of about 300 men.[1] "They give out they are going for Newbern," but Emmet puts the "greatest Confidence" in his information that they "are coming thro' this Place, on their way to the southward."[2] As "This Town, & indeed many parts of the County is much infested with the small pox," he cannot "keep a single man" there and must send this letter to Gen. [John] Butler to forward.[3] ALS (NHi) 1 p.]

1. "Tuesday last" was 24 April. Col. Banastre Tarleton's advance force was ordered to "seize as many boats as possible on the north-east branch of Cape-fear river, and collect them at a place about fifteen miles above Wilmington." (Tarleton, Campaigns, p. 285) The rest of Cornwallis's army left Wilmington on 25 April. ("Von Bose Journal," p. 56)
2. The British were heading north, to Virginia.
3. See Butler to NG, this date, above.

¶ [FROM COLONEL HENRY HAMPTON, Dickson's Ford, "25 miles from Camden," S.C., 28 April 1781. Gen. [Thomas] Sumter asked him to collect provisions for NG's army. Hampton could obtain only "two Waggons" and a limited supply of bacon, which he is sending to NG. To complete the loads, he is sending a supply of corn. Forwards a letter from Sumter that has just arrived.[1] ALS (MiU-C) 1 p.]

1. Hampton forwarded Sumter's letter to NG of 25 April, above, in which he discussed his orders to Hampton.

¶ [FROM THE MARQUIS DE LAFAYETTE, Hanover Court House, Va., 28 April 1781. Learning that Gen. [William] Phillips was preparing for an offensive, Lafayette forced a march with 1,000 men from Baltimore, Md., "towards" Richmond, Va., which he feared would be "a principal object with the Enemy." Describes the initial movements of Phillips's force and the actions of the Virginia militia in opposing them. In a skirmish at Blandford, the Virginia militia, who lost twenty killed and wounded, behaved very gallantly.[1] "Yesterday," the British moved to Osborne's, skirmished with the militia, and destroyed some vessels collected there.[2] They have not yet attempted to cross the [James] River. Steuben, whose troops are on the same side of the river as the British, has fallen back. Lafayette's detachment will be at Hanover, twenty miles from Richmond, in a few hours.[3] "The Enemy are more than double our Force in regular Troops, and their Command of the water gives them great advantages." LS (NjP) 2 pp.]

1. Baron Steuben gave a detailed account of movements by the British and the actions of the militia in his letter to NG of 25 April, above.

2. At Osborne's, on the James River near Richmond, a detachment of British troops commanded by Gen. Benedict Arnold captured and destroyed the remnants of the Virginia State Navy and a number of merchantmen. The Virginia militia witnessed the event but were on the opposite shore of the river, out of musket range, and thus unable to engage Arnold's troops. (Joseph A. Goldenberg and Marion West Stoer, "The Virginia State Navy," in *Chesapeake Bay in the American Revolution*, ed. Ernest M. Eller [Centreville, Md.: Tidewater Publishers, 1981], p. 195)

3. Phillips's and Steuben's forces were on the south side of the James; Lafayette was on the north—or Richmond—side.

¶ [FROM COLONEL HENRY LEE, JR., Long Branch, S.C., 28 April 1781.[1] He is "very unhappy to find that the best designs are so liable to fail thro the negligence of military men. Gen: Sumpter[s] absence is to me extraordinary, the affair of the 25[h] is as astonishing. Surely my dear Gen there is a necessity for an example somewhere."[2] Lee is still with Marion, who has moved to "this place," thirty miles from NG, as a result of NG's orders.[3] Lee is not sure if NG's orders apply to him; he hopes that he will be allowed to "pass the Santee" with Maj. [Pinketham] Eaton and "pursue the conquest of every post & detachment in that country."[4] Otherwise, he believes, "the storming of Cambden [is] unavoidable." If NG plans to storm Camden, Lee wants to be there with him. But if NG finds that his "numbers & discipline" are inadequate, he need only "keep up appearances" at Camden while allowing others to "act vigorously between the Santee & Savannah rivers."[5] The American "operating detachment" should know what NG's route will be in the event of Lord Cornwallis's approach. In Lee's opinion, NG's route should be as far south as possible, so that a junction "may be effected." Tells NG where he thinks Marion should "take post" near Camden.[6] Adds that Marion is "the best hand" to know every movement on the Pee Dee River and from Wilmington, N.C., towards the Pee Dee. Asks NG to send back the express immediately. ALS (MiU-C) 3 pp.]

1. Long Branch was a tributary of the Pocotaligo River, in what is now Sumter County, S.C.

2. As seen at NG to Huntington, 27 April, above, NG did make an "example" of one individual—Col. John Gunby—for the army's defeat at Hobkirk's Hill. Although some of NG's officers have asserted that he viewed Sumter as insubordinate, he did not confront Sumter about his apparent unwillingness to come to the aid of the army. (Gregorie, *Sumter*, p. 155; for more about NG's opinion of Sumter, see note at NG to Sumter, 30 April below.)

3. See NG to Marion, 26 April, above.

4. NG discussed his plans for Lee in a letter to Lee of 29 April, below.

5. As seen at his letter to Lee of 29 April, NG had no plans for storming Camden.

6. NG no longer wanted Marion to "take post" near Camden. (See NG to Marion, 27 April, above.)

¶ [GENERAL GREENE'S ORDERS, Camp, Rugeley's Mill, S.C., 29 April 1781. Each brigade is to furnish six officers to serve as members of a general court-martial "for tryal of Deserters."[1] Lamar Orderly Book (OClWHi) 1 p.]

1. On the outcome of the trial, see NG's Orders of 30 April, below.

¶ [TO FRANCIS KINLOCH. From [Camp, Rugeley's Mill, S.C.], 29 April 1781.[1] Has Kinloch's letter of 6 March.[2] NG had already directed Baron Steuben to parole Capt. [Thomas] Miller to Charleston, but if Steuben has "omitted" to do so, Miller may proceed there and stay until "called for or other ways directed."[3] Df (MiU-C) 1 p.]

1. The place was taken from NG's Orders of this date, immediately above.

2. The letter is above (vol. 7: 404).

3. As seen in ibid., Miller, a prisoner, had been on parole in Virginia. On Steuben's role in the matter, see his second letter to NG of 4 March, above (vol. 7: 390 and n).

*   *   *

To Colonel Henry Lee, Jr.

Dear Sir   [Camp, Rugeley's Mill, S.C., 29 April 1781][1]

Your letter of the 28th has just been received.

You write as if you thought I had an army of fifty thousand Men. Surely you cannot be unacquainted with our ac[tu]al situation. I have run every risque to favor your operations more perhaps than I ought, clearly so, if I had not my own reputation less at heart than the public service in general, and the glory of my friends in particular.

I wrote you an account of the affair of the 25th last evening, and sent Capt Conniers [James Conyers] to conduct the field piece to you and General Marian.[2] The event of the day was contrary to my expectations. Whether it was owing to an order of Col [John] Gunby's, or the misconduct of the Maryland Troops, is now a matter of enquiry.

I took the position on purpose to draw the enemy out, after being fully satisfied that the town could not be stormed, the works being too strong, and the garrison too large to hope for success. I never had an Idea of the kind, unless I found the place very weak. There were not wanting mad caps enough to urge it. Had we defeated the enemy not a man of the party could have got back into town. The sally was what every body wished for, but the event was unfortunate. The loss on either side is not greatly different one from the other. I think the enimy's must have been the greatest. The disgrace is more vexatious than any thing else, tho the disappointment in its consequences, is a capital misfortune: Camden must have fallen had we succeeded.[3]

I am as strongly impressed with the necessity of pushing our operations on the west side of Santee as you can be, but the means are wanting. We want reinforcments. You want detachments; and if you and General Marion seperate you will be both exposd; and I am afraid our little repulse the other day will give fresh hope to the enimy, and damp the spirits of our friends; however the best way to counteract that is, to act vigerously.[4]

In my letter to General Mari[on] of last Evening, I desird him either to detach you, or cross the Santee with you, as he might think advisable, from the information he had of the enemies posts, numbers and situation.[5] I beg you not to think of running great hazards, our situation will not warrant it. If we cannot accomplish great things, we must content our selves in having avoided a misfortune.

General Sumter has got but few Men, he has taken the field and is pushing after little parties of tories towards Ninty Six.[6] Major [Edmund] Hyrne is gone to him, if possible to get him to join us, but this I know he will avoid if he can with decency, for the same reasons that you wish to act seperately from the Army.[7] Should he join us, we shall be strong, and go on with our blockade with security.[8]

I cannot agree with you in opinion that the farther South we go the better. The posts upon the Santee & Congaree should be our great object. I am still afraid whether the Earl will quit his footing in North Carolinia to come to the aid of his posts here.[9]

Mr [Clement] Carrington one of your Officers is here with a party of horse & foot, but most of them are without Arms. They should come on to you, but they are so defenceless that I am afraid to send them. Can you not furnish them with Arms? It is out of our power to do it.

Once more let me warn you to be cautious. Yours

ADf (IHi).

1. The date was taken from the docketing, the place from NG's Orders of this date, above.

2. See NG to Lee, 28 April, above.

3. For more on the battle of Hobkirk's Hill, see NG to Huntington, 27 April, above.

4. As seen in his reply of 30 April, below, Lee continued to operate with Gen. Francis Marion.

5. Marion wrote NG on 30 April, below, that he was returning to the Santee.

6. See Gen. Thomas Sumter to NG, 27 April, above.

7. As seen in NG to Sumter, 30 April, below, Hyrne returned to camp that date with a report from Sumter. NG was implying here that both Lee and Sumter preferred detached service as a means of achieving the personal "glory" that he mentioned earlier in this letter.

8. Sumter did not join NG.

9. When Lord Cornwallis left North Carolina, it was to march his army north, into Virginia.

* * *

¶ [TO LORD RAWDON. From [Camp, Rugeley's Mill, S.C.], 29 April 1781.[1] Is unable to "accommodate" a wounded British officer and therefore has allowed him to go to Camden. Asks that the physician who accompanies the officer be permitted to examine the wound of Captain-Lieutenant [James] Bruff and that Bruff have the "liberty of coming out" if the physician so advises.[2] Df (MiU-C) 1 p.]

1. The place was taken from NG's Orders of this date, above.

2. A captain-lieutenant was an officer who commanded a company or troop at a captain's rank and a lieutenant's pay. (OED) Bruff had been wounded and captured in the battle of Hobkirk's Hill. Rawdon's reply has not been found.

¶ [TO COLONEL JAMES READ.[1] From Camp, Rugeley's Plantation, S.C., 29 April 1781. Read is to go to Salisbury, N.C., and order to camp any "properly armed and equiped" Continental drafts or Virginia militia who have assembled there. If there are any "Smiths and armourers" among these troops, Read should put them to work repairing arms and arrange for "Shops and tools necessary to promote this business." He is also "to take an account" of the baggage and stores at Salisbury.[2] ADfS (MiU-C) 2 pp.]

1. Read, a Continental officer, commanded a North Carolina militia force that had served with NG since shortly after the Southern Army returned to North Carolina from Virginia in February. His regiment was one of the few militia units that fought at both Guilford Court House and Hobkirk's Hill. (Schenck, N.C., 1780–81, pp. 298–99, 391; Guilford Dudley's narrative, in Dann, Revolution Remembered, pp. 216–21)

2. Read replied on 5 May, below.

¶ [FROM MAJOR JOHN DOYLE, Headquarters [Camden, S.C.], 29 April 1781. Replies about Capt. [John] Smith's "Situation" for Lord Rawdon, who has hurt his hand and is unable to write.[1] Rawdon cannot allow Smith "the same indulgence & attention" as the other captured American officers, "who have acted up to the Characters of Men," for this reason: "several deserters & some" American prisoners have reported that Smith "inhumanly put to death" a British officer and three privates after they were capt ured at Guilford Court House.[2] Rawdon has shown no "disrespect" by lodging him in the "Provost." In fact, Smith is in an officer's room, which, "were he not a prisoner, wou'd be as good Quarters as the present Situation of Camden could afford." ALS (MiU-C) 2 pp.]

1. NG had written Rawdon on 28 April, above, to inquire about the treatment that Smith was receiving.

2. The charges were a result of Smith having reportedly killed Col. Duncan Stuart during the battle of Guilford Court House. (Johnson, Greene, 2: 12) NG denied them in his reply to Rawdon of 3 May, below. (For more on the matter, see also Smith to NG, 30 April, below.)

¶ [FROM MAJOR PINKETHAM EATON, [near Rugeley's Mill, S.C.], 29 April 1781.[1] Has just received NG's orders to join Gen. [Francis] Marion and will comply with them "immediately after the troops are refresh[d]."[2] Is about five miles from Rugeley's. Capt. [James] Conyers "got out of the way last night" and did not find Eaton until now. Eaton's men are almost out of meal; asks if the commissary can provide any. ALS (MiU-C) 1 p.]

1. The place was taken from the contents.
2. The orders are in Pierce to Eaton, 28 April, above.

¶ [FROM COLONEL JAMES EMMET, Campbelltown, N.C., 29 April 1781. He wrote NG "yesterday morning" about Lord Cornwallis's movements. Reiterates his belief that the enemy's route "will be through this, to Camden [S.C.]."[1] He will "decamp this night" with three or four men—"& those are all [that are left] in this place"—because "the Enemy comes on most rappidley." Is forwarding this letter by an officer "on Pee Dee," those "here" being "too bad with the small pox to undertake such a journey." Adds that the British were fifty or sixty miles from Cross Creek on 27 April. ALS (MiU-C) 2 pp.]

1. See Emmet to NG, 28 April, above. Cornwallis's army did not march to Cross Creek/Campbelltown or Camden.

¶ [FROM COLONEL THOMAS WADE, [Cheraws, S.C.], 29 April 1781.[1] He wrote NG "a few Line yestrday [not found], respecting the Torys Surprising the Guard, at Col° Kolbs." About forty Loyalist attackers, who were from Drowning Creek, "Kild Col° Kolb and Two other men at his house."[2] About two hours later, an American party that had just arrived with enemy prisoners from "Scots Lake" set off in pursuit, taking some local militiamen with them.[3] They may be able to overtake the Loyalists, who "have no Thought of Being persued." Most men "of this District" are either with Marion "or in plundering parties." Wade is afraid "this Country will be Ruined . . . by the Whigg Torys that form small parties under no Orders and plunder the Country. Within a few days a number of Negroes have been brought in by those partys; and nothing Short of Hanging I believe will put a Stop to that pernisious practice."[4] Has a report that Gen. [Richard] Caswell attacked and defeated a detachment from Lord Cornwallis's army, "with Great Loss on the Side of the Enemy."[5] ALS (MiU-C) 3 pp.]

1. The place was determined from the contents. Wade's letters to NG of 19 and 20 April, both above, were also written from there.
2. On the death of Col. Abel Kolb, see note at Wade to NG, 4 April, above.
3. The party had accompanied enemy prisoners captured at Ft. Watson. (On the capture of the fort and the prisoners taken there, see Marion to NG, first letter of 23 April, above.)
4. By "Whigg Torys," Wade no doubt meant individuals who lacked a strong allegiance to either side.
5. The report was false.

¶ [GENERAL GREENE'S ORDERS, Camp, Rugeley's Mill, S.C., 30 April 1781. In after orders, NG approves the proceedings of a court-martial in which five men were convicted and sentenced to hang for "Desertion[,] joining the Enemy and bearing arms against the United States." NG

would be extremely happy if the Offences of these unfortunate men deserved a punishment less Severe. But Desertion is a Crime so Dangerous to an army that policy has dictated the mode of correction.

The indispensable necessity of giving some serious example, and the recent misfortunes the troops have suffered by the perfidy of some of their unworthy companions forbid the exercise of Lenity, and compel the general to admit the force of Martial Law. The Criminals are to be Executed, according to the Sentences annexed against them, at 4 oClock tomorrow afternoon.[1]

Lamar Orderly Book (OClWHi) 2 pp.]
1. All five—"deserters from our army, who were taken prisoners in the late action"—were executed on 1 May. (Seymour, "Journal," p. 382)

¶ [TO GOVERNOR THOMAS JEFFERSON OF VIRGINIA. From Camp, Rugeley's Mill, S.C., 30 April 1781. Has Jefferson's letter of 5 April "respecting the misconduct of Lt [Epaphroditus] Rudder."[1] NG considers it "a public misfortune that such hot headed youth, have it in their power to injure the public by such imprudent conduct. Let him and every other officer who misbehaves be subject to such punishment as they merit." NG will never "countenance" an officer insulting "Government or its Inhabitants." ADfS (MiU-C) 1 p.]
1. As seen in Jefferson's letter of 5 April, above, the complaint against Rudder concerned his conduct while impressing horses for NG's army.

* * *

To General Thomas Sumter

Dear Sir   Camp at Rugeleys Mill [S.C.] 30th April 1781
Major Hyrne return'd this morning, and soon after, Mr Taylor arriv'd with your letter of the 29th.[1] Both by the Majors report and your letter, I find you think it will be prejudicial to the public service for you to cross the Wateree and join me. Our situation requires it; but as you press so many objections, and I am so desirous to rouse the people in that quarter, I have thought it most adviseable to revoke the order, and leave you at liberty to prosecute your original plan.[2] General Marion, and Coll Lee, had orders to cross the Santee, and one or both undoubtedly will.[3] If both should cross, I am afraid [Col. John] Watson who is now in George Town will throw himself into Camden. If they separate I fear one part will be too weak to oppose him.[4] You will keep yourself informed of both his and Major McArthurs movements, the latter of whom with the Hessian horse, I fear got into Camden last evening.[5] However this is not certain. General Marion has a field piece; but by what I can learn the Fort at Congaree is too strong to be beat to pieces by field Artillery.[6]

In some of my former letters I wrote you to procure if possible a considerable number of Dragoon horses, without which it would be impossible for us to keep the field with our little force. We want a hundred at least; and I beg you take every measure in your power to procure them.[7] Give certificates for the whole, whether taken from

Whig or *Tory* and if any discrimination is necessary, [let] Government make that hereafter.

I am in hopes the Virginia militia will soon arrive in Camp in considerable force, untill when we shall lay a little farther distant from Camden than we have done.[8] Push your operations with great vigor, as no opportunity can be more favorable; and you may rely upon it, the enemy will not be idle, and see themselves insulted on all sides. Much depends upon the present moment. Let me hear from you daily and send me all the provision you can.[9] I mean of bread kind; for Cattle, we have plenty.

Col[l] [Henry] Hampton appears to be a very active officer and deserves credit for his spirited conduct. Present my compliments to him and Col[l] Middleton [Charles Myddleton], and believe me to be with great respect and esteem Your most obedient humble Servant

NATH GREENE

LS (Sumter Papers: DLC).

1. Sumter's letter has not been found. On Maj. Edmund Hyrne's going to meet with Sumter, see Pierce to Sumter, 28 April, above.

2. As seen in his letter to NG of 2 May, below, Sumter began a siege at Ft. Granby. In the opinion of Sumter's biographer, NG had "only pleasant words" for him in this letter because he knew he could not coerce Sumter into joining the army and wanted to save "appearances." (Gregorie, *Sumter*, p. 155) From Sumter's letters of 7 and 13 April, both above, NG had expected him to send reinforcements and actively cooperate in the campaign against Camden. On 23 April, above, NG asked Sumter to secure the sector around Camden "from Ninety Six & Charlestown on the West side of the Wateree"; and on 25 April, following the battle of Hobkirk's Hill, he called on Sumter to join the army "immediately." (See Pierce to Sumter, that date, above.) Meanwhile, in his letters to NG of 25 and 27 April, both above, Sumter outlined the difficulties he had encountered in assembling troops to reinforce the army. Col. William R. Davie, NG's commissary, said in his memoirs that NG, far from approving Sumter's actions, blamed the defeat at Hobkirk's Hill on Sumter's failure to join the army. According to Davie, NG said he would have had Sumter arrested as a "mere . . . freebooter, whose sole object was plunder," except for conditions in the country at that time and the hope that the British might pay "more attention" to Sumter's "rambling expeditions" than "they really deserved." (Quoted in Greene, *Greene*, 3: 257n.)

3. On Henry Lee's and Francis Marion's plans, see their letters to NG of this date, both below.

4. Despite the efforts of Marion and Lee to intercept him, Col. John Watson was able to take his force into Camden. (See Lee to NG, 6 May, below.)

5. Sumter reported Watson's movements in two letters to NG of 6 May, below. He wrote on 2 May, below, that he did not know Maj. Archibald McArthur's whereabouts but thought he could keep McArthur from reaching Camden.

6. On the capture of Ft. Granby, "the Fort at Congaree," see Lee to NG, 15 May, below.

7. See NG to Sumter, 15 April, above.

8. As seen at Jefferson to NG, 30 March, above, few of the militia reinforcements from Virginia were sent.

9. Sumter replied on 2 May, below.

*   *   *

¶ [TO ROBERT WALTON. From Headquarters, Rugeley's Mill, S.C., 30 April 1781. "It is impossible" to comply with the request in Walton's letter of 19 April, which has just arrived. NG is "unacquainted with the value of Tobacco either in Virginia or elsewhere," as that depends greatly on "local circumstances." It would therefore be "improper" to give Walton an order for either money or tobacco. By the time Walton receives this letter, the Virginia legislature "will be siting, and the obstacle" to payment removed. NG will write the governor urging that the drafts "be paid immediately for the reasons" Walton gave.[1] If there is any further difficulty, and if the value of the tobacco "is fixed and a certificate given by the Governor," NG will "give an order on Maryland to one half the amount." But the value Walton has stated appears "enormous, which will make the price of horses intollerable." ADfS (Greene Papers: DLC) 2 pp.]

1. No correspondence on this subject between NG and the Virginia governor, Thomas Jefferson, has been found.

¶ [FROM TRAUGOTT BAGGE,[1] Salem, N.C., 30 April 1781. "The Town and the Country hereabouts" lack many of the "Necessaries" that Bagge, "as a Merchant," used to supply to the inhabitants. Asks NG for a pass so that he can send a wagon or two "with some Commodities" to Pennsylvania or Maryland and bring back "Necessaries." Is afraid to conduct this business "in the common Way, lest the Waggons & Horses or the Loads should be impressd."[2] ALS (MiU-C) 1 p.]

1. Bagge, a merchant in Salem, "was virtually a purchasing agent for the American forces in the vicinity of Wachovia." (*Records of the Moravians*, 4: 1512)

2. NG's reply has not been found; on 14 August, two wagons were sent from Salem to Pennsylvania to bring back "goods for the store." (Ibid., p. 1698)

*   *   *

From Colonel Henry Lee, Jr.

Dear Gen[l]   Swamps of Black River [S.C., 30 April 1781][1]
    Gen. Marion has determined his route towards Santee.[2]
    From hence we march to Benbows Ferry on the Black River, thence to Wright[s] Bluff near Fort Watson, where we cross the Santee. Whether we move down that river or up the Congaree future intelligence will determine.[3]
    You do me great honor in calling the adopted plan of operations mine.[4]
    I have no pretence to such distinction. It gave me great pleasure to know that my sentiments coincided with your intentions, & this honor I claim.
    I am so convinced of the wisdom of the operations, that no disaster can affect my opinion. Hitherto all is well, & nobody to blame but Genera[l] Sumpter. I do not conceive how you can assimilate any part of my conduct to this gentleman[s], especially when you recollect that by my own request I am under General Marion & that next to the Commander in cheif, the com: officer of an expedition has praise.[5]

If we are baffled in our scheme, it will be owing to the [de]lay in creation.

Gen: Marion has wrote you the report concerning Cornwallis.[6]

We have nothing further. I have the honor to be most aff[y] your ob ser

HENRY LEE JUN

LS (Greene Papers: DLC).

1. The letter was docketed "30th or 31st April." There was no 31 April, of course, and the 30th was verified as the date from the contents and from Francis Marion's letter to NG, immediately below.

2. See Marion to NG, immediately below.

3. They marched up the Congaree River to Ft. Motte. (See Marion to NG, 6 May, below.)

4. See NG to Lee, 29 April, above. The "plan of operations" was the campaign against British posts that Marion and Lee were conducting.

5. Thomas Sumter had not come to NG's aid in the days before the battle of Hobkirk's Hill. In his letter to Lee of 29 April, NG said he expected that Sumter would continue to stay away from the army "for the same reasons" that Lee did.

6. The report has not been found.

*   *   *

¶ [FROM GENERAL FRANCIS MARION, Salem, S.C., 30 April 1781. Has NG's letter of the "28h Inst."[1] Had moved to take a position north of Camden, as NG desired, but will "return to Santee," where he hopes "to have an Opertunity of doing something."[2] Has sent eighty men to Rafting Creek "to prevent any provissions being carryed into Camden."[3] Encloses "all the Intelligence" he has been able to obtain [not found]. Will try to intercept Tarleton's cavalry if they come via Georgetown.[4] Col. [John] Watson "must" be at Monck's Corner by now, with at least 600 men and four field pieces.[5] Marion will send a "more perticular Account" of the post at Dorchester, where there are 200 men, in a few days. ALS (MiU-C) 1 p.]

1. NG's letter, dated 27 April, is above.

2. In his letter of the 27th, NG directed Marion to cross the Santee and proceed against "the posts upon the Congaree." That was a change from the order he had sent to Marion on 26 April to cooperate with the army in the vicinity of Camden.

3. Marion was complying with NG's directions to leave a guard near the High Hills of Santee to intercept supplies intended for Camden. (See NG to Marion, 27 April, above.)

4. Col. Banastre Tarleton's troops were with Lord Cornwallis's army, which was in North Carolina, marching toward Virginia.

5. On the movements of Watson, see note at Marion to NG, 6 May, below.

¶ [FROM JOHN MATHEWS, CHAIRMAN OF A STANDING COMMITTEE OF CONGRESS TO CORRESPOND WITH THE COMMANDER OF THE SOUTHERN DEPARTMENT,[1] Philadelphia, 30 April 1781. Encloses a "paper" giving the "latest intelligence" from Europe. The "countenance given by Russia" will encourage Holland to "enter into the war with alacrity and to prosecute it with vigor," creating "another powerful enemy" for Britain. The French, in turn, will be able "to give us more substantial aid."[2] Affairs with Spain also "wear a more pleasing aspect." A French expedition to aid the United States was to have sailed in March; it is thought to be "respectable" in both "troops and Ships."[3] Congress wants NG to look into complaints that many captured British officers are allowed to remain on parole in Charleston, S.C., while the British grant a similar "indulgence" to captured American officers "with a very sparing hand"; NG should "rectify" any "improprieties." Congress also wants NG, who is fully empowered to do so, to negotiate an exchange of prisoners to "relieve as many of ours" as possible "from the horrors of so severe a Captivity."[4] Arrangements should be made "without loss of time as the enemy have already engaged" between 500 and 600 American prisoners for the "West India service," which they enter from "inevitable necessity" and which "forever precludes them from the least chance of returning."[5] Encloses a paper showing "the outrageous malice of the enemy against our officers and the pressing necessity" for decisive measures to "prevent so diabolical a measure as is therein proposed."[6] ALS (MiU-C) 2 pp.]

1. For more on the committee, see Mathews to NG, 27 November 1780, above (vol. 6: 508).

2. The enclosure, which has not been found, was most likely a copy of the *Pennsylvania Packet* of 28 April 1781, containing extracts of two letters from Europe on the subject of Dutch affairs. Both letters indicated that Russia would assist the Dutch in their war with the British. The Dutch, though divided on whether to fight England, had declared war at the beginning of March. (On Great Britain's earlier declaration of war against them, see note at Washington to NG, 21 March, above [vol. 7: 459n].) In May, the Dutch sent their fleet into the Baltic Sea to threaten British trade routes. The British were able to patch together a fleet, and on 5 August, in the fiercest naval battle of the war, they crippled the Dutch squadron and forced it into port. (Mackesy, *War for America*, pp. 394–95) At least one historian contends, however, that by making it necessary for the British to stretch even further their already thin naval forces, the Dutch kept them from effectively countering the French fleet commanded by the Comte de Grasse, which later played a vital role at Yorktown, Va. (Ibid., p. 395)

3. On the expected aid from France, see La Luzerne to NG, 3 April, above.

4. An exchange had been agreed to before NG received this letter. (See Carrington to NG, 8 May, below.) On NG's authority to negotiate exchanges, see Huntington to NG, 31 October 1780, above (vol. 6: 451 and n).

5. Mathews wrote Washington on 2 May that Lord Charles Montagu was enlisting "our Continentals" for service in the West Indies. (Smith, *Letters*, 17: 208) Montagu, a former colonial governor of South Carolina, had returned there after the capture of Charleston and had been allowed to recruit a regiment of American prisoners. Col. Nisbet Balfour wrote Lord George Germain on 1 May that Montagu had finished enlisting his corps; Gen. John Dalling reported from Jamaica on 31 August that the unit numbered 500 men. (PRO 30/11/109; Davies, *Documents*, 19: 207)

6. Mathews enclosed an extract of a letter of 30 March from Balfour to Gen. William Moultrie, the ranking American officer in Charleston, stating that in the absence of a general exchange, the sending of American prisoners to the West Indies could not be "delayed" past the middle of April. (MiU-C) For more on the threat to the prisoners at Charleston, see Cornwallis to NG, 4 February, above (vol. 7: 251).

¶ [**FROM CAPTAIN JOHN SMITH**, Camden, S.C., 30 April 1781.[1] With Lord Rawdon's permission, he informs NG that Smith has been accused by "Some Deserters from our army" of having "Wantingly put to Death" a British captain and several soldiers "a Considerable time after they were made Prisoners" at the battle of Guilford Court House. The report, "tho Quite groundless," has led the enemy to regard him as a "murderor" and to deprive him of "the Common Indulgence granted to officers in Captivity."[2] Asks NG to collect affidavits from several officers, who can affirm his innocence. Adds: "I am Sorry that my Situation is like to give you trouble, tho I am Confident it will not be thought Such."[3] ALS (MiU-C) 2 pp.]

1. Smith, an officer of the Maryland Continental line, had been captured at the battle of Hobkirk's Hill.

2. For more on the allegations and on Smith's treatment by the British, see Doyle to NG, 29 April, above.

3. NG wrote Rawdon on Smith's behalf on 3 May, below.

*   *   *

To General Mordecai Gist

Dear General   Camp near Rugeleys [S.C.] 1st May 1781

Your letter of the 28h of March has arriv'd safe and put a very disagreable end to my expectations of receiving the promised supplies from Maryland.[1]

I rejoice at your recovery from considerations of personal esteem, and consider it as happy for the service, as I do not hear of any other man in the State who is making the least exertions to forward the recruiting business which is so essential to the accomplishment of our military operations and the expectations of our Country.[2]

I shall again address the legislature of the State of Maryland; but what mode of address will rouse a people to a sense of their danger, who for one moment can delay to provide for their security, when the Enemy is at their doors, and destroying their property?[3] The terror imposed upon your Capital by the presence of the British ships in your harbor, and the ravages committed by the Crews of smaller Vessels upon the rich borders of your fine Rivers, are circumstances that would rouse a spirited people to vigorous measures, but from the late conduct of the executive of Maryland we have not much to expect.[4] The method of furnishing recruits by draft for the short time you mention is entirely inadequate to any purpose but that of putting the states to unnecessary expence—procrastinating the war, and rendering the Issue more precarious.[5]

I thank you for your inclosures and intelligence. The horse accoutrements you mention are not yet arrivd, but have been heard of on the way to Camp. I shall give the necessary orders for cancelling your personal obligations for the payment of a ballance of their cost, and will be much obligd to you for all the vouchers you can obtain respecting the business so far as Capt Stiths conduct is concerned.[6]

I wish to know if the Arrangement of Officers of the Maryland line is completed.[7] If it is you will be so obliging as to furnish me with a Copy, and order the Gentlemen of the first and second Regiments to Camp as soon as possible. If it is not completed, you will please to send a sufficient number of Officers to command one Regiment at least, with the first detachment. I am sir with great esteem Your most obedient humble servant   NATH GREENE

NB The southern States must fall if not speedily supported; and if they fall, I think they will [lay?] a train for the failure of all the rest. This is my opinion so help me god.

LS (MdHi).

    1. Gist's letter is above (vol. 7: 476).

    2. Gist had informed NG in his letter of 28 March that he had just recovered from "a long and tedious Indisposition." The rest of the sentence was an indirect criticism of Gen. William Smallwood, who had been ordered to assist Gist in raising men in Maryland. (See NG to Gist, 23 January, above [vol. 7: 172].)

    3. NG most likely referred to his letter to Gov. Thomas Sim Lee of 11 April, above. He apparently did not write the governor or legislature again until August.

    4. The threat to Annapolis and the raids up the Maryland rivers are discussed at Gist's letter of 28 March (vol. 7: 477n).

    5. For the recruiting plan adopted by the Maryland legislature, see Gist to NG, 19 January, above (ibid., p. 151).

    6. As seen in his letter to NG of 28 March, Gist had given "personal Security" to some tradesmen in order to get the horse accoutrements released. He said the tradesmen claimed to have been paid less than half of the $200,000 that "Capt Stith," who had contracted with them, had received from the state treasury for that purpose. Gist concluded the letter by saying he would investigate the matter further and provide NG with evidence to either "Criminate or Acquit" Stith. (MdHi) Capt. John Stith of the Third Continental Dragoons was probably the officer to whom Gist referred. (Heitman, *Register*) No further information has been found.

    7. In his letter to NG of 12 April, above, Smallwood reported on the effort to arrange the Maryland Continental officers.

To the Marquis de Lafayette

My dear Marquis   [Camp near Rugeley's Mill, S.C., 1 May 1781][1]

    I had the pleasure to receive last Evening your long[,] polite and interesting letter of the 17th of April.

    I feel a mixture of pain and pleasure at your return, pain that it has given you so much trouble and pleasure that I shall receive such an important reinforcement at so interesting a crisis. The situation of your detachment was truly distressing and your generosity and exertions to afford them relief must endear you to every Soldeir and lay the public under lasting obligations.[2]

    I will not pain your humanity by attempting a description of the distresses of our little Army. But you may depend upon it that nothing can equal their sufferings but their Merit. We have struggled with innumerable difficulties, and they increase dayly. My force and my Talents are unequal to the conflict. Without more effectual support in the Southern States they must fall and I fear will lay a train to sap the foundation of the Independance of the rest.

    It is my wish that your detachment should halt at Richmond until necessity or further information render other measures necessary. Before this if General Philips still continues in Virginia, I imagine he must have commenced some offensive operations; and you will take upon you the command in that State and conduct the Military operations as circumstances shall dictate to be proper.[3] I have only one word of advice to give you, (having entire confidence in your ability[,] zeal and good conduct), that is not to let the love of fame get the better of your prudence and plunge you into a misfortune, in too eager a pursuit after glory. This is the voice of a friend, and not the caution of a General.

Baron Stuben is desird to give you all the information he can respecting the State of the Department in Virginia. Great care will be necessary to guard against a waste of Stores in that State as the frequent reliefs of Militia is productive of a great consumption of Stores. Such as are coming for the use of this Army, you will please to consider as sacred, and not allow them to be broken in upon, be the ocasion ever so pressing.

Should General Philips be penetrating the Country which I hope he is not, and you by detaining the Pennsylvania line for a few days, have a good prospect of defeating him, you will halt them for the purpose; otherwise let them come directly on, and forward their march all in your power.

I shall always be happy to indulge your wishes, and especially when they agree so perfectly with the public welfare as your desire to command in Virginia. All important transactions which happen within your immediate command, you will transmit an account of both to Congress and the Commander in Chief; copies of which I shall be happy to receive when convenient.

Lord Cornwallis lay at Wilmington the 21ˢᵗ and his Army sickly. Inclosed I send you a copy of an official letter to Congress respecting a little repulse we met with before Camden.[4] You will naturally see the impropriety of having the official account published before it passes through Congress and therefore will only take extra[c]ts from it, to give such information as you may find necessary. We fight[,] get beat, rise and fight again. We have a bloody field; but little glory.

My affectionate regards to Doctor [James] McHenry if he is with you, and to all the Gentlemen of your family. With esteem & affec I am dear Marquis Your Most Obedt humble Sʳ   N GREENE

ADfS (IHi).

1. The date was taken from the docketing, the place from other letters of this date.

2. As seen in his letter of 17 April, above, Lafayette had used his personal credit to obtain needed supplies for his detachment.

3. Gen. William Phillips had begun "offensive operations." (See Lafayette to NG, 28 April, above.)

4. See NG to Huntington, 27 April, above.

*   *   *

¶ [TO GENERAL FRANCIS MARION. From Camp near Rugeley's Mill, S.C., 1 May 1781. NG received Marion's letter of 30 April "last evening." Warns him to "Keep a good look out for Tarlton," who is probably coming via Georgetown but may be on the "uper route."[1] Gen. [Thomas] Sumter is "on the Congarees with a considerable force," which is increasing daily. Marion should "communicate" with Sumter and be prepared to join forces with him "for any capital purpose." NG hopes the artillery arrives before this letter and that Marion will use it "effectually."[2] If Tarleton gets into Camden, Col. [Henry] Lee must immediately join NG's army. NG also fears that Maj. [Archibald] McArthur is on his way to Camden and has "passed" Sumter.[3] "If all those detachments get in[,] the enemy will be strong." The Marquis de Lafayette is on his way south with a large detachment, and the Pennsylvania line is also on the march. "We shall be strong by and by."[4] ADfS (MiU-C) 2 pp.]

1. Col. Banastre Tarleton, who commanded Lord Cornwallis's mounted troops, was accompanying Cornwallis to Virginia. The "uper route" was via Cross Creek, N.C., and the Cheraws region of South Carolina.

2. As seen at Lee to NG, 2 May, below, NG's letters arrived at Marion's camp a few hours before the artillery did. Marion used the field piece in his successful siege of Ft. Motte.

3. On McArthur's whereabouts, see note at Marion to NG, 27 April, above.

4. In the letter immediately above, NG ordered Lafayette and his detachment to remain in Virginia; the Pennsylvania Continental line had not yet marched.

¶ [TO BARON STEUBEN. From Camp near Rugeley's Mill, S.C., 1 May 1781. NG has been "at a loss" to account for Steuben's "long silence at this important crisis, when intelligence is so necessary."[1] As the Marquis de Lafayette has been ordered to Richmond, Va., NG can accommodate Steuben's wish to join NG's army. Steuben should bring with him all the Virginia drafts and dragoons who are "fit for duty."[2] The dragoons in NG's army are "much broke down," and the enemy have a two-to-one superiority in numbers; should NG's army be defeated again and the enemy have a "superior body of horse, nothing less than total ruin must follow." Gen. [Anthony] Wayne, who is on the march with the Pennsylvania line, should follow Steuben to NG's army.[3] Steuben should also bring with him all the stores he can and inform the Board of War about the "deplorable condition respecting arms" in the department. "Unless a new supply can be had, or larger Armouries established for their repairs, we cannot keep the field." [Capt. Nathaniel] Irish should be ordered to "use all possible industry" to repair arms, and Capt. "Prior [John Pryor]" should visit the laboratory "once in every two or three weeks, as nothing tends more to spur industry than attention."[4] Steuben is to give Lafayette "the best information" about affairs in Virginia. NG adds: "I find myself so beset with difficulties that I need the council and assistance of an officer educated in the Prussian school, and perswade myself I shall have in you both the friend and General I want." NG is unsure "in what light our movements will be viewed, but it was dictated by necessity and [was] the only plan that promised any advantage. It is true it was hazardous, and I wish it may not prove unfortunate."[5] He has received the arrangement of the Virginia officers but has not had time to examine it.[6] Asks Steuben to send copies to Washington and the Board of War. "Nothing can exceed our distress for want of platoon officers";

those of the first and second regiments should therefore be "sent out immediately."[7] Col. [Charles] Harrison wants fifty draftees for his artillery regiment;
Steuben should arrange it. Sends compliments to Steuben's aides. LS (NHi)
3 pp.]

1. The last letter from Steuben that NG had received was dated 2 April, above; that of
25 April, also above, had not yet arrived.

2. As seen at Steuben's letter of 2 April, in which he asked to join NG, neither he nor
the troops left Virginia.

3. The Pennsylvania Continental line was still in Pennsylvania. (See note at Washington to NG, 1 June, below.)

4. Irish commanded the artificers who were to establish an armory at Prince Edward
Court House; Pryor had been named commissary of military stores by Steuben. As seen
in Pryor to NG, 30 May, below, his visit to the laboratory disrupted the work there.

5. By "our movements," NG meant his decision to break off pursuit of Lord Cornwallis in North Carolina and move into South Carolina.

6. NG's aide, Lewis Morris, had brought the proposed arrangement from Virignia in
early April. (See Davies to NG, 16 April, above.)

7. In his letter to NG of 18 April, above, William Davies explained why he did not
think NG's request was feasible.

*   *   *

To George Washington

Dear Sir   Camp [Rugeley's Mill, S.C.] May 1st 1781

My public letters to Congress will inform your Excellency of our
situation in this quarter. We fight get beat and fight again. We have so
much to do and so little to do it with, that I am much afraid these States
must fall never to rise again; and what is more I am perswaded they
will lay a train to sap the foundation of all the rest.

I am greatly obliged to your Excellency for ordering the Marquis to
the Southward.[1] I propose to halt him in Virginia until the enemies
plan of operations is better explained. Baron Stuben will join this
Army, he having offended the Legislature of Virginia cannot be as
useful there as he has been. The Marquis is desird to keep your
Excellency advisd of all matters in that quarter as it is too far first to
come to this Army and then be sent back again.[2]

When I was appointed to the command of this Army, I solicited
Congress to give Doctor McHenry a Majority that he might serve me in
the character of an aid. This they refused. I was perswaded when I
made the application of the necessity, and since have felt it most
sensibly. Your Excellency can scarsely tell how happy you are in your
family; and therefore can hardly judge of my situation. I cannot make a
second application to Congress upon the subject, nor should I have
hopes of succeeding if [I] did; but I shall esteem it a peculiar mark of
your Excellencys friendship and esteem if you will interest your self in
the matter and get him a Majority. Your Excellency will judge of the

propriety of my request; and if my wishes has prompted me to ask any thing that dont accord with your opinion or your feelings, I must beg you to decline the measure, and excuse me.[3]

It is a long time since I receivd a line from Mrs Greene. I am afraid they have miscarried before they got to Head Quarters. I am sorry that you had not leisure to call on her on your return from Newport, she would have tho't herself greatly honord, and been peculiarly happy on the occasion.[4] With the greatest respect esteem & affection I am your Excellencys Most Obedient humble Ser   N GREENE
I beg my most respectful compliments to Mrs Washington.

ALS (Washington Papers: DLC).
    1. See Lafayette to NG, 17 April, above.
    2. See NG to Lafayette, this date, above.
    3. On NG's attempt to obtain a commission for McHenry, see NG to Huntington, 30 October 1780, above (vol. 6: 445). As noted there, McHenry did receive the commission in late May—before Washington could have acted—but did not join NG's staff.
    4. On Washington's visit to Newport, R.I., and the reason he was unable to visit Catharine Greene at that time, see Washington to NG, 21 March, above (vol. 7: 459).

                    *   *   *

¶ [FROM GENERAL JETHRO SUMNER, Warren County, N.C., 1 May 1781. He received NG's letters of 19, 21, and 29 April on "the thirtyeth" and will "pay due attention to the contents."[1] Having learned that smallpox was "raging" in Hillsborough and that there was "a large store of provision" at Harrisburg, he changed the site of the general rendezvous for the districts of Wilmington, New Bern, Salisbury, and Hillsborough to Harrisburg. The Halifax and Edenton drafts are to rendezvous at Halifax, but smallpox is reportedly spreading there, too. If that is true, Sumner will also have them assemble at Harrisburg.[2] General Jones, who has returned from Virginia, was unable to obtain arms there. Sumner has been informed that there are 800 stand of arms on their way to NG and that they are probably in North Carolina by now; asks for orders "respecting them," as he does not think the North Carolina government can arm his men.[3] Also doubts that he can obtain arms from Baron Steuben, to whom he wrote "yesterday," because the British have reportedly penetrated to Petersburg, Va., and Steuben and Gen. [Peter] Muhlenberg have retreated to Chesterfield Court House. The Virginia militia are said to be collecting "fast" and "in want of arms."[4] Repeats intelligence he has received concerning the movements of Lord Cornwallis and says he has just heard from Col. [Nicholas] Long, who reports that Cornwallis's army is "on their March to Halifax." Long is removing the public stores from that place, and the district militia have been called "to arms."[5] ALS (MiU-C) 3 pp.]
    1. The letter of 29 April has not been found.
    2. For more on Sumner's efforts to arrange a general rendezvous of Continental drafts, see Sumner to NG, 23 April, above; he wrote NG on 11 May, below, that the troops were collecting "very slow."
    3. Allen Jones, a member of the North Carolina Council Extraordinary, had been sent

to Virginia in early April to try to borrow muskets for the North Carolina Continental draftees. (Abner Nash to Thomas Jefferson, 10 April 1781, Boyd, *Jefferson Papers*, 5: 398) He was told that Virginia had sent all of its spare weapons to NG's army. (Rankin, *N.C. Continentals*, p. 342)

4. In a letter to Steuben of 29 April, Sumner asked for help in equipping the North Carolina drafts. (Steuben Microfilm) For more on the invasion of the Virginia interior by British troops under Gen. William Phillips, see Steuben to NG, 25 April, above.

5. The British were indeed heading toward Halifax, on their way to Virginia. For more on their movements out of Wilmington, see Emmet to NG, 28 April, above. Sumner sent further intelligence in his letter to NG of 8 May, below.

* * *

General Greene's Orders

Camp near Rugeleys [S.C.] Wednesday 2nd May 1781

The court whereof Brigadier Genl [Isaac] Huger is president, appointed to inquire into the conduct of Colonel [John] Gunby in the action of the 25th ulto. Report as follows:[1]

It appears to the Court, that Colonel Gunby received orders to advance with his Regiment, and charge bayonets without firing. This order he immediately communicated to his Regiment, which advanced cheerfully for some distance, when a firing began on the right of the Regiment, and in a short time became general through it. That soon after two Companies on the right of the Regiment gave way. That Colonel Gunby then gave Lt Col^o [John Eager] Howard orders to bring off the other four Companies, which at that time appeared disposed to advance, except a few. That Lt Col^o Howard brought off the four Companies from the left, and joined Colonel Gunby at the foot of the hill, about Sixty yards in the rear. That Lt Col^o Howard there found Colonel Gunby actively exerting himself in rallying the two Companies that broke from the Right, which he effected and the Regiment was again formed and gave a fire or two at the Enemy, which appeared on the Hill in front. It also appears, from other Testimony, that Colonel Gunby at several other times was active in rallying and forming his Troops.

It appears from the above report, that Col^o Gunby's Spirit and activity, were unexceptionable. But his order for the Reg^t to retire, which broke the line, was extremely improper and unmilitary; and in all probability the only cause why we did not obtain a Complete Victory.[2]

Lamar Orderly Book (OCIWHi).

1. The court consisted of Huger, Col. Charles Harrison, and Col. William Washington. (Johnson, *Greene*, 2: 85)

2. For more on the role of Col. John Gunby in the battle of Hobkirk's Hill, see NG to Huntington, 27 April, above.

To the Board of War

Gentlemen   Camp near Rughlys Mill [S.C.] May the 2ᵈ 1781
I have had the honor of your letter of the 30th of March.[1]

I have no doubt of the care and attention, which the Board take in forwarding the Stores in good order. But the distance is so great and the waggoners so unfathful that great abuses prevail on the road; and besides it has been so much the custom for Stores to be stoped on the way by order of the different Governors and officers either commanding or residing in the different States through which the Stores pass that the packages are often broken and issues made without being accounted for. These two last evils I have been endeavoring to prevent ever since I have been in this department. But customs however improper which have receivd a sanction from long indulgence are difficult to correct. Where Stores have been deposited at Posts in North Carolinia I find it has been a custom for the Officers belonging to the State when they happened to be at or near them without being on command to give orders for their issues. I have issued a positive prohibition to this practice and hope to stop it as the Officers in the QM General's department are not to deliver Stores upon the order of any officer unless he is on command, and the nature of his duty requires a compliance.[2]

The best mode of forwarding Stores with security in my opinion will be to establish a chain of posts and have the Stores examined from Post to Post and the Waggon Masters made to account for the deficiences. Where they come such a great distance and issues take place on the road it is next to impossible to find out the abuses which may be practiced upon the public. Private Stores are brought in public Waggons even from Philadelphia. 20 Ream of paper was found in one brigade. I gave orders for the whole of it to be seized for the use of the Army without allowing the owner a shilling and have given directions that this shall be an invariable rule.

The Saddles and harness which was mention'd in my former letter was forwarded from Philadelphia.[3] My information respecting the place and quallity of the Stores were from Col [Edward] Carrington who is a very attentive officer. I believe the horse furniture provided by Cap [John] Stith was very good.[4]

The nature and extent of the war in this Country will consume unavoidably a much greater quantity of Stores than the Northern Army with every possible care and attention, and there are so many emergencies and so much infidelity that there is no preventing it.

The State of our Arms and even the want of Arms is really deplorable and alarming. The Country will be in a defenceless condition soon unless larger and better Armories can be established for the repairs of such as get out of order. I must intreat the Board to pay immediate attention to this business, without which I foresee very disagreeable consequences must follow. We want artificers with the Army exceedingly.[5] A great part of those companies sent by Col Pickering their times of service having expir'd are gone home.[6] Our wants are without number, and our difficultey without end. The war here is upon too unequal a schale [i.e., scale,] the means are totally incompetent to the end, nor can I see a prospect of a change for the better. I perswade my self of the good disposition of the Board to aid me all in their power but I am sensible you have your embarassments also. Col [Otho] Williams will enclose a return of our force which you will see is next to nothing to contend with such a formidable enemy as is and has been employed for the reduction of this Country.[7] Virginia has given us great assistance, but Maryland has neglected us altogether, nor can I hear of any exertions there equal to the pressing emergencey of the Southern States. They fall far short of what I expected and even what they ought to perform agreeable to the federal Union.

Things in this quarter are in a much more disagreeable train than is generally imagined. The Country is inevitably lost if not soon releivd. The well effected have struggled to the last, but they are inevitably ruined and cannot continue their exertions much longer. The carnage which prevails from public bodies and private anaimosities is truly shocking to humanity. The war rages like a fire and devours every thing before it. I have the honor to be with the greatest respect Your Most Obedient humble Serv   N GREENE

ADfS (MiU-C).
    1. The letter has not been found.
    2. See also NG to Board of War, 30 March, above.
    3. See NG to Benjamin Stoddert, 28 February, above (vol. 7: 369).
    4. On the "horse furniture," see also NG to Gist, 1 May, above.
    5. For more on NG's efforts to find men and facilities to repair arms belonging to the Southern Army, see NG to Read, 29 April, above.
    6. On the artificer companies that Col. Timothy Pickering, the quartermaster general, had sent from the North, see Pickering to NG, 23 October 1780 (vol. 6: 427).
    7. The return has not been found.

*   *   *

¶ [CAPTAIN WILLIAM PIERCE, JR., TO GENERAL JOHN BUTLER. From Rugeley's Mill, S.C., 2 May 1781. Acknowledges Butler's letters to NG of 15 and 26 April. NG is "much indebted" to Butler for his efforts "to procure and forward" provisions and to obtain intelligence about the "movements and designs" of Lord Cornwallis. "The former is an object of great consequence, the latter a circumstance of the last importance." There has been a "small change" of "circumstances," which "by no means derange or alter the general plan of our operations."[1] After arriving at Camden, NG decided "to starve the

Enemy out or tempt them" to leave their works. Gives a detailed account of the battle of Hobkirk's Hill. Says it was Col. [John] Gunby's "unfortunate order" that "threw us into disorder and lost us the honor of a Victory"; praises Col. [William] Washington's "heroism and firmness." Believes the enemy suffered "infinitely more" casualties than NG's army. Concludes his report on the battle by saying: "This is a simple state of facts collected from a thorough knowledge of circumstances, and leave you to draw your own conclusions."[2] NG wants "all the intelligence" Butler can provide about Cornwallis's "situation."[3] ADfS (DLC) 3 pp.]

1. Pierce referred to the battle of Hobkirk's Hill, on which he reported in this letter.
2. For more on the battle and Gunby's role, see NG to Huntington, 27 April, and NG's Orders, this date, both above.
3. Butler sent intelligence about Cornwallis's army on 28 April, above, and 4 and 11 May, below.

*   *   *

To Governor Abner Nash of North Carolina

Dear Sir   Camp near Rughlys Mill [S.C.] May 2[d] 1781
I have had the honor of two letters from your Excellency since I wrote you[,] one of the 12th and one of the 7th of April.[1] I thank you for the papers you sent me and for the supplies you are forwarding us. They will I hope arrive seasonably as our Stores are all exhausted.

In my last I informed your Excellency of the object of our movement; and which I am still in hopes will have the effect which we had in contemplation. However this is uncertain as our force is too small to enforce our plan of operations properly. If any thing can save your State from farther ravages it is this movement. But the Virginia Militia which I expected are so tedious in coming out owing to the busy season of the year and General [Thomas] Sumter has failed so much in the force he promised me that I am in the greatest distress.[2] We have had another Action with the Enemy in which we come off second best. Inclosd I send you a copy of my public letter to Congress.[3] But you will see the impropriety of publishing it before it passes that body. Such extracts as you may think necessary for the information of the public about you, you will take from it. The fortune of the day would have been favorable had it not been for Col Gunbies [John Gunby's] order and it was only an error in judgment in him as his courage and activity are unquestionable. War is a critical business and the fate of the day after every possible precaution depends upon the most triffling incident.

I am extreme sorry that your Assembly have not met. Many things are necessary to be done to give proper support to this Army without which it will be impossible for us to hold our ground. I hope you will issue your orders for convening them immediately if you finally fail of making a house in the present instance. The want of the means of transportation distresses us exceedingly.[4] In my last I requested a number of Cavalry horses[;] the service is so severe our horses are almost wore out. The Enemy have a great superiority in the field.[5]

The news from the Northward is that General Clinton is coming with a large force to take a position at New Castle on the Delaware. That a considerable force is coming I believe, but I am perswaded they will enter Chesepeak Bay and land at the Head of Elk.[6]

The Marquis de la Fyette with his detachment and the Pensylvania line are on the march to join the Southern Army. The Marquis will halt in Virginia but the Pennsylvanians will come on.[7]

I can get no certain intelligence of General Philips. Have you heard any thing of him?[8] It is reported here that Lord Cornwallis is embarking his troops at Wilmington; but I doubt the truth of it.[9] I am with Sentiments of the highest respect Your Excellencys Most Obed[t] humble Ser   N GREENE

ADfS (Greene Papers: DLC).

1. Nash's letter of 7 April is above; his letter to NG of 12 April has not been found. NG had written Nash on 13 April, above.

2. On the Virginia militia and Sumter, see notes at NG to Jefferson, 30 March, and NG to Sumter, 30 April, both above.

3. NG's letter to Samuel Huntington of 27 April, above, contains his official report of the battle of Hobkirk's Hill.

4. In his letter to Nash of 3 April, above, NG had delineated a number of problems that he wanted the North Carolina legislature to address, including transportation. As noted at Caswell to NG, 6 April, above, the legislature did not meet again until late June.

5. NG's request for cavalry horses was in his letter to Nash of 13 April, above.

6. As seen at Sharpe to NG, 7 April, above, Sir Henry Clinton did not leave New York City.

7. On Lafayette's orders, see NG's letter to him, 1 May, above. As noted at Washington to NG, 1 June, below, the Pennsylvania line had not yet begun its march to the South.

8. Baron Steuben had sent an account of the latest invasion of the Virginia interior in his letter to NG of 25 April, above; NG acknowledged receipt of that letter in his to Steuben of 14 May, below.

9. The false report that Cornwallis's army was preparing to leave Wilmington, N.C., by water is in Butler to NG, 26 April, above.

*   *   *

¶ [FROM MAJOR RICHARD CLAIBORNE, Richmond, Va., 2 May 1781. He received NG's letter of 16 April on the 26th. Thanks him for his "friendly advice" and says no one "has greater influence" with him than NG. Wishes only that NG could support him "in inforcing it." He received NG's "caution with respect to the Commanding officer in Virginia [Baron Steuben] in the friendly manner in which it was given."[1] Adds:

I have not met him with that spirit of impetuosity which governs him generally; but pursue a very different line of conduct. When he flies out in his fits of execrating every body and every thing, I hear him without emotion. When he moderates I deliberately use arguments and give reasons which he cannot contradict. In short sir my attention to his orders and willingness in executing them as far as I have it in my power bring me off tolerably well. Was I the only person he treats in such a manner I should consider it in a different light from the present; but when I see and hear him attack Governor and Council and Assembly in person and by letter, I might almost be content with a knock or two.

Claiborne has "long since" given the quartermaster general [Timothy Pickering] his "sentiments about the situation of his department here"; Pickering's letters give "satisfaction as to his approbation," but Claiborne receives "no support from that quarter."[2] ALS (Greene Papers: DLC) 3 pp.]

1. In his letter, NG had advised Claiborne "not to get into any dispute" with Steuben.

2. On the "sentiments" that Claiborne had expressed to Pickering, see note at NG's letter to Claiborne of 16 April.

¶ [FROM COLONEL HENRY LEE, JR., "Benbow Ferry on Black River," S.C., 2 May 1781. Has NG's letter "of yesterday [not found]." It "is the first that ever arrived in proper time! The express has done his duty." No "prospects & no difficultys" will keep Lee from joining NG "on the first notice" of Lord Cornwallis's approach, "or of the arrival of the cavalry." On 30 April, Cornwallis was reportedly still at Wilmington, N.C. Lee believes Cornwallis's "pride will urge him to continue the prosecution of his plan for the campaign, however repugnant to the interest of his King." If Cornwallis "adopts this conduct, we must prove to the world, how futile British conquests are, & force mankind to admire the viger" of NG's operations.[1] Nothing will be "wanting" on Lee's part. He is confident "of brilliant success, which will be pleasing in every point of view, but especially so, as it must tend to make happy a General [i.e., NG] struggling without materials, against a well appointed veteran army." Hopes the movement that NG contemplates can be executed.[2] "It will countenance our proceedings, give a face of viger," and facilitate a junction with Lee. General Marion can supply, "if he will," 150 dragoon horses "from his Militia, most of them impressed horses," and can certainly "spare 60 which would be a happy supply."[3] NG should expect to hear from Lee and Marion "in four days."[4] Adds that "Major Eaton Joins this evening."[5] ALS (MiU-C) 2 pp.]

1. Lee believed that Cornwallis would attempt to subjugate North Carolina and Virginia instead of returning to South Carolina. (See also Lee to NG, after 7 April, above.)

2. It is not known what "movement" Lee meant.

3. For Marion's reaction to NG's requests for horses, see his letter to NG of 6 May, below.

4. See Lee's and Marion's letters to NG of 6 May, both below.

5. As seen in Pierce to Maj. Pinketham Eaton, 28 April, and NG to Marion, 26 April, both above, Eaton's detachment of North Carolina Continentals was on its way to Lee and Marion, in company with Capt. James Conyers, who was bringing the artillery they had requested.

¶ [FROM JOSHUA POTTS,[1] Harrisburg, N.C., 2 May 1781. Sends "One hundred and One Pounds Nett" of butter, which was purchased by order of Gov. [Abner] Nash for the use of NG and his aides.[2] Potts has also received about "eight Thousand Weight of good Bacon from Warren County," which he is sending to Salisbury in accordance with Col. [Edward] Carrington's "Directions." ALS (MiU-C) 1 p.]

1. Potts added after his signature that he was an assistant deputy quartermaster.
2. See Nash to NG, 3 April, above.

*   *   *

From General Thomas Sumter

D[r] Sir   Camp at Congrees [S.C.] 2[d] May 1781[1]

Yours of the 30th Ulti[mo] I have Recived.

I am Glad You are So Circumstanced as to permit the Troops With me to Remain in this Quarter, Which I have No doubt but you will find it have an exceeding Good Effect, as it Will tend to increase our force Very much, & Lessen that of the Enemy excessively, & Secoure Resources for our army Which otherways must have been Lost.[2]

Co[l] Hampton has Returnd, Kild thirteen of the Enemies Guard at Fridays Ferry[,] five of a party going to the fort[,] Took a Number of horses & Several Negroes[.][3] The Hessian horses is Gone Downwards Except Twenty five that Crosed from the fort at Motts & Went in to Camden With Maj[r] Doyl [John Doyle].[4]

Co[l] [John] Thomas has Just Returnd from Bush River, Where he fell in With a party of Tories[,] Kild three & Took Twelve Prisoners, four Waggons & Several Negroes.[5] Maj[r] Maxwell Keeps pretty Close.[6] Those at M[r] Motts Very much So. They are Diging for water. Will obtain it With Very Great Difficulty, but may be Cut of[f] from it, with a pice of artillery as it is out Side the fort. I think this place May be Taken with a Sixpounder.[7] Two Regulars & Sixteen Tories Deserted the evening before last. The Tories are Very uneasee & Will Numbers of them Disert if oppertunity Serves. They are Coming in fast from the Country & Will in my oppinion Cheifly Give up if We Can hold our Ground a little longer.[8] I am Not Well informd Where Maj[r] M[c]Arthur is at this Time but have No apprehensions that he Can Git to Camden Without My Knowing it in Time to prevent his Design.[9]

I have Ten waggons on their way to you With Meal, am Doubtfull they will Meet with Great Difficulty in passing the Catawba River[.] If the loading Coud be Recieved by your Commissary any Where below Camden, I Can have Sent forward any Quantity of Meal that you May have occasion for.[10]

I Will use My endeavours to have Some horses procoured Suitable for the Purpose you Intend them. But it will be with Great difficulty if Not impossible to procure any worth While Near hear, as in any part of this State upwards, except in Ninty Six district. I urged Gen[l] [Andrew] Pickens to have Some Got for you. Gen[l] Marian is also in the

Way of Geting Good horses, but how far I May Succeed by applying to him I Know Not.[11] Upon the Whole I fear the Number you Want will Not be Got in this State, that Will Answer the Service. High up in N. Carolina there is a Great many Good horses, & Numbers of thim Carried from this State. The Lead from Newbern has Not yet arived[.] Am Very Scarce of that article & Not well Supplied With powder. If you have it to Spare Shoud be Much obliged to you for a Small Quantity by the Waggons, 2 C^{wt} powder & 3 C of Lead Woud Serve at present.[12] I have the Hon^r to be D^r S^r your most obedt Hbl Servt THO^s SUMTER

ALS (MiU-C).

1. Sumter began his siege of Ft. Granby, on the Congaree River, on this date. (Gregorie, *Sumter*, p. 157)

2. In his letter of 30 April, above, NG had rescinded his order to Sumter to join the army.

3. Col. Henry Hampton's detachment was returning from an expedition to the Wateree River. (See Sumter to NG, 25 April; Hampton to NG, 28 April, both above.) The "fort" was presumably Ft. Motte, near the confluence of the Wateree and Congaree rivers.

4. To create a cavalry force, the British had drafted men from the three Hessian regiments stationed in South Carolina. (Bruce E. Burgoyne, ed. and translator, *Diaries of a Hessian Chaplain and the Chaplain's Assistant* [n.p.: Johannes Schwalm Historical Association, 1990], p. 45)

5. Thomas was one of Sumter's regimental commanders.

6. Maj. Andrew Maxwell was the commander at Ft. Granby.

7. In his letter to Sumter of 4 May, below, NG offered to send a field piece for use in the reduction of Ft. Granby. Sumter proposed using it against Ft. Motte in his second letter to NG of that date, below.

8. Before Ft. Granby was taken, Sumter moved on against the British post at Orangeburg, leaving troops to continue the investment of Granby. (See Sumter to NG, 11 May, below.) On the eventual surrender of the garrison at Ft. Granby, see Lee to NG, 15 May, below.

9. Sumter sent intelligence about Maj. Archibald McArthur's force in his first letter to NG of 4 May, below.

10. NG acknowledged receipt of the meal in his letter to Sumter of 6 May, below.

11. On the horses, see NG to Sumter, 4 May, and Marion to NG, 6 May, both below.

12. NG wrote Sumter on 6 May, below, that he was sending some ammunition.

*   *   *

¶ [FROM COLONEL THOMAS WADE, 2 May 1781.[1] Forwards a letter. Sends intelligence that Lord Cornwallis was in Duplin County, N.C., "and Judged to be on his way to Camden [S.C.] to raise, the Siege"; Wade has sent someone to verify this report.[2] If it proves to be true, Wade "will have Every mill on the East Side of Pee Dee Imediatly Dismantled, and through [i.e., throw] Every Obstickel" in Cornwallis's way. Will give NG "the Erliest Inteligence" that he can. ALS (MiU-C) 1 p.]

1. Wade, who did not give his location, was collecting supplies for NG along the Pee Dee River in North and South Carolina. (See, for example, Wade to NG, 19 and 20 April, both above.)

2. Cornwallis was not heading toward Camden.

¶ [**FROM COLONEL JAMES WOOD,**[1] Charlottesville, Va., 2 May 1781. The Board of War has ordered Wood to detain a physician belonging to the Convention army because the British have held Dr. David Olyphant at Charleston, S.C., following his exchange.[2] Wood is also to inform NG of the board's order.[3] Cy (NN) 1 p.]

1. Wood was superintendent of the prisoners of the Convention army, the enemy troops captured in 1777 at Saratoga, N.Y. (*JCC*, 19: 308)

2. On the detention of Olyphant, see Olyphant to NG, 22 January, above (vol. 7: 170–71). Congress had voted on 11 April to refer a committee report on the matter to the Board of War. (*JCC*, 19: 369)

3. NG replied on 15 June, below.

¶ [**GENERAL GREENE'S ORDERS,** Sawney's Creek on the "West side of Wateree," S.C., 3 May 1781.[1] The army is to "march by the right Tomorrow morning." Greene Orderly Book (CSmH) 1 p.]

1. As seen by the letter immediately below, the army had left its camp at Rugeley's Mill and crossed the Wateree River.

¶ [**TO COLONEL JOHN MARSHEL.** From Camp [Rugeley's Mill, S.C.], 3 May 1781.[1] Marshel's regiment is to remain "on this side" while the army "crosses the Wateree River this morning."[2] He is to "keep parties on all the great roads" leading to Camden from the Pee Dee River and from Charlotte and Salisbury, N.C., and is to order troops and supplies coming to NG's army to cross the Catawba River "twenty or thirty Miles above Camden, or higher up if the fords are favorable." He is to send NG intelligence of enemy activities "up towards Charlotte or Salisbury" and of Lord Cornwallis's movements.[3] ADfS (MiU-C) 2 pp.]

1. The army had been camped at Rugeley's Mill prior to its move to Sawney's Creek, on the west side of the Wateree River, on 3 May.

2. On the reasons for the move, see NG to Huntington, 5 May, below.

3. Marshel replied on 5 May, below.

* * *

To Lord Rawdon

My Lord   Head Quarters May 3ᵈ 1781.[1]

I am informed by Major Doyle in answer to my letter addressed to your Lordship respecting Capt [John] Smith that the reasons of his confinement are certain charges lodged against him by deserters from our army for murdering an officer and three privates belonging to the guards after the action at Guilford.[2] Nothing can be more foreign from truth than the charge and I am surprised that persons whose want of principle and fidelity to any cause or any party should gain such credit with your Lordship as to deprive an officer of an unblemished character of the common indulgence allowed to others in his situation. I have only to observe upon it, that had such charges been made against any of your officers whom the fortune of war had thrown into our hands before I should have treated them with any peculiar marks of indignity I should first have made the enquiry and had the fact better established.

Capt Smith no doubt did his duty in the action but he has too noble a nature to be guilty of such base conduct as you mention, nor did I ever hear of an insinuation of the Kind ⟨in⟩ the army.

It is my wish that the war should be conducted upon the most liberal, national [i.e., rational], and generous principles but I will never suffer an indignity or injury to be offered our officers without retaliation.[3] I am my Lord Your Lordships most obed^t humble Serv

N GREENE

GWG Transcript (CSmH). The word in angle brackets was taken from the ALS (DLC), which is badly damaged.

1. As seen at NG to Marshel of this date, above, NG and the Southern Army changed locations on 3 May.

2. See Doyle to NG, 29 April, above. Smith had been captured in the battle of Hobkirk's Hill. (For more on Smith's situation, see his letter to NG of 30 April, above.)

3. A week later, after the British evacuated Camden, NG is said to have remarked facetiously that Rawdon " 'has left Capt. Jack Smith commandant of the place.' " (See note at Pendleton to Sumter, 10 May, below.) Smith was still a prisoner on parole, however; on 21 May, he left Camden for confinement in Charleston, where, as he wrote a fellow officer, he expected "to feel the Effects of the british tiriny." (Smith to Col. [Otho Williams?], 21 May 1781, MdHi) According to NG's first biographer, Smith was attacked near Charleston by a party of men who "stripped him, bound him, and inflicted on him a barbarous castigation on the bare back." His attackers claimed to be Whigs, so NG could not formally protest the attack or retaliate against a captured British or Loyalist officer. (Johnson, *Greene*, 2: 97)

*   *   *

¶ [FROM THE MARQUIS DE LAFAYETTE, Richmond, Va., 3 May 1781. Is detaining an express with a letter from Washington long enough to give an outline of events since his arrival at Richmond; promises to send a "more Regular account" that evening.[1] He surprised Phillips by the rapidity of his march, causing the latter to retreat and re-embark without attacking Richmond.[2] Fears that Phillips may now move against the iron works at Fredericksburg. Has not received instructions from NG but will try to keep Phillips from joining Lord Cornwallis, who, he believes, "intends Some Expeditions in Virginia."[3] Lafayette's 800 Continentals "find the Climate very warm But do not desert." He will move toward Fredericksburg and Williamsburg and hopes to receive orders from NG. Has done what he "Could at this place"; what the British destroyed "was gone Before" he could "oppose it."[4] ALS [photostat] (ICU) 3 pp. The present location of the manuscript is unknown.]

1. See the letter immediately below; some details mentioned here are discussed in the notes there. Baron Steuben reported on the earlier phase of Phillips's invasion in his letter to NG of 25 April, above.

2. On Lafayette's march to Richmond, see Lafayette to NG, 28 April, above.

3. The British force sailed back down the James River and then reversed its course and returned to Petersburg when Phillips received a letter from Lord Cornwallis on 7 May, informing him that Cornwallis would try to join him there. (Simcoe, *Military Journal*, pp. 115–17; Cornwallis's letter, dated 24 April, is printed in Stevens, *Clinton-Cornwallis Controversy*, 1: 427–29.) Phillips was stricken with typhoid fever during the return to

Petersburg and died there on 13 May; Cornwallis reached Petersburg on the 20th. (Boatner, *Encyc.*, pp. 865, 1152; "Von Bose Journal," p. 57)

4. Gen. Benedict Arnold, whose troops burned a quantity of tobacco at Manchester on 30 April, claimed that Lafayette and his army, across the James River at Richmond, "were spectators of the conflagration without attempting to molest us." (Arnold to Sir Henry Clinton, 12 May, Davies, *Documents*, 20: 144)

¶ [FROM THE MARQUIS DE LAFAYETTE, "Camp on Pamunky River," Va., 3 May 1781.[1] He has informed NG "of the Enemy's movements towards Richmond and the forced Marches" he made to come "to its defense."[2] When he arrived on 29 April, he found the British in possession of Petersburg and Chesterfield Court House.[3] They had taken "part of our Vessels," and their "Command of the Water" and "superiority of regular Troops"—at least 2,300 British to 900 American regulars—"gave them possession of our shore."[4] Knowing that Richmond was their "main object," Lafayette "determined to defend" the town and the public stores and tobacco there, which Gen. [William] Phillips informed him by proclamation "should certainly fall into" British hands.[5] The next morning the British burned warehouses in Manchester.[6] When a party of theirs "ventured on this side," however, they "were timely recalled" and "flew into their Boats" after a charge by "a few" American dragoons.[7] Lafayette collected his forces, knowing that the British had been given orders to attack, but they retreated that night to Osborne's, where they re-embarked.[8] Since their landing at City Point, "(some flour excepted at the Court house) no public property has been destroyed."[9] Cy (Washington Papers: DLC) 3 pp.]

1. Lafayette added details here to the report of activities in the Richmond area that he had sketched out in the letter immediately above.

2. See Lafayette to NG, 28 April, above.

3. On the raid at Petersburg, see Steuben to NG, 25 April, above. At Chesterfield Court House, the British "burnt a range of barracks for *2000 men* and 300 barrels of flour etc." (Benedict Arnold to Sir Henry Clinton, 12 May, Davies, *Documents*, 20: 143)

4. Lafayette referred to the "shore" of the James River. According to one estimate, his force at Richmond, including militia, totaled nearly 3,300 men. (Ward and Greer, *Richmond*, p. 88)

5. In the letter immediately above, Lafayette termed Phillips's proclamation "Bombastic." (Phillips's letter, dated 29 April, is in Idzerda, *Lafayette Papers*, 4: 69–71.)

6. As seen at the letter immediately above, the warehouses contained tobacco. Lafayette said in that letter that the British also destroyed a "Roap work" at Warwick.

7. "This side" was the north side of the James River.

8. It was presumably the presence of Lafayette's force of Continentals and militia in Richmond that caused Phillips to change his mind about trying to capture the town. (Ward and Greer, *Richmond*, pp. 88–89)

9. On the British landing at City Point, see Steuben to NG, 25 April, above.

¶ [FROM GENERAL ANDREW PICKENS, "Camp Near McEl[roees?] Mill," S.C., 3 May 1781. After failing to "fall in with" some parties of enemy militia before they reached Ninety Six, Pickens crossed the Saluda River and united with Col. [Robert] Anderson and a force that Anderson "and the late Colonel [James] McCall had Collected."[1] Learning that "the Georgians were Closely besieging" Augusta, Ga., "which is Said to be very Scarce of Provision, and it was thought could not hold out long," Pickens sent a force under Maj. [Samuel] Hammond "to cooperate with the Georgia Troops on this Side the [Savan-nah] River." Hopes the post at Augusta "will Soon fall."[2] Finds "an almost general disposition among the People to Join us, but there is a great want of Arms." The bearer can give NG "particulars"; asks for orders and "News from the Northward."[3] ALS (DSoC) 1 p.]

1. McCall, who had fought at Cowpens and served with NG's army in North Carolina, had died of smallpox in April. (Waring, *Fighting Elder*, p. 70)

2. Col. Thomas Brown, the Loyalist commander at Augusta, reported on 1 May that he was well-supplied with corn and ammunition and considered his position secure. (Cashin and Robertson, *Augusta*, p. 55) Pickens sent further news of the siege in his letter of 8 May, below.

3. NG replied on 9 May, below.

¶ [TO COLONEL JAMES EMMET, "Head Q. [near Camden, S.C.]," 4 May 1781. Is "obliged" by his letter of 29 April. Begs Emmet to continue to send detailed accounts of Lord Cornwallis's movements "should he not move towards the Cheraws." Cy (MiU-C) 1 p.]

¶ [TO COLONEL HENRY LEE, JR. From "Camp on the West side of the Wateree 7 Miles above Camden," S.C., 4 May 1781. NG received intelligence "last Evening" that Lord Cornwallis was moving rapidly towards Cross Creek, N.C., and is thought to be "coming towards Camden," though "it is possible he may be pushing for our Stores on the upper route."[1] In either case, Lee must join NG's army immediately, bringing with him "the field pieces and all the force detached from this Army." On his march, Lee is to "get all the good Dragoon Horses" that he can.[2] NG's army "moved on this side the River for the convenience of getting supplies." If Lee is on the "East side," he must cross the river or risk encountering Cornwallis. NG will remain "in this neighbour-hood" until he hears from Lee and gets further word of Cornwallis. In a postscript, NG writes that eight days earlier, Cornwallis was fifty miles below Cross Creek, on the east side of the Cape Fear River.[3] LS (CSmH) 2 pp.]

1. The intelligence is in Emmet to NG, 28 April, above. By "Stores on the upper route," NG meant the army's stores that were stockpiled at Charlotte and Salisbury, N.C. As noted at the Emmet letter, Cornwallis was marching to Virginia.

2. As seen in his reply of 6 May, below, Lee decided not to join NG's army imme-diately. NG revoked the orders given here in a letter to Lee of 9 May, also below.

3. In a letter of this date, below, NG asked Gen. Thomas Sumter to forward this letter to Lee. On 5 May, below, NG's aide, Nathaniel Pendleton, fearing that it would not be forwarded, sent a copy directly to Lee. (See Pendleton to Lee, 5 May, below.)

¶ [TO GENERAL FRANCIS MARION. From "Camp on the west side of the Wateree," S.C., 4 May 1781. Gives much of the same information that is in the letter to Col. Henry Lee, immediately above. Adds that he may wish "to fight Lord Cornwallis if our force would warrant it." Wants an account of Marion's strength and an assessment of how willing Marion's men are to "cooperate with us and in the field in time of Action." Has written him several times about dragoon horses, which NG's army needs desperately. Begs him to furnish as many as he can. Adds:

I am told the Militia claim all they take from the Tories: and many of the best horses are collected from the Inhabitants upon this principle. I cannot think the practice warranted either in justice or policy. If the object of the people is plunder altogether, Government can receive but little benefit from them. The horses would be of the highest importance to the public in the regular service.[1]

ADfS (MiU-C) 2 pp.]
1. Hugh Rankin, Marion's biographer, has written that the portion of NG's letter concerning the horses "carried a tone of reprimand, or even of censure." It did "little to soothe" an "irritable" Marion, who was already disturbed by the recent desertion of many of his men. (Rankin, *Swamp Fox*, pp. 201–2) Marion's heated reply of 6 May, below, was the result.

*   *   *

To Joseph Reed, President of the Pennsylvania Council

Camp near Camden on the West side of
Dear Sir   the Wateree [S.C.] May the 4th 1781

I have been in this department near six months and have written you several letters without receiving a line of remembrance.[1] Formerly I us[e]d to flatter my self of holding a place in your friendship, and my being sent to this unfortunate country I hope has not lessened it; for I am sure I never had more need of it in my life, either for consolation or support.

The nature of the war and the circumstances of this Country appear to be little known to the Northward. The strength and resources of these States to support the war have been greatly magnified and over rated; and those whose business and true interest it was to give a just state of the situation of things, have joined in the deception; and from a false principle of pride of having the Country thought powerful have led people to believe it was so. It is true there were many Inhabitants, but they were spread over a great extent of Country, and near equally divided between the Kings interest and ours. The Majority is greatly in favor of the Enemies interest now, as great numbers of the Whigs have left the Country.[2] The produce that is raised in the Country is difficult to collect from the extent of Country in the best of times, and utterly impossible to do it now as all the horses and means of transportation are destroyed. The love of pleasure and the want of principles among many of those who are our friends renders the exertions very languid in support of our cause; and unless the Northern States can give more effectual support these States must fall; and what is worss I am afraid their fall will lay a foundation to sap the liberties of all the rest; for the enemy recruits with great facility in these States; and the service in this quarter is so disagreeable to our Soldiers from the scanty supplies, that many of them enter their [i.e., the British] service.[3] The Enemy have got a much firmer footing in South Carolinia and Geiorgia than is generally believd. Camden[,] Ninty Six and Augusta cover all the fertile parts of these States, and the enemy have laid waste the uper Country in such a manner that an Army cannot subsist in the Neighbourhood of them, and this must secure their posts.[4] Nothing but a superior Army to the Enemies collective force can give relief to this distressed Country, the miseries of which exeeeds all belief. Nor do I beleave any people sufferd greater calamities. The Whigs and the Tories are butchering one another hourly.

The war here is upon a very different scale to what it is to the Northward. It is a plain business there. The Geography of the Country reduces its operations to two or three points.[5] But here it is every where, and the Count[ry] is so full of deep rivers and impassable creeks and swamps, that you are always liable to misfortunes of a capital nature. In collecting provisions and forage we are obliged to send the same guards and escorts, as if the Country was avowedly our Enemies.

Some of the States when ruin approach[es] them, exert themselves; but the difficulties and dangers no sooner subsides, than they sink down into their former sloth and inattention; and seem to be content with the merit of what they have done, without once considering what there is to do. This is the case with Virginia, who exerted her self greatly on the Enemies approach this last winter, but have left us to our selves ever since. North Carolinia did nothing at all until she saw that we would not let the enemy possess the State quietly. There are many good Whigs in the State, but I verily believe the Tories are much the most numerous; and the Whigs are so fond of pleasure that they have but little relish for the rugged business of war. Government is so feeble that it is next to nothing; and the popular plan that influences the Councels greatly weakens the Natural interest of the well affected. The Whigs will do nothing unless the Tories are made [to] do equal duty; and this cannot be effected as the tories are the stronger party, so neither aid the Army.[6] However measures are now taking to raise Men for a year and I am in hopes some will take the field.

Maryland has given no assistance to this Army. Not a man has joined us from that State, and we are discharging her men dayly their times of service being out. She has shamefully neglected us.[7]

You frequently hear of great things from Generals [Francis] Marion and [Thomas] Sumter. These are brave good Officers; but the people that are with them come and go just as they please, and are more allurd from the hopes of plunder than from a desire to serve the public, at least this is the case with many, if not all their followers. Those parties rather serve to keep the dispute alive, than lay a foundation for the recovery of the Country. Dont be decievd in your expectations from this quarter, if greater support cannot be given for the recovery of these States, they must and will remain in the hands of the enemy.

Our Manoeuvers have been various, and the conflict very unequal. We have been twice beaten, the last time by an unfortunate order of Col Gunbies, who orderd the first Maryland Regiment to retire when the enemy were fleeing before them, and the enemy in confusion in all quarters.[8] Victory was certain, and the fall of Camden as certain, as I had taken Measures to cut off the enemies retreat. To induce them to sally was the object of our position, after finding that the works were too strong and the garrison too large to storm with a prospect of succeeding. The event was the most unfortunate that can be imagined, not from the injury we received, but the loss of the opportunity to take the place. Camden seems to have some evil genius about it. What ever is attempted near that place is unfortunate. War is a critical business, and the best concerted plans, subject to disppointments, from the most triffling incidents.

The prospects here are so unpromising, and the difficulties so great, that I am sick of the service, and wish my self out of the Department. When I made this last Movement I expected 2000 Virginia Militia to operate with us, and 1000 Men with Sumter but both have faild me; and I am in the greatest distress. The tardiness of the people puts it out of my power to attempt any thing great. If our good ally the French cannot afford assistance to these Southern States in my opinion there will be no opposition on this side Virginia before fall; and I expect the enemy will possess all the lower Country of that State. The want of subsistence will prevent farther operations in this Country, unless we can take post in the Congarees, where provisions are to be had in great plenty. With esteem and regard I am dear Sir Your most Obed[t] and humble Ser   N. GREENE

ALS (NHi). An ADfS of this letter (MiU-C), differs substantially from the ALS. Some of the differences are discussed in the notes that follow.

1. This was the fourth letter that NG had written Reed since joining the Southern Army in December 1780. Reed finally responded in a long letter of 16 June, below.

2. Interestingly, Nisbet Balfour and Lord Rawdon, the British commanders in South Carolina, were writing at about this time about a "general revolt of the province" and a "dissafection which shewed itself on every quarter," forcing them finally to abandon most of the state's interior. (See Rawdon to Cornwallis, 26 April PRO 30/11/5, and Balfour to Cornwallis, 21 May, PRO 30/11/6. The quotes are from Balfour's letter.)

3. In his draft, NG added that the severity of the service caused officers to use "any pretence to quit the field." Conversely, Balfour wrote just weeks later that unless there were a dramatic turnabout of affairs in South Carolina, not a "single man" would join the British service. (Balfour to Cornwallis, 21 May, PRO 30/11/6)

4. As NG was writing this letter, the British were making plans to abandon all the posts. (Ibid.)

5. NG wrote in his draft that the war in the North "requires neither the genius or application to conduct it there that it does here."

6. In his draft, NG added that North Carolina had only a few militia in the field, "and those the worst in the World for they have neither pride or principle to bind them to any

party or to a discharge of their duty. There are some Counties where there is a good Militia such as the Counties of Ro[w]an and Mecklenburg; but these people have been ruined by their last years exertions and the ravages of the enemy."

7. NG added in his draft: "Delaware has not even answerd my letters."

8. On the battle of Hobkirk's Hill and the order issued by Col. John Gunby, see NG to Huntington, 27 April, above.

To General Thomas Sumter

Camp on the West side of Wateree 7 Miles
Dear Sir   above Camden [S.C.] May 4th 1781.

Last night intelligence arrived that Lord Cornwallis was moving up towards Cross Creek, and it is thought on his way for Camden, but this is altogether uncertain as our baggage and stores upon the upper route may be his object.[1]

The movements of Lord Cornwallis will oblige us to collect all our regular force. You will please to forward the letters which accompany this to Gen[l] Marion and L[t] Col. Lee.[2]

I am glad to hear the people are joining you, but am afraid it is a force little to be depended on as th[ey] will fall off from the first change of circumstances.[3] I should be glad to know what force you have and what Gen[l] Marion can join us with. If our collective strength would warrant an attack upon Lord Cornwallis I should be glad to make it, for defeating him will be next to an entire recovery of the Country, and every thing else a partial business.

If you could possess the post upon the Congaree with a field piece it can be sent you immediately. But then whatever is done must take place immediately as the enemy will in all probability be soon upon our backs.[4]

We shall halt on 25 Mile Creek untill I hear further from you, L[t] Col. Lee and Lord Cornwallis. Send us all the provision you can, and direct it by the route to that place.

We have some Ammunition which we can supply you with provided you can send for it; but if the Field piece should be sent you it may come in the Amunition Waggon.[5]

Do not fail to get us all the good Dragoon horses that you can, for we are in the utmost distress for want of them. Gen[l] Marion I am told has a considerable number of them on which he has mounted his Militia. It is a pity that good horses should be given into the hands of people who are engaged for no limited ti[me].[6] I am Dear Sir Your Most Obed[t] Humble Servant   NATH GREENE

LS (Sumter Papers: DLC).

1. On this intelligence, see note at NG to Lee, this date, above.

2. See NG to Francis Marion and NG to Lee, this date, both above.

3. Sumter had reported in his letter of 27 April, above, that large numbers of men were joining him.

4. As seen at Sumter to NG, first letter of 6 May, below, Sumter wanted a cannon to use initially against the British installation at Motte's instead of Ft. Granby, "the post upon the Congaree."

5. Sumter had requested the ammunition in his letter of 2 May, above.

6. See NG to Marion, this date, above.

*   *   *

¶ [TO COLONEL THOMAS WADE. From West side of the Wateree River, S.C., 4 May 1781. Has Wade's letter of 2 May; asks him to keep forwarding "the most perfect account" of Lord Cornwallis's movements. Wade should send the enclosed letter by express to Col. [James] Emmet, unless "operations of the enemy make it difficult."¹ Cy (MiU-C) 1 p.]

1. NG's letter of this date to Emmet is above.

¶ [FROM GENERAL JOHN BUTLER, Ramsey's Mill, N.C., 4 May 1781. Has a report that on 2 May Lord Cornwallis was on the north side of the Neuse River, ten miles from Smithfield, on a road leading directly to Halifax.¹ "It is given out" that the British will move toward Wake Court House, but Butler doubts that report because they have already crossed the Neuse.² He also has received word that Gen. [William] Phillips has "advanced" as far as Petersburg, Va., and perhaps to the Nottoway River.³ Has another report that an enemy party is moving toward Cross Creek, N.C., but none of Butler's many spies has confirmed this.⁴ He will march for Wake County "this morning" to join "Brigadier G[en. William] Caswell," who has an unknown number of men "in the field." Butler's troops will be "Discharged" on 15 April. Adds in a postscript that he is now "better convinced" that the British are not moving toward Cross Creek. ALS (NjP) 2 pp.]

1. Cornwallis's army crossed to the north side of the Neuse River on 4 May and marched to Halifax, arriving on the 12th. ("Von Bose Journal," p. 57)

2. Cornwallis wrote Gen. William Phillips on 24 April that he was marching to join Phillips at Petersburg but would be "pointing towards Hilsborough, in hopes to withdraw Greene" from South Carolina. (PRO 30/11/85)

3. On Phillips's movements, see note at Lafayette to NG, second letter of 3 May, above.

4. No British detachment was marching to Cross Creek. (See Rowan to NG, 5 May, below.)

¶ [FROM GENERAL WILLIAM SMALLWOOD, Annapolis, Md., 4 May 1781. He received NG's letter of 31 March two days after writing NG on 12 April; hopes his own letter satisfied NG that Smallwood has "not been unmindful of the distressing and critical Situation of the Southern department" and that he has worked to "promote the recruiting Service."¹ He "waved no Opportunity" to direct the legislature's and executive's attention to "important Objects," leaving "Matters upon a smaller Scale" to Gen. [Mordecai] Gist and other officers, who had no more "Power of effecting any thing material" than Smallwood. He did nothing about arranging the Maryland officers because Gist at first refused to accept his orders and then because he decided that it was not an "essential Object, as the present incorporation of the Troops could not be dissolved, 'till a suficient number of Men were raised to admit of a separation of the old Corps." Asks NG to send him the arrangement of the

Delaware officers; Smallwood has not received one from the Board of War.[2] Sends an act of the Maryland Assembly, by which NG will see from it that it is impossible to get recruits in the state except by drafting them.[3] The executive, however, "twice suspended" a draft, so that it began only on 1 May. The draftees will serve only until 10 December, "and for want of Equipment" their term will be "shortened" even more. "The measures of this State, and the whole Continent call loudly for a Revolution, or at least a reform." After receiving NG's letter, Smallwood immediately sent it to the governor and council to "induce" them to convene the Assembly "directly." They refused but have since ordered the legislature to meet on 10 May, when Smallwood will "attend them, and Strain every Nerve to get things put in a better train." Gist has gone to urge the governor of Delaware to "compleat[,] equip, and forward" that state's quota of troops. Gist will also visit the Board of War to "enforce" Smallwood's requests for clothing, arms, and accoutrements, which Maryland cannot provide and without which the troops cannot march.[4] Smallwood will continue to "press" Maryland to provide the clothing and equipment, but he has been told by officials to expect nothing, as the state has no supplies, "Not a Copper in the Treasury," and is "without Credit." Points out that under the recruitment law the draftees "are not to be drawn from the respective Counties until clad." Smallwood sees "nothing but delay and difficulties" ahead but will spare no effort to "surmount them upon the Assemblys meeting." LS (MiU-C) 3 pp.]

1. See Smallwood to NG, 12 April, above.
2. NG said nothing about the arrangement in his reply of 9 June, below.
3. For the recruiting plan adopted by the Maryland legislature, see Gist to NG, 19 January, above (vol. 7: 151).
4. Gist reported on his efforts in Delaware and with the Board of War in a letter to NG of 28 May, below.

¶ [FROM GENERAL THOMAS SUMTER, "Camp at Congrees," S.C., 4 May 1781. Has received intelligence "this Moment" that on 25 April Lord Cornwallis's army was in Wilmington, N.C., with "No accounts of his Moving Soon." Some of the wounded from Cornwallis's army have arrived in Charleston, S.C. The enemy are repairing old works and building new fortifications there. Maj. [Archibald] McArthur was still at Nelson's Ferry when Sumter's informant left Charleston.[1] Small parties of Loyalists are "Troublesom in different parts of the Country," but not enough to "prevent people from Turning out Which they are doing Very well." Sumter has stationed men on the Wateree River to prevent the sending of cattle into Camden. He finds that "Parties of Tories Lyes in the Swamps & when oppertunity Serves Swims Stock over the River." He means to lie as "Close to the post to Night as possible." It has two twelve-pounders, three or four smaller cannon, and a garrison of between 300 and 500 men.[2] He expects to have 500 men with him by next week; other parties, which are en route, will join him later. Needs ammunition. Hopes NG can send back a supply in the wagons that Sumter sent to the Southern Army. Also needs guns, swords, and pistols. Asks NG to inform him of "any thing late" from the northward that is "of Consequence & Not a Secret."[3] ALS (MiU-C) 2 pp.]

1. McArthur, about whose force NG had been concerned, had been ordered not to march to Camden. (Rawdon to Cornwallis, 2 May, PRO 30/11/6)

2. "The post" at Ft. Granby had a garrison of 340 men, including sixty regulars. (Gregorie, *Sumter*, p. 157)

3. NG replied on 6 May, below.

¶ [FROM GENERAL THOMAS SUMTER, "Camp at Ancrums," S.C., 4 May 1781. He just received NG's letter.[1] If Sumter's intelligence is accurate—and he has no reason to doubt it—NG's reports about Lord Cornwallis's movements "are Not Just." Sumter will send his man back to Charleston for additional intelligence and will also send men for the field piece that NG offered.[2] "How far it May Answer is uncertain but I think an attempt Necessary, at any Rate upon the post at Mr Motts," which has a garrison of 108 men and no artillery. The field piece must cross the river within four miles of Motte's, and the roads there are good, "either up or Down."[3] No time should be lost, as the enemy will offer "Less Vigerous" opposition now than "after assistance Might have Nearly arived." ALS (MiU-C) 2 pp.]

1. See NG to Sumter, this date, above.

2. Sumter's intelligence is in the letter immediately above. NG defended the quality of his own information in his first letter to Sumter of 6 May, below.

3. Sumter wrote NG on 7 May, below, that the enemy at Motte's had recently received artillery. After learning that Henry Lee and Francis Marion had the post there under siege, Sumter took the field piece that he obtained from NG and moved against the British post at Orangeburg, which he captured on 11 May. (See NG to Huntington, 14 May, below.)

¶ [GENERAL GREENE'S ORDERS, Camp, Twenty Five Mile Creek, S.C., 5 May 1781. Orders a general court-martial to sit "Tomorrow." Lamar Orderly Book (OClWHi) 1 p.]

¶ [TO GENERAL JOHN BUTLER. From "Camp 25 Mile Creek 7 Miles from Camden," S.C., 5 May 1781. Thanks him for the information in his letter of 28 April and the "enclosures"; Butler should continue to send NG the "earliest intelligence of Lord Cornwallis's movements." If Cornwallis is heading toward Virginia, Butler should have those in charge of public stores at Hillsborough and Halifax, N.C., move them "into the uper Country" and should help to insure the stores' "security."[1] Df (MiU-C) 2 pp.]

1. Cornwallis was heading toward Virginia. As seen at the Marquis de Malmedy to NG, 11 May, below, the British captured or destroyed many of the public stores at Halifax.

¶ [TO JOSEPH CLAY. From [Camp, Twenty Five mile Creek, S.C.], 5 May 1781.[1] NG has authorized Col. [William R.] Davie to contract for stores to relieve "The distress of the sick." The stores are to be delivered to one of Davie's assistants, Mr. [James] Weir, who will certify their arrival. Upon receiving Weir's certificates, Clay should pay the bearer, Capt. [James] O'Hara, in bills of exchange on France. NG gives the prices Clay is to pay for the "Spirits," wine, sugar, and coffee that will be provided. Directs him to settle on a "rate of exchange" with O'Hara; they should consult a third party if they disagree. If Clay does not have "Bills to discharge the account," he should "draw on the Pay Office at Phil[adelphia] for the Ballance." Df (MiU-C) 2 pp.]

1. The place was taken from NG's Orders of this date, above.

*   *   *

To Samuel Huntington,
President of the Continental Congress

Sir

Camp on the West side of the Wateree
near Camden [S.C.] May 5th 1781.

In my last I informed Your Excellency of a repulse we met with before Camden, which I consider the more unfortunate as from every enquiry it appears that the enemy were generally retiring at the time that Col. Gunby ordered the first Maryland Reg^t to take a second position in the rear.[1] This unfortunate order gave the enemy the advantage of the day and totally cut off all hopes of reducing Camden, which could only be effected by taking an advantage of a sally, and the enemy notwithstanding their advantage have never ventured out of their works since, unless it was in small parties to reconnoitre our situation. We continued two days at Saunders's Creek and then retired to Rugley's Plantation for the sake of recruiting our Cattle; from which place we moved on this side the river because we found the enemy drew greater supplies from this quarter than any other, and we could procure supplies for our troops with less difficulty than we could on the East side.[2]

The 2000 Virg^a Militia I have been expecting to join us, have not come out nor can I learn when they will. Capt [Nathaniel] Pendleton one of my Aids de Camp whom I sent from Deep River to hasten their march has returned, and informs me that from the criminal neglect of the County Lieutenants it is altogether uncertain when they will be ready to take the field; and from the cavelling of some but a small proportion can be expected at all.[3] Nothing could be more unfortunate than this delay, and I wish it may not expose us to ruin, as our force is now but little more than three fourths as great as it was at the time we retired over the Dan River.[4] The time of service of many of the Maryland troops is expired, and we are daily discharging them. Sometimes not less than eight or ten in a day, and these some of the best soldiers in the field. Maryland has neglected us altogether, not a Man has joined us from that State since I have been in the Department. Tardy measures are very illy adapted to the dangerous and critical situation of the Southern States, nor can I see any hopes of recovering them unless we can take the field with an Army superior to the Enemys collective force; Whenever an Army takes a position in the Country the enemy will give up their posts & risque an action which must decide who shall possess the open Country.

I can see no place where an Army of any considerable force can subsist for any length of time; and the horses are so destroyed in this Country that subsistance cannot be drawn from a distance. The Country is so laid waste and the means of transportation so unequal to the business of collecting supplies from a distance for an Army, that it is difficult for me to concieve how an Army is to be subsisted in this Country any longer unless it's strength is such as to enable it to take post on the Congaree.

Capt [James] OHara by whom I write is waiting, which prevents my being more explicit upon this subject which in it's consequences will decide the Southern operations. I have the honor to be With great Respect Your Excellency's Most Obedient Humble Servant

NATH GREENE

LS (PCC, item 172, vol. 1: 161: DNA).

1. Col. John Gunby's role in the battle of Hobkirk's Hill is discussed at NG to Huntington, 27 April, above.

2. On the army's move to the west side of the Wateree, see NG's Orders of 3 May and NG to Marshel, 3 May, both above. By "Cattle," NG meant livestock, most of which would have been horses.

3. For more on Pendleton's mission, see NG to Pendleton, 11 April, above. As noted at Jefferson to NG, 30 March, above, only a small number of Virginia militiamen were sent to reinforce the army.

4. NG's army had numbered approximately 1,400 Continentals and 600 militia when it retreated into Virginia in February. (See Proceedings of a Council of War, 9 February, above, vol. 7: 261.) NG's letters to Huntington of 14 and 16 May, both below, reached Congress seven days before this one, and the appeal for men that he made here was lost in the excitement over the military successes that he reported in those letters. (JCC, 20: 620, 658; for an example of the reaction to the latter reports, see Daniel of St. Thomas Jenifer to John Hall, 11 June 1781, Smith, Letters, 17: 309.)

*　　　*　　　*

¶ [CAPTAIN NATHANIEL PENDLETON TO COLONEL HENRY LEE, JR. From Camp, Twenty Five Mile Creek, S.C., 5 May 1781. To make sure that Lee receives it, he encloses, at NG's request, a copy of a letter from NG that Gen. [Thomas] Sumter was asked to forward to Lee.[1] Congratulates Lee on his "success against Fort Watson."[2] ALS (IHi) 1 p.]

1. The letter to Lee of 4 May is above.

2. See Marion to NG, first letter of 23 April, above.

¶ [TO GENERAL JETHRO SUMNER. From "West side of Wateree 7 Miles from Camden," S.C., 5 May 1781. Has just received intelligence that Lord Cornwallis "is in motion," but "his route or destination" is not yet known. If Sumner has any recruits ready for the field, they should join either NG, in case Cornwallis moves toward Camden, or Baron Steuben if Cornwallis goes toward Virginia.[1] "If the enemy are marching Northwardly," the stores at Hillsborough, Halifax, and New Bern should be moved immediately to "the upper Country."[2] LS (RHi) 2 pp.]

1. Cornwallis was headed toward Virginia.

2. Sumner replied on 15 May, below.

*　　　*　　　*

To General Thomas Sumter

Dear Sir   Camp at 25 Miles Creek [S.C.] May 5th 1781

I wrote you yesterday that Lord Cornwallis was advancing into the Country on the East side of Cape Fear River, and was when the Express come away within forty or fifty miles of Cross Creek.[1] His object and future route remains to be explained.[2] Should he come this way or go up into the uper Country towards Salisbury at which place the Virginia Militia are to collect, it would be my wish to collect our force and fight him. On this presumption I beg you to inform me what force you think you could join me with for the purpose; and how far you can depend upon the people you have with you, to fight with regular troops. Much may depend upon a defeat on either side. On the part of the enemy it would be ruinous; on ours it would be a capital misfortune.

Please to inform me immediately whether you can possess the post at the Congarees if a field piece is sent you; and how long a time it will take to effect it. Hasten on the Stores to this Army as fast as you can, and as matters are drawing to a critical crisis, I could wish you would send us twenty or thirty people well mounted to serve with us as Expresses.

What is the strength and situation of the Post at Ninty Six? I could wish to be accurately informed.[3]

Nothing could be more unfortunate than our repulse the other day, which was entirely owing to an order of Col Gunbies, ordering the first Maryland Regiment to take a new position in the rear. This impressed the Regiment with an idea of a retreat, and drew off the second Regiment with it. The Enemy were all in confusion and retiring at the same time. Victory was ours if the troops had stood their ground one Minute longer, and the defeat would have given us full possession of Camden, as the enemy could not have got back into Town.[4] With esteem & regard I am dear Sir Your most Obed[t] humble Se[r]

N GREENE

ALS (Sumter Papers: DLC).
  1. See NG to Sumter, 4 May, above.
  2. Cornwallis was marching to Virginia.
  3. Sumter replied in his second letter to NG of 6 May, below.
  4. On the battle of Hobkirk's Hill and Col. John Gunby's performance, see NG to Huntington, 27 April, above.

*   *   *

¶ [DOCTOR ROBERT JOHNSTON TO JAMES WEIR.[1] From Wateree, S.C., 5 May 1781. Asks Weir, at NG's direction, to receive and keep a specified quantity of stores at Charlotte, N.C., or another safe place. These particular items, which Capt. [James] O'Hara is bringing to Weir, are for the use of the "flying hospital." Weir is to deliver the rest of the shipment to the general hospital.[2] ALS (Nc-Ar) 1 p.]

1. On 15 May, Congress named Johnston to serve as one of two hospital physicians in the Southern Department. (*JCC*, 20: 506) Weir was an assistant commissary. (See NG to Clay, this date, above.)

2. For more on the stores, see ibid.

¶ [FROM COLONEL JOHN MARSHEL,[1] "Camp Flat Rock," S.C., 5 May 1781. At NG's order, he has "taken post and placed guards at every necessary place."[2] Has no information of Lord Cornwallis's or other enemy movements. Has directed that all troops and wagons coming to the army cross the Catawba River at McDonald's Ford, which "is the most convenient for Waggons." Requests ammunition and salt. Has eighty men on duty in his regiment. ALS (MiU-C) 1 p.]

1. This letter, written in a different hand than Marshel to NG, 23 April, above, is signed "Marshall." The usual spelling was "Marshel."

2. See NG to Marshel, 3 May, above.

¶ [FROM COLONEL JAMES READ, Salisbury, N.C., 5 May 1781. He has "repaired to this Place," as NG ordered, and found only fifty unarmed Continental draftees.[1] There are no armorers among them, but he hopes to find some among the draftees who are due to arrive in a few days. If NG does not object, he will set up the armory in some uninhabited houses that he has found close to town, where "the workmen can be more attentive to their business . . . than in Town."[2] The Virginia militia "have not arrived."[3] Encloses a return of "Baggage and Stores" at Salisbury [not found]. ALS (NjP) 1 p.]

1. See NG to Read, 29 April, above.

2. NG replied on 9 May, below.

3. As noted at Jefferson to NG, 30 March, above, most of the expected reinforcement from Virginia was never sent.

¶ [FROM COLONEL ROBERT ROWAN, Campbelltown, N.C., 5 May 1781. Is Happy to report that NG is in "no immediate danger" from Lord Cornwallis, who has "most undoubtedly" marched toward Halifax. Fears, though, that Cornwallis may "return upon us" after being reinforced in Virginia; "the flattering accounts we had lately from the Northward it seems are vanished into smoke."[1] The people in Rowan's area are "in the utmost distress, unprotected" in their "persons and properties." They "see nothing but ruin and desolation" ahead. "A british officer, formerly in the American service, [is] now going at large amongst us, under pretence of a flag, perverting the minds of the people. Others [are] daily expected upon a like errand." Rowan supposes that a "Mr Mallet," who is coming from Wilmington, will receive "every indulgence" because of his connections with "our commanding officer."[2] Many local residents went to Wilmington while Cornwallis was there and succeeded in recovering their slaves. Rowan's wife, however, was "treated with the utmost contempt, nay rudeness, hardly permitted to set her foot on shore." Adds: "It was very pretty the officers said, for a rebel Colonel's wife, to have the assurance to go to their garrisoned Town, & [they] ordered her to quit it immediately, with out holding the least conversation with any person." Rowan will "make no further applications" for his slaves and doubts that there will be any "censure" if he makes "reprisals." Many "rascals" who are now serving the British in Wilmington "have families in this county," in whose behalf he has often interested himself; he has "met with a generous return for it." Asks for instructions concerning the "reception & treatment of flags." Unless something is done, his area "might as well be within british lines," for the enemy "come & go when they think proper." He has seventy pairs of shoes available for the army but cannot get transportation; suggests that NG send "a couple of horsemen with bags" to receive them.[3] Wishes NG health, success, "and if it should be most proper a quick return to this state." ALS (MiU-C) 3 pp.]

1. Cornwallis did not return to North Carolina. By "flattering accounts," Rowan probably referred to the failed plan to try to capture Gen. Benedict Arnold and his army in Virginia. (See above, Steuben to NG, first letter of 4 March [vol. 7: 390].) Not only had hopes for the success of that attempt "vanished into smoke," but a reinforced British army under Gen. William Phillips had now invaded the interior of Virginia. (See Steuben to NG, 25 April, above.)

2. "Mr Mallet" was probably Peter Mallet, a Wilmington merchant, who was suspected of being a Loyalist sympathizer. (See above, vol. 6: 564n.)

3. NG replied on 14 May, below.

¶ [FROM BARON STEUBEN, "Camp. New Kent County, 16 Miles from Richmond," Va., 5 May 1781. The Marquis de Lafayette, who arrived in Richmond two days after Steuben last wrote NG, will inform NG "of the operations of the Army." Steuben will only add to his "last" that none of the stores collected for the Virginia troops at Chesterfield Court House and Petersburg fell into enemy hands.[1] He will stay with Lafayette, who is now in command, "so long as there is any probability of coming to action," and will then "fullfill" NG's instructions to hasten "the Departure of the Levies for the Southward." Lafayette has already agreed to this, and Steuben has ordered Col. [William] Davies to assemble the recruits near Richmond. They will lack arms, cartridge boxes, swords, and blankets; he hopes to get "every thing else" from the state.[2] ALS (RNHi) 2 pp.]

1. Steuben's "last" letter, reporting Gen. William Phillips's invasion of the Virginia interior, was dated 25 April, above. Lafayette had sent further reports on the military situation in two letters to NG of 3 May, above.

2. Steuben again discussed his efforts to assemble and equip the recruits in a letter to NG of 15 May, below.

¶ [GENERAL GREENE'S ORDERS, Camp, Twenty Five Mile Creek, S.C., 6 May 1781. Roll is to be called "every hour to confine the Soldiers to Camp, and prevent Marauding." Lamar Orderly Book (OClWHi) 1 p.]

¶ [TO COLONEL NICHOLAS LONG. From "Camp near Camden," S.C., 6 May 1781. He received intelligence "yesterday" that Lord Cornwallis was "in motion"; NG is "inclind to think" it will be in a "Northwardly" direction. Is "apprehensive" that Cornwallis will take Halifax, N.C., "in his way, as it will distress the Southern operations not a little to break up your Manufa[c]tories of different kinds."[1] Advises Long to move his stores "towards the Moravian Towns" and set up "business anew" there. NG is "too remote" to give "positive orders," but Long should keep the stores safe "at all events."[2] The army is in great need of arms. The repair of arms and the making of cartouche boxes and shoes "are three great objects"; equipment for the cavalry is next in importance. Compliments Long's son, who "behaves with great gallantry upon all occasions."[3] ADfS (MiU-C) 2 pp.]

1. Cornwallis did capture Halifax, N.C., on his way north to Virginia. (See Clay to NG, 11 May, below.)

2. The ."Moravian Towns" were Salem, Bethabara, and Bethania. They were about 140 miles west of Halifax.

3. Nicholas Long, Jr., was a cavalry officer in the North Carolina militia. (*NCSR*, 17: 966)

* * *

To General Francis Marion

Dear Sir   Camp at 25 Miles Creek [S.C.] May 6th 1781

I wrote you day before yesterday that Lord Cornwallis was in motion, and that it was uncertain which way he meant to operate, but in any case it was necessary for us to collect our force for which purpose I had given L[t] Col Lee orders to join the main Army immediately with the several detachments and the field piece.[1]

I am not determined yet what line of conduct to pursue supposing Lord Cornwallis to move Northwardly; and therefore wish you to continue at or near the Congarees so as to prevent supplies from coming to Camden until you hear further from me.[2] I expect more full intelligence toNight which will enable me to decide.[3] Dont forget to give me an account of your numbers; and you would promote the service greatly if you could furnish us with sixty or Eighty good Dragoon horses.[4]

I am sorry for Col Kolbs death and the necessity there is for detaching a part of your Regiment.[5] With esteem & regard I am your Most Obed[t] humble Se[r]   N GREENE

ALS (ScC).

1. See NG to Marion and NG to Henry Lee, both 4 May, above.

2. Cornwallis was moving "Northwardly," toward Virginia.

3. See NG to Marion, 7 May, below.

4. On Marion's "numbers" and the horses, see Marion to NG, this date, below.

5. The death of Col. Abel Kolb is discussed at Wade to NG, 4 April, above. Marion had detached a regiment to pursue the Loyalists who killed Kolb. (Rankin, *Swamp Fox*, p. 199)

* * *

¶ [TO GENERAL THOMAS SUMTER. From "Camp 25 Mile Creek," S.C., 6 May 1781. He received Sumter's two letters of 4 May "last evening." Sumter can "depend upon" NG's intelligence respecting Lord Cornwallis. It is not yet certain whether Cornwallis is going north or south, but NG is "inclined to think" he will "leave every thing here and move Northward."[1] That was the "original plan," and Cornwallis is "too proud to relinquish his object." NG has received "The meal" and has sent ammunition to Sumter in the returning wagons. "Guns, Swords and Pistols we have none."[2] Agrees that "vigorous measures are necessary to strike terror into our enemies and give spirit to our own people." Sumter should be careful to protect the field piece so that the besieged garrisons "cannot possess it by a sally." He should keep NG's army "well supplied with meal." LS (Sumter Papers: DLC) 3 pp.]

1. Cornwallis was moving "Northward," toward Virginia.

2. Sumter had requested the ammunition and the military stores in his first letter of 4 May, above.

*   *   *

To General Thomas Sumter

Dear Sir   Camp 25 Mile Creek [S.C.] May 6th 1781

I am exceeding sorry that Col [John] Watson has found means to get into Camden. This reinforcment if Col [John] Small is with Watson will enable Lord Rawdon to excel us.[1] I am also a little apprehensive for the safety of Lt Col Lees detachment who is orderd to join this Army on this side the river.[2] Should the enemy attempt any thing against you or him you will form a junction; and for this purpose you will advise Col Lee of your situation, and point out to him the safest and best route to form a junction with me. Dont run any great hazard until the Virginia Militia come up, which will enable you to push your operations with rapid[ity] and safety.[3]

You will please to forward the inclosed letter to Col Lee as soon as possible.[4] I am Sir with esteem Your most Obed humble Ser

N GREENE

ALS (Sumter Papers: DLC).

1. Letters to NG of this date from Henry Lee, Francis Marion, and Sumter, all below, contained intelligence of Watson's force reaching Camden. (On Watson's success in the undertaking, see note at Marion's letter of this date.) Watson's detachment added about 500 men to Rawdon's force, making it slightly larger than NG's army. (Balfour to Germain, 1 May, PRO 30/11/109)

2. The orders are in NG to Lee, 4 May, above. As noted there, Lee delayed his march to join NG and was therefore not in danger of being attacked.

3. The Virginia militia were not "coming up." (See note at Jefferson to NG, 30 March, above.)

4. The letter was undoubtedly NG to Lee, 4 May, above. Sumter replied on 7 May, below.

*   *   *

¶ [FROM DOCTOR JAMES BROWNE, "General Hospital at Col⁰ Perkins's in Pittsylvania," Va., 6 May 1781. Since the establishment of the hospital "at this Place," more than 200 soldiers have been returned to NG's army.[1] Browne expects soon to send "sixty or seventy more," many of whom were wounded at Guilford Court House.[2] Even though it has been difficult to acquire provisions, only two men have "died of their Wounds." In compliance with NG's order, three doctors have gone to Charlotte, N.C.[3] Browne will remain "some time longer" to distribute the stores that are daily expected from Petersburg, Va., and to get the remaining patients "fit" for duty.[4] Asks NG to decide the case of the bearer, Robert Wilson, who was appointed commissary of hospitals for the department last August but was arrested in January for "ungentlemanly Conduct." During Wilson's suspension, Doctor Brownson was appointed purveyor.[5] Wilson's arrest was withdrawn on the supposition that he would leave the army after settling his accounts. Instead, he has applied to remain an "Officer of the Hospitals." Since NG has stated in the "strongest" terms "the Impropriety of multiplying Officers," Browne refers Wilson's case to him, reminding NG that Congress has "discontinued Hospital Commissaries" in its arrangement of the hospitals.[6] Browne has "no News from Brownson."[7] Adds in a postscript that he would be happy to have NG "direct a Mode for Settling the Hospital Accounts." ALS (MiU-C) 2 pp.]

1. On the establishment of the general hospital in Pittsylvania County, see note at Browne to NG, 15 April, above.

2. In a letter to NG of 14 May, below, Browne wrote that he had discharged sixty men and sent them to camp.

3. For more about the doctors who were sent to Charlotte, see Browne to NG, 15 April, above.

4. In his letter of 14 May, below, Browne said the hospital's stores had been exhausted.

5. Nothing is known about Wilson's arrest or suspension; on the appointment of Dr. Nathan Brownson as deputy purveyor of hospitals in the Southern Department, see note at NG to Huntington, 14 January, above (vol. 7: 119).

6. The arrangement of the hospital department, which Congress had enacted in September 1780, is in JCC, 18: 878. NG's reply has not been found.

7. On Brownson's whereabouts, see letters to NG from Samuel Huntington, 15 April, and the Georgia Delegates in Congress, 26 April, both above.

¶ [FROM COLONEL JOHN ERVIN,[1] Rafting Creek, S.C., 6 May 1781. Sends intelligence that a British party, "Supposed to be" Col. [John] Watson's, was about "20 miles below Camden on this side the river."[2] Ervin will "reconitre" and send further intelligence. ALS (MiU-C) 1 p.]

1. Gen. Francis Marion had sent a party under Ervin to Rafting Creek, in the High Hills of the Santee, "to awe the Tories and prevent them from sending provisions into Camden." (Rankin, Swamp Fox, p. 193)

2. Ervin's party was on the east side of the Wateree River. On Watson's march to Camden, see note at Marion to NG, this date, below.

¶ [FROM GEORGE FLETCHER,[1] Cross Creek, N.C., 6 May 1781. He has received frequent reports that the British army was advancing "this way" but believes it was only a "large Forrageing party," which moved as far as Duplin Court House and is thought to be returning to Wilmington. If the enemy do approach Cross Creek, Fletcher will inform NG "immediately."[2] The county commissioner, who has collected 100 cattle at Fletcher's order, wants to know what to do with them. Fletcher has "saved about forty barrels of the Pork" that were thrown into the Cape Fear River; the meat would "make very good baccon." Two men have presented him with an order to pay them in provisions for their work as boat builders; Fletcher asks NG for directions. He also asks if he should provide "provision[,] forrage &c" to expresses and others traveling through Cross Creek who are in "great distress" for it. Seeks a pass to permit James Moore and him to go to Wilmington. Fletcher fears being "totaly" ruined if some men there with whom he has done business leave the country. The British also took some of Fletcher's "Negroes" to Wilmington. Only the thought of his family being "distress'd" induces him to trouble NG with this request.[3] Adds in a postscript that he has just received intelligence from a reliable source that "Lord Corn Wallies" has advanced to the Neuse River and is on his way to Halifax. ALS (MiU-C) 3 pp.]

1. As noted above (vol. 7: 4n), Fletcher was the purchasing commissary at Cross Creek.

2. Fletcher sent further intelligence about enemy movements in his postscript to this letter.

3. NG responded to this request and replied to Fletcher's other queries on 14 May, below.

¶ [FROM COLONEL HENRY LEE, JR., "Before Motts Post," S.C., 6 May 1781, 4 P.M. He received NG's letter of 4 May "a few moments" after his arrival at Motte's.[1] Is glad that NG has "passed the Santee."[2] Adds: "Unfortunately we were a day too late. [Col. John] Watson has gone on to Cambden."[3] Lee rejoices to hear of Lord Cornwallis's march; he continues to believe that NG's "⟨plan⟩ is to ⟨cut?⟩ connexion with Virginia."[4] Lee will prepare to pass "the western path" of the Santee but will wait a day or two unless NG orders otherwise. If he does not hear from NG, Lee's "general direction" will be to "⟨march⟩ fifteen miles from ⟨Camden toward Ninety Six⟩." Asks NG to write and "send duplicates."[5] ALS (MiU-C) 2 pp. Parts of the letter are in a number code. In the calendar, the editors have replaced the numbers with the deciphered words and put angle brackets around the words.]

1. Thomas Sumter wrote NG on 7 May, below, that Francis Marion and Lee had arrived at Motte's "yesterday fore noon."

2. NG's army had actually crossed to the west side of the Wateree, a tributary of the Santee River. (See NG to Huntington, 5 May, above.)

3. On Watson's success in reaching the post at Camden, see note at Marion to NG, this date, below.

4. Lee had further discussed NG's "plan" and its relation to Cornwallis's movements in his letter to NG of 2 May, above.

5. As seen in Lee's letter to NG of 8 May, below, NG sent one of his aides to state his "intentions & wishes."

*   *   *

From General Francis Marion

S^r   Mottes Congarees [S.C.] 6th May 1781.

Yourse of the 4th Inst I rec^d & am sorry to Acquaint You that I brought here but one hundred & fifty men, the rest have Dropt away, waried with Duty & I believe Dispirited; in not seeing greater support.

I acknowledge that you have repeatedly mention the want of Dragoon horses & wish it had been in my power to furn[is]h them but it is not nor never had been. The few horses which has been taken from

[Torreys?] has been kept for the service & never for private property, but if you think it best for the service to Dismount the Malitia now with me I will Direct Col [Henry] Lee & Cap[t] [James] Conyers to do so, but am sertain we shall never git their service in future. This woud not give me any uneasyness as I have somtime Determin to relinquish my command in the malitia as soon as you arrived in it & I wish to do it as soon as this post is Either taken or abandoned.[1]

I Shall assist in reducing the post here & when Col. [Henry] Lee returns to you I [will] Take that oppertunity in waiting on you when I hope to get permission to go to Philadelphia.[2]

Our purpose in crossing Santee was to fight [Col. John] Watson but unluckily We was one day to Late. He crossed at Buckenhams Yesterday & is gone toward Camden with about two hundred men & two field p[iece]s.[3]

Severall Droves of Cattle is on their way to you at Rugelys but am affaird they will fall in the Enemy hands.

Col. Lee has rec[d] your Orders & will not be detained by me, he thinks that we are so near you he can at the shortest Notice Join you.[4] I have the Honour to be your Ob s[t]   FRAN[S] MARION

ALS (MiU-C).

1. As noted at NG to Marion, 4 May, above, Hugh Rankin, Marion's biographer, believes that Marion was angered by the tone of NG's letter of that date. That, together with other frustrations, led him to threaten to resign his militia commission.

2. NG replied on 9 May, below.

3. On Watson's earlier movements, see note at Wade to NG, 19 April, above. From Georgetown, where he had retreated after breaking off pursuit of Marion, Watson marched toward the Santee River; his detachment was "much reduced in Number, thro' Casualties, Sickness and a Reinforcement which he had left to strengthen the Garrison at Georgetown." (Rawdon to Cornwallis, 24 May, PRO 30/11/6) He crossed the Santee at Lenud's Ferry, near the river's mouth, and waited for a day or two by order of Nisbet Balfour to cover the possible return of Lord Cornwallis or Banastre Tarleton to South Carolina. Watson's detachment of about 500 men then moved toward Nelson's Ferry, on the Santee. (Balfour to Germain, 1 May, PRO 30/11/109; Balfour to Clinton, 6 May, ibid.; Rankin, *Swamp Fox*, p. 200) Henry Lee later stated that NG's position prevented Watson from reaching Camden "on the usual route from Motte's post." Watson, who was moving up the south side of the Santee, was thus left with two other options, according to Lee: he could cross the Congaree at Motte's and the Wateree below the High Hills of Santee or else cross the Santee below Motte's and move up the north side of the Santee by way of the High Hills. (Lee, *Memoirs*, 2: 70) Guessing that Watson would take the former route, Marion and Lee crossed to the south side of the Santee at Scotts Lake and moved "with celerity" toward Mottes. (Lee, *Memoirs*, 2: 70–71; Rankin, *Swamp Fox*, p. 201) Watson, however, who was now ahead of them, crossed the Santee at Buckenham's—or Buchanan's—a small ferry near the confluence of the Congaree and Wateree, which, he later wrote, had been "left unguarded" because it was supposedly "impracticable" to cross. His detachment then proceeded to Camden "without molestation," though not without difficulty, by a route that required the troops to wade across six creeks, build a sixty-foot bridge over a seventh, and cut "for about a Mile and half through the canes that grow in those swamps." (Watson to unnamed correspondent,

n.d., Clinton Papers, MiU-C) Lee decided in retrospect that if he and Marion had remained on the north side of the Santee "the much desired interception would have been effected: for with horse, foot, and artillery, it was not to be expected that a corps of infantry only could have made good its landing in the face of an equal foe." (Lee, *Memoirs*, 2: 70–71) An angry Marion, according to one of his biographers, believed that changes in NG's orders delayed him and Lee and kept them from intercepting Watson. (Bass, *Marion*, p. 187)

4. See NG to Lee, 4 May, and Lee to NG, this date, both above.

*   *   *

¶ [FROM GENERAL ARTHUR ST. CLAIR, Philadelphia, 6 May 1781. Reports that a detachment of 1,100 Pennsylvania Continentals, commanded by Gen. [Anthony] Wayne, will leave York, Pa., "about" 12 May to join NG.[1] "Could it have been sent earlier," this force "would probably have given" NG a "compleat and decided Advantage over Lord Cornwallis"; the delays, though, were "unavoidable." St. Clair hopes these troops, who are "compleatly equipped," will not be "too late" to help NG "bring an End to the cruel Depredations of the Ennimy." They are to march to Fredericksburg, Va.; Wayne is to select the best route from there to NG's army.[2] "Part of Moylans Reg[t]" will also march soon. St. Clair does not know when the "second Division" of the Pennsylvania line will be ready, but he will do all that he can to speed its departure.[3] Reports that "another Embarkation at New Yorke has been in agitation for some Time, but at present it seems laid aside." It was probably destined "for the Southward."[4] ALS (MiU-C) 2 pp.]

1. As noted at Washington to NG, 1 June, below, Wayne's troops did not begin their march until 26 May.

2. After learning that Cornwallis was moving north, NG instructed the Marquis de Lafayette to use the Pennsylvania troops in Virginia. (See NG to Lafayette, 14 May, below.) The Pennsylvanians did not join NG until early January 1782, after the siege of Yorktown.

3. As seen in NG's reply of 22 June, below, St. Clair was to command the "second Division" of the Pennsylvania line. As noted there, the troops did not begin their march until October.

4. Clinton had hoped for some time to seize the peninsula between Delaware and Chesapeake bays. He was then planning a joint operation, in which a force to be sent from New York would cooperate with Gen. William Phillips's army in subduing the area. As a step toward implementing that plan, he had embarked reinforcements to send to Phillips. (Clinton, *American Rebellion*, pp. 274–80; see also Sharpe to NG, 7 April, above.) The detachment of 2,000 men, commanded by Col. August de Voit, finally sailed on 14 May, after several delays. Clinton would later relinquish his plan for a peninsula campaign after learning that Lord Cornwallis was marching to Virginia and that Phillips's troops were moving to Petersburg to form a junction with him. (Mackenzie, *Diary*, 2: 515–21; Clinton, *American Rebellion*, pp. 280–84; Washington reported the sailing of the troops in his letter to NG of 1 June, below.) The troops from New York arrived at the James River in Virginia about May 22, about the same time as Cornwallis. (Idzerda, *Lafayette Papers*, 4: 201n; Cornwallis acknowledged their arrival in Virginia in a letter to Clinton of 26 May, PRO 30/11/74.) Lafayette assumed they were part of Cornwallis's army. (Idzerda, *Lafayette Papers*, 4: 201n)

¶ [FROM GENERAL THOMAS SUMTER, "Camp at Ancrams," S.C., 6 May 1781. He learned "Yesterday evening" that Col. [John] Watson was crossing the Santee at "Buckenhams Ferry" and sent word to NG.[1] A party of 250 horsemen, which Sumter "immediately" sent after Watson, intercepted the enclosed letters, which show that Watson is recrossing the river and going to Camden by way of the High Hills; he may arrive there "by to morrow Noon."[2] Sumter does not know Watson's strength, but the latter's men are "Much fatigued & hungry." If Watson "gets into Camden, it will Make the enemy more insolent. They take Great pains to magnify their late success."[3] Sumter cannot understand how Watson "past and repassed through the Country to the Eastward" without NG's "having Notice of it." It is now out of Sumter's power to do "any Injury" to Watson. He has recalled his party and is "taking measures to Cross the River."[4] If NG has decided to send a field piece, Sumter will use it "against the post at Motts first."[5] Abstracted from *Charleston Year Book* (1899), Appendix, pp. 16–17.]

1. Sumter's letter of 5 May has not been found.
2. The enclosures have not been found. On Watson's route of march to Camden, see note at Marion to NG, 6 May, above.
3. The "late success" was the British victory at Hobkirk's Hill, which is discussed at NG to Huntington, 27 April, above.
4. Sumter was camped with part of his force on the north side of the Congaree River; he was planning to join the rest of his troops on the south side of the river. (Gregorie, *Sumter*, p. 157)
5. On the field piece, see Sumter to NG, second letter of 4 May, above, and NG to Sumter, 7 May, below.

* * *

From General Thomas Sumter

D[r] Sir   Camp at Congerees [S.C.] 6th May. 1781

I Wrote you this Morning that Col Watsons Was Crosing the Santee yesterday from the West to the East Side[,] that his Route woud be by the Way of the High hills to Camden. Which Information I hope Went Safe.[1]

Lord Cornwallis[s] Moving toWards + [i.e., Cross] Creek is Certainly a Matter of moment and Great exertions Must Consequently be use to oppose the Enemy effectually in every Quarter, otherways our Situation will be More Intollerable than ever.[2]

I have Now with me five hundred Men & officers included. I expect to be Eight hundred Strong by the Middle of the Week. Perhaps in the Corse of the ⟨month⟩ one thousand, But this Number May Not be lasting, as the Distreses of the people Generally are excesive, in So much that at this Time I am ob[li]ged to Support a Great Number of families With Bread While the Men are in the field.[3]

It is hard to Say What Number I Coud Join you with, provided they had to March out of the State. As by that Means the Whole State Would again Devolve to the British, & those Who Remain in it obliged to acceed to their Government. In that Case few woud Leave their families behind, Which would Greatly Lessen the Number that otherways

Might be in the field. For these & other Reasons it is Much to be Wished, that the enemy Coud be Met With here, Where there is the Greater plenty of provision Rather than to Move out of the State, the Necessity or propriety of which I by No Means pretend to Judge.

How far the Militia Coud be Depended upon to act With Regular Troops, I am also at a Loss to Determin, But am Rather of oppinion they Woud Not behaive well as they have Never been accustomed to oppose the enemy openly.

The State Troops Mounted & equiped as Light dragoons I think will in a Short Time, that is when properly Supplyed with arm's be equally as Servicable as the Best horse upon the Continent. The Men I think preferable to any I ever Saw. Near three hundred have Inlisted for ten Months. These Men Will be able to perform Good Service in a Short time.[4]

I Dont think this fort [i.e., Ft. Granby] Coud be taken under many days. This woud depen[d] much upon the use they Can make of their Twelve pound pieces of artillery, Which is Very Short, & Some other Matters, Which I am Not Well Informd of. The post at Mrs Motts I think May be Taken in three or four days.[5] 96 is easier Taken than the Post at this place. The Garrison Consists of about one hundred & Eight men, three, three pounders & Several Swivels, Not very well Supplied with provision. It Woud be a Great acquisition to have these posts, & Woud Tend as much In my oppinion to Bring the War to a Termination, as the Defeat of Lord Cornwallis.[6] I hope his Lordship Will Not Come Very Rapidly upon us.

I think his Circumstances Will Not admit of it. The Country which he has to pass through is against him in every Respect. His delays I think are favourable to us. In a few days I Shall be able to form a better Judgement of these Several matters and Will Write you there upon. I Will have Some men Sent to you for the purpose you mentioned, and Stores Shall be Sent to you as fast as possible.[7] I am D^r S^r your most ob^t S^t THO^s SUMTER

N B I am Concernd my Writing is So bad that it must be with Difficulty you Can Read it. My hand is Still Very Stiff. My Sholder Very uneasie & I fear as the wether grows warmer, Shall be obliged to Retier.[8]   T S

ALS (MiU-C). The word in angle brackets was taken from a transcript of the letter in the Draper Microfilm.

1. Sumter's letter is immediately above. For more on Watson's success in reaching Camden, see note at Marion to NG, this date, above.

2. NG had sent a report to Sumter, which later proved to be false, that Cornwallis was marching toward Cross Creek, N.C. (See NG to Sumter of 4 May, above.) Had the report been true, it might have meant that Cornwallis was returning to South Carolina.

3. In his letter of 4 May, NG had asked Sumter how many men he could bring if NG collected a force to oppose Cornwallis.

4. On the ten-month troops, see Sumter to NG, 7 April, above.

5. On the capture of Forts Granby and Motte, see Lee to NG, 15 May, and NG to Huntington, 14 May, both below. As seen by Lee's letter, the garrison at Ft. Granby did not offer as much resistance as Sumter had anticipated.

6. Sumter greatly underestimated the size of the garrison at Ninety Six, as well as the supply of provisions collected there. (See NG to Huntington, 9 June, below.)

7. On the men, see NG to Sumter, 5 May, above; on the stores, see NG to Sumter, 4 May, above.

8. Sumter was still troubled by the wound he had suffered at Blackstock's Plantation in November 1780. (See above, vol. 6: 581n.)

* * *

¶ [**GENERAL GREENE'S ORDERS**, "Camp Twenty five Mile Creek," S.C., 7 May 1781. John Spitzfathom, an ensign in the Virginia line, is acquitted of charges that he allowed men in his guard detail "to go into the Country a Plundering." He is guilty, however, of "sleeping on Guard" and of allowing "Captain Armstrong to take him and his Guard Prisoners without discovering him."[1] For this offense Spitzfathom is to be cashiered. NG hopes the episode "may serve a Warning to prevent others from falling into the same dangerous negligence." Officers commanding the "out Guards, cannot be too Vigilant, as they have the Lives of the whole Army in charge." In After Orders, the army is to march "by the right" at 4 P.M. Lamar Orderly Book (OClWHi) 3 pp.]

1. The editors believe that "Captain Armstrong" was Capt. George Armstrong of the Maryland line.

¶ [**MAJOR ICHABOD BURNET TO COLONEL JOHN ERVIN**. From Headquarters [Twenty Five Mile Creek, S.C.], 7 May 1781. NG, who has received Ervin's letter, "begs" him to continue to forward every piece of "interresting intelligence."[1] NG wants an "accurate" account of the strength and "situation" of Col. [John] Watson's detachment.[2] ACyS (MiU-C) 1 p.]

1. Ervin's letter is above, dated 6 May.

2. For more on Watson's detachment, see Marion to NG, 6 May, above.

* * *

To General Francis Marion

D[r] Sir   Camp at 25 Miles Creek [S.C.] May 7th 1781.

Colo. Watson I find is on his way to Camden.[1] This is rather an Unfortunate Circumstance as the Enemy will begin to be impudent & to Shew themselves without their works, which they have never ventured upon since the Action of the 25th.[2] Our force divided & the Enemies collected puts matters upon an UnMilitary footing. There is no further Intelligence from Lord Cornwallis, which induces me to beleave that he is marching Northwardly. Major [Edmund] Hyrne will Inform you of my plan Supposing that to be the Case.[3] The Major will Inform you also how far Lieut. Colo. Lee is at Liberty to Continue to Opperate with you against the fort you was Yesterday firing at.[4] I Should be Exceeding Glad to have an Account of the probable operating force you may Expect to Act with you for some Months to Come.

This will Enable me to Judge with more Certainty, the propriety of the plans I have in Contemplation.[5] With Esteem, I am D[r] Sir, Your most obedt. humble Servant NATH[L] GREENE.

Tr (Force Transcripts: DLC).

1. On Col. John Watson's detachment, see Marion to NG, 6 May, above.

2. The "works" were at the British post at Camden; the "Action of the 25th" was the battle of Hobkirk's Hill, which is discussed at NG to Huntington, 27 April, above.

3. For more on NG's plans, see his letter to Henry Lee of 9 May, below.

4. Marion and Lee were besieging Ft. Motte, a British support post on the Congaree River.

5. Marion's report has not been found.

To General Thomas Sumter

Dear Sir   Head Quarters 25 Mile Creek [S.C.] May 7th 1781.

There is no further intelligence from Lord Cornwallis which convinces me he is moving Northwardly.[1] Before I can determine upon any general plan of operations I wish to have that point ascertained.

General [Francis] Marion & Col. [Henry] Lee are operating against the fort at Motts to which place I find you have directed your Artillery. I wish both pieces may terrify the enemy so as to induce them to surrender. Major [Edmund] Hyrne if you are at or near that post will inform you what I have in contemplation.[2] If the people will exert themselves and the Earl is gone to the Northward, I am in hopes this Country may be once more unfettered. But much will depend upon themselves. Be in readiness to join us if necessity should require it, but you may depend upon not being called from the Congarees but from the most pressing necessity; for I am as fully impressed with the advantages of your continuing there as you can be.

I think you underrate the post at Ninety Six, is the fort strong or weak?[3]

Your writing needs no apology, rely upon it I understand you perfectly and meet with no difficulty in reading your letters.[4] On the contrary they are plain[,] clear and intelligible. With esteem & regard I am D Sir Your Most Obed[t] Humble Servant NATH GREENE

LS (Sumter Papers: DLC).

1. Lord Cornwallis was indeed moving northward, toward Virginia.

2. For more on NG's plans, see his letter to Henry Lee of 9 May, below.

3. In his second letter to NG of 6 May, above, Sumter had said he believed the British post at Ninety Six could be captured easily.

4. Sumter had apologized for his handwriting in his second letter to NG of 6 May.

*   *   *

¶ [FROM CAPTAIN WILLIAM PIERCE, JR., Haley's Ferry, N.C., 7 May 1781.[1] He arrived on 5 May "after a severe ride of ninety miles," but has been

unable until now "to ascertain" the movements and "situation" of Lord Cornwallis's army. Cornwallis is reportedly in Duplin County, "on the point of two
roads," one leading to Halifax and the other to Cross Creek. Some think he
will move north and establish a post at Halifax; others say he is only collecting
provisions and "covering the Country" to "prevent the Inhabitants from
driving off their Stock." Although both views carry "an air of probability,"
Pierce favors the former because by moving to Halifax, Cornwallis would be
"conveniently situated" to assist a British party that is reliably reported to have
taken "possession" of Petersburg, Va.[2] Pierce has also learned that the Marquis
de Lafayette, who was at Chesterfield Court House, Va., with his Continentals
and a large force of militia, is preparing to move towards Petersburg.[3] Adds: "I
think you may venture to rest assured that the Enemy do not mean to disturb
you in the South, for they think their Posts too strong to be reduced by the
Army we have there." Pierce will stay where he is to "find out, if possible, his
Lordships particular object."[4] ALS (MiU-C) 3 pp.]

1. On 14 May, below, NG wrote Samuel Huntington that Pierce had been sent to watch
"the motions of Lord Cornwallis."

2. As seen at Rowan to NG, 5 May, above, Cornwallis had begun moving toward
Halifax before Pierce wrote this letter.

3. See Lafayette's report of his operations in his second letter to NG of 3 May, above.

4. If Pierce wrote NG in the following days, no letter has been found. He was back in
camp by 18 May.

¶ [FROM GENERAL THOMAS SUMTER, "Camp Congrees," S.C., 7 May
1781. He forwarded NG's letter to Col. [Henry] Lee as soon as he received it.[1]
Did not know Lee's whereabouts at the time, but has learned since then
that Lee and Gen. [Francis] Marion reached Motte's "yesterday fore Noon."
Motte's is close to where Sumter sent the express. Sends two letters to NG,
which he thinks are from Marion and Lee. Reports that "Two pieces of artillery" were delivered to the enemy at Motte's "on Satuarday [5 May]"; does not
know their "Mettle."[2] ALS (MiU-C) 2 pp.]

1. NG had asked Sumter to forward his letter to Lee of 4 May, above. (See NG to
Sumter, 6 May, above.)

2. In his report on the capture of Ft. Motte, NG listed only one piece of artillery, a
"Caronnade," as having been taken. (See NG to Huntington, 14 May, below.)

¶ [GENERAL GREENE'S ORDERS, "Camp Colonels Creek," S.C., 8 May
1781. Two days' provisions are to be issued to the troops. In after orders of "5
o'Clock," the troops are "to encamp here." Lamar Orderly Book (OClWHi) 1 p.]

¶ [TO GENERAL THOMAS SUMTER. From "Head Quarters Sawneys
Creek," S.C., 8 May 1781. NG has received Sumter's letter of "yesterday," with
the enclosures. "The troops removed to this ground last evening." Has no
further news of Lord Cornwallis's movements. LS (Sumter Papers: DLC) 1 p.]

¶ [FROM COLONEL EDWARD CARRINGTON, [Claudius Pegues's, near
Cheraw, S.C.], 8 May 1781.[1] Sends a copy of the "Cartel for the excha[nge] and
releif of Prisoners of War taken in the southern department," agreed to by
Carrington, as NG's deputy, and Capt. [Frederick] Cornwallis, the British
representative. Encloses a copy of the latter's "powers."[2] ALS (MiU-C) 1 p. The
letter is torn and parts are missing.]

1. The place, which is missing from the letter, was determined from the enclosed cartel. (MiU-C)

2. On the terms of the cartel, see note at NG to Huntington, 10 May, below. The copy of the British representative's "powers" has not been found.

¶ [FROM MAJOR GEORGE DAVIDSON, Rowan, N.C., 8 May 1781. "Through the Sollicitations of several continental Officers," Davidson has delivered a small number of boots and shoes without orders from NG. Asks whether he should forward "all Shoes and Boots" immediately to headquarters or hold them until NG or "Others who may have Authority" apply for them.[1] He currently has idle workers because of a lack of leather but foresees a "flattering Prospect" for a better supply in the future, "as the Havock the Enemy made in our [tanning] Yards begins to be less sensably felt." Has sent Francis Cunningham to camp to see that "particular Care" is taken of the hides of cattle slaughtered there. Cunningham will "cheerfully" receive NG's orders. In a postscript, Davidson asks for a new and more "explicit" appointment if NG does not consider his present powers "ample."[2] ALS (MiU-C) 1 p.]

1. NG's reply, which has not been found, miscarried. (See NG's letter to Davidson of 26 July, which was written in response to another request for instructions from Davidson of 18 July, both below.)

2. NG had appointed Davidson commissary of hides on 14 December 1780, above (vol. 6: 572). Davidson said nothing about his appointment when he wrote NG on 18 July. According to that letter, leather remained scarce.

¶ [FROM MAJOR EDMUND M. HYRNE, Mrs. Motte's, S.C., 8 May 1781. He informed Gen. [Francis] Marion and Col. [Henry] Lee of NG's "sentiments and determination" about "operations of the army."[1] He also discussed "the Carolina line" with Marion. Hyrne finds that his plan cannot be implemented, but he is "not entirely discouraged."[2] Lee has recommended Maj. [Hezekiah] Maham to NG's "notice."[3] Hyrne has known Maham for a long time and holds him in such respect that even though Maham is "not an officer in the line," Hyrne would willingly "wave all considerations of rank" and serve under him. "If any individual in this Country is capable of mounting a Corps, it is Major Maham, he has assidulty, capacity, and a perfect knowledge of the Country— added to this he is in some degree acquainted with the horse service."[4] Marion reports that it is "out of his power to furnish the dragoon horses" for the purposes that NG suggested.[5] Marion will obtain a few for NG's "particular use," however.[6] Hyrne will be delayed until "tomorrow." ALS (MiU-C) 3 pp.]

1. For more on NG's "sentiments and determination," see Lee to NG, immediately below, and NG to Lee, 9 May, below.

2. Hyrne's plan for the South Carolina line has not been found.

3. See Lee to NG, immediately below.

4. On 21 June, below, NG authorized Maham to raise a mounted regiment.

5. NG, who had been strongly pressing Marion to provide dragoon horses for the Southern Army, withdrew that request in his letter to Marion of 9 May, below.

6. As seen in his letter to Richard Caswell of 11 April, above, NG's personal mounts had been stolen.

¶ [FROM COLONEL HENRY LEE, JR., [Motte's Plantation, S.C.], 8 May [17]81. Maj. [Edmund M.] Hyrne has communicated NG's "intentions & wishes" to Lee.[1] If Lord Cornwallis "takes the ⟨road⟩" that NG fears, the

Southern Army can "⟨reduce⟩" South Carolina, provided that NG remains in the state.[2] Any advantage Cornwallis may gain by going north will then "⟨fade⟩" away. Moreover, it will be some time before the British forces can unite. If NG decides to leave the state, Lee believes the Southern Army will be reduced by desertion; asks him to consider how the soldiers would view such a step. If NG thinks it necessary to "detach" cavalry to Virginia, Lee's mounted troops, "with the militia will be fully sufficient here." Adds that only NG can "finish his business soon here."[3] Lee finds himself "deceived in ⟨Marion⟩. He is inadequate & very discontented—this discontent arises from his nature."[4] Lee has a worse opinion of Sumter and thinks a "third person"—"Major Maum [Hezekiah Maham]"—is absolutely needed. Maham could raise a legion equal to Lee's in one month, giving NG "one corps in the state which will be capable to serve you."[5] Sends NG "the strength" of Charleston.[6] If NG takes "post" where Lee recommends, Charleston "invites." Lee is presently trying to "introduce" himself to an acquaintance there and hopes "it will answer." He did not intend to give his opinion on the "principal matter," as his "personal feelings have too much influence" on his views. But he found himself in a "philosophic mood" and "honestly" gave NG his sentiments, which he begs NG to consider before taking a step "so full of importance." Adds beneath his signature: "Things here were [wear] a good countenance. Tomorrow will decide."[7] ALS (MiU-C) 4 pp. Parts of the letter are in a number code. In the calendar, the editors have replaced the numbers with the deciphered words, which are in angle brackets.]

1. On Hyrne's consultation with Lee and Francis Marion, see Hyrne to NG, immediately above.

2. It is clear from NG's reply of 9 May, below, that he thought Cornwallis's army was heading toward Virginia.

3. As seen in his letter to Lee of 9 May, below, NG was considering a plan to take personal charge of the American forces in Virginia and leave a subordinate to command in South Carolina.

4. On Marion's "discontent," see his letters to NG of 6 May, above, and 11 May, below.

5. As noted at Hyrne's letter, immediately above, NG did authorize Maham to organize a mounted regiment. Maham, however, never superseded Sumter or Marion as a leader of the South Carolina forces.

6. Lee's estimate of British forces in Charleston has not been found.

7. On Lee's and Marion's successful siege of Motte's, see NG to Huntington, 14 May, below. As seen there, the British post did not surrender until 12 May.

¶ [FROM GENERAL ANDREW PICKENS, "Cuffy Town," S.C., 8 May 1781. Nothing "material" has happened since he wrote NG on 3 May. Describes his effort to surprise a detachment of Loyalists under Gen. [William] Cunningham and "the remainder of Dunlaps Dragoons," who were camped near Ninety Six.[1] The attempt was foiled after two of Pickens's detachments blundered into each other and exchanged "a few Shot." They did little damage but alarmed the enemy. His troops took some enemy horses, but three of his men, who were captured, "were most Barbarously cut to pieces." Adds: "This seems to be their [i.e., the enemy's] determination with every one who falls into their hands." Pickens finds that the people of the area, "except those who are at Ninety Six," are "determined unanimously" to join the American cause. He is unable to arm them, however.[2] He has just learned that the post at Augusta, Ga., has been "blockaded" by "the Georgians and Some Men under Maj. [Samuel] Hammond." A "very valuable" shipment "of Ammunition[,] Cloathing, &ca," which was on its way up the Savannah River, has also been "intercepted" and has taken refuge at "Galphins Fort at Silver Bluff." The importance of those two posts induces Pickens to leave Colonels [Joseph] Hayes and Robert Anderson in command of the troops near Ninety Six and proceed to Augusta. He expects to be there "tomorrow Morning."[3] Hopes to inform NG soon of the surrender of the Georgia forts, but "at any rate" will do "whatever" he can. This letter will be delivered by Col. John Purvis, who can give a reliable account of the situation "of this Quarter." Purvis is carrying a message "of importance" from Pickens.[4] Adds: "The enclosed fell into my hands yesterday."[5] ALS (NcD) 1 p.]

1. On the earlier defeat of dragoons commanded by Maj. James Dunlap—and the murder of Dunlap himself—see Pickens to NG, 8 April, above.

2. NG addressed the question of arming residents of the Ninety Six area in his letter to Pickens of 9 May, below.

3. Both posts were captured after Pickens's militiamen were joined by a detachment from NG's army. (See Pickens to NG, first letter of 25 May, and Pickens and Lee to NG, 5 June, both below.)

4. In his letter to NG of 12 May, below, Pickens discussed the message carried by Purvis, a militia officer who served under him. (See also McCrady, *S.C. in the Revolution*, p. 229.)

5. The enclosure has not been found.

¶ **[FROM GENERAL JETHRO SUMNER**, Halifax, N.C., 6 May 1781, 4 P.M. By his "best accounts," the enemy are now near Tarboro. Their cavalry routed a party of militia near that place before the main body of Lord Cornwallis's army "was in view." Sumner expects most of the public stores to be "remov'd and out of their way before they get here." Has been able to arm only sixty of the 100 draftees. Gen. [Anson] Jones is "here" with eighty militiamen and expects another 200 from Edgecombe County. Sumner just received word that the enemy is in Tarboro.[1] He has sent an express to Taylor's Ferry, Va., "least some Public Stores from Virginia should Cross, and meet no escort"; has ordered the conductors to wait for further instructions. The counties in the Edenton district will not draft troops for "some time." Sumner will now go to see how many draftees are at Harrisburgh. Expects his express to Baron Steuben to return momentarily.

Harrisburgh, N.C., 8 May 1781, 12 P.M.

Has just arrived "here." [The Marquis de] Malmedy, who joined Sumner on the road, reports that the enemy were very near Halifax on "Monday Morn'g [7 May]." Has just received an express reporting that a "part of the Enemy" was crossing the Tar River at Lemon's Ferry on Saturday morning [5 May]. A small mounted troop has been sent to observe its route. Malmedy reports that the American militia crossed the Roanoke River at Halifax on Sunday [6 May], followed by the draftees on Monday [7 May]. The officer who is to receive the Edenton drafts was ordered six weeks ago to keep his men out of the enemy's way; Sumner hopes he was "very active in ficilitating this manuvre." Sumner saw the governor [Abner Nash] at Warren; he understands that Gen. [John] Butler is near Wake Court House. Hopes in his next letter to give a "full Acct"

of the enemy's strength and route and to report that the militia are "embody'd
and arm'd."[2] Sumner will have the stores "here" sent to Hillsborough if the
enemy "move this way." Has word from Virginia that Gen. [William] Phillips
has "Taken Ship'g" and that the Marquis de Lafayette has moved his force
toward [New] Kent County, Va.[3] ALS (MiU-C) 4 pp.]

1. After crossing Contentea Creek, on the road to Tarboro, Lord Cornwallis's troops
moved westward, bypassing the town. They followed a northwesterly track to Lemon's
Ferry, on the Tar River, where they resumed a northeasterly march toward Halifax.
("Von Bose Journal," p. 57; *The Marches of Lord Cornwallis in the Southern Provinces*
[London, 1787], a map by William Faden, "Geographer to the King") As seen in Butler to
NG, first letter of 11 May, below, the British cavalry took possession of Halifax on 7 May
at 10 A.M. The rest of Cornwallis's army followed slowly, arriving on the 12th. ("Von
Bose Journal," p. 57)

2. Sumner wrote NG again on 11 May, below.

3. As seen in Lafayette's second letter to NG of 3 May, above, Sumner's reports were
incorrect.

*   *   *

Recollection of a Conversation between General Nathanael Greene and Colonel William R. Davie[1]

[Colonel's Creek, S.C., 9 May 1781]

[NG told Davie]: "You see that we must again resume the partizan
war. Rawdon has now a decided superiority of force. He has pushed
us to a sufficient distance to leave him free to act on any object within
his reach. He will strike at Lee and Marion, reinforce himself by all the
troops that can be spared from the several garrisons and push me back
to the mountains; you acted in this quarter in the last campaign, and I
wish you to point out the military positions on both sides of the river,
ascending it to the mountains, and give me the necessary information
as to the prospect of subsistence; you observe our dangerous and
critical situation. The regular troops are now reduced to a handful, and
I am now without militia sufficient to perform the convoy and detachment service, or any prospect of recieving any reinforcements of this
description; Sumter refuses to obey my orders, and carries off with
him *all the active force* of this unhappy State on rambli[ng] predatory
expeditions unconnected with the operations of the Army. North Carolina dispirited by the loss of her regular line in Charleston, stunned
into a kind of stupor by the defeat of General Gates, and held in check
by Major [John Harris] Cruger and the Loyalists makes no efforts of
any kind; Congress seem to have lost sight of the Southern States, and
to have abandoned them to their fate, so much so that we are even as
much distressed for ammunition as men.[2] We must always calculate
on the maxim that *Your Enemy will do, what he ought to do.* W[e] will
dispute every inch of ground in the best manner we can—but Rawdon
will push me back to the mountains, Lord Cornwallis will establish a

William R. Davie, 1756–1820; oil painting by James Sharples
(Independence National Historical Park Collection)

chain of posts along James River *and the Southern States, thus cut off, will die like the Tail of a Snake.*"[3]

"Revolutionary Sketches of William Richardson Davie" (NcU).

  1. In introducing this conversation, which he recorded long after it occurred, Davie wrote:

Being informed that Col° [John] Watson had evaded [Gen. Francis] Marion and [Col. Henry] Lee he [NG] retired up the Wateree to Sawney's Creek on the 7th, and upon the advance of Lord Rawdon, he again retreated on the following day to Colonel's Creek, and on the 9th he took a strong position still higher up the river and this evening sent for me earlier than usual; I found the map on the table, and he introduced the business of the night with the following striking observations, which serve to show the State of his mind at that trying crisis.

Davie's wording makes it appear that the Southern Army fell back from Colonel's Creek to a third defensive position, "still higher up the river," on 9 May; as seen in NG's letters of 9 and 10 May, the army remained at Colonel's Creek.

2. For more on the defeat of Gen. Horatio Gates at Camden, see above (vol. 6: 257–59n). Although Davie clearly wrote "Cruger," he almost certainly meant Maj. James Craig, who commanded the British forces occupying Wilmington, N.C. Cruger, a colonel, was the commander at Ninety Six, in the South Carolina backcountry.

3. In his memoirs, Davie continued:

These are his [NG's] very words, they made a deep and melancholly impression, and I shall never forget them. After expressing an anxious desire to remain as near as possible to aid or cover the retreat of Lee from Fort Motte we recurred again to the map, where I had it in my power from personal knowledge to assure him that the Country abounded in strong military positions, and as to subsistence there would be no difficulty, as we should be falling back on our depots or magazines in N° Carolina; that if he was obliged to retreat further he must permit me to resume my original plan; as I was morally certain a respectable force could be raised in the Western Districts of that State. The interview concluded by his informing me, that he would dispatch an express to Philadelphia in the morning, and requesting me to write to the members of Congress with whom I was acquainted, painting in the strongest colors our situation and gloomy prospects.

In contrast to Davie's comments here regarding NG's state of mind, see NG to Lee, immediately below.

To Colonel Henry Lee, Jr.

Colonel's Creek, [S.C.] May 9th, 1781
"Dear Sir—I have not time to write in cyphers.[1]—Yours of the 8th, by Captain [Thomas?] Davis, was delivered me last evening. We have no further intelligence from Lord Cornwallis, and therefore I am persuaded he has gone northerly. General Philips is at Petersburg [Va.], and our army beaten back; but whether the Marquis or the Pennsylvania line has arrived, I am not informed.[2] Keep this a secret, as it is not known here. We moved our camp night before last, from Twenty-five Miles creek to Sandy creek, five miles higher up the river. Lord Rawdon came out yesterday morning as I expected he would, and I suppose, with an expectation of finding us at the old encampment. I did not like our new position to risk an action in, and ordered the troops to take a new position at this place, four miles still higher up the river, leaving on the ground the horse, the pickets, and light infantry. The enemy came up in front of our encampment, and drew up in order of

battle, but did not dare to attempt to cross the creek; and after waiting an hour or two, retired suddenly towards Camden.[3] Major [Edmund M.] Hyrne having made you fully acquainted with my general plan of operations, it will be unnecessary for me to be more explicit on that head. It gives me pleasure to find that your sentiments so perfectly corresponds with mine, in all the points except the duty of 310, (General Greene).[4] This, I suppose you mean as a compliment upon your general principles, that all men are fond of flattery. But you will give me leave to tell you that if 306 (Lord Cornwallis) is gone to the northward, that great abilities will not be wanted here. The plan being laid, and a position taken, the rest will be a war of posts, and the most that will be left to be performed by the commanding officer until we come to Camden, is to make proper detachments, and give the command of them to proper officers. The plan being laid, the glory will belong to the executive officers executing the business. The benefit resulting from our operations will, in a great measure, depend upon the proper management of affairs in Virginia. If the principal officer in the enemy's interest is there, who should be opposed to him? Which will be more honourable, to be active there, or laying, as it were, idle here? From whence comes our supplies to this quarter, and who is most likely to give timely and necessary support to all parts of the department; one that has but a partial interest, or one that is interested equally in all the parts? I am confident nothing would come to this army, and all things be in confusion, if 310 (General Greene) was not to go to the northward. Therefore, whether taken up in a military, personal, or public point of view, I am decided it is his interest and duty to go; nor can I conceive the great inconveniences will arise from it here you mention. I am confident B———s will arrange matters very well, and 310 (General Greene) will take care to direct him to the proper objects to employ.[5] Much is to be done in Virginia, and without great prudence on our part, matters may be reduced to great extremity there; and depend upon it, the enemy's great push will be against that state, as it may be said in some sort to sever the continental interest asunder. More advantage will result from 310's (General Greene) going than staying; for he can serve them more effectually yonder than here; and vanity will lead him to think that he can oppose the enemy more effectually there than those that will command if he don't go. I perceive that 312 (General Marion) is not satisfied, and I think you are not mistaken respecting 311, (General Sumpter).[6] However be careful, be cautious, be prudent, and above all attentive; this, with men as well as with ladies, goes a great way. It will give me great pleasure to render Major Mayum every service in my power; and if he will repair to head quarters and lay his plan before me of raising a legion, I will give him all the authority I am vested with, and recommend any thing further that may be necessary to give it proper arrangement. I had a very high opinion of Major Mayum from his general character; but that opinion is increased from his late exertions. You have got a new mode of reducing posts, which I think will be no less honourable to the projectors than the mode is new and singular.[7] A general exchange of prisoners is agreed upon; and all our officers in captivity, that cannot be exchanged, are to be paroled. This will be a great relief to the unfortunate captives.[8] God bless you with success, and may your reputation keep pace with your merit is the wish of yours.

"Augusta and the posts below it, are closely besieged, and in all probability will be reduced.[9] At Ninety Six there are symptoms of an evacuation, which I think will take place, if you succeed in the reduction of the posts on the Congaree."[10]

Reprinted from Lee, *Campaign of 1781*, pp. 355–58.

1. Further along in this letter, NG did use number codes for certain names. The editors have followed the style of the printed version, in which the decoded name is given in parentheses immediately after the corresponding number.

2. As NG surmised, Lord Cornwallis's army was marching toward Virginia to form a junction with Gen. William Phillips's force at Petersburg. NG had not yet received the Marquis de Lafayette's second letter to him of 3 May, above, which discussed both Phillips's movements and Lafayette's response. The Pennsylvania Continental line had not yet marched for the South. (See Washington to NG, 1 June, below.)

3. After Col. John Watson succeeded in eluding Lee and Gen. Francis Marion, he reached Camden on 7 May with about 500 men and two field pieces. (See note at Marion to NG, 6 May, above; Marion's and Lee's failure to intercept Watson is also discussed there.) That same night, Rawdon marched out of Camden and crossed the Wateree River, "proposing to turn the flank & attack the rear of Greenes army," which he assumed was still at Twenty Five Mile Creek. Immediately after crossing, Rawdon received word that NG had moved. Rawdon decided to take "the direct road" to the American army's new position behind Sawney's Creek, or Sandy Creek, as NG called it here. (Rawdon to Lord Cornwallis, 24 May, PRO 30/11/6) In a pension application many years later, Guilford Dudley, a militia officer who was serving with NG at this time, recalled that it was more the "mortified" spirit of the American army, which was "yet rather depressed" from the "late repulse before Camden," than any weakness in position that caused NG to fall back again. (Dann, *Revolution Remembered*, p. 222) In fact, Dudley called NG's new position at Sawney's Creek the "strongest" he "ever saw anywhere in South Carolina or perhaps anywhere else." (Ibid.) Rawdon wrote Cornwallis on 24 May that he could not have attacked without "suffering such loss as must have crippled my force for any future enterprize." (PRO 30/11/6) While Rawdon hesitated, NG decided to retire again with most of his army. In Dudley's words:

> In the meantime, on the upper side of the [Sawney's] creek all was in motion, General Greene in person and the adjutant general [Otho Williams] forming our troops on the heights in battle array, my battalion ordered down the hill to cross a narrow, lengthy field in the bottom, not in cultivation that spring, and to post myself in and around sundry deserted houses near the ford of Sawney's Creek under the supposition that the enemy would force a passage, and there to maintain my post as long as I could. This order I received from the general himself on the brow of the hill. But scarcely had I reached the houses before I was recalled. At this moment the general had received information of another crossing place

about two miles lower down the creek, quite convenient for the enemy's purpose of getting at him and attacking him in the rear of his present position on the lofty summits of the hill. This intelligence instantly changed the mind of the general and produced the determination to retrograde again and once more fall back three or four miles to a large creek of still, deep water (Colonel's, I believe it was called), having over it a framed bridge covered with plank. Lord Rawdon, not liking to risk an attack upon his adversary in his strong position on the heights, thought it best to retire into Camden, at the same moment Greene was retrograding. (Dann, *Revolution Remembered*, pp. 222–24)

Rawdon does not seem to have known about the other crossing that Dudley mentioned, for he reported that the creek ran "very high into the Country" and added that if he had attempted to "get round" NG, he would have "wasted" valuable time. Instead, Rawdon returned to Camden "the same afternoon" after first trying to "decoy the enemy into action, by affecting to conceal our retreat." (Rawdon to Cornwallis, 24 May, PRO 30/11/6) The same day that NG wrote this letter, Rawdon announced the evacuation of Camden to his troops. It took place during the night of 10–11 May. (Ibid.; see also Pendleton to Sumter, 10 May, below.)

4. See Lee to NG, 8 May, above.

5. "B——s" was undoubtedly Baron Steuben, whom NG had ordered to join the Southern Army in a letter of 1 May, above. NG did not go to Virginia, nor did Steuben join NG's army.

6. On Marion's discontent, see his letters to NG of 6 May, above, and 11 May, below. Lee had remarked in his letter of 8 May, above, that he had a low opinion of Gen. Thomas Sumter.

7. Lee had recommended that Maj. Hezekiah Maham be allowed to raise a legion in South Carolina. (See Lee to NG, 8 May, above.) On 21 June, below, NG authorized Maham to recruit a mounted regiment. For more on the "Maham" tower, which had been used in the capture of Ft. Watson, at Wright's Bluff, see Marion to NG, first letter of 23 April, above.

8. For the terms of the cartel for the exchange of prisoners, which representatives of NG and Cornwallis had agreed to on 3 May, see note at NG to Huntington, 10 May, below.

9. On the siege of Augusta, see Pickens to NG, 3 and 8 May, both above.

10. Nisbet Balfour wrote Cornwallis on 21 May that "Foreseeing the obvious consequences of the enemys superiority in this province," he had sent orders to Col. John Harris Cruger, the commander at Ninety Six, to "be watchful, & when he heard that Camden was evacuated," to "retreat to Augusta, & so to fall down upon Savannah. This letter he received on the 6th." (PRO 30/11/6) Balfour's instructions may have caused the activity that NG mentioned here. Cruger, however, either did not hear of the evacuation of Camden or chose to remain until he received more positive orders. These were sent but never received because all of the British couriers were captured. Cruger thus continued to occupy the post when NG's army arrived on 22 May to place it under siege. (Rawdon to Cornwallis, 5 June 1781, PRO 30/11/6)

To General Francis Marion

Dear Sir   Camp at Colonels Creek [S.C.] May 9th 1781

I am favord with yours of the 6th. I am sorry the Militia are deserting because there is not greater support. If they were influenced by proper principles and were impressed with a love of liberty and a dread of slavery they wou'd not shrink at difficulties. If we had a force sufficent to recover the Country their aid would not be wanted and they cannot be well acquainted with their true interest to desert us because they conceive our force unequal to the reduction of the Country without their assistance.

I shall be always happy to see you at head Quarters; but cannot think you can seriously mean to solicit leave to go to Philadelphia. It is true your task has been disagreeable; but not more so than others. It is now go[in]g on seven years since the commencment of this war. I have never had leave of absense an hour nor paid the least attention to my own private affairs. Your State is invaded, your all is at stake. What has been done will signify nothing unless we persevere to the end. I left a family in distress and every thing dear and valuable to come & afford you all the assistance in my power, and if you leave us in the midst of our difficulties while you have it so much in your power to promote the service it must throw a damp upon the spirits of the Army to find that the first Men in the State are retiring from the busy scene to indulge themselves in more agreeable amusements.

However your reasons for wishing to decline the command of the Militia & for going to Philadelpha may be more pressing than I imagine. I will therefore add nothing more on this subject until I see you.

My reasons for writing so pressingly respecting the Dragoon [horses] was from the distress we were in. It is not my wish to take the horses from the Militia if it will injure the public service, the effects and consequences you can better judge of than I can.

You have renderd important services to the public with the Militia under your command; and done great honor to yourself and I would not wish to render your situation less agreeable with them unless it is to answer some very great purpose and this I perswade my self you would agree to from a desire to promote the common good.

I wish you success at the fort you are besieging.[1]

Lord Rawden was out yesterday. We had the night before taken a new position on Sanders [i.e., Sawney] Creek and imagine he came out to attack us expecting to find us on the 25 Mile Creek. We did not like the position on Sanders Creek to risque an action in and therefore took a new position at this place leaving the horse[,] light Infantry and Piquets at the old encampment. The Enemy came and drew up on the other side of the Creek but did not attempt to cross; but retird into Camden before night.[2]

We are in dayly expectation of a large reinforcment of Virginia Militia and some Continental troops. When these arrive we shall push our operations with more vigor.[3]

No further news from Lord Cornwallis. With esteem & regard I am Sr Your hu^{bl} S^r   N GREENE

ADfS (MiU-C).

1. Marion and Col. Henry Lee were besieging the British post at Motte's Plantation.

2. For more on Rawdon's advance, see NG to Lee, immediately above.

3. As noted at Jefferson to NG, 30 March, above, most of the Virginia militia force that NG expected to join him never left the state. The "Continental troops" were presumably the Pennsylvania line, which had been ordered to join NG; they, too, would remain in Virginia. (See note at Washington to NG, 1 June, below.)

To General Andrew Pickens

Camp Colonels Creek west side Wateree [S.C.]

Dear Sir   May 9th 1781

Yours of the 3d by Mr Lawrence I have had the pleasure to receive. It gives me pleasure to find the people are still desirous of affording their assistance to expel the enemy notwithstanding all their sufferings. Encourage them all you can and as there is a scarcity of Arms, I would take them from the old and infirm to put into the hands of the young and healthy who are willing to aid the operations. It would be best if you could effect it to get the people to engage for a given time not less than four months. Great things may be done in that time as Lord Cornwallis is in all probability gone Northerly and will afford the people a happy opportunity of recovering their freedom.

Many of the Arms lodged at Guilbert Town taken at Tarltons defeat I am told are in the hands of the people about that place, those should be collected if possible.[1]

Have sent you agreeable to the private Note by Mr Lawrence some powder[,] Lead & flints and would have sent you more could they have found any mode of conveyance.[2] Collect all the force you can and hold them in perfect readiness for the close investiture of Ninty Six which will soon be undertaken. Nothing new from the Northward[,] only troops are coming to the Southward very fast. The Marquis de Lafyette with 1500 Men. General Wayne with as many are on their March southerly. Besides these Virginia and Maryland have both troops on the March to reinforce the Southern Army and 2000 Virginia Militia are collecting at Salisbury to aid our operations and North Carolinia is trying to do som thing, but their efforts will be feeble as they have been so oppressed for some months past.[3] With esteem & regard I am dear Sir Your Most Obed humble Sr   N GREENE

ADfS (MiU-C).

1. American troops had captured 800 stand of arms in "Tarleton's defeat"—the battle of Cowpens. (See above, vol. 7: 160n)

2. Pickens's "private note" has not been found.

3. Neither Lafayette's troops, the Pennsylvania line (which had not yet begun its march), nor most of the 2,000 Virginia militiamen joined NG's army; they would remain in Virginia to confront the British threat there. There were no reinforcements "on the March" from Maryland, either.

*   *   *

¶ [TO COLONEL JAMES READ. From Colonel's Creek, S.C., 9 May 1781. Has received Read's letter of 4 May.[1] NG would prefer to have the armory located within the town of Salisbury, N.C., but if no "suitable buildings" are available there, Read should establish it where he proposed. "Nothing will contribute more to promote the public service than puting this business upon a proper footing; for I think we shall fail more in our Arms than in our Numbers." NG is surprised "at the delay of the drafts and the tardiness of the Virginia Militia." Gen. [Robert] Lawson, who is due in Salisbury on 14 May, should take charge of the militia immediately upon his arrival. If Read is still there, he can then "confine" his attention to the draftees and the armory.[2] Read should ask Lawson to draft for service in the armory any Virginia militiamen who might be useful there. If Lord Cornwallis moves toward Salisbury— and NG does not expect that he will—Read should give the "necessary" orders for the "preservation" of the stores there and at Oliphant's Mill.[3] NG is on the west side of the Wateree River; when Read joins the army, he is to "cross the river at Rocky Mount [N.C.] or highe[r] up." ADfS (MiU-C) 2 pp.]

1. Read's letter, dated 5 May, is above.
2. Neither Lawson nor the Virginia militiamen came to Salisbury. (See note at Lawson to NG, 20 April, above.)
3. Cornwallis did not move toward Salisbury.

¶ [FROM CAPTAIN JOHN HAMILTON TO MAJOR ICHABOD BURNET, Charlotte, N.C., 9 May 1781. NG spoke to Hamilton "some time ago" about purchasing thread for the troops. "This Country" is the best place to obtain it, and he has been offered "any quantity" at "3 hard Dollars per pound." Payment must be in "*hard money*" and must be sent "soon." Hopes for a reply before he leaves for camp on 16 May.[1] ALS (MiU-C) 1 p.]

1. NG's reply has not been found.

¶ [FROM COLONEL THOMAS POLK, Charlotte, N.C., 9 May 1781. Discusses his efforts to expedite the draft in Anson, Richmond, Rowan, and Montgomery counties.[1] In the last of these, all was "confusion & suspense," as all the officers had been "broke," except the "Commanding Colonel," who had "removed to Virginia with his family & a quantity of plundered Property & was not yet returned." Polk arranged to have new officers sworn in and assigned to duty. Gives the number of draftees to be raised in each of the above counties and adds that Mecklenburg is to draft twenty-three men, "besides about 150 now with Gen[l] Sumpter."[2] Polk is setting off for Lincoln, Rutherford and Burke counties, where he understands that nothing has yet been done for the draft. ALS (MiU-C) 1 p.]

1. As seen at his letters to Polk of 14 and 28 April, both above, NG had asked Polk to serve as the temporary commander of the Salisbury militia district and hoped that the state would confirm the appointment. As seen in Polk to NG, 15 May, below, North Carolina officials did not do so.
2. Polk, whose son William was a colonel in one of Gen. Thomas Sumter's South Carolina state regiments, had been helping Sumter to recruit Mecklenburg County men for service in those units. (See Polk to NG, 8 March, above [vol. 7: 413].)

¶ [GENERAL GREENE'S ORDERS, Colonel's Creek, S.C., 10 May 1781. The army is "to march very early Tomorrow morning." Greene Orderly Book (CSmH) 1 p.]

*   *   *

To Samuel Huntington,
President of the Continental Congress

Sir

Camp at Colonels Creek on the west side
of the Wateree [S.C.] May 10ᵗʰ 1781

I do myself the honour to inclose to your Excellency, a copy of the conditions of a Cartel agreed to for the exchange of prisoners in the southern Department; which I hope will meet the approbation of Congress.[1]

The business has been a long time in hand, and many interruptions happened from the operations of the two Armies, and the enemy's insisting upon conditions, contrary to the principles laid down as a rule of conduct for the government of the commissioner on our part.[2] Should Congress wish to have copies of the whole transaction, with the powers and instructions given on each side, and the letters that passed on the occasion at different times, they shall be forwarded.[3]

Many hundreds of our people taken by the enemy, enlist into their service. At the begining of the War, perhaps, this practice was attended with less injury than now. The suffering of our soldiers in captivity in the early part of the war, led many of our officers to encourage the men to enlist, to get an opportunity to make their escape. But soldiers being long in service become more indifferent which side they serve, & having such a plausible pretence to engage in the enemy's service, enter in great numbers; and are found in Arms against us: indeed one third of the force employed in the southern States, if we are to form a judgment from the prisoners we take, are deserters from our Army, & prisoners enlisted from our Captives.[4] A Resolution of Congress declaring that all prisoners, of War, that engage in the enemies service, from whatever pretence, shall be treated as Deserters, if taken in Arms against us; would have a good effect. Should the soldiers enlist with a view to get away, they will embrace the first opportunity, when they know they are to be treated as deserters; and those that are not willing to run that hazard to effect their escape, will continue patiently in captivity: at least I think it would be some check to the practice which now prevails, to the great prejudice of the continental interest.[5] I have the Honor to be with great respect, Your Excellency's most Obedient, humble Servant   NATH GREENE

LS (PCC, item 155, vol. 2: 67, DNA).

1. In his letter to NG of 8 May, above, Col. Edward Carrington had enclosed a copy of the cartel that he negotiated with the British. Under the terms of the agreement, regular troops were to be exchanged for other regulars and militia for militia. The "mode of exchange" for officers was to be "rank for rank" and by rotation according to length of captivity; non-commissioned officers and privates could be exchanged by "particular corps, or particular persons." Non-commissioned officers and privates who had been paroled by means other than the "faith of an" officer were to be considered "liberated,"

while captive officers who could not be exchanged "for want of a similar rank" could be paroled to their homes. Passports to bring supplies to captives were to be allowed, commissaries of prisoners were to be permitted to pass "into the opposite lines," and flags "going with" the prisoners were to be "sacred." The first American prisoners to be released from Charleston were to embark by 15 June for Jamestown, Va., where the first group of British prisoners was to embark by "the first Week in July" for the "nearest British Post." As long as the cartel was in effect, no prisoner was to be "sent from the Continent." (A copy of the cartel, dated 3 May, is in MiU-C.)

As seen in the letter from Otho Williams to Francis Smith, 22 June, below, prisoners included in the cartel were being exchanged by that time. A supplementary agreement, signed on 22 June by Maj. Edmund Hyrne, NG's commissary of prisoners, and James Fraser, Hyrne's British counterpart, declared all militia prisoners on both sides in the Southern Department to be "absolutely & reciprocally exchanged." (A draft of this agreement is in RPAB.)

2. Lord Cornwallis had first proposed a general exchange in his letter to NG of 4 February, above (vol. 7: 251). On the conditions he had "insisted" upon, see Cornwallis to NG, 3 April, and NG to Cornwallis, 9 April, both above. For the instructions NG had given his representative, see NG to Carrington, 11 March, above (vol. 7: 425, 426n).

3. Neither Congress nor the Board of War, to whom Congress referred NG's letter, apparently ever requested "copies of the whole transaction." (JCC, 20: 620; on NG's authority to negotiate prisoner exchanges within the Southern Department, see Huntington to NG, 31 October 1780, above [vol. 6: 451].)

4. For more on the enlistment of American prisoners by the British, see Mathews to NG, 30 April, above.

5. The Board of War sent a copy of NG's letter to Washington on 22 June, requesting his "Sentiments" on the proposal. (Washington Papers, DLC) He replied on 28 June that he approved "very much . . . of such a Resolve of Congress as General Greene recommends." (Fitzpatrick, GW, 22: 280) No evidence has been found that the board sent this recommendation to Congress or that Congress considered such a resolution.

*   *   *

¶ [TO GENERAL ROBERT LAWSON. From Headquarters, Colonel's Creek, S.C., 10 May 1781. Has his letter of 20 April and is happy that Lawson may be "accompanied by those Gentlemen who were formerly" under his command. Lawson's troops are "exceedingly necessary" for the army's operations "against the posts at the Congarees."[1] Asks him to forward them by regiments or battalions as soon as possible. They should obtain supplies and a route of march from the assistant deputy quartermaster at Charlotte, N.C.[2] NG has sent Capt. [James] Read to Salisbury to receive the North Carolina recruits and establish an armory.[3] Asks Lawson to furnish Read with any men from his command who could "be of use" repairing arms. He should proceed to camp after he has sent "the first Regiment."[4] LS (H. DeForest Hardinge, Mercer Island, Wash., 1989) 3 pp.]

1. The "posts at the Congarees" were Forts Motte and Granby, both of which were later captured.

2. Most of the expected reinforcement from Virginia never left the state. (See note at Jefferson to NG, 30 March, above.)

3. Read was both a captain in the North Carolina Continental line and a colonel of militia. (In NG's letter to him of 29 April, above, Read was referred to by the latter rank.)

4. As noted at his letter to NG of 30 April, above, Lawson remained in Virginia.

*   *   *

Captain Nathaniel Pendleton to General Thomas Sumter

Head Quarters Colonels Creek [S.C.]
Sir   May 10th 1781. 11 oClock P.M.

General Greene has this moment received information that the enemy have evacuated Camden.[1] They moved out this morning very early, after destroying the Mill, the Goal [i.e., gaol or jail] and all their Stores, together with many private houses.[2] What may have induced this unexpected and precipitate movement is uncertain; but the General is of opinion that the same motives which has induced Lord Rawdon, to this step, will also induce the evacuation of all the out Posts, which the enemy have at Ninety Six, Augusta and on the Congaree.[3] The General begs you will take such measures if possible, as will prevent Maxwells escapeing.[4]

The Army was to have moved towards Friday's Ferry tomorrow morning. It will move that way still, tho pirhaps, by a different Route and more slowly.[5]

It is uncertain which way Lord Rawdon took his Route. It was either to George Town, or Charles Town, but most probably the latter.[6]

You will please to send an express to the commanding officer before Augusta, & let him know this circumstance, that he may take his measures accordingly; as the General is firmly persuaded they will, if they can, leave all their out Posts.[7] I am, Sir with high respect Yr Mo: Obedt Hble Servt   NATHL PENDLETON

Genl Sumpter will please to send an express immediately to Genl Pickins with a Copy of this Letter.   N.P.

ALS (Sumter Papers: DLC). According to a notation on Pendleton's draft (MiU-C), copies of this letter were sent to both Sumter and Gen. Francis Marion.

1. In his pension application, Col. Guilford Dudley later recalled that he had been invited to breakfast with NG on the morning of 11 May. When he arrived at NG's quarters,

> the general, who seemed to have been expecting me, came to the front door of his apartment and saw me close at hand and ready to dismount at the gate in the upper corner of the yard. At the first glance I thought I perceived in the general's countenance an expression of something of a pleasing and interesting nature, and so there was. With his accustomed politeness he stepped out of the door, his fine manly face wearing the smile of complacency and benevolence so natural to him, and met me at the yard gate, where, hardly taking time to present his hand, his invariable practice whenever an officer visited him, with apparent eagerness asked me if "I had heard the news?"
>
> Struck by the manner of his asking the question, I hastily replied, "No, sir, what news?"
>
> "Rawdon evacuated Camden yesterday afternoon," and added in a facetious way, "[and] has left Capt. Jack Smith [an American officer captured in the battle of Hobkirk's Hill] commandant of the place, in care of his sick and wounded, as

well as ours, and pushed towards Nelson's Ferry on the Santee." This pleasing intelligence the general had but just received himself, no patrols of our cavalry having been on that side of the river for several days, nor down about the ferry the evening before, nor that morning, where they must have seen the conflagration of houses, etc., which Lord Rawdon, in his clemency, thought proper to destroy by fire. (Dann, *Revolution Remembered*, pp. 224–25)

On Smith's situation as a prisoner, see Doyle to NG, 29 April, and Smith to NG, 30 April, both above.)

2. Rawdon wrote Lord Cornwallis on 24 May that he had stayed in Camden with part of his troops until 10 A.M. on 10 May to "cover" the march of his supply train and that he had "destroyed the Works" before he left. (PRO 30/11/6) According to a history of Camden, Rawdon "left almost every . . . building of consequence a heap of ashes," except for Col. Joseph Kershaw's mansion, which had served as British headquarters. (Kirkland and Kennedy, *Camden*, p. 277)

3. In his letter of 24 May to Cornwallis, Rawdon said he decided to abandon Camden when he learned that "the whole interior Country had revolted" and because he was concerned for the safety of Charleston. (PRO 30/11/6) NG was correct in assuming that the British meant to abandon all their interior posts. (See ibid.; Balfour to Clinton, 6 May, PRO 30/11/109.)

4. Maj. Andrew Maxwell commanded the British post at Ft. Granby. Sumter replied on 11 May, below.

5. NG's army marched from Camden on 12 May and reached Friday's Ferry on the 15th. (Seymour, "Journal," p. 383; NG to Catharine Greene, 15 May, below)

6. On Rawdon's movements following his evacuation of Camden, see note at Sumter to NG, 15 May, below.

7. NG apparently had not yet received Gen. Andrew Pickens's letter of 8 May, above, informing him that Pickens was taking command of the siege force at Augusta, Ga.

*   *   *

¶ [TO GEORGE WASHINGTON. From Headquarters [Colonel's Creek, S.C.], 10 May 1781.[1] Sends a copy of the cartel "for the exchange and relief of prisoners taken in this department"; hopes Washington approves of it.[2] LS (Washington Papers: DLC) 1 p.]

1. The place was taken from other letters of this date.
2. On the cartel, see NG to Huntington, this date, above.

¶ [FROM COLONEL HENRY LEE, JR., "Mottes Post," S.C., 10 May 1781. "This post still holds out," despite "every exertion." Its capture "will be accomplished," however, unless Lord Rawdon, who alone could "drive us away," arrives before "tomorrow evening."[1] Lee hopes Rawdon will "not evacuate Camden for two weeks," by which time "things will be properly settled, on this [s]ide of the Congaree."[2] Expects Gen. [Thomas] Sumter to take Orangeburg "by tomorrow."[3] "Nelsons Ferry, Biggins Church & Dorchester must fall next. Then there will be full room for material operation."[4] Encloses Maj. [Hezekiah] Maham's plan. Maham "cannot be spared to wait on" NG with it; Lee urges NG's "closing with the plan, as numbers of indolent fellows might be picked up & made serviceable."[5] NG's "reasons" concerning his "duty" convince Lee that his "idea^s were erroneous." Lee's "personal attachment" to NG led him "to postpone matters dear to" him; asks NG not to order him to "camp" until "things are properly [Lined?] in this country," no matter how "inconvenient personally" his "stay may prove."[6] Asks NG to order the forwarding of clothing for Lee's troops from Salisbury, N.C. Letters from Philadelphia inform Lee "that the army & the country have formed a proper idea" of NG's "exertions." ALS (ViU) 4 pp.]

1. Ft. Motte was captured before Rawdon could come to its relief. (See NG to Huntington, 14 May, below.)

2. As seen in Pendleton to Sumter, this date, above, Camden had already been evacuated.

3. Sumter reported the capture of Orangeburg in a letter to NG of 11 May, below.

4. On the evacuation and destruction of the post at Nelson's Ferry by Rawdon's troops, see Marion to NG, 16 May, below. Rawdon's movements prevented any attempt to capture the British posts at Dorchester and Biggin's Church. The "material operation" Lee had in mind was presumably a drive into the South Carolina low country, as far as the "gates of Charlestown," as NG put it in a letter to John Butler of 24 May, below,

5. Lee enclosed a copy of Maham's plan for enlisting an independent, mounted corps. (The plan is in MiU-C, where it is identified as a memo of this date from Lee to NG.) NG had asked for the plan in his letter to Lee of 9 May, above; on 21 June, below, he authorized Maham to recruit such a corps.

6. NG had given Lee his reasons for planning to remove to Virginia and take command of the opposition to Lord Cornwallis in his letter of 9 May. Lee had expressed reservations about such a move. (See Lee to NG, 8 May, above.) Lee was apparently requesting here that he not be ordered to join NG in Virginia until he had completed his operations in South Carolina. As it turned out, neither NG nor Lee went to Virginia.

¶ [GENERAL GREENE'S ORDERS, "Camp Stoney Creek 4 Miles West Camden," S.C., Friday, 11 May 1781. Maj. [John] Mazaret is to serve as field commissary of military stores for the Southern Army "Until the pleasure of Congress and Board of War be known." Lamar Orderly Book (OClWHi) 1 p.]

*   *   *

To Colonel John Marshel

Sir   Camp Jumping Gully Creek [S.C.] May 11th 1781
You will have heard before this reaches you, of the evacuation of Camden.[1] The enemy were distressed for want of provisions, & it is probable they have quitted Camden in order, the more effectually, to cover their posts to the Southward.[2]

You will please to collect all the militia & negroes you can about the Country, & march into Camden, in order to destroy the works left their [i.e., there]. Let the parapets be level'd, the pallisades cut down, & the Abattes burnt, those at the Ferry as well as those in Town.[3]

It will be necessary to have a Ferry established over the Wateree at where it formerly was, to be kept by Negroes used to the business; you will please to have it done as soon as you possibly can. You will also pay some attention to the Stores left at Camden, assist in having them collected and secured; & do every thing else you may think will further the public service. I am sr &c

Df (MiU-C).

1. On the evacuation of Camden by the British, see Pendleton to Sumter, 10 May, above.

2. Lord Rawdon's reasons for relinquishing the post are discussed at ibid.

3. See also NG to Ross, immediately below.

* * *

¶ [TO ARTHUR BROWN ROSS. From Headquarters [Jumping Gully Creek, S.C.], 11 May 1781. Ross is to collect "all the Negroes" around Camden and "set them to work" destroying the fortifications there until Col. [John] Marshel arrives to take charge.[1] He should inform the people that the "most exemplary punishments will be made on Delinquents" who fail to "send their Negroes." Df (MiU-C) 1 p.]

1. See NG's orders to Marshel, immediately above.

¶ [FROM WILLIAM GRAYSON OF THE BOARD OF WAR, War Office [Philadelphia], 11 May 1781. The board has received NG's letters of 30 March and 4 and 5 April.[1] The members can "readily enter into" his "embarrassments, and the causes which produce them." They are sure that NG will send them regular returns of his army, which are "essential to the good of the service," as soon as possible. They understand the "bad consequences, resulting from the pernicious practice of dealing out the public Stores, indiscriminately to the Militia and Continental Troops." They regret that circumstances force NG "to suffer the continuance of such a measure" and are certain he will dispense Continental stores to the militia only when "essential." They have done everything in their power to forward clothing and stores for NG's army. The amounts have not equalled their "wishes" but were all that "the exhausted state" of their finances would allow. They will never know, however, "what will be sufficient" if stores "are appropriated to different purposes than what they are intended." They have learned that stores are being diverted but have never been able to determine who is responsible "with sufficient accuracy." They ask NG to acquaint them "fully" with the circumstances of the case; want to know what was missing, and by whose authority the stores were "directed to a different channel."

They have forwarded most of the clothing that NG requisitioned for Lee's Legion, except cloaks, which will not be available until supplies arrive from Europe. They have ordered the making of 200 boots, and Washington is sending 300 pairs of leather breeches. The cavalry's other needs "must be deferred" until the board is "in a better situation to relieve them." They send two resolutions of Congress forbidding colonels to send officers to procure supplies for their regiments. This practice has been "attended with great expence" and has produced "no good consequence."[2] Concerning NG's request to increase the pay of the staff departments, the board has no power to authorize such a step. But as NG is "on the spot" and "best able to judge of the propriety of th[e] measure," Congress will no doubt "confirm" whatever he thinks necessary. LS (MiU-C) 3 pp.]

1. Most of the letter is a point-by-point response to the three letters, all of which are above.

2. The resolutions have not been found.

¶ [FROM GENERAL JOHN BUTLER, Wake County, N.C., 11 May 1781. His scouts report that Lord Cornwallis "continues his March towards Halifax." The British dragoons, who are moving ahead of the "Main Body," took possession of Halifax "about 10 oClock on Monday [7 May]." They dispersed a few militiamen there and reportedly killed one resident.[1] The British infantry "make very easy Marches being delay'd by the inhabitants who flock in from all quarters to take paroles." On Wednesday night [9 May], they were twelve miles above Tarboro. Butler "broke up Camp Yesterday," as his men's time of service had expired. He will go to Hillsborough and use his "influence & authority" to complete "the Quota of Continental Troops for this district" by the time of the scheduled rendezvous on 26 May.[2] Has had "various reports" about NG's operations, some "very agreeable & others the reverse." Has not had a letter from NG since 21 April; is anxious for "such intelligence" as NG "may Judge proper to communicate."[3] The two expresses that Butler sent have not returned, nor has he heard anything from them. He will continue to send NG all the intelligence "worthy" of notice. LS (MiU-C) 2 pp.]

    1. The Marquis de Malmedy gave a fuller description of the British capture of Halifax in a letter to NG of this date, below. He also reported a larger number of American casualties.

    2. As seen in Sumner to NG, 25 June, below, the draft was not completed by that date.

    3. Butler heard from NG shortly after finishing this letter. (See Butler to NG, immediately below.) NG replied on 24 May, below.

¶ [FROM GENERAL JOHN BUTLER, "At Col Lanes" [Wake County, N.C.], 11 May 1781, 11 A.M. Since writing NG "this morning," he has received NG's "favour of the 3ᵈ Instant."[1] The expresses who brought it report that another express, who left NG's camp two days before they did, was waylaid at Deep River by eight Loyalists, who took his dispatches, robbed him of his horse and clothing, and beat him badly.[2] ALS (MiU-C) 1 p.]

    1. Butler's letter is immediately above. The one he received, written by NG's aide, William Pierce, is above, dated 2 May.

    2. It is not known which dispatches the express was carrying.

¶ [FROM JOSEPH CLAY, "near Hicks Ford on Meherrin" River, Va., 11 May 1781. Clay has not written sooner for "Want of Conveyance." He had purchased cloth for overalls, leather for shoes, and stockings, all of which he turned over to Col. [Nicholas] Long. The latter had everything "in a train to have afforded to the Army a very considerable supply of these Articles," but many supplies were lost when the enemy captured Halifax, N.C. The supplies had been placed on a boat and were to have been taken across the river to wait for wagons, but the boat was captured after the guards abandoned it. Long is now "conveying what Stores he has saved up the Country" and does not yet know what was saved and lost.[1] Clay would have purchased a larger quantity of cloth had he not been afraid that the enemy would move toward Halifax, little having been done to "check" them. Is now "at a loss how to Conduct" himself. He will come "S'ward" unless NG directs him otherwise or it is "imprudent."[2] Will go to Prince Edward Court House, Va., "for the present" and will leave directions as to where he can be reached. He has paid Long $50,000 since his last letter to NG and now holds $700,000, "besides Bills" of exchange.[3] The bearer will inform NG of the state of the situation "here." ALS (MiU-C) 2 pp.]

1. For more on the loss of stores at Halifax, see note at Sumner to NG, 15 May, below.

2. NG's reply has not been found. On Clay's return to camp, see Polk to NG, 4 June, below.

3. Clay had last written NG on 29 March, above (vol. 7: 482–83).

¶ [FROM THE MARQUIS DE MALMEDY, Williamsburo, N.C., 11 May 1781. North Carolina officials have denied his request to raise another regiment; he again asks to be placed under NG's "immediate command." When he dismissed his troops, most of the "best men" wanted to serve another tour of duty with him.[1] He explained to the governor [Abner Nash] the advantages of placing a well-equipped "body of 120 horse" and "about thousand militia" in the "center of the state" to keep watch of Lord Cornwallis's movements and be ready to reinforce either NG or the Marquis de Lafayette, "as the circumstances would require." The governor referred Malmedy's proposal to his council; Gen. [Richard] Caswell agreed "highly," but Col. [Alexander] Martin "declined positively," and Malmedy is now serving "with the governor, protempore."

Discusses the capture of Halifax by the British. "No precautions to Evacuate the stores" were taken until 5 May. NG may thus "presume the confusion which arose" on the morning of 7 May, when the enemy was sighted. Even "Two days before[,] the field officers of the district would not admitt any propability of Conwalis moving towards" the Roanoke River. Most of the "warlike stores" were captured, "and perhaps the baggage of Colonel [Henry] Lee." Many men were "killed around the town, 17 Continental soldier taken."[2]

North Carolina is "in an unfortunate situation." It has 150 men at Taylor's Ferry, including the new levees; another 150 are expected "here" this day. These men, together with the forty dragoons who accompany the governor, are the only state troops now in the field. Nor is there any "flattering prospect of Exertion where the marquis [i.e., Lafayette] will be wanting of reinforcement." Adds: "The governor wishes to collect forces. He may have informed you of the orders he gave; indeed he does what he can, but Conwalis would have effected his jonction if he does intend it, before the governor might render Essential services."[3] Reiterates his desire to join NG's army "as soon as possible." ALS (MiU-C) 3 pp.]

1. As seen in his letter to NG of 14 April, above, Malmedy's regiment had completed its tour of duty on 26 April.

2. Col. Banastre Tarleton's account of the taking of Halifax supports Malmedy's contention that the American defense was uncoordinated and inept. (Tarleton, *Campaigns*, pp. 287–89) As seen in Joshua Potts's letter to NG of 24 June, below, part of the baggage belonging to Lee's Legion was lost to American looters.

3. As late as 31 May, some ten days after Lord Cornwallis's army had linked up with Gen. William Phillips's detachment at Petersburg, Va., North Carolina had still not brought more regular troops or militia into the field. (Lafayette to Steuben, 31 May, Idzerda, *Lafayette Papers*, 4: 150) In his letter to NG of this date, below, Nash wrote that "little good" could be expected from the militia in the "middle and lower parts of the Country"—the area from which Malmedy presumably thought Lafayette would draw reinforcements.

*   *   *

From General Francis Marion

Sr   Motts [S.C.] 11th May 1781

Yourse of the 9th Inst. came to hand & I assure you I am very serious in my intention of relinquishing my Malitia Command, not that I wish to Shrink from fatigue or trouble, or for any private Interest but because I found Little is to be done with such men as I have, who Leave me very Often at the very point of Executing a plan & their Late infamous behavour in Quiting me at a time which required their service must confirm me in my former Intentions. If I cannot act in the malitia I cannot see any service I can be, to remain in the state & I hope by going to the Northward to fall in some employ where I may have an Opertunity of serving the United States, in some way that I cannot be in this Country.[1]

I rec^d Intelligence yesterday, that Lord Rawden Left Camden the day before yesterday with his whole force and Lay at Swift Creek & Last night was to be at Singletons Mill & mean to retreat over Nelsons Ferry, but I believe it must be only a Large forraging party. I expect to know the certainity of it today.[2]

Genl [Thomas] Sumter is gone against the post at Orangeburg. Our approaches here is almost up to the Enemys abbattis. Today we shall make Lodgement at the foot of their work & make no Doubt we shall carry the post.[3]

I send by Maj^r Heyrne a horse for yourself. He is very tender foot, & must be shod before he can be of use. As soon as it is in my power to procure more I will send them.[4] I have the Honour to be your Ob^t s^t

FRAN^S MARION

ALS (MiU-C).

1. NG is said to have persuaded Marion to continue as a militia commander in a face-to-face meeting at Motte's, shortly after the capture of that post. (Rankin, *Swamp Fox*, p. 208)

2. As seen in Pendleton to Sumter, 10 May, above, Rawdon had abandoned the post at Camden.

3. As seen in NG to Huntington, 14 May, below, the British post at Motte's surrendered on 12 May.

4. For more on the horses, see Edmund M. Hyrne to NG, 8 May, above.

*   *   *

¶ [FROM GOVERNOR ABNER NASH OF NORTH CAROLINA**, Granville County, N.C., 11 May 1781. By intelligence that he has received, Nash is "sertain that Lord Cornwallis with his whole force reached Halifax today."[1] Nash has so advised "the Marquis [de Lafayette]," whose letters to NG he is forwarding "by a Guard of three men." The North Carolina militia "in the middle & lower parts of the Country are so badly armed" that Nash thinks "little good is to be expected of them." The new Continental levies, most of whom are ready to take the field, also lack arms. "How this difficulty is to be got over I cannot see. We must do the best we can." Nash fears Lafayette will be "in some danger," as the enemy's force, "when joined," will be superior to his. Is anxious to hear from NG; has unconfirmed reports of NG's "gaining advantages" over the enemy.[2] ALS (OMC) 1 p.]

1. Cornwallis himself reached Halifax on 10 May, but some of the units in his army did not arrive until the 12th. (See Cornwallis to Gen. William Phillips, 10 May, PRO 30/11/86; "Von Bose Journal," p. 57.)

2. Before he received this letter, NG sent Nash a report of the Southern Army's operations in South Carolina, dated 14 May, below.

¶ [FROM CAPTAIN JOHN PRYOR, Richmond, Va., 11 May 1781. Sends a copy of his appointment as field commissary of military stores for the Southern Department. He appreciates NG's approval of the appointment, and although he fears being inadequate to the demands of the job, he promises to make "constant exertions."[1] As Baron Steuben instructed, Pryor will turn his "whole attention" to "forming and establishing Magazines at such places and of such magnitude and quality" as are needed, "agreeable to estimates." Has appointed a field commissary and conductors for the army in Virginia; hopes soon to appoint such officers for NG's army and have them take charge of "all the prepared Ammunition and other articles of Military Stores" at Prince Edward Court House and move them to NG's camp "by the safest route." When Pryor can obtain a return of military stores at Prince Edward Court House, he will send a copy to NG, with a "state" of the laboratory. The "supply of this Army has been carried on by the State" since Capt. [Nathaniel] Irish relocated to Prince Edward Court House, but Pryor plans "to make it Continental as soon as possible." As Lord Cornwallis is approaching Virginia, Pryor, as "directed," has ordered Irish to move all the stores to "some more remote and secure place." He assumes this has been done.[2] Gen. [William] Phillips is at Petersburg, and "tis supposed" Lord Cornwallis "will meet him there by tomorrow."[3] Lafayette is north of the James River, "10 or 12 miles below this," with his corps, two militia brigades, six field pieces, and two howitzers. The legislature adjourned "yesterday" and will "meet at Charlottesville in a fortnight." The Pennsylvania Continentals reportedly marched from York, Pa., on 8 May.[4] Pryor will not trouble NG with the "minutias" of the "late operations" in Virginia, as Lafayette and Steuben must "have communicated them more properly." Adds that he will give "all attention" to NG's orders and estimates. ALS (MiU-C) 3 pp.]

1. A copy of Pryor's appointment, signed by Baron Steuben, is at MiU-C. As seen in NG to Pryor, 15 June, below, the appointment should have been as deputy commissary general and was thus incorrect. The Board of War, meanwhile, had appointed Thomas Jones to the deputy's position, leaving Pryor without a post. (JCC, 20: 679)

2. The military stores had not yet been moved. (See Irish to NG, 20 May, below.)

3. As noted at Lafayette to NG, first letter of 3 May, above, Cornwallis joined the British force at Petersburg on 20 May.

4. The Pennsylvanians did not march until almost the end of May. (See note at Washington to NG, 1 June, below.)

¶ [FROM GENERAL JETHRO SUMNER, Williamsboro, Granville County, N.C., 11 May 1781. Reports that the British cavalry captured Halifax on 7 May at 2 o'clock; Lord Cornwallis and most of his army were to have arrived there "last even'g."[1] The Continental draftees, few in number, collect "very slow." Most of them lack muskets, and Sumner plans to send them to "the Rear, or to Hilsborough." The Marquis de Lafayette, from whom he requested arms, has none available but has ordered that 400 stand be repaired and sent to Sumner "as soon as possible," along with 20,000 cartridges.[2] Sumner will set off "to day" to join Gen. [Allen] Jones, who has collected 200 militiamen and is marching to Taylor's Ferry. The militia from the different counties "have not made any junction," but the governor [Abner Nash] has assured Sumner that those in Granville and Franklin counties will rendezvous "to morrow" and march toward Taylor's Ferry. Sumner shares Lafayette's fear that Cornwallis intends to unite with [Gen. William] Phillips. Sumner also believes that "greater exertion than we are able to make in this quarter" will be needed to aid Lafayette. Has learned that some arms are being sent "from the northward," but he understands they are crossing "high" on the Roanoke River. He will take them for the draftees should they come within "Reatch."[3] Has accounts of the British "horse crossing at Halifax."[4] Wants to hear from NG.[5] ALS (MiU-C) 2 pp.]

1. On the capture of Halifax by the British dragoons, see Malmedy to NG, this date above. The arrival there of Lord Cornwallis and his army is noted at Nash to NG, this date, above.

2. An abstract of Lafayette's letter, dated 7 May, is in Idzerda, *Lafayette Papers*, 4: 492.

3. Sumner presumably referred to the shipment of military supplies discussed at Compty to NG, 28 April, above.

4. As seen in Sumner's letter to NG of 15 May, below, the British cavalry and "a large part of the Infantry" crossed the Roanoke on 13 May.

5. NG replied on 23 May, below.

¶ [FROM GENERAL THOMAS SUMTER, Orangeburg, S.C., 11 May 1781. Sumter invested "this post" at 7 P.M. "yesterday"; it surrendered at 7 o'clock "this Morning."[1] He captured eight officers, eighty-two privates, a small supply of "Military Stores," and "Provisions plenty But No Conveniency of Moving it."[2] Has just heard that "Camden is evacuated." If so—and if Gen. [Francis] Marion is "Disengaged"—Rawdon's "Retreat Might be Cut of[f], that is he might be prevent[ed] from Crossing at Neilson's Ferry."[3] Maj. [Andrew] Maxwell will be "Taken Good Care off" until Sumter returns.[4] Sumter has examined "this Post" and finds it to be "extreemly Strong"; it would have been very difficult to capture if it had been "obstinately Defended." ALS (MiU-C) 2 pp.]

1. Thomas Young, who participated in the siege of Orangeburg, remembered that Sumter's state troops arrived the night of 10 May. The rest of Sumter's force reached Orangeburg the next morning with artillery. "The field piece was brought to bear upon the house" immediately, "a breach was made through the gable end—then another lower down—then about the centre, and they surrendered." (Quoted in Alexander S. Salley, *The History of Orangeburg County, South Carolina, from Its First Settlement to the Close of the Revolutionary War* [Orangeburg, S.C., 1898], p. 516n; for more on the capture, see NG to Huntington, 14 May, below.)

2. Twenty-eight of the prisoners were Loyalists. They were sent in chains to NG's headquarters on 12 May, but militia guards reportedly murdered thirteen of them along the way. (Levi Smith's narrative, *Royal Gazette* [Charleston], 13–17 April 1782)

3. Marion still had Ft. Motte under siege. No serious attempt was made to cut off Rawdon's retreat.

Thomas Sumter, 1734–1832; oil painting by Rembrandt Peale
(Independence National Historical Park Collection)

4. Maxwell commanded Ft. Granby, where Sumter had begun a siege on 2 May. Finding the fort too strong to attack without artillery, he sent men to borrow a field piece from NG. Leaving one of his regiments to cut off the garrison's supplies, he then took the rest of his command to Orangeburg, some fifty miles to the southeast. (Sumter to NG, second letter of 4 May, above; Gregorie, *Sumter*, p. 157) Before Sumter could return, Henry Lee marched his troops to Ft. Granby and persuaded Maxwell to surrender the post. (See Lee to NG, 15 May, below.)

¶ [**TO GENERAL ROBERT LAWSON**, [12 May 1781].[1] The enemy evacuated Camden "yesterday morning and are collecting their force." It is "indispensably necessary" that the Southern Army be reinforced "as early as possible." Lawson is to forward the militia "by Battalions" by a route that NG gives.[2] Df (MiU-C) 1 p.]

1. The date was taken from the endorsement sheet; NG's location is not known. NG's army was marching on that date to a mill some twelve miles southeast of Camden to support Francis Marion and Henry Lee in the event that Lord Rawdon attempted to lift their siege of Ft. Motte. (Journal of Thomas Anderson, DLC; Lee, *Memoirs*, 2: 73)

2. Only a small part of the militia reinforcement that NG was expecting from Virginia ever joined his army. (See note at Jefferson to NG, 30 March, above.)

¶ [**FROM SAMUEL HUNTINGTON, PRESIDENT OF THE CONTINENTAL CONGRESS**, Philadelphia, 12 May 1781. By an enclosed act of Congress, each state's Continental line is to have no more than one chaplain per brigade, and supernumerary chaplains are to be "certified to the Board of War" and dismissed.[1] A ship from France has brought news of the sailing of a large French fleet, "supposed to be destined for America." On inquiry, Huntington thinks a "very considerable french Fleet" did sail, but its "Destination, Number of Ships & Troops is Matter of Opinion."[2] Adds in a postscript that NG's letter of 31 March "hath been receiv^d." ALS (PPRF) 1 p.]

1. The resolution, enacted on 8 May, is printed in *JCC*, 20: 487–88.

2. On 22 March, a huge convoy left Brest for the West Indies. It included twenty ships of the line, three frigates, and 150 transports carrying 3,000 soldiers and supplies. (Dull, *French Navy*, pp. 217–24; Boatner, *Encyc.*, p. 444)

¶ [**FROM GENERAL FRANCIS MARION**, "before Mottes house," S.C., 12 May 1781. Encloses a letter from Gen. [Thomas] Sumter, who has captured Orangeburg.[1] The post "here" is "Obstinate, and strong[.] Our approaches is now to their Abbittis & hope by tomorrow at furthest to reduce it."[2] Lord Rawdon camped in the High Hills of the Santee "Last night"; he apparently plans to cross the Santee at Nelson's Ferry, where the enemy have assembled boats.[3] Sumter reports that an enemy detachment has "Just come out of" Charleston, but he does not know its "Destination."[4] ALS (NN) 1 p.]

1. Sumter's letter to Marion has not been found, but some of its contents can probably be inferred from Sumter to NG, 11 May, above.

2. As seen at NG to Huntington, 14 May, below, the post surrendered on the 12th.

3. The fires from Rawdon's encampments could be seen from Motte's. That sight braced the post's defenders and led Marion and Henry Lee, who decided that Rawdon was no more than forty-eight hours away from breaking their siege, to attempt to force the post's surrender. They did so by setting fire to the residence of Rebecca Motte, a staunch supporter of the American cause, whose house comprised the strongest part of the British post. (Bass, *Marion*, p. 193; for more on the siege, see notes at NG to Huntington, 14 May, below.) As Marion surmised, Rawdon was heading toward Nelson's Ferry. (See note at Sumter to NG, 15 May, below.)

4. Nisbet Balfour, the commander at Charleston, wrote Lord Cornwallis on 21 May that he had sent 150 men to a "fortified church" at Dorchester. (PRO 30/11/6) This was presumably the enemy movement that Sumter reported to Marion.

¶ [**FROM GENERAL ANDREW PICKENS**, Snow Hill, Ga., [12?] May 1781.[1] He wrote NG by Col. [John] Purvis, who was to report the "Situation of this Country; almost unanimous in our favour but the greatest Want of Arms to

Rebecca Motte, 1737–1815
(Reproduced from Benson J. Lossing, Pictorial Field-Book of the Revolution,
2 vols. [New York, 1860])

make them useful."[2] Purvis was to ask NG for some "regular Troops," who are needed more than ever now that the enemy have evacuated Camden, S.C. Pickens believes Col. [John Harris] Cruger will "endeavour to quit Ninety Six in the Same Manner" that Lord Rawdon left Camden and will march "this Way" to relieve Col. [Thomas] Brown, whose post at Augusta, Ga., "is now Closely besieged." The two would then retreat to Savannah. Should Cruger make such an attempt, Pickens would be forced to "move out of his Way" because many of his men lack arms. If NG can "throw a Sufficient force below" Cruger "on this Side," Pickens believes "the Whole force of the Enemy in this quarter will Soon fall into our hands."[3] Adds that "Powder is as much wanted as Arms." LS (MiU-C) 1 p.]

1. The space for the date was left blank on the letter and appears to have been scratched out on the docketing. What appears to be a "12" has been added to the docketing in another hand. The date of 12 May is consistent with the letter's contents.

2. See Pickens to NG, 8 May, above.

3. Lord Rawdon and Nisbet Balfour had sent orders to Cruger to abandon Ninety Six, but their messages were all intercepted. As noted at Lee to NG, 9 May, above, Cruger was still holding that post when NG's army arrived and began siege operations on 22 May. As seen in NG to Lee, 16 May, below, NG sent some "regular Troops" to assist in the siege of Augusta.

*   *   *

From General Thomas Sumter

Dʳ Sir   Orangeburgh [S.C.] 12ᵗʰ May 1781

I Wrote you yesterday that we were in Possession of the post at this place Since Which I have Not been at Leasure to be More perticuler.

I am Just favoured with Yours of the 12ᵗʰ informing of the evacuation of Camden Which I think a favourable Circumstance.[1] You Need not in my oppinion have the Least Doubts of the Posts above this Not falling or Making their escape, that at the Congrees I think Will be taken proper Care of.[2] No assistance will be wanted there to Keep them Close untill I Return with Troops & field piece. If they Shoud March out & Shoud Prove Superior to the force we have there yet they Cant Get Clear by any means as I am below them.

Before I Return to the Congrees I think to Move towards Santee, and endeavour to Alarm Lord Rawden to prevent his Crossing the River, or Removing the Post from Nielsons Ferry, untill Genˡ Marion & Coˡ Lee are Disengaged as they Might if you thought proper have it in their power to take it.[3] An other Motive I have for Taking a Turn through the Country, is, I find Many people Braking up & Removing to Town, So that if Lord Rawden Shoud Pass the river or take post at Nielson, there is every Reason to beleive the Country will be Striped of every thing that is Valuable.[4] I Wish to Deprive them of as Many horses as possible & prevent the Inhabitance from Moving & Carrying off great Quantities of Stock Which are Now Collecting.[5]

My Movements Will be as Rappid as May be, & I Shall Never be out of the Way of Cuting of[f] the Retreat of the Enemy from any of their frontier posts, as our officers will Know where to Send to me.

My Return to the Congrees will be Speedy. I have the Honʳ to be Dʳ Sir your most obedt Hble Servt   THOˢ SUMTER

ALS (MiU-C).

1. No such letter of this date has been found. Nathaniel Pendleton, NG's aide, had sent word to Sumter of the evacuation of Camden on 10 May, above.

2. Sumter referred to Forts Motte and Granby, the latter of which was at the Congarees.

3. After Gen. Francis Marion and Col. Henry Lee completed their siege of Ft. Motte, NG sent Lee to Ft. Granby. Marion went on to Georgetown shortly afterwards.

4. Rawdon later destroyed the works at Nelson's Ferry and moved closer to Charleston. (Rawdon to Cornwallis, 24 May, PRO 30/11/6)

5. After writing this, Sumter moved to within eighteen miles of Monck's Corner and sent detachments to sweep the country between Wassamassaw and Dorchester. (Gregorie, *Sumter*, p. 159) This effort was so effective that Rawdon later reported he had been "five days within the Santee before a single" Loyalist "came near" his army. (Rawdon to Cornwallis, 24 May, PRO 30/11/6)

To Colonel Henry Lee, Jr.

Dear Sir   Camp at McCords Ferry [S.C.] May 13th 1781

You will march immediately with the van of the Army for the post at Frydays Ferry commanded by Major [Andrew] Maxwell and demand an immediate surrender of that post.[1] As I wish to save the effusion of blood you will inform the Commanding officer of the evacuation of Camden, of the retreat of Lord Rawden towards Charlestown, of the reduction of Fort Mott, and the surrender of the post at Orrangburg and that Ninty Six & Augusta are invested; also of a flying report of a successful naval Engagement to the Northward.[2] You will in addition to this inform him that the Army will be at or near the fort by 12 oClock on the 15th and if he shall obstinately persist in holding the post he must abide the consequences as he will never receive but one summons for its surrendar.

I depend upon your pushing matters vigirously.[3] With esteem & regard I am dear Sir your most Obed^t humble S^r N GREENE

ADfS (MiU-C).

1. Ft. Granby was the post at Friday's Ferry.

2. There was no allied naval victory "to the Northward" at this time.

3. Lee later recalled that NG wanted to bring a quick end to the siege at Granby because he expected Lord Rawdon to try to relieve the post. (Lee, *Memoirs*, 2: 81–82) Rawdon did march to raise the siege but gave up the attempt after receiving a false report that NG's army was moving in the direction of Charleston. (Rawdon to Cornwallis, 24 May, PRO 30/11/6) As seen in his letter to NG of 14 May, below, Thomas Sumter was angered by Lee's taking charge of the siege. (For more on Lee, Sumter, and the surrender of Ft. Granby, see notes at Lee to NG, 15 May, below.)

*   *   *

¶ [GENERAL GREENE'S ORDERS, "Camp Huks Farm," S.C., Monday, 14 May 1781. Announces the capture of the British post at Orangeburg. "The address of Genl Sumpter [Thomas Sumter] upon this occasion, Intimidated the Enemy and Saved him the loss of even a Single Man." Also announces the capture of Ft. Motte through the "Gallant Exertions" of Gen. [Francis] Marion and Col. [Henry] Lee, "who's perservereance in Military Conduct in carrying on the approaches, with great dispatch under many difficulties deserves the highest Encomiums."[1] In after orders, wants a return of all "Deputies and Assistants" in the staff departments, "with the Dates of their Commissions[,] Warrants &c." Lamar Orderly Book (OClWHi) 2 pp.]

1. On the capture of Orangeburg, see Sumter to NG, 11 May, above; on that of Ft. Motte, see NG to Huntington, this date, below.

¶ [TO GEORGE FLETCHER. From [McCord's Ferry, S.C., 14 May 1781.][1] Has received Fletcher's letter of 6 May.[2] Fletcher should put the cattle "in order" by sending them to a "proper range," where they are to remain until needed. The pork should be preserved and stored. "Expresses to and from the army on public business and all parties out under military authority" should be issued provisions and forage "agreeable to the rules and regulations of Congress." The men who were employed in building boats "last winter upon the Pedee" should be paid in provisions. Is sorry Fletcher has "suffered so much" in his "property." NG would give him a "flag" but is "persuaded it would defeat" what Fletcher could "perhaps obtain by some other means." NG will leave the means to Fletcher's "own discression."[3] Df (MiU-C) 2 pp.]

1. The date was taken from the docketing, NG's location from other letters of this date.

2. The remainder of this letter is a point-by-point response to Fletcher's letter of 6 May, above.

3. In a portion of the draft that was crossed out, NG suggested that Fletcher send "a friend to negotiate the business on a flag [of truce to enter the British lines] from the commanding officer in the district"; that method would "affect the business" of getting Fletcher's slaves returned to him "much better than" a flag from NG.

*   *   *

To Samuel Huntington, President of the Continental Congress

Sir

Camp at McCords Ferry on the Congaree [S.C.] May 14th 1781

I wrote your Excellency on the 5th from near Camden, by Captain [James] OHara. On the 10th that place was evacuated by the enemy. They left it with great precipitation, after burning the greater part of their baggage and Stores, and even the private property belonging to the inhabitants. They also burnt the goal [i.e., gaol or jail], Mill & several other houses & left the Town little better than a heap of rubbish. They left all our men, wounded on the 25th amounting to Thirty one and fifty eight of their own and three Officers, who were all too badly wounded to be moved.[1] It is confidently asserted by several people of the place, that the enemy suffered in the late action not less in killed & wounded than three hundred men.[2]

Upon the enemy's evacuation We immediately took possession of the place and the works are leveling, a plan of which is herewith inclosed.[3] Had the Virginia militia arrived in time the Garrison would have fallen into our hands, as they would have enabled us to have invested it on all sides, and the Garrison had neither provision or Stores to hold out a seige.[4] The Detachments below operating under General Marian & Lieutenant Colonel Lee having cut off their supplies, particularly the Article of salt, of which the Garrison were entirely destitute.[5]

On the 9th the Army marched for this place.[6] On the 11th the post of Orangeburg commanded by a Colonel, & consisting of upwards of eighty men, and several Officers, part British, surrendered to General Sumpter, who by his address so intimidated the Garrison in the disposition of his Artillery and troops, as to produce a surrender of a very strong post, without loss of time or men. Great quantities of provision and some other Stores were found at this place.[7] On the 12th Fort Motte surrendered to General Marian. The Garrison consisted of upwards of one hundred and Forty men, 120 of which were british and Hessian, & seven or eight Officers. The place was invested on the eighth, and the approaches carried to the foot of the Abattis before it surrendered. The redoubt was exceeding strong, and commanded by Lieutenant McPherson a very gallant Officer. Great credit is due to General Marian, and the few Militia that continued with him, in the reduction of this post. Lieut Colonel Lee's legion and the detachments serving with him under Major [Pinketham] Eaton, Captains [Ebenezer] Finley of the artillery, & [Edward] Oldham & [John?] Smith of the infantry were indefatigable in prosecuting the Seige. There was taken at the Fort one Caronnade, about 140 stand of Arms, a quantity of salt, provisions, and other Stores; returns of which shall be forwarded hereafter.[8]

When we began our march towards Camden from Deep River, I wrote to General [Andrew] Pickens to endeavour to collect a body of Militia to lay seige to Augusta and Ninety-six, and both places are now invested, and as soon as the Virginia Militia join us, I am in hopes to be able to make such detachments from this Army as will effect their reduction.[9]

The Fort at Fridays Ferry will be invested by tomorrow morning. Lt Colo Lee with his Legion, and some of the detachments serving under him marched for this purpose last evening. The Army marches for that place this morning.[10]

By The last intelligence I had from Lord Rawdon, he was near Nelsons Ferry, where the enemy have a Post; the stores at which were moving to Charles Town, which indicated an evacuation.[11] Generals Sumpter and Marian are watching their motions. If proper exertions are made to prosecute the southern War, the enemy will soon be convinced, that if they divide their forces they will fall by detachments, and if they operate collectively they cannot command the Country.

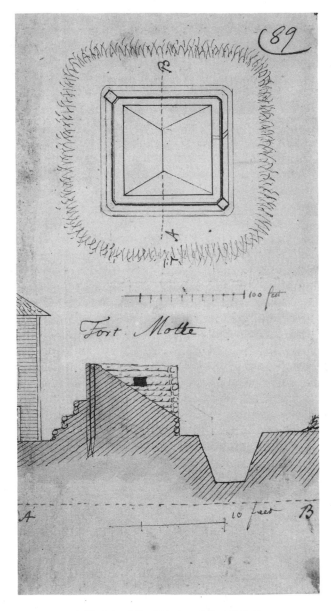

A Sketch of the Works at Fort Motte
(*National Archives*)

Captain Pierce one of my Aids who is out watching the motions of Lord Cornwallis informs me that he is on his March towards Hallifax, from Duplin Courthouse.[12] Should he push his operations in that quarter, I shall leave this Army here under the command of General [Isaac] Huger, to effect the reduction of the remaining posts, & join the Troops collecting to the northward.[13]

Inclosed I send your Excellency copies of several letters found among the Papers of Lieutenant McPherson.[14] I have the honor to be with great respect Your Excellency's most Obedient Humble Servant

NATH GREENE

LS (PCC, item 155, vol. 2: 59, DNA).

1. For more on the evacuation of Camden, see Pendleton to Sumter, 10 May, above.

2. The "late action" was the battle of Hobkirk's Hill, fought on 25 April. For more on the battle and the casualties on both sides, see NG to Huntington, 27 April, above.

3. The sketch of the works at Camden is in PCC, item 155, vol. 2: 161, DNA.

4. NG referred to 2,000 back-country Virginia militia, whom Gov. Thomas Jefferson had ordered to join NG. As noted at Jefferson to NG, 30 March, above, only a small number of those troops ever joined the Southern Army.

5. Henry Lee's and Francis Marion's detachments, "below operating," had cut off supplies coming up the Santee River to Camden.

6. This date was incorrect; the Southern Army did not move from its camp near Camden until 11 or 12 May.

7. For more on the capture of the post at Orangeburg, see Sumter to NG, 11 May, above.

8. Ft. Motte protected McCord's Ferry and was the principal British depot for supplies moving between Charleston and Camden. (Bass, *Marion*, pp. 187–88) A convoy carrying provisions had arrived only hours before Marion and Lee reached Motte on 8 May. It was trapped inside the fort and was captured when the post fell. (Nisbet Balfour to Lord Cornwallis, 21 May, PRO 30/11/6) As seen in Marion to NG, 12 May, above, the siege lines, which had been dug by the American troops and by slaves obtained from local planters, extended by that date to the abatis surrounding the post. As also seen at that letter, the appearance of Rawdon across the Santee River on the night of 11 May left the siege force little time to finish the task. On the 12th, therefore, Lee and Marion decided that in order to force a surrender they would have to burn the new mansion house of Mrs. Rebecca Motte, which occupied most of the works. (Lee, *Memoirs*, 2: 75) The decision was a painful one because the Motte family were "firm" friends of the American cause. According to the most widely repeated version of events, Rebecca Motte readily acceded when Lee informed her of the decision to burn her house and even provided a "bow and its apparatus imported from India" to start the blaze. (Ibid., p. 77) Lt. Donald McPherson, the post commander, tried to counter this stratagem by sending men onto the roof to pull off the blazing shingles, but grapeshot from the American field piece, "posted close to one of the gable ends of the house," forced them back under cover without extinguishing the flames and left McPherson with no choice but to surrender. (Ibid., pp. 78–79) Despite what NG wrote here, the regulars at the post surrendered to Lee, while Marion accepted only the formal surrender of the Loyalists. Some historians see this as evidence of friction between Marion's militiamen and Lee's corps. (See, for example, Rankin, *Swamp Fox*, p. 206.) Any rift that existed must have widened when Marion angrily halted the hanging of a Loyalist prisoner, which Lee had reportedly ordered. (See note at Lee to NG, 16 May, below.)

9. NG's letter to Pickens has not been found, nor did Pickens mention such orders in his letters to NG in April. On the investment of the forts in the area of Augusta, Ga., see Pickens's letters to NG of 8 and 12 May, both above.

10. Ft. Granby surrendered to Lee's troops the next day, before the arrival of NG's troops. (See Lee to NG, 15 May, below.)

11. Rawdon evacuated the post at Nelson's Ferry, blew up its works, and retreated to Monck's Corner, some thirty miles from Charleston. (See Marion to NG, 16 May, below.)

12. William Pierce's letter, dated 7 May, is above.

13. Cornwallis did "push operations" by moving his army into Virginia, but NG did not take command of the American forces there.

14. As seen in note 8 above, McPherson was the British commander at Motte's. The captured papers consisted of several letters addressed to Rawdon. They included one from Josiah Martin, the former royal governor of North Carolina, reporting his decision to sail for England and commenting on Rawdon's decision to leave the army. There were also two letters from Rawdon's uncle, Lord Huntington, in England, in one of which he strongly urged Rawdon to resign from the army. Yet another letter, from an "S.L.," reported on operations in the Caribbean. (PCC, item 155, vol. 2: 147–59, DNA).

To the Marquis de Lafayette

Camp at M Cords Ferry [S.C.] on the Congaree
My dear Marquis   May 14th 1781

I am happy to find by your letters of the 28th and 29th of April that you have arrivd at Richmond at so critical a conjuncture.[1] I am doubly pleased at the event as I had foreseen the necessity and pressed it so effectually.[2] You march with equal rapidity with Lord Cornwallis.

I am so remote from northern intelligence and a change of circumstan[c]es happening so frequent in which the safety of Virginia and North Carolinia seem to be involved that I am not a little embarassed in deciding what advice to give either to you or to Baron Stuben. When I expected no body but General Philips [William Phillips] to operate in Virginia it was my orders to the Baron to join this Army with the Virginia detachment and to you to forward the Pennsylvania line without a moments delay; unless by detaining them a few days you had a good prospect of defeating Philips, in that case you were left at liberty to act as you thought proper.[3]

But as Lord Cornwallis is moving Northerly and General Philips pushing his operations at a point which seems favorable for forming a junction with his Lordship, I think none of the force except the Maryland troops should come this way until the effect of the enemies operations to the Northward is better explained and more fully understood.[4]

Inclosed I send you a copy of my letter to Baron Stuben and it is my wish that you should prevent a junction of the enemy if practicable.[5] Should Lord Cornwallis prosecute his operations to the northward, I shall join the Northern Army after puting things in a proper train here for the reduction of the remainder of the Enemys posts. Since I wrote you before[,] Camden has been evacuated, and the Garrison retird towards Charlestown, Fort Mott taken with 140 prisoners[,] 120 of which were british & Hessian; also Orangburg fort with upwards of 80 prisoners part British; the first surrenderd to General [Francis] Marion the last to General [Thomas] Sumter.[6]

All the other posts are besiegd (except one at Nelsons Ferry which I expect will be evacuated) and must fall unless fortune who is not much our friend plays the gilt again.[7] Had the Virginia Militia come out in time we should have had the Garrison at Camden.[8]

We are in distress in this quarter for want of Arms, not because there is not a plenty but because we have no means of repairing them. I beg you to keep me constantly informed of the situation of things in your quarter and of all official reports. Send copies to Congress and General Washington agreeable to your proposal.[9] Dont be sparing of Expresses as it is of importance to be well informed of our own situation as well as the enemies.

I wish you glory and honor and am with the most perfect esteem your Most Obedient humble ser   N GREENE

ADfS (MiU-C).
    1. The letter of 28 April is above; that of the 29th has not been found.
    2. See NG to Lafayette, 3 April, and NG to Washington, 1 May, both above.
    3. See NG to Steuben and NG to Lafayette, both 1 May, above.
    4. As seen at Gist to NG, 28 May, below, the detachment of Maryland troops was still in Maryland.
    5. NG enclosed a copy of his letter to Steuben of this date, below. As noted there, the British intercepted the original of that letter.
    6. For more on operations in South Carolina, see NG to Huntington, immediately above. NG did not leave South Carolina.
    7. A "gilt" was a thief or burglar. (OED)
    8. On the reinforcement of Virginia militia that NG had expected, see Jefferson to NG, 30 March, above.
    9. In his letter of 17 April, above, Lafayette had asked NG if he should inform Congress of his activities.

*   *   *

¶ [TO GOVERNOR ABNER NASH OF NORTH CAROLINA. From [McCord's Ferry, S.C.], 14 May 1781. Gives a report on operations in South Carolina similar to the one contained in NG to Samuel Huntington, this date, above, with the following additions: the British destroyed their cannon when evacuating Camden; Maj. [Archibald] McArthur has "evacuated" the British post at Eutaw Springs, convincing NG that Lord Rawdon will retreat to Charleston; twelve British soldiers and seventy-six Loyalists were captured at Orangeburg, as were 127 British and Hessians and twenty Loyalists at Motte's. NG expects the "speedy reduction" of the British posts at "Fryday's Ferry [Ft. Granby,] Augusta & Ninety Six" if his army can "continue in the field." Lord Cornwallis will probably "prosecute his first plan," as he is marching northward.[1] NG fears that the "part of N Carolina through which he may march will be much distressed unless Gen' Sumner has collected a body of the Recruits."[2]

NG has directed "The Marquis [de Lafayette] and Baron Steuben to take measures effectually to counteract him"; hopes "in a few days to be able to join them."[3] Df (MiU-C) 2 pp.]

1. In NG's opinion, Cornwallis's "first plan" was presumably a "design to push through Virginia," as NG had written Nash on 6 March, above (vol. 7: 401).

2. As seen in his letter to NG of 11 May, above, Gen. Jethro Sumner did not have "a body of the Recruits" to challenge Cornwallis.

3. See NG to Lafayette, this date, above, and NG to Steuben, this date, below. NG remained in South Carolina.

¶ [TO COLONEL ROBERT ROWAN.[1] From "Camp near McCord's Ferry Congaree River," S.C., 14 May 1781. NG has received his letter of 5 May. The shoes Rowan wrote about are "very much wanted here," and he should forward them "by the firs[t] opportunity." Is surprised at the "latitude which british officers and other[s] take" under flags of truce; the district commander should put a stop to it. "No officer should be the bearer of a flag but upon some special occasion—a frivolous plea to cover an artful design cannot be admissible, and the person is liable to be detained as a prisoner." Affairs in South Carolina "wear a favorable aspect and fortune has taken a turn in our favor." Gives details of American successes.[2] These successes, together with a favorable conclusion to several sieges now under way, for which "the prospect is fair," will give "the greater part of these Southern States . . . releif from the oppression and tyrany of the Enemy." Df (MiU-C) 3 pp.]

1. The recipient's name was taken from the docketing and is confirmed by the contents.

2. On the "successes" in South Carolina, see NG to Huntington, this date, above.

*   *   *

To Governor John Rutledge of South Carolina

Dr Sir   Camp at McCords Ferry [S.C., 14 May 1781]

Camden is evacuated, Fort Mott and Orangburg taken, Ninty Six and Frydays Ferry besieged, and a probability of Nelsons Ferry being evacuated, which will lay open the whole Country, should the uper posts be reduced of which there is a good prospect.[1] From the state in which I find things and the confusion and pers[e]cution which I foresee, I could wish that Civil Government might be set up immediately, as it is of importance to have the minds of the people formed to the habits of Civil rather than Military authority. This is upon the presumption we are able to hold our ground which is altogether uncertain.

I have not time to go into a detail of matters, but you may depend upon it that many unruly spirits will require bridling in this Country to make the people feel a happiness in the success of our arms. For farther particulars of the operations of this quarter I must beg leave to refer you to my public letters to Congress.

I beg my most respectful compliments to Mrs Rutledge and am with the highest respect Your most Obed^t humble S^r   NATH GREENE

ADfS (NcU).

1. NG discussed his army's successes and operations at greater length in his letter to Samuel Huntington of this date, above.

* * *

¶ [**TO BARON STEUBEN**. From McCord's Ferry, S.C., 14 May 1781. Has his letter of 26 April.[1] Is "happy" that Steuben judiciously chose "not to hazard a general action, and yet not permit the enemy to advance without considerable opposition." The conduct of Gen. [Peter] Muhlenberg and his troops pleases NG. "This spirited opposition will have a most happy effect on their future operations." NG is glad to have pressed "so early and so warmly" for the return of the Marquis [de Lafayette], whose "timely arrival" was a result.[2] Lord Cornwallis is moving northward, contrary to NG's "wishes"; NG wants Steuben and Lafayette to prevent, if possible, Cornwallis's junction with Gen. [William] Phillips. The Pennsylvania Continental line, the North Carolina Continental draftees—who should be assembling near Hillsborough and Halifax, N.C.—and "such militia as may be in Arms in the Northern parts" of North Carolina "may join and cooperate in the plan." If a junction cannot be prevented, Steuben should unite "all the force Ordered to the southward, (the Maryland troops excepted) and cooperate with the Marquis to prevent the enemy from penetrating the Country."[3] If Cornwallis marches south, the Pennsylvania line and the North Carolina and Virginia regulars should follow him and join NG's army; Steuben should command the detachment. "But as the season is getting very warm in this quarter, I am inclined to think his Lordship will confine his operations to the Northward." If he does, NG will join the army in Virginia as soon as he has "put things in a train here." He will have his army in South Carolina "complete the reduction of the remaining posts, and hold possession of the Country, which will defeat at once what the enemy have been two Campaigns in accomplishing, at such an expence of blood and treasure."[4] Refers Steuben to Lafayette for "the State of our Operations here."[5] LS (PRO 30/11/105) 4 pp.]

1. Steuben's letter, dated 25 April, is above.

2. See NG to Lafayette, 3 April, and NG to Washington, 1 May, both above.

3. Cornwallis joined forces with Phillips's detachment, now commanded by Benedict Arnold, on 20 May, well before NG's orders could have arrived. This letter, in fact, was intercepted by the British, but Steuben, refusing to acknowledge the new state of affairs in Virginia, continued to prepare his detachment for a march to South Carolina. In a letter to Washington of 18 June, Lafayette blamed Steuben's failure to protect a cache of supplies from a small British raiding force on the Baron's wish "for a journey to the Southward," adding: "The orders to Stay in this State Had Been intercepted But all this Cannot Be an Excuse." (Idzerda, *Lafayette Papers*, 4: 195) Lafayette, to whom NG sent a copy of this letter to Steuben, forwarded it to Steuben on 31 May. (Ibid., p. 150; see also NG to Lafayette, this date, above.)

4. NG remained in South Carolina.

5. NG had sent Lafayette a report on the operations of the Southern Army in his letter of this date. Lafayette gave Steuben a synopsis in a letter of 31 May. (Idzerda, *Lafayette Papers*, 4: 150)

¶ [**FROM DOCTOR JAMES BROWNE**, "General Hospital Pittsylvania," Va., 14 May 1781. Has discharged sixty soldiers and sent them to camp since he last wrote.[1] Encloses a return of "discharged, dead, and deserted," by which NG can calculate the number still at the hospital.[2] Dr. [William] Read will send NG a return from the hospital at Charlotte, N.C.[3] In Pittsylvania, they have exhausted their stores, except for rum, which will also soon be gone. They must send "as far as James River for Flour." As NG directed, they applied to the "Commissaries of Purchase and Issues in Virginia" for "Wine &c," but have received nothing.[4] Upon learning about the battle at Camden, Browne sent a steward to Brunswick, Va., for two pipes of wine that were there.[5] If he gets it, and it "prove palatable," Browne wonders if one pipe "would not be acceptable at Head Quarters." In a postscript, says an officer is needed to "superintend the hospitals, and regulate the Conduct of the Convalescent and prevent Desertion." The one who had been doing this duty left on 1 May. "From the many Removings of the hospitals in this Department," Browne has been obliged to allow the "Mates" to keep one horse each.[6] "This not being warranted by Congress," he would like to know NG's "Sentiments." None of the mates has been paid, and Browne fears they will "leave the service if this Priviledge is denied them."[7] ALS (MiU-C) 1 p.]

1. Browne had written NG on 6 May, above.
2. In the return, also dated 14 May, 146 men were listed as discharged; five had died, and seven had deserted. (MiU-C)
3. Read enclosed a return in his letter to NG of 4 June, below.
4. NG's instructions have not been found.
5. Wine was used in hospitals as a "stimulant to the appetite, a sedative, a diuretic, and merely as a nutritous addition to the diet." (Gillett, *Medical Department*, pp. 7–8)
6. Mates served as assistants to physicians and surgeons. (Ibid., p. 8)
7. NG's reply has not been found.

¶ [FROM COLONEL CHARLES S. MYDDELTON,[1] Orangeburgh, S.C., 14 May 1781. The bearer, "Co[l] Coleson [Jacob Colson?]," has two sons who were "taken at this Post." They had apparently been forced into the British service and "allways acted as Friends to America." Their father was in the American service "for Many Years" and has been "allways esteemed as a good Friend" to the cause. Myddelton, who does not know them personally, was informed of their situation by some inhabitants, whose word is reliable. Asks that Coleson's sons be "Liberated & Orderd to their duty," if NG thinks "propper."[2] ALS (MiU-C) 1 p.]

1. Below his signature, Myddelton, an officer in Gen. Thomas Sumter's brigade, added that he was "Com[r] at Orangeburgh."
2. William Pierce replied for NG on 26 May, below.

*   *   *

From General Thomas Sumter

[Orangeburgh, S.C., 14 May 1781][1]

"I hope it may not be disagreeable to recall Colonel [Henry] Lee, as his services cannot be wanted at that place; and as to his taking command, *as at the post at Motte's*, I cannot believe it would be your wish.[2] And notwithstanding I have the greatest respect for Colonel Lee, yet I could wish he had not gone to that place, as it is a circumstance I never thought of; his cavalry can be of no service there, and may be of the greatest here. I have been at great pains to reduce that post, I have it in my power to do it, and I think it for the good of the public to do it without regulars."[3]

Extract reprinted from Johnson, *Greene*, 2: 122.

1. The date was given by William Johnson; Sumter was at Orangeburg at this time, as seen by his letters to NG of 11 and 12 May, above, and 15 May, below.

2. "That place" was Ft. Granby, the British post at Friday's Ferry. In his letter to Congress of this date, NG referred to Gen. Francis Marion as the commander of American forces in the successful siege at Ft. Motte's. (NG to Huntington, 14 May, above).

3. Lee negotiated a surrender of the post on 15 May. (See Lee to NG, 15 May, below.) Sumter was so angered by Lee's involvement at Granby and by the terms of surrender that he submitted his resignation to NG. (The resignation is in Sumter to NG, 16 May, below; see also the note at Lee to NG, 15 May.)

* * *

¶ [GENERAL GREENE'S ORDERS, "Camp at Andersons Ferry on Cong[a]-ree River," S.C., 15 May 1781. The surrender of the garrison at Ft. Granby "entitles" Col. [Henry] Lee to NG's "thanks" and affords "another Instance of the Success that is attendant on Enterprize and Perseverance."[1] NG also thanks the militia force under Col. [Thomas] Taylor, which "in a great Measure facilitated the Success," and Capt. [Edward] Oldham's company, which is now to rejoin its Maryland regiment after serving with Lee's Legion. Lamar Orderly Book (OClWHi) 2 pp.]

1. On the capture of Ft. Granby, see Lee to NG, this date, below.

* * *

To Catharine Greene

Camp at Frydays Ferry on the
Dear Caty   Congaree [S.C.] May 15th 1781

I have so many and such a variety of calls that I have scarsely time to write you. Since I wrote you of our defeat or rather repulse at Camden the enemy have evacuated that place burnt the greater part of their baggage and Stores and retird with precipitation towards Charlestown.[1] There has also surrenderd to our Army under different commands the fort at Orangeburge, Motts and Frydays with not less than three or four hundred prisoners.[2] Ninty Six and Augusta are both invested and I hope will soon be in our possession after which the enemy will have no post but upon the Sea Coast except at Nelsons Ferry [and?] at Watboo, the former of which I expect will be soon evacuated.[3]

Lord Cornwallis is on his march towards Hallifax in North Carolinia and General Philips is operating in Virginia;[4] I expect therefore to be obligd to move to the Northward not with the force that is here but to collect a force to the Northward to oppose them.[5] Marquis de la Fyette and Baron Stuben are both in Virginia and I pray god they may be

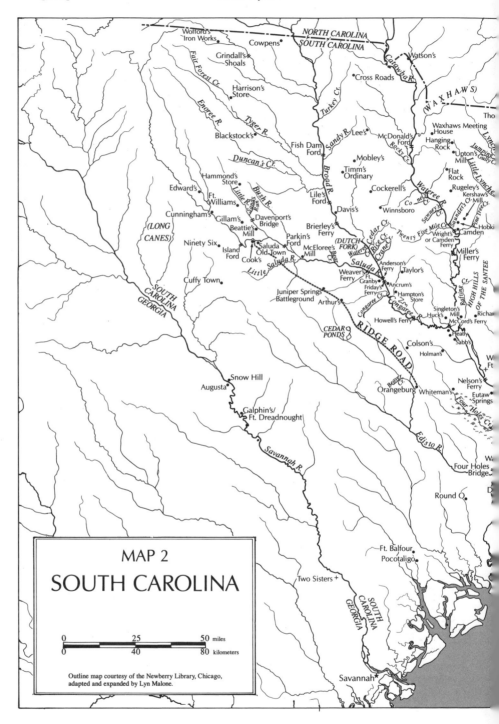

NORTH CAROLINA
SOUTH CAROLINA

Wofford's
Iron Works
Cowpens
Watson's
Catawba R.
Grindall's Shoals
Cross Roads
(WAXHAWS)
Tho
Harrison's Store
Waxhaws Meeting House
Fair Forest Cr.
Enoree R.
Turkey Cr.
Lynch
Sandy R.
Lee's
McDonald's Ford
Hanging Rock
Upton's
Jumping
Gully Cr.
Tyger R.
Rocky Cr.
Blackstock's
Fish Dam Ford
Mobley's
Little Lynche
Flat Rock
Duncan's Cr.
Broad R.
Timm's Ordinary
Rugeley's
Kershaw's Mill
Hammond's Store
Lile's Ford
Cockerell's
Co Cr.
Sawney's Cr.
Hobki
Edward's
Ft. Williams
Bush R.
Davis's
Winnsboro
Wright's or Camden Ferry
Camden
Cunningham's
Gillam's
Davenport's Bridge
Brierley's Ferry
Twenty Five Mile Cr.
Little R.
Beattie's Mill
Cedar Cr.
Rice Cr.
Miller's Ferry
(LONG CANES)
Ninety Six
Island Ford
Saluda Old Town
Parkin's Ford
McEloree's Mill
(DUTCH FORK)
Crane
Saluda
Anderson's Ferry
Taylor's
HIGH HILLS OF THE SANTEE
Cook's
Little
Saluda R.
Weaver's Ferry
Granby
Ancrum's
Cuffy Town
Friday's Ferry
Hampton's Store
Singleton's Mill
Richar
Juniper Springs Battleground
Arthur's
Congaree Cr.
Congaree
Huck's
McCord's Ferry
Howell's Ferry
Heatly
Sabb's
CEDAR PONDS
RIDGE ROAD
Colson's
W
Ft
Holman's
Snow Hill
Nelson's Ferry
Augusta
Beaver Cr.
Orangeburg
Whiteman's
Eutaw Springs
Galphin's/
Ft. Dreadnought
Four Holes Cr.
W
Savannah R.
Edisto R.
Four Holes Bridge

SOUTH CAROLINA
GEORGIA

Round O

Ft. Balfour
Pocotaligo

MAP 2
SOUTH CAROLINA

Two Sisters +

SOUTH CAROLINA
GEORGIA

0   25   50 miles
0   40   80 kilometers

Outline map courtesy of the Newberry Library, Chicago,
adapted and expanded by Lyn Malone.

Savannah

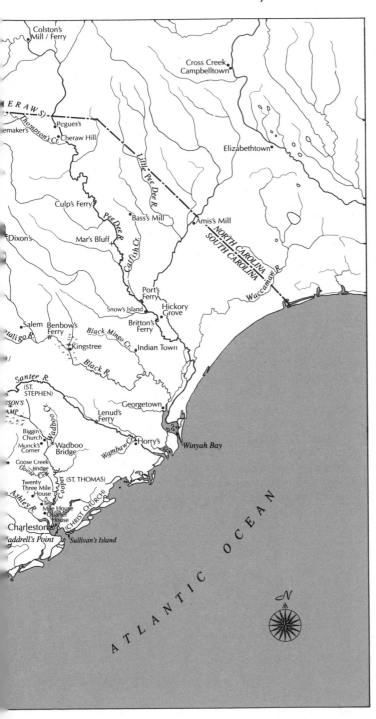

Colston's
Mill / Ferry

Cross Creek•
Campbelltown

(E R A W S) Thompson's Cr. •Pegues's
emaker's •Cheraw Hill
•Dixon's

Elizabethtown•

Culp's Ferry
Pee Dee R.
•Bass's Mill
Mar's Bluff
Catfish Cr.
Little Pee Dee R.
•Amis's Mill
NORTH CAROLINA
SOUTH CAROLINA
Waccamaw R.

Port's
Ferry
Snow's Island •Hickory
Grove
•Salem Benbow's Britton's
Ferry Ferry
uali go R. Black Mingo Cr.
•Kingstree •Indian Town
Black R.

Santee R.
(ST.
STEPHEN)
SON'S
MP
Georgetown•
Lenud's
Ferry
Biggin's
Church
Monck's• Wadboo
Corner Bridge Wambaw Cr. •Horry's Winyah Bay
Goose Creek
Bridge
Goose Cr.
Twenty (ST. THOMAS)
Three Mile
House Cooper R.
Ten
Ashley R. Mile House
Quarter
House (CHRIST CHURCH)
Charleston•
addrell's Point Sullivan's Island

ATLANTIC OCEAN

N

successful in that quarter, that the people may gather strength and confidence. The distress and suffering of many of the poor Inhabitants exceeds all description.

My soul embraces you and I hope before many Months we shall meet and enjoy that happiness which we have so long enjoyed since our connection. God bless you and preserve your health until our meeting. Yours aff

AL (MiU-C).
1. NG's letter to Catharine on the American defeat at the battle of Hobkirk's Hill has not been found. On the battle, see NG to Huntington, 27 April, above; the evacuation of Camden is discussed at Pendleton to Sumter, 10 May, above.
2. On the capture of Orangeburg, Ft. Motte, and Ft. Granby (the post at Friday's Ferry), see Sumter to NG, 11 May, above; NG to Huntington, 14 May, above; Lee to NG, this date, below.
3. The British had two posts in the area of Wadboo Creek: one at Monck's Corner and a smaller one at Biggin Church, about three miles away. As NG anticipated, the British did evacuate the post at Nelson's Ferry. (See Marion to NG, 16 May, below.)
4. On the capture of Halifax, N.C., by Cornwallis's troops, see Malmedy to NG, 11 May, above. Phillips's operations in Virginia are discussed at Steuben to NG, 25 April, and the Marquis de Lafayette's two letters to NG of 3 May, all above.
5. NG did not go to Virginia.

*   *   *

¶ [FROM THE CHEVALIER DE LA LUZERNE, Philadelphia, 15 May 1781. Asks NG's help for two French officers "in the American service," who are imprisoned at Charleston, S.C., and have been reduced to a "dire plight." NG should request that they be paroled to Philadelphia, and "If a few sentiments of humainity remain in our enemies," they must allow it. Hopes NG got La Luzerne's letter of "April the 2nd," with its "sincere compliments on the useful and glorious campaign of this winter," which has earned NG "the esteem and the confidence of your fellow citizens and that of your allies."[1] Expects news from Europe "any moment" about "arrangements" being made in France "for the support of the common cause." Will immediately send it to NG. "Meanwhile, rest assured that His Majesty [Louis XVI] will find his troops put to a good use, in cooperating with a general who was able to accomplish such great things with such small means."[2] Asks NG to forward some letters. LS (MiU-C) 2 pp. Translated into English by Eric Deudon.]
1. La Luzerne's letter, dated 3 April, is above. The "sincere compliments" were presumably those contained in La Luzerne's letter of 10 February, above (vol. 7: 274).
2. On the hoped-for assistance from France, see note at La Luzerne to NG, 3 April, above.

*   *   *

From Colonel Henry Lee, Jr.

Sr   Fort Granby [S.C.] 15ʰ May [17]81
I have the honor to communicate to you the surrender of Fort Granby, & I enclose a copy of the Capitulation.[1] Col Taylor whom I found here with a corps of Militia left by Genˡ Sumpter to annoy &

Henry Lee, Jr., 1756–1818; oil painting by Charles Willson Peale
(Independence National Historical Park Collection)

harrass the garrison had most vigorously & judiciously exerted himself, & has claim to particular attention.[2]

The troops und^r my command after a rapid march from the post at
Mottes reached this place on the evening of the 14^h.[3] The enemy^s
position was reconnoitred, labourers collected, & the line of approaches determined on. During the night a battery was thrown up in
point blank shot of the fort under direction of L^t [James] Heard &
Cornet Lovel [James Lovell] assisted by party^s from Co^l Taylor^s Militia.

Early in the morning of the 15ʰ Cap: [Ebenezer] Finley commenced a cannonade, at the same time the Legion Infantry & Capᵗ Oldhams detachment took a position of support.[4]

Matters being thus arranged, agreable to my instructions I sent the summons which I have the honor to transmit & received the answer annexed.[5]

A few moments after, an interview took place between myself & Major [Andrew] Maxwell & the business was thrown into a train of adjustment.[6]

It is needless for me to say any thing concerning the efforts of the officers & the toil of the troops who have served with me during the late expedition. Your perfect knowledge of every intention, & every exertion of the corps, & your invariable disposition to countenance merit, fully ensure to them every reward they may deserve.

The heads of departments will give in returns of stores, & a list of prisoners will be transmitted to Major [Edmund] Hyrne the Comʸ Genl [i.e., commissary general of prisoners] as soon as it can be made out.[7] I have the honor to be sir with the most exalted sentiments of respect & esteem your most ob ser   HENRY LEE JUN

ALS (MiU-C).

1. A copy of the articles of capitulation is in PCC, item 155, vol. 2: 79, DNA.

2. Gen. Thomas Sumter, who had begun the siege of Ft. Granby, had left a party there under Col. Thomas Taylor to intercept supplies and keep up the siege while Sumter went on to Ft. Motte, where he expected to use the field piece that NG was sending. (Gregorie, *Sumter*, p. 157; see also note at Sumter to NG, 11 May, above; and Sumter to NG, second letter of 4 May and both letters of 6 May, all above.) From Motte's, Sumter went on to invest the post at Orangeburg, the capitulation of which he announced in his letter to NG of 11 May, above.

3. Following the capture of Ft. Motte, NG had ordered Lee on 13 May, above, to march to Ft. Granby and push "matters vigorously" to secure the immediate surrender of that post.

4. On Capt. Edward Oldham's detachment, see NG's Orders of this date, above.

5. Neither the summons nor Maxwell's answer has been found; for the instructions under which Lee was operating, see NG to Lee, 13 May, above.

6. In his memoirs, Lee said he knew Maxwell to have been more fond of plunder than of "military laurels" and to have gathered a considerable "spoil" in the fort. "Solicitous to hasten" the surrender of the garrison, Lee agreed to let him and his men keep their stolen property. Maxwell was given the use of two covered wagons, free from search, to carry his own baggage. Under the terms of the capitulation, Lee also permitted the garrison of some 360 men, mostly Loyalists, to march to Charleston as prisoners of war, under the protection of an armed escort. (Lee, *Memoirs*, 2: 82–85) Sumter, who had expected to take the fort "at his leisure," was incensed at this outcome, as were many of the militiamen who had taken part in the siege. (Gregorie, *Sumter*, pp. 159–60) Some of the latter reportedly "indicated an inclination for breaking the capitulation, and killing the prisoners." According to the contemporary historian William Gordon, they were only kept from doing so by NG's declaration "that he would put to death any one that should be guilty of so doing." (Gordon, *History*, 4: 90; although no document has been found to indicate that NG made such a statement, Gordon obtained much of his

A Sketch of the Works at Fort Granby
(National Archives)

information about the Southern campaign from Otho Williams, who could have been an eyewitness.) Sumter, who had sought Lee's recall from Ft. Granby in a letter of 14 May, above, was not satisfied at the explanation that NG offered in reply and submitted his resignation. (Sumter discussed NG's reply, which has not been found, on 16 May, below, when he offered to resign.)

Some historians have questioned Lee's motives and have blamed him for unnecessarily hurrying the negotiations and allowing Maxwell to surrender on terms that were far too liberal. (Johnson, *Greene*, 2: 122–23; McCrady, *S.C. in the Revolution*, pp. 242–46) Lee, however, claimed that it had been necessary to conclude the operation quickly because he had received word that Lord Rawdon was marching to lift the siege. (Lee, *Memoirs*, 2: 85; on Rawdon's attempt to relieve the post, see note at Sumter to NG, this date, below.) One historian, citing a maxim of Napoleon's that " 'the keys of a fortress are well worth the freedom of the garrison,' " has credited Lee with using "good sense in handling this situation," in which neither side suffered any casualties. (Boatner, *Encyc.*, p. 377) Despite the loss of plundered property, the Americans did gain control of a quantity of public stores, "consisting chiefly of ammunition, salt, and liquor." (Lee, *Memoirs*, 2: 85) NG reached Ft. Granby shortly after its capitulation. According to Lee, he was "delighted with the happy termination," especially "when he saw the strength of the fort." (Ibid., p. 86)

7. A copy of Hyrne's return of prisoners, dated 15 May, is in PCC, item 155, vol. 2: 83, DNA.

*   *   *

¶ **[FROM CAPTAIN JOHN MEDEARIS**,[1] [Wake County, N.C.], 15 May 1781. Upon seeing a letter to Col. [Nicholas] Long, he "made free" to send NG "a few Wayfers Blackball & Pomatum tho Doubt the Goodness of the Latter."[2] Adds in a postscript that he has received "the Stores" from Philadelphia, which he will send "by the Earliest opertunity," together with a barrel of cheese and ten hogsheads of rum. ALS (MiU-C) 1 p.]

1. Medearis was an assistant deputy quartermaster, stationed in Wake County, N.C. (*NCSR*, 15: 450)

2. Blackball, "also called *heel-ball*," was made of hard wax and lamp-black and was used to polish boots and shoes. (*OED*) Pomatum was an ointment used to soften skin. (Johnson, *Dictionary*; *OED*)

¶ **[FROM COLONEL THOMAS POLK**, Salisbury, N.C., 15 May 1781. By an express from Gov. [Abner] Nash that arrived on this date, the command has been given to Col. [Francis] Lock; Polk's orders "Will be no more obaid."[1] He has gone to "all the Countys but those over the mountans[,] Surry & Gilford"; the men, arms, and accoutrements "Will be Nearly Redy in about eight days.[2] The amounition in the Waggons at this Place must [furnish?] the men."[3] Tells NG: "Any thing in My Power is at your Call." ALS (MiU-C) 1 p.]

1. Lock had been named to the command of the Salisbury militia district, which NG had solicited for Polk. (See NG to Polk, 3, 14, and 28 April; NG to Nash, 3 April, all above.) NG replied to Polk on 11 June, below.

2. For more on Polk's efforts to raise and equip draftees, see his letter to NG of 9 May, above.

3. Col. James Read, writing NG from Salisbury on 17 May, below, enclosed an invoice for ten wagonloads of ammunition.

¶ **[FROM COLONEL JAMES READ**, Salisbury, N.C., 15 May 1781. Has NG's letter of 9 May. Reports that there are about eighty North Carolina draftees and

300 Virginia militia "at this place." He "cannot hear where Genl Lawson is."[1] It will be "impossible to get the Arms repaired" if he relies on these troops, so he has employed the four gunsmiths in town to do the work. Has also "made aplication to Col^l Lock," who has promised to send all the armorers he can find "in this neighbourhood."[2] Read has sent to Guilford County for "three hundred Stand of Arms" that were left there. There will not be enough cartridge boxes, but [Col. Thomas] Polk has furnished "fifty Sides of Leather" to have some made. Read thinks more leather can be obtained if necessary; asks NG for instructions. He has been accidentally wounded in his right hand and is obliged to write with his left. ALS (MiU-C) 2 pp.]

1. As noted at Lawson to NG, 20 April, above, Gen. Robert Lawson, who was to have brought a force of Virginia militia to the army, remained in Virginia.

2. As seen in Polk to NG, immediately above, Col. Francis Lock was the new commander of the Salisbury militia district.

¶ [FROM BARON STEUBEN, "Carters Ferry on James River," Va., 15 May 1781. "It is long since" he heard from NG, who has reportedly "given Lord Rawdon a lesson"; asks for "particulars."[1] The Marquis [de Lafayette] will inform NG of military operations. Hopes Lafayette's "exploits may be more brilliant" than his own have been, for Steuben has "not yet learnt how to beat regular troops with one third their number of Militia." He could do no more than save the military stores; "if the Magazines at Prince Edward Court House have not fallen into the Enemys hands," he believes that "every thing is saved, except some provisions."[2] Since Lafayette's arrival, Steuben has turned his attention to raising and equipping the recruits. Only 430 have assembled at the Albemarle barracks, and they are "Unarmed, Unequip'd & without Cloaths"; Steuben does not "expect above 400 more." Counties are not required to "Draft their Levies" as long as they have militia in the field, so "near two thirds of the State will not furnish any Recruits" while "the Enemy continues here."[3] If Steuben is able to obtain 1,000 draftees, "it will be the utmost." His efforts to keep and equip the "few" recruits has drawn "the Censure of many of the great Men here," who say these troops should be sent into the field to "releive" an equal number of militia. "Other wise ones ridicule the distance from the Enemy to which I have sent them, whilst their respective Plantations are exposed."

He regrets that desertion among the recruits "equals that" of the Virginians with the Southern Army. NG's "observation that the Men should be more particularly appropriated to their Officers" has led Steuben to adopt an arrangement, a copy of which he encloses.[4] The captivity of a number of officers and the absence of thirty-five others, "whom two Proclamations have not been sufficient to assemble, prevents any other formation of Regiments."[5] Discusses his plan to fill two regiments. NG has mentioned "the great want of Officers" for the Virginia troops serving with NG's army; Steuben encloses a list "of those who have on various pretenses returnd to Virginia" and then "scatterd" so that "there is no possibility" of assembling them. Adds: "In a word my Dr General I despair of ever seeing a Virginia Line exist." No sooner can he get a few officers and men collected than he begins to hear of "nothing but of furlows for the Officers & of the desertion of the Men." Of the few recruits who have been formed into a regiment under Col. [Thomas] Gaskins, "about 150" are armed. They will be sent shortly to "the Fork of the River," where they can protect the magazines and "at the same time be Disciplined & Equipped." He will also send officers to Albemarle Barracks to collect the recruits there and equip and send them to "the Forks."[6] After he completes these arrangements, Steuben will join and remain with Lafayette until he receives orders from NG. Says: "I must give you notice that from the many difficulties which daily occur & of which I have mentioned only a small part, my presence in this State has become entirely useless." He will "fly" to NG's "immediate command" with "great pleasure" and beseeches NG to summon him "as soon as possible for never was man more disgusted than I am at the Conduct & proceedings in this Quarter."[7] Officers of the "two Regiments of Cavalry" are there "to receive Horses, Arms & other Equipment," but Steuben has no idea how horses are to be acquired. A law enacted by the last Assembly fixes the price of horses at £5,000. "The most indifferent" ones "are now three times that price," so "there is not the least prospect of compleating the Cavalry."[8] Asks NG to "write Government on this subject." LS (Greene Papers: DLC) 5 pp.]

1. Steuben referred to the battle of Hobkirk's Hill, which is discussed at NG to Huntington, 27 April, above. NG had written Steuben an account of the battle on the same day, above, which Steuben acknowledged in his letter of 18 May, below.

2. On Steuben's "exploits" and his efforts to save the army's stores from the enemy, see Steuben to NG, 25 April, above.

3. The law regulating the draft is discussed at Jefferson to NG, 16 January, above (vol. 7: 135n).

4. The enclosure has not been found. For more on the arrangement of the Virginia line and on the problems of discipline that had resulted from the troops not being "more particularly appropriated to their Officers," see NG to Davies, 3 April, above.

5. Steuben enclosed a list, dated 14 May, of Virginia officers who were absent and unassigned. (Steuben Microfilm)

6. Steuben further described his efforts to organize and equip the recruits in letters to NG of 18 and 26 May, both below.

7. Some of the reasons that Steuben's presence in Virginia had become "useless" can be inferred from remarks of Richard Claiborne in his letter to NG of 2 May, above. Writing to NG of 9 June, below, Steuben again asked for orders to join the army.

8. For more on the cavalry regiments and the law for procuring horses, see notes at Jefferson to NG, 24 March, above (vol. 7: 467n).

¶ [FROM GENERAL JETHRO SUMNER, Williamsboro, Granville County, N.C., 15 May 1781. Has NG's letter of 5 May. A letter from the Marquis de Lafayette to Gen. [Allen] Jones gives Sumner little hope of acquiring arms from Virginia. That is because of the incursions there of Gen. [William] Phillips, who is now reported to be marching toward Halifax, N.C., for a junction with Lord Cornwallis, who is still at Halifax. The "rear" of Cornwallis's army arrived there on 12 May.[1] Cornwallis's cavalry and "a large part of the Infantry" crossed the Roanoke River on Sunday [13 May] and is building "works" on the north side.[2] The enemy are said to number between 1,600 and 1,800 men, including 240 to 400 "badly mounted" horsemen.[3] "The Inhabitants" have gone to the British "for protection very fast."[4] Boats on the river have reportedly either been destroyed or taken to Taylor's Ferry.[5] The stores from Halifax and Kingston have been moved to Prince Edward County, Va. Sumner has not seen Col. [Nicholas] Long since the capture of Halifax, so he does not know what was captured or destroyed there "for want of Carriages."[6] Is mortified "at this alarm'g season" to report the strength of his command, which is at "Low Ebb."[7] Hopes soon to have a "more Considerable force, should armes be had." ALS (NNC) 2 pp.]

1. For more on Sumner's unsuccessful efforts to obtain arms from Virginia for the use of North Carolina recruits, see his letter to NG of 1 May, above. Phillips's incursions are reported in Steuben to NG, 25 April, and in Lafayette's two letters of 3 May, all above. Under orders from Gen. Benedict Arnold, who had succeeded the dying Phillips as commander in Virginia, Col. John G. Simcoe had led a detachment to "facilitate" Lord Cornwallis's "passage" into Virginia from North Carolina. (Simcoe, *Military Journal*, pp. 118–20) Simcoe's corps made contact with part of Cornwallis's force near Halifax, N.C., on 15 May and escorted Cornwallis's troops to their junction with Phillips's army at Petersburg, Va., on 20 May. ("Von Bose Journal," pp. 57–58)

2. The "works" protected the boats that transported the British army across the river. (Tarleton, *Campaigns*, p. 289)

3. According to a return of 1 May, Cornwallis had taken a total of 1,435 men with him from Wilmington. (Stevens, *Clinton-Cornwallis Controversy*, 1: 457)

4. By "protection," Sumner meant a parole that left them prisoners and unable to bear arms against the British.

5. According to Col. Banastre Tarleton, the Americans had "damaged or scuttled the batteaux within their power, which were, however, soon repaired by the carpenters of [Halifax] and the pioneers of the army." (Tarleton, *Campaigns*, p. 289)

6. British forces "seized extensive stores of rum, whiskey, bacon and maize" at Halifax and "burnt a quantity of tobacco." ("Von Bose Journal," pp. 57–57a) The Marquis de Malmedy had written NG on 11 May, above, that most of the Americans' "warlike stores" were also captured.

7. Sumner's return has not been found.

*　　*　　*

From General Thomas Sumter

D[r] Sir   Orangeburgh [S.C.] 3 oclock 15 May 1781

I have Just Received accounts that Lord Rawden is Moving upwards from Neilsons Ferry, that at 7 oclock in the evening he was below Co[l] Thompsons about 20 Miles.[1] This account I have no Doubt you have Received before now. I had Several men Reconitering that way. They have Not been as attentive as I Coud have wished. Gen[l] Marion was in the evening Near to the place Where Rawden was last Seen. Which way he [i.e., Marion] has Gone I Know not.[2] I have Repeedly Mentioned to him the Necessity of a Good Lookout towards the ferry, as I expected that Rawden Woud Move as he has if he Meet with No Interruption at the ferry. I allways thought it unfortunate, to send Gen[l] Marion & Co[l] Lee So high up the River after passing it So Near to Neilsons Ferry, a passuage of So Much Consequence and So much in their power.[3] I am Just Going for the Congaree Were [i.e., where] I Will act for the best as far as I am Capaple.[4] I think Rawden may be Stoped before he Gets there if Gen[l] Marion has Gone upwards. I am D[r] S[r] Your Most obd[t] H[le] Servt   THO[s] SUMTER

ALS (MiU-C).

1. Rawdon had marched to Nelson's Ferry following his evacuation of Camden on 10 May. He arrived there late on the 13th and was reinforced by 300 infantry and eighty dragoons. Judging himself to be strong enough to "check" American operations in the Congarees, he marched the next evening toward Ft. Granby, where he hoped to rescue the besieged garrison. (Rawdon to Cornwallis, 24 May; Balfour to Cornwallis, 21 May, both in PRO 30/11/6) Rawdon had not proceeded far when he received intelligence— which later proved to be false—that NG's army was heading toward the low country and Charleston by way of Orangeburg. He immediately reversed direction, moving all the way back to Monck's Corner, where he established a camp. (Rawdon to Cornwallis, 24 May, PRO 30/11/6)

2. For Gen. Francis Marion's whereabouts, see his letter to NG of 16 May, below.

3. In his letter to NG of 12 May, above, Sumter had recommended a "Move towards Santee, and endeavour to Alarm Lord Rawden to prevent his Crossing the River." After capturing Ft. Watson, which was near Nelson's Ferry, Marion and Col. Henry Lee had moved up the Santee and successfully besieged the British post at Motte's. (See NG to Huntington, 14 May, above.)

4. Sumter did not know that Lee had already negotiated the surrender of Ft. Granby, at the "Congaree." (See Lee to NG, this date, above.) In his letter to NG of 14 May, above, Sumter had objected to Lee's presence there; on 16 May, below, after learning of Lee's success, he submitted his resignation to NG.

*   *   *

¶ **[FROM COLONEL THOMAS POLK**, [Salisbury, N.C., about 15 May 1781][1] Ninety "new drafts" and about 300 Virginia militia are "readey to March."[2] The enemy's "last movement," however, makes it difficult to know which direction to send them, especially as Lord Cornwallis is reportedly at Halifax. Polk thinks it "advisable" to hold them "in readyness to march at a minuts warning when they receive" orders from NG.[3] They have had no recent orders from Gen. [Jethro] Sumner. Polk also awaits NG's instructions for ten wagon-loads of clothing and ten more of ammunition, which had been ordered "to this place" on their way to Oliphant's Mill.[4] There are only three Continental officers "of this State" at Salisbury, and it appears "the duty will be neglected" unless Sumner sends more. In a postscript adds that Col. "Jams Reed [James Read]" has injured his hand and is unable to write.[5] ALS (MiU-C) 1 p.]

1. The place was taken from the contents, which also suggest that this letter is of about the same date as James Read to NG, 15 May, above.

2. For more on the "new drafts" and the Virginia militia at Salisbury, see Read to NG, 15 May.

3. NG sent Lewis Morris to Salisbury to direct the draftees and militiamen to the Southern Army. (See NG to Morris, 21 May, below.)

4. On the ammunition, see also Read to NG, 17 May, below. Nathaniel Pendleton sent Read NG's orders concerning the stores on 23 May, below.

5. See Read to NG, 15 May, above.

¶ **[GENERAL GREENE'S ORDERS**. From "Camp Andersons Ferry," S.C., 16 May 1781. A court-martial is to "Sit Tomorrow" to try deserters.[1] Lamar Orderly Book (OClWHi) 1 p.]

1. The results of the trials are given in NG's Orders of 18 May, below.

¶ [TO THE BOARD OF WAR. From "Camp at Ancrums Plantation," S.C., 16 May 1781. Has received the board's letter of 20 April [not found] and is pained to learn that prospects "are so unpromising." Adds: "Under these difficulties I am peculiarly indebted to the board for the attention paid to the southern department." The shipment of clothing has reached "the banks of the Catawba."[1] As the "hot season is coming on," NG will store the 1,700 coats until fall and "dress the troops in Hunting Shirts." His army is "distressed for want of Shoes." The board's willingness to provide "every aid in their power" to make NG's command "honorable and agreeable" deserves NG's "warmest acknowledgements." The war in the South is carried on "under so many disadvantages," however, that "it is next to impossible to render it either honorable or comfortable." Refers the board to his public letters to Congress for an account of military operations. ADfS (MiU-C) 2 pp.]

1. As seen in Polk to NG, about 15 May, above, the clothing was at Salisbury, N.C.

¶ [TO SAMUEL HUNTINGTON, PRESIDENT OF THE CONTINENTAL CONGRESS. From "Camp at Ancram's Plantation," S.C., 16 May 1781. He wrote Huntington "on the 13th" that the army would move "for this Post" the next day, following Col. [Henry] Lee and the "Van."[1] The army arrived "here yesterday about noon," a few minutes after the garrison had surrendered to Lee. Encloses the surrender terms and a return of prisoners and stores taken.[2] LS (PCC, item 155, vol. 2: 71, DNA) 1 p.]

1. The letter to Huntington, dated 14 May, is above.

2. On the surrender of Ft. Granby, see Lee to NG, 15 May, above.

¶ [TO THE MARQUIS DE LAFAYETTE. From "Camp at Ancroms on the Congaree," S.C., 16 May 1781. Reports the surrender of Ft. Granby and its garrison of 300 men—"part British[,] part state regulars and part Militia in the enemies service." Has no time to give details, which can be found in NG's "letters to Congress."[1] Col. [Henry] Lee is marching to Augusta, Ga., as the "Advance" of the army.[2] The rest of NG's troops will march "this afternoon" for Ninety Six. Both posts must fall "unless fortune should play the gilt again."[3] In a postscript, asks Lafayette to inform Gov. [Thomas] Jefferson of "what is going on" and to apologize for NG's not having written; NG "really" has no time to write "without neglecting matters" that claim his "immediate attention." ALS (RHi) 2 pp.]

1. See NG to Huntington, this date, above. The surrender of Ft. Granby is discussed in Lee to NG, 15 May, above.

2. NG's orders to Lee are in the letter immediately below.

3. A "gilt" was a thief or burglar. (OED)

*   *   *

To Colonel Henry Lee, Jr.

Dear Sir   Camp at Ancroms Plantation [S.C.] May 16th 1781
   You will march immediately for Augusta [Ga.] as the advance of the Army which will move by the way of Ninty Six [S.C.] and demand the Surrender of those posts. General [Andrew] Pickens is at that place. You will report your arrival to him and cooperate with him until the army arrives. Inform the commanding officer of the evacuation[,] surrenders and reduction of the posts in this quarter; and that if they refuse to surrender the posts they must abide the consequences. Perform the March as soon as you can without injury to your troops, and make vigorous exertions for the reduction of those posts after your arrival. Should the posts surrender you will take special care that none of the Stores are plunder'd; and make report of all occurrences on the march and after your arrival necessary for me to be informed of.[1]
   Given at Camp at Ancroms Plantation May 16th 1781. NATH GREENE

ACyS (NcD).
   1. See Lee to NG, 22 May, below.

To General Andrew Pickens

                    Camp at Ancrums Plantation on the Congaree [S.C.]
Dear General   May 16th 1781
   I have had the pleasure of your two letters, the first by Col [John] Purvis the last by Capt [James?] Carter.[1] I thank you for the measures you have taken to prevent the escape of the Garrisons of Ninty Six and Augusta. Lt Col [Henry] Lee is on his march as our advance for Augusta and the Army for Ninty Six.[2] If these posts are not evacuated before our Arrival I am in hopes they will both fall. Should they surrender great care should be taken to preserve the Stores for the use of the Army and such Militia as will enrole themselves to serve a limited time not less than four Months. Inform Col [Elijah] Clarke that a great variety of articles are coming from Philadelphia for the use of the Georgia Militia; and I imagine none but those that are engagd for a given time are to be considerd as proper subjects to pertake of the distribution; however I suppose the Delegates from that State have given some particular directions in this business.[3]
   The post at this place surrenderd yesterday; and the Garrison amounted to upwards 300 men regulars and irregulars.[4] The reduction of Fort Motte, and surrender of Orangburge you will have heard of.[5] Lt Col Lee will be with you in about five days and will bring with him a field piece. With esteem & regard I am dear General Your Most Obed[t] humble S[r]   N GREENE

(NcD).

1. See Pickens to NG, 8 and 12 May, both above.

2. NG's orders to Lee are immediately above.

3. See Walton to NG, 5 April, above; no instructions from the delegates have been found.

4. On the surrender of Ft. Granby, see Lee to NG, 15 May, above.

5. On the capture of Ft. Motte, see NG to Huntington, 14 May, above. Gen. Thomas Sumter reported the capture of the post at Orangeburg in his letter to NG of 11 May, above.

*   *   *

¶ [TO GEORGE WASHINGTON. From "Camp at Ancrams Plantation on the Congarees," S.C., 16 May 1781. Reports the surrender of Ft. Granby.[1] As NG is "anxious to push for Ninety Six," he refers Washington to his letter to Congress for details.[2] Says: "I am in distress and our Affairs are in the most critical situation the cause I will explain hereafter."[3] Lord Cornwallis is moving northward. "I hope to God our affairs may not be reduced to extremity in Virginia." LS (Washington Papers: DLC) 1 p.]

1. See Lee to NG, 15 May, above.

2. See NG to Huntington, this date, above.

3. NG's "distress" may have been due to the situation in Virginia, which he mentioned in the following sentences.

¶ [FROM COLONEL HENRY LEE, JR. [Ft. Granby, S.C.], 16 May 1781.[1] Thinking that his troops may encounter a detachment from Lord Rawdon or Ninety Six on the way to Augusta, Ga., he asks that Capt. [Edward] Oldham be assigned to his command.[2] Wants to know NG's route so as to be able to respond to any "disaster." Assumes that NG will be in a position to "intercept" the garrison from Ninety Six if it tries to move toward Augusta. Adds after his signature that he thinks Maj. [Edmund M.] Hyrne should get a written declaration from Maj. [Andrew] Maxwell that the surrender agreement has not been violated, "otherwise litigation may hereafter ensue."[3] Lee also advises NG to write Rawdon about the prisoners taken at Ft. Watson, "ordering them out or exchanged."[4] Thinks "the violation of the capitulation on our part by plunderers" will give "full reason for violation" on the part of the enemy.[5] ALS (MiU-C) 2 pp.]

1. Lee did not give his location, but as seen in his letter to NG of 22 May, below, he was still at Ft. Granby on this date.

2. NG did not reassign Edward Oldham's company of Marylanders to Lee's detachment. (Johnson, *Greene*, 2: 126)

3. On the articles of capitulation signed by Andrew Maxwell, the British commander of Ft. Granby, see Lee to NG, 15 May, above. If Hyrne, NG's commissary of prisoners, obtained such a declaration, it has not been found.

4. NG apparently did not write Rawdon about the paroled garrison of Ft. Watson. Rawdon, however, wrote Lee on 14 May that he would investigate an allegation that prisoners taken there had not strictly "adhered to the terms of capitulation." (Gibbes, *Documentary History*, 3: 70)

5. Nothing more is known about Lee's reference to the plundering of prisoners. Levi Smith, a Loyalist officer who was captured at Ft. Motte, claimed that Lee himself violated the articles of surrender by having several Loyalist prisoners hanged without a

trial. According to Smith's account, the executions stopped only after Gen. Francis Marion personally intervened and countermanded Lee's orders. (Levi Smith's narrative, *Royal Gazette* [Charleston], 13–17 April 1782)

¶ [**FROM GENERAL FRANCIS MARION**, Ferguson's Swamp, S.C., 16 May 1781, 3 P.M. Reports that Lord Rawdon blew up the fort at Nelson's Ferry "yesterday" and has gone to Monck's Corner. Marion hopes to intercept Rawdon's baggage, which was sent by a different route.[1] Adds: "Rawden seems in Great fright."[2] Marion has ordered Col. [William] Harden to join him.[3] Encloses two captured letters.[4] ALS (MiU-C) 1 p.]

1. As seen in his letter of 19 May, below, Marion had only limited success in his attempt to capture the stores belonging to Rawdon's army.

2. As noted at Sumter to NG, 15 May, above, Rawdon had received false intelligence that NG's army was moving into the Carolina low country, where it would be in a position to threaten Charleston. Concern for the safety of the principal British post in South Carolina was probably what caused Rawdon to move as if he were "in Great fright."

3. Harden, who commanded the militia in the area south of Charleston, apparently did not join Marion but went to join the forces besieging the British post at Augusta, Ga. (See Pickens to NG, first letter of 25 May, below.)

4. The enclosures have not been found.

*   *   *

From General Thomas Sumter

Dr Sir   Capt Authers [Arthur's, S.C.] 16th May 1781
I have been Honoured With your Letter of Yesterdays Date.[1]

I am Convinced your Reasons are Cogent & your observations exeedingly Just, & it has ever been the first Wish of my heart to promote & facillitate the publick service.

But with the deepest Regret find the discontent & disorder among the Militia So Great as to leave No hope of their Subsiding Soon.

My Indisposition & Want of Capacity, to be of Service to this Country Induces me as a friend to it to beg leave to Resign My Command, and have taken the Liberty to enclose My Commission Which I hope you will Receive, as I find my inabillity So Great that I Cant without doing the Greatest Injustice to the publick think of Serving any Longer.[2] I have the Honour to be Dr Sir, with the Greatest Respect Your most obedt Hble Servt   THO^S SUMTER

ALS (MiU-C).

1. NG's letter has not been found.

2. For background on Sumter's decision to tender his resignation, see notes at Lee to NG, 15 May, above. NG's reply is in his first letter to Sumter of 17 May, below.

*   *   *

¶ [**GENERAL GREENE'S ORDERS**, "Camp Andersons Ferry," S.C., Thursday, 17 May 1781. The troops are to receive two days' provisions and a half jill of spirits per man; the officers are to have a quart of spirits each. The army will march "by the Right" at 5 A.M. Lamar Orderly Book (OClWHi) 2 pp.]

*   *   *

To Jacob Greene[1]

Camp at Ancrums Plantation on the Congarees
My Dear Sir   South Carolina May 17th 1781

Not a Line have I rec^d from you or one of my [Conversers?] in Rhode Island since I came to the Southward. I hope you have not forgot Me. A Line of Remembran[ce] woud be agreeable and I should be happy to hear how my Friends are and the State of our private concern [shaped?] at this Time.

Mrs Greene wrote me that she intends to set out for this Country in April. I hope she has not as it is impossible for her to come into this Country and she may as well be at home as to be Four or Five Hundred miles from me.[2]

How is my Friend Griffin and his Family?[3] Remember me affectionately to them and all my Brothers and their Families, to your Family and Mother Greene and all other of my Friends in the County.[4]

For the Military Operations in this Quarter I must beg leave to refer you to the Public Prints.[5] Keep up a good Heart and all things will end well as to the Final Establishment of the Independence of the United States. But there will be a great Deal of Distress and much Blood Spilld first. Yours aff^y   N GREENE

Tr (Foster Transcripts: RHi).
1. The recipient was not given, but the contents indicate that it was NG's brother Jacob, as does the fact that all of NG's letters in the Foster Transcripts are to him.
2. Catharine Greene did not leave for the South until December 1781.
3. "Griffin" was NG's cousin and close friend, Griffin Greene.
4. "Mother Greene" was NG's stepmother, Mary Collins Greene.
5. NG's official letters to Congress were printed in newspapers, the "Public Prints." (See, for example, NG's letter of 16 March to Congress, *Providence Gazette and Country Journal*, 21 April.)

*   *   *

¶ [MAJOR ICHABOD BURNET TO GENERAL ROBERT LAWSON. [From Ft. Granby, S.C.], 17 May 1781. NG has directed Burnet to inform Lawson of the "reduction" of the posts at Ft. Motte, Orangeburg, and "this place." Adds: "Six pieces of Iron Ordinance[,] 10 british Officers[,] 205 privates[,] 22 tory Officers & 375 Tories" have been captured. NG is moving to Ninety Six and wants Lawson to march his militia troops to Winnsboro and await orders. In a postscript, adds that Lawson should obtain provisions for his troops.[1] ALS (NcU) 1 p.]
1. As seen at Jefferson to NG, 30 March, and Lawson to NG, 20 April, both above, neither Lawson nor most of the expected reinforcement of Virginia militiamen marched to join NG.

*   *   *

To General Alexander McDougall

Dear Sir   Camp on the Congarees South Carolina May 17th 1781

I received your obliging letter of the 30th of January containing the political remarks upon the State of our affairs; and of your taking your seat in Congress.[1] I think you manoeuverd well to get admission without objection; and in my opinion you adopted the only mode by which it could be effected.[2]

My command here has been the most disagreeable that you can imagine, and you are pretty ingenious in raising difficulties if you give a latitude to invention. The Northern service is nothing at all; and depend upon it you have never seen any thing like war yet. I am sure I never did. The fate of the Southern States has been suspended by a slender thread. Fortune in two instances has been unpropitious.[3] Things here wear rather a better face; but no Country can be in a more critical situation than the Southern States is at this time. The success of General Philips [William Phillips] in Virginia, and the effect of Lord Cornwallises movements to the Northward I am a stranger to. We are at such distance from Virginia and the difficulty is so great in procuring intelligence that I am much in the dark as to the situation of things in that quarter.

We have many broken bones; spilt much blood and gained but little advantage. Disgrace and not glory has been our portion. But we bear it with patience in hopes of better times; and that just allowances will be made by the liberal for the difficulties we have to contend with.

I still wear Mrs McDougalls cockade, and have found great use for your knife. Yours affectionately   CATO[4]

ALS (NHi).

1. McDougall's letter has not been found.

2. On the controversy over McDougall taking a seat in Congress while retaining a military commission, see above (vol. 6: 447n).

3. NG referred to his army's defeats in the battles of Guilford Court House and Hobkirk's Hill.

4. "Cato" was the Roman statesman and opponent of Julius Caesar. In their correspondence, NG and McDougall sometimes used names from Greek and Roman history. (Johnson, *Greene*, 2: 394n; see also NG to McDougall, 30 October 1780, above [vol. 6: 447].)

To General Francis Marion

Dear Sir   Camp at Ancrums Plantation [S.C.] May 17th 1781

Upon consulting Gen[rl] Sumter respecting the mode of raising and paying the 10 months troops which he has been endeavoring to effect for some time past, I find he had mentioned the matter to me by Col Hampton, and that it originated with Governor [John] Rutledge in substance tho not in form.[1] But upon the whole I think it will have its advantages and I find that great care is taken not to apply any Negroe property but such as can admit of no dispute respecting their principles and intentions.[2] As Continental troops can not be had[,] this may be the best substitute which could be adopted. I wish you therefore to give it all the countenance you can until the Governors pleasure is further known in the matter or the State has it in its power to contribute to the support of the war upon a more permanent footing than the Militia service.[3] If we can gain our Country by this means the purchase will be small altho at a high rate upon the common calculation for military service. I am dear Sir your most Obedient humble Ser

NATH GREENE

ADfS (MiU-C).

1. On Gen. Thomas Sumter's plan to pay his ten-month troops with slaves confiscated from Loyalists, see Sumter to NG, 7 April, above. As seen in the notes there, NG did not give wholehearted support to Sumter's plan. According to Sumter's letter of that date, it was Capt. John Hampton who had acted as Sumter's intermediary.

2. NG meant that only the slaves of avowed Loyalists were to be taken.

3. Despite NG's instructions here, Marion refused to have anything to do with Sumter's plan. (Rankin, *Swamp Fox*, pp. 181, 220, 291)

To General Thomas Sumter

Dear Sir   Camp at Ancrams Plantation [S.C.] May 17th 1781

I take the liberty to return you your commission, which you forwarded me yesterday for my acceptance; & to inform you that I cannot think of accepting it, & to beg you to continue your command.[1]

I am sorry for your ill State of health; and shall do every thing in my power to render your command as convenient as the nature of the service will admit.

It is unnecessary for me to tell you how important your services are to the interest & happiness of this Country; and the confidence I have in your abilities ⟨and⟩ Zeal for the good of the service.[2] Your continuing in command will lay the public in general and me in particular, under a very great obligation; & tho it may be accompanied with many personal inconveniences, yet I hope you will have cause to rejoyce in the conclusion of the business from the consideration of having contributed so largely to the recovery of its Liberty.[3] With Esteem & respect I have the honour to be Dear Sir Your most Obedient Humble Servant

NATH GREENE

ALS (Sumter Papers: DLC).

1. See Sumter to NG, 16 May, above.

2. The aide who copied NG's draft (MiU-C) omitted the word "and," which the editors have included in angle brackets.

3. According to his early biographer, William Johnson, NG "ingeniously waves [i.e.,

waives] every discussion that could give pain" in this letter. (Johnson, *Greene*, 2: 124) It was not the only step that NG took to keep Sumter from resigning at this time. According to Johnson, he also "compelled" Col. Henry Lee, whose role in bringing about the surrender of Ft. Granby had precipitated Sumter's resignation, "to apologize to Sumter." (Ibid., p. 123; on the surrender, see Lee to NG, 15 May, above.) Moreover, in his orders to Sumter, immediately below, NG gave Sumter a share of the arms and stores captured at Granby and allowed him to use the Loyalists' slaves who had been taken at the post to compensate his newly raised regiments of state troops, or ten-month men.

To General Thomas Sumter

Camp at Ancrams Plantation on the Congaree [S.C.]

Sir   May 17th 1781

You will continue your command at this place, & form and encourage the militia in all parts of the State, in the best manner you can for co-operating with the American Army.[1] You will carefully watch the motions of the enemy below this place & advise me of all their movements, & should they come out in force towards Ninety Six, you will take such a Route as to effect a junction with us at that Place.

You will have the fortifications at this place leveled, & those of Motts and Orangeburg, if not already compleated, and also those of Camden.

We shall leave part of our spare Stores at this place; should the enemy make any movements this way or towards Ninety Six, you will give the officer having them in charge Orders to move up to Wyms Borough [i.e., Winnsboro] & as much higher up into the Country as you may think necessary.

Such of the negroes as were taken at this Garrison (as are not claimed by good Whiggs, & their property proved,) belonging to the Tories or disaffected you will apply to the fulfilling your contracts with the ten months Troops.[2] Such part of the Arms and stores, as the Commissary General of Military Stores, & the Quarter Master General shall deliver over to you, you will apply as justice & the good of the service shall require.

But above all things pay particular attention to the arranging the militia, as the safety of the Country in a great measure depends thereon.

You will direct General Marian to take such a position, & employ him in such manner as may most effectually anoy the enemy, & at the same time co-operate with us should occasion require it.[3]

Given at Camp at Ancrams Plantation on the Congaree May 17th 1781.   NATH GREENE

LS (Sumter Papers: DLC).

1. "This place" was Ft. Granby. In the letter immediately above, NG had rejected Sumter's offer to resign.

2. On the compensation for the ten-month men, see Sumter to NG, 7 April, above.

3. As seen in Sumter's letter to NG of 7 June, below, Gen. Francis Marion ignored Sumter's orders.

* * *

¶ [FROM COLONEL JAMES READ, Salisbury, N.C., 17 May 1781. He has halted twenty-two wagons carrying ammunition and clothing, as Col. [Edward] Carrington ordered; encloses an "Invoice of Ammunition in ten" of them.[1] Lord Cornwallis is reportedly "moveing about in Warren and Granville Counties" and is said to be heading toward either Prince Edward Court House, Va., or Salisbury, N.C. Read has written to Gen. [Jethro] Sumner, seeking further intelligence. Should Cornwallis move "this way and attempt to gain the upper Road," Read believes the stores at Salisbury should be sent "cross the Mountains."[2] He supposes that NG has issued "fresh Orders respecting this Post" as a result of Cornwallis's movements and the evacuation of Camden, S.C., "which Orders have not arrived."[3] ALS (MiU-C) 2 pp.]

1. For more on the supplies, see Compty to NG, 28 April, above.
2. Cornwallis was heading toward a junction with Gen. William Phillips's army at Petersburg, Va.
3. Nathaniel Pendleton replied for NG on 23 May, below.

¶ [GENERAL GREENE'S ORDERS, "Camp Broad River," S.C., Friday, 18 May 1781. Approves sentences of death for three deserters, who were serving with the enemy.[1] In After Orders, given at "Weavers Ferry, Saluda River," at 6 P.M., the army will march at 3 A.M. Lamar Orderly Book (OClWHi) 3 pp.]

1. The three deserters, "taken at Fort Granby," were executed on 19 May. ("Journal of Lt. Thomas Anderson," Force Transcripts, DLC)

¶ [MAJOR ICHABOD BURNET TO GENERAL FRANCIS MARION. From Congaree, S.C., 18 May 1781. At NG's direction, he informs Marion of the capture of Ft. Granby. NG's army will move toward Ninety Six "this morning." NG has ordered Gen. [Thomas] Sumter to take command at Ft. Granby and "organize" the militia. Marion should continue to harass the enemy, "receive" Sumter's orders, and "arrange" his militia "with expedition." He should also be ready to cooperate with NG's army. ADfS (MiU-C) 2 pp.]

¶ [CAPTAIN WILLIAM PIERCE, JR., TO GENERAL FRANCIS MARION. From [Weaver's Ferry, S.C.], 18 May 1781.[1] NG received Marion's letter of 16 May "this Evening"; thanks him for the intelligence and the intercepted letter. Marion should remain in the "lower Country" and collect intelligence. If the enemy advance "in force," he should join Gen. [Thomas] Sumter until NG orders otherwise.[2] NG's army is marching to Ninety Six; Col. [Henry] Lee has been sent to assist in the capture of Augusta, Ga. ADfS (MiU-C) 1 p.]

1. NG's location was taken from his after orders of this date, above.
2. As seen at NG to Marion, 25 June, below, Marion did not join Sumter when called upon to do so.

¶ [FROM THE MARQUIS DE LAFAYETTE, "Camp Wilton on James River," Va., 18 May 1781. If Lafayette's letters are less frequent than NG expects, he asks NG to take "Account for Accidents that May Befall them." Is anxious to inform NG of "Every transaction," as he serves under him more from "Inclination" than from duty and gains "particular Happiness" in knowing that NG is

"Satisfied" with his conduct. As NG ordered, Lafayette encloses copies of his "official Letters."[1] Considers a "Correspondence" with [Gen. Benedict] Arnold "So very Repugnant" that he cannot answer Arnold's letters. Arnold "is a Very proud Correspondent," and Lafayette cannot "Submit to Such a Stile from the Rascal." Lafayette assumes that "Every Continental Exchange is to Be Settled in one Arangement," but he solicits NG's "Opinion and orders" as to how he should conduct himself in the future.[2]

His last letters informed NG of the "preparations that Were Making" in Virginia.[3] The militia that had been ordered to join NG have been stopped; Lafayette does not think "it is possible to Maneuvre them down to" NG and thinks they "Will Be More Properly Employed in this quarter."[4] He has instructed Gen. [Jethro] Sumner to obtain NG's orders and, in the meantime, to collect the North Carolina levies in the rear of Lord Cornwallis's army, so that "Nothing May Impede their jonction" with NG. Gov. Abner Nash wrote Lafayette that he was sending a large body of North Carolina militia into Virginia. Lafayette agreed that the North Carolina militia from the Roanoke River area should remain "in front of Lord Cornwallis" but advised Nash that other troops should be sent to NG to replace the detained Virginia militia.[5] Lafayette is not certain that Cornwallis will "Come With His whole force." Should Cornwallis set up posts at Halifax, N.C., and Petersburg, Va., and attempt to establish another one "this Way," Lafayette's forces "may at Last Be upon a footing."[6] Whatever the case, it will be NG's "Success and offensive operations" that "Will Relieve the Southern States." NG, therefore, should have "Every possible Reinforcement." Such levies as "the Baron [Steuben] Can Collect Shall march Immediately"; those who are not ready will be sent later.[7] Steuben will also take with him 1,100 stand of arms that recently arrived from Philadelphia. If NG agrees, the North Carolina levies can join Steuben, who will then bring 1,200 "Continental well armed Soldiers" to NG. Lafayette will also send the Pennsylvania Continentals to NG unless they "are of an Immediate use." If he needs them to "either Strike at Arnold Alone, or Receive the Combined Blows of the two Armies," he will not keep them "More than a few days."[8] Adds that "Camden [S.C.] Must fall" unless Cornwallis returns southward; in either case, NG's "object will Be fulfilled."

Lafayette has no news from the "Northward" and no idea what will be determined "at Head Quarters." It appears that "all the troops and all the Blows will Be divided Betwen Virginia and South Carolina."[9] NG's "Late Engagement at Camden is like Every action You Risk—No ill Consequences in a defeat, the Ennemy's Ruin if Victorious.[10] I wish I Had Abilities, and I wish I Had Circumstances that Could Admit of Such opportunities, But With an Expectation of Support Both Continental and Militia, I dare not attak a Superior Ennemy on its own grounds. To Speak truth I Become timid in the Same proportion as I Become Independant. Had a Superior officer Been Here, I Could Have proposed Half a dozen of Schemes."

Has been forced to take time to arrange "Every department in this State." To promote harmony, he shifted [George] Elliot from field quartermaster to field commissary and named one of Lafayette's aides, "Major Langburne [William Langborn]," to be field quartermaster, to the "Great Satisfaction" of the Continental quartermaster in the state. Has gotten the hospitals "in a good train" and "taken Every precaution to prevent Enormous abuses in the Impressings that Had Been for a time Boundless. In Short, my dear General, I Have Arranged Every thing for the Best and took Every Means I Could think of to promote public Wellfare."[11] Has a "Positive Standing order" that supplies destined for NG's army "Be Held Entirely Sacred" and has "positively ordered Every departement Not to Consider us But in an inferior and Secondary light."

Steuben, who had been at Albemarle Barracks, visited Lafayette after receiving NG's letter and will set off "to Morrow Morning."[12] Lafayette has shown him this letter, and the Baron, who is to "put things in the properest Channel" for moving the levies and supplies, seems pleased with the arrangements. They agree on the need to support NG. Steuben "intends Being With the Assembly and Urging a determination upon More Spirited Measures."

Col. [Banastre] Tarleton has reportedly mounted "a Large Body of His Infantry," and [Col. John Graves] Simcoe is seizing every horse "He Could Come Across." Consequently, "We Have Every thing to fear from their Cavalry. They Will over Run the Country and our flanks; our Stores, our Very Camp will be Unsecured." Of the "State Horse" with Lafayette, "ten only are fitt for Duty"; the "Men are Good but Nacked, Unarmed, Dismounted and fatigued to death." Lafayette has given "Every Encouragement, Recommandation, and order" to restore the fitness of this corps. He also has ten dragoons with him from Col. Armand's legion, but their situation is so bad that they "excite Compassion." Besides these twenty men, his only cavalry are a "few Volonteer Gentlemen," who are "very clever But Volonteers." He had some militia horse, but their term of service expired this morning. Happily, Lafayette was able to retrieve "Some Accoutrements furnished" to these militia dragoons "By the public." Steuben had planned to designate the next 100 recruits for the cavalry, but it will take time to "Get them, Cloathe them, Mount them, Arm them, and Maneuvre them"—especially as there are no horses or "Any thing else." Lafayette, therefore, must detain the thirty-two Continental dragoons commanded by Col. [Anthony Walton] White that Steuben sent him, because "We must at Least Have Some patroles"; hopes NG does not "disapprouve."[13] Lafayette has written [Col. Stephen] Moylan to hurry his cavalrymen southward and will "urge" that the legion of the "Duke de Lauzun" be sent to Virginia. He would "Be much more at Ease" if Lauzun, who is Lafayette's "Intimate friend," were with him.[14] Adds that if he could "Wish a Single Man less in the Carolina Army," it would be Col. [Henry] Lee. "But I Hope we will at last get Some Horse from the North ward where they are So very Useless."

[James] McHenry is in Baltimore, Md., presiding over a board of war; the rest of Lafayette's aides send their respects. Lafayette also sends his regards to NG's aides. Adds: "I will not Expatiate on my Situation. You know it and as I Cannot Create Soldiers and Circumstances we Must Chearfully do our Best With the little we Have." In a postscript, says he will send Col. [Otho] Williams an "Exact Return" of his force by the next express.[15] Has "Continentals Near 900 ([dragoons?] included), 34 Artillery men 4 Six pounders 2 Howitzers, Militia forming two Brigades under G^als Mullemberg [Peter Muhlenberg] and [Thomas] Nelson, Numbers ever uncertain But about 1200, will soon Be 1500, the Horse and 50 infantry under Major [William] McPherson, Some militia under Major [Richard] Call." ALS (MiU-C) 8 pp.]

1. NG's orders are in his letter to Lafayette of 1 May, above. Although the enclosures have not been found, Lafayette probably sent copies of his letter to Washington of 17 May and one that he wrote to Congress on 18 May. (See Idzerda, *Lafayette Papers*, 4: 113n; the letters that are thought to have been enclosed can be found in ibid., pp. 108–9 and 494.)

2. In his reply of 9 June, below, NG said the recently negotiated cartel for the exchange of prisoners did apply to Virginia, as Lafayette surmised.

3. See Lafayette to NG, 28 April and second letter of 3 May, both above.

4. For the decision of Virginia officials to stop the militia from joining NG, see note at Jefferson to NG, 30 March, above. As seen in his reply of 9 June, below, NG was unhappy that these troops had not joined him.

5. Lafayette had written Nash on 15 May. The text of that letter is discussed in Idzerda, *Lafayette Papers*, 4: 114n.

6. Cornwallis moved his entire army into Virginia and did not set up the posts.

7. NG had already sent revised orders directing that the Virginia levies should remain with Lafayette in Virginia. (See NG to Steuben, 14 May, above.)

8. Lafayette retained the Pennsylvania Continentals, who did not join NG until after the surrender of Cornwallis at Yorktown.

9. Lafayette undoubtedly meant that he had no information conerning the plans for the upcoming campaign being formulated at George Washington's "Head Quarters." The "troops" and "Blows" he referred to were presumably those of the enemy.

10. On NG's "Late Engagement at Camden," see NG to Huntington, 27 April, above.

11. Despite what Lafayette had done to correct abuses in the mode of impressment, the Virginia legislature enacted a series of resolutions dealing with impressment when it considered his request for additional warrants on 28 May. (Virginia General Assembly, House of Delegates, *Journal* [Richmond, 1828], 2: 4–5)

12. Lafayette was referring to NG's letter to him of 1 May, above.

13. In his reply of 9 June, below, NG approved of Lafayette detaining White and his men.

14. Despite his repeated urgings to French officials and Washington, Lafayette was unable to have Lauzun's Legion assigned to him. (See Lafayette to La Luzerne, 14 August, and Lafayette to Washington, 24 August, in Idzerda, *Lafayette Papers*, 4: 322, 351.)

15. Otho Williams was NG's adjutant general and served as inspector for NG's army. It is not known if the return was sent.

¶ [FROM COLONEL STEPHEN MOORE AND MAJOR JOHN BARNWELL,[1] "Prison Ship *Tor-bay*, Charles Town Harbour," S.C., 18 May 1781. They enclose a letter from Col. [Nisbet] Balfour, which was handed to them "immediately on our being put onboard this Ship."[2] They think Balfour's letter is self-explanatory and that NG will best know "the notice it merits." If any or all are "to be made Victims, agreable to the menaces therein contain'd," they only regret that their "blood cannot be dispos'd of more to the advancement of the glorious cause."[3] Below their signatures, they add that they are writing in behalf of "one hundred & thirty Prisoners."[4] ALS (ScU) 2 pp.]

1. Both were militia officers—Moore from North Carolina and Barnwell from South Carolina; they had both been captured at Charleston in May 1780.

2. In his letter to American militia prisoners of 17 May, Balfour stated that outrages committed against Loyalist prisoners of war by the American forces compelled him to seize and retain the militia prisoners "as hostages for the good usage of all the loyal militia." He added that he intended to "regulate in the full extent" the treatment of the

American militiamen according to that which their Loyalist counterparts received. (Gibbes, *Documentary History*, 3: 72–73)

3. Moore, Barnwell, and other officers wrote Balfour on 19 May, pointing out instances of mild treatment of Loyalist officers and contending that any "outrages" that might have been committed were the result of "private resentment" and were "totally unsanctioned by any American officer." They argued that in the kind of war that was then being fought in the South, British "irregulars" had committed an equal number of "acts of cruelty." Balfour's actions in holding as hostages men who had been "fairly taken in arms, and entitled to the benefits of a solemn capitualation," would increase the "horrors" of the war, they wrote, adding that only their adherence to the terms of their paroles had given Balfour the opportunity to detain them. They said they trusted that "upon equitable proposals being made for our exchange by Gen. Greene, no objections will be raised" and asked that their letter be published in the Charleston newspaper, as Balfour's had been. (Ibid., pp. 76–77) NG did not write Balfour directly in their behalf but relied on the recently concluded cartel to resolve the matter. Edmund M. Hyrne, NG's commissary of prisoners, who was then en route to Charleston, was able to obtain the militiamen's release in an agreement signed 15 June—but only after threatening to revoke the paroles of British officers in Charleston. (McCrady, *S.C. in the Revolution*, pp. 363–64)

4. In this letter to NG, Moore and Barnwell enclosed a "Roll" of the names of the militiamen confined aboard the *Torbay* and the *Pack-Horse*. (The list is printed in Gibbes, *Documentary History*, 3: 75–76.)

¶ [FROM BARON STEUBEN, Wilton, Va., 18 May 1781. Has received NG's letters of 27 April and 1 May. A "Report had before informed us of your having gained that advantage which but for an unfortunate circumstance, you would certainly have had."[1] He feels for NG's "many difficulties & Vexations"; says NG's "general Plan" does "equal Credit to a Victory." If the plan does not succeed as it should, "the fault" lies with "those States" that have failed to give NG what he needs to carry it into execution. As "faults in War seldom go unpunished," those states already "feel the effects of their Indolence." Virginia, in particular, is "a Victim to it," with a "formidable Enemy" in its "heart" and without "the resources" to defend itself. "The Marquis" will inform NG of the state of affairs in Virginia, so Steuben will confine himself to answering NG's letter of 1 May.[2] If NG has not heard regularly from him, it must be because letters have "miscarried." The express service is "extremely neglected," and unless Col. [Edward] Carrington assumes direction of it, NG will "often Suffer for their negligence." Only 500 of the 3,000 expected recruits have "come in." Steuben has sent orders that no time be lost in "Disciplining" and equipping them. He has also ordered that any recruits found at the rendezvous points be sent to him. The 1,100 stand of arms from Philadelphia—"a very seasonable supply"—have "passed" Fredericksburg. He expects to equip and march the recruits in eight or ten days.[3] Lafayette will explain why he decided to retain the sixty cavalrymen serving with Col. [Anthony Walton] White.[4] Lafayette and Steuben have both "represented" to the Virginia Assembly the need to raise 100 more mounted troops, and Steuben has sent an officer to collect equipment for them.[5] Steuben intends to take 300 stand of arms with him for the North Carolina levies, who are to join him "on the Rout."[6] He sent Gen. [Anthony] Wayne a copy of that part of NG's letter concerning Wayne, but believes Lafayette has already ordered Wayne to "Join the troops here."[7] Capt. [John] Pryor has gone to Prince Edward Court House to forward the ammunition and move the laboratory, which is "exposed." Pryor will have the artificers back at work as soon as possible.[8] Everything else in NG's letter "shall be complied with." L (MiU-C) 3 pp. The letter is unsigned, but the docketing indicates that NG received it.]

1. Steuben referred to the battle of Hobkirk's Hill, which is discussed at NG to Huntington, 27 April, above.

2. See Lafayette to NG, this date, above. In a letter to Steuben of 14 May, NG had radically changed the orders he sent Steuben on 1 May, both above.

3. Because of Lord Cornwallis's arrival in Virginia, that state's Continental recruits did not join NG's army.

4. Lafayette discussed his retention of White's dragoons in his letter to NG of this date, above. According to Lafayette's account, there were only thirty-two men serving with White.

5. The additional cavalry was not recruited until August. (See Lafayette to NG, first letter of 12 August, below.)

6. Because of the change of orders mentioned in note 2 above, the North Carolina levies did not join Steuben. As seen at Sumner to NG, 8 April, above, it was not until August that the newly raised North Carolina Continentals reached NG's army.

7. As seen in Lafayette to NG, this date, above, Lafayette directed the Pennsylvania Continentals to serve, at least temporarily, with his forces in Virginia.

8. See Pryor to NG, 11 May, above.

¶ [FROM GENERAL JETHRO SUMNER, Williamsboro, N.C., 18 May 1781. Reports that the enemy crossed the Roanoke River "Tuesday last [15 May]" and are on the road to North Hampton Court House.[1] They sent to Edenton 500 slaves who had been "plunder'd from the inhabitants." Sumner met with a representative from the Marquis de Lafayette to discuss the "number, and Condition" of the North Carolina levies and "a proper Rout for convaying 20,000 Cartridges."[2] He will move his "few drafts" to Warren County, where he will form and equip "the first Rigem[t]" and march it to join Lafayette "immediately."[3] ALS (MiU-C) 2 pp.]

1. Lord Cornwallis's army did cross the Roanoke on 15 May. From there, it marched north, toward Virginia, instead of northeasterly, toward North Hampton Court House, N.C. ("Von Bose Journal," p. 57a)

2. The cartridges were from the munitions laboratory at Prince Edward Court House. (See Mazaret to NG, 3 April, and Pryor to NG, 11 May, both above.)

3. Sumner was responding to NG's orders to him of 5 May, above. As seen in NG to Nash, 9 June, below, NG changed those orders before Sumner could march to join Lafayette.

*   *   *

Colonel Otho H. Williams to General Thomas Sumter

Sir   Camp Saluda River [S.C.] 19th May 1781

The infamous Nicholls proposed to make an attonement for his crimes by discovering some dangerous Enemies to the Country.[1] A party has been out with him and has return'd with old Mr Biarly and some Negroes.[2] The General considers him as a man incapable of doing much good or harm in the Field, except with his plough; and has order'd me to send him to you with the Negroes who are to be disposed of agreeable to the Instructions you have already Received.[3] I am Sir Y[r] mo: Obed[t] Hble Servant   O H WILLIAMS

ALS (Sumter Papers: DLC).
1. On the "infamous Nicholls," see NG's Orders of 20 May, below.
2. "Old M[r] Biarly" was presumably the owner of Briarley's Ferry, on the Broad River.
3. NG's instructions are in his second letter to Sumter of 17 May, above.

* * *

¶ [FROM GENERAL FRANCIS MARION, St. Stephens, S.C., 19 May 1781. Lord Rawdon is still at Monck's Corner; some of his "straggling partys" have been plundering the "neighbours." Marion captured four of Rawdon's boats coming down the Santee River, but they were carrying few stores and were lightly manned. He has learned that Lord Cornwallis was at Halifax, N.C., and that Georgetown, S.C., is "not Evacuated." Wants to "go & Reduce" the post at Georgetown, which is held by only eighty British soldiers and a few Tories. The Loyalists are "very troublesom over Peedee & Waccomaw," but the capture of Georgetown "will make them quiet." He will leave a party to watch Rawdon and to send NG intelligence. Hopes to hear from NG soon, for he must move quickly or the garrison may "Slip through" his hands. The guards he sent with the officers who were captured at Motte's were mistreated. Marion has decided to "retalliate in every instants" for that and for the detention of one of his officers bearing a flag of truce. He will not communicate with the enemy "untill reperation is made" and hopes NG will permit him to "Insult" any enemy officers he captures.[1] ALS (MiU-C) 2 pp.]
1. NG replied on 26 May, below.

¶ [FROM DOCTOR THOMAS TUDOR TUCKER, Charleston, S.C., 19 May 1781. He was to have been exchanged for one of the British surgeons captured near Camden, but "Objections" similar to those that delayed the exchange of Dr. [Peter] Fayssoux have resulted in Tucker's being "wholly set aside."[1] While the British doctors are "doing their Duty" through NG's "Courtesy," the Americans are able to do theirs only "by right of Capitualation." Wonders if the "Impeditments thrown in the Way of the Exchange" are "a proper return" for NG's "Indulgence."[2] ALS (MiU-C) 2 pp.]
1. On the case of Fayssoux, see David Olyphant to NG, 22 January, and Fayssoux to NG, 31 January, both above (vol. 7: 170–71, 229)
2. As seen in Olyphant to NG, 9 June, below, the British relented and permitted the exchange.

¶ [GENERAL GREENE'S ORDERS, "Camp Sandy Run," S.C., 20 May 1781. Orders a court-martial for William Nicholls "this day." The verdict, given in After Orders of the same date, is that Nicholls, of the "Late 6th South Carolina Regiment," is guilty of desertion. NG approves the court's sentence of death by hanging and orders that it be carried out "Tomorrow." Also in the After Orders are instructions for the army to march at 4 A.M. Lamar Orderly Book (OClWHi) 2 pp.]

* * *

To General Andrew Pickens

Camp on the East side of the Saluda [S.C.]
Dear General   May 20th 1781

We are on our march for Ninty Six and shall be within ten miles of that place tonight. By this Lt Col [Henry] Lee must be with you, or near you; and I hope the Garrison at Augusta will be reducd.[1] Great care should be taken to preserve the Stores for the use of the public if you succeed. As this may be a delicate point with you on account of the exorbitant claims of the Militia, I have given Lt Col Lee particular orders on this subject and I beg your acquissence there in.[2]

A detachment from Cunninghams brigade has done much mischief in the uper Country, by murdering the Inhabitants, and burning the [Wofford's] Iron works & many other buildings. Savage cruelty never equaled the conduct of this party.[3]

Lord Rawden since I wrote you has evacuated Nelsons Ferry and blown up the works and retird towards Charles Town. Lord Cornwallis was at Hallifax in North Carolinia a few days since. General Philips is retreating from Petersburg towards Portsmouth and the Marquis de la Fyette is in full persuit.[4] All things wear a favorable aspect in the Southern department. Push your operations rapidly. With esteem I am Sir Your most Obed[t] humble S[r]   N GREENE

ADfS (NcD).

1. As seen by his letter to NG of this date, below, Lee was already at Augusta, Ga.
2. See NG to Lee, 16 May, above, and NG to Lee, 21 May, below.
3. Gen. Robert Cunningham's brigade of Loyalists was stationed at Ninety Six.
4. NG discussed the source of this inaccurate report in his letter to Lee of 22 May, below.

                        *   *   *

¶ [FROM MAJOR JOHN ARMSTRONG, Salisbury, NC., 20 May 1781. He has been waiting two weeks for the "twelve month[s] drafts" he was to collect, equip, and march to Harrisburg. Is "uneasey" about the delay; hopes the troops will be ready by 26 May.[1] Gen. [Jethro] Sumner has ordered him "Verry Pressingly" to obtain NG's "order" for arms, 30,000 cartridges, and flints. As there were no arms at Salisbury, Armstrong arranged for the repair of some that were "much out of order." To obtain the cartridges, he approached Capt. [John] Compty, who was there with ten wagonloads of ammunition and agreed to give Armstrong a supply if NG approved.[2] The quartermaster at Salisbury, who has flints, likewise requires NG's order before giving them up. Armstrong asks NG to send orders for both.[3] "About 300 tories imbodied on Deep River" have "don Som damage" and forced certain local Whigs, including the county colonel, to flee to Salisbury for protection.[4] ALS (MiU-C) 1 p.]

1. Most of the draftees had still not marched when Armstrong wrote NG on 12 June, below.
2. See Compty to NG, 28 April, above.

3. NG's reply has not been found.

4. The Loyalist uprising in the area was not of long duration. Armstrong reported to Sumner on 13 June that "The tories in the Country is all surrendered their selves and glad of the opportunity." (*NCSR*, 15: 481)

¶ [FROM CAPTAIN NATHANIEL IRISH, Prince Edward Court House, Va., 20 May 1781. Reports on the removal of military stores after it was learned that the enemy were within forty miles of Prince Edward Court House and moving that way. There were no teams available from the quartermaster, who had already moved his stores, so Irish obtained ox carts and a few wagons from local gentlemen. "Oxen not being able to hold out more than 15 Miles," he left most of the stores at a house in the country. He also sent four wagonloads to Bedford Court House and intends to take the rest of the supplies there when he obtains additional teams. He retained a "little Powder" at Prince Edward to keep his "People at work on Ammunition" and will stay there with his party until he hears from NG or is forced to relocate.[1]

"Capᵗ Lieutᵗ John Pryor" claims to have been appointed commissary general of military stores, with NG's approval. If that is true, Irish will resign, for the appointment of a "Man both younger in Commission and Appointmᵗ" would be a clear indication that Irish does "not give Sattisfaction"; he was "the first appointed" to the post by the Board of War. Asks NG to explain why he was superseded and for instructions concerning the military stores.[2] ALS (MiU-C) 2 pp.]

1. See NG to Irish, 9 June, below.

2. NG discussed the matter in ibid. and in a letter to Pryor of 15 June, below. By then, as seen in Pryor to NG, 30 May, below, a confrontation between the two men had resulted in a fistfight. In the end, neither of them received the post. The Board of War, which had to approve any such appointment, had already named Thomas Jones to serve as commissary. (See Pryor to NG, 25 July, below.)

¶ [FROM COLONEL HENRY LEE, JR., Augusta, Ga., "Sunday night [20 May 1781]."[1] A deserter from Ninety Six reports that [Col. John Harris] Cruger is planning to "run away with the regulars" while the Loyalist militia "repair home."[2] It is "absolutely necessary" for Lee to have another 100 Continentals at Augusta.[3] ALS (MiU-C) 1 p.]

1. The letter was docketed 24 May, but Sunday fell on the 20th.

2. Neither Cruger nor the Loyalist militia abandoned Ninety Six.

3. NG did not send the reinforcement. (See NG to Lee, 22 May, below.)

¶ [FROM GENERAL FRANCIS MARION, St. Stephens, S.C., 20 May 1781. He just received NG's letters of 17 and 18 May and will "Observe" NG's orders.[1] He wrote NG "Yesterday" that Lord Rawdon was still at Monck's Corner; has not yet learned "what the Enemy is doing" there. British patrols "come ten miles up every day."[2] Most of Marion's militia have gone home for a few days; when they return, he expects to be stronger than ever before. Georgetown, with its garrison of "about" 100 British, has not yet been evacuated. Marion wants "the Liberty of going against it" but will await NG's orders.[3] Lord Cornwallis was reportedly marching to Halifax, N.C.[4] ALS (MiU-C) 1 p.]

1. Ichabod Burnet and William Pierce, aides to NG, had both written to Marion on 18 May, above.

2. Rawdon explained to Lord Cornwallis in a letter of 24 May that he had taken a position at Monck's Corner to "cover those Districts from which Charlestown draws its principal supplies." Rawdon said he was "in readiness" there "to improve" upon any "favorable occurrence" and was resupplying his men, who had "suffered serious distress" as a result of the "interruption of our Communication." (PRO 30/11/6)

3. Marion moved against Georgetown before he heard from NG. He arrived near the town on 28 May. (Rankin, *Swamp Fox*, p. 213)

4. As seen by Jethro Sumner's letter to NG of 18 May, above, Marion's intelligence was not current.

*   *   *

From John Mathews

Dear sir   Philadelphia May 20th 1781

The various accounts we frequently have here, & the want of information from you, puzzles us exceedingly: a thousand conjectures are formed, but your true situation we can learn nothing of. A man arrived here yesterday one Jennette, who says he left you before Camden on the 27 Ulto & that it was expected that place would surrender to you in the course of four or five days. This will serve you as a specimen of the reports I have above alluded to. You may readily suppose our anxiety is not small, when we receive such intelligence, to hear something from the fountain head. We so frequently receive similar intelligence which is soon again contradicted, that we are grown callous, & believe nothing, but what we get officially. I hope we shall soon hear from you, & be relieved from this cruel state of doubt & uncertainty; and I flatter myself when it does arrive, it will be pleasing; tho', I must confess, we have little reason to expect it.[1]

Congress have at last put *the means* in Genl Waynes hands to march, & I have no reason to doubt, but what he is this day on his march.[2] Had this been done six weeks ago, (which might as well have been then done, as three days ago) he would 'ere this have been with you, & in all probability prevented the present movements of the enemy. But whilst we have men at the head of our affairs, who are uniformly opposed to the least deviation from the plain John trot mode of doing business, whose souls are confined within the compass of a nut shel, & who like Dean Swifts, Peter, Jack, & Martin, tremble at the very Idea of doing anything, that is not strictly enjoined them by their *fathers Will* tho' the salvation of the country depended on it.[3] I say whilst we have such Quidnunc politicians to manage our affairs, we must expect nothing vigorous, or decisive, being done. However they have at length in one instance blundered across the Rubicon (but I believe most of them did it with their eyes shut, as Children do, when they walk in the dark, for fear of meeting the Devil in their way.) I mean the vote that was passed, giving powers to Genl Wayne, to press provisions on his march, whenever he wanted them. Perhaps you may laugh at my making such a fuss about this affair, as your army is fed by scarcely any other means. But remember there is no such power *literally* given to Congress by Confederation and to act up to the spirit of it, is a doctrine supposed to be big with many evils, therefore reprobated. I conceive it to be a great point gained, to drive them from this ground; it looks like conceding the point, & that necessity will oblige them to interpret the powers given by the Confederation in their utmost extent, & in my opinion ought upon some occasions, to be strained to answer the great purposes of war. But I apprehend, when these Doughty heroes, have opened their eyes, & looked back on the tremendous gulph they have passed, they will be astonished at their own temerity; & the next they come to, they will make a halt, to examine their tender consciences, whether after having escaped so great a danger with impunity, it would be prudent to tempt their fate again; & most probably, the result will be, that they are sure the Devil must fly away with them, should they sin a second time, & of course they will apostatize. In which case, it will be an Herculian labour to bring them back to the charge.

The backwardness of the States in executing the requisitions of Congress, is intolerable, & when they do, it is in such a loose, discordant manner that their small exertions produce little good, from whence principally arises our embarrassments. It therefore appears to me absolutely necessary, & for the true interest of the union, that the several states should give to Congress Dictatorial powers during the war, & instruct their Delegates to take the most vigorous measures for prosecuting the war. This power is certainly more safely lodged in the hands of such a body as Congress, than any other. The only objection I have to it, is, that I am afraid, they will want spirit to do their Duty, but this may be remidied by spirited instructions. Something like this must soon be done, or I am clearly convinced our affairs will grow from bad to worse, which must end in our utter ruin. Those states that are in perfect tranquillity, & feel nothing of the effects of the war, will I know, be averse to such a measure, therefore I despair of it's being done, but they will too late find, when the house falls, they will inevitably be crushed in its ruins. We must either stand or fall together. However they may amuse themselves with the Idea of sacrificing some for the good of the whole, the hypothesis will prove fallacious, divida et empera, is an axiom that will prove as certain, as it is old. I am My D^r sir with sentiments of the most sincere Esteem & Regard Your most Obed^t serv^t JN^O MATHEWS

ALS (MiU-C).

1. NG's letters to Congress of 22 and 27 April reached Philadelphia with news from the "fountain head" a few days later. (See Mathews to NG, 22 May, below.)

2. Congress voted on 18 May to let Gen. Anthony Wayne impress any provisions and

forage he could not "otherwise" obtain during his march to the South. (*JCC*, 20: 516; Mathews discussed the significance of the resolution later in this letter.) As noted at Washington to NG, 1 June, below, Wayne's detachment did not march until 26 May.

3. Mathews was alluding to Jonathan Swift's satire on the Catholic, Anglican, and Dissenting churches in section 2 of *A Tale of a Tub*. (Jonathan Swift, *A Tale of a Tub*, 2d ed. [Oxford, Eng.: Clarendon Press, 1958], pp. 73–91)

*   *   *

¶ [GENERAL GREENE'S ORDERS, "Camp Cunninghams Plantation," S.C., Monday, 21 May 1781. The troops are to receive and cook two days' provisions and will march "Tomorrow" at sunrise. Lamar Orderly Book (OClWHi) 1 p.]

¶ [TO COLONEL HENRY LEE, JR., "Camp on the road East side of Saluda from Frydays Ferry to Ninty Six," S.C., 21 May 1781. The army will be "within ten miles" of Ninety Six "to Night." NG hopes the garrison there will "fall into our hands" if it has not already abandoned the post. Nelson's Ferry is "evacuated and the place blown up"; Lord Rawdon is retreating to Charleston, which he "says he is determined to guard at all events."[1] Col. [Stephen] Drayton, who just arrived in camp from northern North Carolina, reports that Gen. [William] Phillips has retreated to Portsmouth, Va., that Lord Cornwallis is at Halifax, N.C., with only 1,200 men, and that a French fleet is believed to be "on the coast."[2] Lee is to "push" his operations.[3] He is also to "Cultivate a good understanding with General [Andrew] Pickens and the Militia. Should you succeed[,] take care to preserve the Stores if any are taken. Some of your Legion behaved greatly amiss at the fort at Frydays Ferry [i.e., Ft. Granby]. They sold the Arms and a large quantity of cloth. This is only meant as a hint to have them watched narrowly."[4] ALS (NcD) 2 pp. The letter is torn at the bottom of the first page, and most of one line of text is missing.]

1. As seen in Marion to NG, 20 May, above, Rawdon had encamped at Monck's Corner. He had "blown up" the British works at Nelson's Ferry on 15 May. (See Marion to NG, 16 May, above.)

2. The intelligence that Drayton had brought was faulty. Phillips's detachment, commanded by Benedict Arnold since the death of Phillips, had returned to Petersburg, where it was joined on 20 May by Lord Cornwallis's detachment of more than 1,400 men. (Wickwire, *Cornwallis*, pp. 321, 326) There was no French fleet near the southern coast.

3. Lee had been sent to assist in the capture of the British post at Augusta, Ga.

4. On the problems between Lee's troops and the militiamen at Ft. Granby, see notes at Lee to NG, 15 May, above. At the foot of the present letter, in Lee's hand, is a note: "Not my Legion but some of the detachm[t] from the army." A company of Marylanders under the command of Capt. Edward Oldham had been serving with Lee at the time of the capture of Ft. Granby. (See NG's Orders of 15 May, above.)

¶ [TO COLONEL LEWIS MORRIS, JR. From [Bush River, S.C.], 21 May 1781. Morris is to proceed to Salisbury, N.C., and have the stores that are listed on the enclosed invoice forwarded to "the Island Ford on Saluda River," S.C.[1] The North Carolina draftees and the Virginia militia at Salisbury should accompany the stores. If Morris finds any stores coming from Charlotte, N.C., "without an escort," he should have them halted until "the whole can be brought forward." The troops and stores "must be brought forward as soon as practicable." Df (MiU-C) 2 pp.]

1. The invoice has not been found. The supplies no doubt included those discussed in Compty to NG, 28 April, above.

¶ [TO GOVERNOR ABNER NASH OF NORTH CAROLINA. From Bush River, S.C., 21 May 1781. Fearing that his letter to Nash of the "2ᵈ of April" has "miscarried," NG encloses a copy. His letter to Congress, which was enclosed with the original, has since appeared in "the [news]papers."[1] Cy (MiU-C) 1 p.]
    1. NG's letter, dated 3 April, is above.

¶ [CAPTAIN NATHANIEL PENDLETON TO DOCTOR WILLIAM READ. From Bush River, S.C., 21 May 1781. Read's letter of 4 May [not found] has been received. NG never intended to move the hospital from Charlotte, N.C., to Salisbury and is pleased that Charlotte offers "conveniences" beyond its "situation." Pendleton is to assure Read that measures have been taken to supply provisions and medicines to the hospitals and that "a failure will be owing to want of transportation or negligence in some of the officers employed in the business." Col. [Lewis] Morris will hand Read this letter and tell him the news from the army. "We have been beaten, we have taken 4 strong posts, the enemy have evacuated two, & gone into Charles Town. We have 800 prisoners & we shall have Ninetysix & Augusta in 5 days at farthest." Hopes God will bless Read and "make you happy at the glove makers." Sends compliments to several wounded officers. Tr (GWG Transcripts: CSmH) 1 p.]

¶ [FROM COLONEL ABRAHAM BUFORD, Roanoke, Va., 21 May 1781. He had come "this far" on his way to rejoin the army when he learned that under the new arrangement of the Virginia line, which NG will no doubt approve, he is a supernumerary.[1] "This country" is "much in need of assistance," and Buford has decided to remain in Virginia unless NG directs otherwise.[2] Lord Cornwallis's army by now has joined that of Gen. [William] Phillips, who reportedly died "about five days agoe."[3] Gen. [Anthony] Wayne should soon join forces with "the Marquis [de Lafayette]."[4] ALS (NNPM) 2 pp.]
    1. As seen in his letter to Baron Steuben of 1 May, above, NG had received the arrangement, which he soon put into operation. (See, for example, NG's Orders of 28 May, below.)
    2. No reply has been found.
    3. Cornwallis's army united with Phillips's detachment on 20 May. ("Von Bose Journal," pp. 57–58) On the death of Phillips, see note at Lafayette to NG, first letter of 3 May, above.
    4. Wayne's Pennsylvania troops did not join Lafayette until 8 June. (Nelson, *Wayne*, p. 134)

*   *   *

To Colonel Henry Lee, Jr.

My dear Sir   Ninty Six [S.C.] May 22 1781

Your early arrival at Augusta astonishes me. For rapid marches you exceed Lord Cornwallis and every body else. I wish you may not have injured your troops.[1]

We arrived before this place this morning, and find this place much better fortified and garrison much stronger in regular troops than was expected. We performed the march in as fast a time as we could; but our exertions when compared with yours have no merit.

At present I cannot detach the men you request, but perhaps I can after a day or two.[2] But more of this hereafter. I beg you to accomplish your business at Augusta and the fort below as soon as possible[.][3] Many reasons induce me to wish it which I cannot explain to you at present.

A Gentleman just from Virginia says a hand bill was circulating at Richmond with Charles Thomsons name to it; that the second division of the French Fleet had arrived. It is highly probable they will operate immediately in the Chespeake. Our military operations in Virginia are flattering.[4]

Please to present my compliments to General [Andrew] Pickens and apologize to him for my not writing[.]

I wrote you day before yesterday that Lord Rawden had evacuated Nelsons Ferry and blown up the fortifications.[5] This letter I hope you have received. The Enemy intercepted a letter from General [Andrew] Pickens to me, at the foot of which you made note that gave them great disgust. You insinuate that unless I hasten my march they will slip through my fingers and escape to Augusta.[6] Yours obt   N GREENE
Ask General Pickens what he thinks of offering the Tories a pardon generally if they will come in and join us excepting only murderers and house burners. Overtures of this sort have been hinted by the Tories.[7]

Typescript (GU). The ALS is bound in a copy of Johnson, *Greene* at the University of Georgia Library, which has furnished the editors with a certified typescript.
    1. Lee reported on his march of seventy-five miles in two days in a letter to NG of this date, below.
    2. Lee had requested 100 Continentals when he wrote NG on 20 May, above.
    3. The "fort below" was Ft. Dreadnought (also known as Ft. Galphin), which was twelve miles below Augusta, on the South Carolina side of the Savannah River. (Cashin and Robertson, *Augusta*, p. 56) A detachment of Lee's troops captured it on 21 May. (See Lee to NG, 22 May, below.)
    4. Charles Thomson was the secretary of Congress. The report that the French second division had arrived was false, as were the reports from Virginia that led NG to conclude that affairs were favorable there. (See NG to Lee, 21 May, above.)
    5. NG's letter, dated 21 May, is above.
    6. Pickens's letter has not been found.
    7. Lee replied on 24 May, below, that Pickens would write NG about pardons for the Loyalists; no such letter from Pickens has been found. No pardon was granted, and the Loyalists of the area either accompanied the British army when it left or stayed and sought forbearance from their patriot neighbors, sometimes without success. (See Lambert, *South Carolina Loyalists*, p. 174.)

*   *   *

¶ [GENERAL ISAAC HUGER TO COLONEL LEWIS MORRIS, JR., 22 May 1781.[1] Lord Rawdon is at Monck's Corner, where Huger believes he will remain. The British also have 200 men and two field pieces at Dorchester. All of Huger's "negroes below are taken by the Enemy," and his furniture, livestock, "&c" have been "destroyed." He cannot find anyone to take his slaves to Virginia and is "greatly perplex'd for the Want of Horses," the enemy having taken all of his. Hopes to move some of his slaves on 25 May. Regrets that "Gen'l S[umter]" has taken 150 slaves belonging to Gov. [William] Bull.[2] Huger asks to have some "Papers or letters" forwarded that he is expecting "from the North'd," as well as some coffee and sugar, should a supply arrive at camp. Thinks Sumter could *"render a greater Service"* by *"moving down"* and patrolling "within fifty or sixty miles" of his present position at the Congarees. Printed in *SCHGM*, 34 (1933): 78]

1. The place was not given, but Huger was most likely at his plantation, "Mount Necessity," on the west side of the Wateree River, some seventeen miles above Ft. Motte.

2. Sumter's party had seized the slaves from the former royal lieutenant governor's plantation, near Ft. Motte. Twenty of Bull's slaves were used to help destroy the fortifications at Motte's, and Sumter distributed 160 more slaves among his men. He also reportedly took 6,500 bushels of corn and all of Bull's horses, cattle, and wagons. (Kinloch Bull, Jr., *The Oligarchs in Colonial and Revolutionary Charleston: Lieutenant Governor William Bull II and His Family* [Columbia: University of South Carolina Press, 1991], p. 290)

¶ [FROM COLONEL HENRY LEE, JR., "Camp on Savannah," 22 May 1781.[1] Describes his march to join Gen. [Andrew] Pickens. After leaving Ft. Granby on the 17th, Lee moved rapidly because of a report that affairs were "critical" at Augusta, Ga., and that an enemy relief force was marching there from Ninety Six, S.C. He also knew that NG's "designs" depended on Lee's "timely arrival" at Augusta. Lee's Legion pushed ahead and "reached the vicinity of" Pickens on 18 May; the "N° Carolina corps & the artillery," which followed, reached Pickens's camp early the next day, thanks to the "soldierlike exertions" of Maj. [Pinketham] Eaton. Lee and Pickens decided that Lee would operate against the enemy post at Galphin's plantation while Pickens arranged the "complete investiture" of Augusta. Lee details the disposition of his troops at Galphins, or Ft. Dreadnought, where, on 21 May, Capt. [John] Rudolph, "by the judgement & vigor of his operation compelled a most obstinate garrison to surrender." Sends a copy of Rudulph's report and recommends "this meritorious officer" to NG's "particular attention."[2] Adds that a "large supply of stores" was taken at Dreadnought and that the capture of that post will enable the Americans to "push" measures against Augusta.[3] Lee's troops are now crossing the Savannah River. They will join Pickens and adopt "the most vigorous operations" for the "recovery of Augusta & the liberation of these insulted & distressed people." ALS (NcD) 6 pp.]

1. As seen near the end of this calendar, Lee's troops were then crossing the Savannah River—the boundary between Georgia and South Carolina; Lee may have written this letter from either side.

2. Ft. Dreadnought was the fortified plantation house of George Galphin, a veteran Indian trader, who operated a trading post on the site. (Lipscomb, "S.C. Battles," *Place Names in South Carolina*, 25 [1978]: 29) In his report, Rudulph did not explain how he

forced the surrender of the fort. (PCC, item 155, vol. 2: 107, DNA) According to Lee's memoirs, however, the enemy commander was not aware that a force of American regulars was operating in the vicinity. Taking advantage of a chance to surprise the garrison, Lee sent a militia party to feign an attack on the fort and then retreat. Most of the garrison left the fort to pursue the militiamen, and the legion troops, commanded by Rudulph, quickly cut them off and forced the few men remaining in the fort to surrender. (Lee, *Memoirs*, 2: 90) In his account, Lee said his men suffered only a single casualty, who succumbed to the intense heat; Rudulph called American casualties "trifling" but reported eight or ten wounded. (Ibid.; PCC, item 155, vol. 2: 107, DNA) According to a list submitted by Rudulph, the captured garrison consisted of seventy King's Rangers, forty-two "irregulars," sixty-one slaves (many of them armed), and fourteen armed boatmen. (Ibid., p. 109)

3. According to Lee, the "annual royal present to the Indians" had recently been deposited at Galphin's, and its capture provided many "articles extremely wanted in the American camp," including "Powder, ball, small arms, liquor, salt, blankets, with sundry small articles." (Lee, *Memoirs*, 2: 89 and n)

¶ [FROM GENERAL FRANCIS MARION, St. Stephen's, S.C., 22 May 1781. Since Marion last wrote, Lord Rawdon has gone "to town." Some of Rawdon's troops are reportedly at Dorchester; the rest—about 400—are still at Monck's Corner.[1] The British have evacuated "The Church" and sent all their baggage to Charleston; their cavalry continue to patrol "up the road" eight or ten miles every day.[2] The militia reinforcements that Marion expected have not yet arrived, and he has had to let the men who were with him "go home." He expects to "be strong" in a few days and will "Lay close" to the enemy and harass them—unless NG allows him to proceed against Georgetown, which is "not yett Evacuated."[3] ALS (MiU-C) 1 p.]

1. Marion had written NG on 20 May, above. If Rawdon went to Charleston, it was only for a brief stay; he wrote Lord Cornwallis from his camp at Monck's Corner on 24 May. (PRO 30/11/6) According to the diary of Henry Nase, an officer in the King's American Regiment, a detachment from Rawdon's army marched from Monck's Corner on 19 May and arrived at Dorchester on 20 May. (Nase Family Papers, The New Brunswick Museum, St. John, N.B.)

2. "The Church" was presumably Biggin's Church, which was opposite Monck's Corner on a branch of the Santee River. (McCrady, *S.C. in the Revolution*, p. 331) Contrary to Marion's report, the British continued to hold Biggin's Church.

3. As seen at Marion to NG, 20 May, above, Marion moved against Georgetown before he received permission.

¶ [FROM JOHN MATHEWS, CHAIRMAN OF A STANDING COMMITTEE OF CONGRESS TO CORRESPOND WITH THE COMMANDER OF THE SOUTHERN DEPARTMENT, Philadelphia, 22 May 1781. NG's "dispatches" of 22 and 27 April were "very welcome," as the earlier accounts that Congress had received "served only to confuse, instead of inform." Laments the "unfortunate turn in the action of the 23ᵈ Ultº." It must have been "mortifying" to NG to have victory "snatched" from him "by the blunder of a single man."[1] Not only were "Immediate advantages" lost, but also "the eclat that would have been given to our arms abroad." Mathews does not dare to hope that Camden can still be taken, but he is sure that everything "will be done for the best." Discusses "a very affectionate and friendly letter" that Congress just received from the King of France.[2] It promises "substantial aid" and calls on the United

States in "polite, yet pathetic terms to make every exertion" to secure "our peace & happiness." Mathews adds: "true magnanimity, firmness, & affection run through the whole" of the letter. The French minister will provide details about the aid after he has deciphered and arranged the letters he received.[3] Gen. [Anthony] Wayne will march "tommorow," but Mathews fears Wayne's detachment will be "too late" to help NG.[4] Should Lord Cornwallis and Gen. [William] Phillips combine, as Mathews expects, and "be reinforced with the detachment now gone from N. York—2000 men—I imagine all your feeble efforts must be at an end, & you must seek an Asylum in some other quarter."[5] Washington is now conferring with the commanders of the French expeditionary force at Wethersfield, Conn.[6] Gov. [John] Rutledge will leave for [Washington's] "Headquarters tomorrow" and will return to the South after a short stay there. Mathews wishes NG health and "deserved success." ALS (MiU-C) 2 pp.]

1. The battle of Hobkirk's Hill, which was fought on 25 April, is discussed at NG to Huntington, 27 April, above. The "single man" was Col. John Gunby, whose role in the battle is discussed there.

2. In his letter of 10 March, which was laid before Congress on 23 May, the king said France would use "all the means" in its power to make the United States "triumphant" and assured Congress that it could depend on France's "perseverance." He expressed "sincere affection" for the "United States in general, and for each [state] in particular." (JCC, 20: 527, 556–57)

3. The minister, La Luzerne, sent a "memorial" to Congress on 25 May, in which he announced that France had granted the United States a subsidy of six million livres and would provide another four million in loans. The subsidy was to be used "to act with vigour during the present campaign"; much of it was to be spent for "clothing, arms and ammunition." The funds remaining after these purchases were made could be turned over to Robert Morris, the superintendent of finance. (Ibid., pp. 557–59) La Luzerne also informed Congress that the French court had decided "to alter the destination" of the second division from France, which had been "intended for the defence of the United States." (Ibid., pp. 543–44; see also note at La Luzerne to NG, 3 April, above.)

4. Wayne's Pennsylvania troops did not march until 26 May. (See note at Washington to NG, 1 June, below.)

5. On 9 May, Washington received intelligence that a British detachment had sailed from New York. (Washington to Dayton, 11 May, Fitzpatrick, GW, 22: 72–73) He sent the information, which proved to be premature, to Congress in a letter of 11 May. (Ibid., p. 76) As seen at St. Clair to NG, 6 May, above, the detachment of 2,000 men, commanded by Col. August de Voit, left for Virginia on 14 May.

6. On Washington's meeting with the commanders of the French expeditionary force, see Sharpe to NG, 28 May, below.

¶ [FROM WILLIAM SHARPE, Philadelphia, 21 and 22 May 1781. Reports that Adm. [Marriot] Arbuthnot's squadron sailed from New York on "Monday evening last [14 May]," in company with transports said to be carrying 2,000 troops. On Friday [18 May], this fleet was seen near the "Capes of Delaware, their destination unknown." Only time will tell if their target is the "large quantities of flour (private property) at sundry places on the Delaware" or if they intend to "take post" in Delaware or Maryland or go farther "southward."[1] Supposes that Gen. [Anthony] Wayne has not marched yet.[2] The French "second Division" has not arrived, although it reportedly sailed from

Brest on 20 March. Sharpe fears that it "will come by the West Indies and delay some time."[3] The clothing and stores have not arrived from France, although they reportedly were sent on 27 March. He is "in pain for their safety."[4] The ship carrying Col. William Palfrey to France is believed to have "foundered."[5] Col. [John] Laurens arrived in France safely, but no letters have arrived from him or Dr. [Benjamin] Franklin.[6] Sharpe sends intelligence received from Europe, including: the Dutch are "making great preparations to avenge themselves"; the "northern powers" will "aid" them; the King of Prussia and the "Emperor [of Austria]" have a "jealous & watchful eye on each other"; American affairs in Spain are "flattering," as Lord Germain's secretary has left after spending six months there and "making propositions secretly"; the siege of Gibraltar continues.[7] About 2,000 suits of clothing, sent by Mr. [John] Jay, have arrived in Boston.[8] The use of paper money is "nearly at an end. The old is almost dead, and the new bills have depreciated here from 6 to 10 for one. Taxes in Specie must be obtained and *that* with more punctuality." Mr. R[obert] Morris has been "engaged" to be superintendent of finance, although it will be "some time" before the country "can see and feel the effects of his labor."[9] Is sorry about NG's disappointment of 25 April, when complete victory was in "full view."[10] Admires the "firmness and perseverance" of NG's army, which is constantly exposed to "weariness[,] famine[,] nakedness and the sword." Is pained by NG's "fatigue, trouble and anxiety" and by the fact that NG receives so little support from North Carolina. Hopes the enemy's victory on 25 April "will eventually be similar to that of Guilford C[t] House." In a postscript, dated 22 May, adds that a French admiral and the son of Comte Rochambeau have arrived in Rhode Island.[11] Washington and the French commanders are to meet to "form a definitive plan of the present campaign."[12] Sharpe reiterates his concern that the French second division "will delay" in the West Indies. There has been "Not a word of reinforcements for Gen[l] [Henry] Clinton," and as of early March, the British "grand fleet had not put to Sea."[13] Repeats the news of the failure of the mission of Germain's secretary in Spain; adds that the "Emperor" has proposed to mediate between "the beligerent powers."[14] ALS (NjMoHP) 3 pp.]

1. For more on this report, which proved to be false, see note at Mathews to NG, immediately above.

2. Wayne's Pennsylvania Continentals began their march to the South on 26 May. (See note at Washington to NG, 1 June, below.)

3. As noted at La Luzerne to NG, 3 April, above, the "second division" was never sent to America. However, as seen at Huntington to NG, 12 May, above, a large French fleet sailed for the West Indies on 22 March. Commanded by the Comte de Grasse, it later played a key role in the capture of Lord Cornwallis's army at Yorktown, Va.

4. The shipment of clothing from France had long been expected. (See Mathews to NG, 12 December 1780, above [vol. 6: 565 and n].) As Sharpe feared, the *Marquis de Lafayette*, which was bringing the clothing and other supplies to America, had been captured by the British on 3 May. (Idzerda, *Lafayette Papers*, 4: 235n)

5. Palfrey, a former paymaster general of the Continental army, had been appointed consul to France in October 1780, with instructions, "in addition to his consular functions, to receive and forward all supplies to be obtained in that kingdom for the use of the United States, and to assist in directing our naval affairs." (*JCC*, 18: 976–78) The ship he was on had been lost at sea.

6. Congress had sent John Laurens to France as a special envoy. (For more on his mission, see above, vol. 6: 463n.)

7. On the "preparations" by the Dutch and "aid" for them from the "northern powers," see note at Mathews to NG, 30 April, above.

8. The clothing, which had been sent by John Jay, the American ambassador to Spain, had long since been promised by the Spanish government. (See Wharton, *Revolutionary Diplomatic Correspondence*, 4: 125, 144, 149, 169.) Washington wrote Robert Morris that "about 3000" suits of clothes had arrived, adding that "unfortunately the Coats are scarlet." (Washington to Morris, 13 July, Fitzpatrick, *GW*, 22: 367)

9. On the appointment of Morris as superintendent of finance, see Sharpe to NG, 28 May, below.

10. Sharpe was referring to the battle of Hobkirk's Hill, which is discussed at NG to Huntington, 27 April, above.

11. The Vicomte de Rochambeau and the Comte de Barras arrived in Boston on 8 May. The latter had been sent to take command of the French naval squadron at Newport, R.I., while the former brought instructions for the 1781 campaign to his father, the Comte de Rochambeau. (Kennett, *French Forces*, p. 104)

12. On the meeting between Washington and the Comte de Rochambeau, see Sharpe to NG, 28 May, below.

13. Clinton did not receive a significant reinforcement until Sir Samuel Hood brought a regiment from the West Indies in late August. (Mackesy, *War for America*, pp. 422–23) The British "grand fleet" was presumably the Channel fleet, which had left to relieve Gibraltar on 13 March, thus missing an opportunity to intercept de Grasse's naval force when it sailed for American waters from Brest. (Ibid., pp. 388–89)

14. For more on the possible mediation by the emperor of Austria, see Sharpe to NG, 28 May, below.

¶ [**FROM GENERAL THOMAS SUMTER**, Camp at Ancrum's, S.C., 22 May 1781. "By the last accounts," Lord Rawdon had halted at Monck's Corner; Sumter is not sure if he is fortifying that place.[1] Sumter also has a report, which he doubts, that Lord Cornwallis is "upon his Return this Way."[2] The fortifications at Friday's Ferry, Camden, Motte's, and Orangeburg are "Tolerably well Demolished." Believes the militia, "especially in the disafected Regem^{ts}," will "turn out well," although they have few arms.[3] Col. [Richard] Hampton has returned from a raid to the "Southward." He took a few British prisoners near Monck's Corner, almost captured the commandant of Charleston, and found the residents removing their stock from the reach of the British, as Sumter had directed. Hammond visited Dorchester, Ashley River, Round O, Edisto, "&C," killing one man, taking several prisoners, and destroying a boat. Sumter is preparing to "fix M^r McElrath to his business at this place In preference to Charlotte," as all the materials "are here."[4] ALS (MiU-C) 2 pp.]

1. As noted at Marion to NG, 22 May, above, the British were fortifying Biggin's Church, near Monck's Corner.

2. The report was erroneous.

3. "Disafected Regem^{ts}" were those from districts whose populations had a high percentage of Loyalists.

4. Sumter was setting up an armory at Ancrum's Plantation to make weapons for his troops. (Gregorie, *Sumter*, p. 162)

* * *

To Colonel William Davies

Dear Sir   Camp before Ninty Six [S.C.] May 23ᵈ 1781
I am favord with yours of the 16th and 18th of April and as they arrived only last Evening, I imagine they must have lain long on the road.

Your observations respecting the pernicious consequences of short
inlistments are very just; and I fear with you the evil has got so deeply
rooted as to render it almost impossible to remove it.[1] Our embarassments under the best direction are numerous, but by impolicy they are
greatly multiplied. We have a chequered scene before us. No sooner
does a gleam of hope rise to view than it is shaded with a Cloud of fear.
In the Southern States there is a great struggle for empire and the
Animosity between the Whigs and Tories of this State render their
situation truly deplorable. There is not a day passes but there are more
or less who fall a sacrafice to this savage disposition. The Whigs seem
determined to exterpate the Tories and the Tories the Whigs. Some
thousands have fallen in this way in this quarter, and the evil rages
with more violence than ever. The British they stand idle spectators
and behold with calm phylosophy the horid scene they have set on
foot. If a stop cannot soon be put to those private massacres this
Country will be depopulated in a few months more, as neither Whig
nor Tory can live.

The Enemy have made a sally, and I can add nothing further.[2] But
my best wishes for your health and happiness. Most respectfully
yours   N GREENE

ADfS (MiU-C).
1. See Davies to NG, 16 April, above.
2. For more on the "sally," which took place the morning after the Southern Army
opened its siege of Ninety Six, see note at NG to Huntington, 20 June, below.

*   *   *

¶ [TO STEPHEN HEARD OR THE SENIOR COLONEL OF GEORGIA.[1]
From [Camp before Ninety Six, S.C.], May 23, 1781. Encloses a copy of a letter
from the Georgia delegates in Congress "concerning supplies coming from the
Northward" for the militia of Georgia.[2] These are expected to arrive "in a few
days" and should be sent for "as soon as possible."[3] NG suggests, but does not
"direct," that they be distributed to troops who will be in service four or five
months. ADfS (NcD) 1 p.]
1. Heard, a militia colonel, was president of the state council. (McCall, *History of
Georgia*, pp. 468–69) Col. Elijah Clarke was then the senior colonel in the state. (See NG
to Georgia Congressional Delegates, 22 June, below.)
2. The letter to NG from delegate George Walton, dated 5 April, is above.
3. NG wrote Clarke on 7 June, below, that the stores had arrived; they were delivered
to Clarke. (See NG to the Georgia Delegates, 22 June, below.)

*   *   *

To the Marquis de Lafayette

Dear Marquis   Camp at Ninty Six [S.C.] May 23ᵈ 1781

Your two letters of the 3ᵈ and one of the 7th have been safely receivd, tho the chance was greatly against it, such is the risque and difficulty of conveying dispaches through this Country.[1]

I am convinced by Lord Cornwallis movements that he means to form a junction with General Philips and I fear it will be out of your power to prevent it.[2] Your seasonable arrival at Richmond gave me great pleasure, but your force is quite inadequate to the protection of that extensive Country intersected with rivers as it is.

The destruction of our Stores will be the great object with the Enemy; and should be carefully guarded against. There will be no poss[i]bility of securing them but by throwing them high up into the open Country. I think Staunten over the Mountain will be the most proper place, and have given orders to Lt Col [Edward] Carrington accordingly.[3] Could I have supposd that the Pennsylvania line would have been so tedious in coming on, and that the Virginia drafts so late in taking the field, I should have advisd to this measure before.[4]

General Washington wrote me that the Pennsylvania first brigade was to march the 16 of April. If they did they must be with you before this.[5] Maryland has totally neglected us[.] Not a man has arrivd from that State since I have been in the Southern department. The critical situation of these States and the tardiness of the Legislators and the drowsiness of the people is truly distressing and alarming. However could you hold your ground in Virginia for a few Weeks, I should begin to hope for a change for the better. But by a letter from Major Claiborne and another from Mr McCraw to Col [Edward] Carrington I have reason to apprehend several waggon loads of Stores fell into the enemies hands at Petersburg after they fell down the River; and that all our Stores at Carters Ferry if not those at Prince Edward have been destroyed.[6] Should this be true, it will distress us exceedingly. God avert so fatal a misfortune. Cannot the french fleet be brought to operate with us to the Southward. If they could once get in to Potomack River they would be in perfect security against any force the enemy could employ against them either by land or water. If you think well of it try to bring it about. You have great influence at Court and are not less interested than myself.[7]

My former letters will inform you what is my desire respecting the forces in Virginia and coming from the Northard and how they are to be employed;[8] and you will give the necessary orders accordingly; I dont mean to confine you in any thing but to leave you to act as circumstance may direct. The public has much to hope from your activities and zeal; but I have every thing to fear from the inferiority of your force, which like ours here is but the shadow of an Army.

We have laid siege to this place but the fortifications are so strong and the garrison so large and so well furnished that our success is very doubtful. Augu[sta] is also closely beseiged by a detachment under Lt Col [Henry] Lee.[9] If we are successful here I shall move Northwardly immediately with a part of our force if [not?] all.[10] Since I wrote you before the enemy have evacuated their post at Nelsons Ferry & blown up their works and retreated to Charles Town.[11] Most respectfully yours.   N GREENE

ALS (Greene Papers: DLC).
1. Lafayette's letter of 7 May has not been found.
2. On Cornwallis's forming a junction with Gen. William Phillips's army in Virginia, see note at Lafayette to NG, first letter of 3 May, above.
3. NG's orders to Carrington have not been found. In his first letter to NG of 3 June, below, Lafayette discussed his efforts to move stores in Virginia to safety; it is unlikely, however, that he did so in response to these orders from NG.
4. See note at Washington to NG, 1 June, below, and Steuben to NG, 15 May, above, on delays in the march of the Pennsylvania line and problems in assembling the Virginia drafts.
5. NG referred to Washington's letter to him of 19 April, above. As noted at Washington to NG, 1 June, the Pennsylvania troops did not march for Virginia until 26 May.
6. Richard Claiborne was deputy quartermaster in Virginia; William McCraw was an assistant deputy quartermaster at Peytonsburg, Va. Neither man's letter has been found. In early May, the British captured army stores near Petersburg consisting of nearly 2,000 yards of cloth, 4,000 yards of canvas, and a ton of lead. (Account of Loss of Goods at Petersburg, undated, Boyd, *Jefferson Papers*, 5: 660–61) No supplies were lost from the depots at Carter's Ferry or Prince Edward Court House.
7. Lafayette does not seem to have tried to get the fleet moved to Chesapeake Bay. By the time he received NG's letter, however, he knew that a Franco-American force, including the French fleet at Rhode Island, was planning to attack either the British garrison at New York City or Cornwallis's army in Virginia. (See Lafayette to NG, 20 June and 21 June, both below.)
8. See NG's letters to Lafayette of 1 and 14 May, both above.
9. See Lee to NG, 22 May, above.
10. The siege of Ninety Six lasted until 19 June and failed to bring about the surrender of the post; NG did not take troops "northwardly," to Virginia.
11. NG was relaying reports he had received from Francis Marion in letters of 16 and 22 May, both above. As seen in the note at the latter letter, Lord Rawdon's army had not retreated to Charleston.

To Governor Abner Nash of North Carolina

Dear Sir   Camp before Ninety Six [S.C.] May 23[d] 1781
I am favord with your two letters of the 7th and 11th.[1]

I wish Lord Cornwallis's situation and mine were such as to have obligd him to take the measures he has upon the principles you suppose. But give me leave to tell you they are far otherwise. It was my intention to have drawn him after me and it was his intention I should have followed him. Both have failed in our expectations. I have pursued my plan and he his. I took the measure with a view to transfer the War from your State into this; but tho I have not succeed[ed] in the main point yet the Manoeuver will have its advantages but North Carolinia will smart for it a little; and perhaps under sufferings she will learn wisdom and be better provided to protect her self in future.[2] It would give me great pleasure to afford you every relief in my power; and you may be assurd that I shall chearfully engage every toil and danger to protect you all in my power; but without men and Supplies what can I effect. My utmost exertions has not been wanting to serve you and if you was fully acquainted with my true situation I perswade myself you would think so.

I have written my mind fully to Congress respecting the inability of the Southern States to contend with the force employed against them, and that unless there is considerable assistance afforded them they must fall.[3] My situation is so extremely disagreeable that I could wish to be in a more eligible situation in any other quarter.

We have various reports respecting the Enemies movements in Virginia but without any certainty and as they are not very agreeable I will wait for better information.

I hope measures have been taken to have the horses moved out of the enemies way. If not I fear they will gallop over the State as they please as our Cavalry is greatly diminished by the severity of the service.[4] I have the honor to be with the greatest respect Your Excellencys most Obed humble S^er   N GREENE

ADfS (MiU-C).

1. Nash's letter of 11 May is above; his two letters of 7 May have not been found.

2. NG discussed his reasons for moving his army to South Carolina in his letter to Samuel Huntington of 22 April, above.

3. See ibid.

4. NG had mentioned the need to keep horses away from the enemy in his letter to Nash of 13 April, above.

* * *

¶ [CAPTAIN NATHANIEL PENDLETON TO COLONEL JAMES READ. From "Camp before Ninety Six," S.C., 23 May 1781. Acknowledges Read's letter of the 17th. NG approves Read's plan to move the military stores "over the mountain" if Lord Cornwallis moves toward Salisbury, N.C.; asks him to take measures to "save them from being taken or destroyed."[1] Col. [Lewis] Morris, whom Read will see before he receives this letter, will designate which stores are to be sent to the army.[2] ADfS (MiU-C) 2 pp.]

1. Cornwallis did not move in the direction of Salisbury.

2. See NG to Morris, 21 May, above.

¶ [TO BARON STEUBEN. From "Camp at Ninety Six," S.C., 23 May 1781. Has just received Steuben's letter of 5 May. Refers him to "the Marquis [de

Lafayette]" for details of "operations here." NG has directed that "all the force coming from the Northward (Maryland excepted)," the Virginia "Drafts," and the North Carolina troops under Gen. [Jethro] Sumner be employed "to prevent a junction between his Lordship and General Philips."[1] Says: "I know you will do every thing that can be done or expected; but the means are wanting. We who serve in the southern department are little less than devoted, so unequal is the means to the duty expected of us."[2] Regrets that Steuben set the place of rendezvous "so near Richmond"; fears he will be "interrupted."[3] If the Pennsylvania troops have arrived and the Virginia drafts have been collected—"as they should have been long since"—NG hopes they "will with the Militia in the field have a respectable force."[4] LS (NHi) 2 pp.]

1. See NG to Lafayette and NG to Steuben, 14 May, both above. As seen in the note at Lafayette to NG, first letter of 3 May, above, Lord Cornwallis had already joined forces with the army of the late Gen. William Phillips.

2. As NG used it here, "devoted" means doomed to destruction. (Johnson, *Dictionary*)

3. NG referred to the rendezvous point for the Virginia draftees, which was at Chesterfield Court House, some ten miles from Richmond.

4. As seen at Washington to NG, 1 June, below, the Pennsylvania troops had not yet left Pennsylvania. Steuben did not receive this letter until 17 June. (See Steuben to NG, 19 June, below.)

¶ [TO GENERAL JETHRO SUMNER. From "Camp before Ninety Six," S.C., 23 May 1781. NG has Sumner's letters of 23 April and 7 and 11 May.[1] Is "sorry the Drafts are so tedious in collecting, and that the Article of Arms was not earlier attended to." In "former Letters," NG "desired" all the draftees to collect at Hillsborough or wherever Sumner "might think more convenient." He excluded only those from Salisbury, whom NG will arm and who will join "this Army."[2] Hopes Sumner will comply with NG's instructions and join "the Marquis [de Lafayette] or Baron Steuben, to prevent a junction if possible between his Lordship and Gen' Philips."[3] Has "nothing certain" on enemy movements in Virginia. Lists the enemy posts in South Carolina that have been evacuated or taken. Has captured 700 or 800 "regulars and irregulars, and fifty odd Officers." Expects Ninety Six and Augusta, Ga., to "fall." LS (NcU) 2 pp.]

1. All three letters are above; the second, dated 6 and 8 May, is at the latter date.

2. NG's orders concerning the troops are in his letters to Sumner of 8, 11, 19, and 21 April and 5 May, all above.

3. See NG to Sumner, 5 May, above. The union of the two enemy armies had already taken place.

¶ [FROM DOCTOR JAMES McHENRY, Baltimore, Md., 23 May 1781. Acknowledges NG's letter of 1 May [not found] and "most tenderly" sympathizes with him on his "various distresses and those of my country. Every one here does the same, and thinks of you pretty nearly as I do." Cannot say if NG's "want of success is considered every where in the same light," but is "sure it should."[1] Calls NG's move to Camden, S.C., a "great piece of generalship," regardless of the outcome. To have a "proper efficacy," however, NG must "extricate" himself and his "little army." If NG had "suceeded," the people would have understood that he was moving the war "into what may be called the enemy's country" and diverting the enemy's attention from the upper

South. "Even as it is, I think they must see it." Encloses the "two last Maryland papers," both of which contain "a little" about NG. Supposing that NG was "in a difficult situation," McHenry "took the liberty" to add to the letters that were printed "to prepare the people for such an event as has taken place."[2]

Thinks NG will succeed in his "application through the General," unless Congress anticipates the "business by sending" McHenry a commission before NG's letter arrives. "It is only a Majors, but any thing to place me where I wish to be."[3] McHenry will be joining the Marquis de Lafayette soon, having "got all the shirts ready" for the latter's detachment. Cautions NG that as "a matter of etiquette," Lafayette "will expect" NG to write him "on the subject of borrowing" McHenry.[4] ALS (MiU-C) 3 pp.]

1. McHenry no doubt referred to NG's defeat in the battle of Hobkirk's Hill, which is discussed at NG to Huntington, 27 April, above.

2. An article reporting the destruction of tobacco in Virginia by Gen. William Phillips's army concludes with these sentences concerning NG's siege of Camden: "The great Strength of the Place, it was thought, would not admit of a Storm, and the General's Circumstances were by no Means calculated to continue the Siege, and support himself against the present Combination. Had some men the Command of our little Army at this critical Moment (considering the superior Force of Cornwallis and Philips, [when?] united—their Intentions and his Situation) I would give up the Army and its Commander for lost. But [I?] prophesy that Greene will extricate himself to [the?] Discredit of both Cornwallis and Phillips." (*Maryland Journal and Baltimore Advertiser*, 15 May 1781)

Appended to an account of the battle of Hobkirk's Hill by an officer serving with the Southern Army—undoubtedly Otho Williams—is the following paragraph:

> When I say that our Commander has behaved himself as heretofore, I only barely do him justice. Look back into our Proceedings, with so Little Means, where have you read so much having been done? Let this Man be unfortunate, or let him be successful, in either Case he will be a great Man. When we get more Troops, we will win Battles; and when we have better Means, we will recover lost Countries. If the Southern States should be *overrun*, blame no one in this Quarter. We have done our Duty; would to God I could say the same thing of these States from whom we have been so long expecting Succour. Tell me, you who know something of public Affairs, what Policy is it, that has prevented you from sending us *black Troops*, if you could not get *white ones*; what Policy is it, that has kept from us, as I am told, about 300 new Levies, for near three Months, which might have given us *two* Victories? As soon as 20 or 30 of your Levies had got together, why have they not been forwarded, under proper Officers? Is it the Officers who do not exert themselves on such Occasions, or is it the Government that fall asleep over their Business? Whatever be the Cause, I know who will experience its Effects. We are not many. We have been tried by great Sufferings, and ye all know, whether we have shrunk from our Duty. But the Sufferings we must feel, arise from the Supineness of some of our Countrymen.

(*Maryland Journal and Baltimore Advertiser*, 22 May 1781)

3. In a letter of 1 May, above, NG had asked Washington to try to persuade Congress to grant a major's commission to McHenry, whom NG wanted as an aide-de-camp. McHenry wrote NG on 29 May, below, that Congress had voted him the commission.

4. McHenry repeated this advice when he wrote NG on 29 May, below; he did not join NG as an aide, however.

¶ [FROM COLONEL JAMES MAYSON,[1] Glasgow, S.C., 23 May 1781.[2] Thanks NG on behalf of some "officers Ladys" for his "Politeness and attention" in sending a guard and one of his aides to "wait on" them. Mayson's overseer, who is bringing the Negroes, as NG ordered, will escort Mrs. Mayson's sister back from "the fort."[3] Requests a passport for a trunk. Mayson's son, who would otherwise have waited on NG, has left to join NG's troops. ALS (MiU-C) 1 p.]

    1. Mayson, a South Carolina Continental officer, lived in the Ninety Six district. (Heitman, *Register*; Lambert, *South Carolina Loyalists*, p. 34)

    2. Glasgow was the name of Mayson's plantation. It was located on the Saluda River in present-day Abbeville County.

    3. See Mayson to Pierce, this date, immediately below.

¶ [COLONEL JAMES MAYSON TO CAPTAIN WILLIAM PIERCE, JR., from "Salluday" [Saluda River], S.C., 23 May 1781. Mayson's overseer will bring the "negroes," with "proper tools," as Pierce's letter [not found] directed. The overseer will also collect and bring to camp "all other negros betwixt this and head Quarters."[1] "They will not do much," however, unless they are given provisions. Some of NG's officers, on "misinformation," have taken a Mr. Colcock's horses and most of his corn. Colcock, who has moved to Dorchester "for the sake of his family," was previously plundered by the British, who called him an "Invitteret Rebble." If the corn is not returned, he will lose his crops, "as well as his plantation." Mayson returns a letter for another man, who has left the area and is now believed to be "near the sea coste." Mrs. Mayson will be obliged if NG can arrange to get the enclosed letter to her sister, "who is in the garrison [at Ninety Six]."[2] Adds in a postscript that he has just learned 400 men will join NG "this day."[3] ALS (MiU-C) 1 p.]

    1. The slaves were presumably to be used in digging approaches to the fort at Ninety Six.

    2. See also, Mayson to NG, this date, immediately above.

    3. Presumably these were local militiamen.

¶ [FROM GENERAL JAMES M. VARNUM, Philadelphia, 23 May 1781. Explains that he had not written NG because he feared a letter discussing "Political subjects" might be intercepted, yet one discussing other topics would "be of no great Consequence." In general, "matters begin to take a desirable Turn." Believes "this Campaign" will be "principally" in the South, even though "Common military Principles" would dictate an attack on New York—the enemy's "principal Place of Arms"—during the warm weather and the transfer of troops to the South afterwards. Does not dare to give the reasons for this belief, "for fear of a Discovery." Is concerned about NG's situation—not because of what happened at Camden, which was "chargeable upon the Fickleness of Fortune only," but from the maneuvers of Lord Cornwallis and Gen. [William] Phillips.[1] Is "apprehensive" that NG's lines of communication will be "totally intercepted"; in that case, Varnum "cannot imagine" how NG will supply himself. NG's "military character now stands high," but the "human heart is very fluctuating," and judgments "are always affected" by the last occurrence. "A capitel Misfortune might injure you, altho' you have performed more already for the Service of the Country, than Zenophon."[2] Thinks the British have sent another reinforcement from New York to the South.[3] The Marquis de Lafayette has "few Continental Troops," and

[Gen. Anthony] Wayne's force has not marched from York, Pa., "before to-day." It will be "very fortunate" if NG can join Lafayette and Wayne on the James River.[4] Reports that "Col. [Christopher] Greene and Major Flagg were both killed last Week near Croton [N.Y.] I believe, by a surprise, as very few Men were lost. A Severe Shock."[5] Rhode Island has "about compleated" its Continental line, but the other New England states "are not so forward." Gives the results of an election in Rhode Island. Encloses a letter from Catharine Greene [not found]. Tr (MiU-C) 2 pp.]

1. On the battle of Hobkirk's Hill, which took place near Camden, see NG to Huntington, 27 April, above; on the junction of Cornwallis's and Phillips's armies in Virginia, see note at Lafayette to NG, first letter of 3 May, above.

2. As noted above (vol. 6: 267n), Xenophon led a Greek army to safety in a long retreat through Persia.

3. On the British reinforcement from New York, see the note at St. Clair to NG, 6 May, above.

4. As seen in the note at Washington to NG, 1 June, below, Wayne's Pennsylvanians did not march until 26 May. While Wayne and Lafayette successfully combined, NG did not join them in Virginia.

5. Col. Christopher Greene, NG's cousin, commanded Rhode Island's First Continental Regiment, which was also known as the "Black Regiment" because it included many ex-slaves. Greene and Maj. Ebenezer Flagg were killed on 14 May when the regiment's headquarters at Croton was surprised by DeLancey's Refugees, a mounted Loyalist unit. (Anthony Walker, *So Few the Brave: Rhode Island Continentals, 1775–1783* [Newport, R.I.: Seafield Press, 1981], p. 78)

¶ [GENERAL GREENE'S ORDERS, "Camp before Ninety-Six," S.C., 24 May 1781. Officers are to be "constantly with their Commands" and are not to allow their men to be "absent from their Corps or Duty upon any pretence." Lamar Orderly Book (OClWHi) 1 p.]

¶ [TO THE BOARD OF WAR. From Camp at Ninety Six, S.C., 24 May 1781. Forwards the proceedings of the court-martial of Lt. [John] Townes, which Gen. [William] Moultrie sent for NG's approval. Believing that officers in captivity lack the "authority" to order a court-martial, NG has taken no action. Townes considers himself "injurd in the determination" and has requested that the matter be "laid before" the board and Congress.[1] NG asks the board to inform Townes, who is in Philadelphia at "great expence," that the proceedings have arrived and to give him the enclosed letter.[2] ADfS (MiU-C) 2 pp.]

1. On Townes's court-martial, see his letter to NG of 25 April, above.

2. NG's letter to Townes of this date is below.

¶ [TO GENERAL JOHN BUTLER. From Camp before Ninety Six, S.C., 24 May 1781. Thanks Butler for the intelligence contained in his letters of 4 and 11 May. NG had anticipated that "Lord Cornwallis's pride would force him to the Northward." Gives a "state of matters" in South Carolina. "Near eight hundred prisoners and fifty officers" have been captured. Should Ninety Six and Augusta, Ga., fall, "which is by no means certain tho probable[,] our prisoners will be numerous and the whole country open near to the gates of Charlestown and the people are joining us in all quarters tho much distressed for want of arms." Is pleased that the draft in North Carolina is almost completed. Hopes there will be time enough to equip the North Carolina draftees "seasonably for the support of the Marquis [de Lafayette]" should the "enemy effect a junction as is probable."[1] Tr (GWG Transcript: CSmH) 1 p.]

1. The draft in North Carolina had yielded only a few men and they lacked needed arms and equipment. (See Sumner to NG, 15 May, above.) When they were finally ready to march, these troops were sent to join NG's army in South Carolina, arriving in early August. (See note at Sumner to NG, 8 April, above.)

*   *   *

To the Marquis de Malmedy

Dear Sir   Camp before Ninety Six [S.C.] May 24th 1781
    Your letter of the 11th I have had the pleasure of receiving. It gives me pain that the enemy have it so much in their power to run over the State [i.e., North Carolina] with so little opposition.
    The Legislature would not be persuaded of their critical situation until it was too late to remedy the evil. I am sensible of the critical situation of the Marquis [de Lafayette] and of the impossibility of affording him seasonable aid. However I have taken every measure in my power and at as early a period as the Enemies intentions could be reduced to a certainty, to give him support. If the Stores are left at Hallifax it has been owing to discrediting or the miscarriage of some of my letters which directed the Stores to be held in readiness to move at the shortest notice; and all articles not immediately wanted for the Manufactories to be sent into the uper Country.[1]
    The great scarcity of Arms and other Accoutrements renders it difficult, nay impossible to employ the force of the State to advantage. The plan you proposd would have been eligible had the State the means of raising and equiping her regular force and those you proposed also. But if she could equip only one the regular service should have the preference.
    As our situation is somwhat critical should the enemy effect a junction with each other and move in force this way, I beg you to continue in the Neighbourhood of the place where you are, or take such a position as to be able to give me the best intelligence of their probable plan of future operations. Your general knowledge of war and of the geography of this Country will enable you to dive into their intentions better and earlier than any other person, who has not those advantages tho equal as to natural abilities. I am Sir Your most Obed[t] humble Ser
                                                            N GREENE

ADfS (MiU-C).
    1. NG must have referred here to his letter to Nicholas Long of 6 May, above. Joseph Clay's account of the capture of the stores was more favorable to supply department personnel than Malmedy had been in his letter of 11 May, above. (See Clay to NG, 11 May, above.)

*   *   *

¶ [CAPTAIN WILLIAM PIERCE, JR., TO CAPTAIN MATTHEW RAMSEY. From Camp before Ninety Six, S.C., 24 May 1781. NG has received Ramsey's letter of 4 April and thanks him for the intelligence and for his "care" in collecting the hides left by the army. The army's dragoons need saddles; Ramsey should complete those he is working on and have more made. ADfS (MiU-C) 1 p.]

¶ [TO DAVID ROSS. From Camp before Ninety Six, S.C., 24 May 1781. Ross's "fortune and knowledge in business" enable him to serve the public in many ways, but none "more effectually than in promoting the Iron business." The army is "distressed" for such products. Ross's works are situated "high up the Country," while Hunter's are exposed, difficult to protect, and liable to be destroyed because of their known importance to the army.[1] NG therefore recommends that Ross set up a "Sliting & plating Mill[,] a Gun and Camp Kettle Manufactory. The public can afford to make it worth" his while, and it will greatly serve the country. NG adds: "I shall from time to time give you all the countenance and aid in my power; and shall consider my self under a personal obligation besides." NG was "induced" to write because of Ross's "general character for promoting extensive business" and from Col. [Edward] Carrington's "perswasion" that Ross "wanted only to have it recommended and countenanced" before engaging in this work. NG does not know Ross personally but trusts "our characters are known to each other." Asks Ross to reply.[2] ADfS (MiU-C) 3 pp.]

1. The enemy never disturbed James Hunter's iron works, which were in Fredericksburg, Va.

2. Ross was serving as Virginia's commercial agent. (Virginia, Council of State, *Journals*, 2: 278) Neither his reply nor any evidence that he expanded his iron making operation in Bedford County, Va., has been found.

¶ [COLONEL LEWIS MORRIS, JR., TO LIEUTENANT [RICHARD?] MASON.[1] From Charlotte, N.C., 24 May 1781. By NG's order, Mason, with some "troops from the Hospital," is to escort a brigade of wagons to the Saluda River by a given route. He is to obtain his provisions and forage "upon the road," giving receipts for what he impresses. He is to move quickly and "compactly" and report to NG when he reaches the Saluda. ALS (ScU) 1 p.]

1. The recipient, whose name was given in the docketing as "L' Mason," was presumably Richard Mason, an officer in the North Carolina Continental line.

¶ [TO LIEUTENANT JOHN TOWNES. From Camp before Ninety Six, S.C., 24 May 1781. Has received Townes's letters of 4 March and 25 April.[1] The Board of War has the proceedings of the court-martial and NG's "sentiments upon them."[2] Cy (Washington Papers: DLC) 1 p.]

1. Townes's letter of 4 March has not been found; that of 25 April is above.

2. See NG to Board of War, this date, above; on Townes's case, see his letter to NG of 25 April.

¶ [FROM COLONEL ROBERT ANDERSON, "Camp at Pudenns Quarter," S.C., 24 May 1781.[1] Anderson, who learned of NG's arrival at Ninety Six "Last Evening," had already sent most of his men to the frontier after hearing "of the Indians Murdering." From the account he received, the Indians had "murdered several Families, at least they were in their Power." The alarm was raised by a boy who escaped with "five Small Children Destitute of any other help."[2] When Anderson learned of NG's arrival, he sent some men to obtain "what Waggons could be got" and to collect and drive cattle to the army. Since starting this letter, he has received directions from Col. Edward Carrington to provide forage; he will "Immediately Detach" for that purpose and will use "Every man" to assist in NG's operations.[3] Adds: "I Glory in Giveing my small Assistance to the American Arms, & will do Every thing in my Power"; fears, though, that the "Efforts" of the people in his area "will be Too weak," as they are "much Distress'd" and have had their provisions, forage, horses, and wagons "much taken & Destroy'd" by the enemy. They are "Really at a loss to Know how to do the needfull." Hopes NG will reply by the bearer.[4] ALS (MiU-C) 3 pp.]

1. Anderson, a colonel in Gen. Andrew Pickens's militia brigade, commanded the men Pickens had left in the neighborhood of Ninety Six when he marched most of his force to Augusta, Ga. (See Pickens to NG, 8 May, above.)

2. Nothing more is known about this incident. As seen at Lanier to NG, 27 May, below, a few Cherokee still opposed a negotiated peace and continued to raid and kill.

3. Carrington's letter has not been found.

4. No reply has been found.

¶ [FROM SAMUEL HUNTINGTON, PRESIDENT OF THE CONTINENTAL CONGRESS, Philadelphia, 24 May 1781. Encloses a copy of a resolution of Congress of 15 May, appointing the "principal Officers" of the Southern Army's medical department.[1] Those who are prisoners of war will be "continued" in their "Offices," but their responsibilities are "to extend no farther than to the Troops & Hospitals within the Enemies Lines." Acknowledges receipt of NG's letters of 22 and 27 April. Cy (PCC, item 15, p. 292, DNA) 2 pp.]

1. The medical officers named were: David Oliphant, deputy director; Peter Fayssoux, chief physician of the hospital; James Brown, chief physician of the army; and Robert Johnston and William Read, hospital physicians. (JCC, 20: 506)

¶ [FROM THE MARQUIS DE LAFAYETTE, Richmond, Va., 24 May 1781. Sends a copy of his letter to Washington.[1] The situation in "this Quarter is not very Comfortable." Lafayette will do his best, but he expects that "people who don't judge upon any Rational Scale Will find it Very Strange that I Have not yet Beaten the Ennemy to pieces." He therefore must look for "Approbation" to Washington, NG, and a few friends, who, he hopes, "Will think with me I Could not do Better." Hopes Lord Cornwallis's absence from South Carolina "May be Improved"; it will "Greatly lessen the pain of the lashes we are Going to Receive in this triply invaded State." Discusses his disappointment in the delay of the Pennsylvania Continentals, who have long been expected. He wrote to "General Waine [Anthony Wayne]" when he learned that Cornwallis was moving through North Carolina, asking him to hasten his march; Wayne's answer, dated 19 May, states that the troops will set off on 23 May and hurry as best they can, but gives "No Reasons" for the delay and "No Account of their Numbers."[2] Lafayette has been informed privately that "there Had Been Some difficulty for their Coming that was levelled By a positive order from General Washington."[3] The delay cost Lafayette any opportunity he had of "Striking" at the enemies' detachments before they united. Adds that any chance of receiving "Lord Cornwallis's first Stroke upon Good Grounds and with a decent force is far Remote and Before Waine Comes we Shall Be obliged to take to our

Heels." He has written the governor of Maryland and Gen. [William] Small-wood, "Earnestly Requesting" that they "forward their New levies" and give NG "Every Assistance."[4] Assures NG that no time will be lost in sending on the Marylanders and Pennsylvanians. Lafayette realizes Virginia "Cannot Be upon a footing With the Ennemy," and nothing but NG's conquest of South Carolina can afford it "proper Relief." As Lafayette's opinion agrees completely with NG's, NG can be assured that Lafayette will "ponctually Obey" all of NG's orders. Baron Steuben is with the new levies. He has not yet informed Lafayette of the situation in the department, as he promised, so the "Business" of supplies for NG remains in Steuben's hands. Lafayette has asked him to do all he can to provide "Comfort and assistance" to NG. "When the Ennemy Have pushed me My object will Be as much as possible to Cover the Communication through the Mountain and the Works at Fredericksburg." Thinks a position near the South Anna River might be best for this, but "the Ennemy's Cavalry and Mounted Infantry Are So Numerous that we Cannot Guard Against partizan Strokes." Expects to know the enemy's intentions in a few days; they have not yet established any post, "So that they Over Run But do not Conquer the Country. Before they get Here we will fight a little But by detail." Steuben has asked to have Armand's Legion go with him to join NG. Lafayette will allow this, except for twelve men, who are needed "upon the lines." Those twelve and thirty from White's Regiment are his only cavalry. Gen. [Peter] Muhlenberg and Gen. [Thomas] Nelson are with Lafayette; Gen. [George] Weedon is at Fredericksburg; Gen. [Robert] Lawson commands on the south side of the Appomattox River but "will get very few men. Indeed Had He Been permitted By the Executive to proceed to Carolina I do not Believe He Could Have got any."[5] Sends his compliments to NG's aides. ALS (NNPM) 4 pp.]

1. Lafayette sent NG a copy of his "official" letter to Washington, dated 24 May. (It is printed in *The Letters of Lafayette to Washington, 1777–1799*, ed. Louis Gottschalk, rev. ed. [Philadelphia: American Philosophical Society, 1976], pp. 196–97.)

2. Lafayette had written Wayne on 7 May. An abstract of that letter and the full text of Wayne's reply are in Idzerda, *Lafayette Papers*, 4: 492, 114–15. As noted at Washington to NG, 1 June, above, the Pennsylvania line began its march on 26 May.

3. According to the editors of the *Lafayette Papers*, "No evidence has been found to support this rumor," which George Weedon communicated to Lafayette in a letter of 22 May. (Ibid., p. 130n)

4. Lafayette had written Gov. Thomas Sim Lee of Maryland on 21 May. (Ibid., p. 494)

5. On Lawson and the militia reinforcements that were to have joined NG, see notes at Jefferson to NG, 30 March, and Lawson to NG, 20 April, both above.

¶ [FROM COLONEL HENRY LEE, JR., "Camp before Augusta," Ga., 24 May 1781. Has NG's letter of 22 May and is pleased that NG has reached Ninety Six, which "must fall long before this." The "connexion of Browne[s] & Griersons forts" makes the situation at Augusta "difficult" for the American forces; only Lee's 110 Legion infantrymen are "in any sort calculated" for "sieges & storms."[1] The stores taken at Ft. Dreadnought "are not so valuable or so abundant as report said." Sends Capt. [John] Rudulph's report, a "list of prisoners, stores &c."[2] The militia want a share of the stores. "Their distresses & exertions (at least some of them) entitle them to part." NG should specify what he wants for the army. Gen. [Andrew] Pickens will write concerning the

Loyalists.[3] Asserts: "Sav[anna]h can be taken. 10 day[s] will do." Asks NG to write him "on this point."[4] ALS (NcD) 2 pp.]

1. There were two forts at Augusta. Ft. Cornwallis, which Lee called "Browne[s]," was defended by Col. Thomas Brown and some regulars. It stood near the Savannah River, at the western edge of the original town and near the site of a church. (Cashin, *King's Ranger*, p. 132) In his memoirs, Lee called this fort "judiciously constructed, well finished, and secure from storm." (Lee, *Memoirs*, 2: 92) About three quarters of a mile to the west of this post stood the fortified house of Col. James Grierson, which Lee termed "very inferior" to Ft. Cornwallis. It was defended by Loyalist militiamen. (Ibid.) In contrast to his statement here, Lee said in his memoirs that he was pleased to find two separate forts because a gully, formed by a lagoon that lay between them, made it difficult for the garrisons to support each other. (Ibid.)

2. Rudulph's report is discussed at Lee to NG, 22 May, above.

3. No letter from Pickens to NG concerning the Loyalists has been found.

4. NG replied on 29 May, below.

¶ [GENERAL GREENE'S ORDERS, "Camp before 96," S.C., Friday, 25 May 1781. Col. [William] Henderson is to arrange and command the militia of Ninety Six district until "further Orders." Lamar Orderly Book (OClWHi) 1 p.]

¶ [COLONEL LEWIS MORRIS, JR., TO MAJOR JOHN ARMSTRONG. From Salisbury, N.C., 25 May 1781. [The North Carolina draftees at Salisbury are] to join NG's army immediately by a route that Morris details.[1] As Armstrong is indisposed and cannot go with them, he should give the command to the "next oldest" officer.[2] The Virginia militia will halt at Charlotte until the Salisbury "drafts" arrive.[3] Catalog excerpt (Carnegie Book Shop, *Catalogue #333*, [n.d.], p. 21).]

1. The catalog abstract states that it was Armstrong himself who was being ordered to join NG's army. As can be seen in the next sentences of the calendar, however, Morris was referring to the draftees.

2. As seen in his letter to NG of 12 June, below, Armstrong retained the command.

3. As noted at Jefferson to NG, 30 March, above, few of the Virginia militiamen that NG expected ever joined the Southern Army.

*   *   *

From General Andrew Pickens

Dear General   Griersons fort [Ga.] 25th May 1781

Last Saturday Lieu[t] Colonel [Henry] Lee Arrived at my Camp, and the Infantry of his Legion and one Troop of Horse being detached on the March for Fort Dreadnought at Silver Bluff, Colonel [Samuel] Hammond with his Regiment (except one Company) and what of Colonel [William] Hardens Regiment was with me Marched that afternoon for the Same place, and on Monday evening Cap[t] Roath [Samuel Roworth] Surrendered the fort and Garrison to our Arms, by which a good Supply of Ammunition, with Some Arms and a considerable quantity of Stores and goods fell into our hands.[1] The reduction of this Post enabled Colonel Lee to assemble his force and Cross the Savannah to co-operate with me against the two forts in this town. For the dispatch of business it was determined to establish ourselves in an intermediate position.

A battery erected during the night of the 23ᵈ opened against the upper fort yesterday morning Colonel Lee at the Same instant moved with the Infantry of the Legion, and one Six pounder under Captain [Samuel] Finley, to counteract any Attempts which the enemy might make from the lower fort towards the relief of their friends, while Colonel Clark [Elijah Clarke] with a body of Militia and Captain [John?] Smiths Command marched directly from our battery towards the post which we meant to occupy.[2]

Colonel Grierson who commanded in the upper fort relinquished the post and moved towards the lower fort. Colº Brown who Commands the enemy's forces in this quarter made a movement towards the Succour of Colº Grierson, but was effectually prevented, an Action then took place with Colonel Grierson which ended in a Complete victory on our Side. The Lᵗ Colonel and forty odd are Prisoners and a Major and About thirty others were found dead on the field (without any other loss on our Side but Two men Slightly Wounded,) Some few of the enemy escaped in the Woods, and the Colonel with a few followers were So fortunate as to escape our fire and reach Browns fort in Safety.[3] Two field pieces fell into our hands on this occasion and the Troops took possession of the upper fort without any resistance. During the Action Captⁿ [Joseph] Armstrong of the Legion drove the enemys outposts from the town, and took possession of their redoubts, thus we are fully masters of the Country & Town and have circumscribed Colonel Brown to one fort.

Every Officer and Soldier engaged behaved with great Gallantry and are well entitled to the thanks and esteem of their Country. I have the honour to be with great esteem Dear General Your most obedient humble Servant ANDᵂ PICKENS

ALS (NcD).

1. On the capture of Ft. Dreadnought, see Lee to NG, 22 May, above.

2. On the locations of Forts Grierson ("the upper fort") and Cornwallis ("the lower fort"), see note at Lee to NG, 24 May, above. Lee, in his memoirs, described the arrangement of the American troops in greater detail than Pickens did here. According to Lee's account, Pickens and the militia were to attack Ft. Grierson on its north and west sides, while Maj. Pinketham Eaton's detachment of North Carolina Continental draftees (which Pickens referred to as "Smiths Command") were to skirt a lagoon that lay between the two forts and approach Ft. Grierson from the south. Lee, with his infantry and artillery, took up a position between the forts, ready either to support Eaton's assault or "attend to the movements of [Col. Thomas] Brown, should he venture to leave" Ft. Cornwallis and attempt to "save Grierson." The legion cavalry was positioned near Ft. Cornwallis to attack Brown's rear if he came out of his works. (Lee, *Memoirs*, p. 93) Brown did sally, but only for a short distance, and he "confined his interposition to cannonade," which Lee returned, "with very little effect on either side." (Ibid., p. 94) In the meantime, the American militia advancing on Ft. Grierson, with "Every second man" carrying an

axe, were surprised to encounter no resistance. They quickly cut away the stockade and palisade and mounted the parapet, only to find that Col. James Grierson had evacuated his post from the side nearest to the river and was trying, under cover of the riverbank, to reach the safety of Ft. Cornwallis. (Johnson, *Traditions and Reminiscences*, p. 357) Grierson and a few of his men did reach Ft. Cornwallis, but as Pickens related in the next paragraph of this letter, most of the garrison was overtaken and either captured or killed.

3. Pickens did not mention here that Maj. Pinketham Eaton, one of the American commanders, was killed during the pursuit of Grierson's men. (See Pickens and Lee to NG, 5 June, below.)

*   *   *

¶ [FROM GENERAL ANDREW PICKENS, Grierson's Fort, Ga., 25 May 1781. Has NG's letter of 20 May. Expects the supplies from Ft. Dreadnought to arrive by boat "this day, and in the mean time" has sent two hogsheads of rum to NG.[1] Could send "more" if he had wagons; has asked Col. [Robert] Anderson to send wagons, but fears that Anderson will be unable to provide the number needed.[2] "I have never yet got an Acco' of what was taken, but Shall use every means in my power to prevent any embezlement."[3] Many of the militia, particularly the Georgians serving with Pickens, have been serving a long time and are "almost Naked"; hopes that part of the goods can be "Applied to their relief" but awaits NG's orders.[4] ALS (NcD) 1 p.]

1. On the capture of Ft. Dreadnought and the supplies stored there, see Lee to NG, 22 May, above.

2. As seen by his letter to NG, 24 May, above, Anderson was unable to obtain many wagons.

3. Lee, who was with Pickens, had already sent NG a list of the captured stores. (See Lee to NG, 22 May, above.) Given Lee's comments there about the militia, the failure to provide Pickens with the list may have been intentional.

4. NG replied on 29 May, below.

¶ [GENERAL GREENE'S ORDERS, "Camp before 96," S.C., Saturday, 26 May 1781. "Officers of all Ranks are to take particular notice of Strangers coming into Camp, and to send all Suspicious Persons to Head Quarters." Guards should be "extremely circumspect" to prevent spies from entering camp. Reprimands an officer for allowing "a Man to pass his Guard from the Enemies Garrison." Reports the capture of Forts Dreadnought and Grierson.[1] Ft. Cornwallis is expected to surrender "every Hour."[2] Lamar Orderly Book (OCIWHi) 3 pp.]

1. On the capture of Forts Dreadnought and Grierson, see Lee to NG, 22 May, and Pickens to NG, first letter of 25 May, both above.

2. Ft. Cornwallis, the last of the enemy fortifications in the area of Augusta, Ga., surrendered on 5 June. (See Pickens and Lee to NG, that date, below.)

*   *   *

To General Francis Marion

Dear Sir   Camp before Ninty Six [S.C.] May 26th 1781

I am favord with your letters of the 19 and 20th.

I am surprisd at the enimies conduct towards the party sent as an escort to the Prisoners taken at Fort Mott and the more so as the party was for their protection and at their request.[1] The insult offerd to our people deserves resentment and you have my full consent to treat their officers as they treat ours. But at the same time it is my wish to carry on the war upon the most liberal principles and as correspondent with the laws of humanity as the nature of the service will admit.

If the enemy are making no preparation to interrupt the siege at this place or Augusta and General Sumter dont think himself exposd in consequence of your moving to George Town of which I have desird him to inform you, that I have no objection to your making the attempt you propose. But if Lord Rawden is making preparations for offensive operations which may interupt the sieges now carrying on, or expose General Sumter in his present position, I would not wish you to make the attempt as that is but an inferior object.[2]

Before this reaches you, you will be better informed of the state and intention of the enemy below. The last account I had of Lord Cornwallis he was at Hallifax in North Carolina and seemed disposd to rest there for sometime; probably with a view of concerting a plan for forming a junction with General Philips.[3]

I beg my most respectful complements to Col Horee [Peter Horry] and Major Mayam [Hezekiah Maham] and the rest of the Gentlemen with you. I am Sir with esteem & regard Your Most Obed[t] humble S[r]

N GREENE

ADfS (MiU-C).

1. On the enemy's "conduct" toward the escort party, see Marion to NG, 19 May, above.

2. Marion had already marched for Georgetown without waiting for permission from NG. (Rankin, *Swamp Fox*, p. 213) He reported its capture in his letter to NG of 29 May, below.

3. As noted at Lafayette to NG, 3 May, above, Lord Cornwallis had already formed a junction with the British forces in Virginia.

*   *   *

¶ [CAPTAIN WILLIAM PIERCE, JR., TO COLONEL CHARLES S. MYDDELTON. From Camp before Ninety Six, S.C., 26 May 1781. NG has asked Pierce to reply to Myddelton's letter of 14 May. "It rests entirely with" Gen. [Thomas] Sumter, who is responsible for the prisoners taken at Orangeburg, to decide if any "deserve" to be returned "into the list of American Citizens." Pierce suggests holding "as many of the Militia taken in the fort" as will be needed to exchange for Americans now suffering in captivity. ADfS (MiU-C) 1 p.]

*   *   *

To General Thomas Sumter

Dear Sir   Camp before Ninety Six [S.C.] May 26th 1781.

Your favour of the 22[d] is before me. General Marian writes me that Lord Rawdon lies at Monks Corner and that he wishes for Liberty to attack the enemy at George Town. I have refered him to you for an answer resting the matter upon these two points; that if Lord Rawdon is making no preparations, which has the appearance of interrupting the sieges, now going on here and at Augusta, or if his moving to George Town will not expose you in your present situation, and [intercept?] the arrangement & preparations you are making, he may attempt the enterprise. But if Lord Rawdon intentions appear offensive, or you will be exposed upon his moving, not to attempt it, as it is but an inferior object.[1]

A Fleet is said to have arrived off Charles Town bar. Make the strickest enquiry who, or what they are.[2]

Col⁰ Branum [Thomas Brandon] on his return home, called at this place, & told me he had your Orders to bring such a part of the militia to your aid below. For particular reasons I have desired him to join us with all the force he can collect at this place, to expedite the reduction of it, as soon as possible. My motives I will explain to you more fully hereafter. I am sorry to break in upon your arrangement, but I flatter myself you will be persuaded it is for the good of the service at large tho' it may be a little inconvenient to you for a time.

I am glad you are setting Mʳ McElroy to work. Nothing will strengthen the hands of the Country, like measures for arming the people. The enemy left many things at Camden, should any of the Articles there be of use to you, in this important business, they may be had for the purpose.[3]

As I have no accounts of Lord Cornwallis's making towards this quarter, I persuade myself Major [John] Rutherfords information is without foundation.[4] However if it is true, I shall have information either to day or tomorrow, as one of my aids is gone to Salisbury for that and other purposes.[5]

I beg my complements to the Field Officers of your Command & am with great respect Your most Obedient Humble Servan[t]

NATH GREENE

LS (Sumter Papers: DLC).

1. As noted at NG to Marion, this date, above, Gen. Francis Marion did not wait for permission from Sumter before moving against the British post at Georgetown. Sumter criticized Marion for his action in his letter to NG of 7 June, below.

2. Sumter said nothing about the fleet in his reply. As seen in NG to Sumter, first letter of 10 June, below, a fleet carrying reinforcements had arrived.

3. Sumter had reported his decision to set up an armory at Ancrum's Plantation in his letter to NG of 22 May, above. There he had called the man in charge of the armory "Mʳ McElrath."

4. On the information Rutherford had brought, see ibid.

5. NG had sent Col. Lewis Morris to Salisbury. As NG suspected, the report concerning Cornwallis was false.

*   *   *

¶ [FROM CAPTAIN JAMES MOORE, [Ninety Six District, S.C.], 26 May 1781.[1] Gives "a tru State" of his "present Confinement" on his plantation as a paroled prisoner of war, including details of being "ill used" by the British. Wishes "no longer to Remain Inactive" and asks NG to arrange his exchange.[2] In any event, Moore will consider himself released from his parole when Col. [John Harris] Cruger is no longer in command at Ninety Six. ALS (MiU-C) 2 pp.]

1. It is clear from the contents that Moore's plantation was in the neighborhood of Ninety Six.

2. NG's reply has not been found.

¶ [**FROM BARON STEUBEN**, Albemarle Old Court House, Va., 26 May 1781. Expects to march to NG with 560 Virginia recruits and thirty men from Armand's Legion. Is now trying to equip these troops and speed their departure, but the "Confusion" that Virginia "has been thrown into" causes difficulties. He will outfit them with the arms sent from Philadelphia. Lacks cartridge boxes but has "some old ones" and hopes to get more from Fredericksburg. Will wait for shoes, overalls, shirts, and blankets, but not for coats. Hopes to march by 4 or 5 June.[1] Fears that Maj. [Richard] Claiborne cannot supply the needed wagons. Assumes that the Marquis [de Lafayette] has informed NG of the "State of Affairs."[2] The "arrival of Lord Cornwallis with [Banastre] Tarleton has Spread an universal terror." The enemy have reportedly moved on to Manchester; Lafayette is on the "heights of Richmond." Having no cavalry, Lafayette has detained Col. [Anthony W.] White and about forty dragoons. Steuben has ordered Capt. [John] Stith to collect and equip as dragoons the next 120 recruits who come in after Steuben departs; if the Assembly provides horses, Stith is to assign sixty to each cavalry regiment. All of NG's other orders "shall be obeyed."[3] Proposes a route of march to take to NG's army. As soon as he is on his way, Steuben will send an officer to Gov. [Abner] Nash to "consult" about the route and to insure that the troops and stores that are to join his detachment from North Carolina are ready. Steuben will take 300 stand of arms for the North Carolinians.[4] Asks if NG can "possibly divine" Cornwallis's intentions. Wonders if Cornwallis will allow Steuben's detachment to join NG and if NG can hold his position until Steuben arrives. Is anxious to hear from NG; has not received a letter from him since 1 May— before NG knew that Cornwallis was heading toward Virginia.[5] LS (MiU-C) 4 pp.]

1. As seen in his letter to Steuben of 14 May, above, NG had decided that the draftees should stay in Virginia to reinforce Lafayette.

2. See Lafayette to NG, 24 May, above.

3. Steuben was presumably referring to orders in NG's letter to him of 1 May, above.

4. NG had ordered the North Carolina recruits to join Lafayette. (See NG to Sumner, 5 May, above.)

5. NG's letter to Steuben of 14 May had been intercepted by the British. (See note at that letter.) NG had sent a copy to Lafayette, who forwarded it to Steuben on 31 May. (Idzerda, *Lafayette Papers*, 4: 150)

¶ [**GENERAL GREENE'S ORDERS**, "Camp before 96," S.C., 27 May 1781. Entrenching tools are to be "collected and deposited at Sun-set in the Rear of the New Battery." Lamar Orderly Book (OCIWHi) 1 p.]

¶ [**TO COLONEL LEWIS MORRIS, JR.** From "Camp before Ninety Six," S.C., 27 May 1781. Informs him that two of the forts on the Savannah River have been captured, with few losses on the American side; thirty to forty of the enemy were killed and more than 120 taken prisoner.[1] The capture of the "Main fort" is expected "today at farthest."[2] NG lacks men to push the "approaches here" rapidly. The enemy keep up a "constant firing" and have made a sally that was "beat back with the loss of a Captain and several Men."[3] Asks Morris to "push on the Stores" and "give every necessary order" for those "left behind."[4] Morris is also to bring NG's boots, as the ones he has now are "failing fast and will not hold out Scarcely the Siege." Cy (RHi) 1 p.]

1. On the capture of Forts Dreadnought and Grierson, see Lee to NG, 22 May, and Pickens to NG, first letter of 25 May, both above.

2. The capture of Ft. Cornwallis, the "Main fort" at Augusta, took place on 5 June. (See Pickens and Lee to NG, 5 June, below.)

3. The sally is discussed at NG to Huntington, 20 June, below.

4. Morris was at Salisbury, N.C., to forward stores and reinforcements to the army. (See NG to Morris, 21 May, above.)

¶ [FROM LIEUTENANT JAMES HINDS, "Post near Oliphants Mill," N.C., 27 May 1781. Has sent five wagonloads of ammunition in compliance with NG's order of the 24th [not found]. Assuming that NG "mought not be" aware that a second delivery of ammunition had been made to Hind's post, he sent items that he thought "would be most wanting" at camp. Before the wagons could proceed, he had to impress horses "in room of some that died." Has detained Maj. [John] Mazaret's baggage for lack of orders. ALS (MiU-C) 1 p.]

¶ [FROM GENERAL ISAAC HUGER, "Congaree, Point Necessity," S.C., 27 May 1781. Reports that Lord Rawdon has retreated to Goose Creek Bridge, sixteen miles from Charleston, he has detached 400 men to Dorchester, "where they are intrenching."[1] Gen. [Francis] Marion has gone to Georgetown, leaving Major Maham "on the Enemy's Lines" near Monck's Corner.[2] Huger has moved thirty of his Negroes to Virginia "with the greatest difficulty."[3] LS (CSmH) 1 p.]

1. Rawdon pulled his army back to Goose Creek about 25 May. (Baron von Bose to Baron von Knyphausen, 7 June 1781, Lidgerwood Collection, NjMoHP) According to a letter that he wrote to Lord Cornwallis of 5 June, Rawdon made the move because of a false report that a French fleet was coming to southern waters to assist NG's army; Rawdon wanted to be in position to protect Charleston. (PRO 30/11/6) As seen at Maham to NG, 1 June, below, the British soon reestablished themselves at Monck's Corner.

2. On Marion's move against Georgetown, see his letter to NG of 29 May, below.

3. See Huger to Lewis Morris, 22 May, above.

¶ [FROM MAJOR EDMUND M. HYRNE, Col. [William] Thompson's, S.C., 27 May 1781. He has stopped a "flag of truce" and opened a letter addressed to NG, which contained a "passport" for Hyrne "& nothing else."[1] The bearer of the flag had his "sword & pistols" taken by an American militia officer; Hyrne has promised to return them "if they can be recover'd."[2] Lord Rawdon has moved "from Moncks Corner to Goose Creek"; Gen. [Francis] Marion "cross'd Santee for George Town," leaving Maj. [Hezekiah] Maham "on the enemies lines."[3] "Every man in that part of the Country" has reportedly joined Maham, "three only excepted." Desertion seems to prevail in the British army: sixty-five deserted when the enemy "turnd to go down the Country." Hyrne plans to set out for Charleston "friday next" unless NG orders otherwise.[4] Asks if he should "insist on their *first* exchanging the garrisons &C[a] which have been sent in, notwithstanding the Cartel."[5] ALS (MiU-C) 2 pp.]

1. As seen later in this calendar, the "passport" was to enable Hyrne, NG's commissary of prisoners, to enter Charleston to arrange for the implementation of the recently signed cartel for the exchange of prisoners.

2. Hyrne wrote NG on 1 June, below, that the bearer's horse was also taken from him "on his return."

3. As seen in Maham to NG, 1 June, below, Rawdon soon returned to Monck's Corner.

4. "Friday next" was 1 June; Hyrne was still at Thompson's when he wrote NG on that date, below.

5. Hyrne was referring to the British prisoners who had recently been paroled to Charleston after the capture of their posts in South Carolina. On the cartel, see Carrington to NG, 8 May, and NG to Huntington, 10 May, both above. NG's reply has not been found.

¶ [FROM ROBERT LANIER, Washington, N.C., 27 May 1781. The Cherokee chief has sent deputies "imploring peace," who say that only a few of their nation are still under the influence of the agent for the British. They wanted to "Treat" with the Americans on 10 June, but the commissioners "put off till July 20." Meanwhile, "Seceders are killing people."[1] If permitted to do so, Lanier could "raise a force and make them cede lands." He could also call on tribes "in the Illinois region" to attack the Cherokee; a chief of one of the western tribes "was here last week" and "opened himself" to Lanier "in a long speech." Lanier approves of Colonel Campbell's plans and thinks the frontiersmen would be glad to fight the Cherokee.[2] Excerpt, Stan. V. Henkels, *Catalogue #1005* (1909), p. 36.]

1. The Cherokee leaders, according to one historian, were "war-weary" and aware that the British were losing their power in the southern interior; they "confessed that they had behaved as 'Rogues' to the Americans in following the British" and said they were ready to abide by a new treaty. (O'Donnell, *Southern Indians*, pp. 116–17) The American commissioners postponed the requested conference because of "the actions of a few renegades." (Ibid., p. 117; see also Anderson to NG, 24 May, above.) As noted at NG's letter to the commissioners, 26 February, above (vol. 7: 353n), the conference was held in July.

2. For more on Col. Arthur Campbell's plans concerning the Cherokee, see Lanier to NG, 13 July, below.

¶ [FROM COLONEL CHARLES PETTIT, Philadelphia, 24–27 May 1781.[1] Pettit is "much in arrears" to NG "in the litterary way." He feels negligent when he considers the difficult circumstances under which NG has written to him, but he sometimes appeases his conscience with the thought "that you gratify yourself by disburdening your mind to me on paper."[2] Adds: "This confession at once serves to shew the frailty & the selfishness of human nature." Lack of money in his "public character" has been "a source of perplexity" and has added to the "teazingness of a situation" that "was not pleasant when you left me."[3] Moreover, his "private affairs" have not "been prosperous or even easy." Discusses in detail a number of problems he has encountered in trying to further his, NG's, and [John] Cox's interests in "the furnace" and in two ships, the *Revolution* and the *Congress*, which are being used as privateers; still entertains some hope of future success, but has been so distressed as to wish himself "in almost any other situation."[4] Additional problems have resulted from his decision "last year" to accept in payment "a considerable sum in Loan Office certificates which [now] lie wholly dead both as to principal & interest." Every "difficulty," moreover, has been heightened by the "fluctuating state of money." Discusses the depreciated value of Continental and state paper money and says that "hard money" is frightened "into concealment," leaving almost no "commercial medium."[5]

26 May. Comments on NG's situation: "It was not expected that when you went to the southward you would sleep on beds of roses, and the world was much divided as to the laurels you would gather." Pettit knew that NG's talents would not leave him "empty handed," though he would have to "pluck them from amidst thorns." NG has exceeded even Pettit's expectations, "and tho' contemporaries give you some degree of credit, the full merit of your toils will not be clearly and generally seen in our day." If NG had the "Troops and resources" that "we are often told of, and which the vulgar believe," there would be little to thank him for; "but those who are best informed of your circumstances are the most warmly impressed with the propriety of your having the command in that Country. Envy itself ceases to shew its head in public, and is silenced if not in many instances dissolved." Pettit recently saw NG's "predecessor [Gen. Horatio Gates]," who "behaves with modesty" and "spoke handsomely" of NG to Pettit. Adds: "Indeed I know not of his doing otherwise in other places." Thinks that Gates "feels some degree of gratitude" for NG's treatment of him.[6]

Pettit finds public affairs "really distressing, & some revolution in them seems necessary to our Political existence. The seat of all our difficulties however, is on one point: the derangement of our finances." Revenues "are in a manner extinguished," even though the means of obtaining them are "plentiful" in the North; with "skill & resolution" in drawing them out, "the yoke of war would become easy & the burden light. Most people are sensible of this, but they differ about the measures & modes of obtaining the desireable end." Discusses the political situation in Pennsylvania, which has "grown worse" since NG went south, and relates it to problems with paper money. Efforts by the state to regulate the value of money led to "such a ferment that paper stagnated altogether; for some days the prices of goods were perfectly wild many asking as 10 for one" for recently emitted bills "& others shutting up their stores or refusing to sell at all."[7] The legislature is now assembling, "& the fate of paper money in this State hangs on their determination."[8] In the meantime, the effect of Pennsylvania's currency crisis "extends less or more to all the States, those nearest to us feeling the shock with the most violence. Every individual feels himself injured & looks for some object of resentment, which has whetted the rages of party to a great height." Congress, meanwhile, has "become more enlightened on the subject of finance," but Pettit fears "it will take much time yet to bring the legislatures of the respective states to a proper way of thinking on these subjects." In regard to supplies, Congress can still do nothing except make "recommendations which may or may not be complied with by these sovereign powers."[9] What little funding Pettit can get for his department is through warrants on the states, which he transfers to the deputies. "Respecting our accounts," he and Colonel Hay have drawn up a plan to give commissioners in each district the power to issue certificates to settle accounts. These can either be used in the payment of taxes or "received for specie loan certificates," as the holder chooses. Deputies and agents are then to settle their accounts with the commissioners, "whose certificate is to be our voucher for a final settlem' with them." This plan has been "reported to Congress," which "recommitted it with orders to consult the Financier, & there it yet remains."[10]

27 May. As Dr. [Peter] Fayssoux is leaving "tomorrow," Pettit will write another "sheet." He wishes he were "in better humour" and does not "like the expression" of what he has written thus far, but it may give NG "information." Pettit may soon have an "opportunity" to leave "public business." Colonel Pickering "two months ago" laid before Congress a plan to centralize control of the quartermaster department, "putting the whole under his direction" and abolishing Pettit's position. Pettit was "embarrassed" but did not resign in order to avoid giving "offence and perhaps create enemies." Congress has reportedly referred the matter to "the General [Washington], & have heard nothing of it since." Pettit, however, believes it may now be best for him to resign and expects "this week" to give Congress his "sentiments."[11] Says that Gov. [Joseph] Reed, who "has long wished for a safe" means to write NG "in confidence," may do so "by this opportunity."[12] Reed "has been so sorely galled that his mind is exceedingly soured with his situation, and he looks with great wishfulness to the next election which will set him free." The actions that Reed took in regard to the Pennsylvania line have led "the Officers into improper and unjust notions concerning him, and into a line of conduct towards him" that Pettit considers "ungrateful."[13] Cox "confines himself" to his farm, "which is in a flourishing way, as indeed are farms in general." Prospects are favorable for a good crop, and now that flour can be exported, "it has become plenty at market & at a moderate price."[14] ADf (MiU-C) 10 pp.]

1. Pettit began this letter on 24 May, added to it on 26 May, and finished it on the 27th.

2. NG's letters to Pettit have not been found.

3. In his "public character," Pettit was assistant quartermaster general. (See above, vol. 6: 153n.) He had last seen NG in November 1780, when NG stopped in Philadelphia on his way to the South. (Ibid., p. 501)

4. The "furnace" was an ironworks at Batsto, NJ. (Ibid., pp. 122–23n) For more about the business partnership in which NG, Pettit, and Cox were involved, see above (vol. 2: 310–11n).

5. For more on the state of paper currency in Pennsylvania, see Reed to NG, 16 June, below.

6. Gates, the former commander of the Southern Army, had been in Philadelphia to try to persuade Congress that its resolution of 5 October 1780, relieving him of command, implied an "unwarranted reprimand to his conduct." (Nelson, Gates, p. 258; on Gates's removal from command, see Washington to NG, 14 October 1780, above [vol. 6: 385, 386n].) In response, Congress declared in a resolution of 21 May that it had not removed Gates from command "at large"; thus, as the court of inquiry that had been called for in October could not be "speedily held," he was free to rejoin the army. (JCC, 20: 521–22) Gates, "incensed," declined to do so. (Nelson, Gates, p. 259) NG's treatment of Gates after taking command of the Southern Army is discussed above (vol. 6: 518–19n).

7. Reports reached the British in New York in early May "that there has been some riots there [Philadelphia] lately occasioned by the Continental paper currency, the circulation of which is now entirely at an end. Some of the Mob tarred a dog, and then

stuck him full of Congress paper dollars; and in that condition turned him into the place in which The Congress was sitting." (Mackenzie, *Diary*, 2: 520)

8. The Pennsylvania legislature, in a special session that began on 24 May, enacted "a large tax, half to be payable only in specie, and . . . wiping out the tender laws." The legislature also agreed to turn over most of the unissued balance of the state's last emission of paper money to Robert Morris, the newly appointed Continental superintendent of finance, for use in purchasing Pennsylvania's quota of supplies for the army. According to the editors of Morris's papers, his careful use of this money helped to prevent its further depreciation. (Morris, *Papers*, 1: 181n).

9. On the state supply system, to which Pettit referred, see above (vol. 5: 214n).

10. For more on Pettit's and Col. Udny Hays's proposal, which was meant to facilitate the settlement of quartermaster department accounts from the years when NG headed the department, see Hay to Pettit, 1 May, and Pettit to Samuel Huntington, 2 May. (PCC, item 192, pp. 351, 339, DNA) The proposal was referred to a committee of Congress, and no action was taken. (*JCC*, 20: 474, 500) "The Financier" was Robert Morris. (As seen at Sharpe to NG, 28 May, below, Morris had not yet been sworn in as superintendent of finance.)

11. On 12 June, Pettit sent a letter of resignation to Congress, which accepted it on 20 June and voted at the same time to abolish the post of assistant quartermaster general. (Smith, *Letters*, 17: 339n; *JCC*, 20: 649, 677–78)

12. In his letter of 16 June, below, Reed explained why he had not written to NG at this time.

13. Reed had been strongly criticized for his role in settling the mutiny of the Pennsylvania line. (See above, vol. 7: 118n.) For more on his political situation, see Reed to NG, 16 June, below.

14. Pennsylvania's repeal of its ban on the exportation of foodstuffs needed for the war effort is noted above (vol. 6: 406–7n).

¶ [**FROM DOCTOR RICHARD PINDELL**,[1] Charlotte, N.C., 27 May 1781. Asks if "any Allowance can be made" for the loss of his horse, which was stolen while he was at Cowpens, caring for the "Wounded of Both Armies."[2] He would have mentioned this before but always found NG "engaged in affairs of more moment."[3] ALS (MiU-C) 1 p.]

1. As noted at his letter to NG of 18 December 1780, above (vol. 6: 600n), Pindell was a surgeon in the Maryland line.

2. On the battle of Cowpens, see Daniel Morgan to NG, 19 January, above (vol. 7: 152–55).

3. NG's reply has not been found.

¶ [**FROM COLONEL THOMAS POLK**, Charlotte, N.C., 27 May 1781. Has received NG's letter "by the hand of Coll. [Lewis] Morris" [not found] and will "pay every attention" to the stores "lodged in" the Salisbury district. Is sending four men "northwardly" to "approach as near as possible to the Enemy" and gather intelligence. ALS (MiU-C) 1 p.]

¶ [**GENERAL GREENE'S ORDERS**, Camp before Ninety Six, S.C., Monday, 28 May 1781. Announces the replacement of Maj. [Thomas] Ridley, a supernumerary officer who has been serving voluntarily since the "Arrangement" of his line.[1] Ridley has NG's permission to "go home" and NG's thanks for his service and "good conduct." Lamar Orderly Book (OCIWHi) 2 pp.]

1. Ridley was a Virginia Continental officer. (Heitman, *Register*)

*   *   *

To General Thomas Sumter

Dear Sir   Camp before Ninty Six [S.C.] May 28th 1781

I have nothing new to communicate from this quarter. Our approaches are going on but slowly, owing to the want of men to dig; however I am in hopes of being up to the enemies lines in a few days.[1]

Accounts from the North render the arrangment of your Militia necessary as soon as possible to join in further offensive operations.[2] Equip and prepare yourself as soon as you can. With esteem & regard I am Sir your Most Obed humble Serv[t]   NATH GREENE

ALS (Sumter Papers: DLC).

1. By contrast, the commander of the besieged post, John Harris Cruger, was impressed with the progress made by the besiegers, reporting to Lord Rawdon on 31 May that NG's army was advancing "by regular approaches, working very industriously, as if your Lordship was at hand." (PRO 30/11/6)

2. The "Accounts from the North" were undoubtedly the news that Lord Cornwallis had entered Virginia. As seen in NG's letter to Henry Lee of 9 May and his to the Marquis de Lafayette of 23 May, both above, NG was planning to march with part of his army to Virginia to counter Lord Cornwallis's move. Sumter's militiamen would be needed to replace the troops NG planned to take with him.

*   *   *

¶ [FROM GENERAL MORDECAI GIST, Christiana Bridge, Del., 29 May 1781. Has NG's letter of 30 March and will "repair to Camp," as NG requested, in time to take command of the Maryland line when the detachment from "this state" and Maryland joins it. The detachment, which will march in "a few weeks," will number between 400 and 500 men, including "about 100" recruits from Delaware. These troops, who enlisted some time ago, "have remaind here without clothing and necessaries, or any efforts made by the Executive to procure them."[1] This inattention—especially on the part of the governor [Caesar Rodney]—"cannot be easily accounted for upon any principle of Virtue or patriotism." NG can imagine Gist's "Chagrin and mortification" in dealing with "public bodies" who have "neither inclination or capacity to direct, nor ability or integrity to execute, Yet arrogate to themselves the power of governing military movements." Gist had arranged the Maryland recruits and was waiting only for clothing when the arrival of enemy troops alarmed the state's officials. They "desired" all the Continental troops to be sent to defend "their City [i.e., Annapolis]." Gist refused the request, but the officials then went to Gen. [William] Smallwood, who acceded to it. When Gist confronted Smallwood about this matter, Smallwood asserted that NG had given him verbal orders to "Supercede" Gist's command in Maryland. Gist thereupon "submitted to his direction," furnished him with a copy of NG's "Instructions," and now refers NG to Smallwood for "the returns requir'd."[2] The lack of supplies needed to outfit the recruits led Gist to make a "personal application" to the Board of War; his appeal, though not entirely successful, did result in enough supplies being sent to "assist in expediting" the recruits' march. Encloses an abstract of Congress's proceedings of 23 May.[3] Gist plans to visit the Maryland Assembly, which is now sitting; he and Smallwood will advocate the adoption of a "plan upon proper principles for compleating the quota of Troops for that state."[4] ALS (MiU-C) 3 pp.]

1. The recruits did not march until the end of August. By then, their orders had been changed, and they were sent to join the Marquis de Lafayette in Virginia. (See Gist to NG, 14 September, below.)

2. For Smallwood's version of this incident, see his letter to NG of 4 May, above. Smallwood took credit there for the appeal to the Board of War for supplies, which Gist discussed later in this letter.

3. The abstract has not been found. On 23 May, Congress debated a committee report concerning supplies for the French expeditionary force and ordered the Board of War to lay in provisions from "arrears of the specific supplies." It also ordered payment for Dr. Peter Fayssoux and authorized the removal of the Convention army prisoners to Massachusetts. (JCC, 20: 527–30)

4. NG did not hear again from either Gist or Smallwood until Gist wrote him on 14 September, below. Gist did not mention his efforts to influence the Maryland legislature in that letter.

¶ [FROM SAMUEL HUNTINGTON, PRESIDENT OF THE CONTINENTAL CONGRESS, Philadelphia, 28 May 1781. Sends a copy of an act of Congress of 25 May, concerning "Promotions in the Line of the Army." The plan was adopted "upon mature Deliberation" as one that was "subject to the fewest Objections of any that could be devised" for a "federal Army raised & recruited from so many distinct sovereign States."[1] Notes the promotions of Col. [Tench] Tilghman and Maj. [James] McHenry. There are provisions in the plan for aides-de-camp and for officers held hostage.[2] Encloses Congress's act of 26 May ordering the distribution to several states of NG's letter of 22 April.[3] L (MH) 1 p. The L is incomplete. The last two sentences of the calendar were taken from the copy that Huntington sent to Washington. (Washington Papers: DLC) A comparison of the first part of Washington's copy with that sent to NG demonstrates that the two letters were otherwise nearly identical.]

1. The act stipulated that promotions within infantry battalions "annexed" to a state should be in "the line of such State," while promotions in cavalry and artillery units and in infantry regiments and legionary corps not belonging to a state were to be "regimental or legionary." The act contained a formula for appointing and determining seniority among brigadier generals and stipulated that the senior brigadier was to receive the next available promotion to major general, regardless of whether he served in the infantry, cavalry, or artillery. It also stated that "lieutenant colonels commandants of battalions" were to be considered as no different in grade than "other lieutenant colonels of the line." (JCC, 20: 539–41)

2. NG had requested a commission for McHenry in November 1780. (See above, vol. 6: 445.) The act provided that aides should retain their ranks and be "eligible to command upon detachments" whenever the commanding officer of a department thought "proper." Officers who were "hostages" (i.e., ones who were "liable to be called for by the enemy") who were not "continued" in a state's line were entitled to full pay until "redeemed" and to half-pay for life thereafter. (Ibid., p. 541)

*   *   *

From William Sharpe

My dear General   Phil[a] May 28. 1781

I wrote you on the 22[d] instant by express going to the Marquis De la Fayette. In full confidence that Doc[r] Fassaux [Peter Fayssoux] will hand you this, I will venture a few hints which are necessary for you to know, and may perhaps be communicated more at large by the commander in Chief or some other person.

We have lately recieved dispatches from France.[1] The second division is not to be sent, but an augmentation so as to give the new Admiral de Barrass the superiority; and a powerful diversion is intended in the West Indias.[2] This change took place in consequence of the Dutch war which must be cherrished by France.[3] A subsidy of six millions of Livres is given, part will come in cloathing &c and part to be a fund under the direction of the Com[r] in Chief. I entertain a hope that M[r] Morris is in the way to restore public credit.[4] G[eneral] W[ashington] has had a conferrence with Compte R[ochambeau] on military operations.[5] The enemy have forbid any communications with New York by Flag or otherwise—many conjecture that an evacuation is intended, I am not yet bro[t] into that opinion.[6]

The Empress of R[ussia] and the Emperor have offered their mediation between all the beligerent powers. It hath been accepted by the Court of L[ondo]n with an apparent degree of eagerness. France waits the consent of their ally before a negociation can begin, conferrences will in all probability open within a few months. In the mean time Military operations will be carried on with the greatest vigor against us. In order to make an advantageous peace we ought to be in condition to prosecute the war. Important events are suspended in which the southern States are infinitely interested. Congress will doubtless use their utmost address to Stimulate the States to suitable exertions.[7]

May you my dear Sir and your little army be preserved to enjoy the fruits of your labor and anxiety in a permanent and an honorable peace. With perfect respect & esteem I am my dear General Your Most Ob[t] Humble Serv[t]   W[M] SHARPE

ALS (MdHi).

1. For more on the dispatches, see Sharpe's letter of 21 and 22 May, above.

2. In a memorial to Congress, the French minister wrote that in place of the second division, France would "despatch some vessels of force to join the squadron [at Newport, R.I.] and enable it to put to sea." (JCC, 20: 558) The force that was sent included a fifty-gun man of war and a convoy of fifteen ships that carried supplies and a reinforcement of 600 infantrymen. (Kennett, French Forces, pp. 104, 107)

3. For more on the outbreak of war between the Dutch and British, see note at Joseph Clay to NG, 29 March, above (vol. 7: 482).

4. On the promised financial support, see note at Mathews to NG, 22 May, above. Robert Morris had been elected superintendent of finance on 20 February. Although he did not formally assume his duties until 27 June, Morris was active in formulating policy in the meantime. (Morris, Papers, 1: 5n, 66–68n)

5. Washington had met with Rochambeau at Wethersfield, Conn., on 22 and 23 May and had learned while there that the Comte de Grasse, whose large fleet was bound for the West Indies, might come north during the summer. Washington and Rochambeau decided to concentrate their forces and agreed that a Franco-American operation against the British garrison at New York should be their first priority. They did not rule out the

possibility of a joint attack on Lord Cornwallis in Virginia, however. (Freeman, *GW*, 5: 286–90)

6. The British were undoubtedly trying to keep Washington from finding out that a detachment of 2,000 men had been sent from New York to Virginia. The transports carrying the reinforcements sailed from New York on 13 May. (For more on the British reinforcement, see the note at St. Clair to NG, 6 May, above.) As Sharpe surmised, the British had no intention of evacuating New York.

7. The impetus for mediation had come as much from the belligerents themselves as from Emperor Joseph of Austria and Empress Catharine of Russia, the comediators. The French foreign minister, Comte de Vergennes, faced growing opposition to the war within his own government and feared that the Spanish might be planning to negotiate a separate peace with Great Britain. Taking into consideration some of the military setbacks of 1780 in America and a growing belief that the United States could not survive, he saw mediation as a means to a face-saving peace. Vergennes favored a long-term truce that would constitute de facto recognition of the United States. Such a truce, however, would be on the basis of *uti possidetis*—the principle of combatants retaining the territory they held at the cessation of hostilities—which meant that South Carolina and Georgia would most likely remain under British control. Vergennes's letter of 9 March to La Luzerne, the French minister to the United States, did not spell out this possibility but did state that a truce was possible and that the United States might have to gain the goodwill of the mediators by exercising great moderation in all of its claims and demands—except for independence. (As seen at Huntington to NG, 3 June, and Reed to NG, 16 June, both below, American leaders understood the implications of a negotiated peace.) The British, for their part, hoped to exploit the known hostility of Emperor Joseph and his key advisor, Count Kaunitz, to both the American revolutionaries and the French. They hoped that Austrian enmity toward France, together with support of the British position from Catharine of Russia, whose favor they unsuccessfully tried to obtain by offering her the island of Minorca, would lead to a settlement based on the Peace of Paris of 1763. Under such an arrangement, they would be left free to deal directly and alone with the Americans. In the end, the effort at mediation collapsed when the British refused to participate in any conference at which American representatives were present. (See Samuel F. Bemis, *The Hussey-Cumberland Mission and American Independence*, [Princeton: Princeton University Press, 1931], pp. 106–127, and Richard B. Morris, *The Peacemakers: The Great Powers and American Independence*, [New York: Harper & Row, 1965], pp. 153–90.) The British refusal to participate in the conference did not come until 15 June, and American leaders continued to fear the possibility of an unfavorable, mediated settlement until the spring of 1782. (See, for example, Connecticut Delegates to Jonathan Trumbull, Sr., 29 April 1782, Smith, *Letters*, 18: 476.) In the interim, NG's strategy was profoundly affected by the possibility of a settlement based on *uti possidetis*. He strove to expand the area of American control and reestablish functioning state governments in South Carolina and Georgia.

*　　　*　　　*

¶ [**GENERAL GREENE'S ORDERS**, Camp before Ninety Six, S.C., Tuesday, 29 May 1781. "Fatigue parties" will be taken "by Detail from the Line" and supervised by the officer of the day under the direction of the chief engineer.[1] Lamar Orderly Book (OCIWHi) 1 p.]

1. The "fatigue," or work, parties were to help dig the siege lines. Col. Thaddeus Kosciuszko was the army's chief engineer.

¶ [**TO COLONEL ELIJAH CLARKE**.[1] From before Ninety Six, S.C., 29 May 1781. The need to establish a force in Georgia "upon the most permanent and oeconomical plan induces" NG to ask Clarke to raise and equip a regiment there, to serve at least twelve months. It should be patterned after a Continental regiment, with the troops receiving the "same pay & Clothing" as Continentals. As the state's senior officer, Clarke should appoint the officers and serve as commander until the "pleasure" of the governor is known.[2] He should use the most "efficatious mode"—either drafting or voluntary enlistments—to man it and should apply to NG for any necessary supplies that he cannot obtain.[3] An "arrangement of the Georgia Militia is absolutely necessary for the protection of the good people of that State," so Clarke must also give "attention to that business." Stores for the Georgia militia have arrived; NG suggests that these and the supplies captured at Galphin's be "applied to the use of your Reg^t." Df (NcD) 2 pp.]

1. Clarke (1733–99) was a native of South Carolina who had moved to Wilkes County, Ga., shortly before the war. A militia officer, he had gained a reputation as a leading partisan commander from his participation in a number of frontier skirmishes. (It was his troops who had captured the Loyalist leader, Maj. James Dunlap. [See Pickens to NG, 8 April, above.]) In recognition of Clarke's services, the state of Georgia granted him an estate after the war and used him as both a negotiator and a military leader when threatened by Indian uprisings. Clarke remained popular among Georgians despite some of his postwar activities, including a brief involvement in the schemes of the French minister, Edmond Genêt, and the illegal seizure and fortification of territory belonging to the Creek Nation. He was also accused of having taken part in a British scheme against Florida and in the Yazoo land frauds. (DAB)

2. Georgia did not have a functioning civil government. The last duly elected governor had been Richard Howly, who was then serving as a delegate to Congress. (Coleman, *Revolution in Georgia*, pp. 160–61)

3. Clarke's reply has not been found, but a short time later NG appointed James Jackson as a lieutenant colonel and authorized him to raise a regiment of ten-month men. (See NG to Georgia Delegates in Congress, 22 June, below.) On 21 August, the new government of Georgia ratified NG's action by confirming Jackson's promotion and directing him to raise the Georgia State Legion, a corps of two hundred men. (*Records of Georgia* 3: 25)

¶ [TO SAMUEL HUNTINGTON, PRESIDENT OF THE CONTINENTAL CONGRESS. From "Camp before Ninety Six," S.C., 29 May 1781. Reports that the enemy evacuated Camden, "blew up their fortifications, and destroyed the greater part of their Stores" there. Encloses an intercepted letter to show the enemy's "apprehensions."[1] On 17 May, Col. [Henry] Lee, with "near one third" of NG's army, marched from Camden for Augusta, Ga.; NG and the remainder of his troops moved the next day toward Ninety Six. Sends accounts of an "Action at Augusta" and the surrender of Ft. Dreadnought.[2] Ft. Cornwallis at Augusta is "closely invested," and NG hopes it will "fall in a few Days." LS (PCC, item 155, vol. 2: 91, DNA) 2 pp.]

1. NG enclosed a letter from Lord Rawdon to Nisbet Balfour of 15 May, in which Rawdon announced his readiness to abandon a number of British posts to "secure the main object," Charleston. (PCC, item 155, vol. 2: 95, DNA)

2. The "Action at Augusta" was the capture of Ft. Grierson; the account that NG sent was a copy of Pickens to NG, first letter of 25 May, above. On the capture of Ft. Dreadnought, see Lee to NG, 22 May, above.

* * *

To Colonel Henry Lee, Jr.

Dear sir   Camp before Ninety Six [S.C.] May 29th, 1781.

Your report of the 22d with Captn Rudolphs of the surrender of Fort Dreadnought, I have had the pleasure to receive.[1] Your exertions merit my warmest approbation, and Captain Rudolph and the Officers and Soldiers under his command my particular thanks which I beg you to communicate to them.

The Stores taken I have given General [Andrew] Pickens power to distribute as he may think best calculated to answer the just claims of the Militia and the good of the service at large: If you have appropriated any part of the Stores to the use of your Corps, which I hope you have not, as it will increase prejudicial jealousies, let the things received be part of the continental proportion.[2]

I am happy to hear that you and General Pickens are upon a perfect good footing; and I beg you will cultivate it by every means in your power. He is a worthy good Man and merits great respect and attention; and no Man in this Country has half the influence that he has.

Doctor [Alexander] Skinner has arrived with your Cloathing. But I think it is best for him to halt here untill you join us, which I wish the moment the Post is reduced at Augusta.[3] The object below must rest for the present.[4] My reasons for it you shall know hereafter, and depend upon it they are substantial.[5]

We are pushing on our approaches; but for want of more fatigue Men the Work goes on slow. With esteem and affection I am dear sir Your most obedt hble servt   NATH GREENE

LS (NcD).

1. In his letter to NG of 22 May, above, Lee had enclosed John Rudulph's report of the capture of Ft. Dreadnought. Rudulph's account is noted there.

2. See NG to Pickens, this date, below. In his study of Pickens, historian Clyde Ferguson interpreted NG's remarks here as implying that Lee had under-reported the quantity of goods captured at Ft. Dreadnought. (Ferguson, "Pickens," pp. 211–12)

3. In his letter of 10 May, above, Lee had asked NG to order the forwarding of a shipment of clothing for Lee's Legion from Salisbury, N.C.

4. At this point in the text an asterisk appears. It is a callout to a note in a different hand, which seems to have been added later. The note reads: "Lt. Col. Lee proposed to strike at Savannah after the reduction of Augusta."

5. In his letter of 24 May, above, Lee had proposed a strike at British-held Savannah, Ga. If NG explained the reasons for his decision to Lee, the letter has not been found.

To John Mathews, Chairman of a Standing Committee of Congress to Correspond with the Commander of the Southern Department

Dr Sir   Camp before Ninty Six [S.C.] May 29th 1781

Your favor of the 30th of April was deliverd me at this place Night before last.

Nothing can be farther from truth than Col [Nisbet] Balfours insinuation that I had refusd an equitable exchange of prisoners. The Wickedness and cruelty of the enemy appear in so many different shapes in this Country, that I am not surprisd of their determination to send off our prisoners to the West Indies directly contrary to the conditions of the Capitulation under which they surrenderd.

My feelings as a man and Soldier has ever made me anxious to effect an exchange for our unfortunate captives as soon as possible; and I have ever thought it rather cruel and unjust to hold them in captivity for fear of throwing an additional force into the hands of the enemy tho this has been the case throughout almost every stage of the war.

The Cartel for the exchange of prisoners for the Southern department I hope has arrivd in Congress and will satisfy them that I have not been unmindful of any part of my duty however embarassed with other difficulties.[1]

It is true I believe there are more of the officers belonging to the Enemy on parole than we have. I have parold but few and those generally at the special instance of some of the Southern Gentlemen: However I am clearly of opinion that the only way of geting our officers out on parole is first to let theirs go in; and then their solicitations being added to the demands of our officers for an equal indulgence with theirs generally produces the desird effect. I have ever considerd it a great misfortune that the british officers were shifted about in the different States, they never fail to corrupt a certain circle and raise apprehensions and discontent among the people. For this and many other reasons I have always thought it bad policy not to grant paroles more liberally than has been done. These reasons gave rise to one of the conditions of the cartel for paroling all the officers. If I have mistaken the policy and intention of Congress in this matter I am sorry for it.

Major [Edmund M.] Hyrne is gone into Charles Town to carry into effect the Cartel; and I hope the unfortunate captives will soon be released from the horid situation they have so long languished in.[2]

Our Military operations here you receive an account of in my public dispaches to Congress and the commander in Chief. With the truest esteem I [am] Sir your most Obed humble Ser   N GREENE

ADfS (MiU-C).

1. See NG to Huntington, 10 May, above.

2. Hyrne, the commissary of prisoners, reported on his efforts to "effect the Cartel" in a letter to NG of 1 August, below.

To General Andrew Pickens

Dear Sir   Camp before Ninety Six [S.C.] May 29th 1781

I had the pleasure of receiving your two letters of the 25th day before yesterday.

Your success is flattering, and the gallantry and good conduct of the troops in the defeat of Col [James] Grierson merit both honor and applause and I beg you will please to accept and communicate my thanks upon the occasion.[1]

Before the receipt of your letters I had dispached Major [Ichabod] Burnet one of my aids to consult with you what was best to be done with the Stores that might fall into our hands. The Militia are undoubtedly intitled to a part. One half of every thing except good Arms and Ammunition, I thought might be just to allow the Militia and I should hope would give them satisfaction.[2] However I submit the whole matter to your discretion and leave you to make such a distribution as you may think will be best calculated to answer the just claims of the Militia and afford the Most effectual support to the service. You know the distress of this Army and the necessity there is for laying a foundation for a permanent opposition to the enemy in this quarter, and the Stores which may be necessary for those purposes.

We have sent Eight waggons to assist in bringing forward the Stores; you will have them loaded, and furnish an escort for their safe conduct.

We are pushing our approaches here with all possible diligence and wish you to effect the reduction of the enemies remaining post as soon as you can. Many reasons induce me to wish it which I will explain to you hereafter. With esteem & regard I am dear General Your most obed[t] humble Serv   N GREENE

P.S. All the indian Guns, which are useless to the Army, the Militia may app[ropr]iate to their own use.

ADfS (NcD).

1. On the capture of Ft. Grierson, at Augusta, Ga., see Pickens to NG, first letter of 25 May, above.

2. In his second letter to NG of 25 May, above, Pickens had suggested distributing some of the stores captured at Ft. Dreadnought to militiamen.

*   *   *

¶ [FROM MAJOR THOMAS HILL, [Ninety Six, S.C., 29 May 1781].[1] He considers himself a "private Citizen" under the new arrangement of the

Virginia line. Believes that if a "freeman" is "unhappy in any station and can leave it with propriety," he should be able to do so. With "so much justice on his side," he plans to leave the army, with or without NG's approval.[2] ALS (MiU-C) 1 p.]

1. The date was taken from the docketing; the place was determined from the contents.

2. NG replied on 30 May, below.

¶ [FROM MAJOR JAMES MCHENRY, Baltimore, Md., 29 May 1781. Writes NG before setting out to join the Marquis [de Lafayette]. "Congress have anticipated your intentions and voted that I am no Doctor, (notwithstanding the labor and time I have spent to acquire the profession) but a Major since the last or first (I know not which) of October 1780."[1] As a matter of "etiquette," NG should ask Lafayette, before McHenry joins him, "to borrow me [for] a campaign or so."[2] In the next several days, McHenry will forward the rest of the 340 shirts that "the ladies of this town made a present of" and some rags for the hospital.[3] ALS (Greene Papers: DLC) 2 pp.]

1. Congress had voted to commission McHenry on 27 May. (See Huntington to NG, 28 May, above.)

2. McHenry wrote NG on 12 July, below, that he had changed his mind and would continue to serve with Lafayette.

3. On 27 September 1780, Mary Lee, the wife of Gov. Thomas Sim Lee, had written Washington to inform him that the "Ladies of Maryland" were subscribing "a considerable Sum for the relief of the American Army" and to ask how it might best be used. (Washington Papers, DLC) In his reply of 11 October, and again to Mordecai Gist on 2 January 1781, Washington suggested that the money be used to purchase shirts for the Southern Army. (Fitzpatrick, GW, 20: 168; 21: 49)

¶ [FROM GENERAL FRANCIS MARION, Georgetown, S.C., 29 May 1781. Marion has proceeded to Georgetown, as he announced that he would in his last letter.[1] Immediately after his arrival "Yesterday," he began "to open Intrenchment." At 9 P.M., the enemy "thought proper to step on board of their vessels" and "fell down towards the Bar." Marion then took possession of the town and the enemy redoubt and found some abandoned artillery, which the British had tried to disable. He will stay at Georgetown only long enough to "Levell the works." He will then move "immediatly" to a position near Monck's Corner and take "post."[2] Adds: "The Enemys Leaving this post has saved a great deal of provisions & Stock & prevent the toreys from destroying our friends & Leave them [i.e., "our friends"] at Leasure to persue their planting. It cannot be conceived the Joy this event has given our friends." ALS (CLjC) 1 p.]

1. As noted at his letter to NG of 20 May, above, Marion had marched to Georgetown without waiting for permission from NG or Gen. Thomas Sumter.

2. As seen in Marion to NG, 5 June, below, his stay at Georgetown was longer than he had anticipated.

¶ [FROM GOVERNOR JOHN RUTLEDGE OF SOUTH CAROLINA, Philadelphia, 29 May 1781. Has received NG's letter of 2 May [not found]. The "difficulties" facing NG and the "distresses" of the South are "apparent"; NG's conduct is "justly admired, and gives universal satisfaction." Everyone is convinced that NG has done all he could, and Rutledge is "truly sorry" that

NG has "been so destitute of Means." Adds: "We must not despair." Is confident that the southern states can be recovered and promises to do his "utmost" to "obtain, (if possible,) such Aid as shall compel the Enemy to evacuate them." Is going to Washington's headquarters "to Morrow"; would have gone sooner, but has been detained in Philadelphia. Refers NG to Dr. [Peter] Fayssoux for an account of "publick Transactions here." Rutledge will write NG after he returns from headquarters—or sooner, if he has something "material to communicate." ALS (MiU-C) 2 pp.]

¶ [GENERAL GREENE'S ORDERS, "Camp before 96," S.C., 30 May 1781. Announces the appointment of Lt. John Hamilton as "Deputy Clothier General." There will be an inspection of the clothing belonging to "the Several Regiments," and Hamilton will report the findings to headquarters. Lamar Orderly Book (OClWHi) 2 pp.]

*   *   *

To Major Thomas Hill

Sir   Camp before Ninety Six [S.C.] May 30th 1781
    Your letter of yesterday has been receivd.
    Baron Stubens proposal for incorporating the two Virginia Regiments into one cannot take place, as it will be prejudicial to the service.[1] Lt Col Haws [Samuel Hawes] is sick, and you are much wanted with the Regiment, and it will be very injurious to the service for you to leave it at this time; therefore I hope you will not think of it under these circumstances; especially until the siege is over.
    It is true you are a supe[r]numary officer, but you will remember you are to retire upon half pay and that you are to retire only upon the presumption of there being too great proportion of officers. This being the case to leave the Army at a time when you are wanted and when your service is essential and when you reap all the advantages of those in service during your continuance will not have a good appearance nor will it correspond with that noble spirit of patriotism which has hitherto dignified the conduct of so many of the American Officers; and induced them to persevere in the service of their Country under every possible disadvantage.
    The Cause of your Country[,] the circumstances of the Army and your own honor require your continuance; but it rests with you to decide the part you will act.[2] I am Sir Your Most Obed humble Ser
                                                                    N GREENE

ADfS (MiU-C).
    1. NG had received the proposed arrangement of the Virginia line prior to 1 May. (See his letter to Steuben of that date, above.)
    2. Hill replied on 31 May, below.

*   *   *

¶ **[FROM COLONEL WILLIAM POLK,**[1] Congaree, S.C., 30 May 1781. A number of the militiamen from Virginia wish to "engage into the Ten months service in this State" but cannot obtain permission from their commanding officer. Asks NG for "liberty to recruit."[2] ALS (MiU-C) 1 p.]

1. Polk commanded one of the ten-month regiments organized by Thomas Sumter. The men in those units received confiscated slaves as pay. (See note at Sumter to NG, 7 April, above.)

2. NG replied on 5 June, below.

¶ **[FROM CAPTAIN JOHN PRYOR,** Gen. Robert Lawson's, near Prince Edward Court House, Va., 30 May 1781. Details his meeting, altercation with, and subsequent drubbing of Capt. Nathaniel Irish, whom Pryor has had arrested.[1] The laboratory is temporarily under the direction of John Martin, a recently exchanged South Carolina officer, whom Pryor had named field commissary of military stores for NG's army. Martin was at the laboratory with Pryor to arrange for a shipment of ammunition to NG's army.[2] "The greatest misfortune in this affair" is the loss of "some valuable Artificers," who were "attach'd" to Irish and will not serve under anyone else. Pryor hopes to quickly enlist replacements by offering the "same pay &c &c" given to artificers serving in the North; he believes craftsmen will find service as artificers preferable to "turning out so repeatedly in the Militia."[3]

Baron Steuben had directed Pryor to send Martin with the ammunition to "the Saura Towns" [in North Carolina], where he was to join the levies marching from Virginia to reinforce NG. Pryor has since learned that the levies are under orders to join the Marquis de Lafayette; he must therefore get Steuben to clarify the instructions. In the meantime, Martin will move the stores to New London, Va.[4] Pryor is sure that NG has learned about the junction of Lord Cornwallis's force with that of [Gen. Benedict] Arnold and the arrival of an estimated 2,000 additional British troops from New York.[5] Calls the "want of Arms" in Virginia "a very great misfortune"; estimates that there are "near 3000 wanting repairs." There is a lack of "public workmen," so Pryor has sent the damaged arms to "a dozen different Country Shops" and is now beginning to get "a good many fit for service." Another 1,100 stand of arms, intended for the new levies, have arrived from the North. Pryor will use his "utmost" exertions to "erect" the necessary armories and factories; he should have this completed "shortly," if there are "no more perplexities." Hopes NG will pardon his "long deranged scrale [i.e., scrawl]," for Pryor has "not got over" his "agaitation wth Capt Irish." ALS (MiU-C) 3 pp.]

1. As seen in his letter to NG of 20 May, above, Irish believed that he, rather than Pryor, held the appointment as commissary of military stores in the Southern Department. Irish's version of the confrontation is in his letter to NG of 17 June, below. As noted at Pryor to NG, 11 May, above, the Board of War had already appointed another officer, so neither Pryor nor Irish got the post. In a letter to NG of 5 June, below, Pryor said the incident with Irish would be investigated prior to the holding of any court-martial. It is not known if Irish was ever tried, but according to a memorial that he sent to Congress in 1785, he continued to serve as a captain in the artificer's regiment. (PCC, item 41, vol. 4: 497, DNA)

2. As seen in his letter to NG of 25 July, below, Pryor learned that NG had already appointed Maj. John Mazaret to the post before Martin left for the army.

3. In his letter to NG of 8 July, below, Pryor reported that he had succeeded in recruiting artificers.

4. As Pryor reported to NG on both 8 and 25 July, below, British raids into the New London area prevented the shipment of ammunition to the army.

5. On the reinforcement from New York, see note at St. Clair to NG, 6 May, above.

¶ [GENERAL GREENE'S ORDERS, Camp near Ninety Six, S.C., Thursday, 31 May 1781. Officers are to receive "a Quart of Spirits each." Lamar Orderly Book (OCIWHi) 1 p.]

¶ [CAPTAIN NATHANIEL PENDLETON TO CAPTAIN JOHN JONES. From Headquarters [Camp before Ninety Six, S.C.], 31 May 1781. "From motives of humanity," NG will allow Jones to leave and get his wound treated.[1] Jones is to send a written parole to headquarters and is to designate the place at which he will remain until he has recovered.[2] ADfS (MiU-C) 1 pp.]
   1. Jones, a prisoner, was a former British officer who had been serving in a Loyalist unit. Oddly, his request for the permission granted here was dated 2 June, below.
   2. Pendleton enclosed a model of the parole that Jones was to send. (MiU-C)

¶ [FROM MAJOR THOMAS HILL, [Camp before Ninety Six, S.C.], 31 May 1781. Thinks the "good natured part" of the "world" would readily excuse his leaving the army. Knows his patriotism would not be questioned where he is best known. Nor can he see any advantage to remaining in the service, where he has already exhausted a "considerable part of a small fortune." However, as NG believes it would be "prejuditial" to execute the new arrangement, Hill will continue to "do duty during the Seige."[1] ALS (MiU-C) 1 p.]
   1. See NG to Hill, 30 May, above.

¶ [GENERAL GREENE'S ORDERS, "Camp before 96," S.C., 1 June 1781. Officers commanding fatigue parties are to see that "particular care" is taken of entrenching tools, which are to be "Secured" when "not in immediate use." Lamar Orderly Book (OCIWHi) 1 p.]

*   *   *

To General Andrew Pickens

Dear Sir   Camp before Ninty Six [S.C.] June 1st 1781
   We are in immediate want of a few barrels of powder to compleat the reduction of this place. We shall be in the ditch of the enemies works by tomorrow Night or next day morning and the powder is wanting to blow up the Works. I beg you will send off the powder the moment this reaches you.[1]
   We have nothing new from the Northward or Charles Town, except the arrival of the second division of the french fleet, which is pretty certainly upon our coast, and most probably will strike a stroke in Chessapeak Bay, if not farther south.[2]
   I hope before this reaches you Augusta will be ours.[3] May fortune befriend you is the wish of dear Sir your most Obed[t] humble Ser
                                                        NATH GREENE

ADfS (MiU-C).
1. Pickens replied on 2 June, below. The American lines did not reach the ditch surrounding the fortifications at Ninety Six until 16 or 17 June. (Haiman, *Kosciuszko*, p. 114)
2. The report was false.
3. Pickens and Col. Henry Lee reported the capture of Augusta, Ga., in a letter to NG of 5 June, below.

*   *.   *

¶ [FROM GENERAL ISAAC HUGER, "Near McCord's Ferry," S.C., 1 June 1781, 4 P.M. Is forwarding intelligence to NG and Gen. [Thomas] Sumter that was just received from Maj. [Hezekiah] Maham.[1] Maham is to be reinforced by part of Col. [Charles] Myddelton's regiment and by Marion, who should have joined Maham "this morning."[2] ALS (MiU-C) 1 p.]
1. See Maham to NG, this date, below.
2. Sumter wrote NG on 7 June, below, that he had ordered a regiment to join Maham. Gen. Francis Marion informed NG that he was unable to assist Maham. (See Marion to NG, 5 June, below.)

¶ [FROM MAJOR EDMUND M. HYRNE, Col. [William] Thomson's, S.C., 1 June 1781. He postponed going to Charleston until "tomorrow" in the hope of hearing from NG and "to avoid being in Town [on] the Kings birth day."[1] Will insist on seeing Gen. [William] Moultrie and the American officers at Haddrell's Point before entering "into the exchange."[2] According to someone who recently arrived from Charleston, the British were "much confus'd and embarrass'd" because of "several Rebel privateers . . . on the coast" and because they held "no post but Dorchester out of the Town." Since then, an enemy party of 200 men has "taken post at Moncks Corner."[3] The British "have abandon'd George Town, and 'tis said Lord Rawdon has taken or means to take a position towards Savannah."[4] Colonel Thomson's efforts to carry out NG's order have been "render'd ineffectual by General [Thomas] Sumters Corps," who take "all the valuable horses."[5] Thomson has been able to obtain only "three or four" horses for the dragoons; his "conduct justifies" Hyrne's "opinion of him." The man who brought Hyrne his "passport, had his horse taken from him on his return"; Hyrne will probably "have to apologize on that score."[6] Wishes NG success in his "exertions"; has heard that the capture of Ninety Six will be delayed. ALS (MiU-C) 2 pp.]
1. Hyrne was on his way to Charleston to arrange an exchange of prisoners under the terms of the recently negotiated cartel. (See Hyrne to NG, 27 May, and NG to Mathews, 29 May, both above; on the cartel, see NG to Huntington, 10 May, above.) King George III's birthday was 4 June; Hyrne arrived in the city on 5 June. (Boatner, *Encyc.*, p. 416; Balfour to Cornwallis, 7 June, PRO 30/11/6)
2. Hyrne reported on his efforts to effect the exchange in a letter to NG of 1 August, below.
3. On the British post at Monck's Corner, see note at Huger to NG, 6 June, below.
4. On the evacuation of Georgetown by the British, see Marion to NG, 29 May, above. In a letter of 5 June, Lord Rawdon informed Lord Cornwallis that the royal governor of Georgia, James Wright, had "represented so strongly the want of troops at Savannah," Ga., that Rawdon had sent the King's American Regiment there, even though "at the time we could ill spare them." (PRO 30/11/6) In his diary, Henry Nase, who served in the King's American Regiment, noted that the regiment marched from Dorchester, S.C., on 27 May. Four days later, it sailed from Charleston for Savannah on board a number of

small vessels because, as Rawdon wrote Cornwallis, no "shipping" was available. (Nase Family Papers, New Brunswick Museum, St. John, N.B.; Rawdon to Cornwallis, 5 June, PRO 30/11/6)

5. On NG's orders to Thomson, see Conyers to NG, 14 April, above.

6. For more about the troubles of the messenger who had brought Hyrne a pass to enter British lines, see Hyrne to NG, 27 May, above.

¶ [FROM COLONEL HENRY LEE, JR., Augusta, Ga. [1 June 1781].[1] Has learned from Major Burnet that NG needs Lee and his troops to complete the "present business."[2] Warns that "the strength of this post, the uncommon inertness & disorder of our assistants, the inferiority of our regulars in point of number, & the judicious conduct of the enemy will render the issue of these operations later than you can wish or expect.[3] Our approaches are very near, & I hope tomorrow or the next day will put affairs in a critical situation." Lee "will not pass by any favourable opportunity . . . to finish the matter."[4] Asks about an officer. Adds: "Burnet can tell you of the necessity of civil government in this state & of the propriety in raising at any expense the quota of regulars for its defence."[5] ALS (Dr. John B. Carter, West Columbia, S.C., 1991) 2 pp.]

1. The year was taken from the docketing; the date, 1 June, was derived from the contents. (See also Pickens to NG, this date, below.)

2. NG had sent Maj. Ichabod Burnet, his aide, to "consult" with Gen. Andrew Pickens and Lee. (NG to Pickens, 29 May, above) NG had written Lee on 22 May, above, that the fortifications at Ninety Six, S.C., were much stronger than expected and that Lee should conclude his "business at Augusta" as quickly as possible.

3. The "assistants" were militiamen.

4. When he wrote NG on 4 June, below, Lee hoped to finish the siege of Augusta by the next day.

5. See also Lee's remarks in his letter to NG of 4 June on the condition of civil government in Georgia.

¶ [FROM COLONEL HEZEKIAH MAHAM, St. Stephen, S.C., 1 June 1781.[1] Has learned that Lord Rawdon's army returned to Monck's Corner "yesterday." Rawdon "has sent strong parteys" to collect livestock; Maham fears they will obtain "the gratesst part of them this Way" because his party is too small to "stop any Of their plund[rs]." Encloses a letter and a "Return of Rawdens Comp[y]" [not found].[2] Gen. [Francis] Marion has "not yet Returnd."[3] ALS (MiU-C) 1 p.]

1. No addressee was given, and the salutation reads simply "D[r] Gen[l]." It is not certain, therefore, if the letter was addressed to NG or to Gen. Isaac Huger, who forwarded it to NG. (See Huger to NG, this date, above.)

2. For more on Rawdon's force, see note at Huger to NG, 6 June, below.

3. Marion had gone to Georgetown, leaving Maham with a small party to watch Lord Rawdon's movements. (Marion to NG, 19 May, above)

                        *   *   *

From General Andrew Pickens

Dear General   Griersons Fort Aug[a] [Augusta, Ga.] 1st June 1781

Since I had the honour of Writting you on the 25th Ult[o] nothing material has occur'd here.[1] We are carrying on Works against Fort Cornwallis with what expedition we can though I think our progress is but very Slow. Yesterday Lt Col^o [Henry] Lee and myself Summon'd Col^o [Thomas] Brown to Surrender, but his Answer was that it was his duty and inclination to defend the Post to the last extremity, and as there is reason to think he will make an obstinate defence, and the Season of the year making it so very necessary that as many of the Militia as possible Should be at their farms, I would be happy if the Service would admit of Sending us two hundred regular troops, which if done immediatly would greatly facilitate the reduction of this Post, and enable the Army to Act elsewhere as you Sho^d Order.[2] I find Col^o Brown has more provision than was at first expected, and as his Works are Strong and the Militia far from being Well Arm'd (although better than lately) it will take more time than I could Wish to end the Seige.[3] The Arms we got at Galphins being for the Indian trade are very indifferent.[4]

The eight Waggons you Sent here have been loaded and left the Boats yesterday, a list of what they carry is now inclosed.[5] Fifteen more Arrived this morning and will Set off for the upper Settlement as Soon as I can get a proper escorte, but as there is a considerable quantity of Salt which is a heavy Article, more Waggons will Still be wanted to remove the Whole.

The mode adopted for dividing the Articles taken at Mr Galphins was one third part for the Continental troops, one third for the Militia of South Carolina, and the other for the Georgians, reserving the Arms[,] Ammunition[,] Rum and Salt entirely for publick Service.[6] A Chest of Medicines was Sent with the eight Waggons. They are much in demand, and no Such thing to be had in the country. I can't doubt their being Saved as much as possible. I have the honor to be with great esteeme Dear General, your most obedient, humble Servant

AND^w PICKENS

ALS (David Coblentz, Raphine, Va., 1973).

1. Pickens's two letters to NG of 25 May are above.

2. NG replied on 3 June, below.

3. Pickens and Lee reported the capture of Ft. Cornwallis to NG on 5 June, below.

4. On the arms and stores captured at Ft. Dreadnought (Galphin's Plantation), see Lee to NG, 22 May, above.

5. NG had sent the wagons for some of the stores captured at Ft. Dreadnought. (See NG to Pickens, 29 May, above.) The list that Pickens enclosed has not been found.

6. NG had told Pickens to decide how the items should be distributed. (Ibid.) He wrote Pickens on 3 June, below, that the "division of the stores is perfectly satisfactory."

* * *

¶ [FROM LIEUTENANT FRANCIS SMITH,[1] Camden, S.C., 1 June 1781. He was left to superintend the hospital at Camden and believes he should inform NG of its "present Situation." He has armed nine men from the hospital to serve as guards for the stores and to collect provisions. He lacks orders respecting the British wounded, who do not consider themselves prisoners. Unless instructed otherwise, he will "confine them as fast as they Recover," or else "numbers" will escape.[2] He has also taken charge of a few prisoners who were sent to Camden by Gen. [Francis] Marion. Reports that there were many desertions from Lord Rawdon's army as it retreated to Charleston; as a result, some orderlies in the British hospital have also deserted. Smith has stored "every necessary article" and reports that "the works are chiefly demolished." Gen. [Charles] Scott, who stopped "the other day on his Parole" to Virginia, "is well" and sends NG "his compliments."[3] ALS (MiU-C) 2 pp.]

1. Smith's rank is given in the docketing of Col. Otho Williams's reply of 22 June, below. He was a Virginia Continental officer. (Heitman, *Register*)

2. In his letter to Smith of 22 June, Williams gave orders for dealing with the prisoners.

3. On Scott's parole, see Lee to NG, after 7 April, above.

¶ [FROM GEORGE WASHINGTON, New Windsor, N.Y., 1 June 1781. Has NG's letters of 22 and 27 April, "enclosing Copies of your Letters to Congress." Adds:

> The difficulties which you daily encounter and surmount with your small force, add not a little to your reputation, and I am pretty well assured, that should you be obliged finally to withdraw from South [Carolina], and even from North Carolina, it will not be attributed to either your want of abilities or of exertion, but to the true cause, the want of means to support the War, in them. I feel for your mortification at the loss of the day before Campden, after it seemed so much in your favor, but I hope you will have found that the Enemy suffered severely, as in their publication of the affair, in the New York Paper they confess the loss of 200.[1] The reduction of Fort Watson does honor to General Marian, and Colonel [Henry] Lee.[2]

Washington has "lately had an interview" with Comte Rochambeau at Wethersfield, Conn., at which they reviewed "our affairs" and "finally determined to make an attempt upon New York . . . in preference to a southern operation, as we had not the decided command of the Water." NG will "readily suppose" what prompted this decision: "the inevitable loss of Men from so long a march [to the South], more especially in the approaching hot season," and the "impossibility" of transporting supplies and equipment by land. If Washington is properly supported "by the neighbouring States in *this*, which you know has always been a favorite *operation*," he hopes the enemy will either "be expelled from" their "most valuable possession" on the continent or have to recall troops from the South "to defend it."[3] The French troops "will begin their march this way, as soon as certain circumstances will admit."[4] Washington can only give "outlines" of the plan because of "the dangers to which Letters are exposed." He will keep NG informed "as matters ripen."

He reports that a British detachment of 1,500 to 2,000 men sailed from New York about 13 May. He has advised Baron Steuben of this and asked him to inform NG. Believes these troops are headed to Chesapeake Bay or Cape Fear, N.C.[5] Doubts that they would have been sent to defend St. Augustine against the Spaniards, and "Pensacola we are told has fallen."[6] The Marquis de Lafayette has informed Washington that 800 recruits should be ready to leave Virginia by the end of May.[7] A source from Maryland told Washington that "about 400" from that state "might be expected to march in April."[8] Thinks General Wayne has left Pennsylvania by now—"If no fresh discontents arise among those Troops." Wayne's detachment will be a "valuable acquisition" to NG. "They are cheifly the old soldiers, and compleatly furnished with every necessary."[9] Washington does not have time to answer NG's "private letter" now. He has heard that Mrs. [Catharine] Greene and NG's family are well. Has written her "and mentioned your disappointment in not getting her letters, again requesting they may [be] put under cover to me."[10] LS (NjP) 6 pp.]

1. On the battle of Hobkirk's Hill and enemy casualties in that engagement, see NG to Huntington, 27 April, above.

2. Francis Marion reported the capture of Ft. Watson in his first letter to NG of 23 April, above.

3. For more on the plan to attack New York City, see note at Sharpe to NG, 28 May, above. On Washington's strong and continuing interest in such an operation, see above, vol. 6: 90–91n.

4. The French expeditionary force was at Newport, R.I.

5. On the 2,000-man reinforcement that had sailed from New York on 14 May, see note at St. Clair to NG, 6 May, above. Washington's request to Steuben was in a letter of 16 May. (Fitzpatrick, GW, 22: 91) No letter from Steuben to NG containing this information has been found.

6. A Spanish force compelled the British garrison at Pensacola, Fla., to surrender in early May, ending a siege that had begun in early March. The Spanish did not attack St. Augustine. (See above, vol. 5: 319n.)

7. See Lafayette to Washington, 8 May. (Idzerda, Lafayette Papers, 4: 88). On the hoped-for reinforcements from Virginia, see Lafayette to NG, 18 May, above.

8. As noted at Gist to NG, 29 May, above, the Maryland recruits marched at the end of August to join Lafayette in Virginia.

9. Congress had assigned the Pennsylvania Continental line to the Southern Department in February, following the mutiny of its troops in January and the temporary dissolution of the line. (Washington to NG, 27 February, above [vol. 7: 363]; on the mutiny, see James Madison to NG, 13 January, above [ibid., pp. 116–17].) The first division of Pennsylvania troops, commanded by Gen. Anthony Wayne, finally marched south from York, Pa., on 26 May. (Nelson, Wayne, p. 130; on the second division, which followed at a much later date, see note at St. Clair to NG, 6 May, above.) The reassembling and equipping of Wayne's force had taken longer than expected, and further delays occurred while Wayne sought the pay that his men had been promised in the settlement of the mutiny. (See note at Sharpe to NG, 7 April, above.) Just prior to marching, he had dealt sternly with another threatened mutiny. (Nelson, Wayne, p. 128; see also note at Sharpe to NG, 7 April, above.) As noted at St. Clair's letter of 6 May, when Wayne's force reached Virginia, it joined Lafayette in resisting the British invaders of that state and remained in Virginia until after the siege of Yorktown.

10. In his "private letter" to Washington of 1 May, above, NG had expressed concern that Catharine Greene's letters to him might have "miscarried." Washington told NG in his second letter of 30 July, below: "Your letters to Mrs Greene I have put under cover, and forwarded."

¶ [GENERAL GREENE'S ORDERS, Camp before Ninety Six, S.C., 2 June 1781. Officers of the day are to report to headquarters "every thing of the least consequence that may occur" during their tours of duty. Greene Orderly Book (CSmH) 1 p.]

¶ [FROM COLONEL WILLIAM R. DAVIE, 2 June [1781].[1] Requests some badly needed clothing for a "young Gentlemen" who is serving as an assistant commissary of purchases.[2] LS (NcU) 1 p.]

1. Davie was presumably in or near the army's camp at Ninety Six, S.C.; the year was taken from the docketing.
2. NG's reply has not been found.

¶ [FROM COLONEL WILLIAM DAVIES, Charlottesville, Va., 2 June 1781. Has just returned from "attending" Baron Steuben, who is not ready to march. The enemy's "incursions" have "thrown every thing into great confusion, as well as filled the minds of the people with the greatest discontent particularly with Baron Stuben, as they think he is disposed to leave them without assistance."[1] Virginians are also angry that the new draftees are to leave the state "when their presence is so much wanting in it."[2] Davies thinks it is "dangerous for the secrets of government and the designs of the commanding generals to be so much exposed to the knowledge of the enemy, as they always will be till a proper cypher is adopted." The number of troops commanded by the Marquis [de Lafayette] is "much inferior" to the enemy's force, "and the stores are in great danger." Although the British have been able to overrun the southern states, Davies thinks the fact that they have lost those states "the moment they left" will "have a considerable influence in Europe."[3] Catalog excerpt (Anderson Galleries, *Catalogue #1213* [1916] 1 p.]

1. The anger of Virginians toward Steuben is summarized in a letter from Benjamin Harrison, speaker of the Virginia House, to Joseph Jones, a delegate in Congress. Steuben, according to Harrison, had "600 fine men," whom he would not "carry into action." Harrison continued: "What are his reasons, I know not, but I can assure you his Conduct gives universal disgust and injures the Service much, the People complaining, and with reason, that they are drafted from thier Families at a time when they are most wanted to make bread for them, whilst the Soldiers they have hired at very great expense lay Idle. In short, My Dʳ Sir, his conduct does great mischief and will do more if he is not recalled. . . . I believe him a good officer on the Parade but the worst in every other respect in the American Army." (Enclosed in Jones to Washington, 20 June 1781, Washington Papers, DLC.)
2. As seen in his letter to Steuben of 14 May, above, NG had changed his orders and issued instructions to keep the Virginia levies in the state.
3. An offer of mediation by certain European rulers had raised the possibility that negotiations to end the war would soon begin. (See Huntington to NG, 3 June, below.)

*　　　*　　　*

From Lieutenant Adam Jamison[1]

Camp before Ninety Six [S.C.] June 2ᵈ 1781

A Report of two Negro Children in my Possession

On the 30ᵗʰ of May five Waggons arrived here from Augusta with Commissaries Stores, and Amongst Other Articles, I found two Naked female Negro's, Aged from appearance, one Eight, & the other Six, being Sisters. Upon Enquiry, None of the Men who drove the

Waggons would acknowledge a right in them, or could render any account how the Negro's came in their Possession, which Induced Me to take them into Custody. On Examining the Children next Morning, they told me their Masters name was Johnston, & that the said Waggoners came to their Mrs House (the Master being absent) & brought them off. They don't know where they Lived.[2] I am sir your Obt Servt

A. JAMISON

ALS (MiU-C).

1. Jamison was deputy commissary general of issues for the Southern Army.
2. It is not known what became of the girls.

*   *   *

¶ [FROM CAPTAIN JOHN JONES, [Edwards's House, Ninety Six District, S.C.], 2 June 1781.[1] He is "Dangerously wounded" and without medical care. Seeks permission "to Go to some Doctor." If he recovers, he will return "forthwith" to NG's "lines." He is an officer in a British light dragoon regiment and was wounded while serving as "Capt of the patternol [i.e., patrol] of Ninety Six District."[2] ALS (MiU-C) 1 p.]

1. The place was taken from the contents.
2. In a letter of 31 May, above, Nathaniel Pendleton, NG's aide, gave Jones the permission he requested. It is not known why the reply was dated earlier than Jones's request.

¶ [FROM GENERAL ANDREW PICKENS, Camp before Augusta, Ga., 2 June 1781. Pickens just received NG's letter of "yesterday" and "immediatly Sent off" 150 pounds of powder. Nothing new has happened since yesterday, when he wrote NG "fully." There has been a report that the British at Savannah will try to relieve Augusta; one of Pickens's officers, though, reports that a force that the enemy have collected at Ebenezer is too small to attempt to break the siege. Should Pickens's "requisition of yesterday be granted[,] their intentions would be entirely defeated."[1] ALS (NcD) 1 p.]

1. In his letter to NG of 1 June, above, Pickens had asked for a reinforcement of 200 regulars.

¶ [GENERAL GREENE'S ORDERS, Camp before Ninety Six, S.C., 3 June 1781. The troops are to receive a jill of rum per man and be "held in readiness for Action." Gives a list of officers and temporary officers in the quartermaster department, who "are to be respected accordingly." Lamar Orderly Book (OClWHi) 3 pp.]

¶ [COLONEL OTHO WILLIAMS TO COLONEL JOHN HARRIS CRUGER. From Camp before Ninety Six, S.C., 3 June 1781. The "situation" of the British forces in South Carolina, which Williams details, and Cruger's own "circumstances" leave Cruger "no hope but in the generosity of the American Army." NG has therefore ordered Williams to "demand an immediate surrender" of Ninety Six.[1] "A moral certainty of success" induces NG to "expect a compliance with this summons," which "will not be repeated." If Cruger refuses, he must answer "for the consequences of a vain resistance or destruction of Stores."[2] ADfS (MiU-C) 2 pp.]

1. By 3 June, NG's army had completed the second parallel of its siege lines, which were in the form of an "awkward 'Z,' " and was within sixty yards of the Star Fort, the strongest point of the defenses of Ninety Six. On the same date, American forces also finished building a Maham tower, which allowed their sharpshooters to fire into the fort and made it difficult for the defenders to disrupt the progress of the siege lines. (Cann, "Siege of Ninety Six," p. 7) In view of these developments, NG summoned the garrison to surrender.

2. Cruger's reply is immediately below.

¶ [COLONEL JOHN HARRIS CRUGER TO COLONEL OTHO WILLIAMS,[1] Ninety Six, S.C., 3 June 1781. Has received Williams's letter, conveying NG's surrender demand, which "my Duty to my Sovereign renders inadmissable at present."[2] ALS (MiU-C) 1 p.]

1. Cruger (1738–1807), a member of a prominent Loyalist family, had once been mayor of New York City. He had led a battalion of New York Loyalists to the South in 1778 as part of the expedition that captured Savannah, Ga. Cruger took command of Ninety Six in August 1780 and is best known for his successful defense of that post against NG's siege. After the British evacuated Ninety Six in July 1781, he continued to lead troops in the South, serving as second in command at the battle of Eutaw Springs. Cruger returned to New York City for reasons of health during the summer of 1782 and lived in London after the war. (Cruger, Petition to Parliament, 9 February 1784, Audit Office Papers, 12/20/142-45, Public Records Office, London; Boatner, *Encyc.*; Cashin, *King's Ranger*, pp. 237–38; on the evacuation of Ninety Six, see Pickens to NG, 10 July, below.)

2. On the evening of 3 June, after receiving the surrender demand, Cruger wrote Lord Rawdon, describing the rapid progress that NG's army had made with its siege lines and surmising that "Their great industry is a pleasing indication . . . that Your Lordship is not far off." Cruger added, though, that he had received "no intelligence, No Creature comes in to us." He described his casualties as light: one officer killed and eight soldiers wounded, out of a garrison of "two hundred Militia, & pretty good & Armed & about an hundred old & useless with their Families." Of his rejection of the surrender demand, he said: "We were this day summoned to surrender, & trust to the Generosity of the American Arms, which being rejected a furious cannonading began from three One Gun Batteries." (PRO 30/11/6)

¶ [TO COLONEL HENRY LEE, JR. From Camp [before Ninety Six, S.C.], 3 June 1781. Is sorry that "Mr Brown" gives "so much trouble." The reinforcements that Gen. [Andrew] Pickens requested will be sent in a day or two, as soon as the troops arrive from Charlotte, N.C.[1] "If you are obligd to storm the place it ought to be attempted with a force adequate to the purpose, otherwise a failure may produce disagreeable consequences." Sends intelligence from the "lower Country"; has no news from the "Northward."[2] Capt. [Henry] Archer has returned and brings "further proof of the very great villiany of Maxwell."[3] ALS (NcD) 2 pp.]

1. Col. Thomas Brown's surrender of Ft. Cornwallis apparently took place before the reinforcements were sent. (See Pickens and Lee to NG, 5 June, below.)

2. For the intelligence, see NG to Pickens, immediately below.

3. Maj. Andrew Maxwell, who had commanded Ft. Granby, the British post at the Congarees, was a notorious plunderer. Archer had presumably commanded the guards who accompanied him and his men to Charleston after their surrender. (See Lee to NG, 15 May, above.)

*   *   *

To General Andrew Pickens

Dear General   Camp before Ninety Six [S.C.] June 3ᵈ 1781.

I am sorry to find that you are in want of some additional force to complete the reduction of Fort Cornwallis. Our operations here are in such a situation that we cannot comply with your request until the arrival of the troops now on the march from Charlotte who are expected in either to morrow or next day.[1]

Lord Rawdon is fortifying at Goose Creek with in about 17 miles of Charlestown and at a place called Dorchester. The militia are all rising to a man in all the lower country and only three men has refused.[2] George Town is said to be evacuated.[3] Nothing new from the Northward, from which I conclude all things go well in that quarter. This place will be summoned this day and if it dont surrender we shall be obliged to burn the town to expedite the reduction.[4]

Your plan for the division of the stores is perfectly satisfactory.[5] I beg you will take particular care to have the publick store properly taken care of. With esteem & regard I am dear Sir Your most obedt humble Ser   N GREENE

GWG Transcript (CSmH).

1. Pickens's request for additional troops was in his letter to NG of 1 June, above. The surrender of Ft. Cornwallis apparently took place before the reinforcements were sent. (See Pickens and Lee to NG, 5 June, below.)

2. Col. William Harden had been trying to persuade former South Carolina militia leaders in the coastal region south of Charleston to renounce their paroles and return to the field. (See Harden to Francis Marion, 7 April, Gibbes, *Documentary History*, 3: 49–51.) From NG's comment, it appears that Harden had been successful with all but three of these men.

3. Marion reported the evacuation in his letter to NG of 29 May, above.

4. For the summons to surrender and its rejection by the commander of Ninety Six, see Williams to Cruger and Cruger to Williams, both of this date, above.

5. On Pickens's plan for dividing the captured enemy stores, see his letter to NG of 1 June, above.

From Samuel Huntington, President of the Continental Congress

Sir   Philadelphia June 3. 1781

I have herewith enclosed for your Information, the Copy of an Act of Congress of the 31ˢᵗ Ulto, recommending to the States of Pennsylvania[,] Delaware & Maryland immediately to raise & equip a Number of Troops; the more immediate Design of which is to repel the Enemy now in Virginia.[1]

I am also to inform you we have received authentic Advice, that the Emperor of Germany & Empress of Russia have offered their Mediation between the Belligerent Powers, which was embraced with apparent Eagerness on the Part of Great Brittain, and will probably be accepted on the Part of France & Spain, and we are called upon by our Ally to prepare for negotiation as soon as possible.[2]

This important Intelligence we have communicated to the several Governors, with Caution that it be not disclosed at present, and a most earnest Recommendation that the States make the most vigorous Exertions at this critical Juncture to drive the Enemy from all their interior Posts & if possible to expell them from these States.[3] We have also received a Letter from the King of France under his own Signature, promising us every Aid & Assistance the Situation of Affairs in his Kingdom would enable him to give.[4]

A powerful french Fleet under the Count de Grasse is arrived at Martinique & gave the British Fleet who were waiting for them, a severe Drubbing near that Island on the 24th of April; since which the French have made a Descent on S[t] Lucia & we may soon expect farther Intelligence from that Quarter.[5] I have the Honor to be, with the highest Respect sir Your most obedient & most humble Servant

SAM HUNTINGTON

LS (MiU-C).

1. Citing "the deficiency of the continental regular lines," Congress called on the states to "raise, arm, equip and accoutre for the field" a militia force to serve for three months. Pennsylvania was to raise four infantry battalions, totaling more than 2,000 rank and file, together with an artillery company and a sixty-four-man "corps of horse." Delaware's quota consisted of an infantry battalion and thirty-two cavalrymen. Maryland was to provide two battalions of infantry and a cavalry corps of sixty-four men. (JCC, 20: 583–84)

2. The proposed mediation is discussed at Sharpe to NG, 28 May, above.

3. Huntington informed the states in a letter of 1 June that although France had temporarily rejected mediation until it could hear from its allies, it would eventually "be obliged to enter into a previous plan of negotiation, conditionally for herself & Allies." The United States, according to Huntington, might then be forced into peace negotiations "in a less eligible situation" than "at any other period of the War." He urged the states to make a "great & timely exertion" to "reduce the force of the enemy now operating in our country." The British should be driven out completely, if possible, but should be confined to the seacoasts "at all events," in order to "give as little room as possible to the enemy's claim of uti possidetis, which will undoubtedly be most strenuously insisted on by them in the course of the negotiation." (Smith, Letters, 17: 283–85; see also note at Sharpe to NG, 28 May, above.) In a circular letter of the following day, Huntington asked that this information be kept secret. (Smith, Letters, 17: 286)

4. On the king's letter, see Mathews to NG, 22 May, above.

5. Adm. George Rodney, preoccupied with the plunder he had captured at St. Eustatius, turned over operational command of his fleet to Samuel Hood. Rodney weakened Hood's fleet by retaining four ships of the line at St. Eustatius. In order to protect a convoy that was sailing from that place, he then moved Hood to a less advantageous position for intercepting the Comte de Grasse's fleet. As a result, when de Grasse arrived off Martinique in early May, he was able to maneuver his transports to safety and then to force the withdrawal of Hood's outnumbered fleet to the British base at St. Lucia. (Mackesy, War for America, p. 417) Finding the British well-entrenched there,

de Grasse moved instead against Tobago, which surrendered on 2 June. (Dull, *French Navy*, p. 238)

*   *   *

¶ [FROM THE MARQUIS DE LAFAYETTE, "Camp between Rappahannock & North Anna," Va., 3 June 1781. Fearing that some of his letters to NG may have "miscarried," he repeats an account of "late transactions" in Virginia, including a detailed discussion of the enemy's movements following the junction of their detachments and of his own counter-movements. Lord Cornwallis's army is "vastly superior," and the British have a "Ten to one" advantage in cavalry. Lafayette has therefore moved "back some distance" and refuses "to indulge Lord Cornwallis with an Action."

The enemy's intentions are unclear, but Fredericksburg may "be their object," as they sent more troops than necessary to their garrison at Portsmouth. Lafayette has had all the public stores removed from Fredericksburg that he could, along with "every part of Hunters Works that could be taken out of the way."[1] An enemy strike against Charlottesville is also possible. Lafayette would not be concerned about such a move if he had not just learned that his orders have been ignored and that state stores are being collected there, "least they should mix with the continentals." His orders were so "positive," though, that he hopes "the precious part of the Stores" have been moved to a safer place.[2] He also ordered the removal of stores from Orange Court House. Finally, the report of an insurrection in Hampshire County and Lord Cornwallis's haste to send him a copy of the cartel, with instructions that prisoners be sent to the James River, make him think the British may try to free the Convention army.[3] Luckily, he opened a letter from the Board of War to the governor, directing that the Convention army be moved to New England; Lafayette sent a copy to the officer in charge of the prisoners, requesting "an immediate execution" of the order.[4] Gen. [Daniel] Morgan has moved to oppose the insurrectionists, who are thought to number about 700.[5] The possibility that the British may move toward the Convention army prisoners or attempt to interrupt Lafayette's junction with Wayne has led Lafayette "particularly to attend to" joining forces with Wayne, which will "give us a possibility to protect some part or other of this State."[6] Lafayette was unaware until recently of NG's orders that the "new Continentals and Militia" under Baron Steuben should join Lafayette's army.[7] Steuben had been planning to march south. When Lafayette unites with Wayne, he will be better able to "command my own movements & those of the other Troops in this State."[8] If the junction with Wayne had taken place earlier, "matters would have been very different."

The enemy cavalry numbers 500 men and is growing daily. It is impossible to prevent them from acquiring horses, given the "neglect of the Inhabitants, dispertion of houses, and robberies of Negroes (should even the most vigorous measures Have been taken by Civil Authority)." It is also difficult for Lafayette to reconnoitre the enemy or counteract any of their rapid movements "Under this cloud of light Troops." Dispatches from the governor have been captured; Lafayette notified the governor and Baron Steuben of this immediately. Cy (PEL) 4 pp.]

1. Fearing an attack on his base at Portsmouth, Cornwallis had sent troops there to reinforce it. He had considered an attack on Fredericksburg, but after learning "the present state of Hunter's iron manufactory" there, "it did not appear of so much importance as the stores on the other side of the country." (Cornwallis to Sir Henry Clinton, 30 June, PRO 30/11/74)

2. Having forced Lafayette north of the Rappahannock River, Cornwallis sent Col. Banastre Tarleton to raid Charlottesville. According to Cornwallis, Tarleton "destroyed there, and on his return, one thousand stand of good arms, some clothing, and other stores, and five hundred barrels of powder, without opposition." (Ibid.)

3. On the cartel, see note at NG to Huntington, 10 May, above. No evidence has been found that Cornwallis meant to free the Convention army prisoners.

4. Lafayette's letter of 3 June to Col. James Wood, the officer superintending the prisoners, is printed in Idzerda, *Lafayette Papers*, 4: 160–61. For the letter from the Board of War to Gov. Thomas Jefferson, dated 25 May, see Boyd, *Jefferson Papers*, 6: 15. By late June, the Convention army prisoners had been moved to Pennsylvania. (Joseph Reed to Valentine Eckert and Reed to William Scott, both 27 June, *Pennsylvania Archives: Selected and Arranged from Original Documents in the Office of the Secretary of the Commonwealth*, 1st ser., 12 vols. [Philadelphia, 1852–56], 9: 230, 232)

5. The insurrection began in April 1781, when a mob drove away an agent of the state who had been sent to draft men and impress clothing and beef. The insurrectionists, many of them armed, continued to oppose the draft and impressment laws throughout May and June. Gov. Thomas Jefferson took no direct action initially, but as the rebellion continued to grow, a decision was reached to send a militia force under the command of Gen. Daniel Morgan against the rebels. Morgan quickly and with little bloodshed quelled the uprising and arrested the ringleaders. (Eckenrode, *Revolution in Virginia*, pp. 246–48; Higginbotham, *Morgan*, p. 160)

6. Wayne's detachment of 1,000 Pennsylvania Continentals joined Lafayette on 10 June. (Idzerda, *Lafayette Papers*, 4: xliv) Cornwallis apparently decided that "it was impossible" to prevent the junction. (Cornwallis to Clinton, 30 June, PRO 30/11/74)

7. In his letter to Steuben of 14 May, above, NG directed that the levies should remain in Virginia but said nothing about the Virginia militia staying there.

8. See Steuben to NG, 26 May, above. The detachment commanded by Steuben did not join Lafayette's army until 17 June. (Selby, *Revolution in Virginia*, p. 289)

¶ [**FROM THE MARQUIS DE LAFAYETTE**, [Camp between Rappahannock and North Anna Rivers, 3 June 1781].[1] Having "Renderd Accounts to A General" in his official letter, he now wants to congratulate NG as a "friend." Tells him: "The Generalship of your Manuevre was Independant of fortune. But Success Has Crowned it and Envy Has Been Silenced."[2] Lafayette enjoys NG's "glory" because he "Heartily" loves NG. He hopes that his own conduct, "under difficult Circumstances," is likewise approved. "Now that Waine is Coming," he will not need to "Run so fast," although he has often moved in expectation of Wayne's arrival and has been repeatedly disappointed.[3] Hopes that "a Maritime Superiority will Be on our Side for this Campaign." Guesses that Washington's army would then "Be in Virginia" and that the "North [Hudson] River [would be] not much Better than a post." Has "very old" news that the French army at Rhode Island had "marching orders" and planned an encampment with the American army. Is not sure if Washington has left New Windsor, N.Y., but does know that he has conferred with Comte de Rochambeau.[4] ALS (Greene Papers: DLC) 2 pp.]

1. The date and place were taken from Lafayette's official letter, immediately above.

2. The "Manuevre" was NG's decision to abandon pursuit of Lord Cornwallis and invade South Carolina.

3. On the junction between Lafayette's force and Gen. Anthony Wayne's Pennsylvania Continentals, see note at Lafayette to NG, immediately above.

4. For the basis of Lafayette's hope for a "Maritime Superiority," see Sharpe to NG, 28 May, above. As noted at that letter, Washington and Rochambeau were not planning to move their armies to Virginia.

¶ [FROM COLONEL THOMAS WADE, Richfield, N.C., 3 June 1781. As he has received no instructions to send provisions, Wade concludes that the Southern Army is well supplied and its movements are "uncertain." Advises trading the damaged public corn meal he has "for Something" and to stop further grinding. Wade has "a Quantity" of "Good" cattle ready to move "on the Shortest notice." The boats are not being used, so the superintendent, who "thinks his pay & Rashins for Self & horses are due him daily," is "not wanting." Wade asks NG for directions on this and the other "Subjicts." Also asks if he should continue to purchase corn and cattle. Reminds NG that these items are now "the Risque of the planter," but if Wade purchases them, they become the public's risk.[1] If the Drowning Creek Loyalists were not so "Trouble Sum," he would buy rice for the army and its hospitals and bring it "up by water." Has received accounts that Lord Cornwallis and Gen. [William] Phillips have "formd a Junction in Virginia." ALS (MiU-C) 2 pp.]

1. NG replied on 9 June, below.

¶ [GENERAL GREENE'S ORDERS, "Camp before 96," S.C., 4 June 1781. Appoints an assistant deputy wagon master. Calls for "Returns of Knapsacks on hand" and of the number needed. Lamar Orderly Book (OClWHi) 1 p.]

¶ [TO COLONEL NISBET BALFOUR. From Camp [before Ninety Six, S.C.], 4 June 1781. Encloses a copy of a letter just received from Col. [James] Wood. Hopes Dr. [David] Olyphant will be freed "agreable to the exchange which took place near twelve Months past."[1] Olyphant's "further detention" would only "encrease the distress of Individuals and multiply the calamities of War."[2] LS (NN) 2 pp.]

1. See Wood to NG, 2 May, above.
2. Balfour replied on 12 June, below.

¶ [FROM THE CHEVALIER DE LA LUZERNE, Philadelphia, 4 June 1781. Has received NG's letter of 24 April.[1] Is confident that NG will "do all that is possible" with the "weak" means at his disposal and is "eagerly" awaiting news. The departure of the French "second division" has been unavoidably delayed.[2] La Luzerne cannot go into the reasons in this letter, but he has informed Congress, which "would not do anything else but congratulate the wisdom and prudence of the king."[3] Reinforcements are still expected, but they will be fewer than originally promised.[4] The king, however, has given the United States a "free grant whose dispositions have been entrusted to the Congress."[5] Robert Morris, the superintendent of finance, has been given orders "for its gradual application, so as to meet the needs of the southern army."[6] Assures NG that French assistance "will be effective" and that the king is committed to doing all that he can. If the United States can "hold back the enemy a little longer," their cause will be ultimately successful. Also assures

NG that the "misfortunes and dangers of the Southern states are one more reason for rekindling his Majesty's interest in their favor." Says "future events will show that the United States were quite justified in not allowing themselves to be discouraged by the difficulties of the present situation." LS (MiU-C) 3 pp. (English translation by Eric Deudon).]

1. The letter, dated 28 April, is above.

2. On the failure to send the second division of the French expeditionary force to America, see note at La Luzerne to NG, 3 April, above.

3. A memorandum prepared by the committee of Congress that met with La Luzerne makes no direct mention of the diversion of the second division. Nor is there anything about congressional reaction to the news in the JCC. La Luzerne seems to have tried to put the diversion in the best light possible, saying, according to the memorandum, that the French king's council was "in hopes that the diversions made by the king's arms will prevent the British from making very great exertions against the thirteen United States." (Wharton, *Revolutionary Diplomatic Correspondence*, 4: 456)

4. In his memorial to Congress of 25 May, La Luzerne reported that the French expeditionary force at Newport, R.I., would receive reinforcements and that "some vessels of force" would be sent to enable the squadron at Rhode Island "to put to sea." (JCC, 20: 558)

5. The king had "resolved to grant" the United States "a subsidy of six millions livres." (Ibid.; for more on the subsidy, see note at Mathews to NG, 22 May, above.)

6. Congress resolved on 4 June to turn over to Morris "the disposition and management of that part" of the grant from France that "is to be employed in America." The money was to be used to promote "a vigorous prosecution of the present campaign." (Ibid., p. 597)

¶ [FROM COLONEL HENRY LEE, JR., [Augusta, Ga.], 4 June 1781. He had hoped to inform NG "ere now" of the surrender of Ft. Cornwallis, "but the judicious exertions of Col. Brown, & the unmaterial aid which we receive from our friends ⟨has⟩ continued to delay the issue."[1] Thinks it probable that "Tomorrow" the American forces will "obtain victory," although NG "can have no idea of the conduct of the Militia, which may disappoint again."[2] Sends reliable intelligence that the Spanish captured an enemy post on 10 May and that they are preparing to besiege St. Augustine, Fla.[3] Seeks news of Lord Rawdon. "Should he detach to releive this place give us assistance. I hope you have got 96."[4] In a postscript, Lee adds: "If you do not take on yourself to govern this state, till civil government can be introduced, you will loose all the benefit from it, which your exertions & the public cause have claim to. They [exc]eed the Goths & Vandals in their schemes of plunder murder & iniqu[ity]. All this under pretence of supporting the virtuous cause of America."[5] ALS (NcD) 3 pp. The ALS is torn; the word in angle brackets was taken from a transcript of the letter in the Draper Papers (WHi).]

1. On the "exertions" of Thomas Brown, the British commander at Augusta, see Gen. Andrew Pickens to NG, 1 June, above, and the note at Pickens and Lee to NG, 5 June, below. "Our friends" were undoubtedly the militia troops Lee mentioned in the next sentence; he had also commented on "the inertness & disorder of our assistants" in his letter to NG of 1 June, above.

2. Pickens and Lee reported the capture of Ft. Cornwallis in their letter to NG of 5 June, below.

3. On the capture of Pensacola, Fla., by the Spanish, see note at Washington to NG, 1 June, above. As seen there, the Spanish did not attack St. Augustine.

4. NG gave Rawdon's whereabouts in a letter to Pickens of 3 June, above.

5. In his letter to NG of 1 June, Lee had also mentioned the need for civil government in Georgia.

¶ [FROM JOHN MATHEWS, CHAIRMAN OF A STANDING COMMITTEE OF CONGRESS TO CORRESPOND WITH THE COMMANDER OF THE SOUTHERN DEPARTMENT, Philadelphia, 4 June 1781. Encloses papers containing recently received foreign intelligence; they also show the response of Congress "in consequence thereof."[1] Hopes that NG will take "measures accordingly." Details some "undoubted intelligence" about French operations in the West Indies.[2] Supposes that Washington has informed NG of "his plan of operations."[3] Adds in a postscript that the enclosures are for NG's "private information, & must not on any account be communicated to any other person." Wants to know if his letter arrives safely.[4] ALS (MiU-C) 2 pp.]

1. Among the papers that Mathews sent was a copy of Samuel Huntington's circular letter of 1 June. (A copy of Huntington's letter, bearing NG's endorsement, "From Mr. Mathew, June 4th. 1781," is at DLC.) At the end of Huntington's circular, William Sharpe, another member of the committee, had written: "The foregoing is a copy of a circular letter sent to the executives of the respective states. It may be proper to note that change of circumstances in Europe has altered the plan of sending us the second division as was at first proposed, but the squadron at Rhode Island is to be reinforced so as to be able to put to sea with confidence." (Continental Congress Miscellany, DLC)

2. For more on French operations in the West Indies, see Huntington to NG, 3 June, above.

3. See Washington to NG, 1 June, above.

4. NG replied on 18 July, below.

¶ [FROM GENERAL ANDREW PICKENS, "Camp before Augusta," Ga., 4 June 1781. Has NG's letter of "yesterday." Since Pickens last wrote, "the Militia have exerted themselves better than before." A "Battery for a Six pounder" has been "raised So high at about a Hundred and fifty yards distance" that the piece can "fire over and into" the enemy's post.[1] Pickens expects "to Night" to have two redoubts for riflemen "finished within fifty yards of their Ditch." Hopes the enemy's "fate is not far distant," as "a few days Just now is of great Service to the farmer."[2] Many enemy deserters and "a Number of half Starved Negroes" have "come out." About 150 enemy regulars and militia have collected near "the Two Sisters"; a party of them crossed the [Savannah] River "and killed two Men in Carolina."[3] Pickens will take "all possible care" of the stores; a number of wagons will be needed to transport them.[4] Refers NG to the letters of Col. [Henry] Lee, who "promised" to send NG "the News from the Southward."[5] ALS (ScU) 1 p.]

1. On the Maham tower that the siege force had erected at Augusta, see note at Pickens and Lee to NG, 5 June, below.

2. Pickens had written NG on 1 June, above, that many of his militiamen needed to be on their farms at this time of year. He and Lee reported the capture of Augusta in their letter to NG of 5 June.

3. "Two Sisters" was a bluff on the Savannah River near Ebenezer. The party was presumably the same enemy force that Pickens had mentioned in his letter of 2 June, above.

4. On the stores, see NG to Pickens, 3 June, above.

5. Henry Lee's letter of this date, above, contained "News from the Southward."

¶ [FROM COLONEL THOMAS POLK, Charlotte, N.C., 4 June 1781. Has learned that Continental money no longer circulates in Pennsylvania or Maryland; the "Officers here" also refuse to "receive their Wages in such Money." A draft for Continental bills can therefore be "of no service" to Polk, unless he can use it to liquidate the $100,000 he owes for provisions. He wishes to do so "before the Money becomes disreputable in this Country," using $200,000 that was left in his care.[1] Adds: "If the Money cannot be spared from the Army, I acquiesce, as the People at home may better dispense with it than the Officers & Soldiers."[2] Expects intelligence from the northward "every day."[3] ALS (MiU-C) 1 p.]

1. For more on the depreciation of currency, see Pettit to NG, 27 May, above. Polk had requested a draft to help pay his public debts. (See Polk to NG, 14 January, above [vol. 7: 122].)

2. On Polk's use of his "own Stock," see his letter to NG of 14 January. NG replied on 11 June, below.

3. Polk had sent men to obtain intelligence about Lord Cornwallis's movements. (See Polk to NG, 27 May, above.)

¶ [FROM DOCTOR WILLIAM READ, Charlotte, N.C., 4 June 1781. Encloses a return of the hospital for May [not found]. Is pleased to report that "Col^l Ford after loosing his Arm is doing well, & Capt Bruff who has a long time layed in a dengerous situation is better."[1] The hospital is "doing well," and Read hopes soon to return to duty "a number" of the wounded. Congratulates NG on his "success." ALS (NjP) 1 p.]

1. Benjamin Ford and James Bruff had been wounded during the battle of Hobkirk's Hill. (See NG's Orders, 26 April, and NG to Rawdon, 29 April, both above.)

¶ [FROM ABEL THOMAS AND THOMAS WINSLOW,[1] Long Cane, S.C., 4 June 1781. Thomas, who is "Contending for a [religious] Reformation amongst my Bretheren" and has "nothing to Do with Carnel weapons," requests a "premit" to "Pass among Thy men" with his "Companion." He understands that NG is "a moderate and Considerate man willing to Shew kindness to the inosant." Thomas would gladly plead his "own Cause" before NG because "the great god of heaven and Earth Commanded mee to Leav my dear wife and Children in Pensylvania and to Travel thro maney trobles and Dangers in this South Part of Amaraca in order to Preach the Everlasting Gospel to the Poor." Earlier, he had been "about to Pass through thy Camp in a few Days after thy Seege at [Cambdin?] to a meeting not far from there" when he was turned back by the captain of NG's guard without being able to see NG. Thomas started toward home, but felt "uneasey" and turned around and returned. Tells NG: "I feel Love in my hart To thee and to all men kind." DS (NcD) 1 p.]

1. It is apparent from the contents and from NG's reply of 7 June, below, that Thomas was a Quaker preacher and the author of this letter; Winslow, his "Companion," also signed this letter.

¶ [FROM GENERAL ANTHONY WAYNE, Goose Creek, Cox's Mills, Va., 4 June 1781. He seizes "with avidity" this chance to write NG; "where it may find" NG, he does not know. His detachment is "this far advanced" en route to join NG's army, but "the Intervention of Lord Cornwallis who is said to be in the Vicinity of Fredricksburg will prevent our further progress for some time."[1] Wayne will join the Marquis de Lafayette within "three day's."[2] Wayne brings Lafayette "about 1000 Combatants & Six field pieces." He estimates the enemy's force in Virginia at "Six to eight thousand."[3] Adds: "A second Division of our Line is preparing to Advance."[4] Asks NG to "tell [Henry] Lee, & his boy's I hope soon to take them by the hand." In a postscript, adds that he has "divested the troops of all heavy baggage" and is advancing "with Velocity." ALS (NNPM) 2 pp.]

1. As seen at Washington to NG, 1 June, above, Wayne's Pennsylvania Continental troops had begun their march to Virginia on 26 May. On Cornwallis's move toward Fredericksburg, see Lafayette to NG, first letter of 3 June, above. Wayne's force remained in Virginia until after Cornwallis's surrender at Yorktown in October 1781.

2. As noted at Lafayette to NG, first letter of 3 June, the junction took place on 10 June.

3. On the recently arrived detachment, see note at St. Clair to NG, 6 May, above.

4. As noted at NG to St. Clair, 22 June, below, the second division of the Pennsylvania line did not march for some time.

* * *

To the Inhabitants Upon the Saluda

Camp before Ninty Six [S.C.] June 5th 1781

Mr [John] Lark having represented that a party of Men said to belong to Col Hammons [Le Roy Hammond's] Regiment are murdering and plundering the Inhabitants not in arms in a most barbarous and cruel Manner.[1] It is impossible for me to express my abhorence and detestation of such a practice, and they may be assurd that no endeavour of mine shall be wanting to restrain and check such violences. Those that have been in the British interest and by their past conduct have renderd themselves obnoxious to their Country have now an opportunity in part to atone for their past conduct by joining the American Army and manifesting by their future conduct a sinsere repentence for what is past as well as a desire to promote the true happiness of their Country in future. If any have become obnoxious to the laws, to them they must be answerable. In the mean time it shall be my study upon their behaving properly to afford them all the security in my power from the improper resentments and depradations of individuals or plundring parties. Given at Camp before Ninty Six June 5th 1781   N GREENE

DfS (NcD).

1. For more on the alleged atrocities, see NG to Pickens, immediately below. The Saluda River area is said to have been "the center of loyalism" in the South Carolina backcountry. (Lambert, *South Carolina Loyalists*, p. 110)

To General Andrew Pickens

Dear Sir   Camp before Ninty Six [S.C.] June 5th 1781

The bearer of this[,] Mr John Lark comes at the request of the Inhabitants near Perkins Ford on the Saluda to represent the great distress they are in from the savage conduct of a party of Men belonging to Col

[Le Roy] Hammonds Regiment. The party plunders without mercy and murders the defenceless people just on private peak [i.e., pique?] prejudice or personal resentments shall dictate. Such enormities will soon make the Inhabitants think they are in a more wretched situation than they have been heretofore. Principles of humanity as well as good policy require that proper Measures should be immediately taken to restrain these abuses, heal the differen[c]es, and unite the people as much as possible. To this end all parties ought to be strichtly prohibited under the penalty of capital punnishment from plundering and that no violence should be offerd to any of the Inhabitants let their political sentiments be as they may unless they are found in Arms. If charactors unfriendly to our cause have committed any thing which renders them obnoxious to the laws of the land, let Civil Government hereafter inflict such punnishments as they may think proper. The Idea of exterminating the Tories is not less barbarous than impolitick; and if persisted in, will keep this Country in the greatest confusion and distress. The eyes of the people are much upon you, the disaffected cry for Mercy, and I hope you will exert your self to bring over the Tories to our interest, and check the growing enormities which prevail among the Whigs in punnishing and plund[er]ing as private averice or a bloody disposition stimulates them. I am sensible the most worthless part of the Whigs will think themselves injurd in being restrained; but I am perswaded in doing it you will do honor to the cause of humanity and promote essentially the interest of your Country.[1] I am my dear General Your Most Obed[t] humble S[r]   N GREENE

ADfS (NcD).
1. See also NG's letter to the Inhabitants on the Saluda, immediately above.

To Colonel William Polk

Dear Sir   Camp before Ninety Six [S.C.] June 5th 1781
    Yours of the 30th of May by Capt [John] Linton I have had the pleasure to recieve. I am fully perswaded of the advantage of what you propose; but am afraid of the propriety. Should I give permission for you to engage the Militia in the Southern Service it would disgust the State of Virginia and serve as a pretence not to send any more however pressing the emergency; for the States are more tenacious of having it known that they have men in service, than careful to have them employed to the best advantage. To draw support from the Northward to the Southward is attended with great difficulty under every favorable circumstance; and if by an improper measure owing to the prejudice and tenacity of the States, I should increase this difficulty, I should injure these States and doubtless incur their blame, tho done with the

best intentions and from a desire to serve them in particular. From these considerations I have thought it unadvisable to give the order you request, tho I wish Major Rose would leave the Men to engage if they thought proper.[1] With esteem & regard I am dear Sir Your Most Obed[t] humble Sr   N GREENE

ADfS (MiU-C).
    1. Maj. Alexander Rose commanded a detachment of militia from Bedford County, Va. (*Virginia Magazine of History and Biography* 33 [April 1925]: 214)

*   *   *

¶ [FROM GENERAL FRANCIS MARION, Georgetown, S.C., 5 June 1781. Since capturing Georgetown, he has been busy "Levelling the works & sending the salt in a secure place for the use of the Army."[1] The enemy garrison has retreated only as far as "the bar"; Marion fears they will return and destroy all the provisions in the area should he leave.[2] As the Georgetown area is "the only place" where a "Quantity of subsistance" may be obtained for NG's army, Marion has delayed returning "South of Santee" River. Encloses a letter from Maj. [Hezekiah] Maham giving the situation of the enemy and reporting that they are planning to destroy "every kind of provissions."[3] Maham is too weak to stop them, and Marion cannot provide assistance "Effectually," as "all the militia Expected is not come in." If NG could send him "a few regular horse," Marion could "prevent Great Destructions." Plans to leave a small force in Georgetown and march "tomorrow" to join Maham "over Santee."[4] ALS (MiU-C) 1 p.]
    1. On the capture of the British post at Georgetown, see Marion to NG, 29 May, above.
    2. "The bar" was at the mouth of Winyah Bay, a few miles south of Georgetown. (George C. Rogers, Jr., *The History of Georgetown County, South Carolina* [Columbia: University of South Carolina Press, 1970], p. 143)
    3. Maham's letter was dated 3 June. (MiU-C) Maham had sent NG a similar letter, reporting intelligence, on 1 June, above.
    4. Marion wrote NG from Georgetown on 6 June, below, with additional intelligence, which superseded that given here. NG replied to that letter in his second to Marion of 10 June, below.

¶ [FROM GENERAL ANDREW PICKENS AND COLONEL HENRY LEE, JR., "Camp in Augusta," Ga., 5 June 1781. Their dispatches of "last month" discussed events leading up to their siege of Ft. Cornwallis.[1] "From that period the most vigorous exertions have been used attended with incessant labor to advance our approaches with rapidity." They completed nearly "A perfect circumvallation" of the fort, with "three issues from it communicating with the Enemys fosse." They continue:

> Several batteries were erected, one near 30 feet high, which gave
> us entire command of their Works; and two Rifle Citadels we
> formed within 30 yards of their parapet. In this situation it was
> our determination to have forced a lodgment in the different Cur-
> tains, from which establishment we might with readiness and cer-
> tainty of success have referred the issue of the contest to the
> Bayonet. The judicious, vigilant and gallant conduct of the Gar-

rison deprived us of many advantages which we wished to have seized in the course of our operations, and which would have tended to have shortened the Seige. At 9 oClock in the morning proposals were received from Col° Brown which we have the honor to transmit with the capitulation which took place.[2]

They enclose all "official communications" and returns of stores, artillery, and prisoners taken.[3] They commend the legion cavalry and name a number of officers who distinguished themselves during the siege, including militia colonels "[Elijah] Clarke, Harding [William Harden] and [Samuel] Hammond." They add: "Our loss has not been very considerable, and by no means proportionate to the warmth of the contest."[4] They regret the death of "the amiable and gallant" Maj. [Pinketham] Eaton, who, they suspect, "fell a sacrifice after surrender." A "very pointed correspondence" took place between Lee and Brown on this subject, and "a further enquiry will now commence, and atonement shall be made for the impious deed."[5] Dr. Matthew Irvine, the bearer, rendered "great utility" during this "important operation," in which "the capital of Georgia with a large extent of territory is recovered." Cy (PCC, item 155, vol. 2: 133, DNA) 4 pp.]

1. See Lee to NG, 24 May, and Pickens to NG, first letter of 25 May, both above.

2. As Pickens and Lee indicated, their men dug trenches around the post during the first days of the siege. They then dug toward the fort, so that by the time of its surrender, according to the recollections of a militia captain, it was possible to stand in the trenches and reach into the enemy's works with a hoe handle. (Brown, "Memoirs," p. 33) While the approaches were being dug, the garrison sallied nightly. To protect the trenches, Lee was forced to post troops in them at night. The besiegers also constructed a "Maham tower," which Pickens and Lee referred to here as one of their "batteries." (For more on Maham towers, see note at Marion to NG, first letter of 23 April, above.) They placed a six-pound artillery piece on the tower, which soon disabled the artillery that Brown had available. With the six-pounder commanding most of the interior of the fort, Brown turned to subterfuge in an effort to save his post. He sent a trusted sergeant, posing as a deserter, into the American camp to try to burn down the tower. He also had explosives placed under two houses that he expected to be used to cover the final American assault on Ft. Cornwallis. Both attempts were foiled. Lee, suspecting the sergeant, placed him under guard, while the garrison prematurely detonated the charges under the houses. On 4 June, with an assault by the Americans imminent, Brown sent word that he was willing to discuss surrender terms. He delayed long enough to avoid surrendering on King George III's birthday but agreed to terms early on 5 June. (See Lee, *Memoirs*, 2: 99–115, and Cashin, *King's Ranger*, pp. 133–36; for the surrender terms, see PCC, item 155, vol. 2: 127, DNA.)

3. A return of prisoners and copies of eleven letters that passed between Pickens, Lee, and Brown are in PCC, item 155, vol. 2: 131, 139–46, DNA. No return of the captured stores or artillery has been found.

4. American losses in the siege have been estimated at forty men; enemy casualties were fifty-two killed and 334 captured. (Boatner, *Encyc.*, p. 51)

5. Eaton was killed during the capture of Ft. Grierson, the sister post to Ft. Cornwallis. (See note at Pickens to NG, first letter of 25 May, above.) It was said in the army that Eaton had been "taken prisoner and surrendered up his sword, and afterward put to death with his own sword." (John Armstrong to Jethro Sumner, 13 June 1781, *NCSR*, 15: 481) As nothing more was said about Eaton's death, the investigation, if it took place, presumably found that Eaton was not killed after surrendering.

Andrew Pickens, 1739–1817; engraving by James Barton Longacre
after a painting by Thomas Sully
(National Portrait Gallery, Smithsonian Institution)

¶ [**FROM CAPTAIN JOHN PRYOR**, Buckingham Court House, Va., 5 June 1781. Asks NG to "pardon" his sending a report of the situation in Virginia and the "late operations of the Enemy," but he knows that there has been no communication from the Marquis [de Lafayette] and that the Baron [Steuben] has "scarce time to write." First reports that Capt. [Nathaniel] Irish is "in arrest" while an investigation is conducted prior to a court martial.[1] "The Enemy have from their Superiour vigilence got so much the advantage of us in Cavalry or mounted Infantry that we are not able to set bounds to their progress to any & every quarter of this Country." Details the route of the enemy's two columns since they crossed the James River and the caches of stores they have destroyed. Reports that Lafayette retreated to protect Fredericksburg and form a junction with Gen. [Anthony] Wayne; by last word, Lafayette was "as high as" Orange Court House, with "the Enemies Right Column keeping him in Awe."[2] The left column of the enemy is in a position to threaten Point of Fork, but as Gen. [Robert] Lawson, with 300 militia, has joined Steuben and the 500 new levies there, Pryor believes "the Enemy will not penetrate higher up."[3] Adds that he believes there is no "Object" for attack but Staunton, where some quartermaster stores were sent. Despite this, Pryor has directed Mr. [John] Martin, who has taken over from Irish, to "secreat" the stores from the laboratory "in sundry places as private as possible 'till he hears farther the movements of this party of the Enemy." Pryor is now obtaining wagons to remove the military stores that were "got across the [Fluvanna] River yesterday" and now are "much exposed." Before he left Point of Fork, many of the stores from there had been moved across the river, where they "lay cover'd wth Tents." The enemy's movement has been so rapid that Pryor is sure "many of the Members of the Assembly are taken at Charlottesville where the Assembly were sitting," although he has also heard that they had "previously adjourn'd" to another site.[4] Has word that 2,000 men, "a late reinforcement [to the enemy], have gone up" the Potomac River.[5] Asks NG to excuse his scrawl. Sends his compliments to Col. Edward Carrington and NG's aides. ALS (MiU-C) 3 pp.]

1. For more on the circumstances leading to Irish's arrest, see Pryor to NG, 30 May, above.

2. Lafayette had reported his situation in his first letter to NG of 3 June, above.

3. Col. John Graves Simcoe, with a small British detachment, was able to trick Steuben, whose command numbered 420 Continental levies and 250 militia, into evacuating his position at Point of Fork and abandoning valuable supplies there. (Selby, *Revolution in Virginia*, pp. 279–80)

4. Although they received a warning shortly before Col. Banastre Tarleton's troops arrived in Charlottesville, seven members of the Assembly were reportedly captured. (Tarleton, *Campaigns*, p. 297) The others narrowly escaped, as did Gov. Thomas Jefferson. (Selby, *Revolution in Virginia*, pp. 281–82)

5. As seen at St. Clair to NG, 6 May, above, the reinforcement had not "gone up" the Potomac River.

¶ [GENERAL GREENE'S ORDERS, Camp before Ninety Six, S.C., 6 June 1781. Regimental commanders are to "make a Minute Inspection" of ammunition supplies, "return what is bad," and make sure each man has thirty rounds. Individuals not on duty or "having particular business" should be kept "from entering into the Trenches, or crowding the Batteries; as great confusion may arise from the gratification of an idle Curiosity." In After Orders of 4 P.M., NG announces the capture of the post at Augusta, Ga., and its garrison, including the commander, Col. Thomas Brown, seven other British officers, seven militia officers, 162 British soldiers, 130 militia, and "about two hundred Negro's."[1] The success of the American troops at Augusta "must Serve as a stimulus to their fellow soldiers now employed in the Blockade of Ninety Six." Lamar Orderly Book (OClWHi) 2 pp.]

1. On the capture of Ft. Cornwallis at Augusta, see Pickens and Lee to NG, 5 June, above.

¶ [CAPTAIN WILLIAM PIERCE, JR., TO GENERAL THOMAS SUMTER. From before Ninety Six, S.C., 6 June 1781. NG wants Sumter to forward the enclosed letter to Col. [Nisbet] Balfour in Charleston.[1] Ninety Six has not yet been captured, "nor is it easy" to know when it will be. The town is "closely invested" on all sides. "This Night we shall be within their Abattis and perhaps by To-morrow Noon we shall be operating in their Ditch." Augusta is also still under siege, its commander seemingly "determined to risque the fortune of an escalade."[2] Adds: "Matters are wrought up to a crisis, and must soon be determined." There is "every reason to beleive" that a French fleet is on "our Coast," or soon will be, and assurances have been offered that this will "give us a decided superiority at Sea."[3] The news from Virginia "is of the negative kind: neither good or bad." Gen. [William] Phillips is dead, and [Gen. Benedict] Arnold now commands the British army there. Reports have also been received, which "bear marks of authenticity," of the fall of the British post at Pensacola, Fla., the capture of the outworks at St. Augustine, and a naval defeat that the British have suffered in the West Indies.[4] "All this is important, and must give pleasure to a Man who loves his Country as much as you do." ALS (Sumter Papers: DLC) 3 pp.]

1. NG's letter to Balfour, dated 4 June, is above.

2. As seen in the After Orders of this date, above, news arrived in camp later on 6 June that the post at Augusta had surrendered.

3. On the origin of this expectation, see La Luzerne to NG, 3 April, above.

4. The reports were in Lee to NG, 4 June, above. (See also note at Washington to NG, 1 June, above; on the naval engagement in the West Indies, see note at Huntington to NG, 3 June, above.)

¶ [FROM GENERAL ISAAC HUGER, "Mount Necessity," S.C., 6 June 1781.[1] Encloses two letters from Maj. [Hezekiah] Maham concerning the "motions of the Enemy below."[2] Huger has delayed his departure for camp to learn more about the enemy's movements and "to endeavour to find out their plan." He will set out in the next day or two if his "badly foundered" horse can travel. LS (MiU-C) 1 p.]

1. Mount Necessity was Huger's plantation in the Congarees area.

2. Huger enclosed letters that Maham had written him on 4 and 5 June. (Maham sent letters, identical in content, to Marion, who forwarded them to NG. [See Marion to NG, 5 and 6 June, below.]) Huger also enclosed an undated letter from Charles Myddelton and a report from two British deserters, giving the troop strength of Lord Rawdon's army as 1,340 infantry and 100 cavalry. According to the deserters, an express had arrived in Rawdon's camp on 30 May, "pressing" for a march to relieve Ninety Six because the garrison there "had but ten days provisions left." (All the enclosures are at MiU-C.) Both Maham and Myddelton reported—and the deserters confirmed—that Col. John Watson was then in command of Rawdon's army; Rawdon, according to Maham, was in Charleston, "Very Sick."

¶ [FROM GENERAL FRANCIS MARION, Georgetown, S.C., 6 June 1781. Repeats the substance of his letter to NG of "Yesterday," which was sent by express. Has sent parties into "every part of the country to Collect horses for the Dragoons"; the horses that he has obtained have been delivered to Capt.

[James] Conyers.[1] Encloses "the first Intelligence" he has received of the enemy being reinforced.[2] Has not heard from NG for a long time and assumes that a letter "miscarryd."[3] Adds that he is enclosing a letter from Maj. [Hezekiah] Maham.[4] ALS (MiU-C) 1 p.]

1. In a strongly worded request of 4 May, above, NG had asked Marion to obtain horses for the Continental dragoons.
2. The enclosure has not been found.
3. NG had written Marion on 26 May, above; it is not known if that letter "miscarryd."
4. On the letter from Maham, see note at Huger to NG, immediately above.

*   *   *

To Colonel Elijah Clarke

Dear Sir   Camp before Ninty Six [S.C.] June 7th 1781

The high reputation you have very deservedly acquird by your bravery since the enemy penetrated this Country induces me to address my self to you to use your influence to restrain two very capital evils which rage in this Country and which if not prevented must soon depopulate it. I mean private murders and plundering, they both originate from such a base principle, and are so unworthy the soldier of honor or merit that I can have no charity for those who are guilty of either; and as I am informed both those practices prevail with parties living over the mountains who are carrying away Negroes and commiting other enormities which want checking. Let me entreat you to exert your self as much as possible to stop the progress of this business, and which if not put an end to very soon, I shall be obliged to exercise great severity and inflict capital punnishment on such offenders which I will most assuredly do if they do not desist.[1]

The Georgia cloathing is here, and I wish you to send an escort to receive it as the Waggons are on expence and desirous of returning.[2] I am Sir Your Most Obed[t] humble Ser   N GREENE

ALS (NcD).
1. On the "private murders and plundering," see NG's letters to the Inhabitants upon the Saluda and to Andrew Pickens, both 5 June, above.
2. On the clothing, see NG to Heard, 23 May, above.

To General Andrew Pickens

Dear Sir   Camp [before Ninety Six, S.C.] June the 7th 1781

I am favord with your and Lt Colonels report of the reduction of Fort Cornwallis.[1] I am at a loss which to admire most the bravery of the Garrison or the perseverence of the beseigers. I beg leave to congratulate you upon the occasion and to return you and the brave Militia under your command my sinsere thanks for your exertions upon the occasion.

This post is not yet reduced but must fall in a few days. The Confusion and [dis]order which prevails in Georgia by private murders and plundering parties induces me to wish that you would stay a few days to regulate matters in some way which will restrain those growing evils that will soon if let alone become a National curse.[2]

I have granted permission to Col Brown to retire to Savannah with the regulars belonging to his garrison[,] he being accountable for the number deliverd him.[3] If you think the Militia will be best accounted for in this way as it is difficult to guard them and accompanied with a constant expence you are at full liberty to grant the same indulgence to them, to be receipted and accounted for, and not to appear in Arms until legally exchanged. You will act in this matter as your own prudence may dictate to be necessary.[4] The Stores taken[,] particularly the Rum[,] Salt and Ammunition should be as carefully preservd as possible. I rely upon you entirely in this matter. With the highest respect I am dear Sir Your Most Obed[t] humble Ser   N GREENE
Lt Colonel Lee has just arrivd in Camp and pays you the highest compliments for your extraordinary exertions which serves but to confirm me in what I was before convinced of that no man acts from better motives and few Men have it so much in their power to promote the interest and happiness of this Country as you.

ACyS (NcD)
    1. See Pickens and Henry Lee to NG, 5 June, above.
    2. According to his biographer, "Pickens remained at Augusta until the removal of the prisoners, the disposal of the captured supplies, and the organization of the post under the Patriots." (Waring, *Fighting Elder*, pp. 78–79) NG sent orders to Pickens on 14 June, below, to join the siege of Ninety Six. For more on the "private murders and plundering parties," see NG to Clarke, immediately above, and NG's letters to Pickens and the Inhabitants upon the Saluda, both 5 June, above. Pickens reported the murder of one captured enemy officer and the wounding of another at Augusta in his letter to NG of this date, below.
    3. According to the articles of capitulation, Col. Thomas Brown and his officers were to be paroled and the soldiers were to be "conducted to such place as the commander in chief [NG] shall direct." (Lee, *Memoirs*, 2: 114n) In his letter of this date, below, Pickens said that feelings against the captured troops were running so high that he wanted to send them to Charleston by way of Ninety Six; otherwise, "were they to go for Savannah they would be besett on the road."
    4. In the letter immediately below, Maj. Ichabod Burnet, NG's aide, sent Pickens further orders regarding the prisoners.

*   *   *

¶ [MAJOR ICHABOD BURNET TO GENERAL ANDREW PICKENS. From [Camp before Ninety Six, S.C.], 7 June 1781. If "the Indians and Tories" are to go with Col. [Thomas] Brown, Brown must provide a proper receipt for each one and promise that an equal number of American militiamen will be exchanged for them.[1] The Loyalist commissioned officers must give their paroles separately and go to Savannah with the captured British officers.[2] After the receipts have been taken, "It would be advantageous if desertion should prevail among" the prisoners. Pickens should send to headquarters all unclaimed Negroes who are fit for the "Pioneer or waggon service." DfS (NcD) 3 pp.]

1. Pickens's reply has not been found. For more on the disposal of the prisoners taken at Augusta, see NG to Pickens, immediately above, and Pickens to NG, this date, below.

2. As seen in NG's Orders of 6 June, above, seven Loyalist militia officers had been captured at Augusta.

*   *   *

To Abel Thomas and Thomas Winslow

Gentlemen   Camp before Ninety Six June 7th 1781

Your letter of the 6th is before me.[1] From the good opinion I have of the people of your profession[,] being bread and educated among them, I am perswaded your visit is purely religious and in this perswasson have granted you a pass, and I shall be happy if your Ministry shall contribute to the establishment of morallity and brotherly kindness among the people, than which no Country ever wanted it more.[2]

I am sensible your principles and professions are opposed to war, but I know you are fond of both political and religeous liberty. This is what we are contending for, and by the blessing of god we hope to establish them upon such a broad basis as to put it out of the power of our enemies to shake its foundation. In this laudable endeaver I expect at least to have the good wishes of your people, as well for their own sakes as for ours who wishes to serve them upon all occasions not inconsistent with the public welfare. I am Gentlemen your most obed humble S^r   N GREENE

ACyS (NcD)

1. See Thomas and Winslow to NG, 4 June, above.
2. NG had been "bread and educated" a Quaker.

*   *   *

¶ [FROM GENERAL HENRY KNOX, New Windsor, N.Y., 7 June 1781. Gov. [John] Rutledge affords Knox a "safe" communication that he cannot "decline."[1] Knox has written NG "several notes" but could not offer the "consolation" of "numerous battalions to reinforce your thin legions." Regardless of its effectiveness, the defense of the southern states by NG's "weak force" has established NG's "reputation on the most durable basis." Knox continues:

The Southern States, Congress, & all America, fully believe that had your force been adequate to the service that you would have expelled your titled enemy and all others from the southern States, or at least to have them confin'd in Charlestown.

Your manoevres must have been small under a pressure of difficulties. We have often given you our Sympathy, the only consolation of the poor. Our mutual friend [Gen. Alexander] McDougall, has often exclaim'd, just starting from a *speculating* reverie, "By the laird Knox I pity our friend Greene. He must have had a choice of difficulties. Poor fellow!" You will observe by these circumstan[ces] that we believe your laurel grows [on] a thorny bush indeed!

It will "be better" for NG "when we get a superior force." Rutledge will explain the American plan to relieve NG "by pressing upon" the few troops the enemy "have left in this quarter."[2] If that fails, NG can expect them "all" to join him "in the fall." Asks for a "line" to assure Knox that he still has NG's "love."[3] ALS (MiU-C) 4 pp.]

1. On Rutledge's visit to Washington's headquarters, see his letter to NG of 29 May, above.

2. Knox referred to Washington's plan to attack the British at New York City. (See Washington to NG, 1 June, above.)

3. NG wrote Knox on 7 August, below, but said nothing about Knox's letter or his "love" for Knox.

¶ [FROM GENERAL ANDREW PICKENS**, Augusta, Ga., 7 June 1781. Reports "a very disagreeable and Melancholly affair which happened yesterday in the afternoon": the killing of Col. [James] Grierson by a man who "rode up to the door of a room here where Col° Grierson was confined, and without dismounting Shot him So that he Expired Soon after." The killer "instantly rode off" and escaped, although he was pursued. Pickens has given orders to bury Grierson "with Military honors."[1] Another captured officer, Maj. [Henry] Williams, who was in the same room as Grierson, "immediatly run into a Cellar among the other Prisoners but Standing in view Soon After was Shot at and badly Wounded in the Shoulder."[2] Col. [Thomas] Brown "was also insulted yesterday" by a man whom Pickens "confined." The "people are So much exasperated against Some" of the enemy prisoners that Pickens has sent the prisoners across the Savannah River under the "care of" American troops. He is "fully perswaded were they to go for Savannah they would be besett on the road, but think they may go to Charlestown by way of Ninety Six."[3] To carry the prisoners' baggage and provisions, Pickens has detained four wagons sent by Col. [Edward] Carrington. Asks to have meal sent to meet them on the march. ALS (MH) 2 pp.]

1. Grierson, the commander of Ft. Grierson, at Augusta, had been taken prisoner when it was captured. (See Pickens to NG, first letter of 25 May, above.) He had not received the same treatment as Col. Thomas Brown, who was put into protective custody immediately after the surrender of Ft. Cornwallis on 5 June. (Lee, *Memoirs*, 2: 116–17) According to historian Edward McCrady, "it was assumed [Brown] would be in danger" because of his "notorious character and the barbarities committed by him." (McCrady, *S.C. in the Revolution*, p. 273; among the accusations against Brown was that he had turned over some of his prisoners to Indians for final torture. [Ibid., pp. 260–62]) The American commanders, according to McCrady, "were not aware that [Grierson] too, was scarcely less odious to the Georgians than Browne himself." (Ibid., p. 274) Grierson was said to have told a visitor on the day he was killed "that his life was in danger." (Cashin, *King's Ranger*, p. 137)

In the aftermath of Grierson's murder, NG sent Joseph Clay to Augusta as his personal representative and offered a substantial reward for the capture of the killer. (See NG to Clay and NG's Proclamation, both 9 June, below.) According to one contemporary, the man's identity and motive were known, but no arrest was ever made. (Brown, "Memoirs," p. 32)

2. After the attack, Williams was sent to Savannah, where he recovered from his wound. As in the case of Grierson, the identity of the attacker was known, but he never was arrested. (Cashin, *King's Ranger*, p. 137)

3. On the feelings against Brown, see note 1, above. It was these same prisoners from Augusta whom Col. Henry Lee later marched so near to the post at Ninety Six that the garrison there took it as an "insult" and Col. John Harris Cruger reportedly ordered his batteries to fire, "notwithstanding it enveloped his fellow soldiers." (Lee, *Memoirs*, 2: 118–19; see also Mackenzie, *Strictures*, p. 153.) The prisoners eventually reached Savannah. (William Bull to Lord George Germain, 28 June, Davies, *Documents*, 20: 165) Brown himself was sent there directly, under guard. (Lee, *Memoirs*, 2: 117; Brown, "Memoirs," p. 33)

¶ **[FROM GENERAL THOMAS SUMTER**, Ancrum's, S.C., 7 June 1781. Has NG's letter of 28 May, in which NG mentions having ordered three regiments of Sumter's brigade to join the Southern Army at Ninety Six. Sumter has also learned that a fourth regiment in his brigade is ordered there. NG's summoning of these units has prevented Sumter from making "the Necessary arangements & enquery in to the State of these Regem^{ts}, & the Temper & Designs of the people, & has also Curtaild my force Considerably, but as you have a Call for them, I am Glad they Was in the way of being Servicable."[1] Reports that "the men are Turning out Very well," even though the harvest is at hand. To avoid losing the produce, Sumter has "left perticuler Persons at home Who, is to assist their Neighbours." Col. Richard Hampton has taken his force of "Disafected Orangeburgers" on "an extencive Tour to the Southward." They surprised two enemy parties, killed the commander of one, and captured prisoners, "a Number of Negroes," and horses. "Upon the Whole it may be Said his party has behaived well."[2] Reports on Gen. [Francis] Marion's move against Georgetown and the evacuation of that post by the British. Marion took this step despite Sumter's request that he "Cover the Country & prevent the Enemy from Raveging it."[3] Gives intelligence of enemy activities in the area of Monck's Corner, which appear designed "to Lay waist the Country behind them. They are Collecting all the Stock of every Kind, Distroying the Crops in the field as well as those in the houses." One enemy officer is reportedly under orders "to Burn all the Houses as high as the uper end of St Johns Parrish." There are also parties at Twenty Three Mile House, Wassamassaw, and Dorchester, but Sumter does not expect them "to Move far up the Country." Sumter has ordered several regiments down to "Coopperate with Maj^r [Hezekiah] Maham."[4] Maj. [William Clay] Snipes was surprised a few days ago by an enemy party from Dorchester; only Snipes and "three out of Twenty escaped. It is Said, the Rest was all put to the Sword."[5] Sumter has no dependable news from Virginia. Hopes to hear soon that the siege of Ninety Six has been "happily Terminated." ALS (MiU-C) 4 pp.]

1. In his letter to Sumter of 26 May, above, NG said he had ordered one militia regiment to Ninety Six; the subject was not mentioned again in NG to Sumter, 28 May, above. NG wrote Sumter in his first letter of 10 June, below: "We have but a small part of the Militia Regiments you mention with us."

2. Sumter had also reported on Hampton's activities in his letter to NG of 22 May, above. It is not clear whether the two reports pertained to the same "Tour."

3. See Marion to NG, 29 May, above.

4. On Maham's whereabouts and mission, see note at Maham to NG, 1 June, above.

5. On Snipes, see also the note at Isaac Huger to Francis Marion, 28 January, above (vol. 7: 208).

¶ [FROM GENERAL THOMAS SUMTER, [Ancrum's Plantation, S.C.], 8 June 1781.[1] Sends a "Packet" of "unfavourable" information from Gen. [Francis] Marion.[2] Sumter will send "Several Detachments" close to enemy lines to "bring off all the Stock" if the enemy advance. LS (NNPM) 1 p.]

1. The place was taken from Sumter's letter to William Pierce, NG's aide, immediately below.

2. The "Packet" has not been found. Its contents can be inferred, however, from NG's second letter to Sumter of 10 June, below, and from Marion to NG, 6 June, above.

¶ [GENERAL THOMAS SUMTER TO CAPTAIN WILLIAM PIERCE, JR., "Ancrum's," S.C., 8 June 1781. Sumter has received his letter of 6 June. Will forward the letter addressed to Col. Nisbet Balfour. Although the capture of the posts at Augusta and Ninety Six is "attended with some difficulty," there is "no cause to complain," as "success is likely." The intelligence concerning the Spanish was "very agreeable"; the "strokes" they deliver, Sumter hopes, will "facilitate the peace and happiness of this country." The "conduct" of the enemy seems to corroborate the report that a [French] fleet will soon arrive, for they are "destroying everything the country affords, except what they carry to town." Tr (Draper Manuscripts: WHi) 2 pp.]

¶ [FROM JOHN WILKINSON, Augusta, Ga., 8 June 1781. Two men "deputed by the Board of Justices" will hand this letter to NG and "represent the situation" in Georgia. NG's "attention" will serve the "general good" and will "be for ever respected with gratitude by the State of Georgia."[1] ALS (MiU-C) 1 p.]

1. After consulting with the board's deputies, NG replied to Wilkinson on 13 June, below.

¶ [GENERAL GREENE'S ORDERS, Camp before Ninety Six, S.C., Saturday, 9 June 1781. Commanders of troops not on duty "tomorrow" should apply for "their proportion of Cloathing," which is to be distributed as soon as possible. Careful accounts must be kept of the "issues." Lamar Orderly Book (OClWHi) 1 p.]

*   *   *

To Joseph Clay

Sir   Camp before Ninty Six [S.C.] June 9th 1781

You are desird to repair to Augusta and collect as many of the Militia and Negroes as you can and employ them in demolishing the Works upon the Savannah River. I also wish you to take such measures as may most effectually stop the progress of private murders and plundering. It is my wish you should consult with the principal Officers in

Joseph Clay, 1714–1804
(Reproduced from Collections of the Georgia Historical Society, *vol. 8 [1913])*

the Militia service and with them concert a plan for forming the Militia
of the State of Georgia upon the best footing for opposing the enemies
future attempts for getting possession of the interior Country. I need
not recommend dispach[;] you are acquainted with the necessity and
will exert your self accordingly.[1] Given at Camp before Ninty Six June
9th 1781   NATH GREENE

ADfS (NcD).
   1. With these instructions, NG appointed Clay, the army's paymaster, to serve as his
personal representative in Georgia. (See also NG to Clay, 24 July, below.)

                    *   *   *

¶ [TO SAMUEL HUNTINGTON, PRESIDENT OF THE CONTINENTAL CONGRESS. From Camp before Ninety Six, S.C., 9 June 1781. Announces the surrender of Ft. Cornwallis at Augusta, Ga., on 5 June. Encloses Gen. [Andrew] Pickens's and Col. [Henry] Lee's report on the capitulation, adding that the "very great exertions" of their troops, and especially Lee's Legion, "deserve the highest honor."[1] LS (PCC, item 155, vol. 2: 123, DNA) 2 pp.]
    1. See Pickens and Lee to NG, 5 June, above.

*   *   *

To Samuel Huntington,
President of the Continental Congress

Sir   Camp before Ninety Six [S.C.], June 9th 1781.
    I informed your Excellency in my Letter of the 22^d of April, dated near Camden, that one great object in moving southwardly after the Enemys retreat from Deep River was to oblige Lord Cornwallis to return to South Carolina to protect and defend his Posts. But finding that I failed in my expectation, and that his Lordship moved northwardly instead of Southwardly, I wrote to the Marquis to take the command in Virginia with instructions to halt his own Troops and the Pennsylvanians and if possible to prevent a junction of the Enemy's force.[1] I also wrote to Baron Steuben to collect the Virginia and North Carolina Drafts and co-operate with the Marquis either to prevent a junction or oppose their future operations.[2] If the Pennsylvania Line is as strong as I expect, the Virginia Drafts as numerous as I have reason to hope, and the Virginia Militia do their duty, I am in hopes, notwithstanding the Enemy's collective strength the Marquis will be able to keep a good countenance. I hope he will not hazard a general Action as the Enemy have a great superiority in horse, which may improve a defeat into a route [i.e., rout], and disperse the whole Army.
    Being obliged to halt all the Troops coming to this Army leaves us exceeding weak in this quarter. The Virginia Militia who I have been so long expecting have been countermanded all except 3 or 400, and a great part of those are without Arms, by Governor Jefferson.[3] This is a matter that I could wish Congress would come to an explanation with the States upon. If it is the prerogative of a Governor to order the Militia when engaged upon a continental plan I will never calculate upon them in any future plan of operations. Nothing can be more ruinous to the public welfare, and dangerous to the public safety to have orders issue from partial considerations destructive of the general interest.[4]
    We have been prosecuting the Seige at this place with all possible diligence with our little force, but for want of more assistance the approaches have gone on exceeding slow, and our poor Fellows are

worne out with fatigue, being constantly on duty every other Day and sometimes every Day. The Works are strong and extensive. The position difficult to approach and the Ground extremely hard. The Garrison numerous and formidable when compared with our little force. They have sallied more or less every Night; but have been constantly driven in.

After the reduction of Augusta I collected all the force at this place having got intelligence that the Enemy had got a large reinforcement on the 2ᵈ of this month by the arrival of the Cork Fleet. Doubtless the Enemy will attempt to raise the Seige of this place, and as we are altogether unsupported if they attempt it they must succeed.[5]

Inclosed is General Marions report of the evacuation of George Town.[6] The Enemy now have no fortifyed Posts either in South Carolina or Georgia except Charles Town and Savannah and Ninety Six which we are now at. As fast as we have either taken or the Enemy evacuated their Works I have ordered them levelled which I have reason to hope is accomplished. Since we have got footing in this State and Georgia I have been endeavoring by all the means in my power to collect, arm, and arrange the Militia, but it is a work of time and there are almost insurmountable difficulties. The People are much divided, and every thing in a State of suspence. The Tories are numerous and still laying out in large Bodies. General Cunninghams whole Brigade consisting of five or six hundred Men are in this neighbourhood concealed in the Swamps which renders it difficult to get supplies.[7] The aid we are obliged to give to the Commissaries and Quarter Masters departments makes such heavy drafts from the Line that our remaining force is but a shadow. Nothing has been left unattempted, nor time lost, and I hope whatever may be the event of the campaign Congress will do me the justice to beleive I have done every thing in my power.

Major [Edmund M.] Hyrne is gone into Charles Town to negociate the exchange of Prisoners upon the principles of the last Cartel.[8] The resolution of Congress respecting Doctor Oliphant has been transmitted to Colᵒ Balfour.[9] I have the honor to be with great respect, Your Excellency's most obedᵗ hble servant   NATH GREENE

P.S. Will your Excellency be so obliging as to transmit Copies of my three last Letters to his Excellency Gˡ Washington as my Family are too unwell to copy them?[10]

LS (PCC, item 155, vol. 2: 113, DNA).

1. See NG to Lafayette, 14 May, above.

2. See NG to Steuben, 14 May, above. As noted there, the enemy intercepted that letter, and Steuben did not receive the orders it contained until Lafayette sent him a copy.

3. NG wrote Jefferson about the governor's countermanding of the orders on 27 June,

below. NG softened his criticism there by acknowledging the plight that Virginia had been in at the time.

4. This letter to Huntington reached Congress on 17 July and was immediately referred to a committee consisting of Oliver Ellsworth, James Madison, and John Mathews. (JCC, 20: 755) Their report of 24 July was generally approved the next day, including a suggested resolution to inform NG of Congress's "entire approbation" of the measures he had "pursued for the general security of the southern states." Congress also accepted the committee's recommendation that "so much of the letter of Major General Greene as relates to calling out militia be referred to the committee appointed to consider of the additional powers necessary to be given Congress." (Ibid., 21: 784, 789–90) That committee reported on 22 August. In its recommendations for completing an "execution" of the Articles of Confederation, it called for "one universal plan of equipping, training, and governing the Militia." Congress referred that article to the Board of War. (Ibid., pp. 894–95) If the board submitted a report, it has not been found; nor did Congress ever act on any of the committee's other recommendations, except one concerning the payment of taxes. (Burnett, *Continental Congress*, pp. 508–9)

5. On the arrival of reinforcements for Rawdon's army from Cork, Ireland, see note at NG to Lafayette, this date, below.

6. Marion's report is in his letter to NG of 29 May, above.

7. Gen. Robert Cunningham commanded the Loyalist militia in the Ninety Six district. NG's statement was an exaggeration, as some 200 of Cunningham's men were serving in the fort. (John Harris Cruger to Lord Rawdon, 3 June, PRO 30/11/6)

8. See Hyrne (the commissary of prisoners) to NG, 27 May, above. On the cartel, see NG to Huntington, 10 May, above.

9. On the resolution concerning Dr. David Olyphant, see Wood to NG, 2 May, above.

10. By his "Family," NG meant his military family or aides. In his letter to NG of 30 July, below, Washington acknowledged having received three letters of NG's written in May, which were undoubtedly the ones NG referred to here.

*   *   *

¶ [TO CAPTAIN NATHANIEL IRISH. From Camp before Ninety Six, S.C., 9 June 1781. Has Irish's letters of 20 April and 20 May. Because of the "deranged state of the commissary General of Military Stores department," NG had asked Baron Steuben to consult with the Board of War and appoint someone to "superintend the business." Although NG has "been a long time separated from" his papers and does not recollect the "nature" of Irish's appointment, he has always considered it to be as "Capt of the Artificers." NG has no connection with "Mr Prior [Capt. John Pryor]" but believes him to be "a very deserving young gentleman." Nor has NG heard any complaints against Irish. Believes that Pryor's appointment was considered to be distinct from that of Irish, who has "no reason to complain thereof." The matter must be referred to the Board of War, and if an injustice was done, Irish can "obtain redress."[1] NG is "so remote" from Virginia that he cannot give "particular directions" for the laboratory. Adds: "All that I wish is it may be fixed in some safe place where the business may not be subject to repeated interruption; which cannot fail soon to leave us without a proper supply of Military Stores." Thinks Staunton, Va., may be such a place; NG has recommended that the quartermaster set up his "Manufactories" there.[2] ADfS (MiU-C) 2 pp.]

1. As seen in Pryor's letter of 30 May, above, Irish's resentment over Pryor's appointment had led to a fight when the two men met. As a result, Irish was under arrest and

facing a court-martial. As noted at that letter, the Board of War had already appointed a third individual to the post.

2. As seen in Thomas Smith to NG, 7 July, below, Pryor chose New London, Va., as the site to reestablish the laboratory.

*   *   *

To the Marquis de Lafayette

Dear Marquis   Camp before 96 [S C.] June 9th 1781
Since I wrote you from this place which was on the 23ᵈ of May, I have been favord with your letters of the 10th 18 and 24 of May and 3ᵈ of June with the inclosures.[1] I am exceedingly distressed to find it altogether out of my power to give you the support your situation claims and my inclinations lead to. The moment I discoverd that it was Lord Cornwallis intention to form a junction with the troops in Virginia I countermanded the march of the Pensylvania line and the Virginia drafts to the Southward.[2] If the Pennsylvania line had arrivd in time and the Virginia drafts had been as considerable as I was taught to believe and the Militia as numerous as I had reason to hope and expect from the number and union of the Virginians[,] I was in hopes you would have it in your power to have obliged the enemy to move with some caution and pretty much in a body. I do assure you from duty and inclination I am not less anxious to support you than you me, and I hope the steps I have taken will convince you of it. I am sensible the prosecution of the war to the Southward will have its advantages but Virginia is a capital link in the chain of communication and must not be left to sink under the oppression of such formidable attacks as are making upon her. I am charmed with your resolution and conduct in not hazarding an action. I ever had the highest opinion of your judgment and it affords me the greatest satisfaction to see you despise the hissing murmurs of an ignorant rabble who would precipitate you into ruin, to cover a single farm. Submit to partial evils but by all means avoid a capital misfortune. Dont spare any pains to remove all the public Stores out of the enemies way, and with the utmost exertions and every precaution it will be utterly impossible to effect it fully while the enemy have such a superior body of horse.

The evils which Virginia now feels from a superior Cavalry I have been labouring to convince her of for months past; but the Inhabitants appear to be not less attached to their horses than their liberties and this attachment has embarassed the Legislature exceedingly[,] particularly the Governor who seemed perfectly disposd to give every assistance in his power for forming a good body of horse. At Present there appears nothing left but to form a body of Cavalry in the same way the Enemies doing; and I recommend it strongly, for I am perswaded unless you can get a good body of horse the State will be over run in every part.[3] The people will undoubtedly murmur but when they begin to feel the benefit they will approve the measure. A good body of horse is every thing to an Army that is obliged to act upon the defensive, and you will have little to fear either from a skirmish or even a defeat if you are well coverd with horse, but without you have every thing to apprehend, as the most triffling disorder may be improvd into a route [i.e., rout]. My own experience convinces me of the truth of these observations. You may act from my orders if you apprehend the measure will render you unpopular and prejudice your operations. I am very happy you have detained Col [Anthony Walton] Whites horse. If I did not give orders for the purpose it was an omission in me; for it was my intention they should act with you as soon as I discoverd Tarltons Legion was moving Northerly.

I am glad to hear the Convention troops are orderd Easterly; and the troops you mention to have filed off for the Garrison at Portsmouth I am perswaded are coming Southerly.[4] The Cork fleet with a considerable reinforcement arrivd on the 2d of this Instant at Charles Town. It is said they amount to upwards of 2000 men. It is reported, also that they are advancing this way. If so I expect they will raise the siege.[5] This will be mortifying after the incredible fatigue we have gone through in carrying on our approaches, and the loss we have sustained in the Seige; for the enemy sallies almost every night.

I am exceeding sorry Governor Jefferson countermanded the Virginia Militia. I depended on them for support; and had they been here it would have enabled me to have compleated the reduction of this place before this; and not have wore down my troops in the manner it has. I think it extremely wrong for a Governor of a State to under take from partial views to counteract a general plan; and I wish Congress would come to an explanation with them on this subject; and if it is understood to be their prerogative I will never embark in a plan again that depends upon an order of men who I have not the command of. If the Governors cannot trust their Generals it is a folly to prosecute the war as nothing but confusion will arise from such different sources of authority.[6]

We have reduced all the Enemies posts upon the Savannah and taken in the different garrisons upwards of 700 prisoners near one half of which were regulars. We also took in one of the forts very considerable quantities of Stores. George Town has been evacuated since I wrote and the enemy left behind them a large quantity of Salt and other valuable Stores. I think your arrangement in the quarter masters department were very judic[i]ous, and necessary; and I hope Mr Langburn's appointment will facilitate your operations as he will serve from duty and affection.[7]

I suppose Lord Cornwallis is impatient to get his prisoners. You will see by the Cartel that Virginia is included and I hope it is upon such a footing as to afford more immediate relief to those who have the misfortune to fall into the enemies hands.[8]

I am happy you got over the affair with Arnold in the manner you did; and admire the dignity and Stile of your letter.[9] Lord Cornwallis taking the command will remove your difficulties. I know not whether to consider Philips's death a misfortune or other wise. He certainly had the best knowledge of the Country of any man in the British Army; but as he was opposd to Lord Cornwallis perhaps the embarassments on that score might over ballance the superior knowledge he possessed of the Geography of the State.[10] You will find my Lord a very different man from Philips. You will have no long letters; but look out for forced marches.

Since I found the enemy reinforcing these Southern States, I have orderd the North Carolinia regulars under Sumner to march this way.[11]

I am sorry to hear of the insurrection in Hampshire. Could they behold the calamities of this Country I am perswaded they would never adopt a measure which cannot fail to bring on them infinitely greater miseries than falls to the lot of any people at war who are not divided among themselves. I wish General Morgan may succeed and excerise moderation as men may be often reformed by soft means when persecution will only confirm them in their opposition.[12]

I will write you again in a few days, in the mean time I wish you all possible success which I shall think great if you avoid a misfortune. With the highest esteem and regard I [am] dear Sir Your Most obed[t] humble ser   N GREENE

ADfS (Greene Papers: DLC).

1. Lafayette's letter of 10 May has not been found.

2. See NG to Lafayette, 14 May, above.

3. As seen in Lafayette's letter of 18 May, above, the British were forcibly taking horses from the inhabitants of Virginia.

4. For more on the moving of the Convention army, see note at Lafayette to NG, first letter of 3 June, above. As seen at that letter, the British troops who were sent to Portsmouth, Va., remained there.

5. Lord Rawdon reported to Cornwallis in a letter of 5 June:

> On the 3[d] Ins[t], the Fleet from Ireland arrived; having aboard the 3[d], 19[h], & 30[h] Regiments, A Detachment from the Guards, & a considerable body of Recruits: The whole under the Command of Colonel [Paston] Gould of the 30[h]. L[t] Colonel [Nisbet] Balfour & I, immediately made known to Colonel Gould the powers which your Lordship had given to us for detaining such part of the expected reinforcement as we might conceive the Service required. We represented as our joint opinion, that Two complete Regiments were indispensibly necessary for the safety of the Province at this particular juncture: But difficulties having arisen respecting the seperation of those three Regiments, it has been settled that they

shall all remain here, until your Lordship signifies your pleasure respecting them. . . . I shall march on the 7ᵗʰ towards Ninety-Six, having been reinforced by the Flank Companies of the Three new Regiments. (PRO 30/11/6)

Baron von Bose, who was stationed in Charleston, reported on 7 June to Baron von Knyphausen, the Hessian commander in America, that the Cork fleet, consisting of "62 sail," had arrived on the "2nd Instant" with "about 100 recruits" and "three of the best [British] regiments." (Lidgerwood Collection of Hessian Transcripts, NjMoHP)

6. See NG to Huntington, second letter of this date, above.

7. For Lafayette's appointment of his aide, William Langborn, as field quartermaster, see his letter to NG of 18 May, above.

8. On the cartel arranged between NG and Cornwallis, see NG to Huntington, 10 May, above.

9. Lafayette had discussed his refusal to correspond with the American traitor Benedict Arnold in his letter to NG of 18 May, above.

10. William Phillips, who died on 13 May, had been a close friend of Sir Henry Clinton. That may explain NG's assumption that there was friction between Cornwallis and Phillips. (Willcox, *Clinton*, p. 23)

11. It was not until 18 June that NG sent orders for Gen. Jethro Sumner to bring his troops to the army. (NG to Sumner, that date, below)

12. On the insurrection in the Virginia backcountry, see note at Lafayette to NG, first letter of 3 June, above. As seen there, Gen. Daniel Morgan's militia force easily put down the revolt. The insurgents were treated with moderation, as NG advised. (See Eckenrode, *Revolution in Virginia*, p. 248.)

To Governor Abner Nash of North Carolina

Sir   Camp before Ninty Six [S.C.] May [i.e., June] 9ᵗʰ 1781[1]
I am favord with your Excellencys letter of the 24th of May.[2]

I am surprisd that none of my letters have reached you. I have given you regular information of all our movements and of all material events; and the enemy have been very fortunate to intercept the whole.[3]

All the enemies posts upon the Savannah are reducd, upwards of Eight hundred prisoners upon that river of different Charactors have fallen into our hands. This post is upon the eve of reduction, and must fall unless fortune is our worst enemy.

I am in hopes notwithstanding your apprehensions, the Marquis [de Lafayette] will have a sufficent force to face the enemy tho their junction is formed. The Pensylvania line is certainly with him before this, a detachment from Maryland must have arrivd also, and besides these there is the Virginia drafts which is considerable.[4] These joined to the light Infantry of the Northern Army and the Militia of the State will make a formidable force.

It was my orders to General Sumner to collect and form his troops near Hillsborough and join Baron Stuben or the Marquis as occasion might require.[5] If the situation of the Northern operations will admit of the force under General Sumner to remain in the State I shall be happy to have them employed in protecting it until they are wanted this way;

which I expect will be very soon as a reinforcment is said to have arrivd at Charles Town with in a few days.[6] The first and great object should be to have the regular troops collected[,] equiped and diciplined fit for service. After which they may be made useful at any point. Col Polk refusd the appointment because the Commission did not agree with the appointment. If he had had a commission sent him of a brigadier General he would have accepted; and I am perswaded he is the only man in that district who will do justice to the command. It is true Mr Lock may be more popular but he has no influence in the field equal to the other. Half the men under one is worth more than double the men under the other. Col Polk has been emminently useful in collecting the new drafts. Give me leave to assure your Excellency popular charac- tors are not always the best officers where they are more intent upon pleasing the people than discharging their duty. Your Excellency will pardon the liberty I take in making these observation[s.] I have noth- ing at heart but the good of the service.[7] I have the honor to be with great respect Your Excellencys Most Obed humble Ser   N GREENE

ADfS (MiU-C).

1. NG initially wrote "May 29th 1781" on the draft, but the 2 has been crossed out and a line drawn through May. The docketed date, "June 9th '81," is consistent with the contents.

2. Nash's letter has not been found.

3. NG had written Nash on 2, 14, 21, and 23 May, all above.

4. As seen in Lafayette to NG, first letter of 3 June, above, none of those troops had yet joined his detachment.

5. For NG's orders to Gen. Jethro Sumner, see his letter to Sumner of 5 May, above.

6. For more on the reinforcement, which had arrived in Charleston on 2 June, see NG to Lafayette, this date, above.

7. Nash's reply has not been found, but Thomas Polk did not receive the com- mission he wanted and Francis Lock continued to command the Salisbury district militia.

*   *   *

¶ [A PROCLAMATION. From Camp before Ninety Six, S.C., 9 June 1781. NG announces the murder of Col. [James] Grierson and the wounding of Maj. [Henry] Williams by an "unknown" person. "Such an insult offerd to the Arms of the United States, as well as an outrage committed upon the rights of humanity deserves the most examplary punnishment." NG offers a reward of 100 guineas to anyone who can "discover & secure the perpetrator of this horid crime."[1] He will "treat all persons as murderers that shall be guilty of a like conduct in future." ADfS (NcD) 1 p.]

1. On the murder of Grierson and wounding of Williams, see Pickens to NG, 7 June, above. As noted there, Grierson's killer was never caught.

*   *   *

To General William Smallwood

Dear Sir   Camp before 96 [S.C.] June 9th 1781

I had the pleasure of recieving a few days since your letter of the 4th of May. It affords me great satisfaction to find that no measures have been left unattempted by the Military Gentlemen to reinforce this Army. I confess my not hearing from you for five Months after you left Camp lead me to apprehend that you was not so fully impressed with the critical situation of the Southern States as I expected or being from the scene of action felt our distresses less than we did. What servd to countenance this opinion was my great expectations from your extensive influence which I expected if it had failed of success I should have been informed of it. But not recieving a line from you my fears were alarmed. Pressed with difficulties on every side and ready to sink for want of support, on whom could I depend but those who could feel and reason justly upon my situation? Nothing affords me greater pleasure than to find my apprehensions groundless; and I hope the critical conjuncture of affairs will apologize for thinking myself neglected.

I have carefully read the Law which you inclosed me.[1] It has more form than substance; and appears better calculated to excuse the State than furnish the men. I wish the Legislatures would come to one of two resolutions, either to give effectual support to the Army or give up the dispute. If they have not virtue and resolution enough to make the necessary sacrafices for the support of the cause, it would be better to desist in time than to protract the miseries of war by an ineffectual prosecution of it. Had I known I should have been left without support in the manner I have I most assuredly should have beged to have been excused from accepting the command. I am sensible an empty treasury and a murmuring people create difficultiees which must embarass the wisest Legislature. But I am perswaded the bolder the politicks the more effectual the measure & I am sure let their embarassments be as great as they will they cannot equal those I have had to contend with. An Army to support without money or means and an enemy to contend with more than double nay treble our numbers was a hopeless task.

Not a shilling of money have I had since I came to this department not even to get intelligence with. We have been beaten again and again; but by persevering the Campaign has had its advantages. All the enemies posts in South Carolina and Georgia except Charlestown, Savannah and this we are now at have been either taken or evacuated. This post has been beseiged upwards of twenty days and we are now near the ditch of the enemies works, and I am in hopes to reduce the place in a few days if not interrupted which I have great reason to apprehend as the enemy have got a reinforcment at Charlestown. The place is exceeding strong and the garrison large when compard with our little force which is not equal to the advance of a proper Army to be employed in this Country. Our troops are wore out with fatigue and hardships and the Maryland line greatly reduced.

The operations in Virginia I presume you are better informed of than I am. After I discoverd that Lord Cornwallises intention was to move Northerly, I orderd all the troops coming to this Army (the Marylanders excepted) to join the Marquis [de Lafayette], depending upon a body of Virginia Militia orderd here for support but those have been countermanded by the State, and now I am left entirely without a prospect of any. In this situation matters now stand. God grant our affairs may go well in Virginia. You dont mention a word in your letter respecting the principal matter which you went home upon, which leaves me in doubt how to advise. I mean respecting the Marquis and the Baron.[2]

As I have few leisure moments to write, I beg you to inform the State how matters are here and apologize to them for my not writing as I have it not in my power without neglecting the immediate demands of the service. With esteem and regard I am dear Sir Your most Obedient humble Ser   NATH GREENE

ADfS (MiU-C).
  1. Smallwood had sent NG a copy of the Maryland law for raising the state's quota of Continental troops. For more on the law, see Mordecai Gist to NG, 19 January, above (vol. 7: 151).
  2. Smallwood had gone home to petition Congress in a matter concerning his rank vis-à-vis those of Lafayette and Baron Steuben. (See above, vol. 7: 12n, 89.)

*   *   *

¶ [MAJOR ICHABOD BURNET TO GENERAL THOMAS SUMTER. From [Camp before Ninety Six, S.C.], 9 June 1781. NG asks Sumter to furnish men to collect and drive cattle "for the Army." ALS (Sumter Papers: DLC) 1 p.]

¶ [TO COLONEL THOMAS WADE. From Camp before Ninety Six, S.C., 9 June 1781. Has his letter of 3 June. Wade should dispose of the damaged meal and not "grind or purchase any more" unless he can send it to Charlotte, N.C., "where grain is much wanted." The cattle should be sent to Charlotte and pastured there until further orders; Wade should let NG know where he leaves them. All the enemy posts on the Savannah River have been captured, and NG hopes Ninety Six will fall shortly. Adds: "I hope the Whigs in your Quarter will be able to give a good account of the Tories, especially as George Town is evacuated."[1] ADfS (MiU-C) 2 pp.]
  1. On the evacuation of Georgetown, S.C., by the British, see Marion to NG, 29 May, above.

¶ [TO GEORGE WASHINGTON. From Camp before Ninety Six, S.C., 9 June 1781. NG is "so streightened in point of time," and his aides "are so unwell," that he has asked Congress to send copies of his letters to them to Washington.[1] As soon as he gets a "leisure moment," NG will send a "full and particular account of matters in this quarter." LS (Washington Papers: DLC) 1 p.]

1. See NG to Huntington, second letter of this date, above.

¶ [FROM DOCTOR DAVID OLYPHANT, Charleston, S.C., 9 June 1781. The British have agreed to exchange the surgeons "objected to" earlier, plus another, who is to be exchanged for a British surgeon captured at Wright's Bluff.[1] Olyphant is sending all of them to the army except the senior surgeon, Dr. [Thomas T.] Tucker, who is to accompany "our Sick that goes with the Prisoners to be exchanged in Virginia."[2] Olyphant hopes to rejoin the army soon. ALS (MiU-C) 1 p.]

1. On the detention of the surgeons, see Tucker to NG, 19 May, above.
2. Olyphant enclosed a list of the medical personnel who were rejoining the army. (MiU-C)

¶ [FROM BARON STEUBEN, Charlotte Court House, Va., 9 June 1781. Is "distressed" at not having heard from NG since 1 May. Is en route to join NG with 550 recruits and stores; asks for orders respecting "Rout & Conduct."[1] Is leaving Gen. [Robert] Lawson behind with 600 militia to "prevent the Enemy from ravaging the Country in small parties." The enemy detached [Col. Banastre] Tarleton and [Col. John Graves] Simcoe with 900 infantry and their legions "to take the Stores" from Steuben. They were only able, however, to capture "a few Articles which fell into their hands thro the negligence of the Commissaries & Store Keepers."[2] The enemy have cut Steuben's communications with the Marquis [de Lafayette], from whom he has heard nothing for "Ten days past." Repeats that he is "distressd for want of" orders. Is finding stores "wherever" he goes; asks if he should "bring them on or leave them scatterd in the Country."[3] Fears that letters between NG and him have been "intercepted" and will therefore send a duplicate of this one. Encloses a copy of his instructions to Lawson. LS (MiU-C) 2 pp.]

1. NG's letter to Steuben of 14 May, above, canceling the order to bring the recruits to South Carolina, had been intercepted.
2. In letters to NG of 18 and 20 June, both below, Lafayette gave a different assessment of what Tarleton and Simcoe had accomplished and of Steuben's efforts to oppose them.
3. Before NG could reply, Steuben learned that NG wanted him to join Lafayette. (See Lafayette to Steuben, 13 June, Idzerda, *Lafayette Papers*, 4: 179.)

¶ [TO GENERAL FRANCIS MARION. From Camp before Ninety Six, S.C., 10 June 1781. Acknowledges Marion's letters of 22, 24, and 29 May.[1] Takes "great pleasure" in the enemy's evacuation of Georgetown; shares Marion's view that "it will be attended with many good consequences to that part of the country." After Marion demolishes the works there, he should "take the position" that he mentioned and "act in conjunction" with Gen. [Thomas] Sumter.[2] Augusta has been captured, and NG hopes to inform him soon of "the reduction of this place but we are opposed to many difficulties, and the garrison resists with great obstinacy."[3] Df (NcD) 2 pp.]

1. Marion's letter of 24 May has not been found.
2. As seen in his letter to NG of 29 May, above, Marion planned to move to a position near Monck's Corner. He had finished razing the works at Georgetown even before NG wrote this letter. (See Marion to NG, 5 June, above.)

3. On the capture of the post at Augusta, Ga., see Pickens and Lee to NG, 5 June, above.

*   *   *

To General Francis Marion

Dear Sir   Camp before 96 [S.C.] June 10th 1781
   Yours of the 6th I have recievd with the inclosures. I had information
of the arrival of a reinforcment at Charlestown before your letter came
to hand. Accounts are various respecting their numbers. By private
information the enemy intend to attempt raising the Seige of this place
which I hope will terminate in our favour.[1] Should the enemy attempt
to penetrate the Country I beg you to collect all the force you can and
join General Sumter without loss of time and give the enemy all the
opposition you can until we form a junction with our collective force it
being my intention to fight them, and I wish them to be cripled as
much as possible before we have a general action.[2] Send me all the
information you can get. With esteem & regard I am dear Sir your most
obed humˡ Ser   N GREENE

ADfS (MiU-C).
   1. On the arrival of the reinforcement at Charleston and the British plan to relieve the
post at Ninety Six, see NG to Lafayette, 9 June, above.
   2. See also NG's orders in his two letters to Sumter, this date, immediately below. On
Marion's movements, see Sumter to NG, first letter of 13 June, below.

To General Thomas Sumter

Dear Sir   Camp before Ninety Six [S.C.] June 10th 1781.
   We have but a small part of the Militia Regiments you mention with
us, they have been & still are wanted to compleat the reduction of this
place the Garrison of which defend themselves by the advantages of
the Ground, strength of the Works, and number of the Garrison with
great obstinacy.[1] However I hope it will fall in a few Days, as we are
preparing a mine to blow up their principal Work.[2]
   I am happy to hear the Orangeburg Militia have behaved with such
spirit. This promises well. Go on with the good business of arranging
and arming the Militia as fast as possible.
   All the Enemy's Posts upon the Savannah are reduced. Upwards of
800 Men were made Prisoners of different characters at the several
Posts.[3] Several pieces of Cannon with some Military Stores were
taken. When this Post is reduced the Enemy will have no Posts in the
two southern States, except Charles Town and Savannah. General
Marion had reported the evacuation of George Town before your
Letter arrived.[4]

By a Charles Town Paper of the 2ᵈ, I find a Fleet has lately arrived at that place; and it is said with a large reinforcement.[5] As you do not mention anything of it in your Letter I imagine you have not received an account of it. Please to make particular enquiry into the matter.[6] The Enemy's laying waste the Country in the Neighbourhood of Charles Town, looks like preparing for a Seige, which perhaps they expect on the arrival of the 2ᵈ division of the french Fleet.[7]

Should the Enemy move out in force with a view of raising the Seige of this place, you will give them all the opposition in your power, that their march may be delayed as long as possible and retire before them so as to form a junction w[ith] us, as it is my intention to collect our force and g[ive] them Battle. Reports say the reinforcement amou[nts] to 3000, but it is most probable that it is only a few recruits for the different Corps perhaps to the amount of 7 or 800 Men.[8]

Our force is accumulating in Virginia. The Pennsylvania Line has arrived, and a reinforcem[ent] for the Maryland Line also. Nothing is to be feard from that quarter. Lord Cornwallis had formed a junction with Arnold. General Philips is dead. The People are in high spirits, and all the young Gentlemen in the Country are forming a Corps of Light Horse. Our affairs wear an agreable face in every quarter.[9] With esteem and regard, I am Dʳ sir Your most obᵗ hble servt NATH GREENE

LS (Sumter Papers: DLC).

1. NG was responding in this letter to a number of points raised in Sumter's letter of 7 June, above.

2. The "mine" was a tunnel that NG's troops were digging under the British fortifications. When completed, it was to have been packed with explosives to blast a passageway for an assault on the Star Fort. In a sally on the night of 9–10 June, the British defenders discovered the mouth of the mine. Col. Thaddeus Kosciuszko, NC's engineering officer, who was on the scene, managed to escape but suffered a slight wound in what a British officer called his "'seat of honor.'" (Haiman, *Kosciuszko*, pp. 113–14) Work on the mine continued despite this interruption, as seen by NG's Orders of 15 June, below. By the time NG was forced to abandon the siege, the "mine and two approaches were within a few feet of their Ditch." (NG to Huntington, 20 June, below.)

3. On the capture of the enemy posts on the Savannah River, see Lee to NG, 22 May; Pickens to NG, first letter of 25 May; and Pickens and Lee to NG, 5 June, all above.

4. See Marion to NG, 29 May, above.

5. In a notice dated 2 June, the *Royal Gazette* of Charleston announced the "safe arrival of a large fleet from Corke, with a powerful reinforcement for the Royal Army." The announcement concluded by adding: "Mr. Greene, we are well assured, lately took occasion to announce in General Orders, to his army, that the fleet abovementioned had been captured by the French." (No such order has been found; for more on the arrival of the enemy reinforcement, see note at NG to Lafayette, 9 June, above.)

6. As seen in the letter immediately below, Sumter had already sent news of the reinforcement, which NG received later on this date. Sumter sent further intelligence of enemy movements in three letters to NG of 13 June, below.

7. Sumter had reported on enemy activities outside Charleston in his letter of 7 June, above. On the second division, see La Luzerne to NG, 3 April, above.

8. As seen at NG to Lafayette, 9 June, the reinforcement that remained in Charleston consisted of three British regiments and some "recruits," totaling close to 2,000 men.

9. The Marquis de Lafayette's reports to NG show the situation in Virginia in a less favorable light than NG presented here. (See Lafayette to NG, 18 and 24 May and second letter of 3 June, all above.)

To General Thomas Sumter

Dear Sir   Head Quarters before 96. [S.C.] June 10ᵗʰ 1781.

I recieved your letter of the 8ᵗʰ accompanying a letter from Genˡ Marian.[1] I wrote you this morning respecting the reinforcement mentioned, having got intelligence thereof before the arrival of your letter.[2]

In consequence of the information I put [Col. William] Washington's horse and the Cavalry of [Col. Henry] Lee's Legion in motion.[3] It is my wish if the enemy should advance into the Country that you should collect all the force you can and skirmish with the enemy all the way they advance removing out of their way all the cattle, means of transportation and subsistance. It is my wish to have the enemy galled as much as possible in penetrating the country as it is my intention to fight them before they get to this post. Inform me constantly of the motions and be always in a situation to form a junction with us when you get within three or four days march of this place.[4] Collect all the force you can and give positive orders for Genˡ Marion's force to join if the enemy attempt to penetrate the Country.

The force from Augusta is arrived at this post, and I think when we are collected we can fight a good battle; and if the enemy's force do not exceed 2500 we shall have a fair prospect of victory.[5]

Forward the enclosed to Genˡ Marian, and write Col. Hardman to join you.[6] Every thing depends on defeating the enemy. Reinforcements are coming from the northward but they will not be here in time.[7] With esteem I am Dʳ Sir Your Humble Servant   NATH GREENE

LS (Sumter Papers: DLC).

1. Marion's letter, dated 6 June, is above; NG replied to it on this date, above.

2. See NG to Sumter, immediately above.

3. Lee himself remained at Ninety Six; the legion cavalry was commanded by Capt. John Rudulph. (See Burnet to Rudulph, 14 June, below.)

4. Sumter's reply is in his first letter to NG of 13 June, below. NG wrote Samuel Huntington on 20 June, below, that Sumter's failure to do as ordered prevented him from executing the plan outlined here.

5. The "force from Augusta" was Lee's Legion. (See NG to Pickens, 7 June, above.) On the strength of Rawdon's force, see note at NG to Clarke, 12 June, below.

6. NG enclosed his second letter to Marion of this date, above. As seen in Sumter to NG, first letter of 13 June, Col. William Harden's detachment did not join Sumter.

7. The reinforcements may have been the North Carolina troops mentioned in NG to Nash, 9 June, above.

*   *   *

¶ [**FROM COLONEL WADE HAMPTON**, Granby, S.C., 10 June 1781. Refers to letters that have been returned because the express was "too much alarm'd on the Road to proceed." Says "several Horrid murders" are thought to have been committed along the road from Granby to Ninety Six and Augusta, Ga. On 8 June, two men "on private Business" were beset by "Nine men in arms." They were "Stript & one of them Murder'd in the most cruel manner, by men he never before saw." The other managed to escape. ALS (NcU) 1 p. At least one page is missing.]

* * *

To Colonel James Mayson

Sir   Camp before 96 [S.C.] June 11th 1781

I am favord with your letter of yesterday.[1] I am a stranger to the charges you mention to have been brought against you not having heard of them until you mentioned them. I take up no prejudices nor have I time to investigate the conduct of private charactors. I feel for the distresses of this unfortunate Country, and wish not to add new mesures to private life to swell the list of public calamities. People will be illiberal and it is not prudent to attempt to stop it all together; but to give them such a turn as to be least prejudicial to the happiness of society. If any of the Inhabitants are dissatisfied with your conduct some future day when reason has more and passion and prejudce less influence, you will have an opportunity to satis[f]y the honest and softer part of the community. The horid practice of private murders and plundering which prevail among both Whigs [and] Tories strikes me with horror and asstonishment. My utmost influence is and shall be exerted to [attack?] these enormous evils. If the war must continue it is my wish it should be conducted upon as humane principles as the nature of it will admit. Events in war are uncertain and it is not my wish to place individuals in a more disagreeable situation than I find them to serve temporary purposes. I am Sir Your Most Obedient humble Ser   NATH GREENE

ADfS (MiU-C).

1. NG appears to have been anticipating a letter from Mayson, dated 14 June, below. The reason for the discrepancy in the dates is not known.

* * *

¶ [**MAJOR ICHABOD BURNET TO GENERAL ANDREW PICKENS**, [Camp before Ninety Six, S.C.], 11 June 1781. NG wants a detailed return of prisoners captured at Ft. Cornwallis and a return of arms taken.[1] ALS (MiU-C) 1 p.]

1. The returns have not been found.

¶ [**TO COLONEL THOMAS POLK**. From Camp before Ninety Six, S.C., 11 June 1781. Has Polk's letters of 9, 15, 27 May and 4 June. Warmly thanks him for his efforts to raise, arm, and equip the new levies. Continues:

I am very sorry that those in power cannot distinguish popularity acquird by improper indulgences from that of real merit and important services. The appointment of Mr [Francis] Lock is not less mortifying to me than unjust to you; and I have not failed to tell Governor Nash that I had rather have half the number of Militia with you than double the number with Mr Lock, who I doubt not is a good Citizen but I am perswaded will never make a Soldier.[1] I shall never rest satisfied until I get you at the head of Salisbury District as it is a pity such a valuable Militia should be lost for want of a proper officer at their head.[2]

The army is distressed for money; asks Polk to "suspend" his demands if it can do so "without great prejudice" to himself or "injury" to his creditors. NG will give him "all the justice" in his power and will govern himself by Polk's answer.[3] Col. [William R.] Davie will inform Polk of "all Military matters." ADfS (MiU-C) 2 pp.]

1. See NG to Gov. Abner Nash, 9 June, above.
2. Lock remained as commander of the Salisbury district.
3. In his letter to NG of 4 June, above, Polk, a former commissary for the Southern Army, had asked that his public debts be liquidated. He replied to NG's letter on 16 June, below.

¶ [FROM COLONEL THOMAS POLK, Charlotte, N.C., 11 June 1781. Sends intelligence from Virginia. In a postscript, reflects on the militia and refers to the rapid movements of the enemy. Printed Calendar (Stan. V. Henkel, *Catalogue #1005* [1909]).]

¶ [FROM GENERAL THOMAS SUMTER, [Congarees, S.C.], 11 June 1781.[1] NG will consider him "Very tardy" for not having moved, but the delay was "unavoidable." He is now "upon the point of Moving," but his troops are still not in "Good order." The enemy remain near Monck's Corner. Gen. [Francis] Marion is about to return from Georgetown but has few men. Sumter has heard nothing further of the arrival of a reinforcement in Charleston.[2] Says the return of Col. "Lawrence" and the "Speedy arival of a French fleet & Land forces appears to be probable."[3] Sends news of the military situation in Virginia. Reports that the Virginia militia "Turn out in Great Numbers, So as to Render a Draft unnecessary."[4] They are poorly armed, but muskets "are near hand." The North Carolinians "behaive Infamously." Expects news from Charleston in a few days, which he will immediately forward to NG. In a postscript, adds: "I am unfortunate enough to find that My Indisposition in Creases So fast as Not to have any hopes, from the Nature of it, to be able to Remain with the Troops Many days longer; I Shall in deavour to hold out until you are So Disengaged as to take Measures in consequence of My withdrawing."[5] ALS (MiU-C) 2 pp.]

1. Sumter did not give his location, but NG's two letters to him of 12 June, below, were directed to "Congaree."
2. For more on the British reinforcement, which had arrived in Charleston on 2 June, see note at NG to Lafayette, 9 June, above.
3. In a letter of 6 June, above, William Pierce, NG's aide, had told Sumter that a French fleet was expected soon on the southern coast. (On the origins of this report, see note at

La Luzerne to NG, 3 April, above.) Col. "Lawrence" was undoubtedly Col. John Laurens, whom Congress had sent to France to solicit aid for America. Laurens returned to America on 25 August with $500,000 and two cargoes of military supplies. (Richard J. Hargrove, "Portrait of a Southern Patriot: The Life and Death of John Laurens," in *The Revolutionary War in the South: Power, Conflict, and Leadership*, edited by Robert Higgins [Durham, N.C.: Duke University Press, 1979], p. 199)

4. Sumter was misinformed. Gov. Thomas Jefferson of Virginia had ordered a militia draft and, as seen in Lafayette to NG, 24 May, above, the men were slow to assemble. (Jefferson's order calling out the militia is in Boyd, *Jefferson Papers*, 5: 646.)

5. As seen in NG's reply of 13 June, Sumter continued to suffer from the effects of a wound he had received in an engagement in November 1780. (For more on Sumter's wound, see above, vol. 6: 581n.) Although his condition became worse, Sumter did not retire from the field. (See NG to Sumter, 23 June, below.)

¶ [GENERAL GREENE'S ORDERS, Camp before Ninety Six, S.C., 12 June 1781. Col. [Henry] Lee and the infantry of his legion are to camp on the "West" of Ninety Six and assist operations in that quarter.[1] Lamar Orderly Book (OClWHi) 1 p.]

1. For the role that Lee and his men played during the remainder of the siege, see NG to Huntington, 20 June, below.

¶ [TO COLONEL ELIJAH CLARKE. From Camp before Ninety Six, S.C., 12 June 1781. Gen. [Andrew] Pickens has just handed Clarke's letter of 9 June [not found] to NG, who regrets that his army is so lacking in arms that he has none to spare. There are a number at Salisbury, N.C., but they need to be repaired. If NG can help, Clarke can "rely upon its being done." Suggests taking arms from those who "will not engage for a given time" and giving them to those who will. NG sent a supply of clothing to Clarke "a few days since"; hopes it has arrived and that Clarke will dispose of it as he judges best.[1] Mr. [Joseph] Clay has gone to Augusta, Ga., to have the fortifications leveled and to "form a Council for the establishment of Civil Government in the State."[2] An unknown number of enemy reinforcements has arrived at Charleston, S.C.[3] NG has learned "By private intelligence" that Lord Rawdon is "to march for the relief of this place."[4] NG intends to fight him if the militia join in sufficient numbers. Begs Clarke to be ready to join him on "the shortest notice" with as large a force as possible. "The fortifications at Augusta should all be demolished without loss of time and the public Stores moved farther back into the Country." ADfS (NcD) 2 pp.]

1. In his reply of 19 June, below, Clarke reported the arrival of the clothing, which the Georgia delegates to Congress had sent from Philadelphia. (See also Walton to NG, 5 April, above.)

2. See NG to Clay, 9 June, below.

3. For more on the reinforcements, see note at NG to Lafayette, 9 June, above.

4. Rawdon marched from Charleston with about 1,850 men on the evening of 7 June. (Rawdon to Cornwallis, 2 August, PRO 30/11/6) Another 200 men under Col. John Doyle joined him en route to Ninety Six, increasing the size of his detachment to just over 2,000 men. (Ibid.; McCrady, *S.C. in the Revolution*, p. 292)

¶ [TO GENERAL BERNARDO DE GÁLVEZ, COMMANDER OF THE SPANISH FORCES IN FLORIDA. From Camp before Ninety Six, S.C., 12 June 1781. NG has received reports through "different channels" that the

Spanish have captured Pensacola, Fla., and are now besieging St. Augustine.[1] This intelligence gives "sensible pleasure and affords a most pleasing prospect." NG briefly summarizes the successful operations of his army in "this quarter." As the Spanish and Americans are "at war with a common enemy"— though not allied, as "every American most ardently wishes"—NG suggests that it would be mutually beneficial to capture Savannah, Ga. That place could be taken "in a very few days with a few Ships of force and about 2000 men." While the British hold Savannah, they can "interrupt" Spanish "Southern possessions" and American "Northern" ones and can "influence and employ the Indians to our prejudice." If Gálvez considers the measure "advisable," NG will use "every possible exertion" to facilitate Spanish operations, "being instructed by Congress to cooperate with you in any manner calculated to annoy the common enimy."[2] The capture of Savannah by the Spanish would lay America "under the highest obligation" and, NG hopes, "lay a foundation for a lasting and honorable connection." Hopes to hear from Gálvez as soon as possible and assures him that it would give NG "the highest satisfaction" to unite their arms in the recovery of a post "highly interesting to the public weal of both Nations," but especially to the United States. ADfS (NcD) 5 pp.]

1. Gálvez's forces had captured Pensacola on 10 May but were not besieging St. Augustine. (See above, vol. 5: 319n.)

2. The authorization to cooperate with Spanish forces was in the instructions Congress had given NG when he was appointed commander of the Southern Department. (See Huntington to NG, 31 October, above [vol. 6: 451].)

3. No reply has been found from Gálvez, who, after capturing Pensacola, had sailed to the West Indies to prepare for operations against the Bahama Islands and Jamaica. (Lorenzo G. LaFarelle, *Bernardo De Gálvez: Hero of the American Revolution* [Austin, Tex.: Eakin Press, 1992], p. 47)

¶ [TO LIEUTENANT EDMUND GAMBLE.[1] From Camp before Ninety Six, S.C., 12 June 1781. The "great difficulty" in getting military stores from the "Northward" and the "severe operations going on in this quarter" make it necessary to "set up every manufactory in our power." Col. [James] Read informs NG that leather is available in the Salisbury district and that there are artificers among the militiamen called into service who could make "Cartouch boxes"; the army has little prospect of obtaining these items elsewhere. Gamble should use "every exertion" to "forward the business" and should "set about it immediately."[2] ADfS (MiU-C) 1 p.]

1. Gamble was commissary at Salisbury, N.C. (*NCSR*, 20: 436)

2. Gamble replied on 1 July, below.

*   *   *

To Governor Abner Nash of North Carolina

Sir   Camp before Ninty Six [S.C.] June 12th 1781

This will be handed your Excellency by Col [James] Read who commanded the North Carolinia Militia that Marched from Deep River with us to the Southward. His conduct merits my highest approbation. Lt Colonel Dudly on his return had the misfortune to lose the Colonels baggage in crossing the Country from Pedee to Haw River.[1] The Col [i.e., Read] had the misfortune also to lose his baggage at Hallifax.[2] These losses fall very heavy upon the Colonel as he has been long in the Continental service and of course has sufferd greatly in his private fortune. If Government could find it consistent to make him some allowance for his losses it would be doing but a piece of justice to his merit[,] as few men have a better claim to such an indulgence.[3]

We are prosecuting our siege at this place with all the dispatch our force will admit. But the works are very strong and the place difficult to approach from the make of the ground. We must succeed in time if not interrupted but as the enemy have receivd a reinforcement at Charlestown and Virginia has not afforded me the support I expected should the enemy move out in force they will oblige us to raise the seige.[4] I shall be prepard for all events.

I hope no time will be lost in collecting[,] forming and equiping your drafts. To secure our advantages requi[r]es great exertions.[5]

The force collecting in Virginia under the Marquis [de Lafayette] I am in hopes will enable him to force Lord Cornwallis with a good countenance. However I wish he may not hazard a general action as the enemy is so much superior in Cavalry. Once before I mentioned to your Excellency the absolute necessity of furnishing this Army with forty or fifty good Dragoon horses. I beg leave to repeat the application and to observe it is impossible to give protection to the Country without a large Cavalry.[6]

I must refer you to Col Read for a more particular account of the opperations in this quarter. I am with the highest respect Your Excellencys Most Obed[t] humble Sr N GREENE

ADfS (MiU-C).

1. In a pension application, Guilford Dudley years later remembered losing the baggage wagon under his care to Loyalist raiders commanded by the notorious David Fanning. (Dann, *Revolution Remembered*, pp. 226–27)

2. On the capture of Halifax, N.C., and stores kept there by Lord Cornwallis's army, see Malmedy to NG, 11 May, above.

3. As a result of NG's letter, a joint committee of the North Carolina House and Senate was named on 29 June to consider "the losses sustained by Colo. Reed in his baggage." (*NCSR*, 17: 916) On 12 July both houses approved the committee's recommendation that Read receive "two suits of broad or other cloth, one piece of good linen not exceeding twenty-five yards, six pairs of Stockings, and three yards of Cambreak, all suitable to the office he bears in the Army." (Ibid., pp. 958–59, 961)

4. As noted at NG to Clarke, this date, above, a British relief force was already on its way to Ninety Six.

5. As seen in Sumner to NG, this date, below, the North Carolina Continental drafts were not prepared to take the field.

6. Thomas Burke, Nash's successor as governor, discussed the response to NG's request for horses in a letter to NG of 4 July, below.

To General Thomas Sumter

Dear Sir   Camp before Ninety Six [S.C.] June 12th 1781.
I am impatient to hear from below. If the Enemy should move up this way send Expresses different routes as Letters are frequently intercepted, and intelligence is of the last importance.

Nothing new here. Our approaches are going on with all possible expedition. The Garrison is obstinate and sallies almost every Night, by which lives are lost on both sides. I think they will soon get tired of this business. Give me an account of the force you and General [Francis] Marion will have to operate with us, should the Enemy attempt to penetrate the Country.[1] All the Horse are ordered down to harrass them on their march.[2] But I can hardly persuade myself yet that they will venture out thus far into the Country, at a time when the second Division of the French Fleet is certainly on the coast, and probably near Charles Town.[3] I am D[r] sir Your mo: ob[t] hble serv[t]

NATH GREENE

LS (Sumter Papers: DLC).
1. Sumter answered NG's query in his letter to NG, 14 June, below.
2. For more on the dispatch of the cavalry, see NG to Sumter, second letter of 10 June, above.
3. Lord Rawdon addressed the question of the French threat to Charleston in letters to Lord Cornwallis of 3 and 7 June. In the first, he said he had received "very early" intelligence from a reliable source that NG was expecting the arrival of a French fleet; this information "induced" him "to decline at that time the attempt of farther opposition to General Greene in the Back Country." Cornwallis's "hint" that the French were heading to Rhode Island, however, and the fact that they had not made an appearance in southern waters led him to believe they were not coming. (PRO 30/11/6) On 7 June, when he was about to march for Ninety Six, Rawdon wrote Cornwallis: "the town, & lower districts, are safe against any French Force." (Ibid.)

*   *   *

¶ [TO GENERAL THOMAS SUMTER. From "Camp before 96," S.C., 12 June 1781. The arrival of the "Cork fleet" at Charleston is confirmed. Everyone agrees that the enemy ships brought reinforcements, but opinions differ as to the number. The "Whigs" say there are no more than 1,500 or 2,000 new troops; NG thinks both of those numbers are inflated.[1] In Charleston, it is also being said that part of the reinforcements are to march with Lord Rawdon to relieve Ninety Six. The fact that NG has not heard from Sumter leads him to hope that report is false.[2] NG repeats what he said in his earlier letter to Sumter: that he wants any intelligence concerning the reinforcement forwarded immediately. The "approaches" are going "very well"; only time is needed to complete the siege of Ninety Six, even though the garrison acts "with great spirit. More or less fall on both sides every day." If Rawdon's troops "advance," Sumter should "fight them every day, so as to retard their approach as long as possible. Washington's & Lee's corps will join him in this ⟨n⟩ecessary business."[3] LS (Sumter Papers: DLC) 2 pp. There is a small hole in the LS, and parts of several words were taken from a GWG Transcript (CSmH).]

1. For more on the reinforcement, see note at NG to Lafayette, 9 June, above. As seen there, at least 1,500 men arrived in Charleston.

2. Sumter sent word of Rawdon's march in three letters of 13 June, below.

3. On the dispatch of the Continental cavalry to assist Sumter, see NG to Sumter, second letter of 10 June, above.

¶ [FROM MAJOR JOHN ARMSTRONG,[1] Salisbury, N.C., 12 June 1781. He has been collecting the "Ballance" of the Salisbury district's twelve-month draftees. Has been delayed by "delitory" militia officers and the inability of the armorers to outfit the detachment. Plans to march to NG's army on 20 June with all the draftees—about 200 men—except for "outlyers and deserters." Asks for instructions.[2] ALS (MiU-C) 1 p.]

1. Below his signature, Armstrong added that he was in the Fourth North Carolina Continental Regiment.

2. NG wrote Armstrong on 21 June, below.

¶ [FROM COLONEL NISBET BALFOUR, Charleston, S.C., 12 June 1781. Has NG's letter.[1] Dr. [David] Olyphant was detained after his exchange because of "a civil suit[,] he being considerably indebted here." Olyphant will "certainly" be included in the cartel and will "embark" with the hospital when the cartel is completed in "a few days."[2] Balfour will happily join NG in measures that "mitigate the general horrors of War, or soften the distresses of Individuals."[3] LS (MiU-C) 1 p.]

1. See NG to Balfour, 4 June, above.

2. On the cartel, see NG to Huntington, 10 May, above. NG's commissary of prisoners, Edmund M. Hyrne, was in Charleston to negotiate its implementation. (Hyrne to NG, 1 June, above)

3. In contrast to what he wrote here, Balfour had written Lord Cornwallis on 7 June that under the terms of the cartel he would have to allow the return of the American leaders from Charleston who had been exiled to St. Augustine and to permit "all the very violent and oppressive People to go home upon their Paroles as Militia." He assured Cornwallis that he would "try to put them off that Article [of the cartel] as much as possible." (PRO 30/11/6)

¶ [FROM ROBERT MORRIS, SUPERINTENDENT OF FINANCE,[1] Philadelphia, 12 June 1781. Has learned from Gov. [John] Rutledge that "some hard Money" would be "of essential Service" to NG in the "present Campaigne." The "Tender & penal Laws" make it very difficult to obtain "precious Metals," but he expects the Pennsylvania legislature to repeal its laws on the subject and hopes that other states will do likewise.[2] "Shou'd this be the case and they will levy Efficient Taxes, we may by introducing Oeconomy into the Expenditures and System into our managements still redeem the Public Credit from that desperate State in which it now appears and instead of a deceiving uncertain medium we may again see Solid Coin or Paper that will procure it on demand, passing freely amongst us." Morris has proposed a "National Bank upon a small Capital"; hopes to have enough subscriptions soon to start it up, "well knowing that so soon as the advantages & Conveniences that will result from this institution are plainly seen & felt it may then & perhaps not 'till then, be extended with ease to a Capital more adequate to the great objects we have in view."[3] Rutledge has taken one of the "Subscription papers" and will obtain as many subscribers as he can during his journey and turn over the money he collects to NG. Morris expects Rutledge to have "tolerable good Success" in finding subscribers, "unless the People are destitute of hard Money"; that is the only difficulty Morris meets with "in this City."[4] Morris also has "five hundred Guineas" that NG can use for purposes he "cannot otherwise Accomplish, such as gaining intelligence, &c." NG must use it for the "vigorous prosecution of this Campaigne." If Rutledge cannot get subscriptions to cover "the Sum mentioned," and NG can draw bills on Morris to make up the shortfall, Morris will "pay Such drafts in Specie."[5] ALS (N) 4 pp.]

1. With the nation's finances in shambles, Congress on 7 February had created the office of superintendent of finance. The superintendent was to be responsible for "improving and regulating the finances, and for establishing order and economy in the expenditure of the public money." (JCC, 19: 126) On 20 February, Congress offered the post to Morris, a highly successful Philadelphia merchant and important political leader on both the state and national levels. (Morris, Papers, 1: 4–5) He accepted the appointment on 14 May, and although he would not formally assume the duties of the office until 27 June, he had already begun to function as superintendent. (Ibid., pp. 5n, 62–64)

2. Tender laws set and upheld the value of paper money issued by the states. The penal laws in question set penalties for violations of tender laws. (Ibid., p. 180) Pennsylvania repealed its tender laws on 21 June. (Ibid., p. 147n)

3. Congress on 26 May had overwhelmingly approved Morris's proposal for the establishment of a national bank. As can be seen here, Morris conceived of the bank as "the progenitor of a new financial order in the United States" and had made it the centerpiece of his plan for national economic reform. As he was able to attract only small amounts from private investors, he and some of his associates turned out to be the principal subscribers; Morris was able to use French hard currency, however, to create a stable circulating medium during the last two years of the war. (Ibid., pp. xxi–xxii, 66–68; Boatner, Encyc., pp. 743–44)

4. Rutledge was unable to obtain subscribers. (See NG to Morris, 18 August, below.)

5. NG told Morris in his letter of 18 August: "If I have any opportunity of obtaining Money and drawing bills on you, I shall embrace it. But it is a very uncertain source and therefore I leave you to judge of the prudence of exposing an Army to such contingencies."

¶ [FROM COLONEL CHARLES PETTIT, [Philadelphia], 12 June 1781.[1] Great things were expected of NG, but he has exceeded even "the most sanguine expectations." The Southern Army's reputation has "risen amazingly" and now "stands unrivalled among all the judges of military merit—Envy is silenced"; NG's former "maligners" are "echoing" that "great things were expected" of him when he was appointed.[2] Discusses money troubles and public credit; complains that he sometimes cannot get cash "for a dinner." Printed Calendar (Stan. V. Henkel, Catalogue #1074, Supplement (1912)]

1. The letter is described in the catalogue as unsigned but docketed "from Col Pettit." No place was given, but Pettit lived and worked in Philadelphia.

2. Pettit's assessment of NG's public image here differs markedly from that in his letter of 24–27 May, above.

¶ [FROM GENERAL JETHRO SUMNER, "Camp [Harrisburg, N.C.]," 12 June 1781.[1] The draftees from the various districts are "at last in motion" to the general rendezvous. Few of them have arms, cartridge boxes, or bayonets. Baron Steuben, who presumably has informed NG that he is bringing 1,500 men to the Southern Army, is now at Upper Saura Town. He has brought 300 stand of "fine Arms" for the North Carolina draftees.[2] After Sumner receives the arms, he will march his men to Virginia, as NG ordered.[3] ALS (NjP) 1 p.]

1. Sumner did not give his location, but during this time he was at Harrisburg, the site designated for the rendezvous of the North Carolina Continental draftees. (Rankin, *N.C. Continentals*, pp. 342–43)

2. Steuben was not in North Carolina and ultimately remained in Virginia to serve with the Marquis de Lafayette. (See Steuben to NG, 9 June, above.) The draftees, moreover, did not receive the muskets from Virginia. (See Sumner to NG, 14 July, below.)

3. NG had changed his orders, writing Gov. Abner Nash on 9 June, above, that the North Carolina draftees should wait for him to summon them to South Carolina.

¶ [GENERAL GREENE'S ORDERS, Camp before Ninety Six, S.C., Wednesday, 13 June 1781. "The Enemy are encourraged by a small reinforcement to take the Field again."[1] If their "Temerity" leads them "this way," NG hopes, "by the firmness of his Troops, and the Gallant Militia and State Troops," to not only "complete the Reduction of this place, but to drive them into Town [i.e., Charleston] again." Lamar Orderly Book (OClWHi) 2 pp.]

1. See NG to Clarke, 12 June, above.

*   *   *

To General Thomas Sumter

Dear Sir   Camp before 96 [S.C.]. June 13th 1781

Yours of the 11th came to hand yesterday a few Minutes after I wrote you. As you mention nothing of the reinforcement I hope less is to be apprehended from their numbers than at first was expected.[1] A few days more will terminate the seige here after which if they have a mind for a ramble into the Country we shall be prepard for them.[2]

I am distressed at the increasing pains in your wound. I cannot think of your leaving service without the greatest pain[.][3] Few people in any Count[r]y know how to command and fewer in this than is common. It will be of importance to the public good that you continue to command if you are unable to perform active service, for you may continue to direct tho not execute. Your name will give confidence to our own people and strike terror into the enemy. This appears to me to be the crisis of this Country and nothing should be left unattempted to give a favorable turn to the minds of the people. I wish you better health and am with esteem Your most Obed[t] humble S[r]   N GREENE

ADfS (MiU-C).

1. On the reinforcement, see note at NG to Lafayette, 9 June, above.

2. As seen in Sumter's three letters of this date, below, the enemy had already moved "into the country."

3. As seen in the note at Sumter's letter of 11 June, above, he did not leave the service.

*   *   *

¶ [CAPTAIN WILLIAM PIERCE, JR., TO GENERAL THOMAS SUMTER. From "Camp before Ninety Six," S.C., 13 June 1781. NG has received Sumter's two letters.[1] Sumter is "to throw" himself "in front" of the enemy and order Gen. [Francis] Marion to join him. With Marion's help, he is to "harrass and retard" the enemy's march.[2] The dragoons will "act in conjunction" with Sumter and provide "every assistance."[3] ADfS (MiU-C) 1 p.]

1. NG was presumably acknowledging Sumter's first two letters of this date, below.

2. Sumter wrote Marion on this date, urging him to march toward Ninety Six as quickly as possible. (Gibbes, *Documentary History*, 3: 95) The next day, however, he informed Marion that the "parties that have been discovered, are said to be Tories," and he advised Marion to "halt, until this matter can be clearly ascertained." (Ibid.) Sumter wrote Marion again on the 15th that the enemy appeared to be advancing and asked him to call out more of his brigade and move to where he could readily join Sumter if the enemy's advance continued. (Ibid., p. 96) On the 16th, after deciding that the British were heading toward Ninety Six and not toward his own party, Sumter directed Marion, who was "moving up," to "move with all the force you can." (Ibid., p. 97)

3. As seen at NG to Sumter, second letter of 10 June, above, NG had sent William Washington's and Henry Lee's dragoons to act with Sumter.

*   *   *

To John Wilkinson

Sir   Camp before 96 [S.C.] June 13th 1781

Your favor of the 8th by the honble William Glascock and Col [Andrew] Burns has been deliverd me. Upon a consultation with those Gentlemen I can think of no better mode for the State [i.e., Georgia] to adopt to regulate its internal police or secure it self from the further ravages of the enemy than to form a Council to consist of five or seven of the most considerable charactors in the State whose orders should have the force of Laws.[1] It is necessary that these Men should be persons of good charactors in whom the people will confide with a degree of confidence that no order will be issued but what is calculated to promote the interest and happiness of the State. Unless the Council is formd of such charactors, or the body is not perfectly constitutional, the people will be apt to cavil and by artfully insinuating that measures are dictated by private interest, defeat the good intention of every order issued.

To attempt to regulate the disorders prevailing in the State by constitutional and legal modes of Government will be tedious and ineffectual. The people cannot be got together to form a constitutional body and besides their deliberations will be too slow for the critical situation of this Country, and the emergencies of war are so numerous and various that a Council can adopt measures to the State affairs better than a constitutional power who are not at liberty to depart from the modes and forms prescribed to them.

Tho this Council cannot be considered a constitutional body, yet there should be some form in their election and as many of the people have a voice in the choice as can conveniently be convened together. I mentioned this mode to Mr Clay who left this a few days ago with an intention to consult the people of Georgia upon the measure.[2]

The Gentlemen solicited for a detachment of Continental troops to be made for the protection of your State. At present it is impossible for me to comply with your wishes, nor would it promote ultimately the security of your State. You may rely upon my giving you all the protection in my power; but the people must take measures not only for their own internal security but to aid the Continental Army should it be necessary. Two evils which prevail in all the Southern States should be checked as soon as possible, plundering and private murders. The Country groans under those two evils and if they continue to rage as they have done, it will soon be depopulated. Appointing a Councel, raising a body of regular State troops, forming, arming, and arranging the Militia generally and destroying the enemies fortifications should be the first objects of the peoples attention. I am Sir your Most Obed[t] humble Ser   N GREENE

ADfS (NcD).

1. As seen in his letter to Joseph Clay of 24 July, below, events in Europe led NG to change his mind and call for the election of a legislature. Voting took place in early August. (Coleman, *Revolution in Georgia*, p. 161; on the developments in Europe, see note at Sharpe to NG, 28 May, above).

2. See NG to Clay, 9 June, above.

*   *   *

¶ [FROM JOSEPH CARLETON, SECRETARY OF THE BOARD OF WAR, Philadelphia, 13 June 1781. Sends an extract from the minutes of a meeting of this date, in which the board decided to send copies of the "regulations of the Ordnance Department" to NG, the Marquis de Lafayette, and Baron Steuben.[1] ADS (MiU-C) 1 p.]

1. Congress had adopted the regulations governing the ordnance department in February 1779. (*JCC*, 13: 200–206) The board no doubt sent the copies because Steuben had improperly named John Pryor to be commissary general of military stores for the Southern Department. Under the regulations, the post to which Pryor was appointed was that of a deputy commissary general. As seen in his letter to Pryor of 15 June, below, NG had correctly anticipated that the board would disallow the appointment because of Steuben's error.

¶ [FROM GENERAL THOMAS SUMTER, Ancrum's, S.C., 13 June 1781. Acknowledges NG's two letters of 10 June. Has received intelligence that Col. [John] Doyle marched toward Dorchester five days ago with a large party, intending, some think, to "Interrup" NG's operations.[1] There are 300 of the new levies from Ireland at Monck's Corner; they came with the "late Reinforcement," which reportedly numbered 600 men.[2] Gen. [Francis] Marion is moving "up" from Georgetown but reportedly has few men and little ammunition; Marion himself, though, has not informed Sumter of "any Such Circumstance."[3] Col. [William] Harden is "Not to the Southward" and reportedly has gone to Augusta, Ga.[4] Sumter's command "at this place" will move "this Morning." The Charleston newspaper says peace is likely "to take place immediately."[5] Sumter has reports of "Two Very Considerable Scirmishes" in Virginia, in which the American troops "had the advantage."[6] ALS (MiU-C) 2 pp.]

1. Doyle's troops joined a detachment commanded by Lord Rawdon, which was marching to lift the siege of Ninety Six. (See note at NG to Clarke, 12 June, above.)

2. On the "late Reinforcement," see note at NG to Lafayette, 9 June, above. As seen in a note at NG's first letter of 10 June, above, Sumter's estimate of their numbers was low.

3. By the time Sumter wrote NG on 15 June, below, he had heard from Marion, who confirmed the reports given here.

4. Andrew Pickens and Henry Lee acknowledged Col. William Harden's service at the siege of Augusta in their letter to NG of 5 June, above.

5. Sumter was presumably referring to an extract of a letter printed in the *Royal Gazette* of Charleston in its 6 June issue. The letter, dated 12 March, from an unnamed London correspondent, reported that the rulers of Russia and Austria had "offered their mediation to bring about a general peace," which the English government had "declared its readiness to accept." The writer added that the French and Dutch would be forced to "come in" to the peace effort as well. (For more on the mediation effort, which failed, see note at Sharpe to NG, 28 May, above.)

6. The reports concerning the skirmishes in Virginia were false.

¶ [FROM GENERAL THOMAS SUMTER, Ancrum's, S.C., 13 June 1781. Has received "certain" accounts that an enemy detachment, "judged to be about one thousand horse and foot," was at Four Holes Bridge "yesterday forenoon."[1] Sumter has sent for Gen. [Francis] Marion and has recalled the troops "that had marched" from his own brigade.[2] If the enemy are heading toward Ninety Six, Sumter will harrass them as much as he can; if their detachment numbers only 1,000 men, however, "it is not probable they mean to proceed much farther." Tr (Draper Manuscripts: WHi) 1 p.]

1. Lord Rawdon's detachment numbered more than 2,000 men. (See note at NG to Clarke, 12 June, above.)

2. In his letter to NG of 15 June, below, Sumter discussed his orders to Marion.

¶ [FROM GENERAL THOMAS SUMTER, [Ancrum's, S.C.], 13 June 1781. Has further accounts of the enemy "advancing & Giving out that they are Going for Ninty Six." Sumter believes they must be near Orangeburg. Has received various reports of the size of the detachment: Loyalists say 4,000 men, Whigs 1,200 to 1,500.[1] Expects to know better "to Morrow." Suggests that NG call out the militia regiments of Colonels [William] Brandon, "Keerseys" [i.e., Joseph Kershaw?], and [John] Thomas. Adds: "it is likely a parcel of Good Riflemen Might be got out in time."[2] Tr (Nightingale Transcript: ScHi) 1 p.]

1. As seen at NG to Clarke, 12 June, above, Lord Rawdon's detachment numbered just over 2,000 men.

2. In his reply of 15 June, below, NG said he had called out the regiments.

¶ [TO GENERAL ANDREW PICKENS. From Camp before Ninety Six, S.C., 14 June 1781. NG "This moment" has received intelligence from Gen. [Thomas] Sumter that the enemy are at Orangeburg, on their way to relieve Ninety Six. Pickens should collect all the force he can and join NG, sending word to Col. Elijah Clarke and "Col Jackson [Maj. James Jackson]" at Augusta to also march to NG's army. There is no time to lose, as the enemy were within 120 miles of

Ninety Six "day before yesterday." NG wants to fight them before they get "too near." Wants to hear from Pickens "immediately."[1] ADfS (MiU-C) 2 pp.]

1. As seen in NG's first letter to Sumter of 17 June, below, Pickens himself had joined NG by then, and part of his militia force was expected to reach camp that night.

¶ [MAJOR ICHABOD BURNET TO CAPTAIN JOHN RUDULPH. From [Camp before Ninety Six, S.C., 14 June 1781].[1] Information has arrived "This moment" that an enemy detachment was at Orangeburg on 12 June, marching toward Ninety Six. Rudulph should immediately join Col. William Washington on the "ridge road" leading from Orangeburg to Ninety Six and "act with" him.[2] Emphasizes the need for immediate action. ADfS (MiU-C) 1 p.]

1. The date was taken from the docketing, the place from other correspondence of this date.

2. See also NG's orders to Washington of this date, immediately below. For the location of the "ridge road," see map 2.

¶ [TO COLONEL WILLIAM WASHINGTON.[1] Camp [before Ninety Six, S.C.], 14 June 1781. NG has information that the enemy were at Orangeburg on 12 June, moving "in force" toward Ninety Six. Washington is to march "across the Country" to the "ridge road" and act with Gen. [Thomas] Sumter and the cavalry of Lee's Legion to "harrass" the enemy and "impede their march."[2] He should keep NG "constantly advised" of the enemy's situation. The legion cavalry has orders to act with Washington, and its commander will inform Washington of his route and situation.[3] The "importance" of Washington placing himself "between this post and the enemy" will induce him to make "every exertion." Df (MiU-C) 1 p.]

1. William Washington (1752–1810), a Virginian and a relative of George Washington's, commanded the Third Continental Dragoons. Henry Lee described him as six feet tall, "broad, strong, and corpulent," possessed of a "good humored . . . generous, and friendly" disposition. Washington, according to Lee, did not choose to "bestow much time or application" to the "cultivation" of the "mind." Lee considered him a "Bold, collected, and persevering" officer, "better fitted for the field of battle than for the drudgery of camp and the watchfulness of preparation." (Lee, *Memoirs*, 1: 402–3) Washington had seen considerable service in the North in the first years of the war. Sent to the South in 1779, he had skirmished with Col. Banastre Tarleton's troops in the early phases of the defense of Charleston. Following defeats at Monck's Corner and Lenud's Ferry in the spring of 1780, he withdrew to North Carolina to recruit and re-equip his force; he was not actively involved again in the Southern Army's campaigns until after the battle of Camden. (Ibid., pp. 399–401; Boatner, *Encyc.*) In the months after NG took command of the army, Washington had won victories at Rugeley's Plantation and at Hammond's Store. He had also played important roles in the battle of Cowpens, the race to the Dan, and the engagements at Guilford Court House and Hobkirk's Hill. Later, in September 1781, he was wounded and captured at the battle of Eutaw Springs and sent to Charleston as a prisoner. He met his future wife there and remained in South Carolina after the war. (Lee, *Memoirs*, 1: 401–2) Washington served in the South Carolina legislature but is said to have refused to run for governor "because he could not make a speech." (Boatner, *Encyc.*)

2. As seen in Burnet to Rudulph, immediately above, the "ridge road" ran between Orangeburg and Ninety Six. Rudulph was commanding the cavalry of Lee's Legion.

3. See Burnet to Rudulph, immediately above.

¶ [FROM COLONEL JAMES MAYSON, "Glasgow," S.C., 14 June 1781. Mayson has been subjected to "Callumny." His accusers have "wickedly and unjustly asperced" his reputation "as a prelude to posses them selves" of his property. He has been in public service twenty-three years and has always been his "Countrys friend and soldier." If he has committed any error, it was "through Ignorance and not Intention"; he tried to protect his family and "not to split on the rock" of British "soverenty," where he was "placed" as the result of "Trechery and averice," not "Inclination."[1] If NG considers Mayson a "supernumary Lt Continental Col[onel]"—which Mayson does not—NG must determine the "mode of Investigation." If NG views Mayson in another light, he might suggest a "Tribunal" in which Mayson could confront his accusers.[2] ALS (MiU-C) 1 p.]

1. The nature of the charges against Mayson are not known.
2. See NG to Mayson, 11 June, above, which appears to anticipate this request.

*   *   *

From General Thomas Sumter

Dr Sir   Congaree [S.C.] 14th June 1781

I this Moment Received the inclosed Letter & have Reason to think the Information Good: as I Sent men to View the enemy Wherever they Might be. They have Not Returnd Which Induces me to believe there is None Near, if they Shoud advance you may Rely upon having the Earliest Notice thereof. I Shall halt the Troops which was Marching to fall in the 96 Road ahead of the enemy, except a party of Two hundred horse which I Mean to Detach upon the Same Road but by a Difrent Route, Who Will if the Enemy are Moving fall in with them[,] if they are Not, Will Serve to Disperse the Tories Mentioned by Co^l Myddelton. If the last accounts of the enemy prove to be facts, I Shall this evening pursue my former Intention, that is to March Downwards with My Whole force Which is about Six hundred horse & Two hundred foot. I beg you Will Not be apprehensive that I May be out of place, by this Movement, I Shall make a point of being with you in time if the enemy Shoud advance.[1] I Do Not Know Genl Marions Strength. I Rather think him but Weak & badly armd and Very little ammunition. I have Cald for a State of his Brigade.[2] Co^l Washington is here & Woud have followed the Troops I had ordered to fall in front of the enemy if needfull.[3] I am Dr Sir with the Greatest Respect Your Most obdt Hble Servt.   THO^s SUMTER

NB I have Not a Sheet of Paper. If you Coud Spare a little & woud have it Sent by the bearer I Should be extreemly obliged by it.[4]   T.S.

ALS (MiU-C).

1. The enclosed letter from Col. Charles Myddelton mistakenly reported that Lord Rawdon's detachment had not moved above Four Holes and that only a small party of Loyalists was marching toward Orangeburg. (A transcript of the Myddelton letter is in the Draper Microfilm.) Myddelton's erroneous information helped convince Sumter to cancel his march. Another factor in Sumter's decision was his concern that Rawdon's

actual objective might be Friday's Ferry/Ft. Granby, where Sumter had his headquarters, a supply depot, and an armory. Sumter remained at Ft. Granby until 15 June, when he learned that Rawdon had passed Orangeburg on the road to Ninety Six. He then began to follow Rawdon, but at a pace that allowed the militia units he had ordered to Granby to overtake him. Sumter never gained Rawdon's front, and NG was thus unable to face Rawdon's detachment before it could lift the siege of Ninety Six. (Johnson, *Greene*, 2: 153)

2. Gen. Francis Marion reported his situation, but not his numbers, to NG in a letter of 16 June, below.

3. See NG's orders to William Washington, this date, above.

4. NG sent paper on 17 June. (See NG to Sumter, first letter of 17 June, below.)

* . * *

¶ [GENERAL GREENE'S ORDERS, Camp before Ninety Six, S.C., 15 June 1781. Orders two lieutenants to "Superintend the Fatigue parties in the Mines."[1] Lamar Orderly Book (OClWHi) 1 p.]

1. The "Mines" consisted of a tunnel that was being dug under the enemy's fortifications. (See note at NG to Sumter, first letter of 10 June, above.)

¶ [CAPTAIN WILLIAM PIERCE, JR., TO MAJOR GEORGE DAVIDSON. From before Ninety Six, S.C., 15 June 1781. NG has received Davidson's letter of 11 April and gives him permission to use as many twelve-month levies and militiamen in the factory as he can. If the army has to march, it will need as many shoes as Davidson can produce. ADfS (MiU-C) 1 p.]

¶ [TO CAPTAIN JOHN PRYOR. From Camp before Ninety Six, S.C., [15] June 1781.[1] Has his letters of 11 and 30 May. Does not think the Board of War will confirm Pryor as "Commisary General of Military Stores of the Southern department" because the appointment should have been as "deputy for the Southern department" under the rules governing the Ordnance department. If there is no other objection to the appointment, NG assumes that Pryor will be willing to serve as deputy.[2] Is aware of the "dispute" between Pryor and Mr. [Nathaniel] Irish, who claims that he already holds the post to which Pryor was named. If Irish is right, the Board of War may confirm him and reject Pryor's appointment, although in NG's opinion Irish is only a "Capt of Artificers."[3] NG approves Pryor's appointment of a field deputy for the Marquis [de Lafayette's] force but had already appointed Maj. [John] Mazaret as deputy for his own army before Pryor's letter arrived.[4] The Board of War will also decide this matter, but NG is afraid that the young gentleman whom Pryor named will be disappointed.[5] Adds that Mazaret is "a good attentive officer," who should "prove a faithful and able assistant." Pryor's duties will be fatiguing, but NG hopes his "activity and resource" will overcome every difficulty. Gives a brief summary of conditions in South Carolina and Georgia. ADfS (MiU-C) 4 pp.]

1. The "14th" is crossed out in the draft, and the docketing gives 15 June as the date of this letter. Pryor acknowledged receiving NG's letter of the 15th when he replied on 25 July, below.

2. As noted at Pryor to NG, 11 May, above, the Board of War had already made its own appointment of a deputy commissary general of military stores.

3. On the "dispute," see notes at Pryor to NG, 30 May, above. Irish stated his claim to the appointment in his letter to NG of 20 May, above.

4. NG announced Mazaret's appointment in his Orders of 11 May, above.

5. In his letter of 25 July, below, Pryor discussed the accommodation he had reached with John Martin after learning that NG had given the job to Mazaret.

¶ [TO DOCTOR WILLIAM READ. From Camp before Ninety Six, 15 June 1781. NG has Read's letter of 4 June and is "happy" that the hospital "under all its difficulties is in so fair a way." He regrets that he cannot "attend more to its wants and convenience" because of "our wretched situation." Df (MiU-C) 1 p.]

* * *

To General Thomas Sumter

Dear Sir　　Head Quarters [before Ninety Six, S.C.] June 15th 1781.
I am favoured with your letters of the 13th and 14th.

I cannot persuade myself yet that the enemy mean to pay a visit to this place. If they attempt it and we can collect our force it may prove difficult for them to get forward or backward.[1] Keep in front of the enemy that we may have an opportunity to fight them with our collective strength.[2] Equip and arrange as many of the Militia as you can. Those Regts you mention are ordered out and I expect Genl [Andrew] Pickens will be at the head of the Militia of this quarter.[3] I am Dear Sir Your Most Obedient Humble Servant　　NATH GREENE

LS (Sumter Papers: DLC).

1. The copyist originally wrote "cannot collect" and then apparently tried to obliterate the "not."

2. As noted at his letter to NG of 14 June, above, Sumter misread Lord Rawdon's intentions and allowed Rawdon's detachment to pass him.

3. In his third letter to NG of 13 June, above, Sumter had suggested that NG call out three regiments of Sumter's brigade.

* * *

¶ [TO COLONEL JAMES WOOD. From Camp before Ninety Six, S.C., 15 June 1781. NG received Wood's letter of 2 May and has sent Col. [Nisbet] Balfour a copy of the portion concerning Dr. [David] Olyphant.[1] Has not heard from Balfour but hopes the "determination of Congress will produce the desired effect."[2] Df (MiU-C) 1 p.]

1. See NG to Balfour, 4 June, above.

2. In his reply of 12 June, above, Balfour said that Olyphant would be released from captivity.

¶ [FROM LIEUTENANT JOHN MCDOWELL,[1] "Camp Ninety Six," S.C., 15 June 1781. Wants to resign his commission. Has been troubled for two years with a cough, which "is likely to turn Consumtive," and he is now "unfit for duty." A number of officers have lately joined "this Detachmt."[2] ALS (MiU-C) 2 pp.]

1. Below his signature, McDowell noted that he was in "Colo Hawes Battal[ion]." Samuel Hawes commanded one of the of the Virginia Continental regiments serving with NG.

2. NG's reply has not been found.

¶ [FROM GENERAL THOMAS SUMTER, "⟨Palmer's⟩, Near the Congaree," S.C., [15] June 1781.[1] The enemy is "Still advancing." A party of their dragoons was at Orangeburg "yesterday," and their infantry was "a few M[i]les back." Sumter finds their movement "Very Singuler, if 96 Shoud be their Destination, Not only because they March Very Slow, but Detaches parties. Some of which it is Lightly [i.e., likely] are Not to be Cald in, one of three hundred Said to be Gone to Neilsons Ferry." Sumter is having trouble learning the strength of the enemy detachments and even their whereabouts because the country is "very open" and their cavalry patrol "at a Great Distance" from the column. Gen. [Francis] Marion's estimate, which is "uncertain," is that "their Reinforcement" numbers nearly 2,000 men.[2] Marion is north of the Santee River, trying to collect more men to bolster his small force. Sumter has given him "positive orders" to march with the troops he now has and try to collect more on the way.[3] Marion is out of ammunition; Sumter has none to spare and asks if NG can send Marion a supply.[4] Marion also reports that "a Detachment of three hundred was going to George Town."[5] Sumter has informed Col. [William] Washington of the enemy's movements but has heard nothing of Col. [Henry] Lee.[6] Sumter will do all he can to "Retard the enemys March" and hopes that NG can finish his "business" without interruption, "as it is yet uncertain What the enemes Views are."[7] He received NG's letter of 12 June and has written NG three times "on & Since that Date"; in one letter, Sumter reported that his force numbered 800 men.[8] ALS (MiU-C) 1 p.]

1. The ALS has several small holes in it, and a few words and parts of words are missing, including the name of the plantation from which Sumter wrote and the exact date. A Draper transcript of the letter gives the plantation name as "Palmer's" and the date as the "13th." (WHi) The date on the transcript is probably wrong, however. In his first letter to Sumter of 17 June, below, NG acknowledged receipt of a letter from Sumter of the 15th and then addressed the subjects that Sumter raised here. For that reason, the editors have assigned the date of 15 June to this letter.

2. As seen at NG to Clark, 12 June, above, Marion's estimate was very close to the number in Rawdon's detachment.

3. According to Marion's biographer, Sumter's instructions to Marion "fluctuated between the insistent and the indecisive"; Sumter's "positive" order of 13 June to march was followed the next day by a letter advising Marion to halt until British plans were better known. (Rankin, *Swamp Fox*, p. 216; see also note at Pierce to Sumter, 12 June, above.)

4. In his first letter to Sumter of 17 June, below, NG agreed to send ammunition.

5. Marion did not mention this detachment when he wrote NG on 16 June, below.

6. NG had ordered Washington and the cavalry of Lee's Legion to cooperate with Sumter. (See NG to Sumter, second letter of 10 June, above.) As seen at NG to Sumter, first letter of 17 June, below, Lee's cavalry, which was under the command of Capt. John Rudulph, was still in the Ninety Six area because of "a mistake" in orders.

7. The "business" was NG's siege of Ninety Six.

8. Sumter had written NG three letters on 13 June and one on the 14th, all above; he reported the strength of his force in the letter of 14 June.

¶ [FROM LIEUTENANT WILLIAM EVANS, "Camp [before Ninety Six, S.C.]," 16 June 1781.[1] As his arrest has only been suspended, Evans wants a court of inquiry to resolve the charges against him, which resulted from the "total rout" of a party he commanded on the siege lines.[2] Firing from an unseen American party in their rear caused his men to believe that part of the enemy force was behind them—"a circumstance that seldom fails to confuse Troops." Evans, who ran toward the rear in an attempt to "rally the men," believes his conduct was correct and his intention good. Wishes to be cleared by a court of inquiry as soon as possible.[3] ALS (MiU-C) 3 pp.]

1. Evans served in the Second Virginia Continental Regiment. (See NG's Orders of 4 July, below.)

2. The enemy garrison at Ninety Six was said to have made nightly sallies. (NG to Huntington, 9 June, above) The date of the incident could have been 22 May, however, when an American fatigue party was overwhelmed and sustained a number of casualties. (See note at NG to Huntington, 20 June, below.)

3. For the disposition of Evans's case, see NG's Orders of 4 July.

¶ [FROM GENERAL FRANCIS MARION, "Rocks Plant[n] S[t] Johns," S.C., 16 June 1781. He just received NG's letter of 10 June. On orders from Gen. [Thomas] Sumter, he advanced "thus far" on his way to join Sumter, bringing only his mounted troops because he expected to "be wanted in hast." On 14 June, he received notice from Sumter to halt "untill further Orders." Marion fears that if he leaves "this part of the country," the enemy will destroy all the provisions south of the Santee River. That is the only available supply "(except Waccamaw)" until the new crops are harvested. Has sent Col. Peter Horry to "Quell" the Loyalists on the Pee Dee and will send Maj. [Hezekiah] Maham to disperse a party of Loyalists that has collected at Four Holes. Maham will also push down to the Quarter House and attack a small guard there and at Goose Creek. The enemy has 400 "new raised Troops" at Monck's Corner.[1] Maham skirmished with some "horse men" near there, "without Effect." If Marion can remain where he is and obtain some ammunition, he can keep the enemy party at Monck's Corner "so close in, that they will not be Able to get any Subsistance from the Country." They now have to bring in provisions from Charleston because Marion has had all the cattle driven away. He is also removing cattle from St. Thomas's Parish and the area near Haddrell's Point. Will wait for orders from NG or Sumter.[2] ALS (MiU-C) 2 pp.]

1. The troops at Monck's Corner were part of the British Third Regiment, one of the units that had recently arrived in Charleston from Cork, Ireland. The flank, or elite, company of that regiment had accompanied Lord Rawdon to Ninety Six. (Paston Gould to Lord Cornwallis, 7 June, PRO 30/11/6)

2. As seen in his letter to NG of 25 June, below, Marion received orders from Sumter to move his detachment to the Congaree area.

¶ [FROM COLONEL THOMAS POLK, Charlotte, N.C., 16 June 1781. Has NG's letter of 11 June and is "truly unhappy" that NG should have involved himself "so anxiously in my promotion." Polk hopes that serving his country will never become an "irksom" duty. However, he would never accept a commission "extorted from a reluctant hand" or "exercise it under a jealous invidious Power ever vigilant to disgrace" him and "ever inventive to find some pretext for the purpose." Needs "a supply of money"; thinks a "prudent distribution" of $20,000 "to the most clamorous & necessitous" of his creditors would produce a "temporary calm."[1] ALS (MiU-C) 1 p.]

1. NG replied on 20 June, below.

*   *   *

From Joseph Reed,
President of the Pennsylvania Council

My dear General   Philad. June 16. 1781.

I am to acknowledge & thank you for three Letters received since you left us[,] two private & one publick.[1] I acknowledge the Justice of your Strictures in part & must rely upon your Friendship to excuse this seeming Inattention in not writing you oftner. I call it seeming because it has not proceeded from Want of Affection and Remembrance but in Truth & Fact from the following Cause. To write you common Occurrencies did not deserve your Time or mine. To write confidentially, & on interesting Particulars has become so hazardous that I could not think of it unless some such Opp^y as the present offered. Dr Fayssioux failed me thro a Mistake having taken Mr Pettit's Letters he thought he had the whole & left Town without my Knowledge tho I had laid out for this Opp^y.[2] We have had in this Quarter the most remarkable Disclosures of private Correspondence that could be imagined. Four Mails ha[ve] been carried into New York this Winter & Spring, & Rivington retails out the Letters weekly. Much publick Dissatisfaction & private Enmity has ensued as you will suppose.[3] My Situation you well know does not admit of my running any Risques of adding to the Number of my publick or personal Enemies & this I assure you has been the only Reason of my Silence. However I think Gov. [John] Rutledge will take Care of himself as well on publick as private Account & therefore I with great Pleasure avail myself of the Opp^y to assure you of my unabated Esteem & my most cordial Wishes for your Health Honour & Happiness. I have long thought that the Partialities of the Southern People which I believe exceed any in the World (the Scotch not exceptd) have kept us in a fatal Blindness as to the real Strength & Resources of their Country. To this, some Successes at the Beginning of the War, brilliant indeed for the Season, have very much contributed: But the Systematical Attack made by Sr Henry Clinton & since pursued with Steadiness shews us the Advantages which that Mode of Warfare will eventually have in Country so thinly inhabited, & when the Spirit or Enthousiasm of the Inhabitants is to supply the Deficiency of solid Battalions & the necessary Apparatus of War. I have ever ascribed the Loss of Charlestown with its numerous Garrison to the Defeat of the British Fleet at Sullivans Island, & by the Repulse of Prevost at that Place in 1779.[4] The other Successes on a smaller Scale have also had their Exaggiration & the Ability of the Country to make effectual Opposition has never been given up till lately. Virginia at this Time affords the most remarkable Instance of Imbecillity & Pride that I believe the World ever exhibited, a few thousand Men march uncontrouled & send forth Detachments to any Part of the Country[;] the fine

Horses which could not be spared for the Cavalry of our own Country have served to mount their Enemies & to enable them to traverse the State in every Direction: But it must be acknowledged they are now come to a Sense of their Weakness & I hope their Folly, in [pouring?] the Strength of their Country into the Wilderness & neglecting the necessary Supplys of Arms & Military Stores, but above all of a systematical well form'd Militia.[5] The Aristocratical Manners of that Country do not agree with a military System which too suddenly raises Men into an Equality of Rank & Sentiment arising from Participation of equal Danger. I am perswaded no Country will ever be well armed which has not a good Militia & have been astonished to find how defective they have been in this particular in all the States to the Southward. Maryland last Year compounded for her Militia by raising a Regiment for the War of the meanest Troops I ever saw collected under the Name of Soldiers.

From your Letter by Mr Ohara the same Spirit still remains which I am exceeding sorry for.[6] It is certain that no State has suffered so little from the Enemy & which on many Accounts could do very handsomely, if so disposed. At present they all seem to lean upon Pennsylvania as well to raise Troops, as to feed the Army, support all the Prisoners & furnish almost every Species of Military Stores. We have now Requistions for about 4000 Men to take the Field & I am not without Ideas of going myself; the helpless Condition of the Southern States excites our Pity & Contempt. Pity for their Distresses & Sufferings & Contempt for their Pride & Imbecillity.

I have often my dear General deplored your Situation, to be placed in a State of Responsibility with so little Means of effecting any Thing decisive. To be at the same Instant beset by the Enemy & Want of every Species is a Condition reserved for American Generals: But it must be your Consolation as it is your Glory that you have conducted yourself so as to draw The Admiration of every one & excite a well ground Confidence in your Abilities that if you cannot preserve the Country it is because it cannot be [preserved?]. I can assure you without Flattery (of which from our long Acquaintance & Friendship you will not suspect me) that you stand very high in publick Esteem. Would to God it would operate in some effectual Support to enable you to close the Scene with final Sucess & Honour. If you will permit me in the Freedom of Friendship I would mention two particulars which some People here carp at; they are so easily corrected that my Regard for you will not let me be quite silent. They insist that you hold the Militia in Contempt & are too much inclined to attribute Failures to them. I do not now recollect particular Instances from which this Infrence is drawn, but such an Idea has taken Place, indeed the Manner in which your Dispatches after the Battle of Guilford describe the Failure compared with that of the Affair before Camden when the Maryland Continentals failed you has added some Force to the Remark.[7] My Sentiments of Militia have been ever pretty much the same but I see plainly that the Avarice & Indolence of the great Body of the People of America will never allow them to support a permanent Force equal to the Defence of the Country & that of course we must give up the Contest or cherish the Militia. The Sucesses which they have obtained to the Northward, at Kings Mountain & elsewhere seem also to give them some meritorus Claims. The Jealousy which has taken Place, especially in this State between the Continental Troops & them very much resembling the Behaviour of the Regulars & our Provincials last War keeps up an Attention to this Point & tho it may be forgivin in the inferior Officers, depend upon it, the Bulk of the Country resent any Indignity attempted towards them.[8] In short at this Time of Day we must say of them as Prior of a Wife, "Be to their Faults a little blind And to their Virtues very kind."[9] I know how natural it is & how difficult to avoid exculpating ones self from supposed Errors by pointing out the real Conduct & Circumstances of Things. It is my own Failing & from which I have suffered more than any other Error in my publick Conduct. After much Experience I find it makes numerous Enemies & carries very little Conviction or Information to People in general who will not give themselves Time to go beyond the Surface of Things. Your private Letters are not allways made a good Use of here, that is, they are shown with too much Freedom so that I have frequently expected to see them in Print. I have often known them copied & handed about with as little Reserve as they would have done a News Paper. This is neither doing you Justice or serving the Publick as you undoubtedly express yourself on those Occasions with a Freedom which you would not do if design'd for the publick Eye. I now refer to private Letters you have wrote to Members of Congress. Besides in the great Hurry of Business, Confusion of March &c it is scarce possible to avoid either in publick or private Dispatches some Inaccuracies. Rivington has been very saucy with you on this Score on your Letter after the Affair of Guilford, tho it appeared to me rather obscure than inaccurate.[10] Congress observe inviolably the Rule of printing Letters as received which I think rather too rigorous as it is almost impossible in certain Circumstances for the most correct Penman wholly to avoid Inaccuracies.

You will naturally wish to have some Estimate from me of our Manners & Principles & a View of our Situation as Ruled & Rulers the former necessarily precedes the Latter. And indeed my dear General I am sorry to be obliged by the all powerful Voice of indisputable Facts to acknowledge that the Independance of the Country seeming to be pretty well established: a Passion & a raging one too for Gain has evidently taken Place of those Considerations which were formerly deemed so honourable & so necessary. Every Attempt to check it produces the vilest Abuse of publick & private Character. The Paper Money has fairly run its Race & Gold & Silver are now the only Medium of Commerce, but will you believe me when I inform you that the Publick can get none of it, No not a shilling, the Merchant[,] the Farmer, the Tradesmen have all closed their Hands. And we are at this Moment in a State of the most shameful Imbecillity tantalized with the Show of Plenty which never was more conspicuous & yet destitute of the Means of procuring the smallest Articles. Not an Ounce of Provision[,] not a single Recruit, not a Particle of military Stores can be procured. The Auri sacra Fames has taken universal Possession & our Legislatures seduced from their Duty by the vile Popularity which every great & good Mind must despise dare not attempt any Thing vigorous.[11] And where Authority ought to supply the Place of Enthusiasm & support private Virtue we behold it dwindled to a Shadow. Congress is not supported by the People, not as our Tories flatter themselves that the Cause is less rever'd or their Persons respected but because dire Necessity has compelled them so often to promise without the Means of Performance & that they have so little in their Disposal. Their Officers are badly paid[,] their Contracts unperformed & every Man of independent Spirit flies from their Service as from a Thankless Bondage. It is a mortifying but not less just Observation that the same Men & the same Authority shall be respected & applauded with a full Purse which is calumniated[,] reprobated & slighted with an empty one. I have ever thought Congress possessed of some of the most estimable & virtuous Characters this or any other Country can boast & that few publick Bodies could have displayed more Ability & Honesty in their arduous Work. Mr Deanes Affairs & his Associates only excepted in which Corruption & Party undoubtedly had too great a Share & which will one Day stamp the Proceedings of that Congress with indelible Infamy.[12] But the Age of Miracles has ceased[.] Congress cannot support Armies, establish the civil Business of a great Empire & conduct a War with one of the greatest Powers on Earth without Means. Poor & destitute, how unjust is it in us to blame them for not doing what they have not Power to do. The present Congress tho not composed of the greatest Men of the Country is much less contaminated with Party than most of their Predecssors & I verily believe if the baneful Influence of New York[,] that hotbed of Calumny & seditious Interference with the Business & Characters of others[,] could be suppressed Congress would soon rise into more Dignity & Consequence but they have Sown the Seeds of eternal Discord between the Southern & the Northern States & those Characters of the Middle who could not be brought to think that every

Vice & Wickedness that can disgrace a People were the Characteris-
ticks of the New England States.[13] General Washington complains of
us all. Engross'd by military Concerns he has not Time or Opp^y to
know the real State of the Country or the Difficulties which environ
Men in civil Life. He will allways deservedly possess a great Splendor
of Character but I am of Opinion it has seen its Meridian. And it is not
improbable he may one Day as we now have Reason complain of
Ingratitude & unkind Return of essential & disinterested Services. The
Affairs of Europe have borne an Aspect generally very favourable,
they do so now, but it seems pretty clear to every observing Character
that our good Ally [i.e., France] means to keep us between Hope &
Despair. The finishing the War in America is so obvious that it is
impossible to miss it by Accident. The Enemy are so confined &
depend so necessarily upon naval Movements that a decisive Superiority for a few Weeks would do the Business. In one Respect they are
right: We are not yet even yet so weaned from Great Brittain as to
afford them the full Benefits of the Alliance. You tell me the Tories are
most numerous with you: I believe I might justly say so of Pennsylvania but they are dastardly cowardly Wretches who confer neither
Credit or Strength on any Cause to which they are attached. Their
Leaders are chiefly Men of great Fortune who first sought that Side as
the safest. The same sordid Spirit & mortified Pride actuates them.
They have neither the Courage nor Ambition which elevates Men to
great Designs & makes them useful to the Cause they espouse. The
New England States have made great Exertions to raise Men but to do
it for the War was impracticable nor have they for temporary Service
had the Success to which they were entitled. Gen. Washingtons Ranks
are thin. Recruiting with us is at an End except for hard Money & large
Bounties neither of which we can compass. However never to despair
of the Commonwealth is the first Duty & Principle of a good Citizen &
with all our Infirmities[,] Failures & even Vices I have no Doubt we
shall be finally safe in the Arms of Independance. Great Brittain cannot stand it much longer, her Exertions now are rather the strong
convulsive Efforts of a Delirium than the fixed & permanent Force of
regular Health & System. But it is our Duty at this Time above all
others to make the most capital Exertions. It seems a universal Opinion & but too probable that she will push a Uti Possedetus & thereby
keep Possession of some of the States till a more favourable Opp^y offers
to recover the whole.[14] This in our Situation would be Ruin & a failure
of the great Object of so much Blood & Treasure. We are too corrupt to
bear a Contact with her & "deliver us from Temptation" was never a
more necessary & proper Prayer. The Southern States in this Respect
would sooner & better serve her Views & I fear Aristocratick Virtue
less likely to support the desirable Opposition than any other. I can

continue to tell you by Way of Digression that you are much more a Favourite with these Gentlemen than when you first went into Command. What a Pity it is that Minds otherwise truly estimable can see Merit with so much Difficulty when separate from the Splendor of Pomp & Fortune.

While I think of it let me beg you to perserve [i.e., preserve] as much as possible regular & authentick Accounts of what has passed & may pass in your Department with a general Sketch of Characters who make any considerable Figure with you. I am about giving som[e] little Essay towards a History of the present Revolution & I would wish to have my Materials as perfect as possible. I think I can give a pretty good Account of the Campaigns in 1775, 1776, 1777 & 1778. Since that Period my Knowledge of military Affairs has been more confind. To the Southward I must depend very much upon you. The little Observation I have made of our own Affairs has destroyed all the Credibility of History: & I am satisfied that one half of what we read & perhaps more is nothing but an agreeable Romance framed according to the Fancy of the Historian & the Materials good or bad which he has accidentally collected. Many a Victory has been gained I firmly believe contrary to the Will & Judgment of the General who has swallowed the undeserved Praise with as little Compunction as if it had been gaind by the Skill of his Maneovres & the full Exertion of his own Talents & Judgment. If I should live to finish what I have begun I shall certainly strip every Jack Daw of his borrowd Plumage, which I can the better do as I have no Pretensions to Plumes of any kind myself, beyond what a Volunteer of subordinate Fame can lay Claim to.[15]

I flatter myself you take so much Interest in my Welfare as to wish to know how I have got along, & I will tell you in a few Words. Every Artifice has been used by the implacable Faction which agitates Pennsylvania to ruin my Peace, destroy my Character, lessen my Influences & embarass my Administration.[16] Having given them the Credit of Industry I can neither applaud their Talents, approve their Morals, or say any Thing favorable of their Designs[.] I have been alternately the Subject of gross Abuse & extravagant Panegyrick; I deserve neither[.] I am an honest servant of my Country but I know I have made many Mistakes in which my Head not my Heart was to blame. At my Age it was unpardonable to expect that Honesty & disinterstedness, a sincere Regard to the publick Interests & very little to private should lull the Monster Envy & that a wicked mercenary Sett of Men should admire or approve what they could never imitate. The vain Task of pleasing all because I wish'd to serve all I have now given over & have learn'd to be content with the Approbation of my own Mind which I have never yet lost & the Popularity which *follows*, for I certainly never shall go in Pursuit of it. The Artifices of my Enemies have succeeded pretty well in setting the Officers of the Pennsylvania Line against me: It was my ill Fortune to be called to suppress a Mutiny which if they had not occasioned they certainly were unequal to the Task of overruling or conciliating.[17] Gen. [James] Potter & myself settled it in the best Way we could but because without any other Assistance we did not subdue by Force 1500 well armd & disciplined Soldiers we were abused. Gen. [Anthony] Wayne, Col[os] [Richard] Butler & [Walter] Stewart gave Offence to their Brethren by continuing with the Mutineers, they had Address enough to transfer the Illwill to myself & what you may think surprizing is not less true that after reciving for 2 Years the most unbounded Acknowledgm[t] of the Troops (I mean the Officers) I am at this Time perhaps the least respected Governour of the whole 13 States in the Army. I mention these Things to show you how little Dependance is to be put on the Opinions of the Day, & how illy provided he must be for future Contingencies who depends upon the capricous Humour of others: But after all & after repeated gross & illibral Attacks of every Kind from Meanness to Treason[,] for great Pains has been taken to prove me in the Interests of the Enemy[,] I am still in good Health & Spirits not disgusted with the Service of my Country tho ready to give Place to any Man who can serve it better. The Amor Patriae, Laudumque immensa Cupido is as predominant as ever & my first & great Wish is to see the Days of Peace & Independance.[18] The Body of the People continue my Friends because they believe that I am (as I truly am) theirs. Of this I have given the most unequivocal Proof because I have consented to watch for 3 Years that others might sleep, to be poor that they might grow rich. But tis Time I should correct myself. What can the political Feuds of a State, the private or publick Scandal of a single Character be to a General surrounded with every Kind of Difficulty?

I am astonished when I review the Sheets I have wrote, but they will serve to prove what I wishd to convince you of that I neither can neglect or forget you. No my dear General this is impossible[.] Every Day adds to my Regard for you because every Day shows me how few there are [in] The World who really derives or can enjoy the real Pleasures of Friendship. Adieu every kind Wish attends you from Your sincere Friend & Obed. Hbble Serv[t]   JOS: REED
My particular Regards to Col. [Henry] Lee. If I can I will write him per this Opp[y] but as it is uncertain assure him of my continued good Wishes & Esteem. Compliments & Remembrance to [Maj. Ichabod] Burnet and your new Family with others who are Well wishers.[19]

ALS (MiU-C).
    1. NG had written private letters to Reed on 9 January and 18 March (vol. 7: 84; 448) and a public one of 30 March, all above. Reed had probably not yet received NG's letter of 4 May, above.

2. Charles Pettit, writing on 24–27 May, above, had informed NG that Dr. Peter Fayssoux was to leave Philadelphia on 28 May.

3. James Rivington published a Loyalist newspaper in New York City. His printing of intercepted letters, including one in which Washington strongly criticized the commanders of the French expeditionary force, did create "publick Dissatisfaction & private Enmity." (On the Washington letter, see Freeman, *GW*, 5: 278–81; the comments of various delegates to Congress about letters of theirs that were also intercepted and published can be seen in Smith, *Letters*, 16: *passim*.)

4. On the capture of Charleston, S.C., on 12 May 1780, see above, vol. 5: 558n. As seen there, the Southern Army, numbering some 2,650 Continentals and more than 1,000 militia, was captured when the city fell. In 1779, a British fleet and invasion force had been turned back at the entrance to Charleston harbor when they were unable to silence the guns of the American fort on Sullivan's Island. (Boatner, *Encyc.*, pp. 197–205) Although Reed seems to have viewed the episode involving Gen. Augustine Prevost's force as a significant American victory, Prevost's only aim in invading the South Carolina low country from Savannah, Ga., had been to force Benjamin Lincoln, the American commander in the South, to abandon his own attempt at recapturing Augusta, Ga. Prevost had not intended to move against Charleston but had continued to the gates of the city after meeting little resistance. When Lincoln moved his army to protect the South Carolina capital, Prevost returned to his base at Savannah. (For more on the episode, see above, vol. 7: 74n.)

5. The "Wilderness" was George Rogers Clark's campaign in the Old Northwest.

6. Reed was apparently referring to NG's letter to him of 9 January.

7. NG's official report on the battle of Guilford Court House is in his letter to Samuel Huntington of 16 March, above (vol. 7: 433–36); his report on the battle of Hobkirk's Hill, or Camden, is in NG to Huntington, 27 April, above.

8. The "last war" was the French and Indian, or Seven Years' War, in which there was ill-feeling between British regulars and Americans serving in provincial regiments. (Fred Anderson, *A People's Army: Massachusetts Soldiers and Sailors in the Seven Years War* [Chapel Hill: University of North Carolina Press, 1984], p. 25)

9. Reed was paraphrasing two lines from "An English Padlock," a poem by Matthew Prior (1664–1721): "Be to her virtues very kind / Be to her faults a little blind." (*The Literary Works of Matthew Prior*, ed. H. Bunker Wright and Monroe K. Spears, 2 vols. [2d ed., Oxford, England: Clarendon Press, 1971], 1:229).

10. The error was in NG's letter to Washington of 10 March, a copy of which was sent to Congress. (See note at that letter, above [vol. 7, 423n].)

11. "Auri sacra Fames" translates as sacred hunger for gold.

12. On the affair involving Silas Deane, see above, vol. 3: 104–5n.

13. It is not known why Reed held such a low opinion of the New York delegates to Congress. New York, in fact, was unrepresented in Congress between 2 May and 31 July. (Smith, *Letters*, 17, xxii)

14. On the principle of *uti possidetis*, see note at Sharpe to NG, 28 May, above.

15. In printing this letter, Reed's grandson and biographer added a footnote: "Mr. Reed does not seem to have made any further progress in this design, his ill-health at the close of the war no doubt preventing it." (William B. Reed, *Life and Correspondence of Joseph Reed*, 2 vols. [Philadelphia, 1847], 2: 359n)

16. The Pennsylvania elections of October 1780 had left the state's two factions, the Radicals and the Republicans, "almost balanced" and had led to increased factional bickering, in which Reed, as leader of the Radicals, was a frequent participant. (Brunhouse, *Pennsylvania*, pp. 88–120; quote on p. 90)

17. For more on the mutiny of the Pennsylvania Continental line and Reed's role in the settlement, see note at James Madison to NG, 13 January, above (vol. 7: 117–18n).

18. "Amor Patriae, Laudumque immensa Cupido" translates as love of country and boundless desire for commendation.

19. Reed was referring to NG's aides, his military "Family."

From General Thomas Sumter

Dr Sir   Congaree [S.C.] 16th June. 1781

I have this Moment Recieved yours by Capt Linton and at the Same Instant Certain accounts that the enemy are or Rather was Twelve Miles above Orangeburg Last Night.[1] Their Number in all probabillity Near fifteen hundred, Command^d by Lord Rawden, they have a Considerable Number of Cavalry, Said four hundred, & eight field pieces. There is Scarce a Doubt but 96, is the place of their Destination. I am Just Moving upwards have been Detaind for Some men to Join from below; Which are Not yet Come. I will Do every thing in My power to Retard their March.[2] I have Given Co^l Washington Notice of their Movement, & Co^l Lee also who I have Just been informd is in the fork of Saluda & Broad Rivers and May Join the other Troop on their way up with ease.[3] Genl Marion has Crossed the Santee & is Moving up but at a Great Distance and but weak.[4]

The Enemy Take Great pains to Collect the Militia upon their March. They are Not Very Sucessfull.

I have Great hope your business will be Compleated before they arive. I am Dr Sir your most Obedt Hble Servt   THO^s SUMTER

ALS (OMC).

1. The letters carried by Capt. John Linton were probably those of NG and William Pierce to Sumter, both 13 June, above.

2. As noted at Sumter to NG, 14 June, above, Sumter's concern that Rawdon might attack his headquarters at Friday's Ferry had delayed his march; his slow pace when he did move kept him from overtaking the British column. Sumter was likewise unable to join NG in time to prevent the relief of Ninety Six by the British.

3. Lee's cavalry was commanded by Capt. John Rudulph. NG's instructions to him are in Burnet to Rudulph, 14 June, above.

4. Marion reported his whereabouts and situation in his letter to NG of this date, above.

*   *   *

¶ [GENERAL GREENE'S ORDERS, "Camp before 96," S.C., Sunday, 17 June 1781. The North Carolina troops serving with Lee's Legion are to join Capt. [Griffith] McRee. An ensign is appointed for the legion. Lamar Orderly Book (OClWHi) 1 p.]

*   *   *

To Colonel Elijah Clarke

Dear Sir   Camp before 96 [S.C.] June 17th 1781

We have certain information from below, that Lord Rawden is moving up with a considerable body of Men to raise the siege of this place. It is my wish to meet him; and I doubt not of victory if the virtuous

Militia collect and fight with their usual gallantry. Come on then my good friend, and bring Lt Col Jackson with you, with all the good troops you have collected.[1] Let us have a field day; and I doubt not it wi[ll] be glorious. No time is to be lost, [be] here by to morrow evening at farthest. Send me an Express with an account of the numbers you will bring and the time you will be with us.[2] I am sir Your humble Ser

N GREENE

ADfS (MiU-C).

1. NG's letters of this time contain refer to James Jackson sometimes as a major and sometimes as a colonel. (See, for example, NG to Sumter, immediately below, and NG to Pickens, 14 June, above.) As seen in his letter to Georgia's delegates in Congress of 22 June, below, NG had appointed Jackson a colonel in charge of raising a legionary corps; the Georgia state government did not confirm the rank until 21 August. (*Records of Georgia*, 3: 25)

2. Clarke, who was at Augusta, Ga., addressed the questions raised here when he wrote NG on 19 June, below, although he had not received this letter. By "field day," NG meant a battle.

To General Thomas Sumter

Dear Sir   Camp before 96 [S.C.], June 17th 1781.

Your favor of the 15th was delivered me last Evening. As the Enemy continue to advance, and as the late reinforcements by General Marions account are much more considerable than I expected, it is highly probable they mean to raise the Seige here.[1] The tardiness with which they advance may be owing to the difficulty of getting Provisions and means of transportation, knowing that the ridge affords little or no Forage or Provisions of any kind, except Cattle they may be providing a Stock to bring them here.[2] The detachments that are made are perhaps employed in collecting Provisions, forage and Carriages.

Their detaching is rather a proof that they have something extensive in view, and that their force is not inconsiderable.

I wish it could be ascertained what is the amount of the reinforcement that came in the other Day. Try to possess yourself of Prisoners, and learn what Troops are out on this expedition; the names of the Corps, and the commanding Officers.[3]

Captain Rudolph who commands the Cavalry of Lee's Legion was only thirty miles from this last Evening, having delayed his march through a mistake of his orders. He is now ordered to march and join [Col. William] Washington with all possible dispatch.

Ammunition begins to get scarce with us, but I will try to forward a supply of 7 or 8000 Cartridges. By the Bearer we send you some Paper.[4] Let the Militia be constantly galling the Enemy. General [Andrew] Pickens is here, and part of the Militia will be in this Evening, as soon as they arrive he will advance to support you.

I expect also Col° [Elijah] Clarke and Major [James] Jackson with the Georgians to join you.[5] Do not neglect any opportunity to annoy the Enemy, and retard their advance.[6] I am dear Sir Your most ob^t hble serv^t NATH GREENE

ALS (Sumter Papers: DLC).
   1. Sumter had written NG on 15 June, above, that Gen. Francis Marion estimated the enemy's reinforcement at 2,000 men.
   2. As seen in Burnet to Capt. John Rudulph, 14 June, above, NG had anticipated that Lord Rawdon would advance toward Ninety Six on the Ridge Road leading from Orangeburg to Ninety Six.
   3. Before receiving this letter, Sumter sent intelligence that had been obtained from some prisoners. (See Sumter to NG, this date, below.)
   4. In his letters to NG of 14 and 15 June, both above, Sumter had asked for paper for himself and ammunition for Marion.
   5. Neither Clarke nor Jackson joined Sumter.
   6. As noted at Sumter to NG, 14 June, Sumter was unable to overtake Rawdon or slow his march.

To General Thomas Sumter

Dear Sir   Camp before 96 [S.C.] June 17th 1781.
   I am favoured with yours of the 16^h Inst. Where can the enemy have collected such a numerous cavalry as you mention? Certainly they must be Militia Horse.[1] I wrote you so fully this morning and in my former letters that it is unnecessary for me to add. I can only express my wishes to have the Militia constantly employed in galling them as they advance. Send the best account you can in your next the force you will have to oppose the enemy besides your State troops, Col Washington[s] detachment & Lees Cavalry.[2]
   It will be impossible to reduce this place for several days to come. There appears therefore no chance of effecting it's reduction unless we can first beat the enemy.
   Detach a small party round into the enemy's rear to cut off supplies and pick up straglers.[3] I am Dear Sir Your Most Obedient Humble Servant   NATH GREENE

ALS (Sumter Papers: DLC).
   1. In regard to the origin of his "numerous cavalry," Rawdon wrote Lord Cornwallis on 3 June that "some of the principal Inhabitants" of Charleston had "made a Subscription amounting to near Three Thousand Guineas" to equip a "Corps of Dragoons." Realizing that he could only raise such a corps by drafting troops from the infantry, and wanting to retain a connection with South Carolina because of the gift, Rawdon "ordered the Royal S. Carolina Reg^t to be converted into Cavalry." (PRO 30/11/6) He appointed Maj. John Coffin, a Loyalist from Massachusetts, to command the new unit, which numbered about 150 men. (Lambert, *South Carolina Loyalists*, p. 218; McCrady, *S.C in the Revolution*, p. 292)
   2. Sumter sent the estimate in his letter to NG of 18 June, below.
   3. As seen in his letter of 18 June, Sumter sent Col. Charles Myddelton with a force of

200 men to harass Rawdon's rear. Myddelton's command was soon routed, suffering heavy casualties. (See Sumter to NG, first letter of 19 June, below.)

*   *   *

¶ [FROM COLONEL WILLIAM DAVIES, Staunton, Va., 17 June 1781. "The enemy have at length driven us over the mountains; their superiority in cavalry is so great that there is scarcely any security below." The militia "on this side" have turned out in "such numbers" that the enemy have been forced back. "The same extreme," however, now is operating "that has so often injured us."[1] He continues: "At least twice as many militia are taking the field as are necessary; a few weeks over, and the harvest as well as a weariness of campaigning it will thin that army into a very small handful besides the continentals, and then the enemy will return upon us when we shall not be able to oppose them."[2] Lord Cornwallis expected NG to follow him to Virginia. Davies and the people of the state, "Distressed" as they are, "applaud" NG's actions, although "for a while they fondly hoped that [Col. William] Washington or [Col. Henry] Lee might have been spared to their assistance." Baron Steuben has "unfortunately become universally unpopular, and all ranks of people seem to have taken the greatest disgust at him, and carry it to such a length as to talk of applying to Congress for his recall. A very little, however, has raised all this clamour; but at all events his usefulness here is entirely over."[3] Davies wishes to know what supplies NG needs from him.[4] The "old continental money is entirely useless here, and every kind of paper currency will be capitally affected." Virginia must rely on "specific taxes" to support the army; "new money" should probably be used to pay the troops, "if so much can be procured." Davies finds it infinitely difficult to do his duty, more from the "false regulations of the legislature than from any other cause." With judicious management, the "great supplies which the laws bring in" could go further to support the army than the "present arrangements afford any prospect of." Has drawn up a plan, which he will send at the "next opportunity."[5] ALS (MiU-C) 3 pp.]
  1. In a letter of 18 June to Washington, the Marquis de Lafayette reported that there were 2,000 Virginia militiamen in the field. (Idzerda, *Lafayette Papers*, 4: 195) As seen at Lafayette to NG, 21 June, below, Cornwallis's reason for moving back toward the coast was to embark troops to send to New York.
  2. By 1 July, Lafayette complained to Thomas Nelson, the new governor of Virginia, that the militia were leaving in such numbers that he would be unable to counter any future advance by the British. (Idzerda, *Lafayette Papers*, 4: 228–29)
  3. For more about the complaints against Steuben, see Lafayette to NG, 20 June, below.
  4. NG replied on 17 July, below.
  5. If Davies sent his plan for the "establishment of the [Virginia] War Office" to NG, it has not been found. (There is a copy of the plan in a letter of 18 June from Davies to the governor of Virginia. [See *Calendar of Va. State Papers*, 2: 166–69.])

¶ [FROM CAPTAIN NATHANIEL IRISH, Prince Edward Court House, Va., 17 June 1781. Irish expects "soon to go to the Northw^d." Capt. John Pryor, who was appointed commissary general of military stores by Baron Steuben, visited Irish and gave him "many Peremptory and unnecessary Orders." Irish agreed to give up the stores in his care if Pryor obtained an order from "any

Gen[l] Officer" but refused to "serve under" Pryor or "obey him." They quarreled, Pryor "Struck" Irish, and they "fought and was parted." Pryor then went to Gen. [Robert] Lawson, who ordered Irish's arrest "without hearing" his version of events.[1] Irish is now going to the Marquis [de Lafayette] to request a trial. He is confident of acquittal but will not return to duty afterward. He will go to Philadelphia instead to settle his accounts and retire if necessary.[2] Pryor has appointed a field commissary for NG's army despite being told that NG had already named Maj. [John] Mazaret to that post.[3] Pryor's appointee, John Martin, has "care of" the stores that Irish "deliver'd up"; Irish sends a partial return of them.[4] Adds: "There seems to be but little Discretion used or care taken of Stores[,] Men &c." NG may fault Irish for not obeying an officer who was "set" over him, but Irish believes his reasons were "good," although "too tedious to trouble" NG. The chief reason was that serving under Pryor would make Irish "unworthy" of his command and appointment. Presumes that Pryor, who is "Artfull," has friends at camp. Congratulates NG on his successes and hopes NG's name will "ever be terrible" to the enemy. ALS (MiU-C) 2 pp.]

1. Pryor's version of the incident is in his letter to NG of 30 May, above. As noted there, neither Pryor nor Irish was confirmed as commissary of military stores for the Southern Department.

2. There is no record of a court-martial. As seen in Irish to NG, 11 January 1782, below, the Board of War sent Irish back to the Southern Department to oversee the Continental laboratory in Virginia.

3. See NG to Pryor, 15 June, above.

4. The return, dated 30 May, is at MiU-C.

¶ [FROM COLONEL JOSIAH PARKER,[1] Isle of Wight, Va., 17 June 1781. Reports the whereabouts and strength of the Marquis de Lafayette's force, Baron Steuben's detachment, and Lord Cornwallis's army. Forwards a report that [Col. Banastre] Tarleton has crossed the [Appomattox?] river with 1,000 dragoons "to intercept" [Col. Henry] Lee & [Col. William] Washington and "retake" NG's prisoners. Steuben has probably informed NG of this report, but Parker thinks it his duty to do so in case Steuben has not done so or his letters have been intercepted. Tarleton has "so many fine horses tis allmost impossible to say where his career will end."[2] Tarleton has dispersed the Virginia legislature at Charlottesville, but it is now reconvening at Staunton.[3] Gen. [Alexander] Leslie "is strong at Portsmouth."[4] Parker's men, who have just recently "taken the field," are only strong enough to "prevent small depredetations," but he is "geting Them in a pretty way."[5] Not knowing where to find NG, Parker has asked Gen. [Allen] Jones to forward this letter "with all haste." If NG has "leisure," Parker would like to hear from him; sends "Compliments" to his acquaintances.[6] ALS (MiU-C) 1 p.]

1. Parker, a former colonel in the Fifth Virginia Continental Regiment, commanded the militia of Isle of Wight County. (Boyd, *Jefferson Papers*, 4: 72n)

2. Tarleton was accompanying Cornwallis's army as it moved toward Portsmouth. (Tarleton, *Campaigns*, p. 352)

3. For Tarleton's scattering of the Virginia Assembly, see Pryor to NG, 5 June, above.

4. On a separate page, Parker sent a list of the units thought to be at or near Portsmouth under Leslie's command. They contained an estimated 1,580 infantry, 50 dragoons, and an artillery company.

5. Lafayette reported to Washington on 20 July that Parker's detachment numbered 300 men. (Idzerda, *Lafayette Papers*, 4: 256)

6. No reply has been found.

¶ [FROM GENERAL THOMAS SUMTER, "Martins Ferry upon the Saluda River," S.C., 17 June 1781. Has just arrived at "this plaice" and received NG's letter of 15 June. The enemy encamped last night at "the Seader Ponds," halfway between Ft. Granby and Ninety Six. Sumter has taken prisoners, who "prevary in their accounts," but he believes Lord Rawdon's detachment numbers about 1,500 men.[1] They have "one hundred & fifty Good horse, & [another] Two hundred Very indifrent, from three to Nine field pieces, their Teams Very Sorry, the army appears to be Subsisted Cheifly upon beef." Sumter has sent 100 state dragoons and 100 mounted infantry to join Col. [William] Washington, who will have more than 330 men to slow Rawdon's advance.[2] Sumter also sent a party of 200 to harass Rawdon's rear "and thereby weaken" the enemy's front; that will give Washington "Greater advantages."[3] The party sent to the enemy's rear is to join Washington if needed. Sumter has halted to wait for three of his regiments to "Come up." As soon as they arrive, he will march "With all Speed" on NG's "Trail." Gen. [Francis] Marion is also "Coming on." Provisions and forage have been stockpiled for Marion, so Sumter expects him to "be up in three Days." Sumter has left ammunition for Marion but has none for the militiamen who may join him.[4] ALS (MiU-C) 1 p.]

1. Rawdon's detachment numbered slightly more than 2,000 men. (See note at NG to Clarke, 12 June, above.)

2. In a pension application, John Chaney later recalled serving as a militia horseman with Washington in the attempt to slow Rawdon's march: "We [were] always encamping at night, and making fires, with the appearance of intending to remain until morning and fighting, but soon after making our fires, marched on all night (halting to sleep in daytime just after crossing a river or suitable place to gain advantage of ground)." Chaney detailed a skirmish in which Washington's troops were involved. (Dann, *Revolution Remembered*, pp. 230–31) Washington was unable to slow the enemy's march enough to allow NG either to collect a force and fight Rawdon's troops or complete the siege of Ninety Six before they arrived.

3. As seen in Sumter to NG, first letter of 19 June, below, the detachment sent to harass the enemy's rear was defeated and dispersed.

4. On 24 June, NG received word that Marion had advanced only as far as the Congarees. (See NG to Lee, 24 June, below.)

*   *   *

General Greene's Orders

Camp before 96 [S.C.]. Monday 18th June 1781

The General takes great pleasure in acknowledgeing the high Opinion he has of the Gallantry of the Troops engaged in the attack of the Enemies Redoubt.[1]

The judicious and alert behaviour of the Legion and those Commanded by Captain [Robert] Kirkwood, directed by Lt Colonel [Henry] Lee, met with deserved Success. And there is great reason to beleive that the attack on the Star Battery, directed by Lt Coll [Richard] Campbell, would have been equally fortunate, if the brave Lieutenants Duvall [Isaac Duval] and Sellden [Samuel Seldon], had not been unluckily wounded: Their conduct merits the highest Encomiums, and must insure them per[pe]tual Honor.

The loss of the amiable Captain [George] Armstrong, and the Dangerous wound received by the Intrepid Captain [Perry] Benson, are to be regretted: Their names cannot be forgotten, while acts of Heroism, are held in Estimation.

The good conduct of the Officers and Men, who Served the Artillery, at the several Batteries meritted attention. The consummate bravery of all the Troops engaged, and the animated disposition of those that were ready to engage, gain'd them the applause of their freinds, and the respect of their Enemies. The General presents his thanks most Cordially to both Officers and Soldiers, and hopes to give them an earlier opportunity of Reaping the Fruits of their Superior Spirit by an attack in the open Field, upon the Troops now lead on by Lord Rawdon. Major [Henry] Hardman will take Command of the first Maryland Regiment 'till further orders.

The Army will be prepared to change Camp Tomorrow Morning by Sun-rise.

Lamar Orderly Book (OClWHi).

1. Fearing that the reinforcements led by Lord Rawdon would arrive before he could complete the siege of Ninety Six, NG on this date tried and failed to take the post by storm, effectively ending the siege. His report of the assault is in his letter to Samuel Huntington of 20 June, below.

To Colonel John Harris Cruger

Sir   Camp before 96 [S.C.] June 18th 178[1]

The flag officer of yours today represented that our prisoners in your possession are in the greatest distress for want of water.[1] I perswade my self you cannot wish to torture human Nature where it cannot contribute to the safety of your garrison. I have to propose therefore that you permit our prisoners to come out of the garrison, their exchange dependant upon the fate of it. I mean this to include the Militia taken in arms as well as the regular troops. I will account for the prisoners either in the general exchange or send in an equal number as soon as they can be collected. I flatter my self a proposal so reasonable and so consonant to the principles of humanity will meet with a ready compliance. None of the prisoners shall appear in arms until legally exchanged.[2] I am Sir Your humble Ser   N GREENE

ADfS (MiU-C). The second page of the draft contains two small drawings, one apparently a fragment of a topographical sketch of a river or stream and the other a well-drawn profile of an unidentified face. These drawings may have predated the draft, as the text seems to have been written around them.

1. Most of the prisoners had been captured during the attempt to storm Ninety Six. (See NG to Huntington, 20 June, below.)

2. Cruger replied on 19 June, below.

*   *   *

¶ [TO GOVERNOR ABNER NASH OF NORTH CAROLINA. From Camp before Ninety Six, S.C., 18 June 1781. Col. [Stephen] Drayton will give Nash and Gen. [Jethro] Sumner a "more particular" account of affairs "in this quarter" than NG can "communicate by Letter."[1] Df (MiU-C) 1 p.]

1. On Drayton's presence at camp, see NG to Lee, 21 May, above.

¶ [TO BARON STEUBEN. From Camp before Ninety Six, S.C., 18 June 1781. Has Steuben's letters of 15, 18, and 26 May. As NG is "pressed for time," and his aides are "much indisposed," he refers Steuben to "the Marquis" for details of NG's operations.[1] LS (NHi) 1 p.]

1. NG sent detailed reports to the Marquis de Lafayette on 9 June, above, and 23 June, below.

¶ [TO GENERAL JETHRO SUMNER. From [Camp before Ninety Six, S.C., 18 June 1781].[1] Has his letters of 15 and 18 May. Hopes that Sumner has a "large body" of draftees ready for the field. Baron Steuben has promised to send 300 stand of arms to equip them.[2] Changes his earlier orders to Sumner, so that instead of joining the Marquis de Lafayette, who has been reinforced and is now operating at a distance from North Carolina, Sumner's men should now be "equiped and marched" to NG's army.[3] Enemy reinforcements are coming from Charleston "to relieve this post," and Sumner's troops "are essentially necessary to secure the advantages we have gained."[4] Sumner should march via Salisbury and Charlotte, N.C., and join the army "by the nearest route." The troops at Salisbury have been "ordered on," and NG hopes the men who are leaving the army "this day" to escort wagons and prisoners to Salisbury can return with them.[5] "There is a deficiency of Sub-altern Officers with those troops." Df (MiU-C) 1 p.]

1. The place was taken from other letters of 18 June, the date from the docketing.

2. See Steuben to NG, 18 May, above. The arms apparently were never sent. (See Sumner to NG, 24 July, below.)

3. The orders for the North Carolina troops to march to Virginia are in NG's letters to Sumner of 5 and 23 May, both above.

4. Sumner wrote NG on 14 July, below, that he had a force about ready to march.

5. On the troops at Salisbury, see Morris to Armstrong, 25 May, and Armstrong to NG, 12 June, both above.

¶ [FROM COLONEL SAMUEL HAWES,[1] [near Ninety Six, S.C.], 18 June 1781.[2] Encloses a letter that he received from Baron Steuben [not found]. Hawes is now "so weak," and "a return of" his fever would be "so dangerous," that he does not think he can move. Asks that his "waiter" be allowed to stay with him. Is sorry to trouble NG, but his "situation is singularly disagreable." Asks NG to give orders to the waiter, who "will inform" Hawes of them "to night."[3] ALS (MiU-C) 1 p.]

1. As seen in NG to Huntington, 27 April, above, Hawes commanded the Second Virginia Regiment.

2. Hawes's location was deduced from the contents.

3. The army was preparing to march. (See NG's Orders of this date, above.) NG's

reply has not been found, but as seen in the Orders of 19 June, below, Maj. Smith Snead was given temporary command of the regiment.

¶ [FROM THE MARQUIS DE LAFAYETTE, "Allens Creek 22 Miles from Richmond," Va., 18 June 1781. Because of the "precious" nature of the arms and stores "arriving" from Philadelphia, the importance of uniting with Gen. [Anthony] Wayne, and "other strong reasons" mentioned in his "last," Lafayette's "first object" was to check the progress of Lord Cornwallis. The latter had taken a position from which he could either return to the James River or "gain our Northern Communication."[1] Meanwhile, Colonel Tarleton's detachment had moved against Charlottesville, where the legislature was sitting, but Tarleton "was disapointed in his purpose by proper information being given" the lawmakers. Tarleton did capture 150 stand of arms and a "small quantity" of powder.[2] Col. [John Graves] Simcoe, with another enemy detachment, "said to be four Hundred Dragoons and mounted Infantry," attempted to capture the stores at Point of Fork. Baron Steuben, who was there with 500 "new levies and some Militia," received "notice" of Simcoe's approach and removed his men and the stores. Simcoe "hazarded a great deal" and sent "a few Men" across the river to destroy the stores that had been left behind; "our loss was inconsiderable."[3] The main British army, meanwhile, moved to the Point of Fork, intending to strike the magazine at Albemarle Old Court House. Lafayette, having united with Wayne and the Pennsylvanians, "made forced marches" and succeeded in getting "between the Enemy and our Stores." Cornwallis then "returned towards Richmond where he now is."[4] Steuben has orders to "return this way" and join Lafayette.[5] In a postscript, sends intelligence that an enemy fleet of "35 Sail" anchored in Hampton Roads on 17 June; it is thought to be "the Fleet which sailed from hence 13 days ago. Only 4 [vessels] appear to have troops on board."[6] LS (NNPM) 2 pp.]

1. See Lafayette to NG, first letter of 3 June, above.

2. As noted at Lafayette's letter to NG of 3 June, the British claimed to have destroyed a greater number of supplies in Banastre Tarleton's raid on Charlottesville than Lafayette admitted here. Tarleton also claimed to have captured seven members of the Assembly. (Tarleton, *Campaigns*, p. 297) Although Thomas Jefferson, who was just ending his term as governor, was able to avoid capture at his home at Monticello, one historian has written that his flight marked "the lowest point of the war" in Virginia. (Selby, *Revolution in Virginia*, pp. 281–82)

3. In his memoirs, Simcoe gave a detailed account of the raid of 4 June on Point of Fork. (Simcoe, *Military Journal*, pp. 121–28) He described the capture and destruction of quantities of materials that Steuben had left behind and conjectured that Steuben "must have believed that the whole of Earl Cornwallis' army were in pursuit of him, or he would have scarcely abandoned such a quantity." (Ibid., p. 128) In a letter to Washington of this date, Lafayette called Steuben's conduct "Unintelligible" and concluded: "This affair Has Chagrined me But the Inclosed Copy [of this letter to NG] will Show you that I Avoid Reflecting on the Man who ought to Have Better Managed our affairs." (Idzerda, *Lafayette Papers*, 4: 194–95) When he wrote NG on 20 June, below, Lafayette gave a much more candid assessment of Steuben's conduct than he had here, saying: "I did Not choose to Be too Severe in My public letter and Request this May Be private to Yourself."

Steuben, according to one of his biographers, had acted in the belief that it was still his primary duty to march his force of Continentals to NG's army. Having been warned by intelligence reports that he might be trapped between two approaching columns of the enemy, he determined to retreat by marching southward, toward the Carolinas. (Palmer, *Steuben*, pp. 276–80; see also Steuben to NG, 9 June, above.) In his letter to NG of the 20th, Lafayette said: "our loss was not very Considerable But will Show a great deal in Newspapers." The losses at Point of Fork also resulted in an uproar against Steuben in Virginia. Lafayette wrote Washington on this date that "Every man woman and Child" in the state was "Roused Against" Steuben, whom he no longer knew "where to employ . . . without Giving offense." (Idzerda, *Lafayette Papers*, 4: 194) Several members of the state council were said to believe that Steuben should be hanged for his conduct, and the legislature, in a resolution that Lafayette chose to ignore, called on him to investigate the loss of the stores. (Chase, "Steuben," pp. 245–46; on the feelings against Steuben, see also Davies to NG, 17 June, above.)

4. On the uniting of Lafayette's and Wayne's forces, see note at Lafayette to NG, first letter of 3 June. Tarleton, who had been ordered to strike first at the magazines and then try to intercept Steuben, wrote that the expedition "was countermanded" when it was learned "the stores were removed from Albemarle court house, and that the Baron Steuben had made a circuitous move, in order to form a junction with the American army." (Tarleton, *Campaigns*, p. 299)

5. Lafayette wrote NG on 20 June, that Steuben had joined him.

6. For more on the enemy fleet, see Lafayette's letter of 20 June.

¶ [FROM CAPTAIN JOHN RUDULPH, "Edward Larman's 1 Mile from the ridge road from Congree to Agusta between Saluda & the road," S.C., 18 June 1781, 5 P.M. He received NG's letter of 17 June [not found] twelve hours after it was written and marched immediately, proceeding to within twenty-four miles of Orangeburg. A party that he sent to find Col. [William] Washington reported that the enemy had left Orangeburg on the morning of 15 June and marched for Ninety Six via Juniper Springs. Not "satisfy'd" with this information, Rudulph sent another party to locate either Washington or the enemy. He sends a messenger from that party for NG's "examination"; the messenger's report led Rudulph to return "to this place." Rudulph's troops "rode all night to get dow[n] & now almost all day to get back[.] My horses had had water only once & not a mouthful of grain yet." He will cross over to the Saluda road, which runs between Ninety Six and Congaree, to get "between the enemy & 96." Gives the enemy's location and promises to send "every intelligence." Has captured "15 or 18 Arm'd Tories" on their way to join Lord Rawdon. Has heard nothing of Washington or Gen. [Thomas] Sumter. A "man of Coll Middletons who was in action against the enmy this morn⁸" says Washington "left the Congrees yesterday morng."[1] Rudulph is "amaz'd" that he has not heard from Washington "ere this." ALS (MiU-C) 2 pp.]

1. On the action involving Col. Charles Myddelton's detachment, see Sumter to NG, first letter of 19 June, below.

*   *   *

From General Thomas Sumter

6 Miles from Wrights Nearly opposite Millers Ferry [S.C.]

Dr Sir   18th June 1781

I Received your of the 15th this fore Noon. I wrote you yesterday that I had Detached with Co^l [William] Washington Two hundred State horse. Yesterday morning I Detached in the Rear of the enemy upwards of two hundred More: the Whole are under off[ice]^rs that will I hope Make them usefull. The Detachment I Sent in the Rear of the enemy I have [Sent?] to, to Join Co⁻ Washington in fron[t.]¹ I have Wrote to him upon this occasion as he May Imploy them for the best. I am Now Sending of[f] an other Detachment which Will Join him to Night or in the Morning. Have been Detaind to get up Some Detachments of Militia that has been thrown behind in consequence of bad intelligence Respecting the enemies Movements. I have been obliged to order Some force to the Congaree to Repell the Tory prisoners Taken there.²

Having a prisoner Just Taken from the enemy a Sutler formerly Sergᵗ Majʳ Who is intelligent, I Can Now Give you Some account of the Troops which Lord Rawd[on's] army is Composed, i[.]e[.] the Troops he Commanded at Camden, Co⁻ Watsons [John Watson] & Majʳ McArthers [Archibald McArthur] Commands[,] 250 hessians, 6 Companies of New Levies, & a Small Detachment to the 63ᵈ & 7ᵗʰ Regemᵗˢ, about 60 Hessian Horse, 40 Yourk Volunteers, 4 Troops of other horse from 40 to 60 in a Troop, five pieces of Artill'y, & a Number of Tories— Several hundred but Dont Know any thing Near their Number[.] He [i.e, the prisoner] is a Scottish Man and Makes his account as Large as he Can. I have No Doubt the Companies he says is not Very large, he Cant tell the Number of Watsons & McArthers Detachments perhaps 600. I Shall proced with all Dispatch[.] The foot are Very Troublesom, And will push them hard So as to place them in the way of being Servicable. As to My self I Can afford you but Little. I Send an off[ice]ʳ Who I wish to Return to me again. I am Dʳ Sʳ your Most obdt Hble Servt

THOˢ SUMTER

NB I am this moment favoured with yours of 17ᵗʰ[.]³ I Shall have With me but about three hundred Militia, or little upwards about 400 the Whole Chiefly Now Detached, and is acting aginst the enemy as you wish & has been ever since they past Orangeburg. I have ordered out all the Militia of My brigade except the Four Fork Regemᵗ which you Wrote was ordered out.   T S

ALS (MiU-C).

1. As seen in Sumter to NG, first letter of 19 June, below, this detachment, commanded by Col. Charles Myddelton, was ambushed and defeated on 18 June.

2. Sumter referred to prisoners taken at Ft. Granby, the capture of which is reported in Lee to NG, 15 May, above. He presumably meant that Loyalists from the neighborhood of the fort who had been captured and paroled had broken their paroles and would have to be subdued.

3. See NG to Sumter, second letter of 17 June, above.

*   *   *

¶ [GENERAL GREENE'S ORDERS, Camp before Ninety Six, S.C., Tuesday, 19 June 1781. The army will march at 5 P.M.¹ Accurate returns are to be made "this Afternoon" of the killed, wounded, and captured of each corps since

22 May.[2] In After Orders, Maj. Smith Snead will command the Second Virginia Continental Regiment until further orders.[3] Lamar Orderly Book (OCIWHi) 1 p.]

1. The "5" was taken from the Greene Orderly Book, CSmH. In the Lamar book, a blank space was left for the hour.

2. NG enclosed a return of his army's casualties during the siege in his letter to Samuel Huntington of 20 June, below.

3. For background concerning this order, see Hawes to NG, 18 June, above.

¶ [FROM COLONEL ELIJAH CLARKE, Wilkes County, Ga., 19 June 1781. Has NG's letter of 12 June. He and all of the Georgians offer their "Hearty & unfeigned thanks" for the clothing, which has arrived. He was in Augusta when NG's letter arrived and would have marched already except for "the Hurry of Business & being some Distance from home." Will move at the "shortest Notice" but requests permission to leave troops behind to guard the public stores, which otherwise "will draw the Enemys attention," and to man "Strong scouting parties Ranging dayly on the frontiers of this County." The scouts are needed to protect against "Outliers & Indjans," who frequently come "Burning[,] Robing & Destroying the peaceable Inhabitants of this Country whereby Our friends in General is the Greatest Sufferers."[1] Clarke has "heard" that Lord Rawdon is retreating. ALS (NjP) 2 pp.]

1. NG's reply is immediately below.

¶ [TO COLONEL ELIJAH CLARKE. From [Camp before Ninety Six, S.C.], 19 June 1781. Has Clarke's letter "of this day."[1] Lord Rawdon is advancing "to relieve" Ninety Six and was at Little Saluda River "last night," making it necessary to collect "our force as much as possible." Clarke should join Gen. [Andrew] Pickens near Ninety Six, leaving a "sufficient guard for the public stores and the scout" that Clarke mentioned. Df (MiU-C) 1 p.]

1. Clarke's letter is immediately above.

¶ [FROM COLONEL JOHN HARRIS CRUGER, "96," S.C., 19 June 1781. Proposes to exchange the American prisoners he holds for an equal number of British soldiers.[1] Gives his word that the American prisoners have "met with every mark of attention & humanity." Cruger visited them "this morning" and "order'd them Water, which & what else we have for the Comfort of unfortunate Men they shall not want." ALS (MiU-C) 1 p.]

1. NG's reply to this proposal has not been found.

¶ [COLONEL OTHO H. WILLIAMS TO COLONEL JOHN HARRIS CRUGER. From Camp before Ninety Six, S.C., 19 June 1781. NG proposes a truce to allow both armies to bury their dead who "fell yesterday between the Lines and within the Trenches."[1] NG relies on Cruger's "promises" of "Humanity & attention" to the wounded Americans he has captured.[2] ADfS (MiU-C) 1 p.]

1. The action of 18 June is discussed at NG to Huntington, 20 June, below.

2. See Cruger to NG, immediately above. Cruger's reply to Williams is immediately below.

¶ [COLONEL JOHN HARRIS CRUGER TO COLONEL OTHO WILLIAMS, Ninety Six, S.C., 19 June 1781. Assures NG that "every attention" will be paid

to the captured American soldiers. Cruger will send out for burial the bodies of those who were killed "within our Abattis."[1] ALS (MiU-C) 1 p.]
1. See Williams to Cruger, immediately above.

* * *

To General Andrew Pickens

Dear Sir Camp before 96 [S.C.], June 19th '81.

The little opportunity we have had to collect the Militia and the regular force to a point, since I got authentic intelligence that the enemy were moving up in force to raise the seige of this place, will put it out of our power to meet them to advantage for a day or two. But you may give the Inhabitants the strongest assurances that it is my intention to maintain our footing in this State; and I am perswaded if the well affected Inhabitants exert themselves upon this occasion the enemy will be obliged to retire from this quarter and if the activity of the Militia equals my expectation we may render it difficult if not impossible for them to effect it.[1] The reinfor[c]ements the enimy have recievd at Charlestown are inconsiderable and totally inadequate to holding this vast extent of Country.[2] Our horse will be continually hovering round the enemy during their stay in this Neighbourhood and prevent their plundering the Country. I am dear Sir Your Most Obed[t] humble Ser NATH GREENE

ADfS (MiU-C).
1. As seen in the note at NG to Lee, second letter of 25 June, below, Lord Rawdon had already decided to evacuate Ninety Six.
2. On the enemy reinforcements, see note at NG to Clarke, 12 June, above.

* * *

¶ [CAPTAIN WILLIAM PIERCE, JR., TO GENERAL THOMAS SUMTER. From Camp before Ninety Six, S.C., 19 June 1781. NG wants Sumter to halt at "General [Robert] Cunninghams Plantation on the East side of Saluda River" and refresh his troops. If NG's army does not join him there, Sumter will receive further instructions.[1] ALS (Sumter Papers: DLC) 1 p.]
1. See NG's two letters to Sumter of 20 June, below.

* * *

¶ [GENERAL ISAAC HUGER TO COLONEL LEWIS MORRIS, JR., [Mount Necessity, S.C.], 19 June 1781. Acknowledges NG's letter [not found] and sends a letter and a newspaper containing information that NG "may wish to see." Huger is "so sick" that he must leave his "pen for the Bed." Will write NG as "soon as able." ALS (Peter Agnew, Port Washington, N.Y., 1988) 1 p.]

¶ [FROM BARON STEUBEN, Hanover County, Va., "25 Miles from Richmond," 19 June 1781. He did not receive NG's letter of 23 May until 17 June, while he was en route to join the Marquis [de Lafayette]. He arrived at Lafayette's camp "this morning"; has not yet seen Lafayette, who "advanced last Night with the Continental troops about 10 Miles" but is expected to return "this Evening." Forwards a letter from Washington to NG, which Steuben mistakenly opened.[1] Has been told that Cornwallis received dispatches from New York just before he began to "retire" and that thirty-five British vessels have arrived. This intelligence seems to confirm Washington's belief that Cornwallis is to be "called back to defend New York."[2] Col. [Richard K.] Meade sends similar information from near Richmond. All of this is "only conjecture," however. The enemy are at Richmond; Lafayette will "fully" inform NG of their "Operations."[3] No additional recruits have arrived, and Steuben's detachment is reduced to about 420 because they "desert so fast which they will do whilst they can do it with such impunity." Hopes that a change of administration may produce "a Change of Measures." Gen. [Thomas] Nelson is the new governor, and "the Council is materially changed[;] from this we have certainly more to hope than to fear." Is anxious to hear of "the success" of NG's operations. People "here are amused with a fine Tale of a large French Fleet having captured Seven Regiments off Charles Town."[4] In a postscript, adds that he did not receive a letter from NG between 1 and 23 May; asks for copies of any that NG may have written him during that time.[5] LS (MiU-C) 3 pp.]

1. From Steuben's later comments in this letter, he was undoubtedly forwarding Washington to NG, 1 June, above.

2. As seen in the note at Lafayette to NG, 21 June, below, Cornwallis was not recalled.

3. Lafayette wrote NG on 20 June, below.

4. The "tale" was not true.

5. NG's letter to Steuben of 14 May, above, was intercepted by the enemy. As noted there, Lafayette received a copy and sent it to Steuben.

*   *   *

From General Thomas Sumter

Dr Sr Dutch Settlement Near Wrights [S.C.] 19th June 1781

I Wrote you last Night by Capt [David?] Glenn. Since Which I have the Disagreeable account of Co^l Myddeltons being Defeated[.] The persons Who brings the accounts Was in the action & Says Co^l Myddelton fell in with the enemies Rear, about ten oclock yesterday Morn^g, a few Miles above the Junaper and Took an off^r & Several other off^{rs} prisonr, & having Sent them off under a Guard, Drawd up his Men and Wated to Recieve the enemy, Who opposed to his front about 200 Mounted infantry Which he ingaged. At the Same time their Cavalry Charged him in flank & Rear, & Soon broke him to pieces but Not without Considerable oppossision, but for the want of Swords While So Mixed had a Very unequal Chance. I Cannot give any account of the loss but there is Reason to think it was prety Considerable.[1] The Whole Dispearced, the Co^l got off, I Dunte Know the fate of any other off^r.[2] I am Very Sorry to find the post at 96 Cant be Reduced before the approach of the enemy. The Raising the Siege is a Disagreeable Circumstance, but in My oppinion Will not prove So disadvantageous as Some May think it, if you Can avoid a Defeat, they are in a fair way to loose More than they will gain by Saving the Garrison, & all their Suposed advantages may prove Real Injuries. This I think there is every probabillity of. I Mentioned to you that My Malitia force was about three hundred, that is What are arrivd exclusive of the Detachment Left at the Congaree Where there is Nearly an equal Number Left unarmd. Co^l Tates [Samuel Tate] & Two other Regem^{ts} in the lower part of My brigade has Not Joind me on account of the Tories Coming up.[3] This Militia I have out Now are Not Valuable, as it is the first Tour of Duty they have ever been upon with Me & are Deserting fast, upwards of a hundred & fifty has Left me already, at Diferent Times. Several Last Night Some of Which was upon Guard & Carried off Some of the prisoners. I have ordered the other Classes out & if it was Not for harvest being upon hand Shoud before this have had a Considerable force but there is Scarrce a possibillity of Geting Men that has been Much in the field out, untill that is Saved. I have heard nothing of Genl [Francis] Marion for Some days, but upon the Whole if you are Not able to fight the enemy to advantage Just Now, I think you will before long if the Westeren Militia behaive well, & I have No fear of Lord Rawdon over Runing the Country, While your army is Safe.[4] I hope to have the pleasure of Seeing you Soon When I will Indeavour to point out, Some Disadvantages the Enemy Labour under. I have Several Waggon Loads of Corn Meal I Can furnish with if you are in Want for the army.[5] I am D^r S^r your Most obedt Hble Servt   THO^s SUMTER

ALS (MiU-C).

1. Col. Charles Myddelton had commanded a party of some 200 men. (See Sumter to NG, first letter of 18 June, above.) As seen in the letter immediately below, only forty-five of his troops could be collected after they were ambushed on 18 June by enemy cavalry commanded by Maj. John Coffin. The engagement took place near Juniper Springs, in the fork of the Augusta and Ninety Six roads. (McCrady, *S.C. in the Revolution*, p. 298; Gregorie, *Sumter*, p. 166)

2. Myddelton did escape, but four of his officers and twenty or thirty of his men were killed or captured. (Rawdon to Cornwallis, 2 August, PRO 30/11/6)

3. According to Sumter's biographer, the movements of Rawdon's detachment roused "the recently scourged Tories," who began to reorganize. (Gregorie, *Sumter*, p. 165) It was against this general menace, and not any particular Loyalist force, that the regiments of Sumter's brigade were directed.

4. According to Marion's biographer, Marion deliberately failed to write Sumter and attempted instead "to lose himself lest he be forced to make the junction with Sumter." (Rankin, *Swamp Fox*, p. 221) NG apparently did not receive a report of Marion's whereabouts until 24 June. (See NG to Lee, 24 June, below.)

5. NG and Sumter do not seem to have met; in a letter of 23 June, below, NG asked him to forward the cornmeal to the Southern Army.

*   *   *

¶ [**FROM GENERAL THOMAS SUMTER**, "Wrights," S.C., 19 June 1781. His spies report that the enemy dragoons "Recrossed" [the Little Saluda River]. They gathered corn, which they left at a mill and will collect again when they cross "tomorrow."[1] The dragoons "Gave Notice" to the inhabitants to "go in" to see Lord Rawdon, who was "Lying by to day to Receive them"; they "Carreid" several "Country people" to Rawdon's camp. Sumter has small parties watching the movements of the enemy dragoons and the mill where they left the corn, but he has "Detached all the best" of his mounted troops and is able "to Do but Very little." Col. [Charles] Myddelton and Col. "R[ich-ard] Hampton" have returned with forty-five horsemen. "Their Loss Cannt yet be assertained[,] their horses Chiefly Tyered."[2] Sumter will detach all the men he can "to Ly Near the Enemy &c," but his infantry "Complain Much[,] are Very Troublesum & Deserts hourly." An entire regiment has "gone back" because parties of Loyalists are "Coming up the Country." Col. [Thomas] Taylor, who is at "the Congaree," is "Very apprehensive" and believes he will be forced to move the stores. The workmen there have already "Broke up."[3] Sumter, who has received a report of the capture of Ninety Six, is impatient to hear from NG.[4] Believes his estimates of the enemy's force "are perfect"; they have been corroborated by "all the prisoners Taken."[5] Wonders if NG wants him to move toward Broad River "& haisten in the Militia, &c."[6] A number of his horses lack shoes and cannot travel. "In fact I find Myself So encumbered with Rubish that I am Rendered Doubly unhappy, as I Cant Render you that assistance I Coud Wish." He had planned to cross the [Saluda] River "tomor-row," but his "Retreat to Day" will mean he cannot "effect it Now under Two Days."[7] ALS (MiU-C) 2 pp.]

1. For more on the whereabouts of Lord Rawdon's force, see William Washington to NG, immediately below.

2. On the defeat of Myddelton's detachment in the action at Juniper Springs, see note at Sumter to NG, immediately above. As seen there, four of Myddelton's officers and twenty to thirty of his men were killed or captured.

3. The workmen were from the armory that Sumter had established at Ancrum's Plantation in the Congarees. (See Sumter to NG, 22 May, above.)

4. The report was false.

5. Sumter's estimates of Rawdon's force are in his letter to NG of 17 June, above.

6. NG sent Sumter instructions in letters of 20 June, below.

7. As seen in NG to Sumter, 23 June, below, Sumter did not cross the Saluda.

¶ [**FROM COLONEL WILLIAM WASHINGTON**, "Samuel Savages," S.C., 19 June 1781. Reports that the enemy at 10 A.M. were "two Miles this Side of the Little Saluda"; expects them to reach Old Saluda Town "This Evening." Capt. [John] Rudulph, who has just joined Washington and "has had Parties" in the enemy's rear, estimates their force at "near" 2,500 men.[1] ALS (MiU-C) 1 p.]

1. Rudulph commanded the cavalry of Lee's Legion; Rawdon's force at this time numbered 1,700 infantry and 150 cavalry. (Rawdon to Cornwallis, 2 August, PRO 30/11/6)

¶ [**GENERAL GREENE'S ORDERS**, "Camp 5 Miles East of Saluda River," S.C., Wednesday, 20 June 1781. Although "the Siege of 96" has been raised, NG "has great hopes that the measures taken to reduce that post, will Ultimately have their effect." He thanks Col. [Thaddeus] Kosciuszko for "planing and prosecuting the approaches," which "would have gained infallible Success, if time had admited of their being compleated." Also thanks several other individuals and "all the officers of the Line, and of the different Departments"; acknowledges "the Patience and Fortitude of the Troops." Lamar Orderly Book (OClWHi) 2 pp.]

¶ [TO MAJOR THOMAS HILL. From "Camp before 96," S.C., 20 June 1781. Thanks Hill, who is leaving the army; acknowledges his "merit" for remaining at NG's "request" after becoming a "supernumery."[1] ADfS (MiU-C) 2 pp.]
    1. See NG to Hill, 30 May, and Hill to NG, 31 May, both above.

*　　*　　*

To Samuel Huntington, President of the Continental Congress

Sir　　Camp at Little River near Ninety Six [S.C.], June 20th 1781

In my Letter of the 9th I informed your Excellency that the Enemy had received a considerable reinforcement at Charles Town, and that I was apprehensive they would march out and interrupt our operations.[1] On the 11th I got intelligence that they were advancing. I immediately detached all the Cavalry with orders to General Sumter to collect all the force he could and keep in their front, and by every means in his power retard their march. Either from bad intelligence or from the difficulty of collecting his force he permitted the Enemy to pass him at the Congaree before he got his troops in motion: afterwards he found it impracticable to gain their front.[2] It was my intention to have fought them before they arrived at Ninety Six, could I have collected a force sufficient for the purpose. But it is almost impossible to draw the Militia out of one District into another.

We had pushed on our approaches very near to the Enemys Works. Our third parallel was formed round their Abattis. A mine and two approaches were within a few feet of their Ditch. These approaches were directed against the Star Fort which stands upon the left of the Town as we approached it from the Saluda.[3] On the right our approaches were very near the Enemys Redoubt; this was a strong Stockade Fort with two Block Houses in it. These two Works flanked the Town which is picketted in with strong Picketts, a Ditch round the whole, and a Bank raised near the height of a common parapet.[4] Beside these fortifications were several little Flushes in different parts of the Town, and all the Works communicated with each other by covered ways.[5] We had raised several Batteries for Cannon, one upwards of 20 feet high within one hundred and forty yards of the Star Fort to command the Works, and a rifle Battery also within thirty yards to prevent the Enemy from annoying our Workmen. For the last ten

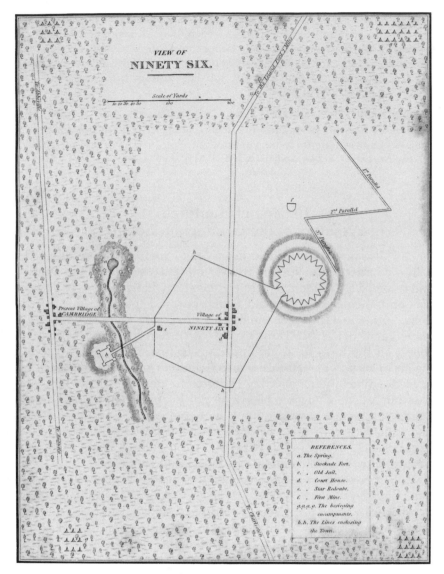

View of Ninety Six
(Reproduced from William Johnson, Life and Correspondence of
Nathanael Greene, *2 vols. [Charleston, S.C., 1822])*

Days not a Man could shew his head but he was immediately shot down, and the firing was almost incessant Day and Night. In this stage of the approaches I found the Enemy so near us that it would be impossible to reduce the place without hazarding a storm; this from the peculiar strength of the place could only be warranted by the success of a partial attempt to make a Lodgment on one of the Curtains of the Star Redoubt, and a vigorous push to carry the right hand Work. The disposition was accordingly formed and the attack made. Lieut' Col° Lee with his Legion Infantry, and Captain [Robert] Kirkwoods light Infantry made the attack on the right, and Lieut' Col° [Richard] Campbell with the first Maryland and the first Virginia Regiments was to have stormed the Star Redoubt, which is their principal Work, and stands upon the left. The parapet of this Work is near twelve feet high and raised with sand Bags near three feet more. Lieut' [Isaac] Duval of the Maryland Line, and Lieut' [Samuel] Selden of the Virginia Line led on the forlorn hope, followed by a party with hooks to pull down the sand Bags, the better to enable them to make the Lodgment. A furious Cannonade preluded the attack. On the right the Enemy were driven out of their Works and our people took possession of it. On the left never was greater bravery exhibited than by the parties led on by Duval and Selden, but they were not so successful. They entered the Enemys Ditch and made every exertion to get down the sand Bags, which from the depth of the Ditch, height of the parapet, and under a galling fire, was rendered very difficult. Finding the Enemy defended their Works with great obstinacy and seeing but little prospect of succeeding without a heavy loss, and the issue doubtful, I ordered the attack to be pushed no further.[6] The behaviour of the Troops on this occasion deserves the highest commendations, both the Officers that entered the Ditch were wounded, and the greater part of their Men were either killed or wounded. I have only to lament that such brave Men fell in an unsuccessful attempt. Captain [George] Armstrong of the first Maryland Regiment was killed, and Captain [Perry] Benson who commanded the Regiment was wounded at the head of the Trenches. In both attacks we had upwards of 40 Men killed and Wounded; the loss was principally at the Star fort and in the Enemys ditch, the other Parties being all under cover. The attack was continued three quarters of an hour, and as the Enemy were greatly exposed to the fire of the Rifle Battery and Artillery they must have suffered greatly. Our Artillery was well served, and I beleive did great execution.[7]

The Troops have undergone incredible hardships during the Seige, and tho' the issue was not successful I hope their exertions will merit the approbation of Congress. Had the Virginia Militia joined us agreable to order our success would have been compleat.[8] The seige has been bloody on both sides from the frequent sallies that the Enemy made. The Garrison behaved with great spirit, and defended themselves with judgment and address. Inclosed is a List of our killed and wounded during the Seige; and I am persuaded the Enemy's are not less.[9]

We continued the Seige untill the Enemy got within a few miles of us[,] having previously sent off all our sick, wounded, and spare Stores. It is mortifying to be obliged to leave a Garrison so near reduced, and I have nothing to console me but a consciousness that nothing was left unattempted that could facilitate its reduction.[10]

It will be my endeavor in our future movements to oblige Lord Rawdon to move down into the lower Country, and to evacuate Ninety Six. But my force is so small that I can hardly flatter myself with the hopes of success. Our movements to the Southward have been attended with very great advantages, and had not this reinforcement arrived so soon, or the Virginia Militia failed me the Manoeuvre would have been crowned with compleat success. Had we not moved this way this Country would have been inevitably lost, and all further exertions would have failed. Besides which the Enemy would have it in their power to detach a greater force from this quarter and hold the Country in subjection, than we have employed to bring about the revolution. But our present situation is truly distressing, and while the Enemy continues to pour in reinforcements, and we are left without support, it is no difficult matter to foresee the issue of the present struggle.

I have once before informed Congress that a very large majority of the People from inclination were in the Enemys interest. My own experience and observation confirms it. In the district of Ninety Six I verily beleive there are five for one against us. The Tories swarm around us and render it extreme difficult to get either forage or subsistance for our Troops. We contend with the Enemy upon such an unequal footing that I have nothing less to expect than disgrace and ruin.[11] But whatever fate may attend our operations I hope Congress will be persuaded that I have spared no pains to render them successful. You know the strengths, constitution, and provision made for this Army, from which you can easily judge of our prospects. In Virginia I hope we shall contend with the Enemy upon a more equal footing, but they will over-run all the southern States unless we can keep up a superior Cavalry. I have left myself exceedingly weak here, to prevent the Enemy's gaining an advantage there. I have the honor to be with great respect Your Excellencys most obedient hble serv[t]

NATH GREENE

LS (PCC, item 155, vol. 2: 175, DNA).

1. See NG to Huntington, second letter of 9 June, above.

2. See NG's first letter to Gen. Thomas Sumter of 10 June, and his first letter to Sumter of 12 June, both above. Historian Edward McCrady, usually a strong defender of Sumter, has conceded that "inaction" by the South Carolinian was a factor in the inability of American forces to impede Rawdon's march to relieve Ninety Six. (McCrady, *S.C. in the Revolution*, p. 296) Sumter feared that Rawdon intended to retake Ft. Granby, where Sumter had established his headquarters, a supply depot, and an armory. He positioned himself to protect Ft. Granby and was unable to gain Rawdon's front. (Rankin, *Swamp Fox*, p. 217) While NG was restrained in his comments about Sumter here, he was less so in private. In a letter written in 1811, Pickens, who himself was critical of Sumter and Marion for not slowing the British advance, recalled: "The night the siege was raised at Ninety Six, I asked Gen'l Green if he knew the cause of their not harassing the enemy, or their not joining the army. He was much irritated, and expressed himself in a manner I had not heard him before or after." (Pickens to Henry Lee, 25 November 1811, Draper Microfilm, VV, 1: 108)

3. The decision to concentrate siege operations against the Star Redoubt was made after NG, his aide Nathaniel Pendleton, and Thaddeus Kosciuszko, the army's chief engineer, closely reconnoitered the post during the night of 22 May, at the beginning of the siege. According to William Johnson, NG's early biographer, they ventured close enough to the enemy's lines to be fired on by sentinels. (Johnson, *Greene*, 2: 143) NG has been criticized for his decision to act against the Star Redoubt. Critics have contended that he should have directed operations against the garrison's water supply, a spring protected by a stockade, which NG mentioned later in this paragraph. (See, for example, Lee, *Memoirs*, 2: 119 and n.) Kosciuszko later justified the decision to act against the Star Fort on the grounds that it was the "Strongest post" in the Ninety Six complex and "Comanded" the remaining fortifications. NG's army, according to Kosciuszko, did not have enough men to undertake siege operations against both the Star Redoubt and the other forts, and according to intelligence that NG had obtained, the British had wells in all their works and could not "be distresed" by cutting off "the spring." (Haiman, *Kosciuszko*, pp. 111–12, 115; the manuscript of Kosciuszko's observations is at MdHi, but several pages have been lost. A comparison of Haiman's printed version with what remains of the manuscript copy shows that Haiman's transcription is accurate.) The same night that he examined the works, NG sent a party to construct a battery, protected by arrow-like works called fléches, close to the enemy's lines; the British attacked and destroyed the battery the following day. British accounts indicate that the battery was constructed a mere seventy yards from the Star Redoubt, demonstrating overconfidence and contempt for the garrison on the part of the Americans. (Mackenzie, *Strictures*, pp. 146–47) William Johnson, who agreed in regard to the distance, maintained that the battery was constructed at a point where an undulation of the ground left it protected from enemy artillery. The battery was thus in a good location to begin the siege lines had it not been too close to the fort, a fact that NG realized after the enemy's sally. (Johnson, *Greene*, 2: 143) According to Kosciuszko, the works were constructed about 150 yards from the redoubt, and only the inexperience of the American troops in siege warfare and the fact that they began digging with the "night far advanced" allowed the enemy's sortie to succeed. (Haiman, *Kosciuszko*, p. 112) Whatever the reason, after losing men and entrenching tools and having the work destroyed, NG ordered the building of a new battery some 300 to 400 yards from the Star Redoubt and behind a ravine, which afforded protection. (Johnson, *Greene*, 2: 143; Haiman, *Kosciuszko*, p. 112; in a note, Haiman gives the different estimates of the distance and their sources.) Protected by this battery, sappers began digging siege lines toward the redoubt in the form of a rough Z. By 6 June, the second parallel, or middle leg of the Z, was completed. (Haiman, *Kosciuszko*, p. 113) Progress was "slow," Kosciuszko wrote, because "the Ground was so hard." (Kosciuszko to Horatio Gates, 29 July 1781, Gates Microfilm) As the siege lines

neared the Star Redoubt, the sappers came under more concentrated and destructive fire from sharpshooters and artillery in the garrison. As seen further along in this paragraph, NG's men constructed elevated artillery batteries and later, on 14 June, a thirty-foot tower for riflemen. (Haiman, *Kosciuszko*, pp. 113–14; Mackenzie, *Strictures*, p. 151, estimated the tower to be forty feet high.) A British account of the siege agrees that the elevated artillery batteries and especially the riflemen in their tower did "great execution" at first. (Mackenzie, *Strictures*, p. 151) Cruger, however, successfully limited the effectiveness of the tower by raising the height of the redoubt's walls with sandbags. By 17 June, when NG decided to assault the redoubt, his men were within six feet of the ditch surrounding the Star Fort. They had burned at least some of the enemy's abatis and had partially completed a tunnel, which was supposed to extend beneath the walls of the redoubt and be used to blast a passageway through them. (Otho H. Williams, "Notes and remarks on the History of the War in S. Carolina," n.d., MdHi; NG to Sumter, 10 June, above.)

4. The advance on the "right" against the stockade fort began on 30 May, when NG's force was augmented by large numbers of militiamen "from the adjacent Countys." (Haiman, *Kosciuszko*, p. 112) Progress against this part of the installation quickened when Lee's Legion arrived at Ninety Six from Augusta, Ga., on 8 June and Henry Lee took command of operations against it. Using cannon brought from Augusta, Lee increased pressure on the stockade and finally forced the enemy to abandon it completely on 17 June with an assault that NG discussed later in this letter. (Mackenzie, *Strictures*, p. 155)

5. In Greene's draft of this letter (MiU-C) the word "flushes" is crossed through and "fletches" is written above it. Both words were variations on fleches, which were simple field works consisting of two breastworks that were dug so as to meet at an angle of not less than 60 degrees. (Scott, *Military Dictionary*)

6. According to a British account that was printed in the Charleston *Royal Gazette* on 27 August, the assault was stopped by means of a counterattack from the redoubt. The author of this account asserted that the fort's defenders had been unable even to lift "their heads above the parapet," which was "effectually commanded" by rifle fire from the Maham tower, "not more than forty yards from the redoubt." Cruger was thus forced "to send out a party and attack them in the ditch." Roderick Mackenzie described this sally as follows: "Two parties . . . issued from the sally port in the rear of the Star, they entered the ditch, divided their men, and advanced, pushing their bayonets till they met each other. This was an effort of gallantry that the Americans could not have expected. General Greene, from one of the advanced batteries, with astonishment beheld two parties, consisting only of thirty men each, sallying into a ditch, charging and carrying every thing before them, though exposed to the fire of a whole army." (Mackenzie, *Strictures*, pp. 159–60)

7. According to Kosciuszko, one American officer and thirty rank and file were killed in the assault. (Haiman, *Kosciuszko*, p. 114; see also NG to Sumter, first letter of this date, below.) During the entire siege, NG's army lost fifty-seven killed, seventy wounded, and twenty missing. ("Return of the Killed, Wounded & Missing during the Siege of Ninety-Six," PCC, item 155, vol. 2: 165, DNA; that total did not include South Carolina militiamen who served with the army during the siege.) In a letter to his brother of 23 June, Otho Williams mentioned that the Maryland brigade had lost one officer killed and another seriously wounded during the siege. Those losses, added to the casualties among Maryland officer from earlier engagements and from incapacitation due to illnesses, left "not officers enough remaining to command the small remnant of our Veteran Troops." (MdHi) British casualties in the assault are not known, but for the entire siege they reportedly numbered twenty-seven killed and fifty-eight wounded. (Boatner, *Encyc.*, p. 808)

Thaddeus Kosciuszko, 1746–1817; oil painting by Jacob Ruys
(Independence National Historical Park Collection)

8. As seen at Jefferson to NG, 30 March, above, Virginia officials had countermanded the order to send 1,500 militia to join NG because of the British invasion of the state.

9. On the casualties suffered by NG's army, see note 7, above. The return that NG enclosed is discussed there.

10. NG was probably correct in saying that the garrison was close to surrendering. Not only had the American siege lines reached the fortress walls, but the attack on 18 June had left the only source of water under American guns. Some water was obtained only

by sending out naked African-Americans, "who brought a scanty supply from within pistol shot of the American pickets, their bodies not being distinguishable in the night from fallen trees, with which the place abounded." (Mackenzie, *Strictures*, p. 156) Despite "extreme" suffering, the garrison held out until Lord Rawdon's relief force arrived on 21 June.

11. The problems that NG's army experienced in obtaining provisions and forage may have resulted from the activities of Gen. Robert Cunningham's mounted Loyalist corps, who, according to William Johnson, had "dispersed themselves in small parties over the country, and lying concealed in the thickets, were ever on the alert to waylay convoys and couriers. This they could do in great safety in the disaffected settlements in that neighbourhood, especially as all the cavalry and mounted infantry of the American army found full employment elsewhere." (Johnson, *Greene*, 2: 141) Despite NG's assertion that the area was heavily and actively Loyalist, Cruger "had little good to say about the loyalists in the vicinity of his post," while Rawdon informed Cornwallis even before he left to relieve Ninety Six that the post could not be maintained. (Lambert, *South Carolina Loyalists*, pp. 172, 173; Rawdon to Cornwallis, 5 June, PRO 30/11/6) As noted at NG to Lee, second letter of 25 June, below, the Loyalists and their families accompanied Cruger when he evacuated Ninety Six in July.

To Colonel Thomas Polk

Dear Sir   Camp at Williams Fort [S.C.] June 20th 1781
Your observations are very just respecting your appointment under a jealous authority watching to take advantage of you.[1] But that objection is not sufficient to excuse you from rendering your further services to your Country in this time of universal distress providing I can bring the Governor to grant you a commision. Should I be so happy I beg you to hold it for my sake if not for his.[2]

As you have the money in charge left with you by Mr [Joseph] Clay, Make up of such sums as you may find necessary. Dont draw for a greater sum than one hundred thousand dollars if you can avoid it. I am dear Sir your Most Ob^d humble S^r   N GREENE

ACyS (NcD).
1. See Polk to NG, 16 June, above.
2. In his letter to Gov. Abner Nash of 9 June, above, NG had criticized the appointment of Col. Francis Lock as commander of North Carolina's Salisbury militia district and described Polk as "the only man in that district who will do justice to the command." NG apparently did not press the matter further and began to direct orders and requests concerning the Salisbury district to Lock. (See, for example, NG to Lock, 21 June, below.)

To General Thomas Sumter

Dear Sir   Head Quarters before 96 [S.C.] June 20th 1781.
I have recieved your Letter of yesterday, and am in hopes the enemy have not persued your troops.[1] It is however an additional reason for collecting our force as early as possible. Should not the enemy move after you I beg you will march up and join us.[2] I am Dear Sir, Your Most Obedient Humble Servant   NATH GREENE

P.S. We make two attempts on the 18th one to escalade their small redoubt, the other to form a lodgement in the parapet of their fort. The form[er] succeeded but we lost about 30 Men in the latter and failed.[3]

LS (Sumter Papers: DLC).
1. See Sumter to NG, first letter of 19 June, above.
2. In the letter immediately below, NG again asked Sumter to join him.
3. On the attempt to storm Ninety Six, see NG to Huntington, this date, above.

* * *

¶ [TO GENERAL THOMAS SUMTER. From "Head Quarters 5 miles on the road from Saluda to the Fort at Williams's," S.C., 20 June 1781. At 8 A.M., the enemy were "three miles below Saluda Old Town on the south side of the river advancing towards Ninety Six." Colonels [William] Washington and [Henry] Lee are "on that side of the river." The enemy party that "crossed below, must have been after forage."[1] NG wants to combine forces "to give the enemy the most effectual opposition"; asks Sumter to join him "near" Williams's.[2] LS (Sumter Papers: DLC) 2 pp.]
1. On the enemy party that had crossed the Saluda River, see Sumter's second letter of 19 June, above.
2. See also NG to Sumter, this date, immediately above. NG changed this order in a letter to Sumter of 23 June, below.

* * *

From the Marquis de Lafayette

Clel Dandriges's 23 miles from Richmond [Va.]
My dear General   20h. June 1781[1]

An official letter writen three days ago Contained Every Intelligence down to that time.[2] I Have But Little to add as a public officer—But as a private friend will make more Intimate Communications. I am affraid Many of My letters to You Have Been Lost. The Last I Have Received Was dated 23 May Before Ninety Six.[3]

Since I wrote You the Ennemy Have Remained at Richmond and I Have formed a jonction With the Baron.[4] The Evening Before Last I Received Information that the Ennemy about 700 in Numbers were Within 12 miles of us. General Müllemberg with the Light Corps was Sent to Cut them off and to Make Sure work of it. The Continental Line Moved down With Unloaded arms. The party proved to Be Tarleton's who I am told Intended to Surprise Müllemberg. But Some Rascals Having Given them Information of our Movement they precipitately Retreated to Richmond.[5]

I am told the transports lately Arrived were Empty. At all events we May Conjecture they Come either to Carry in Newyork Stores or to Carry of[f] a Reinforcement to Newyork.[6] I Have just Now Received Intelligence that the Ennemy were Employed Yesterday in Crossing the River.[7] A letter from General Washington to me informing that if

Newyork was not Reinforced that place Should Be attaked and that if the Bulk of the British efforts was in Virginia He would Come Here with the french and a part of the American Army Has Been taken Near Morristown. This must determine the Ennemy either to throw a Reinforcement [into] Newyork or to Come with all their force in this State.[8] In a word I think the Whole Seat of War, the whole force of the British, that of the french and that of General Washington will Be in Virginia or that we will Have But little to do in this Part of the world. Newyork Had 4500 Regulars and 3000 Militia. They Now are perfectly Acquainted with the General's project Against them.[9] 2000 men who Have Sailed long ago are not Arrived Here.[10] Lord Cornwallis fell down to Richmond where He Burnt Some tobacco which one would think He Had Rather preserved if He was not in Some Hurry.[11] On the other Hand I am of opinion that the Conquest of the Southern States was their Main object—That they thought You Could not take Carolina and No opposition would Be made in Virginia. But peremptory orders May Have Come from Sir Henry Clinton. This as Yet is a Mistery. So Soon as we Can explain I Shall advise you of it. In the Mean time I Cannot Help Being Confidential with you on the Affair of our Stores.

Repeated orders Had Been Given not to Have Any Arms at Charlotte Ville. The Assembly Made a demand of arms for their own defense. State directions Against My knowledge Brought there what they Considered as State property. They Began to Establish a State Laboratory—The whole for fear State Stores Should Mix with Continental ones. The letter advising me of it Came the Very day Tarleton Had gone. Our loss was trifling, the Assembly Had twelve Hours to adjourn to Staunton. But they left the Arms and were No less dilatory in their Motions than they Had formerly Been in their Resolutions.[12]

Repeated orders Had Been given that No Stores Be left At the Point of Fork But what Had Waggons and Boats to transport them. Instead of it they Attracted Stores there, and tho' I Could not get one Single Shoe, it Has Happened that the Ennemy Have found Many Articles— But that of Waggons and Boats Had Been Neglected.

The Baron Had 500 Regular New levies By His own Account and More By Account of others. The whole of the Militia under [Gen. Robert] Lawson Had Been ordered there, Some Had arrived. Simcoe Had no more than 400 men, Half of whom dragoons. The troops and Stores were Crossed on the South Side of the River which a fresh Rendered Very difficult. Simcoe Had no Boats and By a Sum of Monney Induced a Soldier to Swim over who Reported the Baron was gone. 15 or 20 men were with difficulty Contrived over who destroied the Stores. Had the Baron Held 24 Hours Every one of the Articles Might Have Been Carried up as High as Albermale Old Court House where they did not venture. Instead of it He went to Staunton River 15 miles from the Point of Fork and Crossed it. General Lawson with the Militia left Him. His New levies deserted. All Virginia was in an Uproar against Him. The Ennemy Laughed at Him. And I Cannot describe to You what My Surprise Has Been—But I did Not choose to Be too Severe in My public letter and Request this May Be private to Yourself.[13]

Our loss there Consists of State Stores. Arms out of Repair, and State Cloth are the two important Articles. They Have thrown the Arms into the Water and our people are taking them up. Part of the Stores will also Be Saved. Some pieces not mounted fell into their Hands. Part of the Country people Have Been Active Against us. Upon the whole our loss was not very Considerable But will Show a great deal in Newspapers.[14] Had they attaked the Magazines at Albermale Old Court House the Stroke would Have Been Severe.[15] A lucky March through a Road little used Gave us a position to defend them. The delay of the pennsylvanians and disappointements Arising from it Has Been Very Unfortunate. They do not exceed 700. The light infantry 800. Nothing from Maryland. The Virginia New levies 400. General [Daniel] Morgan expected with Riflemen But not Arrived and the Harvest time is Near at Hand.[16] 70 Horse of [Col. John] Moylan are on their Way. Adieu, My dear general, with Every Sentiment of affection and Respect I Have the Honor to Be Your Most obedient Humble Servant   LAFAYETTE

ALS (MiU-C).

1. Lafayette was writing from the home of Col. William Dandridge, at Allen's Creek on the south side of the South Anna River. (Idzerda, *Lafayette Papers*, p. 521n)

2. See Lafayette to NG, 18 June, above.

3. NG had written Lafayette on 9 June, above.

4. On Lafayette's plan to form a junction with Baron Steuben's detachment, see his letter of 18 June.

5. According to Gen. Peter Muhlenberg's biographer, Muhlenberg's force, "thrown a little too far forward," was "snapped at" on 18 June by Col. Banastre Tarleton's cavalry; a timely reinforcement by Gen. Anthony Wayne caused Tarleton to veer off. (Paul A.W. Wallace, *The Muhlenbergs of Pennsylvania* [Freeport, N.Y.: Books for Libraries Press, 1950], p. 225) Tarleton claimed that Muhlenberg's troops "evaded the blow by an early retreat." (Tarleton, *Campaigns*, p. 300)

6. On the arrival of the British ships, see Lafayette's letter of 18 June. This fleet, which had brought reinforcements for Lord Rawdon's army to Charleston, S.C., had proceeded to the Chesapeake with victualers, a detachment of the British Regiment of Guards, and recruits for other regiments serving with Cornwallis. (Clinton, *American Rebellion*, pp. 307, 532)

7. The "Ennemy" crossing of the the river was by a detachment under the command of Col. John Graves Simcoe, which had been operating along the south bank of the James River, clearing it of any American militia parties that might "annoy" the passage of boats. These troops moved to the north side of the James the night of 19 June and rejoined the main British army in Richmond. (Simcoe, *Military Journal*, p. 129)

8. In a letter to Lafayette of 31 May, which was captured between headquarters and Morristown, N.J., Washington had discussed his plans and options for the coming

campaign. (Idzerda, *Lafayette Papers*, 4: 153–54 and n) Washington enclosed a copy of that letter in his to Lafayette of 4 June, saying that the original had been "carried—it is supposed—into New York." (Ibid., p. 168) After learning the contents of the captured letter, Sir Henry Clinton ordered Lord Cornwallis to send reinforcements to New York. (Clinton to Cornwallis, 8 June, *Clinton-Cornwallis Controversy*, 2: 14–17)

9. For more on Washington's plan to attack New York City, see note at Sharpe to NG, 28 May, above.

10. As noted at St. Clair to NG, 6 May, above, the British reinforcements from New York had arrived in Virginia on about 22 May. Lafayette mistakenly though this fleet had brought Cornwallis's baggage from North Carolina and was unaware that 2,000 troops from New York had disembarked and joined Cornwallis. (Idzerda, *Lafayette Papers*, 4: 201n)

11. Cornwallis arrived in Richmond on 16 June and left the night of 20 June. While there, he reportedly burned 2,000 hogsheads of tobacco, various stores and supplies, and "a number of houses." (Ward and Greer, *Richmond*, pp. 92–93)

12. On Col. Banastre Tarleton's raid at Charlottesville, see Lafayette to NG, 18 June.

13. For more on the raid at Point of Fork and the anger over Steuben's conduct, see Lafayette to NG, 18 June.

14. According to a report of the raid in James Rivington's *Royal Gazette* of 18 July, Simcoe destroyed "about three thousand three hundred stand of arms (then under repair), some salt, harness, &c. and about one hundred and fifty barrels of powder." In the same report, Tarleton was said to have destroyed at Charlottesville "one thousand stand of good arms, some clothing and other stores, and between four and five hundred barrels of powder, without opposition."

15. See Lafayette to NG, 18 June.

16. Gen. Daniel Morgan joined Lafayette on 7 July with between 300 and 400 militia from the Virginia backcountry—far fewer than the 2,000 men he had been expected to bring. (See McHenry to NG, first letter of 4 July, and Lafayette to NG, 4–5 July, both below; Higginbotham, *Morgan*, p. 165)

*   *   *

¶ [**FROM COLONEL HENRY LEE, JR.**, "Near Ninety Six," S.C., 20 June 1781. Proposes changes in his corps to make it "doubly servicable." The cavalry would "continue as light dragoons," while the infantry would be mounted on "hardy" horses and would be issued dragoon swords and "carbines with bayonets." This change would "encrease the cavalry" but "not decrease the Infantry." One officer, "if supported by congress," could quickly equip the new unit, "as common saddles will do & holsters are not wanted." The horses "will be cheap to purchase," and many suitable ones could be found in the "Quarter Master⁵ yards."¹ ALS (MiU-C) 3 pp.]

1. NG forwarded Lee's proposal to Congress in a letter to Samuel Huntington of 23 June, below. The outcome is noted there.

*   *   *

From Major James McHenry

Head Quarters Col Dandrege's house 23 miles
My dear General   from Richmond [Va.] 20 June 1781.

I am here with the Marquiss [de Lafayette]. I arrived in time to close his chapter of marches, which you will read at large in his dispatch.¹

The enemy's force, according to our best information, is about 4,000, including a fine body of cavalry. Our regular army, not above 1900, nearly one third of which is in new levies. No body of militia, you know, without a sufficient cover in cavalry, is to be depended on. Our militia makes about 3000.

With this force, I found the strongest disposition in the Marquiss to attack. A partial success, I argued would not drive Cornwallis into Portsmouth. A general one was not to be expected. A partial defeat, on our part, would give his Lordship an opportunity of establishing himself on the Potomack, and to incircle the resources of Virginia. A general defea[t] would put every thing in his power; a post in Maryland, and, perhaps, lose to us, every thing you had with so much difficulty gained. [Gen. Anthony] Wayne was impetuous, and the Marquiss loved glory, but then, he was reasonable, and possessed a prudence which the other thinks he can do without. Under these circumstances, I thought it my duty to divert the Marquiss from the idea of attack to that of defense; to seize favorable moments, but not to give any. I hope I have succeeded. I think it necessary, however, that if I have done right, you will confirm it with as much expedition as possible. No time is to be lost, lest military ardor should be too powerful for reason. But, contrive your advice in such a manner as to drown any suspicion of my interference. I have no time for detail, nor is there occasion, as you must perfectly comprehend the business.[2]

I wrote you two letters before I left Baltimore inclosing some news papers which spoke of your proceedings. The letters spoke also of an etiquette necessary in borrowing me from the Marquiss.[3]

Your reputation can scarcely be higher. Take care of it. Adieu my dear General   JAMES McHENRY

The Marquiss I presume writes you the enemies movements of yesterday.[4]

ALS (MiU-C).

1. See Lafayette to NG, this date, above.

2. In a letter of 22 July, below, NG congratulated Lafayette on having avoided "a general action" and strongly urged him to continue exercising prudence.

3. The letters that McHenry referred to, dated 23 and 29 May, are both above. NG replied on 24 July that he preferred to have McHenry stay in Virginia and moderate Lafayette's "military ardor."

4. See Lafayette to NG, this date.

                    *   *   *

¶ [FROM MAJOR JAMES MCHENRY, [Col. William Dandridge's house, twenty-three miles from Richmond, Va.], 20 June 1781.[1] Begs NG's "politeness" to the bearer, Capt. [John] Swan, a "brave officer." Adds in a postscript that a "misunderstanding" between [Gen. William] Smallwood and [Gen. Mordecai] Gist "respecting command" may delay the forwarding of the Maryland levies. "The sooner this dispute is settled the better. Gist you know is the most active man." It would "avoid offence" if NG gave Gist orders to "forward the new levies."² ALS (MiU-C) 1 p.]

1. McHenry's location was taken from the letter immediately above.

2. For more on the dispute between Smallwood and Gist, see Gist to NG, 28 May, above. In a letter to Gist of 19 July, below, NG ordered him to forward the men.

¶ [GENERAL GREENE'S ORDERS, "Camp William's Spring," S.C., 21 June 1781. "The Troops are to clean their arms & accoutrements, to wash their Cloathes; and to Cook their Provisions as soon as Possible." Rolls are to be called frequently and no passes issued; those who leave without permission "must be punished in the most exemplary manner." Capt. [Robert] Kirkwood's troops are to join Col. [William] Washington's detachment; the Virginia light infantry company will join its brigade. Lamar Orderly Book (OClWHi) 2 pp.]

¶ [TO MAJOR JOHN ARMSTRONG. From Camp, Williams's Fort, S.C., 21 June 1781. A "considerable reinforcement" has enabled Lord Rawdon to "raise the siege of 96." Otherwise, NG's army would "have compleatly reduced the place" in less than "four days more."¹ The enemy now have a "superior force" and will probably try to "push" the Southern Army. NG wants Armstrong to bring him the troops collected at Salisbury, N.C.² He outlines a route of march for Armstrong to take toward Ninety Six. If Armstrong learns that NG is moving "towards the Congaree," however, he should "file off that way." Adds: "The reason why I put it upon this footing, is expresses are often taken and altho I may write you it may miscarry."³ ADfS (NjP) 2 pp.]

1. On the lifting of the siege, see NG to Huntington, 20 June, above.

2. See Armstrong to NG, 12 June, above.

3. NG reported the arrival of Armstrong and his men in a letter to Andrew Pickens of 28 June, below. At the time of the junction, NG's army was moving "towards the Congaree" River.

¶ [TO COLONEL FRANCIS LOCK.¹ From "Camp near 96," S.C., 21 June 1781. Informs Lock that the siege of Ninety Six has been lifted.² Expects the enemy to "endeavor to keep the field and try to cover and hold all the lower Country." NG wishes to prevent that and entreats Lock to join him with the force of 800 or 1,000 "good Militia" that has reportedly been collected to reinforce the Marquis de Lafayette or "for some other purpose." Adds: "This is absolutely necessary as all the troops coming from the Northward have been halted in Virginia to oppose the enemy in that quarter." Asks Lock to reply "as soon as possible."³ Also asks him to take "special care" in guarding "upwards of an hundred prisoners" who have been sent to Salisbury under the command of Capt. [Griffith] McRee.⁴ Lock should "forbid the practice of paroling the Men," for "It will signify nothing to take prisoners if more care is not taken of them." ADfS (MiU-C) 3 pp.]

1. As seen in Polk to NG, 15 May, above, Lock was the new commander of the Salisbury, N.C., militia district.

2. See NG to Huntington, 20 June, above.

3. No reply has been found. The troops were still at Salisbury when an angry NG wrote Lock on 30 July, below, admonishing him to do his duty in spite of popular resistance in his district.

4. On the sending of the prisoners to Salisbury, see NG to Sumner, 18 June, above.

¶ [TO COLONEL HEZEKIAH MAHAM.[1] From Camp near Ninety Six, S.C., 21 June 1781. NG has wanted Maham to "raise a Corps of horse" for some time but has deferred, waiting for the return of Gov. [John] Rutledge, who could have "taken this matter up under the authority of Government." Now that "the enemy are indeavoring to increase their Cavelry," no more time is to be lost. Sends Maham a "Lieutenant Col commandants" commission and authorizes him to raise and equip a corps of 160 rank and file quickly and under the best terms possible.[2] The men, who must agree to serve for more than a year, will be paid "not less" than the Continental cavalry.[3] The new corps is to be divided into four troops, with a complement of commissioned and noncommissioned officers, which NG outlines. Maham should appoint only "active good officers." He is to "impress all the good dragoon horses" he can find. They can be taken from either "friends or enemies" as long as they are not already "in public service." Maham should make special efforts to get horses from the "neighbourhood of Charles Town[,] altogether in the power of the enemy." NG begs him to "exert" himself.[4] ADfS (MiU-C) 4 pp.]

1. Maham (1739–1789), who had been an overseer before acquiring a plantation of his own, had seen active service as a militia officer since 1776 and had commanded cavalry in Gen. Francis Marion's brigade since shortly after the fall of Charleston. (*Biog. Directory of S.C. Senate*, 2: 1035–37) The so-called Maham tower, which he designed and built during the siege of Ft. Watson, had brought him favorably to the attention of NG and other Continental officers. (On the tower, see Marion to NG, first letter of 23 April, above.) Edmund M. Hyrne and Henry Lee had both recommended Maham for a command such as NG offered him here. (See their letters to NG of 8 May, both above.) Maham had also submitted a plan of his own for raising a corps of horse, which Lee had forwarded to NG. (Lee to NG, 10 May, above) NG's appointment of Peter Horry to raise a similar corps eventually led to a sharp dispute between Maham and Horry over rank. (*Biog. Directory of S.C. Senate*, 2: 1036; on Horry's appointment, see Horry to NG, 28 June, below.) In March 1782, the two cavalry units were combined under Maham's command, but "he soon was taken ill and withdrew to his plantation." While there, he was captured by Loyalists. He was paroled but was unable to serve again. (*Biog. Directory of S.C. Senate*, 2: 1036–37) Known for a "quick temper," Maham is said to have been arrested on one occasion after the war because he had forced a deputy sheriff to "eat and swallow" papers that the latter was trying to serve on him. (Ibid., p. 1036; Johnson, *Traditions and Reminiscences*, p. 291) He was elected to several terms in the South Carolina General Assembly. (*Biog. Directory of S.C. Senate*, 2: 1036)

2. See also NG to Maham, 22 June, below. As seen in note 1, above, NG also commissioned Col. Peter Horry to raise a corps of cavalry at this time.

3. On the pay of Continental cavalry, see note at Horry's letter of 28 June.

4. Maham wrote NG on 19 September, below, that he could not yet "mount more than forty" dragoons.

¶ [TO GENERAL JETHRO SUMNER. From Camp, Williams's Fort, S.C., 21 June 1781. As NG feared, Lord Rawdon came "out in force" and relieved Ninety Six; in another "four days," the post would have had to surrender to NG.[1] Believes the British will now "attempt to recover their lost possessions." NG is determined to "maintain our ground in these States at all events" and wants Sumner to join him with as large a reinforcement as possible.[2] LS (MiU-C) 2 pp.]

1. On the lifting of the siege, see NG to Huntington, 20 June, above.
2. Sumner replied on 14 July, below.

*   *   *

From the Marquis de Lafayette

My dear General   C^{lel} Dandriges 21st June 1781
To My Great Satisfaction I Have a Safe Opportunity. I Eagerly Embrace it, and will make Some Communications of the most private Nature.

You Remember I told you Count de Rochambeau was too Sanguine. A Reinforcement will Come But not Very large. Some Ships will escort it and By this time I think they are arrived. Towards the End of the Campaign we May Hope for more.[1] Cloathing is Sent to us. On this article and that of arms I am Satisfied. Hard Monney Has Been Given and permission to draw for more. But not So plentyfully as our Estimate demanded. It will However Have the Greatest Influence in Military Expeditions.[2] The Minister and Mr. Moriss are very [well?] Satisfied with each other and are gone to Head quarters where the disposal of the Monney will Be Settled By General Washington.[3]

Newyork if not Reinforced will Be the object. But the ennemy Cannot defend it and Conqeur the Southern States. Upon their Movements depends General Washington's Determination. In Case the Ennemy prefer the Southern States to Newyork the Grand Army will Come Here. There would Be then A Northen Army in Virginia—a Southern Army in Carolina. The Ennemy know that the General Had Rather attak Newyork than to March the Combined Army this Way.[4] A few days will determine if they will Be Satisfied with Keeping a post in Virginia or if the whole force is Bent to the Conquest of the Southern States.

Propositions of peace Have Been Made and A Mediation offered. France's answer is that they Must above all Consult America. Spain Says nothing Can Be done without France. Congress are now debating on that Matter which is Still a profound Secret.[5] The king of France Has wrote to Congress an Affectionate letter, and assured them that American Independency was an object to which He would Stik at Every danger and every expense, and that all the Ressources of France Shall Be employed to Support it.[6]

The Ennemy's plan Must Be to Secure the Southern States. They will persuade that over Running is possessing. Your Successes are of more Importance than you Had Hitherto Believed. At this period they May decide American Independency.[7]

I am told Savahana May Be easily taken. If it was the Case the Noise of it would Make a Marvellous effect.[8] Would to God we Might take Charlestown. The Stores that Have Been Lost are not Considerable and Cannot affect your operations.[9] Arms out of Repair are the principal article and a greater Number of arms in good order is Coming from Philadelphia.[10] But the Ennemy on one Hand and Some of our public officers on the other will Say we Lost great deal. The fact is that Before the Loss I could not obtain any thing.

While I am writing I Hear the Ennemy Have Evacuated Richmond and Gone the Road to Bottom's Bridge. I Have ordered the Light Corps to pursüe and By all means to try to Strike at them. What Lord Cornwallis Means I do not know But this Retreat will not Read Well in Newspaper.[11] I follow and one Would think I pursüe Him. But as the fate of the Southern States depends on the preservation of this Army, if Mylord chooses to Retreat I Had Rather Loose Some Share of glory than to Risk a defeat By which Virginia would Be Lost. Perhaps the Ennemy Mean to Establish a post at Williams Burg. Perhaps Mylord will Return to you and Send the Remainder to Newyork.[12] In Case I Suspect any thing of the kind I Shall order Back General Sumner and Send on the Pennsylvanians to you.[13] I Have Requested the Gentlemen Bearer of these dispatches to go as fast as thcy Can. I aprehend this Intelligence may perhaps alter your plans to Come into the State. Adieu, My dear General, Most Respectfully and affectionately Yours

LAFAYETTE

(This letter is for you alone.)

ALS (InU-Li).

1. On the reinforcement that had been expected from France, see La Luzerne to NG, 3 April, above. On 16 June, a force of 400 recruits did reach the French expeditionary force at Newport, R.I. (Idzerda, *Lafayette Papers*, 4: 204n)

2. On the supplies and subsidy that France was to provide, see note at Mathews to NG, 22 May, above.

3. La Luzerne left Philadelphia to visit Washington's camp in early July. By then, Robert Morris, the superintendent of finance, had already spent more than one-third of the money he was expected to have available. He did not accompany La Luzerne, informing the minister in a letter of 2 July that Congress had inundated him with "Multiplied business." (Morris, *Papers*, 1: 210)

4. On Washington's preference for a campaign against New York City, see his letter to NG of 1 June, above.

5. La Luzerne wrote Congress on 26 May that Great Britain had accepted an offer from Russia to mediate among the warring powers of Europe. He said that although the king of France wanted to act with "the consent of his allies," it might be necessary to enter into negotiations before a reply from Congress could be received. (The letter is in *JCC*, 20: 560–62.) On 15 June, Congress appointed John Adams, Benjamin Franklin, John Jay, Henry Laurens, and Thomas Jefferson as ministers plenipotentiary, with powers to participate in any negotiations. (Ibid., pp. 652–54; on the mediation attempt, see also note at Sharpe to NG, 28 May, above.)

6. For more on the king's letter, see Mathews to NG, 22 May.

7. It was anticipated that Great Britain would base its claims in any negotiations on the principle of *uti possidetis*. On the effects such a claim could have had on the southern states, see note at Sharpe to NG, 28 May.

8. In his letter to NG of 24 May, above, Henry Lee had given a similar argument in advocating an attack on Savannah, Ga. As seen in his reply to Lee of 29 May, above, NG was unwilling to make such an attempt.

9. Lafayette had written NG on 20 June, above, about the stores lost to British raiders.

10. Lafayette was undoubtedly referring to 2,000 stand of arms that the Board of War had sent from Philadelphia in early June for the use of Continental troops in Virginia. (See Board of War to Lafayette, ca. 12 June, Idzerda, *Lafayette Papers*, 4: 178.)

11. With Lafayette's troops following him, Cornwallis retreated to Williamsburg, arriving on 25 June. According to his biographers, he had "completed his raiding" and was preparing to receive orders from Sir Henry Clinton. (Wickwire, *Cornwallis*, pp. 334–35)

12. Clinton had already sent orders to Cornwallis to forward some 3,000 troops to New York. Cornwallis, in turn, requested permission to go to Charleston. (Clinton to Cornwallis, 11 June, and Cornwallis to Clinton, 30 June, Davies, *Documents*, 20: 158, 168; Clinton, *American Rebellion*, p. 309) In the end, it was decided that both he and the troops would remain in Virginia.

13. As seen in his letter to Gen. Jethro Sumner of 18 June, above, NG had already ordered the North Carolina Continental levies to join the Southern Army in South Carolina. The Pennsylvanians remained in Virginia until after the successful conclusion of the siege of Yorktown in October.

*   *   *

¶ [**FROM WILLIAM SHARPE**, Philadelphia, 21 June 1781. Has NG's "very obliging letter" of 5 May [not found] and feels "the greater obligation" when he considers "the very little time" NG has for "private" correspondence. The "picture" that NG gives "of the miseries of the inhabitants of the southern States" is "well founded" and "confirmed by every account" Sharpe has received. He agrees with NG's view that "a permanent body of troops, at least, equal to the collective force of the enemy" is needed before "hope of recovering and defending" the southern states can be entertained. Asks: "What are we to do? The states which are apparently secure from the invasion of the enemy, look with too much indifference upon those which are suffering and unable to make a vigorous opposition." He could say more but expects Gov. [John] Rutledge, who is "minutely acquainted with every circumstance of our affairs," to brief NG. Adds that the "sufferings and perseverence" of NG and his army "demand the gratitude of every individual." ALS (PHi) 1 p.]

*   *   *

To the Georgia Delegates in Congress

Gentlemen   Head Quarters [Bush River, S.C.] June 22ᵈ 1781

Your favor of the 5ᵗʰ of April covering a memorandum of Stores for the State of Georgia has been recieved; and I am happy to inform you that the articles were safely delivered at Augusta to Col Elijah Clarke the eldest Colonel then in the State.[1]

I sincerely congratulate you on the reduction of the Enemy's posts in The upper part of Georgia.[2] This fortunate circumstance would give security to a great proportion of the State if government could be established. I lament the confusion and inhamunity [i.e., inhumanity] which takes place—the daily scenes of the most horrid plundering and murder which can only be accounted for by the great lengths to which personal animosities are carried and the want of civil authority. The assistance of every respectable citizen is necessary to check and prevent them. I have recommended the appointment of a Committee or Council to Govern untill the Civil Officers can be constitutionally chosen.[3] I have given an appointment of Lt Colonel to Major Jackson who is endeavouring to raise a Reg^t for 10 Months.[4] The appointment of the Officers [is] to be subject to the approbation of the State of Georgia. He has recruited near 100 Men and I am in hopes he will be able to compleat the Corps.

I must beg leave to refer you to my public letters for the state of affairs.[5] I have the honor to be Gentlemen Your Most Obed^t Humble Servant

Df (NcD).

1. The letter, written by delegate George Walton, is above; see also Clarke to NG, 19 June, above.
2. NG was referring to the capture of Forts Dreadnought, Grierson, and Cornwallis, the last two of which were at Augusta.
3. See NG to Wilkinson, 13 June, above.
4. For more on James Jackson's appointment, see note at NG to Clarke, 17 June, above.
5. NG's "public letters" were those to Samuel Huntington, the president of Congress. (See, for example, NG to Huntington, 20 June, above.)

To the Chevalier de La Luzerne

Sir   Camp at Bush River [S.C.] June 22^d 1781

I have had the honor of your letters of the 3^d of April and 15th of May. It affords me the highest satisfaction to hear that the second division is approaching these distressed States.[1] The division among the people and the art and address of the enemy render the task of the well affected extreme burthensome[.] I have communicated to Governor Nash such parts of your Excell^{ys} letter as you recommended and I hope some preparations will be made for a plan of cooperation.[2] Virginia I think affords the greatest object for the first operations. Lord Cornwallis's Army, and the fleet and Garrison at Portsmouth would be much in our power if the french fleet with a large land force was to enter Chesapeak Bay. The Marquis [de Lafayette] could join his force in the general plan and nothing could afford him equal pleasure.

The letter and bill addressed to Col Leimoi shall be forwarded the first opportunity and as all the Amercan officers in the Southern department not exchanged are to be liberated on parole by Articles of a Cartel lately settled between Lord Cornwallis and my self it will be unnecessary to ask it as a favor.[3]

We have it from pretty good authority that Pensacola is taken and that St Augustine is beseiged.[4]

The Enemy has rather lost ground in the Southern quarter lately. If the Marquis is able to preserve a good countenance in Virginia I shall be happy[.]

I thank your Excellency for your complement upon the conduct of the Army at Guilford. If it meets the approbation of my Country and that of our good ally I shall be made compleatly happy.

I must beg leave to refer your Excellency to my letters to Congress for the particulars of the operations in this quarter. Fortune is our Enemy or very much the friend of the British otherwise the garrison of Ninty Six must have fallen into our hands. Nothing but a reinforcment which arrived at Charles Town could have saved it and had it been only four days latter their fate was inevitable. I have the honor to be with the highests respect Your Excellencys Most Obedient humble Ser

N GREENE

ADfS (MiU-C).

1. As noted at La Luzerne to NG, 3 April, above, plans were changed and the second division of the French expeditionary force was never sent to America. A French fleet, however, did arrive in Virginia from the West Indies in time to take part in the siege of Yorktown.

2. NG's letter to Gov. Abner Nash of North Carolina, containing the intelligence that La Luzerne had sent NG on 3 April, has not been found.

3. "Col. Leimoi" was Jean Baptiste Joseph, Chevalier de Laumoy, one of two French prisoners La Luzerne had asked NG to help. (See La Luzerne to NG, 15 May, above.

4. Pensacola, Fla., had been captured by a Spanish army; St. Augustine was not under siege. (See above, NG to Galvez, 12 June, and vol. 5: 319n.)

*   *   *

¶ [TO MAJOR HEZEKIAH MAHAM. From "Head Quarters, South Carolina," 22 June 1781. Maham is hereby appointed a "Lieutenant Colonel Commandant of a Battalion of Light Dragoons for the State of South Carolina, to be employed in the service of America."[1] DS (NN) 1 p.]

1. For more on the appointment, see NG to Maham, 21 June, above.

¶ [TO GENERAL ARTHUR ST. CLAIR. From Bush River, S.C., 22 June 1781. Has his letter of 6 May. Is happy to hear that "so respectable a body" of 1,100 men is marching to reinforce the Southern Army.[1] Would be especially pleased if "the second brigade" were also ready to march and if St. Clair were "at the head." NG relies on St. Clair's "assiduity and attention" to insure that everything is done to "forward the business."[2] The Southern Army is in a critical situation; it has been reduced "to a mere shadow from hard service and severe action," while the enemy are still "formidable in the field." Despite its "difficulties," NG's army has "been favoured with some very important successes." The enemy "are divested of all their posts" in Georgia and South Carolina except Savannah, Charleston, and Ninety Six. "The last was closedly beseiged for near thirty days" and was about to fall when Lord Rawdon came to its

relief. NG laments the failure to capture this post, which "is of great consequence to the enemy." His army was "exposed to excessive labor and an-
noyance in the attempt. But these disappointments we shall ever be subjected
to while the enemy continue masters of the Sea; and our force and means are
so incompetent." ALS (O) 3 pp.]

1. Gen. Anthony Wayne's brigade of Pennsylvania troops was already serving with
the Marquis de Lafayette in Virginia.

2. St. Clair's detachment finally marched from Philadelphia to join Washington's army
in Virginia on about 6 October. (St. Clair to his wife, 16 October, William H. Smith, ed.,
The St. Clair Papers: the Life and Public Services of Arthur St. Clair, 2 vols. [Cincinnati, 1882],
1: 560)

¶ [TO COLONEL ISAAC SHELBY. From "Camp at Bush River in the District
of 96," S.C., 22 June 1781. Ninety Six, the last "interior" post held by the
British, was relieved by Lord Rawdon four days before it would have fallen.
"To secure the advantages of our past successes it is necessary we should
drive the enemy into the lower Country." NG asks Shelby to join the Southern
Army "in a few days" with 1,000 "good rifflemen well armed and equiped
fit for action." NG, who is "deeply interested in this application," believes
Shelby has enough "influence" to provide the army with the needed "support." By bringing a reinforcement, Shelby will serve the public and place both
NG and the state of South Carolina "under very particular obligations"; NG
will happily and publicly acknowledge Shelby's "merit and services." NG
relies on Shelby's "zeal and patriotism." Hopes to see him soon.[1] ALS (CSmH)
3 pp.]

1. Shelby, a militia officer from the frontier area of North Carolina, replied on 2 July,
below.

¶ [COLONEL OTHO H. WILLIAMS TO LIEUTENANT FRANCIS SMITH.[1]
From Camp, Bush River, S.C., 22 June 1781. Those British prisoners of war who
are "sufficiently Recover'd" are to be sent from the hospital at Camden to
Charleston in groups of ten or twelve. Col. James Postell will provide a militia
escort. The prisoners are already "accounted for in Exchange." ALS (MiU-C)
1 p.]

1. Smith had sought instructions regarding the prisoners in his letter to NG of 1 June,
above.

*   *   *

To General James M. Varnum

Dear Sir   Camp at Bush River [S.C.] June 22ᵈ 1781

I am exceedingly obliged to you for your letter of the 23ᵈ of May; for
besides the pleasure of hearing from you it brought me an account
of the health of Mrs [Catharine] Greene who I was happy to hear
had relinquished her project of coming to the Southward as there
is no resting place for her on this side Pennsylvania. The feeling
manner in which you express your self for my success and safety
deserves my warmest acknowledgments. Your apprehensions are well

grounded when you take into consideration the unequal footing we are contending with the enemy. Our movements to the Southward have been attended with various success, and had it not been for a reinforcement which arrivd at Charles Town the success would have been compleat.

Foreseeing the difficulties you mention in Virginia, I halted all the force coming Southward to prevent the enemy from gaining an advantage in that quarter; and have reason to hope the Marquis [de Lafayette] will keep a good countenance; unless the enemies superior Cavalry should plunge him into a misfortune. The importance of Cavalry I have been indeavoring to impress all the Southern States with. But their attachment to their horses prevented any good consequences resulting from the representations. This Country exhibits human nature in every shape that imagination can form. You know little of war to the Northward or of its baneful effects upon the morals of the people[.]

Had I not come into this Country the Southern States had been inevitably lost; and the enemy would have sent a greater force from hence to the Northward than we have had opposd to them here. Detachments were forming for the purpose when I came into the State.

I know peoples expectations allways keep ahead of the greatest possible exertions. Was our difficulties fully known, I perswade my self Congress would be fully satisfied with the conduct of this Army. I am confident never was more done with less force under equal disadvantages.

I am happy to hear your prospects brighten in Congress. But I fear your difficulties there is little less than ours in the field.

The long looked for second division I fear will not arrive timely to our relief.[1] New York is the great place of Arms and would be the first object if it was not for the time it will take to effect its reduction[.] But I think the greatest stroke may be struck in Virginia. If the fleet was to run immediately into Chessapeak Bay and land a force sufficient to cut off Lord Cornwallis's retreat and possess the Shipping and Garrison at Portsmouth. All this might be effected in a short time and would pave the way to still greater success. But I fear fortune has nothing so flattering in store for us. England makes great exertions; and I admire their politicks in point of boldness and decision, tho I abhor their injustice and cruelty. I beg my complements to Mrs [Martha] Varnum. Most respectfully Yours   N GREENE

ADfS (MiU-C).

1. As seen in his letter of this date, above, to the Chevalier de La Luzerne, the French minister, NG had received a false report that the second division of the French expedi-

tionary force was en route to America. The French force that later participated in Cornwallis's capture at Yorktown, Va., had been sent to the West Indies with instructions to assist operations in the United States if its commander, the Comte de Grasse, deemed it advisable.

To George Washington

Sir   Camp Bush River [S.C.] June 22ᵈ 1781.

Your Excellency's Letters of the 19th & 21ˢᵗ of April, I have had the honor to receive.[1]

Nothing would afford me greater pleasure than to have it in my power to oblige Major McPherson; especially as it will afford me an opportunity of obliging your Excellency at the same time.[2]

Inclosed is a copy of my Last Letter to Congress.[3] Copies of my former Letters I desired the President of Congress to forward you which I hope you have received.

We are anxiously waiting the arrival of the second division of the french Fleet.[4] Virginia affords the most inviting object; Lord Cornwallis's Army, and the Garrison and Shipping at Portsmouth. The whole may be taken in three Weeks or less while New York and Charles Town will produce a long[,] tedious and uncertain seige. I hope the Marquis [de Lafayette] will be successful in Virginia. What I mean by success is to avoid a capital misfortune. Your Excellency will see by my Letters to Congress I have left the command of all the force, coming Southward with the Marquis. My fears are principally from the Enemys superior Cavalry. To the Northward Cavalry is nothing from the numerous fences but to the Southward a disorder by a superior Cavalry may be improved into a defeat, and a defeat into a route [i.e., rout]. Virginia and North Carolina could not be brought to consider the Cavalry of such great importance as they are to the security of an Army, and the safety of a Country.

Before this I hope the New England States have filled up their Regiments.[5] Nothing but drafting can lay a permanent foundation for the liberties of America; and with it we have little to fear even from a failure of our finance. I am with great respect Your Excellencys most obedient hble servᵗ   NATH GREENE

LS (Washington Papers: DLC).

1. Washington's letters, dated 19 and 22 April, are both above.

2. For the request concerning Maj. William MacPherson, see Washington to NG, 22 April.

3. NG enclosed his letter to Samuel Huntington of 20 June, above.

4. As noted at NG to La Luzerne, this date, above, the second division of the French expeditionary force was never sent to America.

5. The New England states had not filled their regiments. (See note at Washington to NG, 27 February, above [vol. 7: 365n].)

From Colonel Henry Lee, Jr.

Major [Robert] Gillam[s] Farm [S.C.]
Sir   June 22 [1781] 10 O'clock PM

Lord Rawdon reached Ninety Six yesterday at two o'clock. The baggage of the army was not up this morning at sunrise. It halted six miles short of 96 on the road by Moores. The Tories join fast. The troops have little or no meal. The hand mills are at work. This will be but a scanty supply. I do not beleive his Lordship has more than 2000 horse[,] foot & artillery including the garrison under Col. [John Harris] Cruger & encluding the inhabitants who have or may join.[1]

It is said that they talk familiarly of burning 96: that being done they mean to follow you; another report is, that after destroying the town & works, & refreshing their troops they will loose no time in returning south.[2]

If you can possibly draw to you Marian [Gen. Francis Marion] with 400, Sumpter [Gen. Thomas Sumter] with 500, [Gen. Andrew] Pickens & [Col. Elijah] Clarke with 500, & arrange them so as to form your baggage guards & staff guards out of those militia who will not fight, preserving a distinct corps under good officers the good militia, & so form the cavalry as to give to [Col. William] Washington & myself each 100 with swords, keeping a one troop of Militia horse for patrole duty you will assuredly possess the country, disgrace the enemy & may eventually ruin his Lordship. At all events preserve the appearance of fighting: I am sorry you have retired so far.

M[r] [Ferdinand] Neal whom I detached last evening sent me in a prisoner on whose report I have formed this let[r].[3] He is still out. I hope to be favored with your ⟨answer⟩ by the instant return of ⟨the⟩ bearer & shall be much o⟨[bliged]⟩ by an inkstand & ink.[4]

An additional reason for collecting the militia is that in their present dispersed state they indulge themselves in every species of rapine & plunder. Col [Edward] Carrington has a le[r] [i.e., letter] for L[t] [James] Heard of my Cavalry. I beg he will send it by this conveyance. Yours inviolably   HENRY LEE JUN[R]

ALS (MiU-C). The words in angle brackets were taken from a Draper Transcript (WHi).

1. Lee's estimate was apparently close to the actual size of Rawdon's force. (See McCrady, *S.C. in the Revolution*, p. 301.)

2. On British plans for Ninety Six, see note at NG to Huntington, 20 June, above. Gen. Andrew Pickens reported on the impending evacuation of the post in his letter to NG of 10 July, below.

3. See Lee to NG, immediately below.

4. NG replied on 24 June, below.

*   *   *

¶ [FROM COLONEL HENRY LEE, JR., [22 June] 1781.[1] Gives estimates, based partly on intelligence obtained from prisoners, of the troop strength of the various corps commanded by Lord Rawdon. Reports that "Invalids & Militia are left at Ninety Six. Very few Torys with the army. They have neither blankets, knapsacks nor waggons with them, nor have they a change of shirts. Not a single waggon in the artillery have tumblers for ammunition. They move tomorrow at day-break. They have no provision but flesh, they do not Cook [Its?] meal nor have they any liquor. If you can but collect you will get the army."[2] Adds that Rawdon's "provision train, military stores &c" are on their way to Charleston. Based on the reports of two deserters from NG's army, the enemy believe they will "overtake" NG "this day. They will push tomorrow."[3] If NG is "hurried," Lee asks him to leave "some Infantry." He will defend "such posts as may be proper" to impede Rawdon's advance. Is afraid that NG "will loose by desertion unless the greatest care is taken." On a second page, he recapitulates the numbers of enemy troops and gives totals in two columns. The first column, presumably taken from the prisoners' reports, gives the total British force as 2,450; the second, which is apparently Lee's own estimate, puts the available enemy force at 1,800. ALS (MiU-C) 4 pp.]

1. This letter, undated and docketed "June 24ʰ," appears to contain the intelligence on which Lee based his troop estimate in the letter immediately above; the editors have chosen 22 June as the probable date.

2. NG replied on 24 June, below.

3. On the deserters from NG's army, see ibid.

¶ [GENERAL GREENE'S ORDERS, "Camp Bush River," S.C., Saturday, 23 June 1781. The army will march immediately. Lamar Orderly Book (OClWHi) 1 p.]

*   *   *

To Catharine Greene

Dear Caty   Camp Little River [S.C.] June 23ᵈ 1781.

The very great distance we are apart and the frequent miscariages of letters induces me to write you [by?] every opportunity. Since I wrote you before the Enemy have taken the field and obliged us to raise the siege at Ninty Six. The two Armies now lay within about Twenty Miles of each other.

In your last you press for my consent for your coming Southerly in the Fall.[1] Most assuredly you have my permission providing the state of matters here will afford a prospect of comfort and security. Unless things are in this situation I perswade my self you would not wish to expose your self to the dreadful condition which many experience of being robed[,] plunderd and privately murdered. My dear you can have no Idea of the horrors of the Southern war. Murders are as frequent here as petty disputes are to the Northward. I should be the most unhappy man alive if you was here exposd to these dangers. I beg you will not entertain a thought so unworthy my motives as to suppose that I magnify the evils to discourage your coming. It is from the purest affection and I should consider my self little less than your murderer if any misfortune should attend you and I had concealed the state of things from you. The Gentlemen in this quarter think themselves extreme happy if they can get their wives and families into some place of safety.[2]

In your next I beg you to give me a history of our private affairs in company with Griffen and Jacob.[3] What has become of the Flora frigate, has she taken any prizes?[4]

How is Nancy Varnon, is she married or in the way of it?[5] Please to present my most affectionate regards to her, and to all our family & friends. I am sorry to hear of the death of poor Col Greene & Major Flagg.[6] Yours Aff   NG

ALS (NjP).
    1. Catharine's letter has not been found.
    2. The records of the Moravians show that throughout the month of June prominent families from South Carolina and Georgia who had fled to Virginia in 1780 were again on the road, passing through Salem, N.C. This time they were trying to return home because of the "unrest" in Virginia. The Moravian recorder added: "but the circumstances which they thought favorable have changed before they finished their journey, they cannot reoccupy their former plantations, and do not know where they shall turn, and many men, formerly rich, have become very poor, so that during this month our sympathy has often been aroused." (*Records of the Moravians*, 4: 1696) Catharine did not leave Rhode Island for the South until December.
    3. Catharine's reply has not been found. NG was a partner in a firm that included his brother Jacob and his cousin Griffin Greene.
    4. As noted at NG to Catharine, 18 March, above, the *Flora* was still outfitting. (Vol. 7: 447n)
    5. For more on Nancy Vernon, a longtime friend of NG's and Catharine's, see note at Vernon to NG, 13 November 1780, above (vol. 6: 481). As seen there, she did not marry until after the war.
    6. On the deaths of Col. Christopher Greene and Maj. Ebenezer Flagg at the hands of Loyalists, see note at Varnum to NG, 23 May, above.

                    *   *   *

¶ [TO SAMUEL HUNTINGTON, PRESIDENT OF THE CONTINENTAL CONGRESS. From "Head Quarters [Little River, S.C.]," 23 June 1781. Encloses a proposal to make Lee's Legion "more extensively usefull."[1] If Congress approves, NG asks that the Board of War put this plan into "immediate execution."[2] LS (PCC, item 155, vol. 2: 187, DNA) 1 p.]
    1. See Henry Lee to NG, 20 June, above.
    2. Congress received this letter on 3 August and that same day directed the Board of War "to take order." (*JCC*, 21: 828) The board replied on 9 August that on the "lowest calculation" the amount needed to carry out the proposal "so far exceeds any funds that we have any knowledge of that can be appropriated to that use, that we dare not undertake to carry the proposed plan into execution until Congress should be informed of our situation." (Ibid., p. 852) Congress next appointed a committee, which submitted its report on 14 August. (Ibid., pp. 853, 861) Nothing seems to have been done until

29 September, when Congress issued orders to NG to arrange the legion as proposed and to the Board of War to provide the needed arms and accoutrements by taking what "can be spared from the military stores" or by arranging with the "Superintendent of Finance" to acquire them. (Ibid., p. 1026)

* * *

To the Marquis de Lafayette

Camp at Bush River in the Neighbourhood
Dear Marquis   of 96 [S.C.] June 23ᵈ 1781

What I apprehended has taken place. I wrote you on the 9ᵗʰ that the enemy had receivd a considerable reinforcment at Charles Town and that I expected they would march out in force and interrupt our operations. On the 11th I got intelligence of their advancing. I took every measure in my power to retard their march by detaching our Cavalry and ordering General [Thomas] Sumter to collect all the force he could and throw himself in their front. But he neglected it either for want of intelligence or from the difficulty of collecting his force: for the Militia of this Country will fight only in their own Counties and Districts, and it is with great difficulty they can be got out of them.[1]

Our works were in such forwardness that in four days more we could have compleated the reduction of the place. But finding we should not have time we made an attempt upon two of their works. One we carryed[,] in the other we failed. We lost between forty and fifty Men in the two attempts, and the enemy sufferd as much or more.[2] We retird from before the place on the 19th But not until the enemy got within a few Miles of it. Had the Virginia Militia come on under General [Robert] Lawson we should have compleated the business before the seige could have been raised.[3] But our poor fellows were all wore out being on duty almost Night and day for upwards of twenty days.

We want reinforcments in this quarter but I am afraid to call upon you as I fear you are not less embarassed and oppressed than we are. What a Herculean task we have! To contend with a formidable enemy with a handful of men. In your operations you have one advantage which we have not, that is you are free from Tories. Here they are as thick as the trees and we can neither get provisions or forage without large guards to protect them. They even steal our horses within the limits of our Camp.

I was surprised at receiving a letter from the Baron Stuben dated the 9th of this instant at Charlotte wherein he informs me he is coming on with his detachment. Surely there must have been some great obscurity in the manner of my orders or they must all have miscaried.[4] However I still hope the Baron will receive orders from you timely to prevent his marching out of the way; and as the enemy operate in two divisions perhaps his present position may be as good a one as any that could be chosen.[5] My greatest fears are from your want of Cavlry; and unless you can increase it the Country must and will be over run and the greater part of our Stores lost.

It was my intention to have come to the Northward with the greater part of our Cavalry if the enemy had not receivd a reinforcement here which enables them to take the field; and they are increasing their Cavalry by every means in their power and have a greater number than we have, tho not of equal goodness. We are trying to increase ours. Enlarge your Cavalry ⟨or⟩ you are inevitably ruined. Dont pay any regard to the murmurs of the people. They will bless you when they find they derive security from them. Let your Army be as light as possible and have your Stores kept at a great distance that you may not be cramped ⟨in your move⟩ments. Avoid a general action if possible while the enemy have such a superior Cavalry. A defeat to you in that situation may prove your ruin.

I am indeavoring to oblige the enemy to evacuate 96 and to manoeuver them down into the lower Country. But my force is so small that I am afraid I shall not be able to effect it. With esteem and regard I am dear Marquis your most obed humble Svt   N GREENE

ALS (InU-Li). As the ALS is incomplete, the last two paragraphs were taken primarily from the ADfS (MiU-C); the words in angle brackets are from a GWG Transcript (CSmH).

1. NG was being restrained here in his criticism of Sumter; on his private reaction to Sumter's and Marion's failure to slow the British advance, see note at NG to Huntington, 20 June, above.

2. On the attempt to storm the works at Ninety Six, see NG's letter to Huntington of 20 June.

3. The reasons for the Virginia militia's failure to join NG are discussed at Jefferson to NG, 30 March, above.

4. As noted at Steuben's letter of 9 June, above, NG's orders were intercepted.

5. On Lafayette's orders to Steuben, see Steuben to NG, 9 June.

*   *   *

¶ [TO MAJOR JAMES MCHENRY. From "Little River in the district of 96," S.C., June 23 [1781]. Finds that "fortune is my enemy, or at least not much my friend." The British were reinforced at Ninety Six, forcing NG to abandon the siege there.[1] He would have fought the enemy relief force, but his army, which is "all we have to depend upon," is "too small to hazard an action." The war is "upon such unequal terms in this country" that NG has "nothing better to expect than disgrace and ruin," unless his friends can "convince the sensible part of mankind, that it is not the misapplication but the want of means" that causes "our misfortunes." NG is sure that the latter "will be the case." Adds: "Greater abilities might improve our force to greater advantage; but, as for me, I can do no more than I have done. If my conduct is not satisfactory, I shall submit with pleasure to public censure." Excerpt, taken from McHenry to Gov. Thomas Sim Lee of Maryland, 11 July (MdHi).]

1. See NG to Huntington, 20 June, above.

¶ [TO THE MARQUIS DE MALMEDY. From [Bush River, S.C.], 23 June 1781.[1] Malmedy is to proceed to Salisbury, N.C., and "forward" the Continental recruits there to the army. He is also to inspect the armory, suggest needed "alterations," and "hasten" the march of the Salisbury militia if they are "embodying." He should next go to Gen. [Jethro] Sumner and the governor of North Carolina, "point out the necessity" of sending reinforcements speedily, and help them "expedite the business." He should also inform the governor and legislature of the need for some "good" cavalry horses.[2] Df (MiU-C) 2 pp.]

1. The place was taken from the letter immediately below, which Malmedy carried to Gov. Abner Nash.

2. Malmedy reported to NG on 29 June and 10 July, both below.

* * *

To Governor Abner Nash of North Carolina

Sir   Camp Bush River [S.C.] June 23ᵈ 1781.

The present moment is of such vast importance to our safety that no means ought to be left unattempted to recover the sinking hopes of the People.[1] I have had the fullest assurance of a powerful assistance this Campaign from our good Allies the French, and would wish some great exertions might be made to render a co-operation formidable and respectable.[2] You sir will have it in your power to do something, and I have such confidence in your patriotism as to expect it. The People will I hope readily yield to any measure that may serve to promote their happiness, and safety; especially at this time when you have no Enemy among you to cramp the powers of Government.[3] The first necessary steps in my opinion would be to collect all the Drafts in the State, Arm and equip them, and fix upon some general plan to keep up a Regular force. Experience must now convince every Man that Militia are not calculated to protect an invaded Country, Men are apt to sink under difficulties, and will sacrifice every thing to their ease and convenience unless their duty is made professional and honorable.

Colonel Malmady will have the honor of delivering you this Letter, and will give you the necessary information respecting the operations of the Campaign.[4] We have been generally successful, but fortune has in several instances proved unfriendly. I have the honor to be Your Excellencys most obedient servant   NATH GREENE

Df (MiU-C).

1. A struck-through portion of the draft immediately following this sentence reads: "Our efforts of late have been so feeble that the weak minded will naturally conclude that we are unequal to the struggle, without appealing to the true cause which has brought about all our misfortunes."

2. For more on the hoped-for assistance from France, see La Luzerne to NG, 3 April, and NG to La Luzerne, 22 June, both above.

3. NG apparently did not consider the British force occupying Wilmington, N.C., a threat.

4. See NG to Malmedy, immediately above. Thomas Burke, the new governor, answered this letter on 4 July, below.

* * *

¶ [TO GENERAL ANDREW PICKENS. From "Indian Creek," S.C., 23 June 1781. The enemy left their "sick, invalids and bagga[g]e" at Ninety Six and crossed the Saluda River "this morning." Pickens should collect his force and join NG's army as soon as possible at Fishdam Ford on the Broad River; NG wants to assemble a force to "operate more effectually" against Lord Rawdon. Pickens should order "The waggons" to move "to that place" by a safe route.[1] "The enemy being unincumbered will perhaps move with rapidity." Df (MiU-C) 1 p.]

1. The "waggons" were the Southern Army's baggage train, which Pickens had been ordered to lead to safety. (Ferguson, "Pickens," p. 232) Pickens's family and personal belongings initially accompanied the train, but he decided to send them back to his home, only twenty miles from Ninety Six, to demonstrate to the people in the area his confidence that NG's army could protect them. Historian David Ramsay credited Pickens with setting an example that saved the Ninety Six area from depopulation and prevented mass desertion from the militia. (David Ramsay, *The History of the Revolution of South-Carolina, from a British Province to an Independent State*, 2 vols. [Trenton (N.J.), 1785], 2: 246)

¶ [TO GENERAL WILLIAM SMALLWOOD. From "Camp at Bush River," S.C., 23 June 1781. "The importance of the Cavalry and light troops in the Southern war" has led NG to try to put Lee's Legion "upon as good a footing as possible." He asks Smallwood to assist Capt. [Henry] Archer in obtaining the "remainder of the horses" voted by the Maryland Assembly. If Congress approves the proposal to mount the legion infantry, NG also wants Smallwood to furnish fifty Maryland draftees to "serve in that Corps."[1] NG would not trouble him with "this business" but supposes from Smallwood's last letter that Gen. [Mordecai] Gist is either in Philadelphia or in Delaware.[2] Smallwood is influential and can "effect the business sooner and with more ease than any other."[3] NG wants Gist to join the Southern Army if Maryland raises enough draftees to "form a tolerable brigade" and if Smallwood has "leisure to conduct" the business that NG left in Gist's charge.[4] ADfS (MiU-C) 3 pp.]

1. On the proposal, see Lee to NG, 20 June, and NG to Huntington, this date, both above.

2. See Smallwood to NG, 4 May, above.

3. When he wrote NG months later, Smallwood apparently said nothing about Archer, the draftees, or the horses. (See NG to Smallwood, 12 November, below.)

4. As seen in Gist to NG, 14 September, below, Gist was only then preparing to march from Maryland to join in the siege of Yorktown.

¶ [TO BARON STEUBEN. From "Head Quarters Bush River," S.C., 23 June 1781. Has Steuben's letter of 9 June; hopes Steuben has received NG's of 14 and 23 May and 17 June. Wants the "Cavalry and Virginia recruits" to "act with" Steuben under the command of the Marquis [de Lafayette], whose orders Steuben is sure to receive before this letter arrives.[1] The troops from

Maryland and North Carolina are to join NG's army.[2] The stores should be "deposited in places of security" and a return sent to NG. The enemy have been reinforced in South Carolina and have obliged NG to lift the siege of Ninety Six.[3] "This circumstance has brought us into the field and the fate of this Country is to be decided by an action if his Lordship [i.e., Lord Rawdon] thinks proper to contend for that object." LS (NHi) 2 pp.]

1. In a letter of 13 June, Lafayette had ordered Steuben to join him. (Idzerda, *Lafayette Papers*, 4: 179)

2. The Maryland troops did not join NG until after the siege of Yorktown.

3. See NG to Huntington, 20 June, above.

*   *   *

To General Thomas Sumter

Dear Sir   Camp on Bush River [S.C.] June 23ᵈ 1781.

Colᵒ Polk has been with me and represented your situation.[1] I am sorry to find the Militia fall off in the manner they do. At present I can determine on no precise plan of operations. My object will be to oblige if possible the British Army to retire from the district of Ninety Six. Lieutᵗ Colᵒ [Henry] Lee will move down into the lower Country, and I wish Colᵒ Middleton [Charles Myddelton] to join and move down with him.

We shall move towards Liles Ford on Broad River. You will continue in the neighbourhood where you are, and collect and arrange the Militia as fast as you can. Should the Enemy move towards us we will form a junction.[2] Genˡ [Andrew] Pickens is collecting a considerable force. I am in hopes to see you in a Day or two. If you have any Meal which you would send to this Army it would be very acceptable.[3]

It is my opinion that you had better attempt to equip one half your State Troops as Infantry, the other as Cavalry. Perhaps you may get good Horses for one half, but it will be impossible for the whole. I only suggest it, you will act in the matter as you may think necessary.

Colᵒ Polk informs me your health is getting worse, and your Wound more troublesome.[4] I am sorry on yours, my own, and the public's account, as it will be a great misfortune, especially in our situation. Where is General Marion?[5] With esteem and regard I am dear Sir Your most obedᵗ hble servᵗ   NATH GREENE

LS (Sumter Papers: DLC).

1. Col. William Polk commanded a regiment of ten-month men serving under Sumter.

2. In the letter immediately below, NG sent revised orders to Sumter.

3. Sumter had offered to send cornmeal. (See his first letter to NG of 19 June, above.)

4. Sumter was still troubled by a wound he had received in November 1780. (See note at NG to Sumter, 15 December 1780, above [vol. 6: 581n].)

5. On Gen. Francis Marion's whereabouts, see NG to Lee, 24 June, below.

*   *   *

¶ [CAPTAIN WILLIAM PIERCE, JR., TO GENERAL THOMAS SUMTER. From "Camp on Indian Creek [S.C.]," 23 June 1781, 4 P.M. Intelligence has just been received that the enemy have crossed the Saluda River "and mean to make this Army their particular object."[1] NG wants Sumter to collect his troops immediately "and march with all possible expedition" to join the Southern Army at Fish Dam Ford. "The present moment is important, and no time must be lost." ALS (Sumter Papers: DLC) 1 p.]

   1. For more on the enemy's movements, see note at NG to Lee, 24 June, below.

*   *   *

To George Washington

Dear Sir   Camp at Bush River [S.C.] June 23^d 1781

   Your friendly letter of the 18th of April affords me peculiar satisfaction.[1] If my conduct meets your approbation it will console me amidst the hissing murmurs of ten thousand of the ignorant rabble. The honor you did me in the appointment is an additional motive to exert my self to the satisfaction of the public. My public letters will inform your Excellency of the situation of things here. Our Movements Southward have been attended with great advantage as a stay to the hopes and expectations of North Carolinia and Virginia. For if this Army had moved Northerly[,] Virginia would have been considerd as a frontier State and her prospects must have been much more gloomy and her exertions of consequence much less. My fears for the Marquis [de Lafayette] are all alive, tho I have left him all the force coming to the Southward. I am in a distressed situation myself, but am afraid to call for any aid from the Northward. If the enemy continues to reinforce the Southern Army on their part, and we receive little or none on our side, our ruin is inevitable. I shall keep the peoples hopes alive all in my power; but what can I do without men?

   I am greatly oblige to you for the trouble you give your self in forwarding my letters to Mrs [Catharine] Greene. I must increase the obligation by soliciting a continuance. I hope Mrs [Martha] Washington is with you as her situation at home in the present confusion of Virginia would be rather disagreeable. Please to present my respectful compliments to her and to the Gentlemen of your family.[2] Most respectfully yours   N GREENE

ALS (Washington Papers: DLC).
   1. Washington's letter, dated 19 April, is above.
   2. The "Gentlemen" of Washington's "family" were his aides.

*   *   *

¶ [FROM SAMUEL HUNTINGTON, PRESIDENT OF THE CONTINENTAL CONGRESS, Philadelphia, 23 June 1781. Encloses three acts of Congress. The first, dated 13 June, asks the states to make up the depreciation in the salaries of officers in the hospital department, as was previously done for officers of the line.[1] The second, of 16 June, sets regulations for granting furloughs and gives the form that department commanders are to use for furloughs and discharges. It was passed at Washington's request.[2] The third act, of 18 June, sets out "new Regulations" for the clothing department and repeals previous regulations for the clothing and hide departments that are "inconsistent" with the new arrangement.[3] NG's dispatches of 5, 10, 14, and 16 May have been received. Gov. [John] Rutledge, who will deliver this letter, can give NG "particular Intelligence from this Quarter."[4] LS (MiU-C) 3 pp.]

1. Huntington gave a nearly verbatim rendering of the act, which is printed in *JCC*, 20: 637. On Congress's actions in behalf of the line officers, see notes at General Officers' Memorial to Congress, 15 November 1779, above (vol. 5: 77n).

2. The act is printed in *JCC*, 20: 656–57. In addition to providing the form and wording for furloughs and discharges, it greatly restricted who could grant them and provided that any noncommissioned officer or soldier who failed to present his furlough or discharge to the nearest magistrate within ten days of his return home was to be "apprehended and treated as a deserter."

3. The act arranging the clothing department is in ibid., pp. 663–67. Under the new arrangement, the states were not to charge clothing purchased for the army against their accounts with the United States. All state appointments and state regulations pertaining to the department were abolished as of 1 September, and clothing held by the states was to be turned over to the Continental clothier general. The issuance of clothing was to be regularized, and careful records were to be kept; only those soldiers who had enlisted for at least one year were to receive clothing. (See also Risch, *Supplying*, pp. 280–81.)

4. As seen by his letter to NG of 29 May, above, Gov. John Rutledge of South Carolina had been in Philadelphia to seek support for the Southern Army and for his state.

*   *   *

From Colonel Henry Lee, Jr.

Saturwhite's farm between Davenports & Cook[s] [S.C.]

D[r] Sir   23[d] June [17]81

I should have wrote you sooner, but could not get ink; I am at length accidentally supplied pro tem: I had hopes, my messenger would have furnished me agreable to my yesterday[s] request.[1]

L[t] [Ferdinand] Neal returned last night: he spent the whole day around 96: where Lord Rawdon lay[s] encamped. I have not heard from his lordship this morning, but beleive he has not, nor can he move.[2]

I am much at a loss to form an opinion concerning the strength & intentions of your adversary. Nor can I account for his movements. He seems to be very fearful. For notwithstanding he must have heard; indeed he did hear by express from Col. [John Harris] Cruger of your raising the siege, he did not march on the direct road by Browns which was the route nearest you, but moved on a left road, & marched into Ninety Six from the Augusta quarter. He has left his baggage behind him, it was not in last evening, nor can I possibly learn where he has left it. I am now near Cooks mill to which place I moved in the expectation that I might find out the baggage & strike at it.[3]

His Lordship has no provision, nor has he taken any measures to get any, only by handmills. This informs me he must soon move. If he does I think, I shall be able to distress him.

I have no objection to the junction of Col° Hampton.[4] Yours truely

HENRY LEE JR

ALS (MiU-C).

1. See Lee to NG, first letter of 22 June, above.

2. As seen by Pierce to Sumter, this date, above, Lord Rawdon did move in pursuit of NG's army.

3. As seen at NG to Lee, 24 June, below, Rawdon's baggage reached Ninety Six before Lee could attack the wagons carrying it.

4. Col. Wade Hampton's detachment joined Lee on 28 June. (See Lee to NG, 29 June, below.)

*   *   *

¶ [GENERAL GREENE'S ORDERS, Camp, Broad River, S.C., 24 June 1781. In After Orders, given at 7 P.M., the troops are to receive a "jill of Rum per man" and are to "March tomorrow Morning." Lamar Orderly Book (OClWHi) 1 p.]

*   *   *

To Colonel Henry Lee, Jr.[1]

Dear Sir   Broad River [S.C.] June 24th 1781

It is next to impossible to draw the Militia of this Country from the different parts of the State to which they belong.[2] Marion is below. Pickens I can get no account of, and Sumter wants to make a tour to Monks Corner; and all I can say to either is insufficent to induce them to join us. I have again written to Pickens and Sumter, and hope they may bring forward their force.[3] Every body seems engagd in moving their families, which is attended with great inconvenience at this time.

I believe we have little desertion. Col Williams's Servant was one of the deserters that went to the enemy day before yesterday. He was detected in plundering and made his escape for fear of punnishment.[4] Every precaution is taken to prevent desertion as far as is in my power. But the officers of the army are by no means as careful as they ought to be.

If the British Army is in the distress you represent, they cannot they will not follow us far this morning, nor am I of opinion they will pursue farther.[5] Our Army is on the march for Sandy Run towards the Cross Roads on the route to the Catabaw Nation. At the ford on Broad River I have left your Infantry, [Capt. Robert] Kirkwoods Infantry and a hundred picked Virginia Militia under Major Ross [Alexander Rose].

The Enemy may be stoped a whole day at this pass. However there is a ford a mile or two above where horse & foot may pass but no carriages can cross there. It is a new ford lately found out except that there is no ford for ten or twelve Miles either above or below.

Capt Pearce set off for Charlotte yesterday to hasten on the Militia collecting there, and to press forward the troops under Baron Steuben and General [Jethro] Sumner.[6] I expect Major Armstrong with 200 men will join us every day.[7]

If the Militia are left behind to Garrison Ninty Six, I am much inclind to believe, they will garrison it in future with Militia. By this mode they the enemy will oblige the people to hang together and to provide ways and means for the support of the garrison. The regular troops will keep the field in a collected force. This was a part of their plan [illegible] conquer with the British troops and garrison with the Militia or Tories engagd in their interest.[8] And could they effect this plan they must succeed in the reduction of the Country. Yours aff   N GREENE

I have this moment got a letter from General Marion. He is at the Congaree, and writes that Major Mayum [Hezekiah Maham] is left below at Monks Corner who says a large fleet was seen at the Bar at Charlestown on Saturday last.[9] I am afraid it is another reinforcement from New York or Chessapeak Bay most probable the latter place, as the Marquis wrote me part of Lord Cornwallis's troops, had filed off for Portsmouth, and that he could not conjecture for what purpose, unless it was to embark for the Southward. However the fleet may be our friends instead of our enemies.[10]

By a letter from Gov Nash last evening [Adm. George] Rodney is certainly defeated in the West Indies and St Lucia taken.[11]

ALS (NcD).

1. The recipient was identified from the contents.

2. NG was replying to Lee's two letters of 22 June, above.

3. See NG to Pickens, and Pierce to Sumter, both 23 June, above.

4. For more about the desertion of Col. Otho Williams's servant, Benjamin Dominique, see Williams to NG, 5 July, below.

5. Rawdon wrote Lord Cornwallis that at the time he reached Ninety Six he had no intention of pursuing NG's army, which "had then so much the start" that he thought pursuit with his "fatigued troops would have been hopeless." But after receiving word that NG "had halted within sixteen miles of Ninety Six in a strong position behind Bush River & learning that he [i.e., NG] had still some Waggons with him," Rawdon "resolved to try once more to bring him to action." Leaving behind "every kind of baggage even the Packs of the Men," he marched from Ninety Six on the morning of 23 June. (Rawdon to Lord Cornwallis, 2 August, PRO 30/11/6; see also NG to Pickens, 23 June, above.) Crossing the Saluda River that night, he continued in a northeasterly direction to Duncan's Creek, or "the Fords of the Enoree" River, some forty miles from Ninety Six. (See NG to Sumter, 25 June, below; Rawdon to Cornwallis, 2 August.) He called off the advance there because his troops were "overcome with fatigue" and he saw "no further prospect of getting up with" NG. (Rawdon to Cornwallis, 2 August) On 25 June,

Rawdon began his return to Ninety Six, arriving there probably late on 26 June or early on the 27th. (See Lee to NG, 26 June, below.)

6. See Pierce to NG, 26 June, below.

7. In his second letter of 25 June, below, NG reported the arrival of Maj. John Armstrong with a force of North Carolina Continentals.

8. The British destroyed their works at Ninety Six and evacuated the post; they did not leave a garrison there. (See Williams to NG, 5 July; Henderson to NG, 6 July; and Pickens to NG, 10 July, all below.)

9. As seen in his letter of 25 June, below, Marion had written NG on the 22nd. That letter has not been found.

10. Nothing is known about the fleet that was reportedly sighted at Charleston. On the sending of some of Cornwallis's troops to Portsmouth, Va., see Lafayette to NG, first letter of 3 June, above.

11. The letter from Gov. Abner Nash of North Carolina has not been found. As noted at Huntington to NG, 3 June, above, the Comte de Grasse had arrived in the West Indies in late May with a large naval convoy and had won an engagement with a British squadron. The British-held island of St. Lucia proved "too heavily garrisoned to be stormed." (Dull, *French Navy*, p. 238)

* * *

¶ **[FROM JOSHUA POTTS**, Halifax, N.C., 24 June 1781. At the request of Col. [Nicholas] Long, who is with the legislature, Potts writes to say that NG's letter to Long of 6 May arrived "a few Days ago." It was impossible to comply with NG's wishes because they were forced to move "a considerable Distance up Roanoke River" by the enemy's approach to Halifax. "At some Risk, attended with much Difficulty & Fatigue," they removed and saved most of the public stores and would have lost little, if any, had it not been for "a Number òf People acting in the Quartermaster's Department," who "undertook, without proper Orders, to command & give Directions." At the "Instigation" of these people, "considerable Property of the Public was ransacked," including Col. [Henry] Lee's baggage, much of which has since been recovered. Seventeen barrels of gunpowder, which could have been safely removed, were also destroyed by order of some "Officious Gentlemen."[1] Encloses a return of "Stores saved" and a copy of a request from Gen. [Jethro] Sumner, which, if complied with, will leave them unable to supply NG's army with "such Articles as have been, and are required."[2] If Sumner calls "all the Continentals & twelve Months Men into the Field shortly," as he says he will, Long will be unable "to furnish Much, if any Thing More." Long requests orders concerning those Continentals and draftees who have been serving with him as artificers and "may be called away shortly." Militia officers say that "if Artificers be taken from them, they expect to be supplied with Necessaries from our Manufacture." Therefore, unless NG sends orders soon to insure that Long has enough men to "carry on the several Branches of Business performed as usual at this Place," NG's requests for supplies "cannot be answered; and, of Course, our Mechanical Operations must cease."[3] Encloses an invoice and the route to be taken by four wagons, "now setting off" for NG's army.[4] Was unable to provide "Cartouch Boxes or Canteens," as he recently sent all that he had to Sumner. Cannot get the returns needed for "A General Account of Stores within this State."[5] There is a "considerable

Quantity of Stores" at some "Remote Stations," which were recently sent from other posts, particularly Halifax. Asks NG to "excuse this Entensive Letter." ALS (MiU-C) 4 pp.]

1. In his letter to NG of 11 May, above, the Marquis de Malmedy gave an account of the loss of stores at Halifax that was less flattering to the supply officers.

2. Both the return, dated 16 June, and the letter (Sumner to Long, 12 June) are in MiU-C. In his letter, Sumner upbraided Long for drawing too many artificers from Sumner's brigade and ordered him to return three individuals "who you Maintain were to be Employed in Shoe Making." As "the shoes, are to follow the Cannons," he told Long, it would "Answer the real Intention of the drafts by the State" to call "those Employ'd in that Manufacture to the field." Sumner said he expected to receive 200 or 300 men shortly and would then call back nearly "all the Twelve months men you have."

3. NG's reply has not been found. His feelings about the use of troops as artificers are apparent from a letter of 19 July, below, in which he instructed Sumner to assign to the armory in Salisbury any draftees who might be armorers.

4. The invoice, dated 23 June, is in MiU-C.

5. In his letter to Long of 18 January, NG had requested monthly returns; Long had described the difficulty of getting the information from other supply officers in his letter to NG of 21 March, both above (vol. 7: 141, 457–58).

¶ [GENERAL GREENE'S ORDERS, "Camp Timms Ordinary," S.C., 25 June 1781. The troops are to receive and cook their next day's provisions. Officers will oversee the execution of this order and "be prepared to march at Sun-Sett."[1] Lamar Orderly Book (OClWHi) 1 p.]

1. As seen by the letter immediately below, NG changed his plan and remained at Timm's Ordinary for several days.

¶ [TO COLONEL HENRY LEE, JR. From "Camp at Timms Tavern," S.C., 25 June 1781. NG has been informed "that the Enemy are retiring." This is "nothing more" than he expected, as can be seen in his "letter of this morning" to Lee.[1] Adds: "If you can annoy them on their return you will act as the circumstances may render necessary." Gen. [Thomas] Sumter and Lee are both to move into the "lower Country."[2] Lee should act as his "judgment may direct."[3] NG expects Gen. [Francis] Marion, who is in the Congarees, to join in Sumter's "plan of operations."[4] The Southern Army will "move towards the Wateree and prepare to take post upon the high hills of Santee." Lee should order Capt. [Robert] Kirkwood's troops to join Col. [William] Washington; Lee can either send the infantry and the 100 Virginia militiamen to NG or, if necessary, take them with him.[5] "Dont neglect to take all the good horses you may come across; give receipts for all you take to both Whigs and Tories." A detachment of North Carolina regulars "will join" NG "to morrow."[6] Governor [Abner] Nash has "talked with" a man who "saw the engagement between Admiral [George] Rodney and Count duGrass [De Grasse]. The particulars he is not fully acquainted with but the defeat was general and the French left masters of the sea."[7] NG will "hold here to morrow" and then move towards the Santee River.[8] ALS (Brian Riba Associates, 1989) 2 pp.]

1. NG no doubt referred to his letter to Lee of 24 June, above. The movements of Lord Rawdon's army are noted there.

2. NG sent orders to Sumter in a letter of this date, below.

3. Lee reported his movements to NG in a letter of 29 June, below.

4. See NG to Marion, this date, below.

5. NG had left Kirkwood's troops and the Virginia militia with Lee to slow Rawdon's advance. (See NG to Lee, 24 June, above.) Lee wrote NG on 30 June, below, that Kirkwood was still with him.

6. As seen in NG's second letter to Lee of this date, below, the North Carolina detachment reached the army on the 25th.

7. For more on the engagement, see note at Huntington to NG, 3 June, above.

8. The army did not march until 29 June. (See NG's Orders of that date, below.)

¶ **[FROM COLONEL HENRY LEE, JR.,** [25 June 1781].[1] The enemy have halted at the Enoree River and "are grinding corn & wheat." Lee, who is at the Broad River, has an advance party near the Enoree. Asks for "particulars of Rodneys defeat."[2] ALS (MiU-C) 1 p.]

1. The date was taken from the docketing; no place was given.

2. NG sent Lee details of the naval engagement between British Adm. George Rodney and the Comte de Grasse in the letter immediately above.

*   *   *

To Colonel Henry Lee, Jr.

Dear Lee   [Camp, Timms Tavern, S.C.] 25th June 1781[1]

I have just recie[v]ed your two letters of this day.[2] In my last I gave you full liberty to act as you thought proper; and circumstances dictated to be necessary. Sumter is on the march for the Congaree, and will prepare to go still lower down. Let your movements be correspondent with his, so far as you may find them consistent with the good of the service. We shall remain on this ground to morrow after which we shall move to the point agreed on.[3]

I think the enemy will have a hard struggle in evacuating 96. I am rather inclind to think they will garrison it with Tories if they can get provisions. If the enemies reinforcements are as large as is represented they will try to take post at the Congarees; and nothing but the fear of our Army will prevent it.[4] I cannot think it prudent while the British Army is in the field and we want to reduce them to the necessity of retiring into the lower Country, to detach any part of our horse. It is not only necssary to have a superior Cavalry but a very great superiority. By keeping our selves collected we may effect what we wish; but by dividing we may defeat the whole. Sumter and Marian are collecting their force;[5] and the Militia from Roan and Mecklenburge are collected in considerable force.[6] [Maj. John] Armstrong has joined us this afternoon with the North Carrolinia regulars. A detachment of Continental Troops has come up.[7] If [Gen. Andrew] Pickens joins us with a considerable force it will be my wish to force Lord Rawden to an action.

Letters from Virginia to day but nothing new. General Morgan with a large body of Virginia rifflemen are forming a junction with the Marquis, General Cadwallauder [John Cadwalader] also with 2000 Maryland Minute Men have formed a junction with the Marquis. The people in that quarter are in high spirits and a defeat and capture of the Earl [Cornwallis] is strongly talked of. But this you know will require hard blows. Some of the Southern Army is much wished for, I mean the Legi[on] and the gallant Col Lee.[8] Yours Aff   N GREENE

ALS (MH).

1. As noted at NG's first letter to Lee of this date, above, his location remained the same until 29 June.

2. Only one letter from Lee of this date has been found. (See immediately above.)

3. On the points addressed in this paragraph, see also NG to Lee, first letter this date, above, and NG to Sumter, this date, below. Lee reported his movements in a letter to NG of 29 June, below.

4. Even before he marched to relieve Ninety Six, Lord Rawdon had decided not to try to hold the post with British troops because of the impossibility of supplying it. (Rawdon to Cornwallis, 5 June and 2 August, PRO 30/11/6) Shortly after arriving at the fort on 21 June, he called in the principal Loyalist leaders and gave them a choice either to defend the area themselves, aided by a small force that Rawdon would leave and occasional relief from a British post in the Congarees area, or to resettle the area's Loyalists on plantations in the South Carolina low country. Rawdon informed Cornwallis that the Loyalists chose resettlement in order to gain security against "the savage cruelty of the Rebel Militia: After which the Men proposed to embody to make incursions into the disaffected Settlements." (Rawdon to Cornwallis, 2 August, PRO 11/30/6) As seen in Pickens to NG, 10 July, below, Col. John Cruger Harris took the Ninety Six Loyalists and their families with him when he evacuated the post on 10 July.

5. See Gen. Francis Marion to NG, this date, below.

6. As seen at NG to Col. Francis Lock, 21 June, above, NG had a report that Lock, the local militia commander, had collected some 1,000 "good" militia in his district. The Marquis de Malmedy, who was sent to forward these militiamen, reported to NG on 29 June, below, that Lock had furloughed the men to their homes.

7. It is not known which unit, in addition to the troops that Maj. John Armstrong brought from North Carolina, had "come up"; NG most likely referred to troops returning to his army from detached duty.

8. The source of NG's information is not known. The report that "Maryland Minute Men" had joined the Marquis de Lafayette was false. For more on the militia force commanded by Gen. Daniel Morgan, see note at Lafayette to NG, 20 June, above. As seen there, Morgan brought far fewer militiamen than had been expected.

To General Francis Marion

Dear Sir   Camp on Sandy Run [S.C.] June 25th 1781

I am favord with your letter of   dated at the Congarees.[1] The enemy have obligd us to raise the seige of 96 when it was upon the eve of surrendering.[2] It was my wish to have fought Lord Rawden before he got to 96 and could I have collected your force and those of Generals [Thomas] Sumter and [Andrew] Pickens I would have done it; and I am perswaded we should have defeated him. But being left alone I was obligd to retire. I am surprisd the people should be so averse to joining in some general plan of operation. It will be impossible to carry on the war to advantage or even attempt to hold the Country unless our force can be directed to a point, and as to flying parties here and there they are of no consequence in the great events of war. If the people will not be more united in their views they must abide the consequences for I will not calculate upon them at all unless they will agree to act conformable to the great plan of recovering all parts of the Country and not particular parts.

General Sumter is preparing for a manoeuver down into the lower parts of the State, and he requir[e]s your aid to carry it into effect. You will therefore call out all the force you can and cooperate with him in any manner he may direct.[3] With esteem and regard I am Sir Your humble S^er   N GREENE

PS Count de Grass has defeated Admiral Rodney in the West Indies and taken St Lucia. These are facts and you may propagate them.[4]

ADfS (MiU-C).

1. The letter, which has not been found, was no doubt one that Marion wrote NG on 22 June. (See Marion to NG, this date, below.)

2. On the lifting of the siege, see NG to Huntington, 20 June, above.

3. See NG to Sumter, this date, below. Marion wrote NG on 28 June, below, that he had marched to Singleton's Mill in response to orders from Sumter and would wait there to hear from NG.

4. On the source of NG's information about the engagement between Adm. George Rodney and the Comte de Grasse in the West Indies, see NG to Lee, 24 June and first letter of 25 June, both above.

*   *   *

¶ [MAJOR ICHABOD BURNET TO GENERAL THOMAS SUMTER. From Fish Dam Ford, S.C., 25 June 1781. The army will march "this morning on the Charlotte route." Lord Rawdon camped "last evening beyond the Ennoree; his troops are greatly fatigued & without bread." NG wants Sumter to join him "as early as possible" so that they can give Rawdon "very effectual opposition."[1] ALS (Sumter Papers: DLC) 1 p.]

1. NG halted his retreat after learning later on this date that Lord Rawdon's army was no longer in pursuit. (See NG to Lee, first letter of 25 June, above.) He also changed his orders to Sumter. (See immediately below.)

*   *   *

To General Thomas Sumter

Dear Sir   Camp on Sandy Run [S.C.] June 25th [1781]

The enemy have retird. They come no farther than Duncans Creek.[1] I wish you to file off towards the Congaree and prepare to carry into execution the plan you had in contemplation into the lower Country.[2] No time is to be lost and you will endeavor to spirit up the people as much, as you can by informing them I am on the march that way. General Marion is at the Congarees, you will give him such directions as may be necessary to carry into effect the great object of the Maneuver.[3] I Shall move on towards the Waterree. I hope General [Andrew] Pickens will bring on a considerable reinforcment: and if the reinforcments from North Carolinia and General Stuben join us, we shall be strong to effect what we please.[4] Your Manufactory of Swords and Arms I think you had better send to Charlotte [N.C.] as it is highly probable the Congarees will be the seat of action.[5] If you can carry into execution what you proposd of sending the provision over the Santee it will be securing a great point. I am dear Sir Your Most Obedt humble Sr   N GREENE

ADfS (MiU-C).

1. On the enemy's retreat, see note at NG to Lee, 24 June, above.

2. NG was changing the orders that Ichabod Burnet had sent to Sumter on this date, immediately above. NG wrote Henry Lee on 24 June, above: "Sumter wants to make a tour to Monks Corner." This was presumably the same plan as the "Dog Days Expedition," which Sumter carried out some three weeks later.

3. On this date, above, NG sent orders to Francis Marion to cooperate with Sumter in the expedition. Sumter did not move into the "lower Country" immediately; he wrote NG on 2 July, below, that he had had "to take a Turn" through some of the regiments of his brigade.

4. On the expected reinforcement from North Carolina, see NG to Sumner, 18 June, above. As seen in his letter to Baron Steuben of 23 June, above, NG wanted Steuben to send along the Maryland Continental recruits when they reached Virginia.

5. Sumter had set up an armory at Ancrum's Plantation on the Congaree River. (See Sumter to NG, 22 May, above.)

*   *   *

¶ [FROM GENERAL FRANCIS MARION, "Ancrums Congarees," S.C., 25 June 1781. Marion wrote NG on 22 June [not found] to inform him of his "Arrivall in Consequence of Gen[l] [Thomas] Sumters Orders." He brought "few men" but expects more to join him "tomorrow." Maj. [Hezekiah] Maham, who was left to watch the enemy's movements, sends word that Col. [Alexander] Stewart's detachment of 250 men departed from Monck's Corner "Last Tuesday [19 June] & marched to Dorchester[,] report Say to Join the Army."[1] The British have 300 infantry and fifty dragoons posted at St. John's Church.[2] Charleston lacks "fresh provissions." Marion is "uneasy" in his present location, as he lacks intelligence of enemy movements and of NG's wishes for him.[3] If the enemy cross the Broad River and NG retreats toward Charlotte, N.C., Marion "may be hemed in between this & the Watteree Rivers." ALS (MiU-C) 2 pp.]

1. As seen at NG to Lee, 29 June, below, Stewart commanded the British Third Regiment, which had been sent from Charleston to reinforce Lord Rawdon.

2. Col. James Coates, with his British Nineteenth Regiment and mounted infantry of the South Carolina Rangers, had fortified the parish church of St. John, Berkeley, also known as Biggin Church. It stood on the Cooper River, about a mile and a half from Monck's Corner, and was a key post in maintaining the British line of retreat down the east side of the river. (Lipscomb, "S.C. Battles," *Place Names in South Carolina* 25 [Winter 1978]: 31; see also Sumter to NG, 2 July, below.)

3. NG sent orders to Marion in a letter of this date, above.

¶ [FROM JOHN MATHEWS, Philadelphia, 25 June 1781. Encloses newspapers containing "current news of this quarter." Gov. [John] Rutledge can give NG "other particulars," except such as Mathews "dare not communicate" to either Rutledge or NG. Mathews hopes Rutledge's presence will produce the "good consequences" that NG expects.[1] If NG can "maintain the ground" he has gained "with such infinite labour, & honor," he should see his "exertions crowned with" success—"that is, order, & all the tranquillity that a state of war can admit of, restored to a g[r]ievously distressed country." ALS (MiU-C) 1 p.]

　　1. Rutledge, who was then about to return to South Carolina from Philadelphia, reached NG's headquarters about 1 August. (See NG to Sumter, 1 August, below.)

¶ [FROM GENERAL JETHRO SUMNER, "Camp Harrisburg," N.C., 25 June 1781. Sends a return of draftees "collected at this place." When those from the New Bern district arrive, Sumner will form a second regiment. (The first will consist of the North Carolina troops now with NG and those from the Salisbury district.) An officer is to bring the draftees from the Wilmington district to the general rendezvous; orders have been given for a "diligent Officer" to remain at the site of each district rendezvous to receive the draftees from counties that have not yet delivered them. Sumner received NG's letter of 23 May on 20 June and will "pay due respect to the contents." He will march "as soon as possible" to join Baron Steuben in Virginia.[1] Sends intelligence of the situation in Virginia. Maj. [James] Craig, at Wilmington, "continues his Ravages for thirty and forty Miles up Cape Fear with little or no Opposition." The governor [Abner Nash] sent Sumner orders a few days ago "to march all the drafts collected to Duplin County." Sumner chose not to "alter the Rout before orderd" for several reasons: that this would be "incompatible" with his orders from NG; that some draftees had not yet "come up"; that the enemy party did not exceed 120 men; and that more than 200 American militiamen were reportedly near the enemy.[2] Congratulates NG on the Southern Army's successes in South Carolina and Georgia. LS (MiU-C) 2 pp.]

　　1. In a letter of 23 May, above, NG had ordered Sumner to march his troops to Virginia. NG had since changed that order and now wanted the North Carolina draftees to join him. (See NG to Sumner, 18 and 21 June, both above.) On 14 July, below, after he had received the new orders, Sumner wrote NG that his troops were about to march to join the Southern Army. They arrived in early August. (Rankin, *N.C. Continentals*, p. 346)

　　2. Duplin County was the scene of the "Ravages" by Maj. James Craig's raiders. As seen in the preceding note, Sumner still thought he was to march his draftees to Virginia.

*　　　*　　　*

From General Thomas Sumter

D[r] Sir　　　　　　Davis' 5 Miles below Liles Foard [S.C.] 25 June 1781

　　I have Received your Letter of this Date by Which I find the enemy Wear Persuing you untill late yesterday & I lament Exceedingly that We have No better prospect of Making a Stand.[1] Every Man of Co[l] Taylors Regem[ts][,] Winns[,] Tates & R. Hampon have absentd themselves except a few Who are upon Command.[2] By the Inclosed from Gen[l] [Francis] Marion you will find No assistance is to be expected from him, at least Not Soon.[3] I have Requested him to Return into his Brigade & there use every possible effort to Collect a force. I have also Given the Co[ls] in the Lower Part of My Brigade orders to immbody their Regem[ts] & March to the High Hills[,] Camden &c. This I thought expedient as I was Convinced they Coud Not or Woud Not March up through the fork to Make a junction with me.[4] If any Movement downwards Shoud be though[t] Necessary, I Woud beg leave to Say the Sooner it took place the beter it woud be as it Woud Stop hundreds that will otherways be out of the State & by our Decreasing & the enemies Increasing I am apprehensive Nothing of an extencive Nature will be in our Power.[5] I am Moving towards the Cross Roads Where I Shall be happy to Receive your farther Commands. I am D[r] S[r] your most obedt Hble Servt   THO[s] SUMTER

ALS (MiU-C).

1. See Burnet to Sumter, this date, above.

2. Colonels Thomas Taylor, Richard Winn, Samuel Tate, and Richard Hampton commanded regiments in Sumter's brigade.

3. The letter from Marion that Sumter enclosed has not been found, but it presumably contained much the same information as Marion to NG, this date, above.

4. According to Sumter's biographer, the militia of the "lower regiments would not risk marching through the Tory settlements of the Dutch Fork while the British army was so near." (Gregorie, *Sumter*, p. 168)

5. On the "Movement downwards," see NG to Sumter, this date, above.

*   *   *

¶ [FROM JOHN WHITE,[1] Salisbury, N.C., 25 June 1781. He has come this far "from Congress, with a charge" for Mr. [Joseph] Clay, the deputy paymaster general.[2] In the "present State of affairs," he believes it would be "imprudent" to proceed any farther. He will remain at Charlotte until Clay returns there or until he receives orders from NG; hopes NG approves of this.[3] Forwards several letters that he brought for NG. ALS (MiU-C) 1 p.]

1. White signed himself "Escorte of the Continental Board of War."

2. As seen in White's letter to NG of 1 July, below, the "charge" that he brought was $67,000 in new-emission money.

3. NG replied on 30 June, below.

¶ [GENERAL GREENE'S ORDERS, "Camp Timms Ordinary," S.C., Tuesday, 26 June 1781. The troops are to draw and cook one day's provisions, wash their clothes, and clean their weapons. The army will march "tomorrow Morning." In After Orders, given at 6 P.M., the order to march is canceled. Lamar Orderly Book (OClWHi) 2 pp.]

¶ [TO CAPTAIN WILLIAM THOMSON.[1] From "Camp at Timms Tavern," S.C., 26 June 1781. Gives him permission to return home. Praises his "patriotism and zeal" in staying with the army after his regiment was reduced and he became "subject to the command of others of inferior rank."[2] Warmly acknowledges Thomson's "good conduct" and the "importance" of his service. Wishes him "health and happiness." ALS (Bruce Gimelson, Chalfont, Pa., 1979) 1 p.]

1. Thomson, or Thompson, as his name is usually spelled, had been a captain in the Virginia State Regiment of Artillery. (Boyd, *Jefferson Papers*, 4: 541)

2. The state regiments had been reorganized in accordance with an act of the Virginia Assembly of 1 January 1781. The artillery regiment had been reduced to one company. (Advice of Council respecting Consolidation of the State Regiments, 6 February, Boyd, *Jefferson Papers*, 4: 536–37)

¶ [FROM COLONEL HENRY LEE, JR., 26 June 1781. Lord Rawdon continues his rapid retreat; Lee expects him to reach Ninety Six "this evening or early in the morning."[1] Believes Rawdon will stay there only two days to destroy the post before marching to Charleston.[2] "It will be happy" if NG's route of march can "give the color of a pursuit, & cause a suspicion" that NG will "visit" Charleston. If NG approves, Lee will "make a flourish around 96" and watch the enemy on their first day's retreat. He will then join Sumter, as NG ordered, "or act as circumstances & the state of my horses may require." He will send his infantry down the Tyger or Enoree River toward Friday's Ferry. When they are on a line with Motte's, they will "file off" either to join NG's army or to rejoin Lee at Motte's.[3] He would like [Gen. Andrew] Pickens to pursue the enemy's rear "while this game is playing in front." Reports that "Desertion prevails [among the enemy]" and "will increase." Rawdon's army, including Loyalists and the Ninety Six garrison, "will amount to 2,000 effective."[4] Rawdon is going to England after he reaches Charleston; his regiment of 300 men is ordered to Long Island, N.Y.[5] Suggests that [Capt. Robert] Kirkwood remain with Maj. [Alexander] Rose.[6] "It will render appearances better & will save you some little provision." Hopes the enemy intend to "confine themselves to the low country"; their plan should be apparent by the time NG reaches the Santee River. "The state of Virginia claims your attention"; suggests sending [Col. William] Washington "slowly" in that direction. Washington could impress mounts, fatten the ones that he has, and collect men along the route of march. If things turn out "as we hope," NG could then "readily follow" with the infantry of Lee's Legion. Lee's cavalry is "sufficient here, & the State cavalry may be made so before" NG leaves the state. Cavalry is needed in Virginia. NG could write—and Washington could report—that Lee's horsemen are also coming to Virginia.[7] ALS (MiU-C) 2 pp.]

1. For more on Rawdon's movements, see note at NG to Lee, 24 June, above.

2. As noted at NG to Huntington, 20 June, above, Rawdon had decided to evacuate Ninety Six even before he reached the post. On his departure and, later, that of the garrison, see Lee to NG, 30 June, and Pickens to NG, 10 July, both below.

3. Lee again reported on his plans in a letter to NG of 29 June, below. As noted there, changing circumstances quickly led to a different plan.

4. For more on Rawdon's estimated troop strength, see Lee to NG, 2 July, below.

5. Rawdon wrote Lord Cornwallis from Charleston on 2 August that he was leaving the army and returning to England because of the "total failure" of his health. (PRO 30/11/6) He sailed from Charleston on 21 August. (Nisbet Balfour to Cornwallis, 2 October, PRO 30/11/109)

6. For NG's orders concerning Kirkwood, see NG to Lee, 24 June and first letter of 25 June, both above; and Lee to NG, 30 June, below.

7. NG did not send any of his cavalry to Virginia or go there himself.

¶ [**FROM CAPTAIN WILLIAM PIERCE, JR.**, Charlotte, N.C., 26 June 1781. Encloses several letters that he "took the liberty of breaking open." Baron Steuben "has certainly" joined the Marquis [de Lafayette] by now.[1] Pierce will "go no further" unless NG directs. The weather is "warm," and his horses are "fatigued," but he will "chearfully undertake anything" to "serve" NG.[2] [Col. Francis] Lock is reportedly "on an expedition to Wilmington, but as the scheme seems rather farcical," Pierce will instruct Lock, in accordance with NG's orders, to join the army.[3] Will also write Gov. [Abner] Nash and Gen. [Jethro] Sumner "to-morrow."[4] Continues: "The sentiments of the People seem favorable, they wish you success, and talk of joining you with as much composure as the Councils of our Country do in establishing a plan for raising the Continental Army. They talk of turning out in large numbers, and boast of the great exploits they intend to do, but as they are Militia I cannot help thinking of the *Ragout*.[5] ALS (PHi) 2 pp.]

1. See Steuben to NG, 19 June, above.

2. Pierce's orders have not been found. As seen in Pierce to Nash, 27 June, below, NG had undoubtedly sent Pierce to North Carolina during the retreat from Ninety Six to expedite the movement of reinforcements and supplies to the army. He was back in camp by 1 July. (See Pierce to Carrington, that date, below.)

3. Pierce's letter to Lock has not been found; in a letter of 21 June, above, NG had asked Lock to send reinforcements to the Southern Army. On the proposed expedition to Wilmington, see Sumner to NG, 25 June, above. As seen by the Marquis de Malmedy's letter to NG of 29 June, below, the report that Lock had gone to Wilmington was false.

4. See Pierce's letters to Nash and Sumner, both 27 June, below.

5. Ragout was a dish usually consisting of meat cut into small pieces, stewed with vegetables, and highly seasoned. (*OED*) Pierce's use of the word here is not clear. As noted at Malmedy to NG, 29 June, below, North Carolina militia reinforcements did not join NG's army for some time.

¶ [**GENERAL GREENE'S ORDERS**, "Camp Timms Ordinary," S.C., 27 June 1781. Appoints two men to serve as ensigns in the Fourth North Carolina Regiment "till the pleasure of the State is known." Francis Cunningham, assistant deputy commissary of hides in the Salisbury district, is "to Secure the Hydes of the Cattle Slaughtered in Camp." Lamar Orderly Book (OClWHi) 1 p.]

*   *   *

To Governor Thomas Jefferson of Virginia[1]

Sir   Camp near the Cross Roads between Broad River
and the Catawba [S.C.] June 27th 1781.

The tardiness, and finally the countermanding of the Militia ordered to join this army has been attended with the most mortifying and disagreeable consequences.[2] Had they taken the field in time and in force we should have compleated the reduction of all the enemy's out posts in this Country; and for want of which we have been obliged to raise the seige of 96 after having closely beseiged it for upwards of twenty days and when four days would have compleated it's reduction. For want of the Militia the approaches went on slow and the seige was rendered bloody and tedious. My force has been unequal to the operations we had before us, but necessity obliged me to persevere, tho' under every disadvantage; and we should have been finally successfull had not the enemy recieved a large reinforcement at Charles Town generally agreed to amount to 2000 Men, which enabled them to march out and raise the Seige.[3]

The place might have been taken ten days sooner if our force had been equal to the labor necessary to facilitate it's reduction. Every post the enemy held either in S Carolina or Georgia have been taken or evacuated except Charles Town[,] Savannah and Ninety Six, and our success would have been compleat had our force been equal to the plan. However I hope the operations this way will be accompanied with many advantages. Certain it is, the enemy were about to detach from this quarter to Lord Cornwallis a greater force than we have had operating here. The reduction of their posts, destruction of the stores, their loss in killed, wounded and prisoners together with the increase of our friends and the decline of theirs are matters highly injurious to the enemy's interest and favourable to ours. And the operations would have been rendered still more so had the militia come forward agreeable to my application and your first order.[4]

The high respect which I ever wish to pay to the prerogatives of every State induces me to question with all due defference the propriety of your Excellency's order for countermanding the Militia which were directed to join the Army. No general plan can ever be undertaken with safety where partial orders may interrupt it's progress; nor is it consistant with the common interest that local motives should influence measures for the benefit of a part to the prejudice of the whole. I concieve it to be the prerogative of a Governor to order the force belonging to a State as he may think necessary for the protection of it's inhabitants. But those who are ordered out upon the Continental establishment are only subject to the orders of their Officers. Without this just & necessary distinction there would be endless confusion and ruinous disappointments. I only mention these things to avoid a misunderstanding in future. I have no wish for command further than the interest and happiness of the people are concerned, and I hope every body is convinced of this from my zeal to promote the common safety of the good people of these Southern States. I feel for the circumstances of Virginia, and if I had been supported here in time, I should have been there before this with a great part of our Cavalry.[5] But though I have not had it in my power to join the army, I hope your Legislature are convinced that I have left nothing unattempted to afford you all possible protection. You may remember in some of my former letters that I had solicited the Commander in Chief for the return of the Marquis [de Lafayette] with his detachment to the Southward from a persuasion you would be oppressed, and I have great reason to believe it had the desired effect.[6] The moment I got intelligence that Lord Cornwallis was moving Northwardly I gave orders for the Marquis to halt and take the Command in Virginia and to detain the Pensylvania Line and all the Virginia drafts.[7] With this force aided by the militia I was in hopes the Marquis would have been able to have kept the enemy from over running the State.

The importance of Cavalry and the consequences that might follow the want of it, your Excellency will do me the justice to say, I early and earnestly endeavoured to impress upon your Legislature, and they must blame themselves if they experience any extraordinary calamities for the want of it.[8] You would have been in a tolerable situation had your Cavalry been sufficiently augmented, and the last reinforcement from N. York had not arrived.[9] This gave the enemy such a decided superiority that there appears nothing left but to avoid a misfortune untill reinforcements can be got from the Northward. I have the highest opinion of the abilities of the Marquis and his zeal, and flatter myself that nothing will be left unattempted to give all the protection to the States that his force will admit. Your Militia are numerous and formidable and I hope if Gen[l] [Daniel] Morgan is out with them, they will be usefull.[10] Tho' Virginia is oppressed she is not a frontier State to the Southward, which would have been the case had I not moved this way, and all the force in North & South Carolina and Georgia would have been lost. Besides the disagreeable impression it would have made upon the nothern States to see those to the Southward over run. To divide the enemy's force as much as possible I have ever considered as favourable to our purposes, as it enables us to imploy a greater body of Militia and to more advantage.

My heart is with you, and I only lament that the cross-incidents in this quarter have prevented hitherto my pursuing my inclinations that way. I have the honor to be with great respect Your Excellency's Most Obedient Humble Servant   NATH GREENE

LS (Vi)
1. In this letter and in one to Jefferson of 29 June, below, NG was writing to Jefferson on official business and was assuming that he still was governor. Jefferson's term had legally ended on 2 June, and he did not function in the office after the British raid on Charlottesville on the 3rd. The legislature, whose members had scattered during the raid, finally elected Gen. Thomas Nelson to replace him on 12 June. (Selby, *Revolution in Virginia*, pp. 281–83)
2. On Jefferson's rescinding of the orders to Virginia militia to join NG, see Lafayette to NG, 18 May, above.
3. For more about the lifting of the siege at Ninety Six, see NG to Huntington, 20 June, above.

4. For the "application" and "first order," see NG to Jefferson, 23 March, above (vol. 7: 466), and Jefferson's reply of 30 March, above.

5. NG had written the Marquis de Lafayette on 23 May, above, that he would march to Virginia with part or all of his force if he succeeded in reducing the posts in South Carolina.

6. In his letter to Jefferson of 6 April, above, NG had said he hoped Washington would approve his orders to Lafayette not to "think of leaving Virginia in her present distresses but to march his Infantry by Alexandria [and] Fredricksburg to Richmond."

7. See NG to Lafayette, 1 May and 14 May, both above.

8. See NG to Jefferson, 1 January, above (vol. 7: 35).

9. On the "last reinforcement," see note at Washington to NG, 1 June, above.

10. On Morgan and the militia, see note at Lafayette to NG, 20 June, above.

*   *   *

¶ [TO GENERAL ROBERT LAWSON. From "Camp near the Cross Roads between the Catabaw & Broad River," S.C., 27 June 1781. Has received Lawson's letter of 14 May [not found]. Would have answered sooner but learned from that letter and from the Marquis de Lafayette "that the Militia orderd to the Southward was countermanded."[1] Repeats the complaints and criticisms that are seen in the letter to Thomas Jefferson, immediately above. Emphasizes that "before a force is granted for the service at large, the Executive has it in their power to determin whether they will furnish the force or not but after the order is given out, they can have no power over those troops; otherwise a general and an Army might be sacrificed." Wonders if Jefferson believed NG would ignore Virginia; outlines what he has done to protect the state. Adds: "The Governor I perswade my self, did not advert to the consequences or he would not have broke in upon my plan." Fears that the Virginians' lack of cavalry, which NG "foresaw long since" and "endeavored to impress upon your Legislature," will give the enemy "an advantage that will be accompanied with no small distress to the poor inhabitants." Continues:

> I have done all in my power to give protection in every quarter, but the efforts of the States have been by no means equal to the emergency; and therefore they must patiently submit to the misfortunes which their own tardiness have brought upon them. My utmost exertions shall be continued and I am ready and willing to encounter every danger and hardship to afford relief to this distressed Country. But without support what is to be done? I wish to be in Virginia; but whether it will be practicable for me to leave this Country at present I cannot fully determin.[2]

ALS (MH) 5 pp.]

1. On the countermanding of the orders, see Lafayette to NG, 18 May, above. As seen in his letter of 20 April, above, Lawson had expected to lead a contingent of Virginia militiamen to reinforce NG.

2. Although NG had briefly conisidered taking personal command in Virginia, he remained with his army in South Carolina.

¶ [CAPTAIN WILLIAM PIERCE, JR., TO GOVERNOR ABNER NASH OF NORTH CAROLINA. From Charlotte, N.C., 27 June 1781. NG is "retreating before Lord Rawdon with a force much inferior to" Rawdon's 2,000 men. "In all probability," NG will be "on the borders of North Carolina" by the time this letter reaches Nash.[1] NG "begs" Nash to "rouze the People" to his "immediate aid." Pierce says: "If a timely support is given us I know the General means to fight his Lordship." If help is not given, North Carolina could again become "the Theatre of War," and its "People will feel the miseries entailed on supineness and indifference." NG has asked Pierce to repeat his requests for dragoon horses.[2] Without cavalry, it is "utterly" impossible "either to secure your Camp, or operate with any probable hopes of success in the Field." With 200 "good" horses, the Americans would have "a decided superiority" and could "confine the Enemy to narrow limits."[3] Reports that "nothing material" has happened—not "even a skirmish"—since the siege of Ninety Six was raised. ADfS (MiU-C) 3 pp.]

1. NG had halted his retreat on 25 June. (See NG to Lee, first and second letters of 25 June, above.)

2. Previous requests for cavalry horses are in NG's letters to Nash of 13 April, 2 May, and 12 June, all above.

3. Thomas Burke, Nash's successor as governor, replied to NG on 4 July, below.

¶ [CAPTAIN WILLIAM PIERCE, JR., TO GENERAL JETHRO SUMNER. From Charlotte, N.C., 27 June 1781. NG wants Sumner to march "immediately" to join him with all the troops he has and any more he can collect along the way.[1] ALS (Nc-Ar) 1 p.]

1. Sumner wrote NG on 14 July, below, reporting on his efforts to forward troops to the Southern Army.

ℵ   ✦   ✶

To General Anthony Wayne

Camp near the Cross Roads between Broad River
Dear Sir   and the Catabaw [S.C.] June 27th 1781

A few days since I had the pleasure of your letter of the 4th. The reciept of it gave me double pleasure, I was happy in hearing from you, and happy to find you at the head of a 1000 choice fellows. I hope the Marquis [de Lafayette] will receive great support from your Corps. That the enemy are strong in Virginia I have too much reason to believe. I wish our prospects in that quarter were more flattering. But I hope to avoid a capital misfortune; and rest assured that both you and the Marquis will do every thing that is to be expected from Men.

We in this quarter have our ups and downs. We are somtimes retreating and somtimes advancing. Fortune is not our friend or rather our means are incompetent to the business we have to execute. More I believe was never done by an equal force than has been by this Army. Lt Col [Henry] Lee has provd himself this campaign what I always knew him to be that is one of the first Officers in the World. This will be handed you by one of his *Pets* who will be very happy in an opportunity to take you by the hand;[1] for you must know you are the Idle [i.e., Idol] of the Legion; and both Lee and my self have wished for you most heartily many a day. I hope we shall soon meet; and in meeting take an opportunity to give the Noble Earl [Cornwallis] a Southern breakfast.

I beg my most respectful complements to the Gentlemen of your brigade. I must refer you to Capt Rudolph [John Rudulph] for further particulars of the State of matters in this quarter. Yours affy

N GREENE

ALS (PHi).

1. The "pet" was Capt. John Rudulph, whom NG mentioned by name near the end of this letter.

*   *   *

¶ [FROM THE BOARD OF WAR, War Office [Philadelphia], 27 June 1781. Encloses a resolution of Congress for "furnishing the Continental Army with provisions by Contracts."[1] The board estimates that the Southern Army needs 31,137 rations per day. The estimate does not include rations for the troops from South Carolina and Georgia, as those states could not be expected to supply provisions by contract. The estimate is on a "large Scale," assuming that when there are deficiencies in a state's quota of men, as specified by Congress in its resolution of 3 October 1780, they will be made up for by calling militia into service. NG should inform the board where provisions "should be deposited," in "what proportions," and what steps should be taken "to cover and secure the Magazines."[2] The members are "apprehensive on this last Account," as the "greatest precaution" should be taken "in Countries actually invaded." They acknowledge NG's letter of 24 May, with the proceedings of Lt. [John] Townes's court-martial. They inform NG that "a quantity of Cloathing" is being sent to his army from Philadelphia and enclose an invoice. An officer is conducting these stores, and they hope "no person will be permitted to open them" along the way, "as has been frequently practised in similar Instances."[3] DS (NjGbS) 2 pp.]

1. The enclosure was probably a copy of a resolution of 22 May, in which Congress directed the Board of War to "estimate the supplies necessary for the northern and southern army in rations . . . and that proposals be taken in for supplying these at a stipulated price in gold and silver, by a contract or contracts, from the 1st of July next to the 1st day of January, 1782." (JCC, 20: 525–26) The policy of contracting for supplies was new, although the idea had been under consideration for some time. (Risch, Supplying, p. 244) It was a key part of the plan of Robert Morris, the new superintendent of finance, to bring costs under control. (Morris, Papers, 1: xxi)

2. NG replied on 19 September, below.

3. An invoice signed by Jacob S. Howell, dated 6 July, detailing the contents of twenty-six packages of clothing sent to the Southern Army under the care of Lt. [John?] Gordon, is at MiU-C.

¶ [FROM THE MARQUIS DE LAFAYETTE, "Mr. Tyree's Plantation 20 Miles from Williamsburg," Va., 27 June 1781. He informed NG in his letter of the 18th "of the Enemy's retrograde movement to Richmond where they made a stop. Our loss at the Point of Fo[rk] chiefly consisted of Old Arms out of repair and some Cannon, most of which have been since recovered."[1] The enemy advanced on the 18th, apparently "to strike at a detached Corps commanded by Gen^i [Peter] Muhlenberg." The light infantry and the Pennsylvanians, under Gen. [Anthony] Wayne, forced them to retire.[2] Baron Steuben's corps joined Lafayette the next day. Then, "on the night of the 20th Richmond was evacuated."[3] Lafayette's "light Parties" followed the British and "fell in with them near N[ew]. Kent Court House." Lafayette's army, though, "was Still at a distance and Ld Cornwallis continued his rout[e] towards Williamsburg." Later, "within Six Miles of" that place, an American advance party commanded by Maj. [William] McPherson, consisting of fifty dragoons and an equal number of infantrymen who had been mounted behind the dragoons, overtook Col. [John Graves] Simcoe's corps, which was covering the British "rear and right flank." The Americans charged, killing "about 60" and wounding "One Hundred."[4] Encloses a return of American casualties.[5] Says "the whole British Army came out to save Simcoe, and on the arrival of our Army . . . returned to Williamsburg.[6] The post they now occupy is strong and under protection of their shiping, but upwards of One Hundred miles from the Point of Fork." Lafayette has informed "the Executive of this Commonwealth that the seat of Government might be again reestablished in the Capital."[7] Cornwallis has received a reinforcement from Portsmouth. LS (NNPM) 2 pp.]

1. On the British raid at Point of Fork, see Lafayette's letters to NG of 18 and 20 June, both above.

2. For more on this incident, see Lafayette to NG, 20 June, above.

3. See Lafayette to NG, 21 June, above.

4. The skirmish took place on 26 June near Spencer's Ordinary. (Selby, *Revolution in Virginia*, pp. 289–90) It ended when Simcoe, who had gained a momentary advantage, left the field, fearing that Lafayette and the rest of the American army might be close at hand. The British reported much smaller casualties than Lafayette claimed. According to Cornwallis, "the enemy, though much superior in numbers, were repulsed with considerable loss." (Cornwallis to Sir Henry Clinton, 30 June, PRO 30/11/74) Simcoe called the skirmish "an honourable victory" for the British, "earned by veteran intrepidity." (Simcoe, *Military Journal*, p. 135) The Americans remained in possession of the field, however, winning what one historian has termed "an important psychological victory." (Selby, *Revolution in Virginia*, p. 290)

5. Lafayette reported losing nine killed, fourteen wounded, one captured, and thirteen missing. (PCC, item 156, p. 155, DNA) Simcoe, who claimed to have captured thirty-two Americans, said Lafayette reported only the losses among his Continental troops but also had "a great many" militia casualties, "exclusive of the prisoners." (Simcoe, *Military Journal*, pp. 135–36)

6. Simcoe, retreating toward Williamsburg, encountered Cornwallis, who was coming to his aid. According to Simcoe's account of the incident, he then returned to Spencer's Ordinary to recover his wounded. (Ibid., pp. 135–36)

7. In a letter of 26 June to Gov. Thomas Nelson, Lafayette recommended that the state government return to Richmond. (Idzerda, *Lafayette Papers*, 4: 214)

¶ [FROM CAPTAIN WILLIAM PIERCE, JR., Charlotte, N.C., 27 June 1781. Encloses a letter from "Col° Davis [William Davies]," which Pierce "broke open."[1] Davies's letter is "rather old and the news stale," but the express who brought it reports that "Sir Henry Clinton is arrived in Virginia with a reinforcement."[2] Pierce adds: "Possibly it may be so, but our force accumulates so fast in that quarter that they begin to dread us." ALS (MiU-C) 1 p.]

1. It is not known what letter of Davies's was enclosed.

2. The report was false.

¶ [**GENERAL GREENE'S ORDERS**, "Camp Timms Ordinary," S.C., 28 June 1781. Appoints a court at the request of Col. [John F.] Grimké to investigate Grimké's reasons for leaving Hadrell's Point, where he had been held as a prisoner of war.[1] A court-martial is appointed to try the "Keeper of Live-Stock" and any other prisoners brought before it.[2] Lamar Orderly Book (OClWHi) 2 pp.]

1. The results are reported in NG's Orders of 29 June, below.

2. For the findings of this court, see NG's Orders of 4 July, below.

*   *   *

To General Andrew Pickens

Dear General   Camp near the Cross Roads [S.C.] June 28th 1781

I have been impatiently waiting to hear from you and the Waggons in your quarter. Not a line have I receivd since we parted at Ninty Six. The enemy made a push after us, and we retird at our ease. They were so much distressed for want of provisions that they soon gave over the pursuit.[1] The Militia in Salisbury District will soon afford us a large reinforcment. I expect Col [Isaac] Shelby will also bring to our aid a very considerab[le] force.[2] Major [John] Armstrong has joined us with a reinforcment of North Carolinia regulars. General Sumter[,] Col Lee and Washington are moving down towards Orrangburg.[3] I wish to know where you are and what for[ces] are with you.[4] It is not certain what the enemy mean to do with Ninty Six. If they leave a Garrison there we are in a situation to invest it immediately. But unless they can collect provisions which I think they cannot, if you are active in your quarter, they cannot hold the place; nor do I believe they dare attempt it. We shall wait near this place until the enemies intentions are further explained.[5]

General Washington has laid seige to New York with a large Army. Lord Cornwallis is retreating in Virginia owing to a very great host of Militias taking the field.[6] I have official inform[a]tion of the defeat of the B. fleet in the West Indies from Congress.[7] I have also several other interesting and agreeable pieces of intelligence; which I am not at liberty to explain for fear this letter should fall into the enemies hands and defeat what is now carrying into execution. I am Sir Your humble Ser   N GREENE

ADfS (MiU-C).

1. On the pursuit of NG's army by the British after the lifting of the siege of Ninety Six, see note at NG to Lee, 24 June, above.

2. Neither the militia from Salisbury nor Shelby's frontiersmen joined NG until much later. (See notes at NG to Lock, 21 June, above, and Shelby to NG, 2 July, below.)

3. See NG's letters of this date to Thomas Sumter, Henry Lee, and William Wash-

ington, all below. NG asked Sumter to detach Col. Charles Myddelton to cooperate with Lee and Washington.

4. Pickens wrote NG on 30 June, below.

5. Lord Rawdon wrote Lord Cornwallis on 2 August that he decided to withdraw the garrison from Ninety Six because of the impossibility of obtaining provisions. (PRO 30/11/6)

6. On the planned campaign against New York, see Sharpe to NG, 28 May, and Washington to NG, 1 June, both above. The Marquis de Lafayette had written NG on 21 June, above, that Cornwallis was retreating.

7. See note at NG to Lee, 24 June, above.

*　　*　　*

¶ **[FROM CAPTAIN DAVID HOPKINS,**[1] Baltimore, Md., 28 June 1781. The Board of War, to whom he applied for a promotion to major in the First Regiment of Light Dragoons, has directed Hopkins to "address" NG because the unit is "immediately" under NG's command. He requests "an order for a commission." Discusses his claim to the promotion. Expects to be employed in organizing the "300 horses" that Maryland is now raising for the cavalry; asks that NG's reply be directed "to this place."[2] Reports that "about 100 persons" have been "taken up" in Maryland within the past five days for conspiring to release the Convention army prisoners; General Lee is said to have been the instigator.[3] ALS (MdHi) 2 pp.]

1. Hopkins signed himself a captain in the Fourth Regiment of Light Dragoons.

2. NG's reply has not been found.

3. The number of arrests was greatly exaggerated here. One of the ringleaders of the Loyalist plot reportedly claimed that 6,000 men had been secretly recruited for service with the British. Only seven men were arrested, however, three of whom are thought to have later been executed. Reports filed by Maryland officials said nothing about an attempt to release the Convention army prisoners, nor did they in any way implicate former Continental Gen. Charles Lee. (See Dorothy M. Quynn, "The Loyalist Plot in Frederick," *Maryland Historical Magazine* 40 [1945]: 201–10.)

¶ **[FROM COLONEL PETER HORRY,** High Hills, S.C., 28 June 1781. He returned to Gen. [Francis] Marion's camp yesterday to find NG's letter of 21 June, containing "a Commission."[1] Thanks NG, adding that he will readily undertake anything NG proposes that will benefit the country. In accepting, however, he does not relinquish his "Claim" to be "Continued on the Continent' Infantry of this State." Will do his "Utmost" to complete NG's plan, but is "afraid men cannot be had for Less bounty than what General Sumter has Given and by what methods I could Obtain Negroes for that Purpose I Am at a Loss. The negro Given by Gen' Sumter is Equal to a Dollar per day to Each private[.] I have no money in hand, nor Authority to take Tories negroes, and without something in hand few am afraid will depend on Promises. However I will try it on the Usual bounty & Pay Given by Congress."[2] Marion will help Horry and can supply him with money borrowed "on the faith of the Country, but will not Suffer negroes to be Seized on or taken out of his Brigade." Asks NG what the pay of Continental dragoons is and whether he may impress clothing for his regiment.[3] Horry will "Put men to make Swords & Saddles Immediately" and will equip the troops "as fast as" he can raise them. He will continue to serve under Marion until he has "a sufficient Number to Act."

Thinks the regiment should include a major, an adjutant, and a sergeant major, which NG did not mention in his "formation." Asks for a quick answer.[4] ALS (MiU-C) 2 pp.]

1. NG's letter has not been found, but his proposal to Horry must have been similar to the one he made to Col. Hezekiah Maham to "raise a Corps of horse" for the army. (See NG to Maham, 21 June, above.)

2. Thomas Sumter had offered confiscated slaves as bounty to the troops of his mounted corps. (See note at Sumter to NG, 7 April, above.)

3. In his letter to Maham of 21 June, above, NG had said that the pay of recruits was to be no less than that of Continental dragoons. In 1778, Congress had established the rate of pay for those troops at $8 ⅓ per month. (JCC, 11: 541)

4. Maj. Ichabod Burnet replied for NG on 2 July, below.

¶ [FROM GENERAL FRANCIS MARION, "Singletons Mill High Hill Santee," S.C., 28 June 1781. "In Consequence" of Gen. [Thomas] Sumter's order, which he received the evening of 26 June, Marion "marched for this place." Will wait there for NG's orders, which he wishes to have "as soon as possible." Has 400 men and expects more to join him "in a day or two." ALS (MiU-C) 1 p.]

1. NG replied on 2 July, below.

¶ [GENERAL GREENE'S ORDERS, "Camp Timms Ordinary," S.C., "Morning," 29 June 1781. The army is to "march by the Right." Lamar Orderly Book (OClWHi) 1 p.]

¶ [GENERAL GREENE'S ORDERS, "Camp Bigg Spring Rockey Creek," S.C., 29 June 1781. A court of inquiry has found that Col. [John F.] Grimké's confinement by the British freed him from the terms of his parole. As Grimké "did not enter into any new Contract with the Enemy either Verbal, or Writen," after his release from confinement, he was "perfectly" justified in escaping.[1] The commissary is to "issue a Canteen of Spirit to each Officer, and a jill to each NonCommisd Officer and Soldier this Evening." Lamar Orderly Book (OClWHi) 2 pp.]

1. The court of inquiry had been convened in accordance with NG's Orders of 28 June, above. Grimké, captured at Charleston in May 1780, had been on parole until Col. Nisbet Balfour, the British commander at Charleston, charged him and another American officer with having "written letters to an adherent of the American cause in Beaufort," behind British lines. Balfour had both men placed in "close confinement." (McCrady, S.C. in the Revolution, pp. 354–55; see also Moultrie to NG, 3 April, above.) Released from that situation after the signing of the prisoner-exchange cartel in May, Grimké soon escaped. He made his way to NG's camp and requested a court of inquiry into his conduct. (McCrady, S.C. in the Revolution, p. 356)

¶ [TO GOVERNOR THOMAS JEFFERSON OF VIRGINIA.[1] From "Head Quaters near the X Roads," S.C., 29 June 1781. Capt. [John] Rudulph of Lee's Legion "comes to Virginia" to augment the cavalry of that "usefull and necessary Corps." Jefferson must decide what help Virginia can provide, but NG assures him that "whatever aid is given" will "promote the service, and the force so formed shall be employed in Virg[a] while the State continues to be oppressed."[2] ALS (Vi) 1 p.]

1. As noted at NG to Jefferson, 27 June, above, NG did not yet know that Gen. Thomas Nelson had succeeded Jefferson as governor.

2. For more on Rudulph's mission, see NG to the Marquis de Lafayette, immediately

below. No reply has been found. On 30 July, the state council, at Lafayette's request, authorized Rudulph to impress 100 horses. (Virginia, Council of State, *Journals*, 2: 368) That must have been the only aid the state was willing to provide, for Lafayette wrote Rudulph on 22 August that Virginians "would consider it a sacrilege" if any new recruits were turned over to Rudulph. It was "entirely out of the question," moreover, to obtain "accoutrements" in Virginia. (Idzerda, *Lafayette Papers*, 4: 318n)

¶ [TO THE MARQUIS DE LAFAYETTE. From "Head Quarters near the Cross Roads between Broad River & the Catabaw," S.C., 29 June 1781. Introduces Capt. [John] Rudulph, who has been sent "to procure horses and rifflemen" for Lee's Legion. That unit and [Col. William] Washington's corps "are of great importance to the service and deserve every possible encouragement." NG asks Lafayette to give Rudulph all the assistance he can "without interfering with the claims and pretentions of the other Corps of horse now forming in Virginia." If necessary, Lafayette should arrange for Rudulph to obtain warrants for impressing horses and "such sums of money" as he needs.[1] "What ever force" Rudulph raises will "be employed in Virginia while that State continues to be so hard pressed." Rudulph can inform Lafayette about NG's "operations." ADfS (MiU-C) 2 pp.]

1. Lafayette wrote NG on 12 July, below, that Rudulph had "Arrived Yesterday." On Lafayette's efforts to assist him, see note at NG to Jefferson, immediately above.

* * *

To Colonel Henry Lee, Jr.

Head Quarters [near the Crossroads, S.C.]
Dear Sir June 29th 1781

By a deserter who came into Camp last evening, I learn the enemy have 16 Waggon load of stores of different kinds moving up from Charles Town upon the Orangburge road under an escort of 400 Men & forty horse for the use of Lord Rawdens Army.[1] He left them at Four Holes about five and thirty miles below Orangburg on Sunday last, and says they could not march more than eight or ten Miles a day; and adds they were very sickly and much dissatisfied.

I have directed Col Washington to move down to Ancrums Plantation upon the Congaree and Col Middleton to join them at that place[.][2] If you are in a situation to form a junction with them, I think you may take the whole of this escort with great ease. I beg you will take measures therefore without loss of time for forming a junction with them at that place or advertize them where it may be effected to more advantage. Or if you think your force equal to the attempt and that the opportunity may be lost in waiting for a reinforcement, in that case you will move as farther information may dictate to be necessary. As your collective force joined to those of Washington and Middleton will effect the business with out risque I wish you not to hazard too much to effect it alone. But at any rate you will inform Col Washington what route you will move and what you would wish him to do.[3] I shall send duplicates of this letter for fear one should miscarry.

I have the pleasure to inform you by letters receivd yesterday from Virginia that Lord Cornwallis is retreating and the Marquis pursuing. General Washington joined by the French Army has laid seige to New York with an Army of 15000 men.[4] I have also official information from Congress of the defeat of Admiral Rodney in the West Indies.[5] I have several other interesting peices of intelligenc[e] which are flattering to our interest; but I am not at liberty to disclose them at present.

I rely upon your prudence and activity and am yours Aff

N GREENE

NB. Part of our reinforcements have arrived & the remainder are near.[6]

ALS (CSmH).

1. Col. Alexander Stewart was to have brought the Third British Regiment to join Rawdon at the Congarees on 3 July. Stewart, however, had mistakenly been "stopped in his march by orders from Charlestown & recalled to Dorchester." (Rawdon to Lord Cornwallis, 2 August, PRO 30/11/6; see also William Washington to NG, 2 July, below.)

2. See NG to William Washington, this date, below, and NG to Charles Myddelton, immediately below.

3. Upon hearing that Rawdon was marching toward the Congarees with a force of 500, Lee decided to "advance towards" him. (Lee to NG, 30 June, below) Some days later, NG again ordered Lee to intercept Stewart's column. (NG to Lee, 4 July, below) When Rawdon began to move toward Orangeburg, both Lee and Washington concentrated their efforts on trying to cut him off. (See Lee's two letters to NG of 3 July and Washington to NG, 5 July, all below.) In the end, only Gen. Francis Marion's militiamen had the opportunity to intercept Stewart, who skillfully avoided a trap that Marion had set for him and joined Rawdon at Orangeburg on 7 July. (Marion to NG, first letter of 8 July, below.)

4. On Cornwallis's retreat toward Williamsburg, see Lafayette to NG, 20 June, above. George Washington's plan for a joint, Franco-American attack on New York was never implemented. (On the plan, see Sharpe to NG, 28 May, and Washington to NG, 1 June, above.)

5. NG had written Lee about the naval engagement in his letter of 24 June, above.

6. On the reinforcements, see NG to Lee, second letter of 25 June, above.

*   *   *

¶ [TO COLONEL CHARLES MYDDELTON. From Camp [near the Cross-roads, S.C.], 29 June 1781. Orders him to join Colonels Lee and Washington in intercepting "an escort with a quantity of Stores" for Lord Rawdon, which is now on the road to Orangeburg.[1] NG has written Myddelton directly because General Sumter may not be present to receive NG's letter on the subject.[2] If Sumter is not there, Myddelton should "move down," leaving the "next oldest officer" in command of Sumter's troops. NG will send the "tin Cannisters and ammunition" that Myddelton requested. ADfS (MiU-C) 2 pp.]

1. For more on the "escort" and NG's orders to Henry Lee, see the letter immediately above. NG's letter to William Washington, this date, is below.

2. See NG to Thomas Sumter, immediately below.

¶ [TO GENERAL THOMAS SUMTER. From Headquarters [near the Cross-roads, S.C.], 29 June 1781. Sends Sumter much the same intelligence as that contained in NG's letter to Henry Lee, this date, above. Asks him to have Colonel Myddelton's regiment join Washington and Lee in intercepting an enemy detachment now on the march to Orangeburg; by combining, the American "force may be equal to the attempt without risque."[1] Tells Sumter: "The sooner you can move your whole force towards the Congaree the better." NG has not heard from General Pickens and does not know "whether the enemy will attempt to evacuate or hold 96."[2] Believes, however, that "we are in the most convenient situation for investing" that post if they try to retain it. LS (Sumter Papers: DLC) 2 pp.]

1. For more on the enemy detachment and NG's orders to the two officers, see his letters of this date to Lee, above, and William Washington, immediately below. See also NG to Charles Myddelton, immediately above.

2. As noted at NG to Huntington, 20 June, above, Lord Rawdon had decided to evacuate Ninety Six before he reached it. Andrew Pickens reported the garrison's preparations for departure in his letter to NG of 10 July, below.

¶ [TO COLONEL WILLIAM WASHINGTON. From [near the Crossroads, S.C., 29 June 1781].[1] Captain "Conners [James Conyers]" last night brought in a deserter from "the escort coming up to Orrangburge."[2] NG approves of Washington's plan to move down to Ancrum's Plantation and has directed Col. [Henry] Lee and Col. [Charles] Myddelton to join Washington there.[3] If Washington finds that an attack on the enemy is warranted without waiting for Lee, NG wants him "to do it." If there is a timely prospect of forming a junction, though, it would be better to wait, as there would be less "risque of a defeat."[4] NG relies on Washington's "prudence and activity"; reminds him that his "horses are low in flesh and should be indulged as much as possible." Tells him to stay in contact with Lee. NG will "continue" in the same neighbor-hood "for some days."[5] ADfS (MiU-C) 2 pp.]

1. The date was taken from the docketing, the place from other letters of this date.

2. For more on the deserter and the "escort," see NG to Lee, this date, above.

3. No letter from Washington on this subject has been found, but Conyers, who was a member of Washington's corps, may have told NG of the "plan." NG's orders to Lee and Myddelton are in letters of this date, above.

4. NG had given similar advice to Lee in his letter of this date. As noted there, NG's detachments did not intercept Alexander Stewart's force.

5. As seen in his letter to Gen. Andrew Pickens of 28 June, above, NG was waiting to learn whether the British would leave a garrison at Ninety Six or evacuate the post.

¶ [FROM COLONEL HENRY LEE, JR., "Camp between the Ennoree & Bush Rivers on the Old Saluda Road," S.C., 29 June 1781. As NG has placed his "trust" in Lee, with no "particular instructions," Lee thinks it proper to inform him "of the line of conduct" he has "determined to pursue."[1] His "first object" is to "impress" the people with "the superiority" of NG's "arms" and to convince them that Lord Rawdon's retreat to Charleston, which Lee takes "for granted," is a result of Rawdon's "disinclination to risk an action."[2] To this end, Lee is moving toward Ninety Six. On 27 June, he detached Capt. [Joseph] Eggleston to Ninety Six with a party of dragoons, hoping that Eggleston will "find the enemy in a dispersed position" and "strike where prudence may direct." Lee hopes thereby "to hold up the idea of our superiority, to intimidate the disaffected," and to learn Rawdon's "real situation and intention." If Rawdon moves "without leaving a post behind," Lee plans to "gain his front," possibly joining with Gen. [Thomas] Sumter to do so, and keep "a party of horse" in Rawdon's rear. If Rawdon leaves a garrison at Ninety Six that is "equal to an attempt," Lee will use his infantry to attack it and will pursue the "fugitives with the horse." That is the outline of his plan, but "circumstances unforseen may cause an alteration."[3] Thinks his presence may have caused Loyalists to postpone a muster that was to have taken place "yesterday." There are "many deserters from the enemy," although Lee himself has not yet seen any. One deserter told Col. [Wade] Hampton, who joined Lee "yesterday," that "96 will be destroyed, that Lord Rawden will embark for England, his reg[t] will go to Long Island," and that three other regiments will sail to New York.[4] "If this is the case you will have a peaceable autumn." Lee's cavalry is "shoing & refreshing"; it is doing "very well for provision" but lacks rum and salt. Adds in a postscript that he understands NG is "strongly reinforced & marching for Friday[s] Ferry." ALS (MiU-C) 4 pp. A few words that are illegible because of a crease in the ALS were taken from a Draper transcript (WHi).]

1. Lee referred to the instructions in NG's first letter to Lee of 25 June, above.

2. Rawdon was still at Ninety Six. He left Ninety Six on 29 June and moved toward the coast with some 900 men. (See Lee to NG, 30 June, below.) He halted at Orangeburg, however, instead of proceeding to Charleston. (See note at Marion to NG, 7 July, below.)

3. Lee had not yet received the new orders that NG sent him on this date, above. Lee's subsequent movements are noted there.

4. On the evacuation of Ninety Six, see Pickens to NG, 10 July, below. As noted at Lee to NG, 26 June, above, Rawdon did leave the army to return to England. The British regiments remained in South Carolina.

¶ [FROM THE MARQUIS DE MALMEDY, Salisbury, N.C., 29 June 1781. Col. [Francis] Lock has "furloughed his militia at home," having received "no farther direction from the governor."[1] At NG's "request," Lock is now ordering them out again and promises to have 800 men at Charlotte in seven days.[2] Captain "McKree [Griffith McRee] is to be relieved" and go "immediately to head quarters."[3] Malmedy is waiting for an express to forward NG's letters to Virginia. He will then proceed immediately "to the assembly."[4] ALS (MiU-C) 1 p.]

1. NG had sent Malmedy to hurry a detachment of Salisbury district militia to the Southern Army. (See NG to Malmedy, 23 June, above.)

2. The sending of militia reinforcements from Salisbury continued to be delayed. (See, for example, Malmedy to NG, 10 July, and Lock to NG, 10 August, both below.) In a letter to Lock of 30 July, below, NG implied that the militia colonel had been "criminally negligent."

3. McRee had commanded a detachment escorting prisoners of war to North Carolina. (NG to Lock, 21 June, above)

4. In a letter to NG of 10 July, below, Malmedy reported on his dealings with the North Carolina legislature.

¶ [FROM MAURICE SPILLARD, Caswell County, N.C., 29 June 1781. [Capt. William] Pierce, in a letter of 18 April, said that NG would allow Spillard to go home after Spillard's baggage arrived.[1] Spillard has sent NG "two letters for

Camden," requesting that the baggage be forwarded.[2] He has had no answer and assumes that NG's "hurry of buisness" has kept him from writing. Because of his "distressed situation," Spillard has sent the bearer to "beg" that he be allowed to go home and to find out if Lord Rawdon has sent the baggage. Adds that his lack of clothing "is truely distressing[;] not having the second change therefore must Render my situation for so long a journey alarming if my Baggage is not sent me." Asks to "go to procure" the baggage.[3] ALS (MiU-C) 2 pp.]

1. In Pierce's letter, above, nothing was said about Spillard going home.
2. See Spillard to Pierce, 27 April, above.
3. No reply has been found.

* * *

General Greene's Orders

Camp Bigg Spring [S.C.] Saturday 30th June 1781

Every endeavour is to be used to keep the present Encampment as clean as Possible. Vaults are to be dugg immediately and Centinels from the Camp guards posted, to prevent the common uncleanly customs, by which the Camp is generally rendered disagreeable and unwholesome.

The Officers in the Several Branches of the Staff departments will pay particular attention to this Order.

The Rolls are to be called every two hours, to prevent Marauding, and absentees, must be Severely punished.

The Arms and accoutrements must be prepared for a general review tomorrow, and it is expected the Men will have their Cloaths Clean.

Lamar Orderly Book (OCIWHi).

* * *

¶ [TO JOHN WHITE. From "Camp at the Cross Roads," S.C., 30 June 1781. Has his letter of 25 June. Mr. [Joseph] Clay is at Augusta, Ga., and will probably not return "in less than a fortnight." NG can better decide whether White should "come to the Army" if White will explain his business with Clay.[1] ADfS (MiU-C) 2 pp.]
1. White replied on 1 July, below.

¶ [FROM COLONEL HENRY LEE, JR., "Camp on the Wateree Creek[,] Hamptons Store," S.C., 30 June 1781. He received NG's letter "yesterday evening & instantly moved in the direction" NG "commanded."[1] Does not know if Col. [William] Washington has crossed the Broad River. Capt. [Robert] Kirkwood received Washington's orders "yesterday" to join Washington, but NG's letter of 29 June has "induced" Lee to keep Kirkwood "least an opportunity of striking might be lost . . . for want of force." Wants NG to inform Washington of this, "least a stupid jealousy may arise." Lee considered Kirkwood to be under his orders because of the letter Lee wrote NG "from Tyger

River" and NG's reply.[2] Such "confusion in orders must detrement the service." Capt. [Joseph] Eggleston has sent intelligence "that Lord Rawdon is on his march to the Congarees (Fort Granby)[;] whether he means to establish a post or not is uncertain."[3] Rawdon has fewer than 500 men with him; [Col. John Harris] Cruger "has the Cheif force at 96 & has detached the main body of it to Long Cane."[4] The small force that Rawdon has with him leads Lee to believe another enemy party "has marched for Augusta." A Loyalist officer, who "joined" Lee "this moment" after mistaking Lee's troops "for the British," confirms the division of the enemy's forces and the size of Rawdon's detachment. Lee expects Rawdon either to establish himself at the Congarees or march to Charleston, "having und[r] him those troops reputed to be under orders for N York."[5] Adds: "If you can advance to the Ennoree & detach Washington to 96, it is probable you will baffle their schemes, save the country & perhaps gain an oppertunity of injuring the enemy capitally & I beleive you will collect your militia the sooner. I would not permit them to hold 96."[6] Lee will "advance towards" Rawdon. With the addition of Col. [Wade] Hampton's detachment, which is to join him today, he may be strong enough to attack Rawdon. Expecting NG to advance, Lee plans "to keep between 96 & Fort Granby on the Saluda." Asks for writing paper and wafers. ALS (MiU-C) 4 pp.]

1. See NG to Lee, 29 June, above.

2. It is not known which exchange of letters had led Lee to consider Kirkwood as still being under his orders. NG had ordered that Kirkwood's troops be sent to join Washington in his first letter to Lee of 25 June, above.

3. Lee had sent a party under Eggleston toward Ninety Six. (Lee to NG, 29 June, above)

4. Lee revised his estimate of Rawdon's troop strength in his letter to NG of 2 July, below. On the raid on Long Cane by troops from Ninety Six, see note at Henderson to NG, 6 July, below.

5. Rawdon later wrote that he had marched a "small force" of "800 Foot & 60 Horse" to the Congarees in the expectation of meeting Col. [Alexander] Stewart's force. He had left Cruger at Ninety Six with "the more active part of my force." Rawdon's purpose in making the move was to see if "a feint . . . against [NG's] Stores could not decide Greene to fall back as far as Charlottesburg [i.e., Charlotte, N.C.]." That, in turn, would have left Rawdon free to send a reinforcement to Lord Cornwallis, as Cornwallis had wanted him to do as soon as "the Convoy" arrived at Charleston. (Rawdon to Cornwallis, 2 August, PRO 30/11/6) As noted at NG to Lee, 29 June, above, Stewart's troops, instead of advancing to join Rawdon, were mistakenly ordered back toward Charleston. They did not meet Rawdon until later, at Orangeburg.

6. NG decided to march in pursuit of Rawdon. (See Pierce to Carrington, 1 July, below.) On Washington's movements, which were also related to Rawdon's, see Washington to NG, 2 July, and NG to Washington, 3 July, both below. The British had already decided to evacuate Ninety Six. (See note at NG to Huntington, 20 June, above.)

¶ [FROM GENERAL ANDREW PICKENS, "Camp near Grindels Sholes," S.C., 30 June 1781. Has NG's letter of 23 June and is marching to join the Southern Army with "Between four and five hundred Men." He found it necessary to leave NG's wagons behind but has "brought on the Horses."[1] Has reports of Lord Rawdon's "Return to 96," but no other intelligence.[2] Asks for intelligence and directions as to where to join NG.[3] LS (MiU-C) 1 p.]

1. During the retreat from Ninety Six, Pickens had taken charge of the wagons carrying the Southern Army's baggage. (See note at NG to Pickens, 23 June, above.)

2. On Rawdon's return to Ninety Six after unsuccessfully pursuing NG's army, see note at NG to Lee, 24 June, above.

3. See Pickens to NG, 3 July, below.

¶ [GENERAL GREENE'S ORDERS, "Camp Bigg Spring," S.C., 1 July 1781. In After Orders, given at 5 O'clock, the army is to be ready to march "tomorrow morning" at 3 A.M.[1] Lamar Orderly Book (OClWHi) 2 pp.]

1. On the purpose of the march, see Pierce to Carrington, immediately below.

¶ [CAPTAIN WILLIAM PIERCE, JR., TO COLONEL EDWARD CARRINGTON. From "Camp near the Cross Roads," S.C., 1 July 1781. The army will march "to-morrow Morning towards Fridays Ferry on the Congaree" to "intercept Lord Rawdon," who is marching "either to take Post on the Congaree or to form a junction with the new Troops moving up" from Charleston.[1] NG wants Carrington to forward stores for the army's "use on the route to Camden."[2] ADfS (MiU-C) 1 p.]

1. On Rawdon's movements and purpose, see note at Lee to NG, 30 June, above.

2. As seen in Pendleton to NG, this date, below, Carrington was in North Carolina.

¶ [TO COLONEL FRANCIS LOCK. From "Camp at the Cross Roads," S.C., 1 July 1781. Capt. [William] Pierce, NG's aide, has informed Lock "of the necessity of reinforcing this Army."[1] The need "increases every hour as the enemy are indeavoring to reesta[blish] their posts in this State." Lock's state, North Carolina, will want to keep them from doing that. NG continues: "Let me beg of you therefore to march to our assistance as large a reinforcment as possible and I doubt not but we shall drive the Enimy into Charles Town." NG's army is "moving towards the Congaree"; NG wants Lock "to march directly to Camden."[2] ADfS (MiU-C) 2 pp.]

1. See Pierce to NG, 26 June, above; as noted there, Pierce's letter to Lock has not been found.

2. Lock's reply has not been found. For more on the effort to obtain a militia reinforcement through him, see Pierce to NG, 26 June, and Malmedy to NG, 29 June, both above.

* * *

To General Francis Marion

Dear Sir   Camp at the Cross Roads [S.C.] July the 1st 1781

I am favord with your letter of the [blank] ultimo dated at the Congaree.[1] We shall march from this towards the Congaree in the morning. I wish you to have in readiness all the force you can possibly collect to join us at that place. Should an opportunity offer to give the enemy a blow in conjunction with General [Thomas] Sumters troops and those with Col [William] Washington you will give all the assistance in your power. My last intelligence was that Lord Rawden was moving towards the Congaree with only 400 Men.[2] If so he may be defeated with great ease. Dont spare any pains to collect your force as it is my determination to give the enemy battle the moment I can collect our force. Have [your] men equiped and ready for action that no time may be lost when a junction is made of our forces.[3] I am with esteem Your Most Obed humble S[r]   N GREENE

ADfS (MiU-C).

1. The letter from Marion was undoubtedly that of 25 June, above.

2. On Rawdon's movement toward the Congarees and his troop strength, see note at Lee to NG, 30 June, above. As seen there, Rawdon's detachment numbered almost 900 men.

3. NG wrote Marion on 2 July, below, again directing him to join the army.

*   *   *

¶ [FROM LIEUTENANT EDMUND GAMBLE, Salisbury, N.C., 1 July 1781. NG's letter of 12 June arrived in Gamble's absence. "The Gentleman that undertook the Business" complied with NG's orders "as far as lay in his power." Gamble has a supply of leather, which he will have made into cartridge boxes.[1] He wants NG to direct Col. [Francis] Lock to provide some "good Workmen, & a few Express Riders." Gamble has received "Spirits" for the army's use and wishes to know "as Soon as Possible" if he may give it "Out to Traveling Officers[,] Artificers &c." He is being "Constantly preplex'd, & the Officers Must & will have it, & are Much Offended" when he tries to "deny" them.[2] ALS (MiU-C) 1 p.]

1. For more on this matter, see Gamble to NG, 10 July, below.

2. NG replied on 16 July, below.

¶ [FROM CAPTAIN NATHANIEL PENDLETON, Charlotte, N.C., 1 July 1781. As NG requested, he has sent the two wagons carrying NG's baggage to the army. The escort consists of a sergeant and eight men—"all that could possibly be armed from the Hospital." They are also bringing "some Waggons loaded with meal"; Pendleton hopes they "arrive safe." Although he has not "re-established" his health, he is getting stronger and hopes to rejoin NG with Col. [Edward] Carrington, who left "this morning for Oliphants."[1] ALS (MiU-C) 1 p.]

1. The nature of Pendleton's health problem is not known. He was back in camp by late July. (See Pendleton to John Mazaret, 26 July, below.)

¶ [FROM LIEUTENANT NATHAN SMITH,[1] "Camp Big Spring," S.C., 1 July 1781. Encloses his commission and asks permission to resign. He has found, "upon trial," that his constitution is "very inadequate to the fateague of Active Duties," leaving him "no Longer able to Disscharge" his responsibilities.[2] ALS (MiU-C) 1 p.]

1. Smith was an officer in the Fourth Maryland Regiment. (Steuart, *Maryland Line*, p. 133)

2. NG's reply has not been found. Smith repeated his request in a letter to NG of 22 July, below.

¶ [FROM JOHN WHITE, Charlotte, N.C., 1 July 1781. Has NG's letter of 30 June. Is sorry to have given NG "so much troble" at "a time like this"; he thought he had informed NG that he is carrying $67,000 of the new emission.[1] His "horse is verary tired." Hopes NG will "dispence" with his coming to camp and send someone to receive the money.[2] Adds in a postscript that he has an escort, which is "on pueblick Expences" and is "verary" costly. ALS (MiU-C) 1 p.]

1. See White to NG, 25 June, above.
2. NG's reply has not been found.

¶ [GENERAL GREENE'S ORDERS, "Camp Lee's Farm," S.C., 2 July 1781. The troops are to draw and cook one day's provisions "and be ready to march at 5 O'Clock." In After Orders, given at 5 O'Clock, the troops are to receive a gill of spirits each and "march tomorrow Morning if fair." Lamar Orderly Book (OClWHi) 1 p.]

¶ [MAJOR ICHABOD BURNET TO COLONEL PETER HORRY. From Headquarters [Lee's Farm, S.C.], 2 July 1781.[1] NG has received Horry's letter of 28 June. Horry will "not invalidate any claim" he has to "Rank in the Federal Army" by accepting the commission. He should "nominate" a major and an adjutant for his corps and fill the ranks "as early as possible." He is to impress such clothing as he may need. NG "fully relys" on Horry's "exertions to accomplish the business." ADfS (MiU-C) 1 p.]

1. The place was taken from NG's Orders of this date, immediately above.

¶ [TO GENERAL FRANCIS MARION. From Headquarters, "Lee's old place," S.C., 2 July 1781. NG received Marion's letter of 28 June "this moment." Lord Rawdon is reportedly "moving towards the Congaree"; NG's army is also marching "to that place." NG wants Marion to join the army near Friday's Ferry "as early as possible," bringing "a plentyfull supply of provision" with him.[1] Hopes Marion received NG's letter "of yesterday." Cy (MiU-C) 1 p.]

1. On Marion's efforts to reach the army, see William Washington to NG, 4 July, below.

¶ [FROM COLONEL HENRY LEE, JR., "Broad River West Side," S.C., 2 July [1781], "12 O Clock." Lord Rawdon reached Ft. Granby "Last night." Capt. Joseph Eggleston, who followed him closely, obtained intelligence from a prisoner about the strength of Rawdon's force and of the troops who were "left at 96." The numbers in various units with Rawdon total 420 men. In addition, there are an estimated 150 in a "Hessian detachment," 300 in flank companies, and 400 in the Third Regiment, which "was to join last night with the convoy of provision." Potentially, Rawdon has 1,270 men, but Lee considers "the above computation large."[1] At Ninety Six, Col. [John Harris] Cruger has 800 men, including the "sick & wounded," all of the Loyalists, and the artillery.[2] The enemy cavalry is "part with Lord Rawdon, part with" Cruger. Its "dragoon horses are all ruined, the troops sickly & starved." Lee is within twelve miles of Ft. Granby and will join Col. [William] Washington "this evening." They will "harrass his Lordship perfectly, & fight him if we can."[3] Advises NG to "move to Cooks Mill on the Saluda[.] By this you can readily assemble your force, & ruin the enemy."[4] Adds in a postscript that he considers Cruger to be the proper "object[;] had we not better all join you, & a few harrass Lord Rawden." Lee will deal with a dispute over "precedence" between two lieutenant colonels. ALS (MiU-C) 3 pp.]

1. The Third Regiment, the reinforcement commanded by Col. Alexander Stewart, had been delayed and did not join Rawdon at Ft. Granby. (See Lee to NG, second letter

of 3 July, below, and notes at NG to Lee, 29 June, and Lee to NG, 30 June, both above.) By including the "Hessian detachment," which "Lt General de Bose" had loaned to Rawdon for the expedition to Ninety Six, and the flank companies, which had also accompanied him there, the size of Rawdon's detachment, as given by Lee, totaled 870. That estimate is close to the number of troops—860—that Rawdon informed Lord Cornwallis he had taken with him. (Rawdon to Cornwallis, 2 August, PRO 30/11/6) It is not known why Lee considered the "Hessian detachment" and the flank companies to be separate from Rawdon's force.

2. NG wrote Sumter on 3 July, below, that Cruger had between 1,200 and 1,400 men. (See NG's first letter to Sumter of that date.) On 17 July, NG reported that Rawdon had left close to half of his troops at Ninety Six. (See NG to McKean, 17 July, below.) If so, Cruger's force would have numbered some 1,000 to 1,200 men.

3. Lee and Washington had still not joined when Washington wrote NG on 5 July, below.

4. In his second letter to NG of 3 July, below, Lee gave his reasons for offering this advice, which NG apparently chose to ignore.

¶ [FROM COLONEL ISAAC SHELBY, Sullivan County, N.C., 2 July 1781. He received NG's letter by express "yesterday" and has "consulted the most Principle officers in this quarter."[1] To bring the number of men that NG requested would leave the frontier "greatly exposed" until a treaty can be negotiated with the Cherokee nation. That cannot be done before 20 July, when a number of their leaders will arrive.[2] The harvest, which is "just now on hand," is "an other Obstacle," as is the fact that a "great Number" of the "best men" from the area are now with Col. [Elijah] Clarke in Georgia. Shelby, therefore, cannot bring more than half the number that NG requested—"& those not before the 15th." Nor can he get help from his "near Neighbours" in Virginia, who "are just about to March" against Lord Cornwallis. He is "deeply interested in complying" with NG's request, both because he wants to aid "our suffering freinds" in South Carolina and because a "reverse of fortune to the Southward will again draw on this quarter the resentment of our old inveterate enemies the Cherokees." He will therefore make the "utmost exertion" to bring those men who can be spared. He will notify NG when he is ready to march.[3] ALS (CSmH) 2 pp.]

1. See NG to Shelby, 22 June, above.

2. On the proposed treaty with the Cherokee nation, see Lanier to NG, 27 May, above.

3. Shelby wrote NG on 3 August, below, that the negotiations with the Cherokee had been completed and that he had 700 well-mounted riflemen ready to move. Their march was delayed, however, and it was not until well into the fall that they arrived in South Carolina. (See Marion to NG, 2 November, below.)

¶ [FROM GENERAL THOMAS SUMTER, "Co^l [Samuel] Watsons 15 Mile from X [Cross] Roads," S.C., 2 July 1781. Has received NG's letter reporting the movement of the enemy detachment "towards Orangeburg."[1] Hopes these troops will be "interupted" before they can join Lord Rawdon, as NG intends. Sumter "thought it Necessary to take a Turn through the uper Regemt^s" of his brigade, and as a result, four regiments are nearly ready to march. He is at "Great Disadvantages" for "Want of arms." Has set several artificers to work, but "Material for Making of Swords are extreamly Scarce." He will go to Camden via the Waxhaws to expedite the manufacture of the swords and will "Meet with the Troops between the Water[ee?], & Congaree, on friday [6 July]," when he will be ready to "Execute the Plan Purposed, if thought Necessary."[2] Has intelligence from Col. [Hezekiah] Maham that Col. [Alexander] Stewart's detachment marched from Monck's Corner and was reinforced at Dorchester on its way to Ninety Six.[3] Another detachment from Charleston is at Biggin's, "Near Monks Corner."[4] Also gives the size of the enemy guard detachments at the Twenty Three Mile House and the Ten Mile House.[5] Maham confirms that the enemy troops are "Very Sickly." Sumter would have been happy to have met NG before returning to the Congaree, "but the Want of arms, & the Doubts of the Workmen at Camden Not being well Imployd, Induced" him to go directly there, where he expects to arrive "thursday [5 July]." Two of his officers will go "with, or immediately after the Militia of this Place." Is pleased that Gen. [Andrew] Pickens is expected to join NG "to day."[6] The militia from Mecklenburg County, N.C., have "orders to imbody & March immediately," but Sumter is not sure where.[7] ALS (MiDbEI) 2 pp.]

1. See NG to Sumter, 29 June, above.

2. On 29 June, to try to prevent a junction between Rawdon and the detachment moving toward Orangeburg, NG had called on Sumter to move his force to the Congaree as quickly as possible. (Ibid.) Replying to Sumter on 3 July, NG again urged him to "form a junction with us as soon as possible." (NG to Sumter, first letter of 3 July, below)

3. Stewart's detachment was the one mentioned at the beginning of this letter; it was on its way to form a junction with Rawdon at Orangeburg. (For more on Stewart's force, see note at NG to Lee, 29 June, above.)

4. On the detachment at Biggin Church, see note at Marion to NG, 25 June, above.

5. These posts guarded the main road from Charleston to Monck's Corner and the Santee River.

6. Pickens reached the army on the 6th. (Huger to NG, 6 July, below)

7. For more on the militia from the Salisbury district, which included Mecklenburg County, see Malmedy to NG, 29 June, above.

¶ [FROM COLONEL WILLIAM WASHINGTON, "Camp near Col: Tailor's," S.C., 2 July 1781. Lord Rawdon reached "the Fort below Friday's Ferry [i.e., Ft. Granby] last Night about 11 O'Clock." Washington thinks Col. [Henry] Lee "is mistaken" about Rawdon's numbers and thinks his own sources' estimate of 1,000 to 1,200 men in Rawdon's force is "tolearble just."[1] Rawdon also has "about eighty Cavalry in horrid Order." Washington is glad that NG is moving "this Way"; he thinks Rawdon "will run away or loose his Army if not reinforc'd." As Rawdon's detachment "must be inferior" to NG's force when the latter is collected, "the most important Object" for Washington and Lee is to prevent a junction between Rawdon and Col. [Alexander] Stewart's regiment, which was camped at "Four-Hole Bridge last Friday [29 June]."[2] Has asked Col. [Hezekiah Maham?] "to keep a watchful Eye" on Stewart and "take such a Position" that they can form a junction of their own and intercept him.[3] If "practicable," Washington will "keep Possession of the North Side of the Congarees."[4] ALS (MiU-C) 2 pp.]

1. Lee had written NG on 30 June, above, that Rawdon had no more than 500 men with him; in his letter to NG of this date, above, he had given numbers closer to Washington's. On the force with Rawdon, see also the note at Lee to NG, 2 July.

2. For more on Stewart's detachment, see notes at NG to Lee, 29 June, and Lee to NG, 30 June, both above.

3. The manuscript is torn, and the officer's name is missing; the editors believe it was Maham, who had been tracking Stewart's movements. (See Sumter to NG, immediately above.)

4. NG replied on 3 July, below.

¶ [GENERAL GREENE'S ORDERS, "Camp Cockerells Farm," S.C., 3 July 1781. Publishes an extract of a resolution of Congress regulating the promotion of officers in the Continental army. The resolution mandates that paroled officers who are not continued in service are to receive "full pay for Life afterwards," just as "Reduced" officers are, and recommends that the states make good the depreciation in the pay of those officers who are "Hostages."[1] Lamar Orderly Book (OClWHi) 6 pp.]

1. The resolution, adopted 25 May, is printed in *JCC*, 20: 539–41.

*   *   *

To General Thomas Sumter

Head Quarters near Weymborough [Winnsboro, S.C.]
Dear sir   July 3ᵈ 1781.

Your Letter of yesterday overtook me on the march for the Congaree.[1] I doubt not many advantages will result from your visiting the upper Regiments; but I fear the opportunity for striking the Posts at Monks Corner and in that Neighbourhood is past.[2] Lord Rawdon is moving down towards the Congaree, and it is said to take the Post at Fridays Ferry.[3] He has about 1200 Men with him besides the force I mentioned in my former Letter, coming up thro' Orangeburg, which I suppose has formed a junction with him as he was at the Juniper Springs last Saturday [30 June].[4] Colº [John Harris] Cruger and Majʳ [John] Doyle are left at 96 with about 12 or 1400 Men.[5] From the present disposition which the Enemy are making it appears they intend to hold 96, and reestablish themselves at Augusta and the Congarees.[6] It is of the greatest importance that we prevent it, if possible. For this purpose I wish to draw all our force together at or near Fridays Ferry, and oblige the Enemy to give up the Post, fight us in detachment, or collect their force to a point. If our force is separated we can affect nothing. If it is collected we can oblige the Enemy to keep theirs collected; and that will prevent their establishing their posts again; a matter highly interesting to these States, as I shall inform you when we meet, from the peculiar circumstances of foreign affairs.[7] Having given you a state of matters, I beg you will form a junction with us as soon as possible. I have already directed General Marion to meet us at Fridays Ferry without loss of time.[8]

The Militia of Salisbury district have orders to march for Camden, and from thence they will join us.[9] General [Andrew] Pickens is on the march to form a junction with us, and I hope it will be effected to Day or to-morrow.[10] This is an important crisis in the affairs of this Country;

and I am hazarding every thing to give them a favorable turn, and with your immediate aid, I am in hopes to effect it. If we could get the Enemy from 96 and the Congaree into the lower Country it would be gaining a great point. With esteem and regard I am sir Your humble serv   NATH GREENE

LS (Sumter Papers: DLC).
    1. Sumter's letter of 2 July is above.
    2. In a letter of 25 June, above, NG had asked Sumter to lead a force into the "lower Country."
    3. Colonels Henry Lee and William Washington reported Rawdon's arrival at Ft. Granby, near Friday's Ferry, in letters to NG of 2 July, above. After receiving Washington's letter, NG wrote Sumter again on this date, with greater urgency. (See the letter immediately below.)
    4. The letter to which NG referred was his to Sumter of 29 June, above. The detachment was the one commanded by Col. Alexander Stewart, which did not join Rawdon until 7 July. (For more on Stewart's detachment and its progress, see note at Lee to NG, 29 June, above.) As noted at Lee to NG, 30 June, Rawdon's force numbered about 900 men.
    5. As noted at Lee to NG, 2 July, above, Cruger's force probably numbered between 1,000 and 1,200 men.
    6. The British did none of these things.
    7. NG referred to the possibility of mediation by certain European powers to end the war on the principle of *uti possidetis*—i.e., of combatants retaining the territory they held at the cessation of hostilities. (See note at Sharpe to NG, 28 May, above.)
    8. See NG to Marion, 2 July, above.
    9. As noted at Malmedy to NG, 29 June, above, the militia reinforcements from the Salisbury district of North Carolina did not march for South Carolina until months later.
    10. On Pickens's efforts to reach the army, see his letter to NG, this date, and Huger to NG, 6 July, both below.

To General Thomas Sumter

Dear Sir   Camp at Cockrells [S.C.] July 3^d 1781
    Since I wrote you this morning I have got a letter from Col [William] Washington, who is at Col Taylors on the Congaree, informing me of the arrival of Lord Rawden at Frydays Ferry last Night about 11 oClock.[1] This is what I expected; and not a moments time is to be lost in collecting our force to that place otherwise his Lordship will fix himself so firmly, that there will be no possibility of moving him.[2] Than which nothing can be more injurious to the interest and happiness of this Country. Had I a force sufficient to authorise an attempt without you, I would not delay a moment; but unfortunately for our cause I have but a shadow of a force, much less than you imagine. I write you thus plainly that you may not be deceivd by common report. I wish you not to go by the way of Camden if it will delay you a single hour.[3] I am with great esteem Your most Obedient humble Servant
                                                    NATH GREENE

ALS (Sumter Papers: DLC).

1. See NG to Sumter, immediately above, and Washington to NG, 2 July, above.

2. Washington reported on 4 July, below, that Rawdon's troops had left Ft. Granby (Friday's Ferry).

3. In his letter of 2 July, above, Sumter had said he was going to Camden before joining NG. He replied on 4 July, below.

*   *   *

¶ [TO COLONEL WILLIAM WASHINGTON. From "Camp at Cochrans Plantation," S.C., 3 July 1781. NG expected Lord Rawdon to be "at the Congarees," as Washington's letter "of yesterday confirms" that he is.[1] NG will march to Winnsboro "to Night" and will leave the army's baggage there so that his troops can "move rapidly." Gen. [Francis] Marion, who has "a very considerable force," is to join NG at Friday's Ferry.[2] Gen. [Thomas] Sumter, who "is about thirty miles" in the army's rear, has been asked to join as soon as possible.[3] NG also expects "a very considerable reinforcment" of militia from North Carolina to join him.[4] Gen. [Andrew] Pickens is near, and NG expects him to arrive at camp "to Night."[5] As soon as this force is collected, NG intends to "push" Rawdon. Meanwhile, he wants Washington and [Col. Henry] Lee, from whom he has not heard "since day before yesterday," to prevent Rawdon from "receiving reenforcments or crossing the Congaree." Adds: "A few days, I hope will put his Lordship in our power." Washington should collect as much of "the force" operating along the Congaree River as possible and "guard against a surprize." If Rawdon crosses the Congaree, Washington should inform NG and Marion as soon as possible. Asks him to send an express to let Lee "know how matters stand."[6] ADfS (MiU-C) 4 pp.]

1. Washington's letter of 2 July is above.

2. See NG to Marion, 2 July, above.

3. See Sumter to NG, 2 July, and NG's two letters to Sumter of this date, all above.

4. As seen at Malmedy to NG, 29 June, above, the militia reinforcement that NG expected was not sent.

5. On Pickens's arrival, see Huger to NG, 6 July, below.

6. Washington reported on Rawdon's movements in letters to NG of 4 and 5 July, both below.

¶ [FROM COLONEL HENRY LEE, JR., "Legion Camp on Saluda," S.C., 3 July 1781.[1] Describes how Capt. [Joseph] Eggleston's detachment followed Lord Rawdon to Ft. Granby.[2] Lee, in the meantime, moved along "the west side of the Broad River" and encamped on 2 July "thirteen miles from the enemy." Knowing "the distressed state of the British army, & having learnt that his Lordship had left a body of his Cavalry at 96," Lee sent reinforcements to Eggleston and ordered him to "gain the forage country & to seek an opportunity for striking at the enemy⁵ foragers." Eggleston "crossed the enemy undiscovered, & took a judicious position two miles in their front." On the morning of 3 July, his scouts saw "the main body of the British horse" advancing. Preparations were made, "& the enemy presuming on a militia prize pushed on with vigor." The enemy dragoons "were met with great gallantry, & were in a few moment⁵ entirely defeated, & pursued to the picquets of the [British] army." Eggleston's men captured three officers and forty-five privates, as well as their horses, arms, and accoutrements; only "one man escaped." Praises Eggleston, who in turn compliments the "exertions" of several of his officers and the "zeal" of his men.[3] Lee believes this event "must tend to encrease the distress of the enemy, & to damp the spirits of their soldiers at this critical juncture." Lee will "be in front of his Lordship tomorrow morning," unless Rawdon "moves this night." Reports that "the convoy has not joined."[4] Hopes to "detain" Rawdon so that NG can "reach him." Has ordered the grinding of grain. If NG can get boats, he should cross the Congaree at Howell's Ferry; Lee has asked Col. [William] Washington to write NG "on this head."[5] ALS (MiU-C) 4 pp.]

1. Lee originally wrote the date as "June 3ᵈ," but he or someone else crossed out June and wrote "July" immediately below it. The letter is docketed "July 3ᵈ," a date that is consistent with the contents.

2. On Eggleston's mission, see Lee's letters to NG of 29 and 30 June and 2 July, all above.

3. According to the account in his memoirs, Lee had learned during the operation against Ft. Granby in May that "only the rich settlement south of Friday's ferry could afford sufficient forage for the British." He therefore expected them to send foragers there and "determined to avail himself of the probable chance to strike." (Lee, *Memoirs*, 2: 135) Eggleston's troops were hidden when a foraging party, "consisting of fifty or sixty dragoons and some wagons," approached "the very farm to which [he] had directed his attention." (Ibid., pp. 135–36) The surprise was complete, and the enemy was routed "without any loss" among Eggleston's men. (Ibid., p. 136) According to Rawdon, his dragoons had gone out to forage "contrary to express order"; their loss enabled the Americans "to watch very closely all the Avenues to our Camp." (Rawdon to Lord Cornwallis, 2 August, PRO 30/11/6) On 8 July, Lee wrote to offer the "horses taken the other day" to Hezekiah Maham, who had been commissioned to raise a new regiment of mounted men. Only thirty horses were then available, Lee wrote; "the rest are lost." He also offered Maham "saddles[,] bridles & pistols," if they had not already been "stolen." (ViHi)

4. For more on Lee's plans, see the letter immediately below. Rawdon did not stay at Ft. Granby. Learning of "the Enemy's design" to converge on his position at the Congarees, he "resolved to march immediately" and meet Col. Alexander Stewart and the reinforcements from Charleston—the "convoy" mentioned in this letter—farther downcountry, "at Orangeburgh, or wheresoever he might be advanced." (Rawdon to Cornwallis, 2 August, PRO 30/11/6) For Lee's reaction to Rawdon's movement, see note at the letter immediately below.

5. No letter from Washington "on this head" has been found. NG replied to Lee on 4 July, below.

¶ [FROM COLONEL HENRY LEE, JR., [Camp on the Saluda River, S.C., 3 July 1781].[1] In his letter of "yesterday," Lee presumed that NG "would not think of moving to the Congaree, as it was probable before you could get up Lord Rawdon would march."[2] Lee "also presumed that the 3ᵈ regt had joined," but he learns "this morning that it is not up."[3] Now, hoping that NG is on his march, Lee intends to "throw" himself "between his Lordship & Stuart & to break down bridges, &c."[4] As Col. [William] Washington is on the "east side," he can "send any letʳ" for Lee.[5] ALS (MiU-C) 1 p. One or more pages may be missing.]

1. The date was taken from the docketing, the place from the letter immediately above.

2. See Lee to NG, 2 July, above.

3. As noted at the letter immediately above, Rawdon decided to move toward Orangeburg to meet Col. Alexander Stewart's Third Regiment, which had been delayed in its march to join him. The junction of the two British detachments took place on 7 July.

4. According to Lee's later account, his troops were able to pass to "the enemy's front" without being detected, although they had to make a dangerous maneuver in doing so. They destroyed a bridge over Congaree Creek, posted guards there, and "encamped one mile in the enemy's front, expecting hourly to hear of the advance of the corps" under Gen. Thomas Sumter and Gen. Francis Marion. (Lee, *Memoirs*, 2: 138–39) According to Rawdon, Lee left a "considerable" force at the creek and felled trees to block the fords. Despite those obstacles and the "violent" noontime heat, Rawdon was able to get his advanced troops across "after the exchange of only a few ineffectual shots"; his main force then crossed the creek in "security." (Rawdon to Lord Cornwallis, 2 August, PRO 30/11/6) For the remainder of that day and again on the following day, Lee kept his position in front of Rawdon's column. At Beaver Creek, some thirty miles from Friday's Ferry/Ft. Granby, Lee, who still had not heard of any other American forces nearby, gave up "any further struggle to hold the enemy's front" and turned aside; Rawdon proceeded to Orangeburg. (Lee, *Memoirs*, 2: 140–41)

5. In his memoirs, Lee said he heard nothing of Washington or the other American commanders during his retreat before Rawdon. (Ibid., pp. 139–41)

¶ [FROM GENERAL ANDREW PICKENS, "Turkey Creek," S.C., 3 July 1781. He received Maj. [Ichabod] Burnet's letter of 1 July [not found] "Yesterday Evening" on the Broad River and set out as quickly as possible. Gives the route he will take unless NG directs otherwise. Hopes to join NG "with all possible Expedition," bringing the "Waggon Horses" with him.[1] The people along his route of march are reportedly "turning out to a Man"; he believes they will "Act with Spirit on the Occasion." LS (CSmH) 1 p.]

1. On Pickens's arrival at the army, see Huger to NG, 6 July, below.

¶ [GENERAL GREENE'S ORDERS, "Wynsborough," S.C., 4 July 1781. The troops are to receive thirty rounds of cartridges per man, and most units are to prepare to march "as Light as possible at 4 O'Clock P.M." The North Carolinians and the Virginia militia will escort the "non-Effectives," the "Women and Children," and the "Heavy Baggage."[1] NG reports the defeat and capture of a "Body of the British Cavalry" by "part of the Cavalry" of Lee's Legion, commanded by Capt. [Joseph] Eggleston. The officers and men in Eggleston's command "merit applause."[2] Lt. [William] Evans is released from arrest. His "Subsequent conduct" has convinced NG that "the cause for which he was arrested was occasioned by an error of judgement in a peculiar Circumstance, and not by the want of that fortitude which is requisite in an Officer."[3] The findings of a court-martial held 28 June are given in After Orders. David Allison, "Keeper of Live Stock," was found guilty of appropriating hides for "Sale to his own private advantage" and sentenced to make good the loss, forfeit his pay, and be dismissed from the service; NG approves the sentence. A sergeant and two privates from the Second Virginia Regiment were found guilty of desertion and sentenced to receive 100 lashes each. These sentences are to be carried out immediately. Below the After Orders is a note that the army "marched and encamped this Night at Cedar Creek." Lamar Orderly Book (OCIWHi) 4 pp.]

1. For more about these orders, see NG's letters to John Armstrong and Henry Lee, this date, both below.

2. On the action, see Lee to NG, first letter of 3 July, above.

3. For background, see Evans to NG, 16 June, above.

¶ [TO MAJOR JOHN ARMSTRONG. From "Camp Wynsborough," S.C., 4 July 1781. He is to command the troops left to guard the baggage and stores and is to "move by slow, easy marches towards Camden." The "Stages" of his march should be determined by the availability of provisions and forage. He should not cross the Wateree River without further orders unless a detachment of the enemy approaches; in that case, he should cross and advise NG of his "movements and Situations." NG recommends "the Strictest Discipline among the Troops and the greatest care of the Stores and Baggage."[1] Cy (MiU-C) 2 pp.]

1. For background on Armstrong's assignment, see NG to Lee, immediately below.

* * *

To Colonel Henry Lee, Jr.

Dear Sir   Head Quarters Wynnsborough [S.C.] July 4th 1781

I am favord with your three letters of yesterday.[1] Capt Egglestons enterprise merits the highest encomiums; and I beg you to return him, Capt [James] Armstrong, and Mr [William] Winston and the troops under their command my particular thanks for their great gallantry and good conduct.[2] I have done it in the general orders of the day, and will not fail to mention it to their advantage in my public dispaches. The success was as compleat as any thing of the kind I ever heard of.

We are in our march for the Congaree. Generals Sumter[,] Marion and Pickens have orders to meet us there as soon as possible.[3] We shall leave our baggage at this place and come with the troops as light as possible; and I make no doubt if the Militia Generals are active in forming a junction with us we shall give a good account of Lord Rawdon. If you and Col. [William] Washington can keep Major Stewart from joining Lord Rawden the work we [i.e., will] be easy.[4] At any rate I shall want to know how matters stand on my arrival which I expect will be next day after to morrow at farthest. Indeed I believe I shall come down this evening with a proper escort to form an opinion to what point it will be best to move the troops to. This will be gaining time if a change of the route should be necessary.

I had letters from General Washington and the Marquis yesterday. New York is beseiged and the Noble Earl is retreating in Virginia with no small haste.[5] All things in the North wear an agreeable face. Publish it among the people. Yours aff   N GREENE

ALS (RHi).

1. Only two of the letters have been found.

2. On the defeat and capture of a party of British cavalry by Capt. Joseph Eggleston's troops, see Lee's first letter to NG of 3 July, above.

3. NG's orders to Francis Marion, dated 1 July, and to Thomas Sumter, dated 29 June, are above. His instructions to Andrew Pickens have not been found.

4. For more on the movement of the British detachment commanded by Col. Alexander Stewart, see note at NG to Lee, 29 June, above.

5. NG had received George Washington's letter of 1 June, above. As seen there, a siege of New York was being planned but was not actually underway. In a letter to NG of 20 June, above, the Marquis de Lafayette reported that Lord Cornwallis was retreating.

From Governor Thomas Burke of North Carolina

[Wake County Court House], State of North Carolina
Sir   July 4th 1781[1]

Your Several Letters of 11th, 18th & 23d ulto and one from Mr Pierce your aid de Camp of 27th ulto to my predecessor in office were laid before the General assembly.[2] On the first, they Requested me to take measures for procuring the forty dragoon Horses which you Require and I gave immediate orders to the Quarter master to obtain them by purchase, or impressment if Necessary. I hope they will soon be in Readiness, at least as soon as can be effected without funds, of which I find the State utterly destitute.[3] On the others they have passed an act of which an Extract is inclosed, and I have Issued the orders therein directed.[4]

These, Sir, are not the aids which I deem effectual and which it is my wish to be impowered to give, but they are Such only as are now in my power. Whether the General Assembly will make adequate Provision for the defence of the State, and assistance of the common Cause is yet problematical.[5] But I will venture to assure you that what ever they Shall put in my power Shall be exerted with all the vigor[,] industry and dispatch of which I may be found Capable and if I can Supply any defects by my personal Influence or personal presence neither Shall be with held.

The extreme derangements in every department and the incredible imbecility of every power of Government open to me the most gloomy prospects at my very entrance upon my Office. Disciplin must be introduced, and even an habitual negligence and disregard of Orders must be Corrected. Civil Government must be Reestablished, and enabled to Correct and Restrain the most licentious abuses which are now raging in this Country. The Revenues must be arranged, and in a word the Strictest attention and most Inflexible vigor must be applied to our affairs.[6]

But altho I shall find employment Sufficient for my Tallents in this arduous Scene, yet nothing Shall divert my attention from the War, and the Assistance which it may be in my power to Render. I hope even to partake with you in the labors of the field So Soon as I shall have put the Civil business in proper train. The Principal object with me will be to have force and Supplies always in readiness, and to be able at any time to Cooperate with Efficiency in any of your General Measures and I hope we Shall be able to Establish So good an Intelligen[ce] with each other that I shall have timely notice of your wants either of Supplies or Success.

By my private advices from Congress I learn that we are no longer to expect the Second Division, but that Some Ships of the Line are to be added to those already on our Coast to Render that Squadron Superior to the British. The Du[t]ch war has Occasioned this change in the disposition of the French forces for, I suppose, Holland must be protected by France until her own preperations are made. A mediation, it Seems is again on the Tapis offered by Austria and Russia. The proposal is agreeable to Britain, France must consult her allies, and the *Uti possiditis* is held up, by Britain but rejected by France: this, With the Raising the blockade of Gibraltar is the Sum of all the European News which has Reached me.[7]

Lord Cornwallis, of whose movements I suppose you are well informed, had retreated to Williamsburg, and we have Some Reports of General Gregory's having been Surprised at his post but nothing Authentic.[8]

I shall be happy, Sir, to keep up a Constant Communication with you, and Shall give the most Satisfactory information in my power Relative to our affairs. I have honor to be with Respect and Esteem S[r] your very ob[t] humb[l]   THO[s] BURKE

ALS (NNPM).

1. Burke was with the North Carolina legislature, which was then in session at Wake County Court House.

2. Burke had been elected to succeed Abner Nash on 25 June. The letters from NG to Nash that Burke laid before the Assembly are above; the one referred to as being of 11 June carries the date 12 June. William Pierce's letter to Nash is also above.

3. The legislature had instructed Burke to appoint "some prudent & proper Officers to procure, or purchase, or if necessary, to impress Forty Horses suitable for Dragoon Horses, and send them to General Greene as soon as may be." (*NCSR*, 17: 824–25)

4. The extract, which has not been found, was undoubtedly of an act of 4 July, entitled "An Act for raising Troops out of the Militia of this State for the defence thereof, and other purposes." (Ibid., 24: 384–87)

5. On 5 July, Burke wrote the members of the Assembly complaining that the bill under consideration for organizing the state's militia would "delay the execution of necessary orders and destroy all vigor and energy." (Burke to the General Assembly, 5 July, Burke Microfilm)

6. To the legislature, Burke was even more blunt, informing them in his acceptance speech that the state was:

> every where unprepared for defense, without arms, without discipline, without arrangements, even the habits of civil order and obedience to Laws, changed into licentious contempt of authority and a disorderly indulgence of violent propensities. Industry is intermitted, agriculture much decayed and commerce struggling feebly with almost insuperable difficulties. The public money is unaccounted for, the taxes uncollected or unproductive, the individuals creditors

to the public for years past, and the Treasury totally unable to make payment. (Burke to the General Assembly, 29 June, Burke Microfilm)

7. On 4 June, William Sharpe, a delegate to Congress from North Carolina, had sent Burke a letter containing much the same intelligence that Sharpe had sent to NG on 28 May, above; it is discussed there. (Sharpe's letter to Burke is in Smith, *Letters*, 17: 296–97.)

8. Gen. Isaac Gregory, a North Carolina militia officer, had been guarding the route from Portsmouth, Va., into North Carolina through the Great Dismal Swamp. In a letter of 6 July, he reported that his command had been surprised by a superior British force but had withdrawn successfully, with only a "Trifleing" loss. (Gregory to James Blount, Burke Microfilm) In his letter to NG of 10 July, below, Burke reported that the British force that attacked Gregory had pulled back toward Portsmouth and that Gregory had regained his former position.

From Major James McHenry

Head Quarters [twenty miles from Williamsburg, Va.]
4th July 1781.[1]

Since I wrote you confidentially by Capt[n] [John] Swan, this army has not increased.[2] Both continentals and militia are less in number. But notwithstanding this, the spirit I so much dreaded is constantly discovering itself. I make representations, my dear General; I point out the necessity of waiting the accomplishment of our expected succours. Morgans reinforcement of about 300 militia, the junction of Sumner, who marched from Harrisburg with near 600 draughts, the 31st of last month, and the additional force in Militia, from this State after the harvest is closed.[3]

Could you be spared from the great objects in which you are engaged, I should be happy, and releived from a thousand inquietudes which I now suffer. At least, let the Marquiss have your advice, if he cannot have your presence. And, let him be sure of his strength before he consentingly hazards at one cast, more, perhaps, than a State.[4]

Our van-guard is within twelve miles of Williamsburg, and our main body, within twenty. It would seem as if his Lordship were not quite at his ease; and that we had puzled him with appearances. But his Lordship is an old gamester, and this may be only a trick to draw in a young one. Still however there are circumstances that favor an evacuation of his present post; but in this case, it is difficult to say where he is going. If he is to be commander in chief, as is reported, he will be more anxious for New-York, than if he remains a secondary character.[5]

Let me hear from you, my ever dear General, for I know you do not wish me with you at this critical moment; although, were I with you, I might gain a little reputation, which is more than can happen to me here. Most sincerely I am your affectionate friend   JAMES M[C]HENRY

ALS (NNPM).

1. The location was derived from the contents.

2. See McHenry's letters to NG of 20 June, above.

3. Gen. Daniel Morgan's detachment joined Lafayette's army on 7 July. (Higginbotham, *Morgan*, p. 165) As seen at Pierce to Gen. Jethro Sumner, 27 June, above, the North Carolinians were not marching from Harrisburg, N.C., to join the Marquis de Lafayette.

4. For more on McHenry's concerns about Lafayette, see his first letter to NG of 20 June.

5. On the movements of Lafayette's and Lord Cornwallis's armies, see Lafayette to NG, 4 and 5 July, below. Cornwallis was not preparing to replace Sir Henry Clinton as commander of British forces in America.

* * *

¶ **[FROM MAJOR JAMES MCHENRY,** Headquarters [twenty miles from Williamsburg, Va.], 4 July 1781.[1] Recommends a Mr. Carlyle, who expected to be appointed a cornet in William Washington's regiment and is "full of zeal." Asks NG to help Carlyle obtain the appointment. If Carlyle does not receive it, he "intends playing the volunteer until something offers in the line of the army." NG could use him as an aide "for a few days."[2] Catalog excerpt (Mary A. Benjamin, *The Collector #841* [1975], p. 17).]

1. McHenry's location was taken from the letter immediately above.

2. In his first letter to McHenry of 24 July, below, NG said he would "pay particular attention" to Carlyle.

¶ **[FROM GENERAL THOMAS SUMTER,** "Near the Hanging Rock," S.C., 4 July 1781. Has received NG's two letters of 3 July, which convince him "that the Greatest Injuries Will Result from Lord Rawdens reestablishing himself in the Country." That appears to be Rawdon's "Design if not Vigerously opposed." Although NG did not want Sumter to "go [by] Camden," he is now "So far advanced" in that direction that it will make "Little Difrence . . . in Point of Time." He has "Much occasion" to go there on "account of arms & Some Detachments that are gone on" and because he needs to give "Some Directions." He will proceed, hoping that NG "will not Disaprove." No time will be lost, and "great succes" will result from "the Tyersum Round" Sumter is taking. ALS (MiU-C) 1 p.]

¶ **[FROM COLONEL THOMAS WADE,** "Pee Dee," 4 July 1781.[1] Will "Indevour to Comply" with the orders in NG's letter of 9 June. Cannot obtain teams to transport provisions to Charlotte, N.C., but has sent "a drove of Beaves" there. He decided to keep another "parcel" of steers "in fine pastures on Pee Dee" after learning that the "pasturage wass ordnary" around Charlotte; has enough men to move them "on the Shortest Notice." Asks for instructions as to the "Laying in" of salted meat and flour for the army's use "this fall." If NG wants to have that work done "on the Pee Dee," Wade needs to know now so that coopers can season timber for the barrels and he can collect "a Quantity of Salt." He understands that Gen. [Francis] Marion has "Secured" a supply of salt from Georgetown and "Lodged" it "in Sundry places" along the Pee Dee. Marion has sent no instructions about what is to be done with it. Wade believes he can obtain a "boat Load of Rice from George Town, which would be of Great Servis to the Hospitals." While he continues to serve as purchasing commissary for South Carolina, he will always be ready to execute NG's orders, as his commission puts him under both NG's and Gov. John Rutledge's direction.[2] In a postscript, he asks NG to send paper and flints, as the Loyalists "are very Troubelsom Towards Cape Fear Rivers on Drownding Creek and Little Pee Dee." On "Saturday last [30 June]," half of Wade's regiment marched against the Loyalists, who had defeated a detachment of Bladen and Cumberland County militia "a few days" earlier.[3] ALS (MiU-C) 4 pp.]

1. As a North Carolina militia officer who also served as purchasing commissary for the state of South Carolina, Wade operated along the Pee Dee River in both states; his location at the time he wrote this letter is not known.

2. As seen in Wade's letter to NG of 9 August, below, NG asked him to come to camp, presumably to discuss the matters that Wade raised here.

3. On 12 July, Isaac Williams, a resident of the area in which the Loyalists had embodied, wrote Gen. William Caswell that "Between Two and five Hundred" of them were collected near the "Raft Swamp." He said that 150 horsemen sent by Wade had arrived, but the local militia had not assembled as ordered. (NCSR, 15: 525–26)

¶ [FROM COLONEL WILLIAM WASHINGTON, "Capt Howell's," S.C., 4 July 1781. Has intercepted a letter from [Col. Alexander] Stewart to Lord Rawdon, by which Washington learns that Stewart is marching to join Rawdon. Washington will cross the Congaree at Howell's Ferry and join [Col. Henry] Lee, who is "eight or ten Miles below the Enemy." Gen. [Francis] Marion has written that he will cross at McCord's "To-Morrow" and join Washington and Lee with 400 mounted men. Washington has asked Col. Henry Hampton, who was "left to Guard the Fords," to give NG the "earliest Information of the Enemy's Movements." Has just learned that the enemy "mov'd down the River from Fort Granby this Evening at one O'Clock."[1] ALS (CSmH) 1 p.]

1. Because of extreme heat, Rawdon marched at night. As noted at Marion to NG, first letter of 7 July, below, even with such precautions, some fifty of Rawdon's men died of heat exhaustion.

*   *   *

From the Marquis de Lafayette

Camp 20 Miles from Williamsburg [Va.]
My Dear General   4h July 1781[1]

Here is once More a Safe Opportunity to write which I am Happy to Embrace and will inclose a public letter of Mine wherein you will find an Account of His Lordship's Retrogade Movements.[2] Your desire was that I should Hold My Ground in this State. We were Happy enough as to Recover Every part of Ground But what is under An Immediate protection of Shipping.[3] Our numbers are very Small But our Movements are offensive and we Appear Eager for action. We Never Encamp in a Body, and our Numbers are Much Exagerated.

What Has Been lost at the Point of Fork is in Great Measure Recovered. Little will Be lost, including the Baron's popularity in Vir-

The Marquis de Lafayette, 1757–1834; oil painting by Charles Willson Peale
(Independence National Historical Park Collection)

ginia.[4] The Assembly Have Resolved that I should Be Requested to order an Enquiry into the Conduct of the officers at the Point of Fork. But I Have Enough to do to Enquire into Lord Cornwallis's intention, and will Have the Honor of Refering the Assembly to your Superior Authority.[5]

That Lord Cornwallis Meant to Go to Frederiksburg is a Certainty, the More Certain as we Have Intercepted a letter from the Captain of a vessel to His Lordship wherein He Says He was sent into Rappaanack from Portsmouth on purpose to establish the Correspondance.[6] That Lord Cornwallis knew we Should follow Him, and of Course He Could Hope for an action is clearly proved By Tarleton's letter—So that His Virginia Campaign will not do much in favor of His Cause abroad.[7] Had we Beat Him, we Might Have Acquired More Honor. But Had we Been Compleatly Beat this State was lost, and your Expeditions Interrupted.

The light infantry is about 800[,] the pennsylvanians not 700, the Virginia Continentals 400. The Militia Reduced Amazingly and as the Harvest time is Coming will Vanish into Nothing.[8] Morgan was to Come with 2000 men. He is not arrived and will not Bring more than 400.[9] Our Cavalry is allwaïs on the Same footing, or to Speak Better we Have No Cavalry. I Have taken great pains to procure Some. Expect in a few days 80 Maryland gentlemen. Have Some expectations of 60 from [Col. Stephen] Moylan's dragoons and 40 of [Maj. John] Nelson.[10] Have ordered C[lel] White [Col. Anthony W. White] and Major [Richard] Call to Collect accoutrements and Shall Mount a part of the New levies. But My prospects are distant, My losses instant, and danger very Near at Hand. I do However put on a good face. There is no detachement from the Ennemy But what a detachement Marches against them and they generally Retire. Children Sing when they are affraïd.

The Ennemy are Extremely Cautious. Many a Nights I give Myself the pleasure of Having their Army turned out.[11] I Have taken the Best precautions I Could for the Security of my flanks, and for look out parties upon the Rivers. There is a Small Corps in Glocester County—an other about Portsmouth. By keeping the Ennemy in check we prevent their making detachements and forraging on the other side of the Rivers.

Should the Appearance we put on deter them from Establishing a post any where But at Portsmouth—Should your Conquests and the Combined expedition Recall their operating Army, my first object will Be to know what Rout they take. At all events I Shall make it my Business to afford you Speedy Support. There are Some indications of an Embarkation—not So many However as is generally Believed.[12] A few days will explain the intentions of Lord Cornwallis. I wish we May Again Induce Him to Run from us least I Should Be obliged to Run from Him.

By a letter from C[lel] [Josiah] Parker I Hear G[al] [Gen. Isaac] Gregory Has Been defeated—But no particulars. Should this affect North Carolina you May depend upon Speedy Intelligences. But I presume it is Nothing But a Scarmish.[13]

The french Army is, I am assured, Arrived in the Eastward.[14] So is the Alliance and a forty guns ship By my Name Carrying Cloathing and Supplies of Every kind for us.[15] But it is an age Since I Heard from that part of the world. As to you, My dear general, it is only By public Report I Hear Augusta is taken, and Ninety Six in a fair way to Make a *paragraph*.[16] I Heartly partake your glory. Your popularity is now to the Highest pitch. You are the general every Body Speacks of, and every one prides in your Maneuvres. Happy I shall Be to Have Made a Run way diversion provided you think I Have Maneuvred Right. The paragraphing Rage does often Seize me, But Since I am first in Command I Became a Great Coward.

Should I undertake the History of departements there would Be No end. The Quarter Master wrote me He could do nothing, and again wrote me He could not even answer for my engagements as there was no Monney. He is very clever, very zealous, But Has no means, and of Course is very Cautious.[17] The Commissary departement is Headed By Mr Brown to whom I Say every Morning that He Shall Be Hanged.[18] The Medical departement Has lately Been put in pretty good order. There is an immense waste of provisions, of ammunitions, of Every thing. I do what I Can, But Cannot do what I wish. In a word, My dear general, I Manage Matters for the Best, try to Correct abuses, get angry five or Six times a day, and I Hope you will Be Satisfied at least with my Good Intentions.

I Have not as Yet Received the Cartel from You. Lord Cornwallis Sent it to me. I owe Him the justice to Say that His Correspondance Has Been frank and polite. We Have not Received any prisoners from Charlestown. But upon His Requesting that fifty who were in the Neighborbood of Camp Be Sent to Him, I the More Readily Agreed as By the Miscarriage of your directions we are not able to Comply with the Cartel in the first week of july. But I was the first who proposed an Enterview of Commissaries, the first who Made a delivery of prisoners So that appearances will Be in our favor.[19]

5ʰ july

Before I Seal this I must tell you that Yesterday I Have Received intelligence that Williamsburg is Evacuated. Lord Cornwallis Retired to James Town Island.[20] It is Said the light infantry and 76ʰ Regiment are going to Newyork with His Lordship who takes the Chief Command.[21] The Remainder is to Stay at Portsmouth. But I fancy this last part of the Intelligence is not Right and a Good Number of them Must Be destined to you.[22] I Have wrote [Gen. Jethro] Sumner that He was to join you with Speed and Shall Immediately Send the supply of arms that He wants. At all events (unless Portsmouth Can Be taken By a Coup de Main) I Shall forward to you the pennsylvania[ns,] Virginia Continentals and if possible Some Militia.[23] Circumstances will direct me But My Heart and My duty will make your Support the first

Business I Shall attend to. Requesting My Compliments to your family and My other friends I Have the Honor to Be With the most Sincere Respect and affection Yours   LAFAYETTE

ALS (NjMoHP).

1. Lafayette began this letter of 4 July and finished it the next day.

2. It is not known what letter Lafayette enclosed; his to NG of 27 June, above, described the "Retrograde Movements" of Lord Cornwallis's army.

3. In his letter to NG of 27 June, above, Lafayette had reported that Williamsburg, to which the enemy had marched after a series of raids in the interior, was strongly defended "and under protection of their shiping."

4. On the loss of supplies at Point of Fork and Baron Steuben's unpopularity in Virginia, see Lafayette to NG, 18, 20, and 27 June, all above.

5. For the resolution, which had been prompted by Steuben's retreat from Point of Fork, see Virginia General Assembly, House of Delegates, *Journal* (Charlottesville, [1781]), pp. 47, 49. Lafayette wrote Gov. Thomas Nelson on 31 October, at the conclusion of the Yorktown campaign, that the situation in Virginia before he was "joined by General Washington put it wholly out of my power" to conduct an investigation. (Idzerda, *Lafayette Papers*, 4: 435) NG, meanwhile, wrote Steuben on 17 September, below, that he was "confident of the propriety" of Steuben's conduct.

6. The letter has not been found; the captain had been sent to establish contact with Loyalists in the vicinity of Fredericksburg, presumably intending to gather intelligence. (B. Edgar Joel to George Weedon, 22 June, *Calendar of Va. State Papers*, 2: 179–80) Lafayette had left Gen. George Weedon to defend the Fredericksburg area against a possible incursion. (Ward, *Weedon*, pp. 196–99) As he indicated earlier in this letter, Lafayette was not sure what Cornwallis intended to do.

7. According to the editors of the *Lafayette Papers*, the letter referred to was one that Col. Banastre Tarleton had written Cornwallis on 13 June, during the British army's march to Williamsburg. (Idzerda, *Lafayette Papers*, 4: 235n) In that letter, which was captured and published, Tarleton stated that Lafayette's "design" was "to follow" him. He said he would inform Cornwallis if Lafayette did "not keep a proper distance" and that he would try to "strike at" any detachments from Lafayette's force. (The letter is printed in ibid., p. 183.)

8. Lafayette told the governor in a letter of 1 July: "Many and Many men are Daily Deserting—But it is Next to Impossility to take them in their flight through the Woods." At the same time, many other militiamen were going home because their terms of service had expired, "and You Might as well Stop the flood tide as to Stop Militia whose times are out." (Ibid., p. 228)

9. On the force that Gen. Daniel Morgan brought to Lafayette, see note at Lafayette to NG, 20 June, above.

10. Nelson's corps had joined Lafayette by 16 July; it was not until 12 August that a party of Moylan's dragoons, forty in number, arrived in Lafayette's camp. (See Lafayette to Morgan, 16 July, Idzerda, *Lafayette Papers*, 4: 251 and n; Lafayette to NG, first letter of 12 August, below.)

11. Lafayette meant that he had sent parties to harass the British outposts and to force Cornwallis's army onto the alert and deprive its soldiers of sleep.

12. The "Combined expedition" was the planned attack on New York City by Franco-American forces; on the expected "Recall" of part of Cornwallis's army, see note 21, below.

13. For more on Gregory's defeat, see note at Burke to NG, 4 July, above.

14. French troops under the Comte de Rochambeau had marched from Newport, R.I., to join Washington's army near New York; the junction took place on 6 July. (Fitzpatrick,

GW, 22: 332; Evelyn M. Acomb, ed., *The Revolutionary Journal of Baron Ludwig Von Closen, 1780–1783* [Chapel Hill: University of North Carolina Press, 1958], pp. 90–91.)

15. The *Marquis de Lafayette* had been captured at sea. The *Alliance*, which had escorted her from France, reached Boston on 6 July. (Idzerda, *Lafayette Papers*, 4: 235n)

16. On the capture of Augusta, Ga., see Pickens and Lee to NG, 5 June, above; NG had reported the lifting of the siege at Ninety Six, S.C., in his letter to Lafayette of 23 June. By "*paragraph*," Lafayette presumably meant achieving favorable notice in the newspapers and from Congress.

17. Maj. Richard Claiborne, the deputy quartermaster for Virginia, wrote Lafayette on 13 June that his department could not make itself "liable where there is no prospect of support." Claiborne would therefore "decline all purchases and Contracts until I am furnished with money or some other means to pay off the old debts, and to proceed in the business." (Idzerda, *Lafayette Papers*, 4: 181)

18. On John Browne, see Pendleton to Browne, 18 and 21 April, both above.

19. The terms of the cartel for the exchange of prisoners are discussed at NG to Huntington, 10 May, above. Cornwallis enclosed a copy of the cartel in a letter to Lafayette of 26 May. (Idzerda, *Lafayette Papers*, 4: 134) The further correspondence between the two that Lafayette reported here is in ibid., pp. 167–68, 196–97, and 218–19. In his third letter to Lafayette of 17 July, below, NG sent "directions" concerning the prisoners who were being sent to Virginia from Charleston.

20. For more on Cornwallis's movements, see Lafayette to NG, 8 July, below.

21. Cornwallis did not take the "Chief Command," nor were British troops sent from Virginia to New York; Sir Henry Clinton revoked his orders recalling them. (Wickwire, *Cornwallis*, p. 347)

22. Cornwallis did not send these troops to South Carolina.

23. For more on Sumner and his North Carolina Continentals, see Sumner to NG, 25 June, above. The other troops mentioned by Lafayette remained in Virginia.

* * *

¶ [FROM MAJOR JAMES MCHENRY, 5 July 1781. Since he last wrote, the enemy have left Williamsburg, Va., and are reportedly "retiring" to Jamestown.[1] The information concerning [Lord] Cornwallis and his army "is drawn from a deserter"; the Marquis [de Lafayette] will furnish "details."[2] There is a report that [Gen. Isaac] Gregory "has lost the important post that opens into [North] Carolina."[3] If Cornwallis is to be the commander in chief, McHenry thinks "he will not take his cavalry to New-York" but may plan "a serious force against" NG.[4] McHenry has told Lafayette that the Pennsylvania troops should "move to" NG "the moment the intentions of the Enemy" are known.[5] ALS (NNPM) 2 pp.]

1. McHenry's two letters of 4 July are above.

2. See Lafayette to NG, 4 and 5 July, immediately above, and 8 July, below.

3. See Burke to NG, 4 July, above.

4. Cornwallis was not to become the British commander in chief.

5. See also Lafayette's comments on sending the Pennsylvanians to NG in his letter immediately above.

¶ [FROM COLONEL WILLIAM WASHINGTON, Howell's Ferry, S.C., 5 July 1781. Lord Rawdon "is running away[;] he was on his March near Beaver Creek early this Morning."[1] Washington will immediately cross at McCord's Ferry. He will "fall in" with [Gen. Francis] Marion and [Col. Henry] Lee and "get up with" Rawdon as soon as possible.[2] ALS (MiU-C) 1 p.]

1. On Rawdon's march from Ft. Granby to Orangeburg, see notes at Henry Lee's two letters to NG of 3 July, above.

2. As noted at Lee's second letter of 3 July, above, Rawdon reached Orangeburg before the American forces could unite to stop him.

*   *   *

From Colonel Otho H. Williams

Dr General   Thursday 12 o'Clock [5 July 1781] Rice Creek [S.C.]¹

Dominique, whose offense you know, just now arrived from Ninety Six, which he left late the Evening before last.² He was taken into service by Major Green [Joseph Greene] who was about to send him attendant on Mrs Green (who is going with an Escort) to Charles Town. He informs me that the Garrison is fed upon boild Corn which is very scarce and fresh Beef. Col^l [John Harris] Cruger had intelligence the Day before Yesterday that your army was recrossing Enoree and that Col [Henry] Lee was advancing by a private rout thro the Woods in consequence of which orders were issued about Twelve o'Clock for the Troops to prepare to march at a moments Warning.³ He [i.e., Dominique] saw, and assisted in the Demolition of part of their works, all their swivells were broke before he came away. Our militia have pursued theirs to the Walls of their fortifications. Captⁿ Stone intercepted a Convoy of Provisions, routed the Party & cut their Horses out of their Waggons. Lord Rawdon made a Detachment to Georgia with which most of our Deserters were sent.

Dominique says he stroll'd into the Country the Day he left me and was taken up by the Inhabitants and that four Days afterwards he was taken into the Garrison, That Major Greene offer'd him his choice of going to the Provost or waiting on him. He said he wo^d [would] prefer waiting on him, but that if he Sho^d [should] be taken I wo^d hang him. The major said there wo^d be no danger of that as he sho^d go immediately with Mrs Greene to Charles Town, and then with him to N. York. Captⁿ [Thomas] French and other Officers talk'd also of going to N. York.⁴ He understood that a part of the Troops were to march to Augusta and the others immediately to Cha: Town.⁵ Genl [Robert] Cunningham was in the Garrison but left it about the time Lord Rawdon left it.⁶ They have a great many Militia[;] some of them are averse to going to Cha: Town.

Domminique is very circumstancial and consistant in his reports, and as he has been so expeditious in his return I have pardon'd him which I hope you will excuse.

An Express went this morning in search of Genl [Andrew] Pickens with your orders.⁷

We halted here half an Hour to refresh and are again form'd to recommence our march. Genl [Isaac] Huger proposes to Halt and Cook at Crane Creek—3 miles.[8] Prosperity crown your hopes. I am D^r G^l mo truly Yrs

O. H. WILLIAMS

ALS (MiU-C).

1. The date was taken from the docketing.

2. Benjamin Dominique, Williams's servant, had deserted at Ninety Six. (NG to Lee, 24 June, above)

3. For Lee's movements, see his two letters to NG of 3 July, above. Cruger commanded the troops remaining at Ninety Six.

4. On the report that several enemy regiments were to be sent to New York, see Lee to NG, 29 June, above.

5. When the troops from Ninety Six evacuated that post, they marched to join Lord Rawdon at Orangeburg.

6. On Rawdon's departure from Ninety Six, see Lee to NG, 30 June, above. Cunningham had commanded the Loyalist militia in the Ninety Six area.

7. NG's orders to Pickens have not been found.

8. As seen in his letter to Lee of 4 July, above, NG had gone ahead of the army to decide where it would "be best to move the troops." Huger commanded the army in his absence.

*   *   *

¶ [FROM COLONEL WILLIAM HENDERSON,[1] Pacolet River, S.C., 6 July 1781. Has used "Every Exertion" to collect men since arriving "in this Quarter." Hopes to have 200 "by tomorrow Night" but did not expect "Such Difficalties" in raising them. "If the Spirit of plundring Ware held Up: they Would Turn out With Alacrity but finding that To be Discountenanc^d makes them act With Reluctance." Henderson sent "Sum Confidential persons" to gather intelligence "near the Enemy on Little River." He reports the whereabouts of the enemy light horse and the Loyalists, few of whom have "colected." Col. [John Harris] Cruger reportedly has marched "with a partie for Long Cane Settlement" to lay waste to the country.[2] About 1,500 men are still at Ninety Six; the rest, under Lord Rawdon, have marched "Down the Same Road the[y] cum up."[3] Henderson concludes that all of the enemy troops are going to move "Dow[n] the Cuntry" because "they Indis[c]riminatly Destroy all the Grane & Standing Corn" on their march and because of information he has received about the "Tories Who are in a shocking Situation." Rawdon informed the Loyalists in the area that he was unable to protect them "in such a vast Exstent of Cuntry" and ordered them to "Remove below the Congerees." Henderson believes "a Considirable Number Will Bite at the bate." This is confirmed by "private" letters of Loyalists, directing their families to sell their property and be ready to move "under the Cover of a Scout that is to Cum up for that parpose in a few Days."[4] Henderson will try to "frustrate there Designs." He has also learned that the enemy have destroyed nearly all of the works at Ninety Six. They are gathering "all the Live Stock they can," including "all the horses that is to be Got."[5] Henderson cannot get men to march from this area "So Long as it is threton^d To be Laid Waist. Indeed there is but Very few men[;] the Cuntry is allmost Depopilated." He will come to camp after the bearers of this letter return. Asks for powder, lead, and salt. Will transmit any important intelligence he obtains. ALS (MiU-C) 2 pp.]

1. Henderson was a South Carolina Continental officer. (Heitman, *Register*)

2. Greene's first biographer described the raid reported here as a "last opportunity" for Cruger and his troops to wreak "vengeance on the unfortunate whigs." (Johnson, *Greene*, 2: 163) According to a Loyalist source, however, the detachment was sent "to bring away the Loyalists and their families" of the region. (Chesney, "Journal," p. 24) As seen in Gen. Andrew Pickens's letter to NG of 19 July, below, reports of damage in the Long Cane region were exaggerated.

3. As noted at Lee to NG, first letter of 3 July, above, Rawdon's force was marching to Orangeburg.

4. For more on British strategy in regard to Ninety Six and the Loyalists living nearby, see also the note at NG to Lee, second letter of 25 June, above, and Pickens to NG, 10 July, below.

5. Col. Otho Williams also sent intelligence about the destruction of the works at Ninety Six in his letter of 5 July, above. In his letter of 10 July, below, Pickens reported that the Loyalists at Ninety Six had "Collected all the waggons and horses" they could, as well as "Provisions of Every Kind."

¶ [FROM GENERAL ISAAC HUGER, "Camp 1 1/2 mile from Friday's Ferry," S.C., 6 July 1781. "The army arrived at this place in the cool of this morning"; it will stay until NG's "pleasure is known." The troops are "washing and refreshing" and will be "in perfect readiness" to march wherever NG "may think proper."[1] Gen. [Andrew] Pickens arrived with 300 men "this morning." Pickens cannot immediately undertake the "business" that NG ordered because his "horses are so much reduced." Pickens will send men toward Ninety Six to watch the enemy, however, and will probably write NG "by this conveyance."[2] Huger has spoken with Colonel [Thomas] Taylor and is confident that Taylor, assisted by Major [Robert] Forsyth, will furnish the desired quantity of provisions if he is "not too soon interrupted by the movement of the army."[3] LS (MiU-C) 3 pp.]

1. NG's reply has not been found, but Col. Otho Williams wrote NG on 8 July, below, that the army had marched to Howell's Ferry after receiving orders from NG during the afternoon of the 7th.

2. From Pickens's letter to NG of this date, immediately below, it is clear that the "business" that NG had ordered him to pursue was that of "discovering the enemys movements" around Ninety Six.

3. In a letter to Gen. Thomas Sumter of 7 July, William Pierce, NG's aide, explained that NG had asked Taylor, a regimental commander in Sumter's brigade, to collect provisions for the Southern Army because Taylor's men "were better able to serve this Army from their knowledge of the Country." (Sumter Papers, DLC; see also Forsyth to NG, 8 July, below.)

¶ [FROM GENERAL ANDREW PICKENS, "Colonel Taylors House," S.C., 6 July 1781. Has NG's letter "of yesterday" [not found]. Is glad the enemy "are moving downwards"; hopes NG can make their march "at least a Troublesom one." Pickens's horses are "much worn down from the long march" and from a lack of forage along the way; they are "intiarly unfit to perform the service of discovering the enemys movements or even to gett out of their way should they prove too powerfull for us."[1] He has therefore sent a small party to the Ninety Six area "to make discoveries and if possible find out the movements and intention of the enemy." Pickens also expects "hourly" to hear from other parties, which have been "on the same business" for days.[2] When he marched, he left 100 men behind to cover the country and harass "our foes" and asked Col. [Elijah] Clarke to act with and support these scouts. "If the Enemy are moving downwards," he believes he will have a "better chance of falling in with them" by staying where he is and resting his horses for a few days than by moving "upwards." He will halt "in this Neighbourhood" and await NG's orders.[3] Will try to get expresses to Colonels Clarke and [James] Jackson of Georgia and will do all in his "power to harass the enemy and to gain intiligence." ALS (MiU-C) 2 pp.]

1. As seen in the letter immediately above, Pickens had reached camp that day.

2. In a letter to NG of 10 July, below, Pickens sent the intelligence that his parties had gathered in the Ninety Six area.

3. NG's reply has not been found. When he wrote NG on 10 July, Pickens had moved a short distance up the Broad River, to Dutch Fork.

¶ [FROM GENERAL THOMAS SUMTER, Camden, S.C., 6 July 1781. He arrived "yesterday" to find "little Work has been Done and things Generally in Disorder."[1] He intended to set out for NG's camp "this Morning," but because of the "Movements of the enemy & the Troops having" crossed the river, he "thought it probable" that NG would want him to "Pass the river also." He will proceed a short distance and await "farther orders."[2] Has written "Co^l [Edward] Lacey &c" to "wait upon" NG for orders and "March downwards. . . with all possible Expedition" if NG thinks proper.[3] About 250 enemy troops have marched from Biggin Church to the Santee River. Sumter is unsure of Lord Rawdon's "Intentions," as it still appears that Col. [Alexander] Stewart "Means to Move up & Join him."[4] If the American mounted troops can collect, Sumter believes Rawdon "May be Made Very uneasie & forced to Retreat or Run the Risque of the [British] Posts below Suffering." Expects to know better soon "the Movements[,] Strength & Dangers of the enemy." Thinks the reinforcement was "little Short of eighteen hundred men."[5] ALS (MiU-C) 3 pp.]

1. On Sumter's purpose in going to Camden, see his letter to NG of 2 July, above.

2. Lord Rawdon's and NG's armies had crossed the Congaree. When he wrote NG on 8 July, below, Sumter was at Russell's Ferry, on that river. For NG's "farther orders," see his letter to Sumter of 7 July, below.

3. Capt. William Pierce wrote Sumter on 7 July that Lacey had orders to rejoin Sumter. (Sumter Papers, DLC) Some of Lacey's troops had reached Sumter when he wrote NG on 8 July, below.

4. On Stewart's junction with Rawdon, see Marion to NG, first letter of 8 July, below.

5. The "reinforcement" to which Sumter referred was probably the force that had accompanied Lord Rawdon to relieve Ninety Six. As seen in the note at NG to Clarke, 12 June, above, Rawdon's detachment at that time numbered about 2,000 men.

¶ [FROM COLONEL OTHO H. WILLIAMS, "Camp Crane Creek," S.C., 6 July 1781. Encloses a report on Maj. [Henry] Hardman, who as "Field Officer of the Day" on 4 July "not only neglected but, positively Refused" to do his duty. Believes that an example must be made "to Reestablish subordination[,] the basis of Discipline."[1] ALS (MiU-C) 2 pp.]

1. No evidence has been found of disciplinary action against Hardman, a Maryland Continental officer.

* * *

To General Thomas Sumter

Dear Sir   Mrs Motts [S.C.] July 7th 1781

Lord Rawden is retiring towards Charles Town[;] the Cavalry of the Army and part of your State Cavalry with General Marians [Francis Marion's] Militia are at and in the neighbourhood of this place and will go in pursuit of him. The infantry of our Army will follow from Ancrums this afternoon; and all the rest of your State troops at that place. You will please to collect all your Militia and the remainder of the State troops and follow on to give us support should it be necessary. Where this will meet with you I cannot tell and therefore leave you to take such route as you may think proper to bring you to a point of support in the shortest time.[1]

I have reason to hope that 96 is or will be evacuated.[2] I rely upon your exerti[on]s and hope it will be in your power to give us great assistance. I am with great esteem Your Most obe[t] humbl Ser

N GREENE

ALS (Sumter Papers: DLC).

1. Sumter discussed his whereabouts and his plan to join NG when he replied on 8 July, below.

2. On the evacuation of Ninety Six, see Pickens to NG, 10 July, below.

*   *   *

¶ [FROM MAJOR JOHN ARMSTRONG, "Camp on the Watarees 16 Miles Above Camden," S.C., 7 July 1781. The command that NG has given him is the "most disagreeable" he has ever had.[1] Two-thirds of the Continentals are sick, and the rest are needed to "take care of the Baggage"; the Virginia militiamen are either sick or "in Such Order" that Armstrong cannot "Command them to Duty." The militiamen insist their time of service is up and are determined to go home; their officers say they cannot stop them because they desert at night. Armstrong has talked to the militiamen, and they have agreed to stay until NG's orders are received. They are willing to escort the prisoners, "exspecting it will be Northwardly." It is the only "Service they can be put to at This Time," as they refuse to do any duty "in Camp."[2] Bread is scarce. Armstrong must send parties out to thresh wheat. He sent twenty men with a guard to the hospital in Camden. Thirty-eight prisoners taken by Capt. [Joseph] Eggleston arrived in camp and were put into "the Provost this Evening."[3] Armstrong's detachment is camped at a "Wasted Plantation," which affords excellent pasturage for the horses. No troops have joined him since he left Winnsboro. He has examined the returns and finds that "Rations are Drawn" for 450 men even though he has only 100 fit for duty. Promises to "strickly adhere to & Observe" NG's orders. ALS (Greene Papers: DLC) 2 pp.]

1. In a letter to Armstrong of 4 July, above, NG had given him command of the army's heavy baggage, prisoners, and invalids.

2. As seen in Armstrong to NG, 10 July, below, the express carrying one of his letters to

NG—probably this one—returned without delivering it. When he wrote on the 10th, Armstrong again asked NG for advice concerning the militiamen.

3. On the capture of these men, see Lee to NG, first letter of 3 July, above.

¶ [FROM GENERAL FRANCIS MARION, "Sabbs Plant[n]," S.C., 7 July 1781. Prisoners taken by one of Marion's detachments report that Lord Rawdon's troops are "so fatigued they cannot possible move." The prisoners say three of Rawdon's regiments were "going to Lay down their Arms & they believe they will today if they are orderd to March."[1] The enemy have no idea that an American force is "near them & they straggle three miles from Camp." Col. [Alexander] Stewart was four miles west of Four Holes the "day before yesterday"; his horses are "so poor they cannot proceed to join Rawden." Marion will move toward Stewart and attempt "to do something with him or at least prevent him from Joining Rawden."[2] Marion will also follow Rawdon to Dorchester and is sure he can "take a number of prisoners." If NG wants to attack Rawdon, Marion will be "on the Orangebourg Road at or near Walnut Hill."[3] ALS (MiU-C) 2 pp.]

1. The march from Ninety Six to Orangeburg in sweltering heat was so taxing for Rawdon's troops that according to a contemporary British source, some fifty of them died from heat exhaustion along the way. ("Annual Register—1781," p. 865) Col. Alexander Stewart's troops, who reinforced Rawdon at Orangeburg, were so "fatigued" and "discontented" that it was "some weeks" before they were again "in a condition to move." (Johnson, *Greene*, 2: 206)

2. Marion was unable to prevent the junction. (See Marion to NG, first letter of 8 July, below.)

3. Walnut Hill was the name of Henry Hyrne's plantation in modern-day Colleton County.

¶ [FROM GENERAL FRANCIS MARION, "Whitemans on Foreholds 13 miles from Orrangebourg," S.C., 7 July 1781, 4 P.M.[1] Marion was not sure whether NG intended to advance "against the Enemy," so he sent a party to Orangeburg to "pick up" British stragglers. They will rejoin him "Seven miles below" Orangeburg on the road to Charleston, where Marion will await orders from NG. ALS (MiU-C) 1 p.]

1. "Foreholds" was Four Holes, a creek and swamp east of Orangeburg.

¶ [FROM ROBERT SMITH, [Charlotte, N.C.], 7 July 1781.[1] "A small quantity of Salt" is owed to the inhabitants for making shirts and overalls for the army.[2] Smith has none available, and the people "are in Great Need." Asks for an order on "Sume Person that Can Deliver it." Encloses an account to show what is due.[3] ALS (MiU-C) 1 p.]

1. "R Smith," as the letter was signed, was most likely Robert Smith, the assistant deputy quartermaster at Charlotte. (See above, vol. 7: 68n.)

2. For more on the clothing, see NG to Smith, 7 January, above. (Ibid., p. 67)

3. The account showed that eighteen and three-fourths bushels were still owed to the inhabitants. NG's reply has not been found.

¶ [FROM THOMAS SMITH,[1] "New London[,] Bedford County," Va., 7 July 1781. The "very great disorders" that the enemy have caused in Virginia have led John Pryor to reestablish the "Laboratory &c" at New London. "With dificulty," Smith has gotten the "works in such a train" that he can now "venture to assure" NG that orders for "Arms, Ammunition and Accoutrements will be complyed with in a short time." Capt. Bowen Price, the commissary of military stores at New London, will receive NG's orders. ALS (MiU-C) 1 p.]

1. Smith noted after his signature that he was deputy commissary general of military stores.

¶ [TO MAJOR JOHN ARMSTRONG. From "Head Quarters at Beaver Creek," S.C., 8 July 1781. NG has an unauthenticated report, which cannot be totally dismissed, that the enemy have sent a party from Ninety Six to "strike at" the baggage.[1] Armstrong is to cross the Wateree River and move toward the High Hills of the Santee. If pursued, he should "take a strong position where there is a number of buildings and where a body of horse cannot act and there draw up your waggons and horses in such a manner as the fire from the houses will cover them. This [is] easily effected with a little resolution and spirit." If Armstrong is in "danger," he is to inform the army immediately, and a "body of Cavalry" will be sent to "relieve" him. If there is "the least danger" of the baggage being captured, he is to burn NG's papers. If he meets the Salisbury militia, which is marching to Camden, he should put the baggage "under their protection."[2] He is to send a mounted party to obtain intelligence and "use every precaution and hazard every danger to secure the baggage to the last extremity."[3] ADfS (MiU-C) 4 pp.]

1. Armstrong commanded the party that was taking the army's baggage and stores to Camden. (See NG to Armstrong, 4 July, above.)

2. As seen at Malmedy to NG, 29 June, above, militiamen from the Salisbury, N.C., militia district were not en route to Camden.

3. Armstrong replied on 12 July, below.

¶ [CAPTAIN WILLIAM PIERCE, JR., TO GENERAL THOMAS SUMTER. From Howell's Ferry, S.C., 8 July 1781. NG has written Gen. [Isaac] Huger that "an opportunity may shortly offer to strike at Lord Rawdon."[1] Sumter is therefore to hold himself "in the most perfect readiness to co-operate." In compliance with NG's instructions, Huger also asks Sumter to provide fifteen or twenty men acquainted with the Orangeburg road to reconnoiter the country between Juniper Springs and Orangeburg. "The object is important, and no delay can be admitted." Much depends on the success of the army's operation, and "much credit will be the reward of those who exert themselves at this very interesting and important crisis." Reiterates "that General Greene expects" Sumter to be in "perfect readiness to co-operate with this Army," which will halt at "Beaver Creek for to Day perhaps."[2] ALS (Sumter Papers: DLC) 2 pp.]

1. NG's letter to Huger has not been found.

2. See Sumter to NG, this date, below.

¶ [FROM MAJOR ROBERT FORSYTH, Howell's Ferry, S.C., 8 July 1781. Will try to comply with NG's orders contained in the letter of Gen. [Isaac] Huger.[1] Expects to get three wagons from Col. [Thomas] Taylor; another ten, which are bringing salt from Charlotte, N.C., will be sent to Thompson's Mill "to get loaded." The troops have enough meal "in their Knapsacks for this Day and Tomorrow." Forsyth has also brought a three-day supply of meal and two hogsheads of spirits across [the Congaree River] and has enough additional supplies within his "Reach" that NG can "reckon on at least" 10,000 jills of spirits and eight days' worth of meal. Forsyth will "pick up" beef along the route of march, for he can find "no Militia that will pay the necessary attention to driving" livestock. Assures NG that he will use his "utmost exertions to provide every thing for the comfort of the Troops" within his "Power." ALS (MiU-C) 2 pp. The bottom of the first page is cut off and missing.]

1. Huger's letter conveying NG's orders to Forsyth has not been found.

¶ [FROM MRS. HARRIOTT PINCKNEY HORRY, [Hampton Plantation, St. James Parish, S.C.], 8 July 1781.[1] Seeks a permit to ship rice from Santee to Charleston. The proceeds from the shipment are to be used to support her son, who is in England to be educated. She trusts that the "Education of American Youth" is a "Matter of sufficient Importance" to "excuse" her for bothering NG. Adds that when exportations were stopped, "an exception was made with respect to such property as should be exported for the maintenance and Education of Youth."[2] AL (MiU-C) 1 p.]

1. Harriott Pinckney Horry was the wife of Daniel Huger Horry, whose estate was later amerced because of his Loyalist sympathies and who had taken their son to England for the schooling that she mentioned in this letter. (Frances Leigh Williams, *A Founding Family: The Pinckneys of South Carolina* [New York: Harcourt Brace Jovanovich, 1978], pp. 33, 185–86; Harriott Pinckney Horry to NG, 12 January 1782, below) Their plantation was on Wambaw Creek, a tributary of the Santee River. (Samuel G. Stoney, *Plantations of the Carolina Low Country*, rev. ed. [Charleston: Carolina Art Association, 1964], pp. 59–60)

2. In 1779, the South Carolina legislature had passed a law prohibiting the exportation of "all kind of provision" and other specified articles from the state. The governor and commander-in-chief were given some latitude in the enforcement of this ban, but the terms of the law contained no specific exemption such as Horry claimed here. (South Carolina, *Statutes at Large*, 10 vols. [Columbia, 1836–41], 4: 480–81) NG's reply has not been found; in her letter of 12 January 1782, Horry again sought permission to send a load of rice for her son's support, assuring NG that the money would not benefit her husband, who "will have left England long before anything she sends could reach" him there.

¶ [FROM THE MARQUIS DE LAFAYETTE, "Ambler's Plantation opposite James Island," Va., 8 July 1781. Reports the movements of Lord Cornwallis's and his own armies since 4 July, when the British evacuated Williamsburg. Describes an action that took place on 6 July, which began when an "advanced Corps" under Gen. [Anthony] Wayne attacked the British pickets "close to" the enemy encampment. When Wayne's "Van Guard" attempted to capture an enemy cannon, "the whole British Army came out, and advanced to the thin Wood occupied by Gen[1] Wayne." Although Wayne's force numbered fewer than 800 men, "at sight of the British Army the Troops ran to the rencoutre. A short skirmish insued with a close[,] warm and well directed fire; but as the Enemy's right and left of course greatly outflanked ours; I sent Gen[1] Wayne orders to retire half a Mile," to where the "Light Infantry Battalions had arrived by a rapid move." The American troops remained there until "some Hours in the night." After the action, Lord Cornwallis's army retreated first to James Island and then to the "South side of the [James] River." Gen. [Peter]

Muhlenberg occupied the ground they evacuated. In the course of their retreat, the enemy abandoned "A Number of valuable Horses." They also suffered heavy casualties, which they have taken "pains" to conceal. Sends a
return of Wayne's losses. Is happy that no officer was killed, although many
were wounded. Most of the field officers had their horses killed, and the teams
of two field pieces were also killed, making it impossible to "move them unless
Men had been sacrificed. But it is enough for the Glory of Gen' Wayne and the
Officers and Men he commanded[,] with a reconnoitring Party only to have
attacked the whole British Army, close to their incampment; and by this severe
Skirmish hastened their retreat over the River."[1] Cy (MiU-C) 3 pp.]

1. In this letter, Lafayette was offering a positive view of what had been a defeat for his
army. In the battle of Green Spring Farm, as the action was called, Anthony Wayne fell
into a trap that Cornwallis had set. Believing that he was engaging only Cornwallis's rear
guard, Wayne pushed forward until he discovered that the entire British army had been
posted just out of sight; they outnumbered his men by four or five to one. As they
advanced and threatened to cut off Wayne's detachment completely, he brashly formed
his troops and ordered a charge that momentarily checked the British advance. The
overwhelming superiority of the British force soon broke Wayne's lines, and confusion
and flight followed. Lafayette, who had been suspicious of the stubbornness with which
the British "pickets" defended their position and had discovered the trap just before
Wayne fell into it, ordered up the rest of his army, which had been camped five miles
away. When Wayne's men, now thoroughly disorganized, reached these troops at
Green Spring Farm, they stopped and reformed. (Gottschalk, *Lafayette*, pp. 264–67)
Because darkness was approaching, Cornwallis called off the attack. Nor did he renew it
the next day, writing afterwards that to do so would have delayed his detachment's
march to Portsmouth and its embarkation for New York. (Cornwallis to Clinton, 8 July
1781, Stevens, *Clinton-Cornwallis Controversy*, 2: 59) While Lafayette publicly praised
Wayne, he was privately critical of the "serious blunders" of his subordinate, saying that
only the fact that the British had retreated made it appear in the newspapers to have
been an American victory. (Nelson, *Wayne*, p. 137) The casualty figures support a claim
to victory by the British, who had eleven killed, sixty-six wounded, and one missing,
while the Americans suffered losses of twenty-eight killed and 111 wounded and
missing. (British casualties are in MacKenzie, *Diary*, 2: 564–65; the American casualty
report is in PCC, item 156, p. 173, DNA.)

¶ [**FROM GENERAL FRANCIS MARION**, "11 Miles from Orangbourg,"
S.C., 8 July 1781, 1 A.M. Marion just received NG's letter of "Last Evening."[1]
He moved "here" to intercept Col. [Alexander] Stewart, but Stewart "pass
yesterday & made a Junction with Ld Rawden with 300 Infantry & 50 Cavel-
dry."[2] Rawdon does not seem to be getting ready to move, but Marion hopes to
have "a better Account" soon. He has seemingly dependable information that
the British troops at Dorchester mutinied and that thirty men were killed and
sixty wounded.[3] "Two prisoners taken yesterday" report that Rawdon's men
were ready to "Lay down their Arms & was fatigued, that the most of them
was Exceedingly Discontented."[4] Has sent an officer to give NG "every perticular" and to report Marion's intended movements. Marion cannot learn of
any enemy post "from here to Dorches[ter]." Will write again "in a few
hours."[5] ALS (MiU-C) 2 pp.]

1. NG's letter has not been found.

2. According to his biographer, Marion marched in pursuit of Stewart at 1 A.M. on
8 July. Stewart, through luck or advance knowledge, used a less-traveled road parallel-

ing the one that Marion took. He passed Marion undetected. (Rankin, *Swamp Fox*, pp. 222–23)

3. Nothing is known about the reported mutiny.

4. On the prisoners and morale in Rawdon's army, see also Marion to NG, first letter of 7 July, above.

5. See Marion to NG, immediately below.

¶ [FROM GENERAL FRANCIS MARION, "Whitemans," S.C., 8 July 1781, 8 A.M. He received NG's letter of 6 P.M. "yesterday" [not found]. Col. [Peter] Horry has returned with three captured sutlers' wagons carrying rum and wine.[1] Horry, who confirms that Col. [Alexander] Stewart has joined Lord Rawdon, was unable to take prisoners or obtain "further intelligence." Marion did not stay where he said he would because his "horses has starved Since Yesterday Morning."[2] He will proceed to a local mill and await orders. ALS (MiU-C) 1 p.]

1. On the contents of the captured wagons, see Marion's second letter to NG of 9 July, below.

2. See Marion to NG, second letter of 7 July, above.

* * *

From Captain William Pierce, Jr.

Camp on the South side of Congaree opposite to
Sir   Howels Ferry [S.C.] July 8th 1781

General Huger was honored with a Letter from you dated yesterday about sun-rise this Morning.[1] He desires me to inform you that he shall note its contents, and execute your commands as far as he has it in his power. The Army having crossed the River during the Night he proposes to proceed immediately to Beaver Creek, where it will halt for your further orders. We are at a loss for a full construction of your Letter. You desire the General to inform himself of the movements of Col° [John Harris] Cruger and that in case the junction between his Lordship [i.e., Rawdon] and himself is likely to be speedily formed, to recross the River; without saying how far he is to advance, or where to fix his position.[2] This circumstance applied to the subsequent part of your Letter wherein you tell him not to force a march, serve to embarrass us very much. However the General has determined to move to Beaver Creek at which place he may be found, and from which place he intends to write you.

General Pickens is written to, to reconnoitre the Road between Juniper Springs and Orangeburg and General Sumter will also receive information of our situation and instructions how to act. He is gone down the River; we know not his object, but leave you to judge of his intention by the inclosed Letter.[3] The means of obtaining intelligence we are deprived of for want of Dragoons, but nothing will be left unattempted I am convinced, to put matters upon the best and most advantageous footing.

Wherever you strike we wish you success and pray for the opportunity of improving the advantage. I have the honor to be sir Your very obᵗ servᵗ   Wᴹ PIERCE Jᴿ

NB General Huger wishes that a party of Colᵒ Middletons [i.e., Charles Myddelton's] Men may reconnoitre the lower Country about the Congaree in case Sumter should not come up in time.

ALS (MiU-C).

1. NG had left his army late on 4 July or early on the 5th and had joined Col. William Washington's detachment in order to scout Lord Rawdon's situation and coordinate operations against him. (Johnson, *Greene*, 2: 159–60) His letter to Gen. Isaac Huger, whom he had left temporarily in command of the Southern Army, has not been found.

2. On Cruger's junction with Rawdon, see note at Williams to NG, this date, below.

3. The orders to Pickens, who was with Huger, have not been found. (See Pickens to NG, 6 July, above.) Those to Gen. Thomas Sumter are in Pierce to Sumter, this date, above. Pierce presumably enclosed Sumter's letter of 6 July, above.

*   *   *

¶ [FROM CAPTAIN JOHN PRYOR, Charlottesville, Va., 8 July 1781. Details his activities since undertaking his "Offices." Has just learned that the Board of War "cannot approve" his appointment because it had already appointed Thomas Jones to the post. Until Jones or his representative arrives in Virginia, Pryor will continue "unremittingly to promote" a department that has been "horridly neglected." Hopes "at least, [to] be secured" in the "sundry contracts and engagements" he has entered into and that the money he has "borrowed and advanced for the department" will be "accounted for."¹ Pryor long since appointed the bearer, John Martin, to be field commissary of military stores for NG's army. Martin's delay in joining the army was explained in a previous letter.² The removal of the laboratory from Prince Edward Court House to Bedford Court House has "stagnated the preparations" of ammunition, but a number of artificers have been recruited, and Pryor's deputy is arranging matters in such a way that "a littl time" should "produce sufficient supplies."³ The enemy did far less damage than he feared when he last wrote NG.⁴ The only military stores that were lost were 400 ½ barrels of powder and 200 good muskets, all state property. The British have retired to Williamsburg; the Marquis [de Lafayette] is about "20 Miles above." Gen. [Daniel] Morgan is expected to join Lafayette with 2,000 men, and that should enable Lafayette to attack.⁵ "As yet, littl or nothing has been done." ALS (MiU-C) 2 pp.]

1. In his reply of 19 August, below, NG pledged that Pryor's "engagements" and just debts while serving as deputy commissary of military stores would be honored.

2. In Pryor's letter to NG of 5 June, above, he had informed NG that Martin had been assigned temporarily to oversee the Continental laboratory in Virginia. As seen in Pryor to NG, 25 July, below, Martin did not bring this letter to NG or serve as the army's field commissary for military stores.

3. See Thomas Smith to NG, 7 July, above.

4. See Pryor to NG, 5 June.

5. As noted at Lafayette to NG, 20 June, above, Morgan brought a much smaller force with him. On the movements of Lord Cornwallis's and Lafayette's armies, see Lafayette to NG, this date, above.

¶ [**FROM GENERAL THOMAS SUMTER**, "Near Russels Ferry," S.C., 8 July 1781. Has received NG's letter of "yesterdays Date." Col. H[enry] Hampton and the state troops will "pass the River after & will Move on with Genl [Isaac] Huger," as NG ordered. Sumter will remain "here" until the regiments of Colonels [William] Hill and [William] Bratton arrive, as he hopes they will "this Day." He will then "Instantly follow" the army.[1] Some of the troops in the regiments commanded by Colonels [Edward] Lacey and [Richard] Winn have already joined. All of these units together would comprise "a pretty Detachment." Sumter assures NG that he will "press forward with all Possable Dispatch the Moment" he can "Comply with What appears to be" NG's "Design." Thinks Lord Rawdon's situation is "Certainly against him, & probably So favourable an oppertunity of attacking him Might Never offer again provid[ed] the Troops Moving Were Collected." ALS (MiU-C) 2 pp.]

1. Sumter joined Gen. Francis Marion and Colonels Henry Lee and William Washington on 9 July. (Lee, *Memoirs*, 2: 141) The combined force, according to Otho Williams, "formed a very respectable little army." (Williams to Nathaniel Pendleton, 16 July, Gibbes, *Documentary History*, 3: 105)

¶ [**FROM MAJOR JOHN WARD**, [near Camden, S.C.], 8 July 1781.[1] The militia troops he commands insist that "agreeable to" Gov. [Thomas] Jefferson's "Promise their Time is undoubtedly Expir'd." They refuse to remain as guards for the baggage but have "unanimously agreed" to escort the prisoners "to any Part of Virginia" that NG desires and to serve until that duty is completed. If NG approves, he should send instructions to Major Armstrong. Ward promises to perform his "Duty with all Diligence."[2] Adds in a postscript that "Several" militiamen have "already left." ALS (MiU-C) 1 p.]

1. The place was taken from Maj. John Armstrong's letter of 7 July, above, in which Armstrong also discussed the militiamen's situation.

2. NG apparently accepted Ward's offer. (See NG to Maj. Alexander Rose, 23 July, below.)

*　　　*　　　*

From Colonel Otho H. Williams

Dr Genl　　　Howells Ferry [S.C.] Sunday [8 July 1781] 9 o'Clk A.M.

I had the Honor to inform you by my Letter of the 6th Ins^t that Dominique had return'd from 96, which he left last Tuesday Evening.[1] He says Provision was extremely scarce, That orders were issued for marching at a moments warning, That the Officers Baggage, the stores &c were packing up: and that He understood part of the Troops were to march to Augusta and Part immediately to Charles Town.[2] All this is coroborated by an Old hand who went into 96 Wednesday Morning and came off about Noon, with this addition that the Star Fort was Actually Demolished[,] that they coverd in the Trenches Iron & other articles which co^d not be Transported.

In consequence of your Letter which G^l Huger rec^d about 3 oClk P.M. Yesterday[,] the army march'd last night to this Place.[3] We arrived about 11 oClock and have been crossing ever since in three Small Canoes and a very Old Flatt which just now Sunk. We have got the Flatt on shore and the Artificers are about repairing Her. I do not know if it is possible to procure any other means of transportation at this Place. The army will march immediately to Bever Creek.

Gen⁰ Sumpter has gone down and Gen⁰ Pickens up the other side of the River.[4] The latter intended to cross Broad River last night and Saluda (at Widow Weavers) this morning. G⁰ Huger has wrote to G⁰ Pickens this morning to attend to the motions of Col⁰ Cruger and to send him intelligence.[5] He has no other dependance having no militia Horse with him. Cruger can not arrive at Orangeburgh before tomorrow night if I am right inform'd of the Distance.[6]

We are at much loss for information respecting the motions of the relative parts of our Army, as well as for better instruction in Geographical knowledge. Orangeburgh I understand is 20 or 25 miles from this Ferry and about 90 from 96. But where you are, or where you expect to pick up Col⁰ Stewart I have no intelligible Idea.[7]

I wish you cou'd rejoin the Army before it comes into any critical circumstance. I am D⁰ G⁰ Mo truly & affectionately Yrs

O.H. WILLIAMS

ALS (MiU-C).

1. Williams had reported the return of his servant, who had deserted to the enemy, in his letter to NG of 5 July, above.

2. See note at Williams's letter of 5 July.

3. On NG's letter to Isaac Huger, which has not been found, see Pierce to NG, this date, above.

4. On Sumter's whereabouts, see his letter to NG of this date, above.

5. Huger's letter to Pickens has not been found; for the intelligence that Pickens gathered concerning the march of Col. John Harris Cruger from Ninety Six, see Pickens to NG, 10 July, below.

6. Cruger joined Rawdon at Orangeburg on 14 July. (Rawdon to Cornwallis, 2 August 1781, PRO 30/11/6)

7. As seen in Marion to NG, this date, above, Col. Alexander Stewart's troops had successfully evaded attempts to intercept them and had joined Rawdon at Orangeburg on 7 July.

*   *   *

¶ [GENERAL GREENE'S ORDERS, "Camp Beaver Creek," S.C., 9 July 1781. The troops are to receive and cook meat "for tomorrow" and meal "for up to the 11th Inclusive." They are to be ready to march "tomorrow" at 3 A.M.[1] The men in Gen. [Thomas] Sumter's brigade are to discharge and clean their weapons "this afternoon." Lamar Orderly Book (OClWHi) 1 p.]

1. As seen in NG's Orders, 10 July, and in NG to Marion, second letter of 10 July, both below, the army did not march at that time.

¶ [MAJOR ICHABOD BURNET TO COLONELS HENRY LEE, JR., AND WILLIAM WASHINGTON. From [Beaver Creek, S.C.], 9 July 1781.[1] NG wants their troops to draw and cook provisions for "tomorrow." In the morning, they are to "gain the front of the Army," which will move to Orangeburg. ADfS (MiU-C) 1 p.]

1. The place was taken from NG's Orders of this date, immediately above.

¶ [FROM GENERAL FRANCIS MARION, "Holmons," S.C., 9 July 1781. Has NG's letter of 8 July [not found]. Marion's men and horses were "so fatigued" that he could not "proceed" as NG ordered until "this morning," when he sent Maj. [Hezekiah] Maham, with 100 men, to watch the enemy's motions. Maham will report to NG before he rejoins Marion, who will then be ready to join the army wherever NG directs.[1] ALS (MiU-C) 1 p.]

1. For the intelligence that Maham obtained, see note at Marion to NG, immediately below.

¶ [FROM GENERAL FRANCIS MARION, "Holmans," S.C., 9 July 1781. 8 P.M. He received NG's letter of 8 July [not found] at 5 P.M. Will unite with the Southern Army where and when NG wishes. If NG is moving to Orangeburg by way of the east side of Beaver Creek, Marion can join him on the march and save twenty miles. Sends intelligence that Maj. [Hezekiah] Maham obtained from two prisoners, who appear "very Intelligent."[1] Lord Rawdon's army "keep so close that no stragglers are to be seen." Only two hogsheads of rum, a small cask of wine, and two small barrels of "Shrub" were captured in the wagons.[2] Marion will await NG's orders at Whetstone Mill, to which he will move "tomorrow morning for the Advantage of subsistance & forrage."[3] ALS (MiU-C) 1 p.]

1. The report gave information about the composition and numbers of Rawdon's force, which the prisoners estimated to total 1,150 men, exclusive of Col. [Alexander] Stewart's regiment. The prisoners said they expected Rawdon to "march up for the Congarees in a few Days" because provisions were scarce at Orangeburg. They also reported that Rawdon would relinquish his command and leave for Charleston in a few days. (The intelligence is with Marion's letter, in MiU-C.)

2. On the capture of the wagons, see Marion to NG, second letter of 8 July, above. "Shrub" was "a prepared drink made with the juice of orange or lemon (or other acid fruit), sugar and rum (or other spirit)." (*OED*)

3. See Pierce to Marion and NG to Marion, both 10 July, below.

¶ [GENERAL GREENE'S ORDERS, "Camp Beaver Creek," S.C., Tuesday, 10 July 1781. The troops are to receive beef and meal, which they are to cook "this afternoon, and be prepared to March at a Moments warning." Lamar Orderly Book (OClWHi) 2 pp.]

¶ [CAPTAIN WILLIAM PIERCE, JR., TO GENERAL FRANCIS MARION. From "Camp at Beaver Creek," S.C., 10 July 1781. The army is "on the point of a very important move" and waits only for Marion's arrival. NG wants Marion to "hurry" his march and join the army at a convenient place on the Orangeburg road. He expected Marion to arrive last evening and "held the Army in readiness to move" at 3 A.M.[1] "No steps can or will be taken untill we hear from you. Every moments delay is dangerous." ADfS (MiU-C) 1 p.]

1. See also NG to Marion, immediately below.

* * *

To General Francis Marion

Dear Sir   Head Quarters at Beaver Creek [S.C.] July 10th 1781
  Your two letters of the 9th dated at Holmans were both receivd this morning.

  Letters are so subject to miscarry either by the delay or unfaithfulness of the expresses that I fear to hazard a movement which depends on conveyance of letters punctually. In my letter wrote at Heallys I desird you to meet me at this place.[1] Had it been deliverd punctually we could have marched this morning to attack Lord Rawden. We were to march this morning at 3 o Clock and only waited for you; but not hearing from you until some hours after the time appointed to march, I was obligd to pospone the march until tomorrow morning when we shall march for Orrangburg on the briddle road, and I wish you to join us with out fail at Colstons on the bridle road to which place we shall march. But should the enemy advance this way you will form a junction with us between this and that place, or at our Camp here, according as the movements of the enemy may permit. Let nothing but the enemies retiring prevent your joining us. And should they retire you will follow them.

  Inclosed I send you our order of battle and you will please to have the necessary dispositions made accordingly in your brigade, that we may be prepard for action the moment we meet as there can be no doubt of the enemy moving towards us, the moment they get intelligence of our advancing if they wish to fight us.[2] Have all your Men supplied with a proper quantity of ammunition, they ought to have if possible Eighteen or twenty rounds a man. With esteem & regard I [am] Sir your humble Ser   N GREENE
NB Capt Pearce wrote you this morning to join us here, but as you are contrary to my expectation at so great a distance, I think it best to shorten your march by form^g a junction at Colstons.[3]

ADfS (MiU-C).
  1. NG's letter has not been found.
  2. The order of battle has not been found.
  3. See William Pierce to Marion, immediately above.

To Thomas Walters

               Head Quarters on Beaver Creek near Orangburg [S.C.]
Sir   July 10th 1781
  I am informed you have a press with a compleat set of tipes for printing. Nothing will contribute more to the recovery of these Southern States than a proper channel to convey intelligence to the people; for want of which they are kept in ignorance and subject to every British imposition. If you will remove your press to Charlotte or Sal-

lisbury [N.C.] and open the business of printing I think you will render an essential service to your Country and you may depend upon my giving you every possible encouragement so as to render it beneficial to your interest; and I am perswaded Governor [John] Rutledge in behalf of the State of South Carolinia will do the like.

I shall be happy to hear from you on the subject as soon as possible.[1] I am sir Your humble Sr   N GREENE

ADfS (MiU-C).

1. Neither Walters's reply nor any evidence that he ever operated a press in North or South Carolina has been found. NG wrote John Mathews on 18 July, below, that a printing press was "exceedingly wanted" in the Carolinas.

*   *   *

¶ [CAPTAIN WILLIAM PIERCE, JR., TO CAPTAIN WILLIAM R. WITHERS.[1] From Headquarters [Beaver Creek, S.C.], 10 July 1781. If possible, he is to purchase at Georgetown the articles listed on the enclosed invoices, using bills on Congress, payable in specie.[2] He is to impress the items if necessary. ADfS (MiU-C) 1 p.]

1. Pierce wrote "Captain Wethers" at the bottom of the draft, but the letter was probably intended for William R. Withers, a Georgetown resident and South Carolina militia officer.

2. The invoices have not been found.

¶ [FROM MAJOR JOHN ARMSTRONG, "Camp Watree 8 Miles above Camden," S.C., 10 July 1781. Since he last wrote, forty Virginia militiamen have deserted.[1] A detachment from "Colo' Lasseys horse," which Armstrong sent in pursuit, failed to overtake them.[2] Armstrong's men are "getting Sick Verry fast." The express he sent with a letter to NG has returned without delivering it.[3] He fears that the Virginia militia will desert *en masse* and that he will not have enough men to mount a camp guard or to guard the prisoners. He does not know what to do. "I am Sure if the whole armey had been pick⁴ You Could not got a more disorderly Crew[;] plundering and Stealing is in full Perfection and dun in Such a Manor that we Cannot come to the knowledge of it." He cannot depend on "Lasseys" men to guard the prisoners because "they will not be Confin⁴ to Camp." Asks for advice.[4] He is using his North Carolina troops to forage, thresh wheat, and serve as guards and pickets. No additional men from North Carolina have joined him since he left NG's army. He sent twelve of his own sick and ten British sick and wounded to Camden "this day." ALS (MiU-C) 1 p.]

1. On desertion among the Virginia militiamen, see also Armstrong to NG, 7 July, above.

2. Col. Edward Lacey's regiment was part of Gen. Thomas Sumter's South Carolina militia brigade.

3. Armstrong probably referred to the letter mentioned in note 1, above.

4. As seen in NG's letter to Maj. Alexander Rose, 28 July, below, NG allowed the militiamen to escort British prisoners of war to Virginia. They had earlier expressed their willingness to do such duty. (See Armstrong to NG, 7 July, and Ward to NG, 8 July, both above.)

¶ [FROM GOVERNOR THOMAS BURKE OF NORTH CAROLINA, [Wake County Court House], "State of North Carolina," 10 July 1781.[1] Sends the "Resolves" of the legislature for remounting NG's cavalry; cannot "promise that the measure will prove effectual."[2] Adds: "On the Contrary, I am persuaded if this business be no better executed than such is, usually, when Committed to so many independent Commissioners, very little dependence ought to be put in its Success." As the commissioners are not "public officers," Burke cannot "Compel them to a diligent and expeditious discharge of thier duty" or "punish them for Neglect or misbehaviour." He doubts that many horses can be obtained "for Certificates" and thinks the "Notoriety" of the measure will make impressment impossible. Does not want the army's operations "deranged by too great a Reliance on this State for Horses." Suggests that Virginia can furnish "much better" ones, more speedily and more certainly. Burke will do all that he can, however. Asks if there is a better place than Hillsborough to collect "those from the lower districts." Says in a postscript that Gen. [Isaac] Gregory "was forced to abandon his post, but the Enemy being called off to reinforce Ld Corwallis, he has regained it."[3] ALS (CSmH) 1 p.]
   1. On Burke's location, see note at his letter to NG of 4 July, above.
   2. Burke enclosed a copy of the law, which had been enacted on 7 July, naming six men to be commissioners and directing them to acquire 160 dragoon horses. They were to offer "generous prices" for the horses and were to resort to impressment if necessary. Commissioners who failed to act were to be replaced. (The copy of the law, dated 7 July and signed by Alexander Martin and Thomas Benbury, is in MiU-C.)
   3. On Gregory's actions, see Burke to NG, 4 July, above.

¶ [FROM LIEUTENANT EDMUND GAMBLE, Salisbury, N.C., 10 July 1781. Has four men making cartridge boxes, as NG requested.[1] As he will soon exhaust his supply of leather, NG must give him "An Order on" the commissary of hides if "this Business" is to continue. Col. Malmedy, who arrived in Salisbury "Yesterday," informs Gamble that he is inspecting "the Manufactorys at the Different Posts" at NG's order. Malmedy says he is "to Equipt Such Troops on their way to Join" NG's army. That is contrary to the orders that Col. [Edward] Carrington gave Gamble "Respecting the delivery of stores"; seeks clarification.[2] ALS (MiU-C) 1 p.]
   1. See NG to Gamble, 12 June, above.
   2. See also the Marquis de Malmedy's letter to NG, this date, below. NG replied to Gamble on 16 July, below.

¶ [FROM COLONEL HENRY LEE, JR., [near Beaver Creek, S.C.], 10 July 1781.[1] "Presuming that the order of March" is to be the same as that of "yesterday," and that it does not matter if his men arrive "this night or tomorrow Morning," Lee will remain where he is until "two o'clock."[2] Extract from Stan. V. Henkel, *Catalogue #997* (1909).]
   1. The extract does not give Lee's location, but the contents suggest that he was not far from the Southern Army's camp at Beaver Creek.
   2. Lee probably meant that he planned to march at 2 A.M.

¶ [FROM THE MARQUIS DE MALMEDY, Salisbury, N.C., 10 July 1781. He intended to bring the enclosed letters to NG but has been detained in Salisbury because of "Circumstances" concerning NG's instructions.[1] Assumes that "Governor Bourke" will inform NG of the North Carolina legislature's resolutions to provide "Reinforcements" for the army and the "Speedy Purchase of Forty Horses."[2] Since Burke last wrote, Malmedy has asked the legislature for 150 more horses. Both houses approved the request and ordered a committee to "determine on the Means of Procuring them Expeditiously to the Satisfaction of the People." Malmedy left before they reported, but several legislators "intreated" him to "Assure" NG "that no pains Should be Spar'd, to Comply with" the request.[3] Malmedy previously informed NG that he had ordered the sending of arms that were being stored at Charlotte to Salisbury for repairs "in case they might be wanted for the use of the N° Carolina Troops."[4] When the legislature voted to reinforce NG with 500 militiamen from the Hillsborough district, "Some Objection was made against it from the difficulty of Arming them." To silence that objection, Malmedy promised to supply 400 stand of arms and cartridge boxes. He thought he could take the arms from Salisbury and Charlotte, as well as from the Virginia militiamen who are soon to be discharged, and use them to arm the Hillsborough militiamen and some of Gen. [Jethro] Sumner's men. He has been "Very Much disappointed," though. There are only 285 muskets at Salisbury, of which only 120 are fit for use. That total may include the muskets that Malmedy saw at Charlotte, which could have been sent to Salisbury in the interim. He finds, moreover, that Col. [Edward] Carrington's "late Order" to the quartermaster "not to deliver any Stores Whatever without" NG's or Carrington's "positive Order" will "Delay for a Considerable time, the Equipment & march of the Troops." Carrington's orders did not "even discriminate the Commanding Officer of a body of Troops, on his way to the Army." Malmedy fears that sending for such an order "might disappoint" NG's operations. He also thought that NG's instructions to him might have "Mitigated" Carrington's earlier orders. Accordingly, he has ordered the quartermasters in the area to forward the arms in their keeping to Salisbury, where they are to be "immediately Repaird." Malmedy will deliver them to the officers of detachments on their way to the army, who will be strictly accountable for the arms.[5] He has also requisitioned the commissary for supplies for the militia. He encloses the latter's reply and asks NG to send orders to the commissary. Does not understand why Col. [Francis] Lock failed to march on 4 July, as promised. Malmedy "urg'd him again," and Lock has agreed to "Send positive Orders, to the Col° of the Countys to Collect immediately their Respective draughts & Send them to" Waxhaws Creek. Malmedy will bring to headquarters the first 300 men who assemble and will command them and any troops who follow until Governor Burke takes the field. Asks NG to "contenance" this arrangement. Explains his reasons for having the militiamen rendezvous in the Waxhaws: that it is the "most neighbourhingh place" to the "Low counties" of the Salisbury militia district; that supplies can easily be collected there from the inhabitants, who are "chiefly" disaffected, thus sparing the resources of friendlier areas; and that the Waxhaws is a good "intermediary place" to various points in South Carolina. If NG agrees to the establishment of a "temporary post & store" in the Waxhaws and to the militia holding its rendezvous there, Malmedy will "survey" the area in a few days.[6] He left Gen. [Jethro] Sumner, with 500 rank and file, at Guilford

Court House "yesterday." Having been asked to "provide for" the "march" of these troops, he has directed Sumner to move via the Waxhaws, to which place NG should send further orders for Sumner.[7] Malmedy has "spared no pains" and hopes his "proceedings" are agreeable to NG. "Capt [i.e., Lieutenant] Gamble" had to write part of this letter because Malmedy was so "indisposed by the fatigue & the heat" that he "cannot write as I should wish." LS and ALS (MiU-C) 4 pp.]

1. It is not known what letters Malmedy enclosed.

2. Gov. Thomas Burke had written NG on 4 July, above, reporting the legislature's actions.

3. On the bill to acquire additional dragoon horses for the use of NG's army, see Burke to NG, this date, above.

4. The letter has not been found.

5. Lt. Edmund Gamble also questioned NG on this date, above, about the discrepancy between Malmedy's orders and the standing order from Carrington. NG replied to both Gamble and Malmedy on 16 July, below.

6. NG gave Malmedy permission to establish a point of rendezvous either in the Waxhaws or at Camden, "as first ordered." (See NG to Malmedy, 16 July.) The Salisbury militiamen did not join Malmedy. (See Malmedy to NG, 29 June, above.)

7. NG's letter to Sumner of 19 July, below, contained no mention of the Waxhaws.

¶ [FROM GENERAL FRANCIS MARION, Colston's, S.C., 10 July 1781, 6 P.M. He received NG's letter "of this days date" and has come to Colston's "agreeable thereto."[1] It was impossible to comply with NG's order of "yesterday" [not found] to join the Southern Army. Marion received the order forty miles from Beaver Creek, and his horses were exhausted from "being two days without forrage or Grass." If his "last letter" had found NG "yett at Middletons," Marion could have learned whether he had permission to shorten his march.[2] He has heard nothing from Orangeburg "today" but expects to receive intelligence by "morning." His men have only six rounds of ammunition each. ALS (NcU) 1 p.]

1. Both NG and his aide William Pierce had sent orders to Marion on this date, above. Marion was probably replying to NG's letter.

2. See Marion to NG, second letter of 9 July, above.

¶ [FROM GENERAL ANDREW PICKENS, "Camp at Bear Creek," Dutch Fork, S.C., 10 July 1781, 10 P.M. Capt. [Joseph] Towles, who was sent to gather intelligence from Ninety Six, has just returned with the information that as of 1 P.M. "yesterday" the wagons there were "Loaded with the Baggage, & the Horses Geer'd."[1] According to a trustworthy man whom Towles sent into the post to make inquiries, the enemy are to march "this morning," and "all the Families who Expected Brittish protection was Required to move Below Orrangeburgh, or be Deem'd as Enemies & Treated as Such." The spy was able to talk with Col. [John Harris] Cruger, who informed him that "they Intended to Lay all the Contry above [Orangeburg] in ashes." Cruger asked the spy which route—that by "Little Saludy to the Juniper" or the Ridge road—was better provided with water and forage. The man replied that the former was "the best watered, but he believed there was no furrege on Either." The Loyalists have collected "all the waggon & horses" they could and "Provisions of Every Kind."[2] They have also reportedly "burn'd manny houses in Long-

Cains & Drove off all the Cattle[,] Sheep[,] hogs &c."³ They are now "Chiefly out prepareing their Families to move," some of whom are understood to be meeting the army "this day or night near Saludy Old Town," while others are to join "at Little Saludy." Pickens will send other parties to gather intelligence. He will do all he can to harass the enemy on their march, but his horses are "Reduced by the heat" and by "want of Furrage."⁴ LS (MiU-C) 3 pp.]

1. See Pickens to NG, 6 July, above.

2. NG's first biographer described this Loyalist evacuation as "not unlike the pictures of the Exodus." (Johnson, *Greene*, 2: 163)

3. On the raid on Long Cane, see Henderson to NG, 6 July, above.

4. As noted at Williams to NG, 8 July, above, Cruger's force joined Lord Rawdon's army at Orangeburg on 14 July. It appears from his letter to NG of 19 July, below, that Pickens was unable to give Cruger's column much trouble before he broke off pursuit.

¶ [**FROM CHARLES THOMSON**,¹ Secretary's Office [Philadelphia], 10 July 1781. Samuel Huntington has requested a "leave of absence" for reasons of health.² Congress has named Thomas McKean to replace him as president.³ LS (MiU-C) 1 p.]

1. Thomson was secretary of Congress.

2. Huntington, the president of Congress, wrote Washington on this date that his health was "much impaired by long Confinement & Application." (Smith, *Letters*, 17: 391)

3. Samuel Johnston, a delegate from North Carolina, had declined the appointment before it was offered to McKean. (*JCC*, 20: 732–33) As noted above (vol. 2: 425n), McKean was both a delegate from Delaware and chief justice of the Pennsylvania Supreme Court.

INDEX

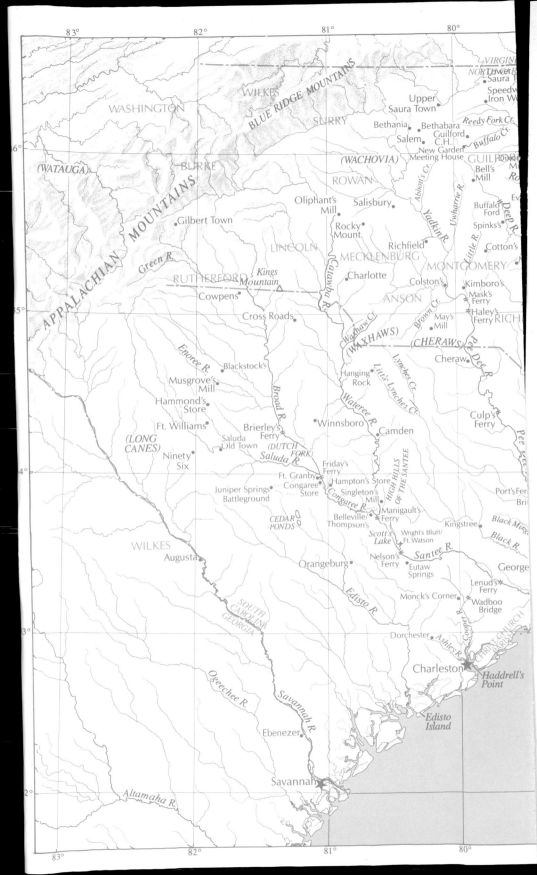